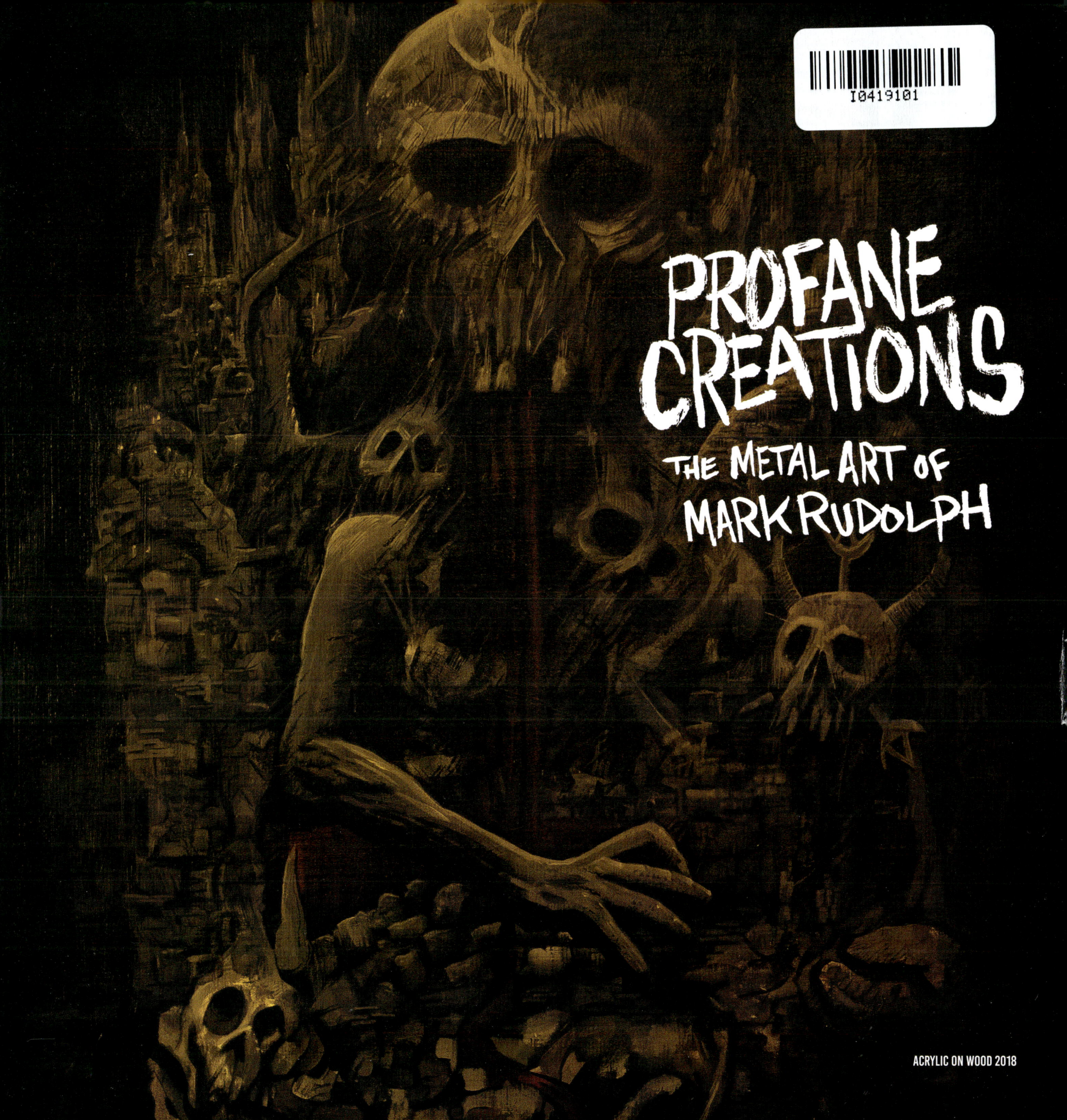

PROFANE CREATIONS

THE METAL ART OF MARK RUDOLPH

ACRYLIC ON WOOD 2018

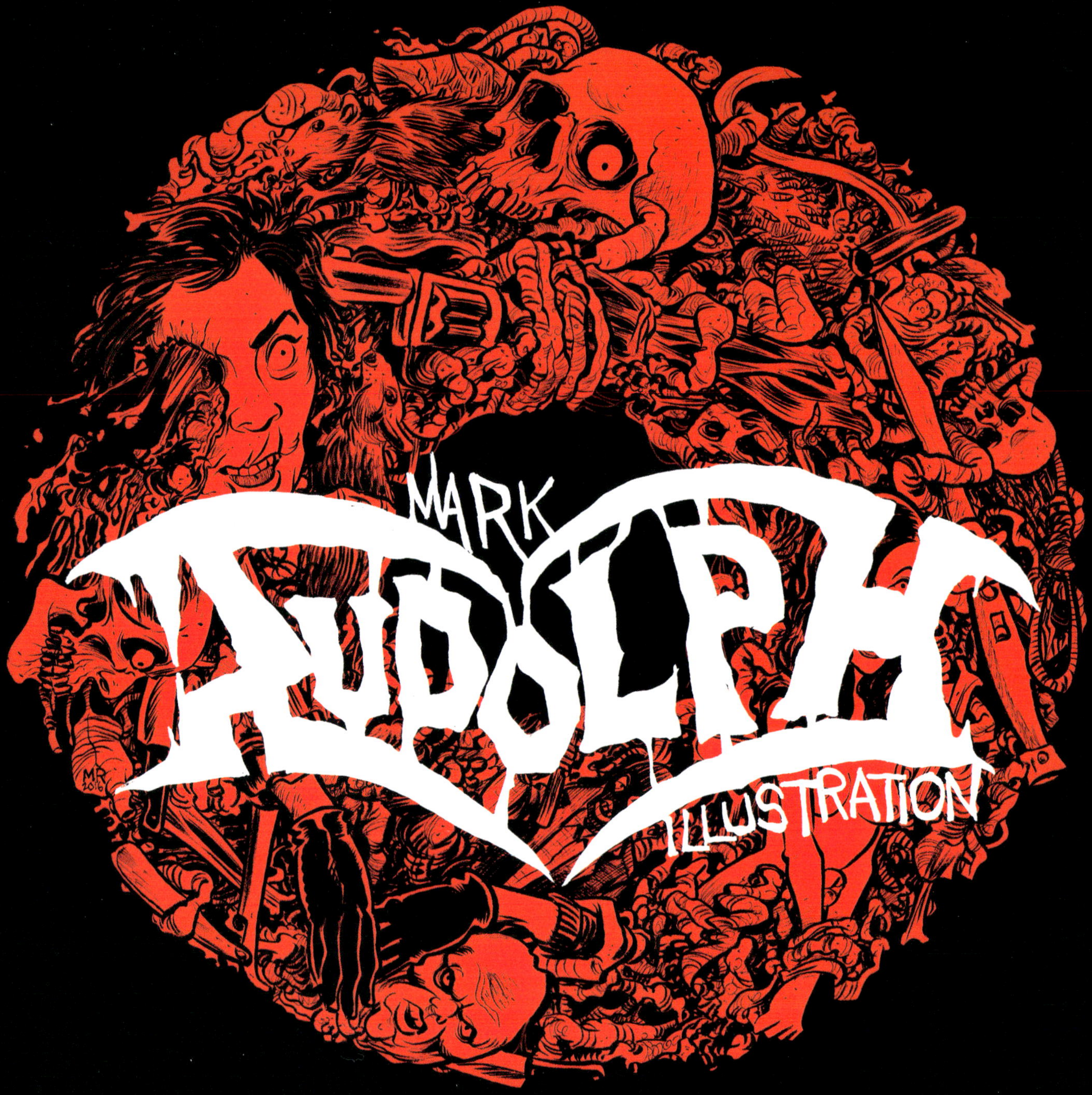

MARK RUDOLPH ILLUSTRATION

PUBLISHED BY DEAD SKY PUBLISHING, LLC
MIAMI BEACH, FLORIDA

COVER AND DESIGN BY MARK RUDOLPH
ISBN: 978-1-63951-185-3
FIRST EDITION: NOVEMBER 2024
PRINTED IN TÜRKIYE

JEREMY WAGNER – PUBLISHER / PRESIDENT
STEVE WANDS – PUBLISHER / CHIEF CREATIVE OFFICER
KRISTY BAPTIST – EDITORIAL / CONTENT MANAGER
ANNA KUBIK – EDITORIAL / TRAFFIC MANAGER

SPECIAL THANKS TO: LISA KRAUSE, MOM & DAD, CHRIS DICK, JASON HUNDEY, ALBERT MUDRIAN
AND JEREMY WAGNER FOR ALL YOUR SUPPORT THROUGHOUT THE YEARS.

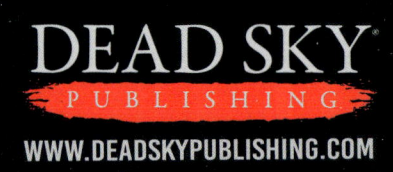

WWW.DEADSKYPUBLISHING.COM

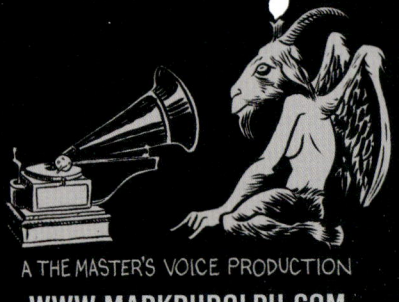

A THE MASTER'S VOICE PRODUCTION
WWW.MARKRUDOLPH.COM

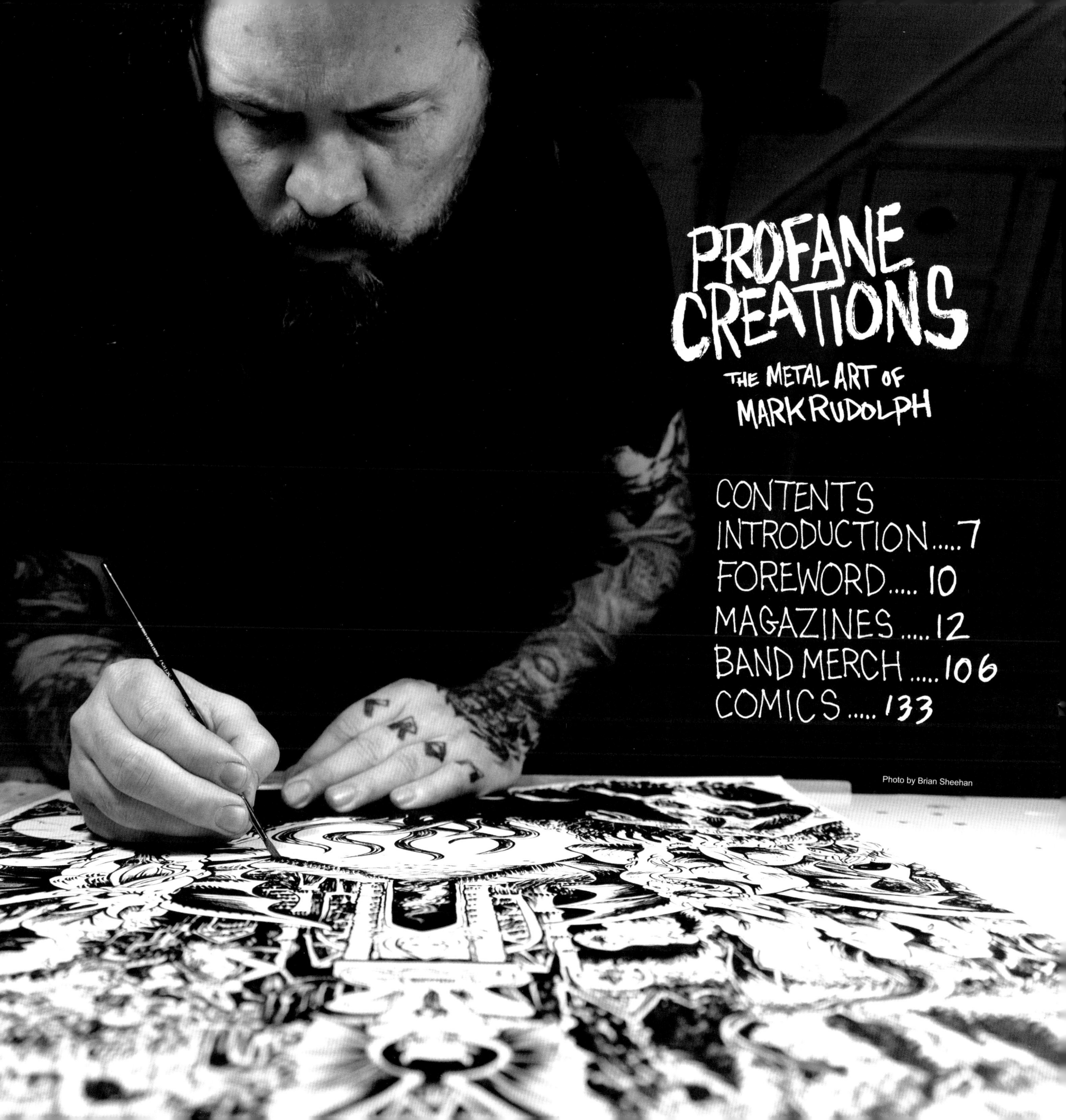

PROFANE CREATIONS

THE METAL ART OF MARK RUDOLPH

CONTENTS

Photo by Brian Sheehan

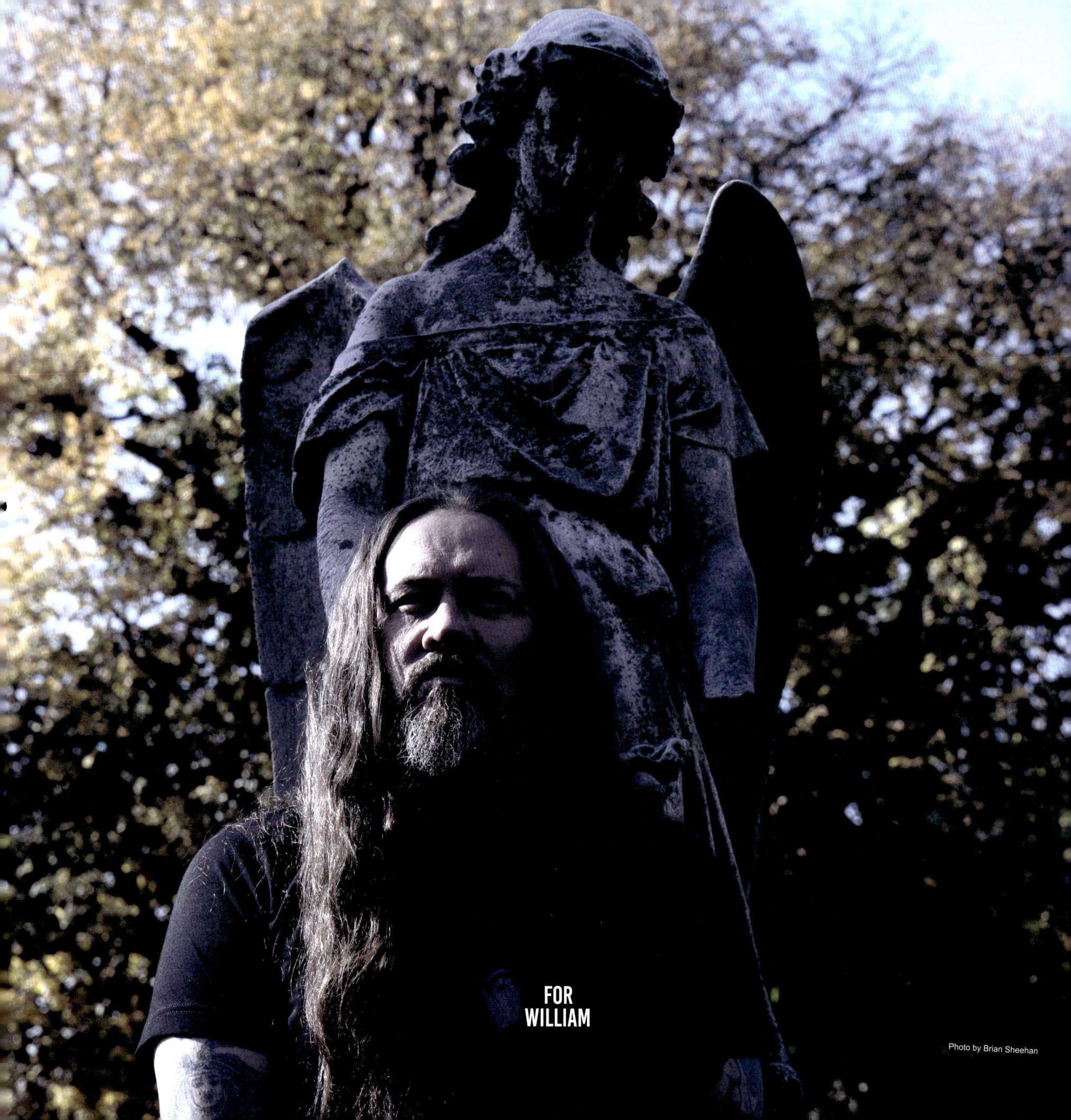

FOR
WILLIAM

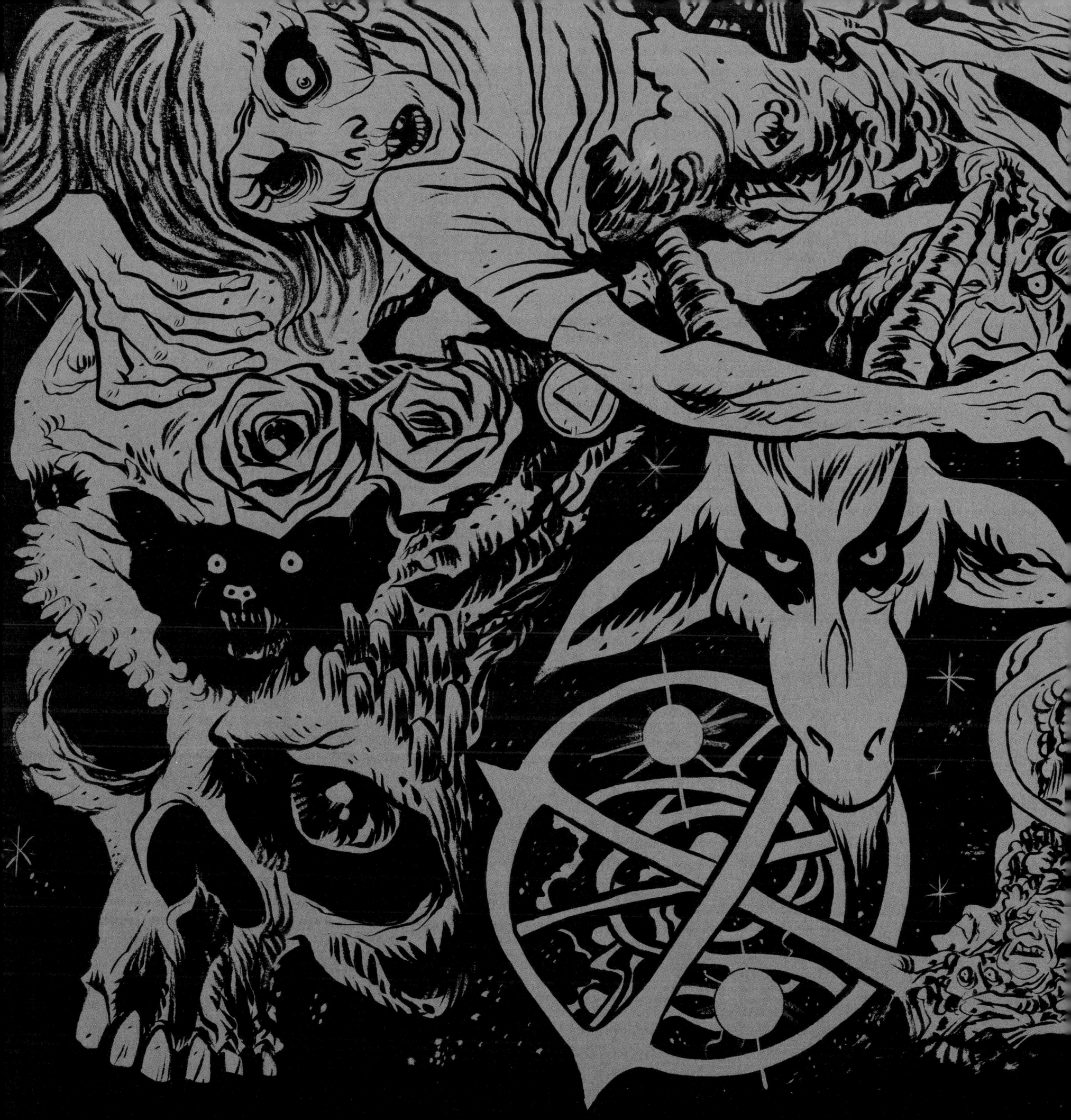

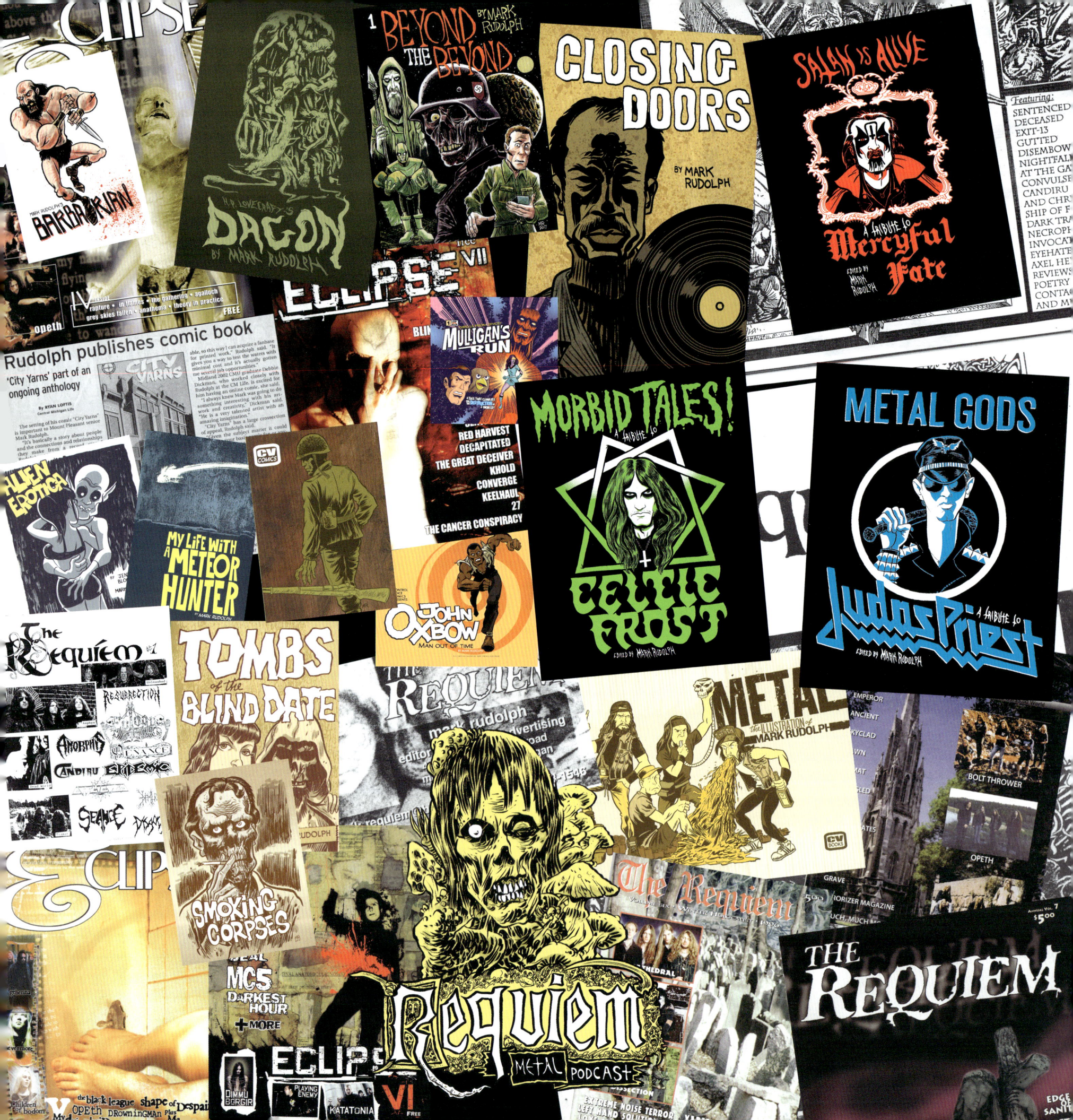

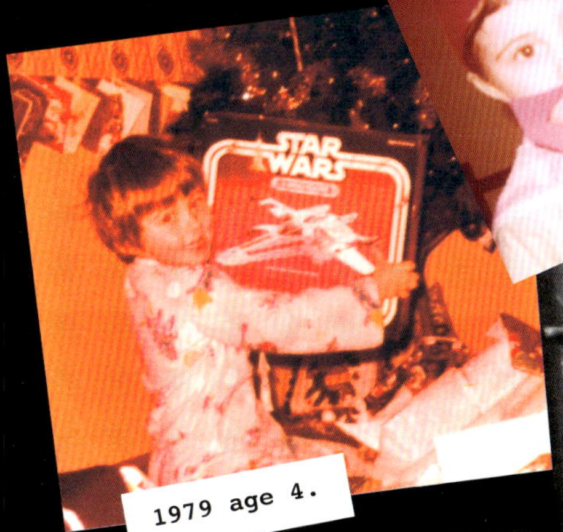

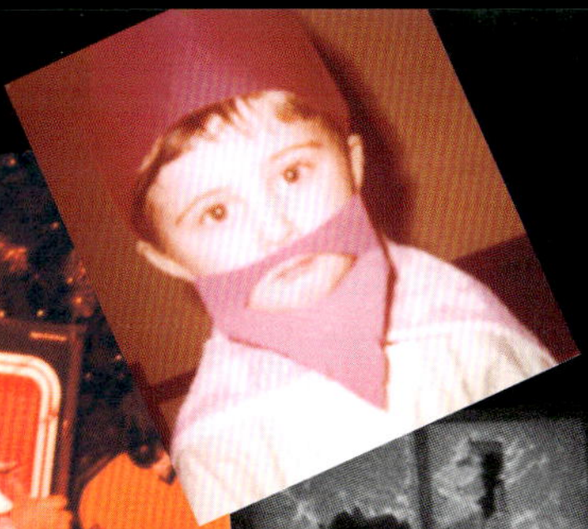

1979 age 4.

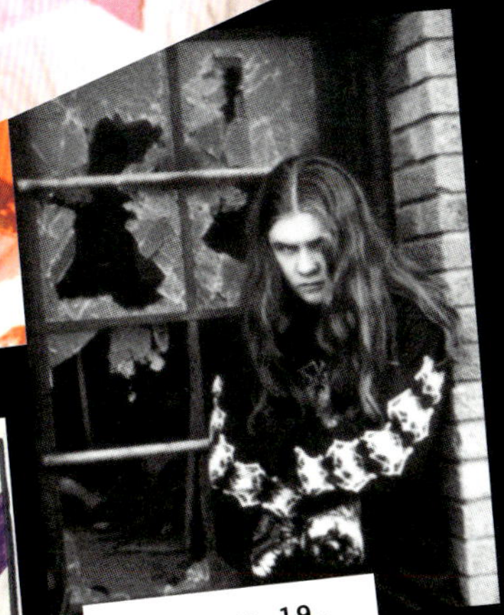

1994 age 19.

2022 age 47.

COMIC BOOKS & DEATH METAL

AN INTRODUCTION

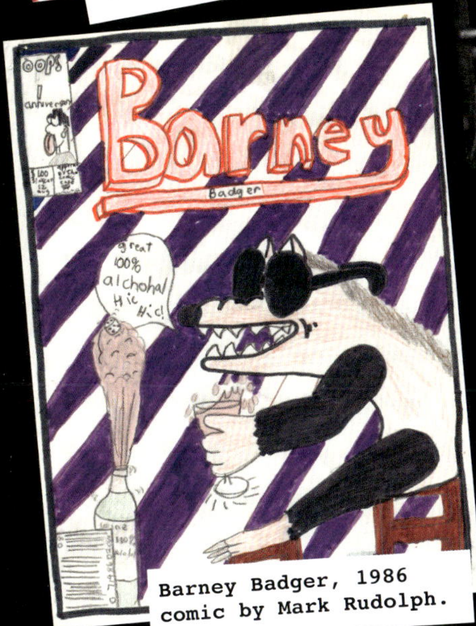

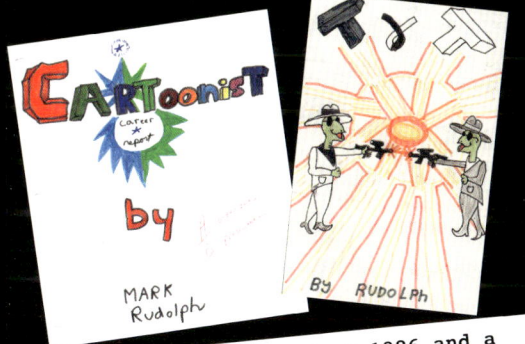

Barney Badger, 1986
comic by Mark Rudolph.

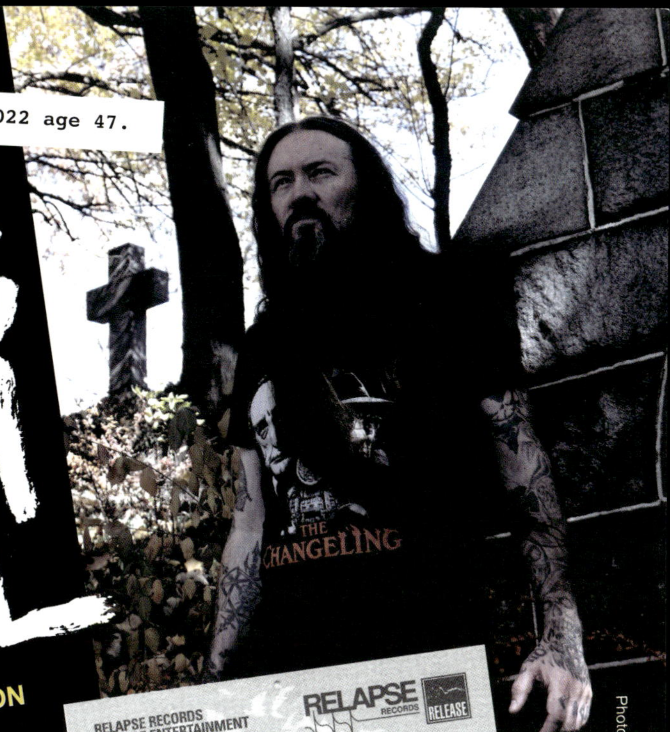

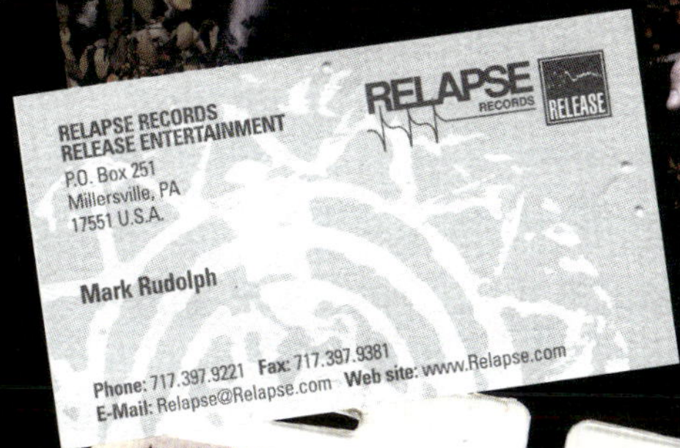

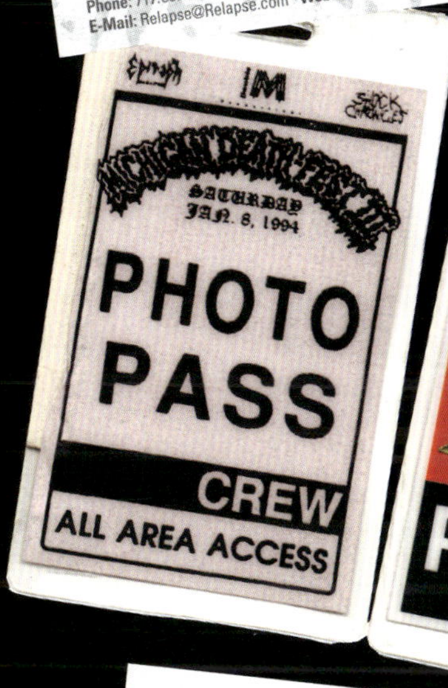

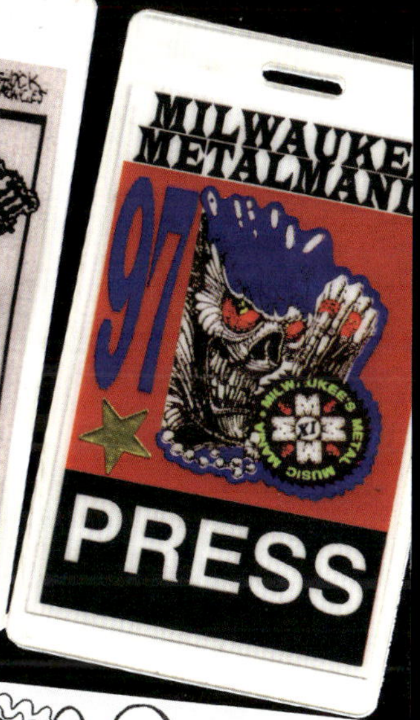

A career report from 1986 and a
Spy Vs Spy ripoff comic from 1987.

1987 drawings.

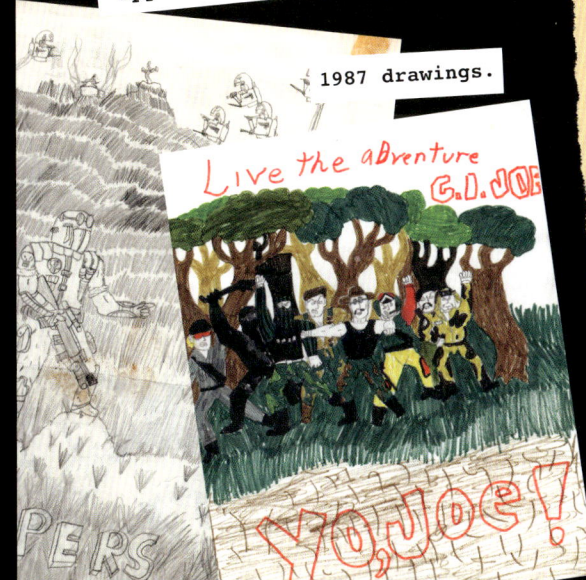

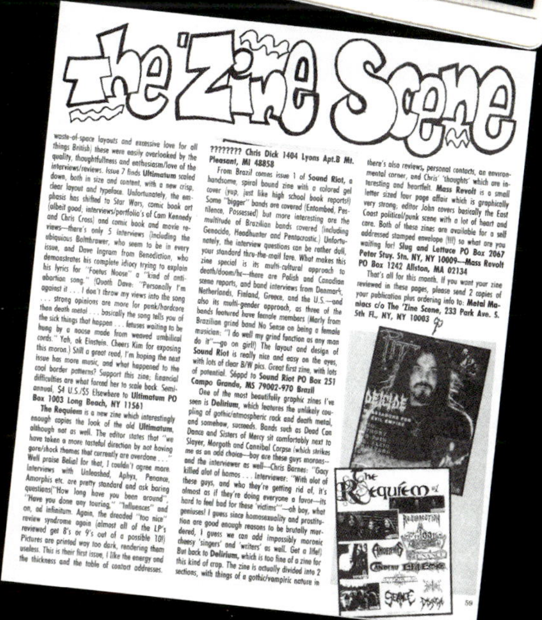

I was born in Jackson, Michigan in the winter of 1975, but lived my formative years in a small college town about two hours north of that, Mount Pleasant. Not much topography, but the pleasant part was right. It was a great place to grow up. My dad worked for the university and my mom stayed home to raise me during my early years before she went back to school and became a public school teacher. Education was important in our family and always encouraged.

We lived on an acre surrounded by farmland on one side and a golf course on the other. The rural environment and solitude really fostered my imagination. My time was spent either outside playing and exploring or inside pouring over comic books and drawing.

For the first nearly six years of my life I was an only child. I was a shy kid and was more comfortable alone than playing team sports or hanging with a crew. The things I was drawn to were more solitary pursuits and comic books were a very early outlet for me. The art style was aspirational; It took me into my 20s before I could even begin to understand the complexities of the arcane drafting tools that the pros used. Early on it was just about the wild imagination and worldbuilding, but I was hooked.

I wouldn't feel the pull of anything that strong again until I was in highschool. Sure, I was into horror movies and collecting toys and all that kind of crap, but nothing demanded me to be involved like death metal did. It was the early days of the scene. Death and Obituary had just put out their second albums and the excitement was palpable.

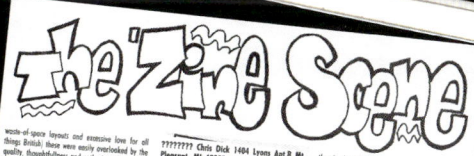

PHOTO PASS
CREW
ALL AREA ACCESS

MILWAUKEE METALMANIA
97
PRESS

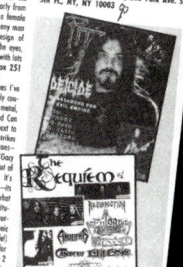

Photo by Brian Sheehan

The 'Zine Scene

When I first started highschool I was a big comic book fan and music was important, but it was more of a background interest. I was listening to Metallica, Megadeth, Warrant, Def Leppard and the like. I knew I dug aggressive music, but I was only being exposed to the bands that were on the radio. Nothing deeper than that. After a chance meeting in an English class, metal became all I cared about.

Enter Christopher Dick. We had totally opposite personalities: he was outgoing and boisterous and I was quiet and reserved, but a powerful friendship was forged in that classroom. We were both crazy for metal and the class became a game of one-upmanship. It was an obsession. Our time was spent listening to records, talking about said records and pouring over thanks lists and liner notes to try and find out more about the bands. We were in Mid-Michigan and there were only a handful of people we knew that were listening to this stuff. The magazines at the drugstore didn't even touch the extreme bands, so we had a major metal information deficit.

That was until we discovered the Hard N Heavy Grindcore Special issue VHS. It was a revelation. Bands we adored like Napalm Death, Paradise Lost and Bolt Thrower were featured both in an interview portion as well as live performances and music videos. Looking back this pivotal discovery directly led to us creating a fanzine of our own, The Requiem.

For nearly a decade the fanzine ruled our lives. Through college, working at a newspaper and eventually accepting a design job at Relapse records, it was always there. Until it wasn't. That's when I focused on comics again in college and created a graphic novel as my thesis project, all the while working at New Moon Records. That experience broadened my musical tastes and opened my mind to worlds that I never knew existed. Many life-long friendships formed around the store.

Most importantly was the one with Jason Hundey. Jason was a few years younger than Chris and I, but he matched our enthusiasm

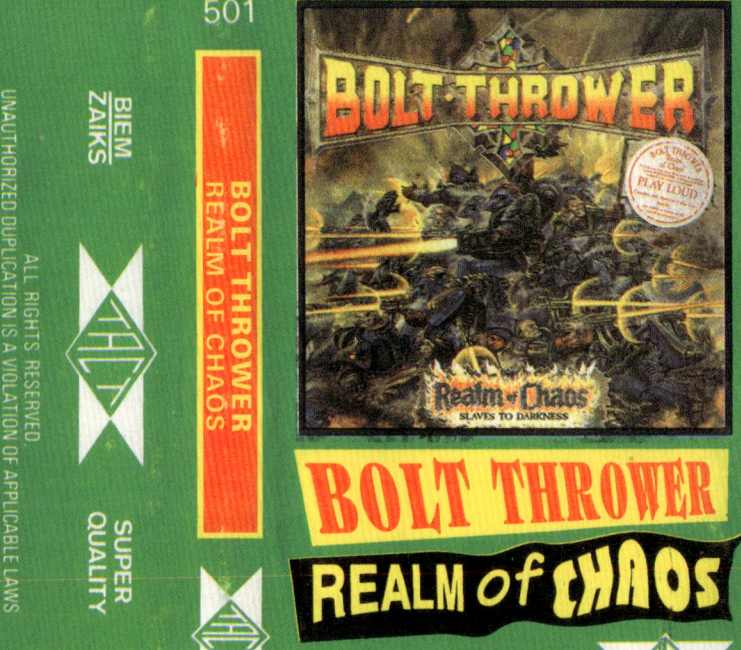

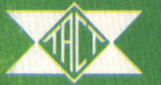

The album that changed my life.

and our unquenchable thirst for music discovery and history. Fast forward a few years and the three of us were working on another metal magazine together and for the last 15 years, Jason and I have been doing a podcast, named after the old fanzine, The Requiem Metal Podcast.

This book is the culmination of over 30 years of love for two things that did not seem like they'd ever work together, but became something all their own in the process. I hope you enjoy the ridiculous fun within these pages. It's the thrill of a lifetime to have the opportunity to present this work to you. I thank each of you from the bottom of my metal heart for your support.

December 2024

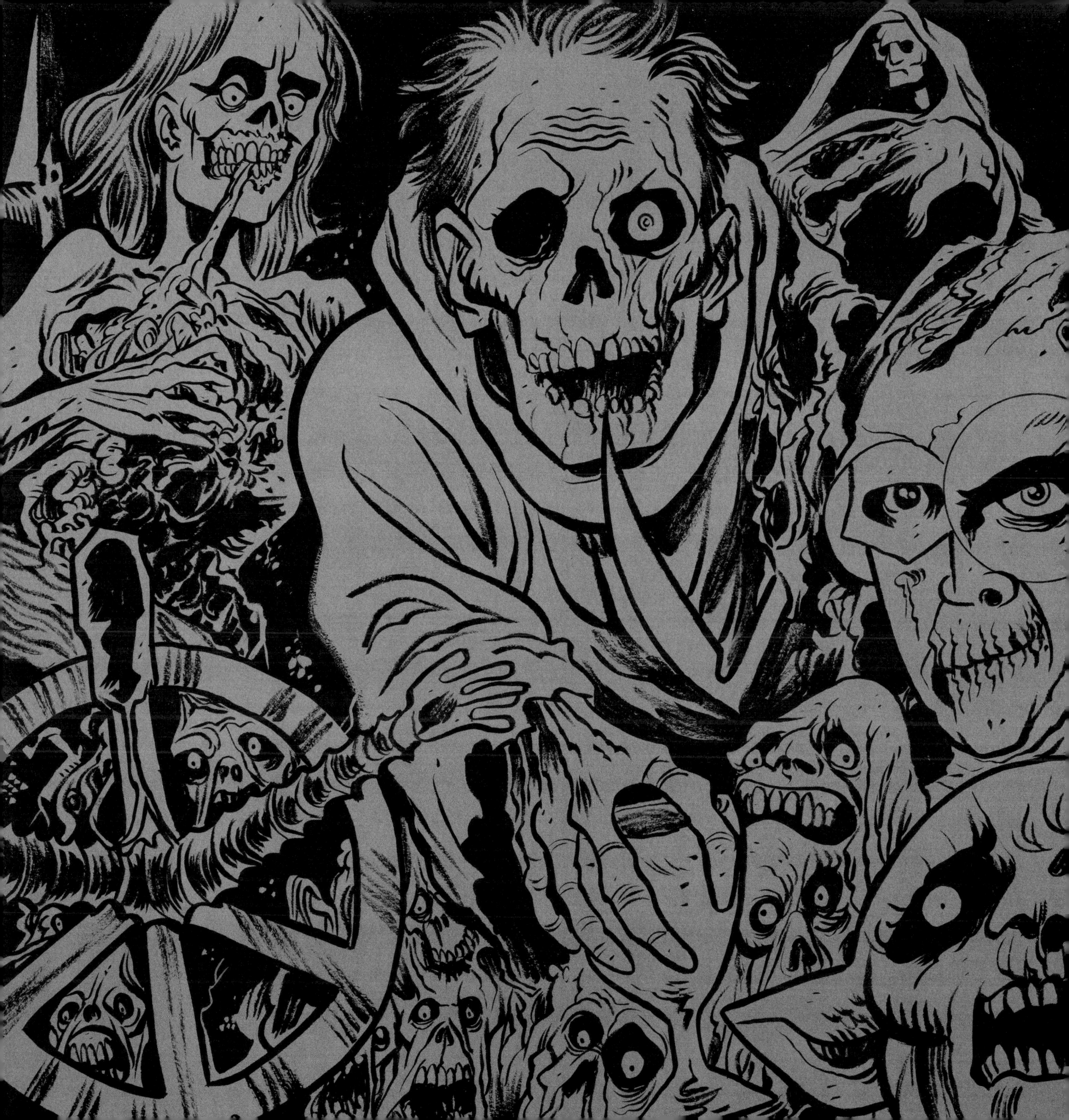

FOREWORD

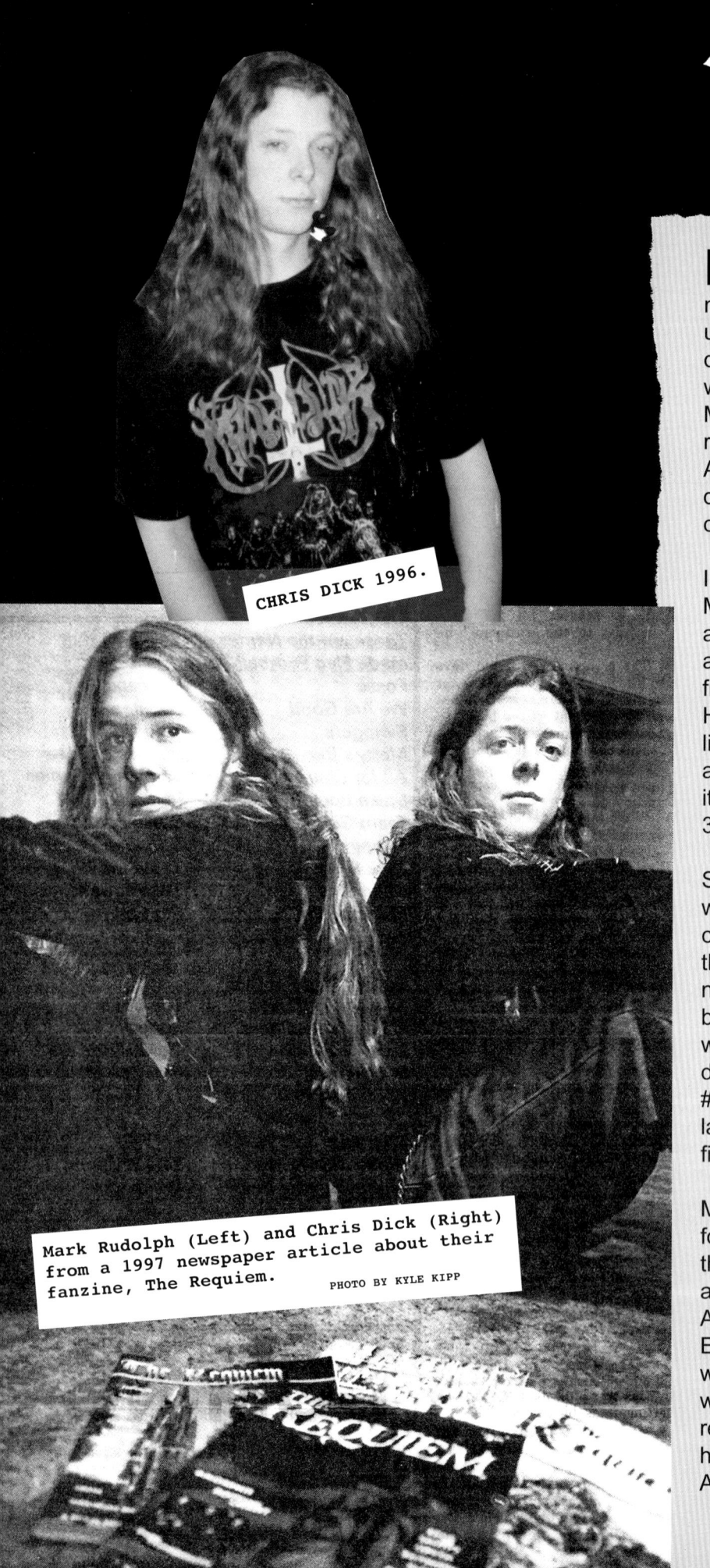

CHRIS DICK 1996.

Mark Rudolph (Left) and Chris Dick (Right) from a 1997 newspaper article about their fanzine, The Requiem. PHOTO BY KYLE KIPP

I've known Mark for longer than I haven't. In a world of uncertainty, that's more than special. We weren't childhood friends, but in our mid-teens fate put us together. We could've easily not been friends. Our personalities are quite different. Yet, in the vortex of small-town America, there's fellowship in those who dare to cut across the grain. We were both odd-men-out on parallel tracks. Mark was the artist-type. Not recreationally either. His earliest pieces—that I remember—were line art stabs at escaping the mundanity of small-town America. I could tell he wanted out. The people, places, and things he had drawn (and was willing to show me) said more than my then-friends could ever muster.

I know I tried to interpret, boil down, and figure out Mark. Sometimes I got him. Most of the time, I didn't. That's probably typical of new relationships. During an utterly boring English class in 10th grade, Mark and I found a bond. He was absolutely engrossed in comic books and graphic novels. I was the furthest from. I was insanely into thrash metal and death metal. Mark was into Metallica. He was already in front of the gateway, I probably thought. He just needed a little shove. Must've been in the spring of '91 when Mark, staring at the cover art for Bolt Thrower's "Realm of Chaos (Slaves to Darkness)," jumped through it. I mean, there was Death, and then there was Bolt Thrower. Our journey, now 31 years in the making, started there.

So close were we that we started a fanzine, The Requiem, out of nothing. We were in high school study hall, pouring over all the death and doom metal we could acquire. There were fanzines, too. I think we looked at one another, in the dark recesses of naivety, and thought, "Yeah, we can do this, too!" We had no idea what we were doing, but we did it. The Requiem, in many respects, became the vehicle for Mark to not only show off his skills—publishing anything was a big deal—as an artist, but also as a budding and talented designer. From drawing a memorable caricature of Dismember's Matti Kärki (in The Requiem #2) to setting up his first desktop publishing computer, he became, in my eyes, larger than life. I had a lot of respect (and a little bit of jealousy) seeing Mark find and, of course, expand on his potential.

Mark eventually worked for Relapse Records, where he designed materials for Amorphis, Neurosis, and more. High school Mark would've never imagined that. His post-record label career arc was directly in line with his passion for art and music. We reconvened on another publishing venture Eclipse Magazine. Again, his excellent visual aesthetic was brought to the fore. It wasn't long after Eclipse Magazine folded that Mark truly realized the subtle art of commerce. I witnessed Mark learn how to hustle. Difficult lessons no doubt. Through hard work and reputation alone, he had bands, magazines, other artists, and even restaurants hitting him up. I was beyond stoked for Mark when he told me he had lined up a piece for long-time favorites Carcass. Since then, he's added Autopsy, Coalesce, Pig Destroyer, Broken Hope, and a host of others to his list

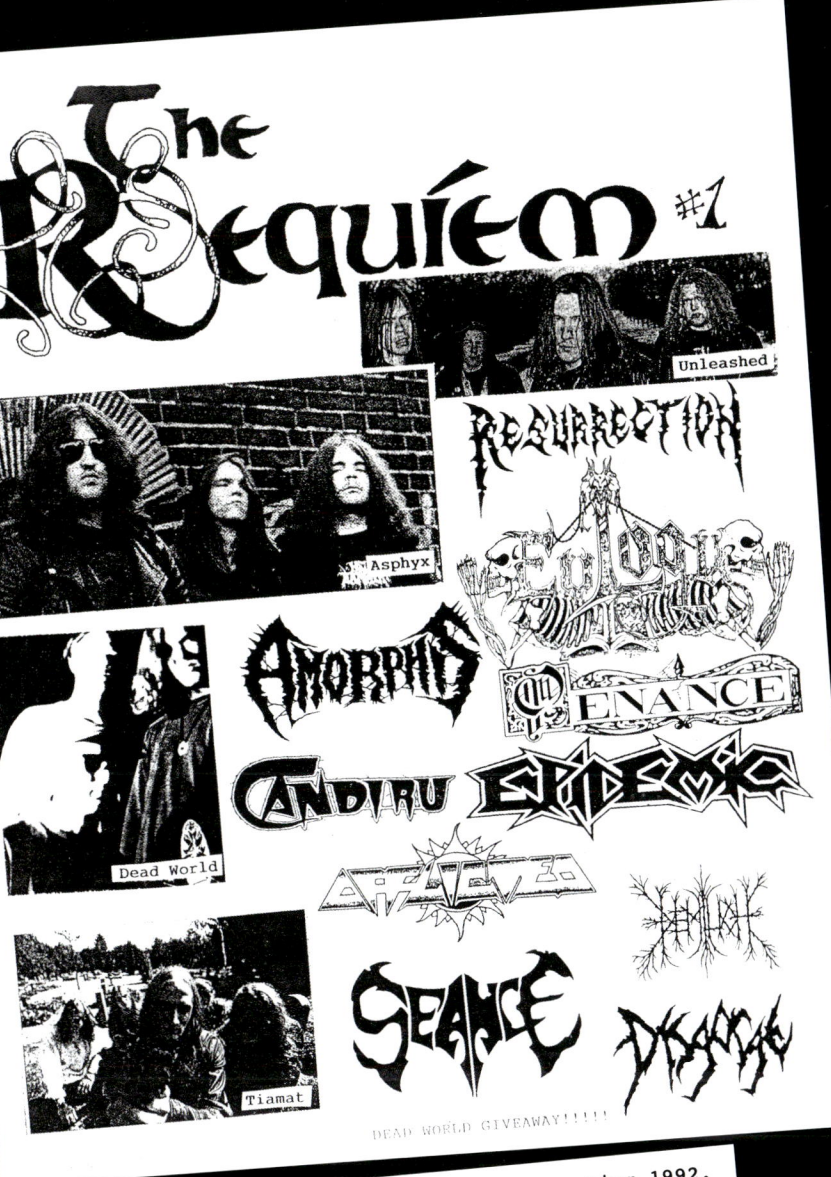

First issue of The Requiem 1992.

of prominent co-conspirators.

Mark's most impressive work is his own publications. His Dagon book is unbelievable. There's undeniable adoration for old-school sci-fi in his Beyond the Beyond book. And, I don't think I could even write this if it wasn't for his record store reverence in Closing Doors, a heartfelt eulogy to New Moon Records, a place that gave us both employment and opportunity for musical (and personal) growth. But his most accomplished books to date are the tributes to metal legends Celtic Frost, Mercyful Fate, and Judas Priest. I can't begin to tell you how great it was to see coverage in mainstream media on Mark's work as an artist, and of course, fan of metal. That these books dovetailed into and out of his illustrations for Metal Hammer, Blood Of Gods 'zine, and of course, Decibel Magazine– where he's contributed incredible covers and innumerable Lead Review pieces–has defined Mark's work and his upward trajectory.

To understand Mark you have to know and appreciate the depth of his art. It took me half of my adult life to realize this. I couldn't be more grateful that I got there. Mark's a true friend and a brother for life. Hail!

Chris Dick
October 2024

Chris Dick holds a major in Journalism from Central Michigan University, but that's not what put him on the path he's on today. That, in fact, would be The Requiem 'zine. From there, he established Eclipse Magazine (now defunct), worked at Relapse Records as slinger of Internet Marketing, co-founded DigitalMetal.com (now defunct), founded Teethofthedivine.com, served as Content Director for Mediaguide, Inc., spent time as a staff writer for Metal Maniacs, spearheaded Candlelight Records USA's web presence, and has been happily entrenched at Decibel Magazine for 16 years (and counting). Besides metal, he's a Senior Manager, Ingest Systems at Xperi. And, yes, Chris still buys CDs.

The rest of the run of Requiem.

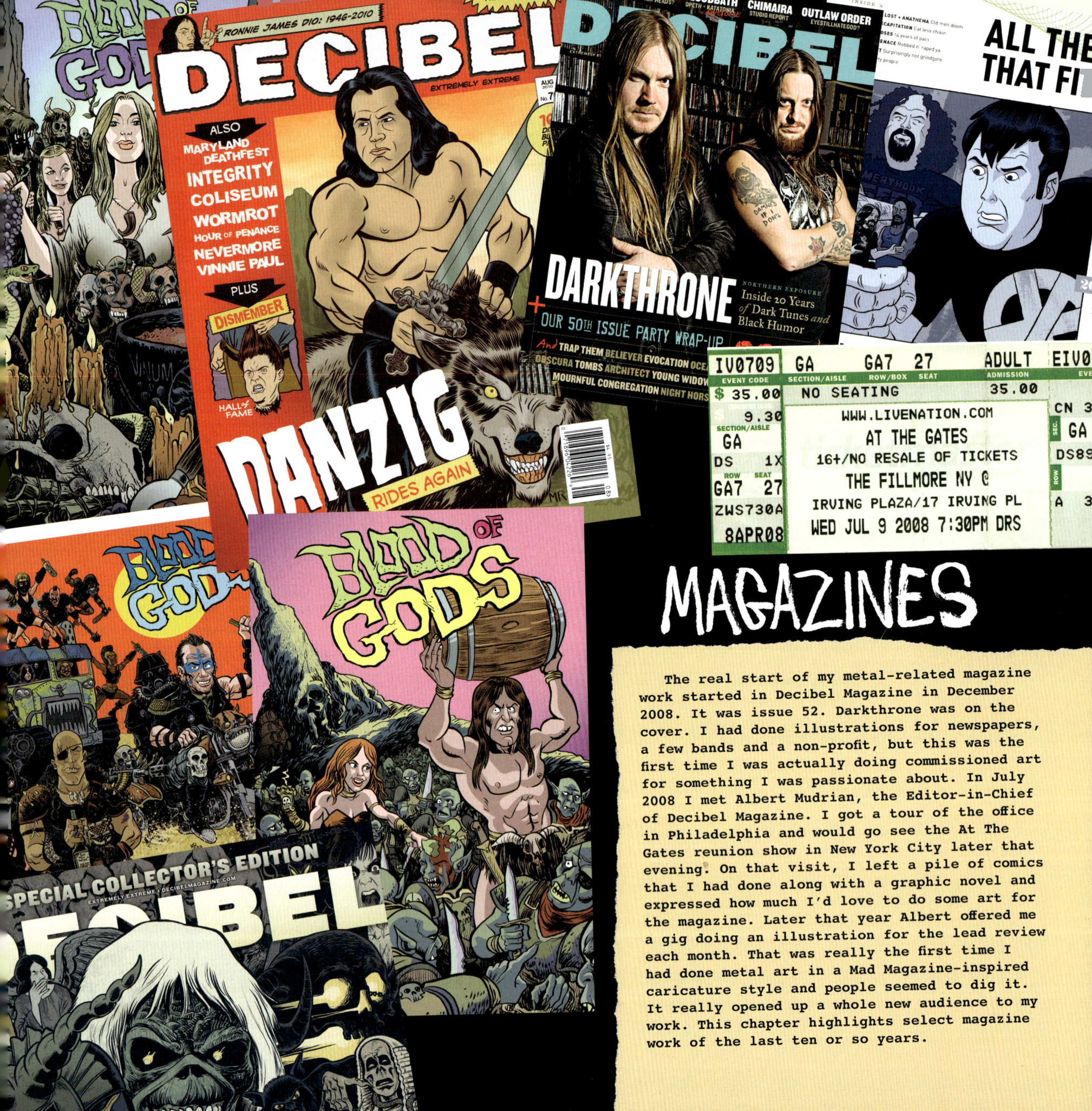

MAGAZINES

The real start of my metal-related magazine work started in Decibel Magazine in December 2008. It was issue 52. Darkthrone was on the cover. I had done illustrations for newspapers, a few bands and a non-profit, but this was the first time I was actually doing commissioned art for something I was passionate about. In July 2008 I met Albert Mudrian, the Editor-in-Chief of Decibel Magazine. I got a tour of the office in Philadelphia and would go see the At The Gates reunion show in New York City later that evening. On that visit, I left a pile of comics that I had done along with a graphic novel and expressed how much I'd love to do some art for the magazine. Later that year Albert offered me a gig doing an illustration for the lead review each month. That was really the first time I had done metal art in a Mad Magazine-inspired caricature style and people seemed to dig it. It really opened up a whole new audience to my work. This chapter highlights select magazine work of the last ten or so years.

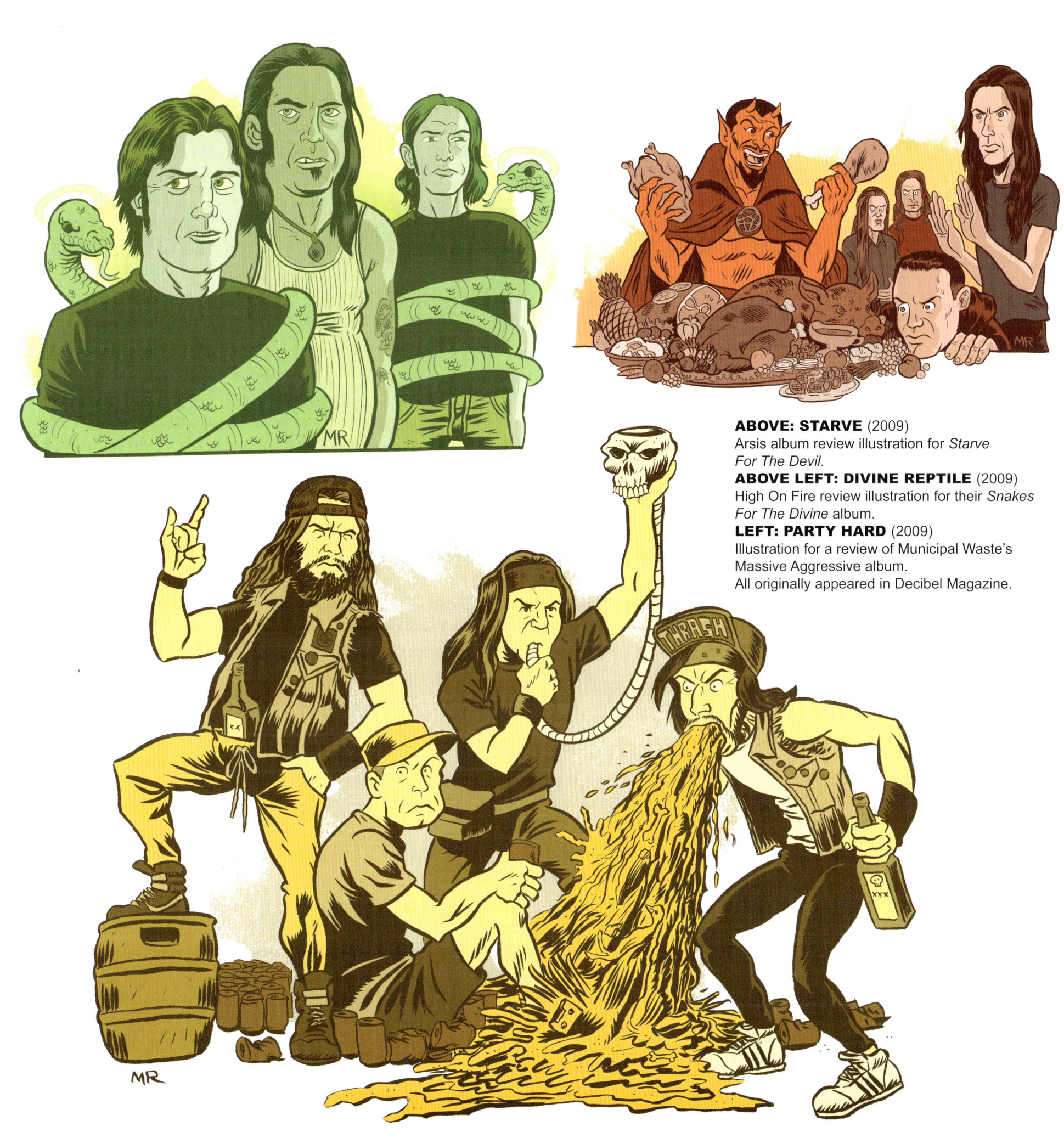

ABOVE: STARVE (2009)
Arsis album review illustration for *Starve For The Devil.*
ABOVE LEFT: DIVINE REPTILE (2009)
High On Fire review illustration for their *Snakes For The Divine* album.
LEFT: PARTY HARD (2009)
Illustration for a review of Municipal Waste's *Massive Aggressive* album.
All originally appeared in Decibel Magazine.

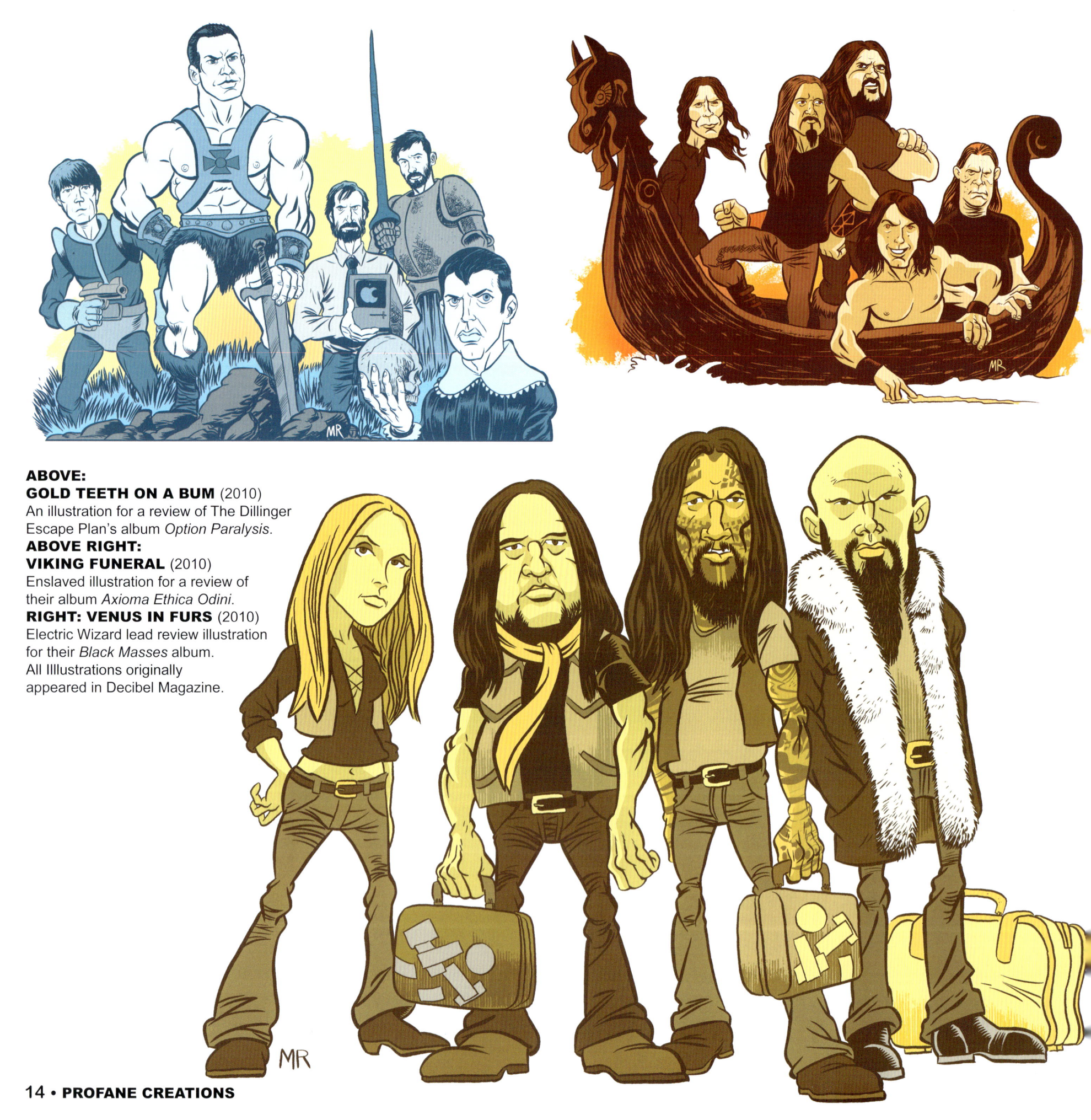

ABOVE:
GOLD TEETH ON A BUM (2010)
An illustration for a review of The Dillinger Escape Plan's album *Option Paralysis*.
ABOVE RIGHT:
VIKING FUNERAL (2010)
Enslaved illustration for a review of their album *Axioma Ethica Odini*.
RIGHT: VENUS IN FURS (2010)
Electric Wizard lead review illustration for their *Black Masses* album.
All Illlustrations originally appeared in Decibel Magazine.

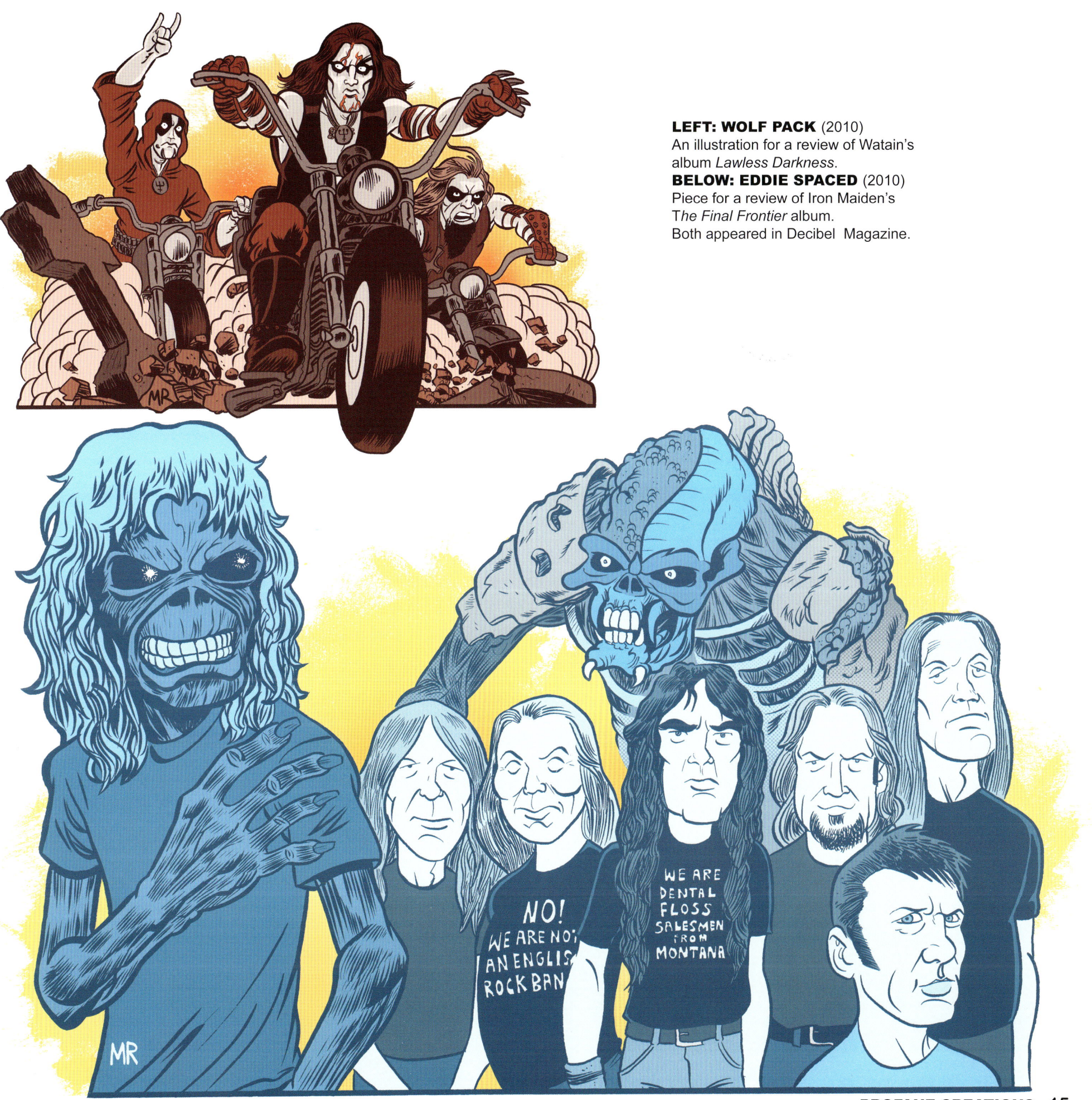

LEFT: WOLF PACK (2010)
An illustration for a review of Watain's album *Lawless Darkness*.
BELOW: EDDIE SPACED (2010)
Piece for a review of Iron Maiden's *The Final Frontier* album.
Both appeared in Decibel Magazine.

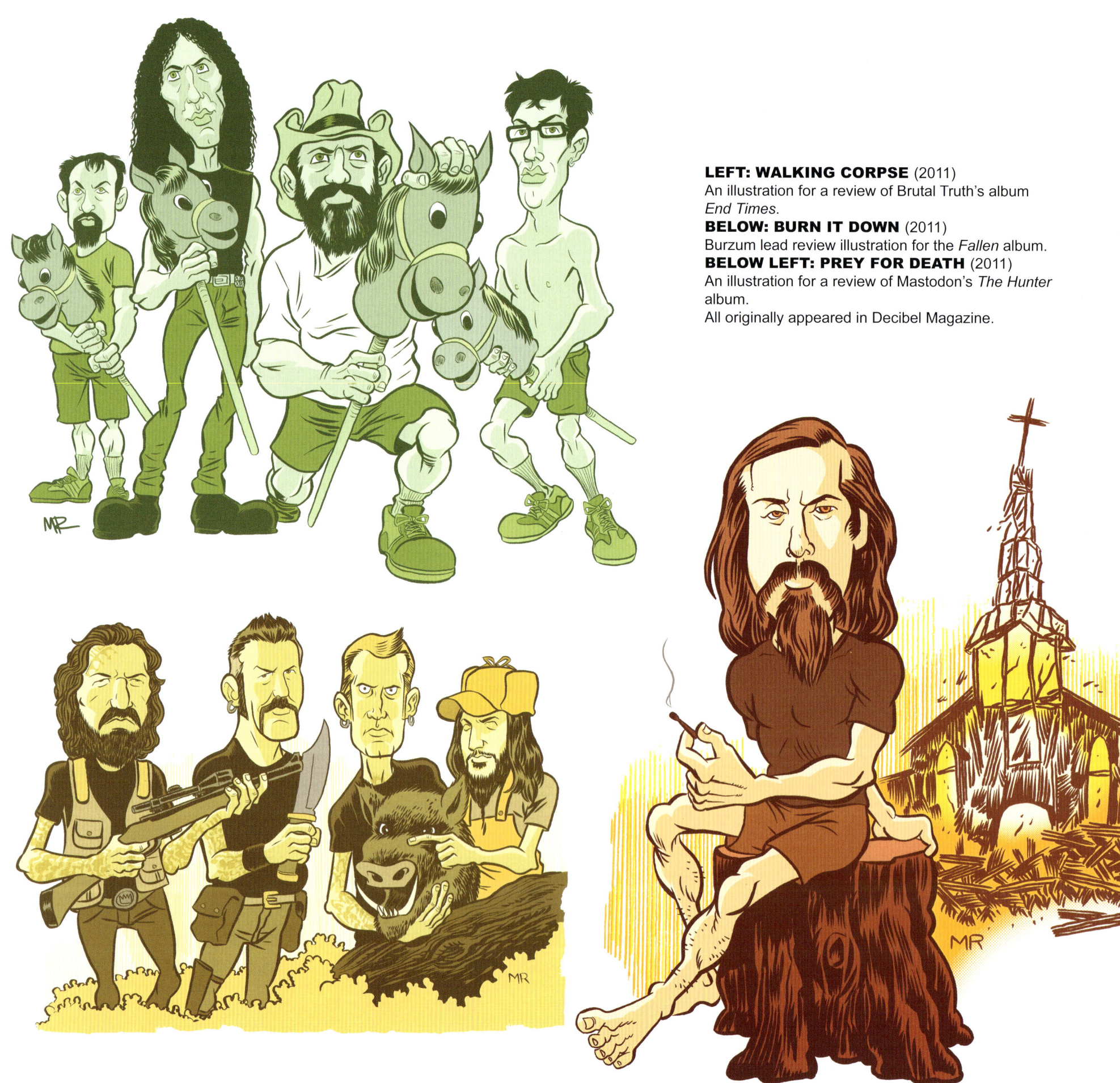

LEFT: WALKING CORPSE (2011)
An illustration for a review of Brutal Truth's album *End Times*.
BELOW: BURN IT DOWN (2011)
Burzum lead review illustration for the *Fallen* album.
BELOW LEFT: PREY FOR DEATH (2011)
An illustration for a review of Mastodon's *The Hunter* album.
All originally appeared in Decibel Magazine.

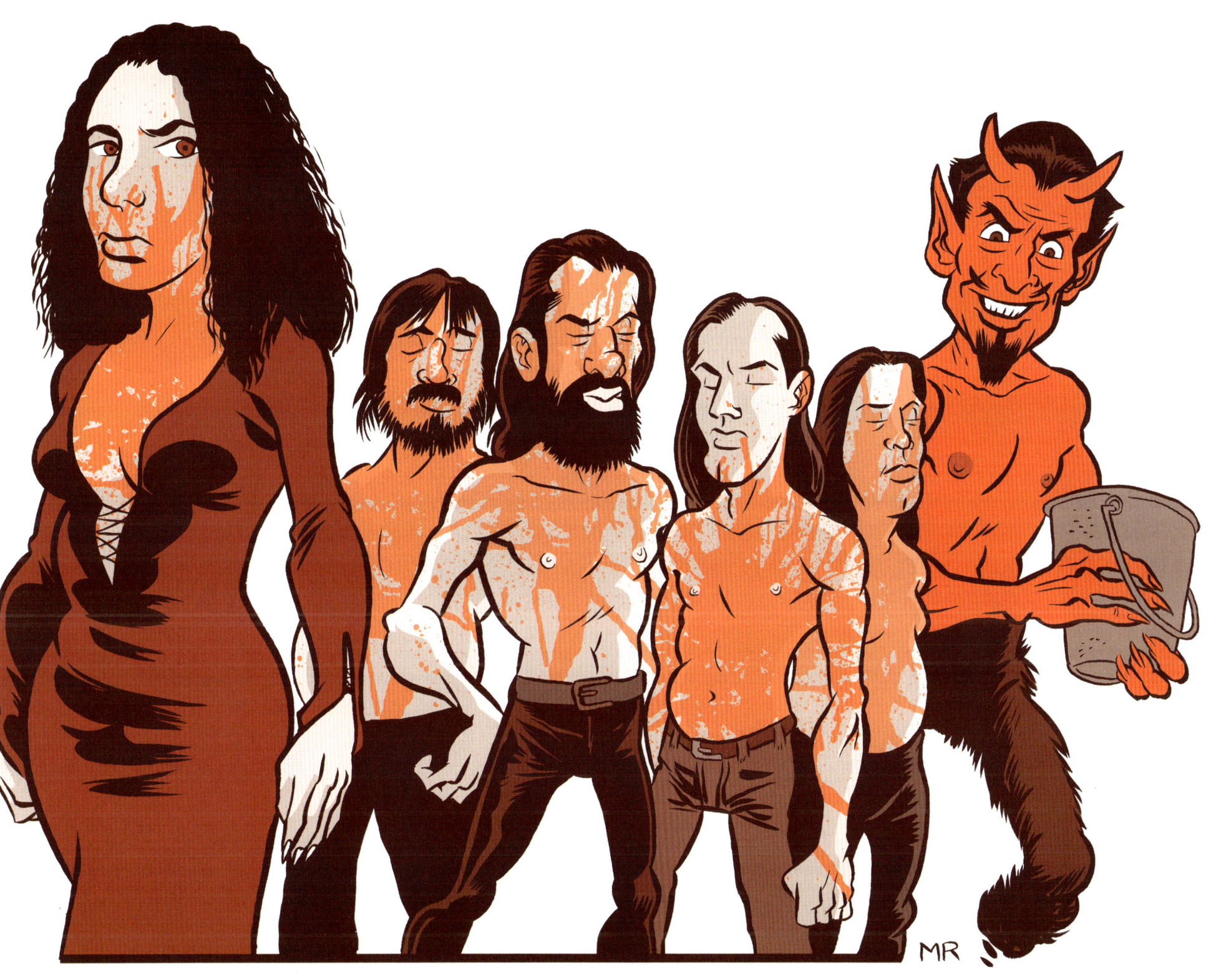

BLOOD FOR THE MASTER (2011)
Illustration for a review of the album *The Thousandfold Epicentre* by The Devil's Blood. From Decibel Magazine.

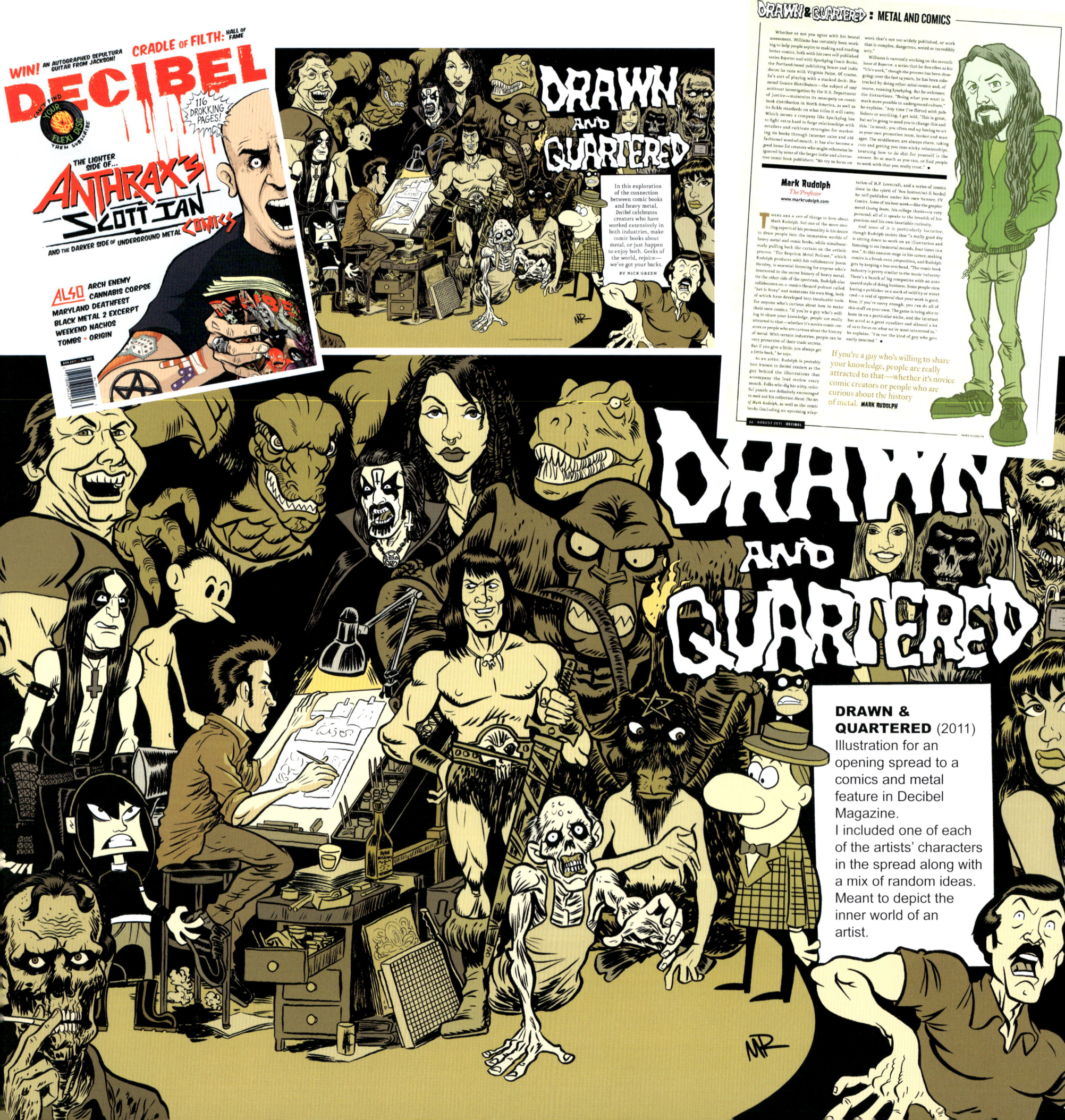

DRAWN &
QUARTERED (2011)
Illustration for an
opening spread to a
comics and metal
feature in Decibel
Magazine.
I included one of each
of the artists' characters
in the spread along with
a mix of random ideas.
Meant to depict the
inner world of an
artist.

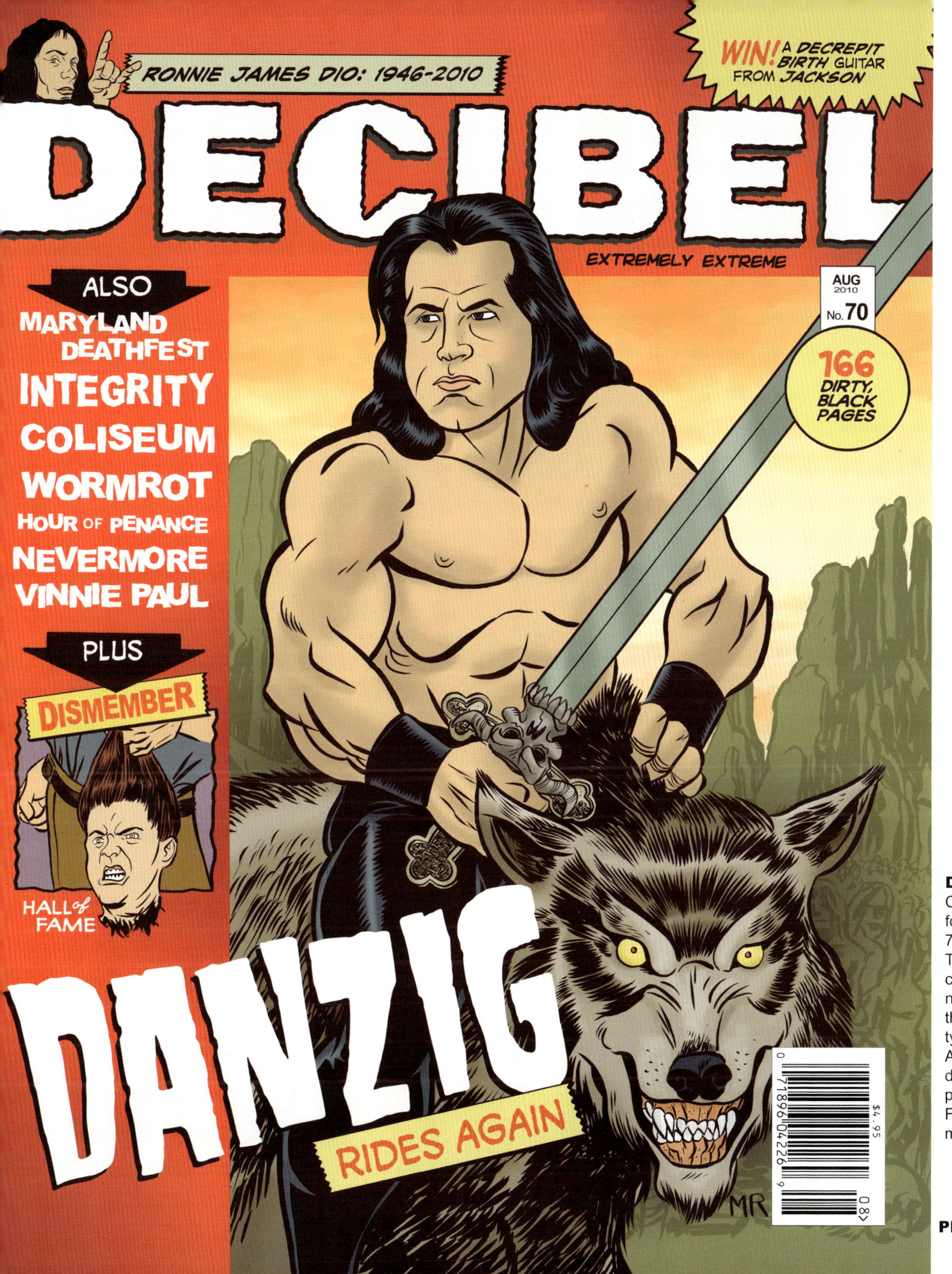

DANZIG (2010)
Cover illustration and design for Decibel Magazine number 70. August 2010.
This was the first in a series of covers I did for Decibel. It was nice that I was able to change the logo and handle all the typography for the cover. Around this same time I also did another Danzig-related project for The Henry & Glenn Forever and Ever anthology mastermined by Tom Neely.

PROFANE CREATIONS • 19

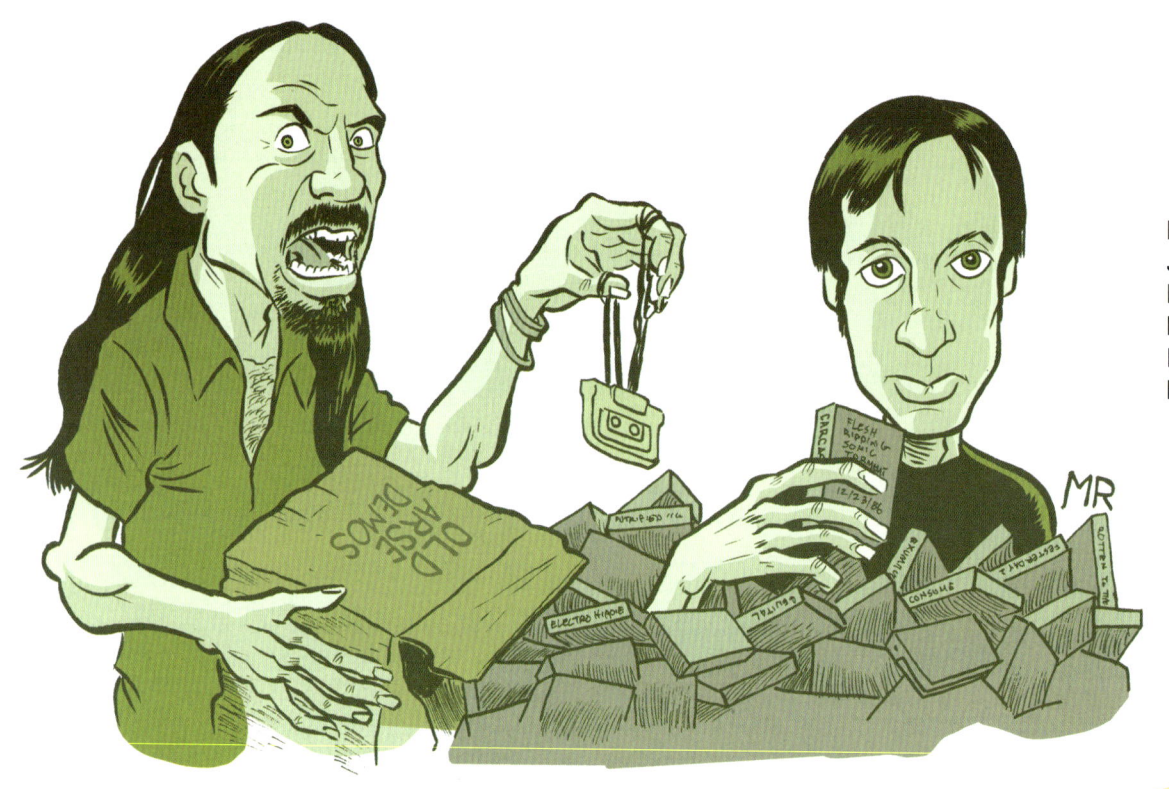

LEFT: CARCASS DEMO TAPES (2012)
Jeff Walker and Albert Mudrian Ilustration for the Southpole Dispatch column written by John Darnielle. Decibel Magazine.
BELOW: THE END IS NEAR (2012)
Illustration of Venom's Cronos from his column that appeared Metal Hammer UK about the end times.

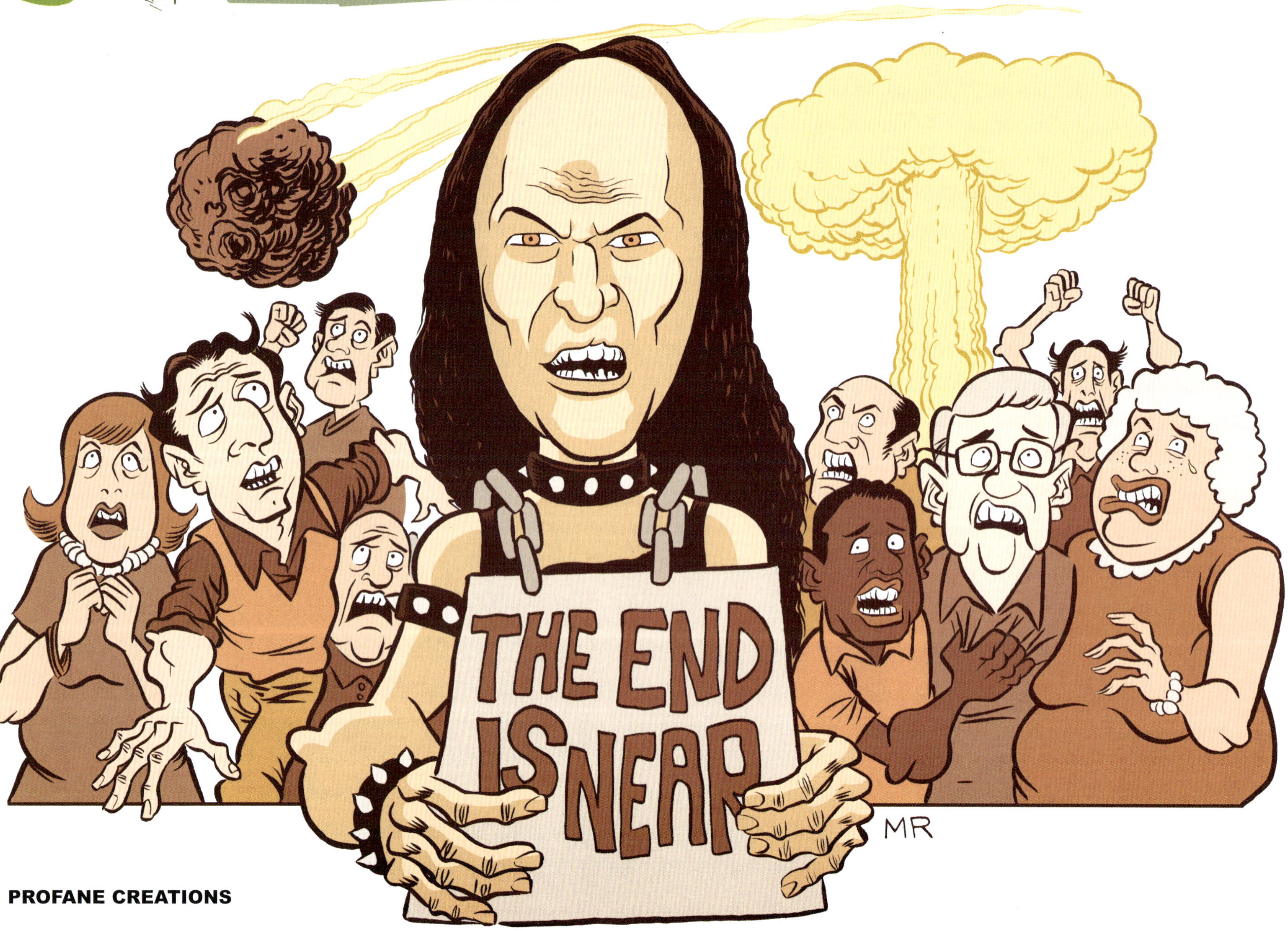

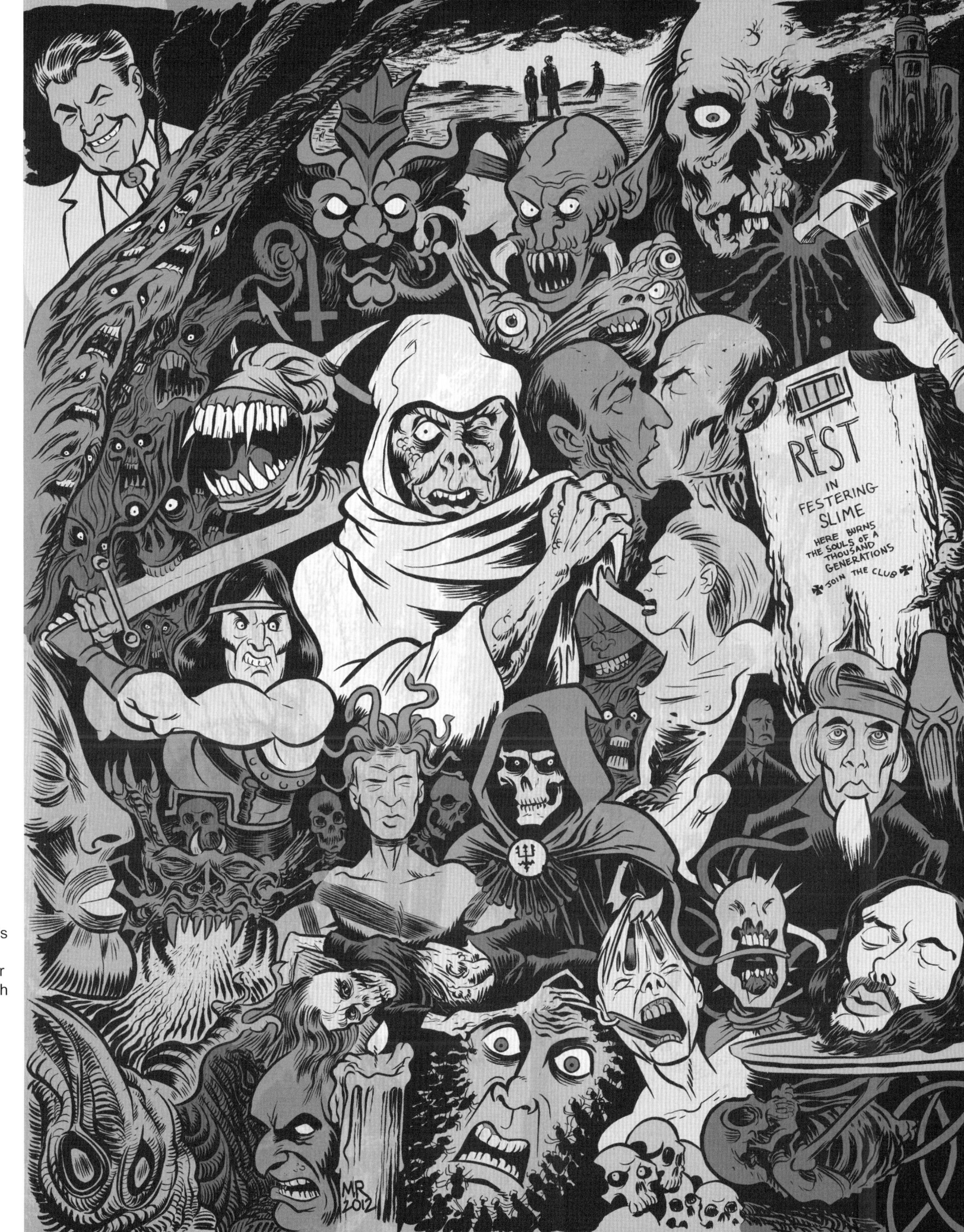

DEATH METAL (2012)
Cover illustration for Decibel's special Death Metal issue. A montage of 34 different cover elements of the top 100 death metal albums of all time.

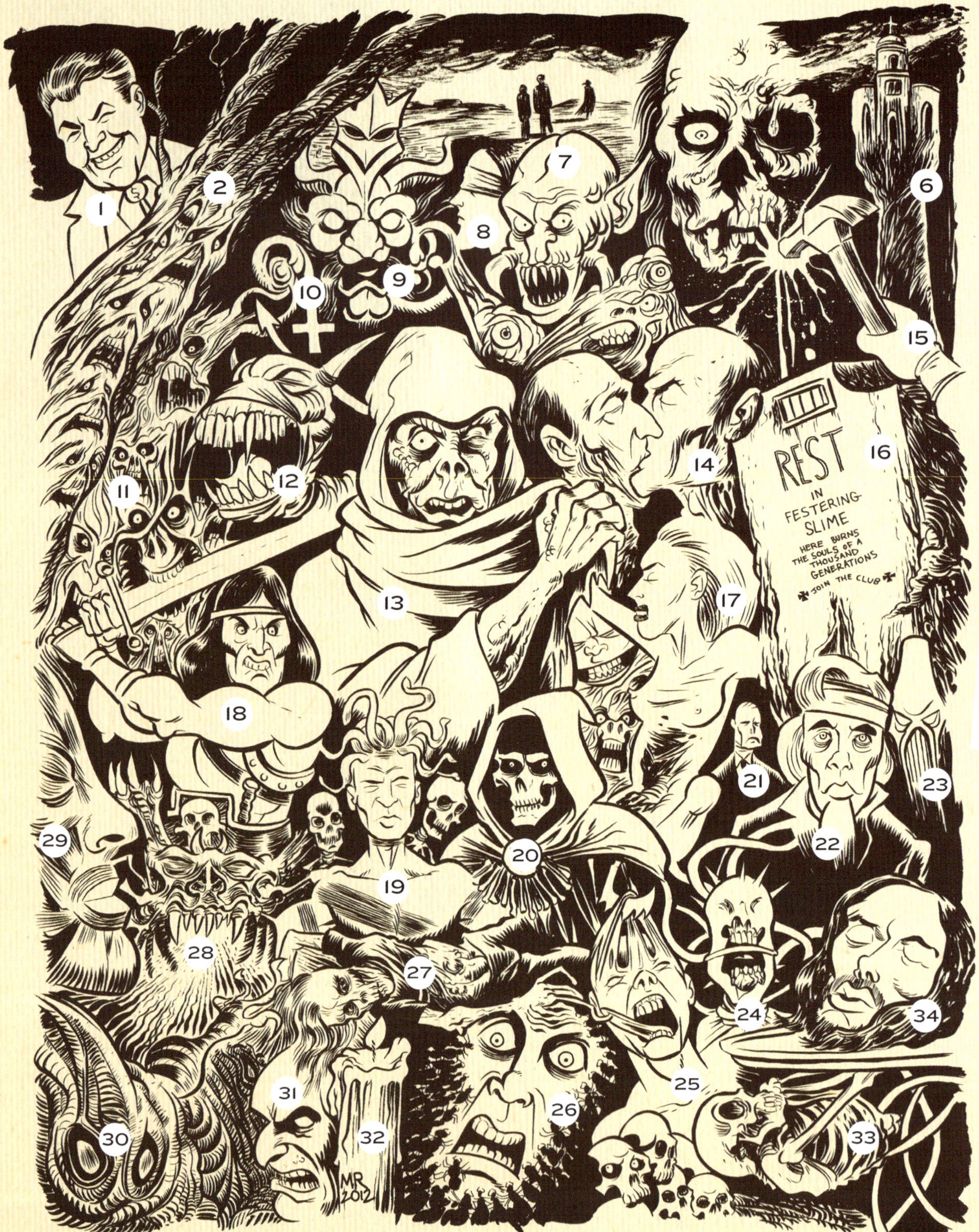

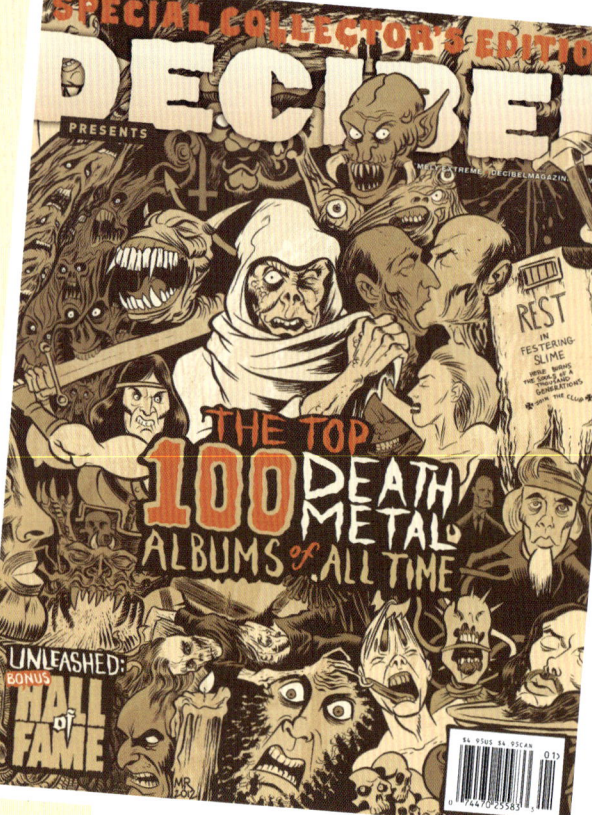

1. DEATH - Spiritual Healing
2. OBITUARY - Cause of Death
3. IN FLAMES - The Jester Race
4. DARKTHRONE - Soulside Journey
5. REPULSION - Horrified
6. GRAVE - Into the Grave
7. MASSACRE - From Beyond
8. EUCHARIST - A Velvet Creation

9. DEICIDE - Deicide
10. POSSESSED - Seven Churches
11. MORBID ANGEL - Altars of Madness
12. AUTOPSY - Mental Funeral
13. DEATH - Leprosy
14. PUNGENT STENCH - Been Caught Buttering
15. CARCASS - Necrotiscism...
16. ENTOMBED - Left Hand Path
17. CANNIBAL CORPSE - Tomb of the Mutilated

18. BOLT THROWER - Warmaster
19. RIPPING CORPSE - Dreaming with the Dead
20. DISSECTION - Storm of the Light's Bane
21. DECEASED - Fearless Undead Machines
22. DYING FETUS - Destroy All Opposition
23. DEMILICH - Nespithe
24. VADER - De Profundis
25. AUTOPSY - Severed Survival
26. PESTILENCE - Consuming Impulse

27. OBITUARY - Slowly We Rot
28. DISMEMBER - Like an Everflowing Stream
29. NAPALM DEATH - Harmony Corruption
30. ASPHYX - The Rack
31. BLOODBATH - Nightmares Made Flesh
32. MORBID ANGEL - Covenant
33. TIAMAT - The Astral Sleep
34. CRYPTOPSY - None So Vile

RIGHT: THE VOYAGE HOME (2012)
An illustration from a column by Joseph Duplantier from Gojira discussing Greenpeace's efforts to save the whales. Originally appeared in Metal Hammer UK.

BELOW: DEAD END STREET (2012)
Lead review illustration for the Katatonia album *Dead End Kings* from Decibel Magazine.

BELOW RIGHT: BORN AGAIN (2012)
A piece that accompanied Janne "JB" Christoffersson of Grand Magus column about his love of Black Sabbath. Originally appeared in Metal Hammer UK.

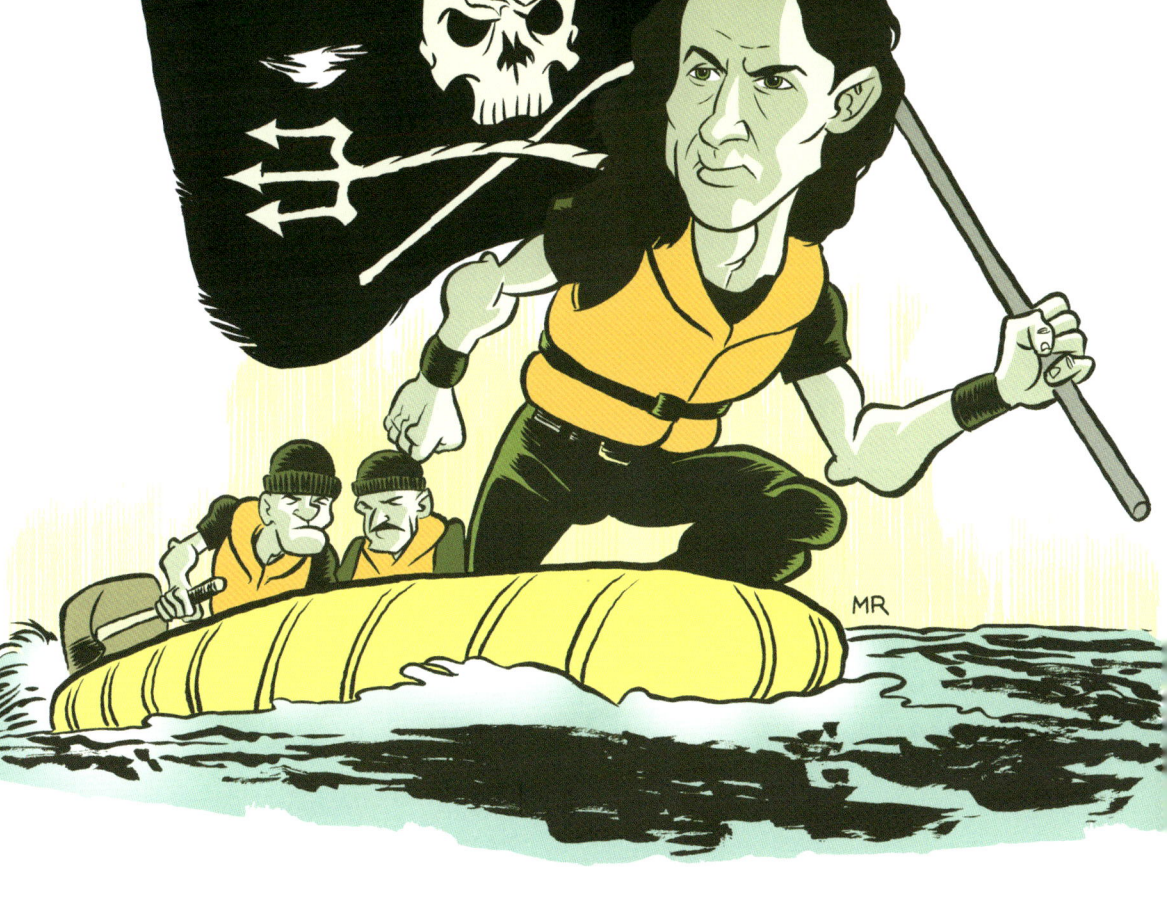

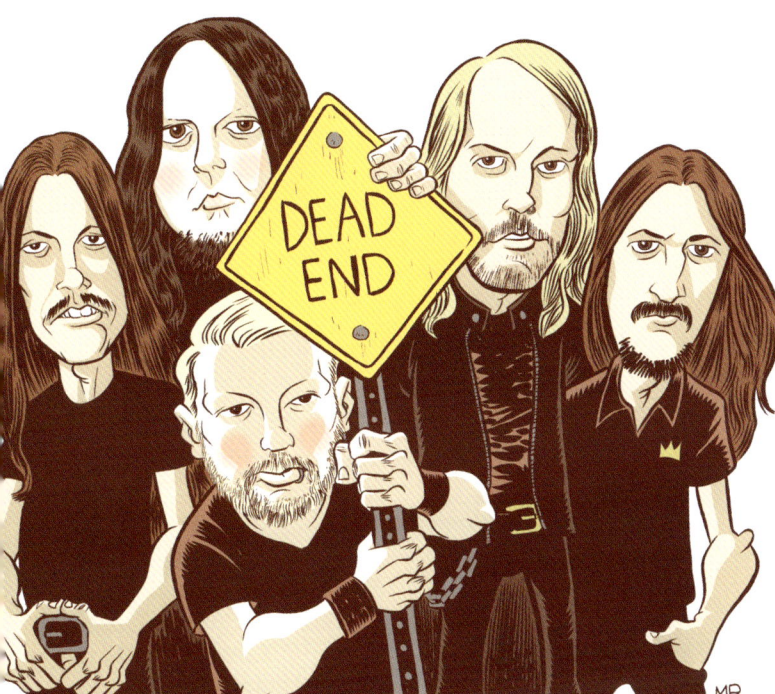

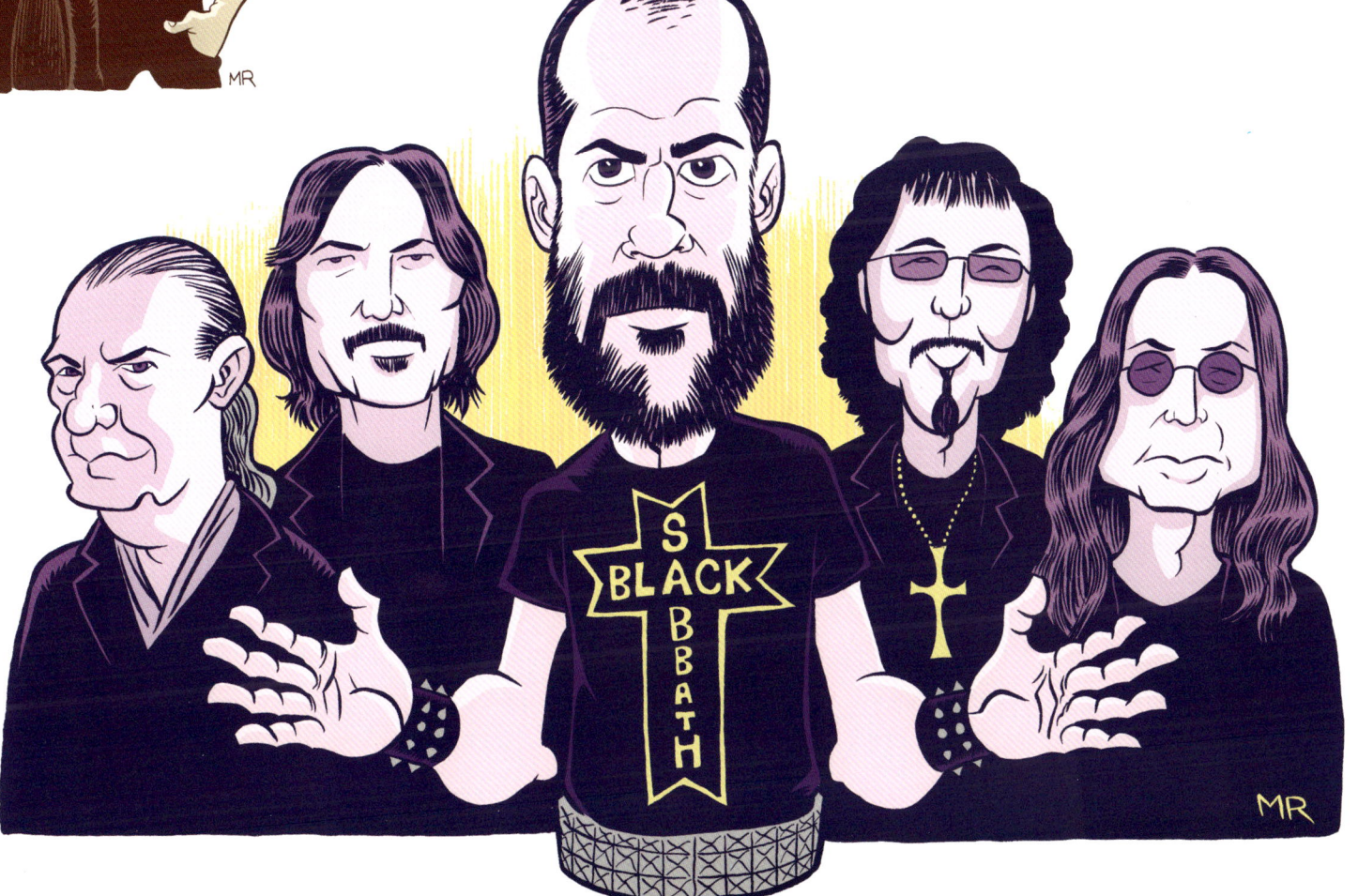

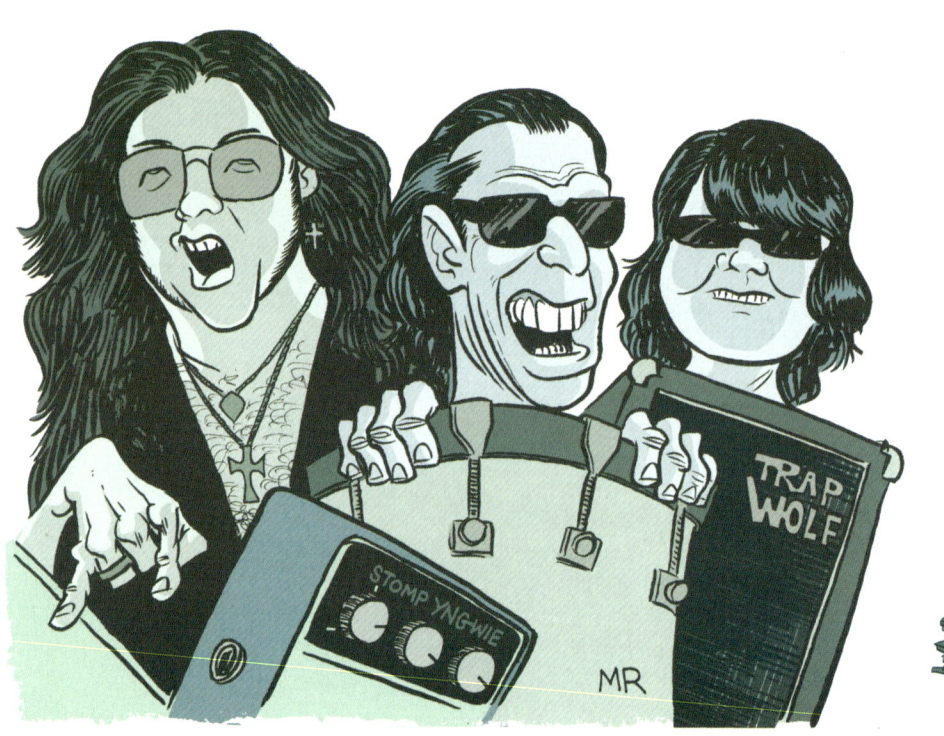

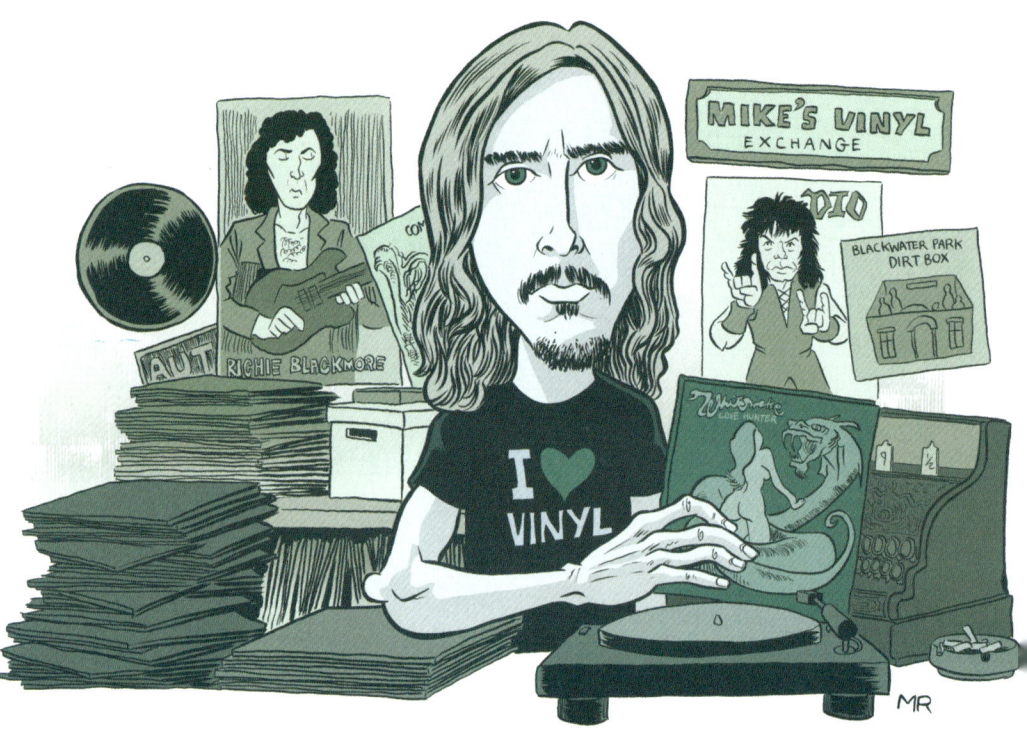

ABOVE LEFT: YNGWIE, THE HORSE & THE WOLF (2012)
A Southpole Dispatch illustration featuring Yngwie Malmsteen, Alex Van Halen and Guitar Wolf. Originally appeared in Decibel Magazine.

ABOVE: SLIDE IT IN (2012)
Mikael Akerfeldt from Opeth illustration from his Metal Hammer UK column about his love of vinyl records.

BELOW: POLYRHYTHMS (2012)
A piece that accompanied the lead review for Meshuggah's *Koloss* album.

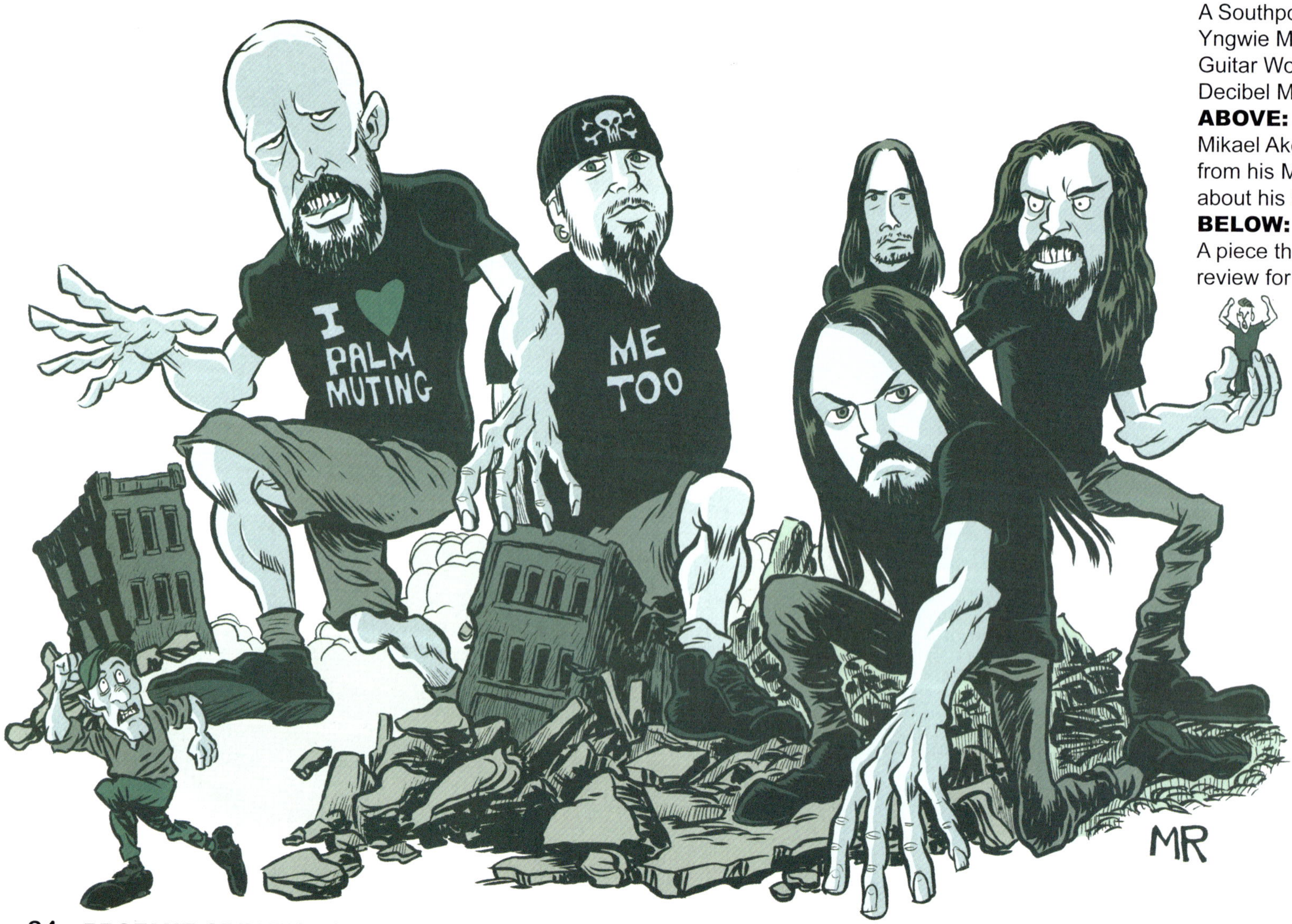

RIGHT: BURN THE WITCH (2012)
Lead review illustration for Pig Destroyer's *Book Burner* album.
BELOW: THE GLORIOUS END (2012)
Illustration for a review of Paradise Lost's *Tragic Idol* album.
Both appeared in Decibel Magazine.

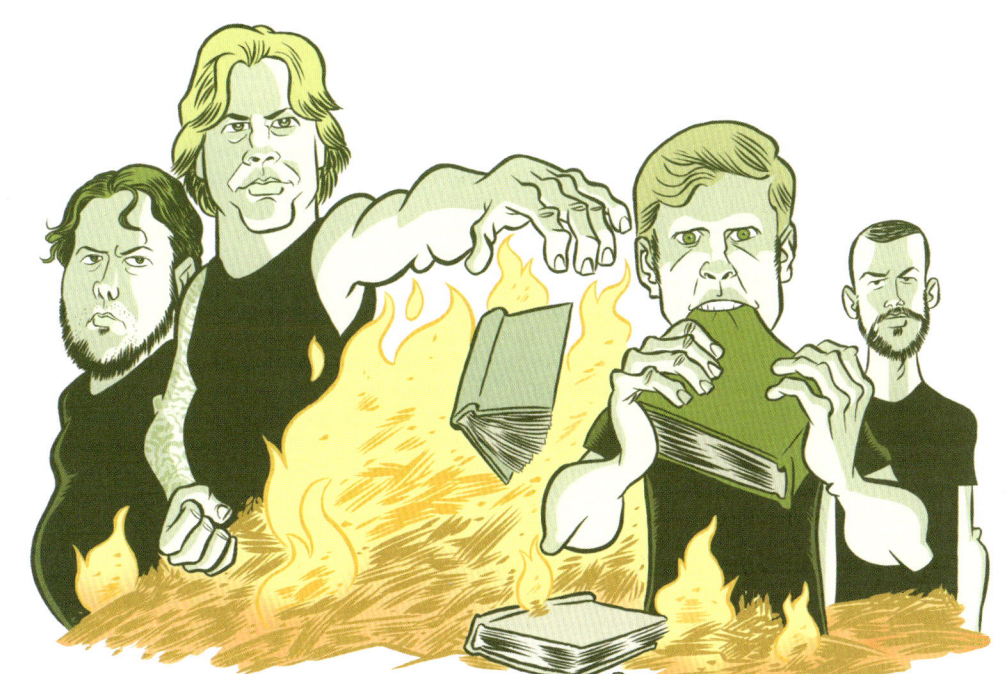

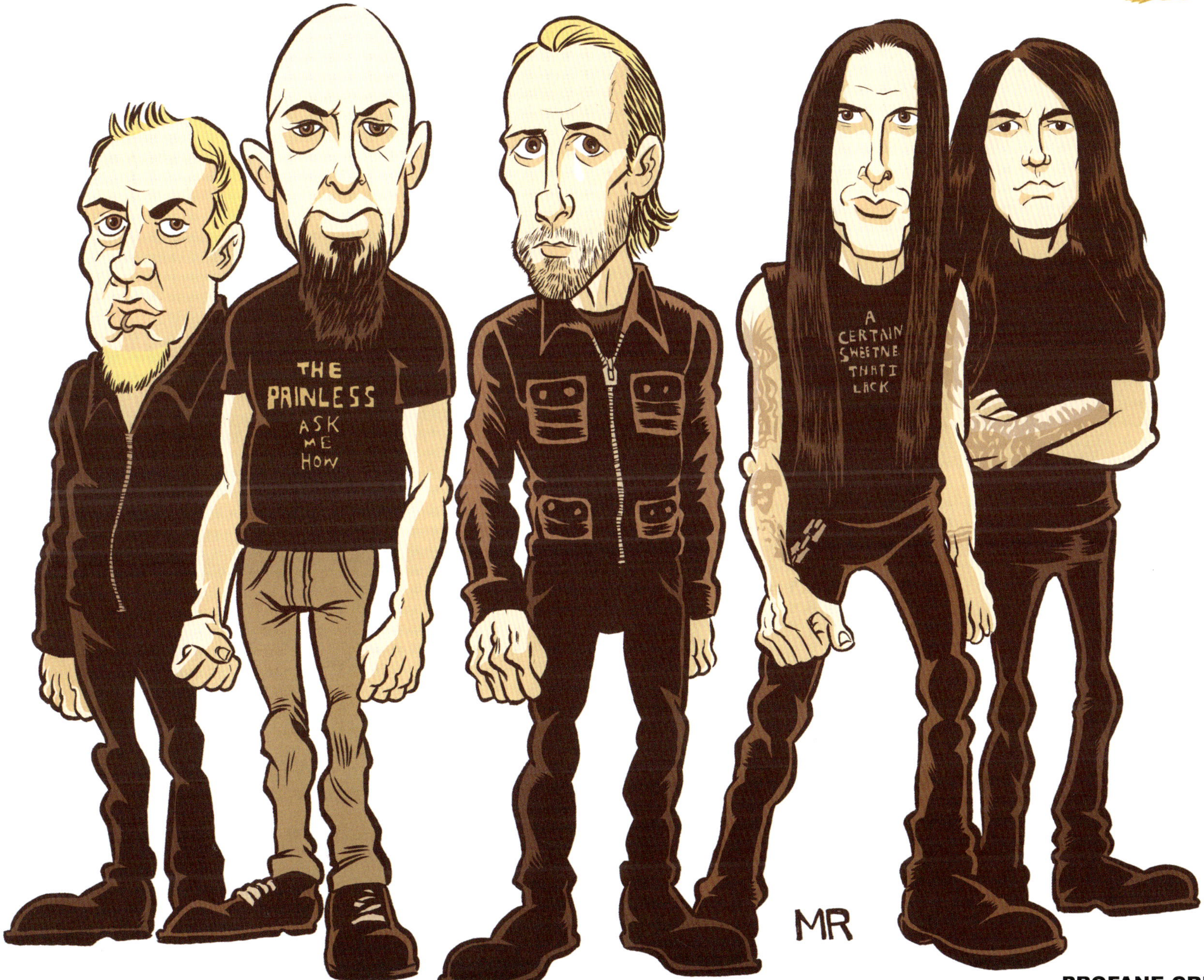

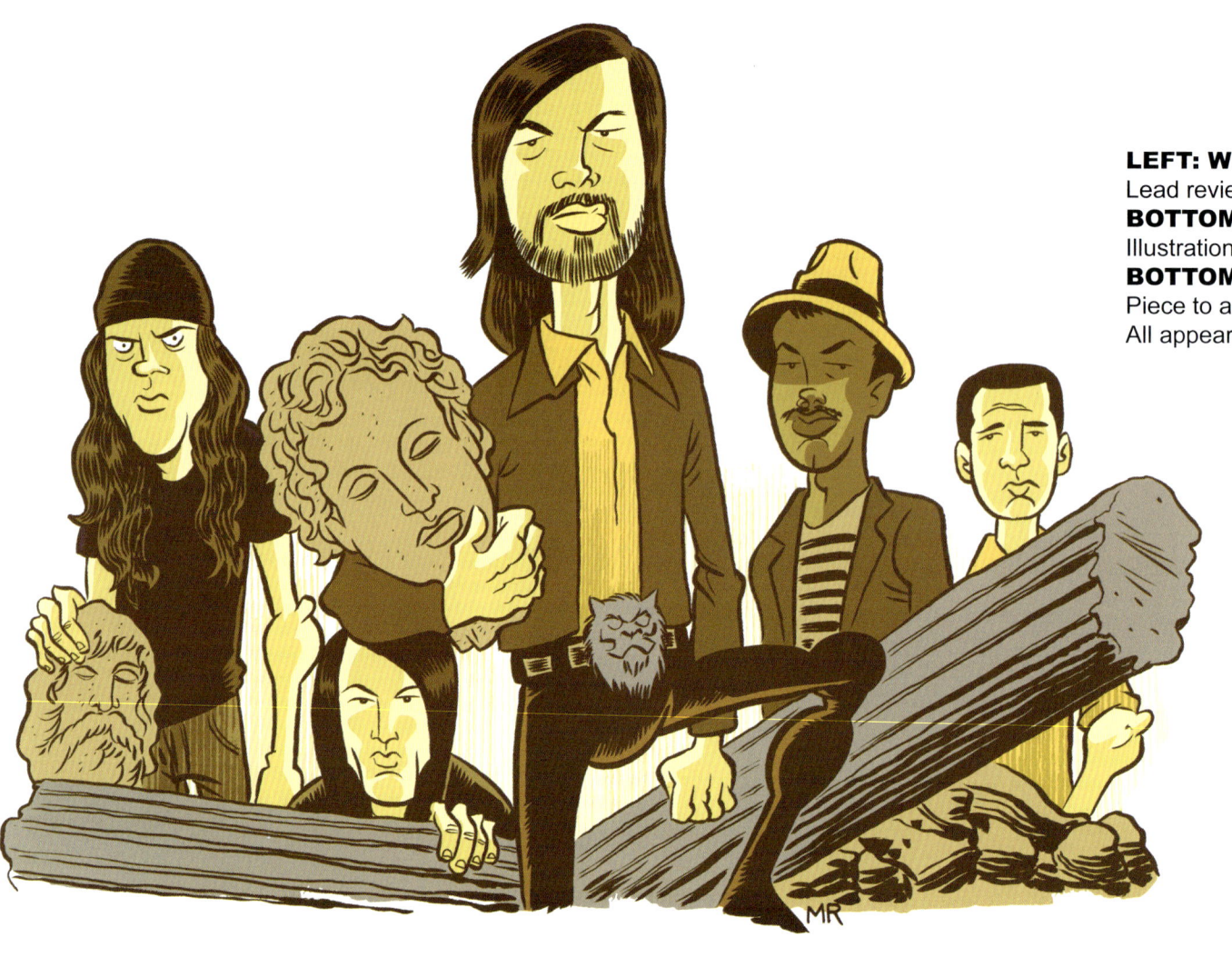

LEFT: WITCHFINDER (2012)
Lead review illustration for Witchcraft's *Legend* album.
BOTTOM LEFT: STEEL SURGERY (2013)
Illustration for the review of Carcass' *Surgical Steel.*
BOTTOM: CANNIBALL CORPSE (2013)
Piece to accompany a Southpole Dispatch column.
All appeared in Decibel Magazine.

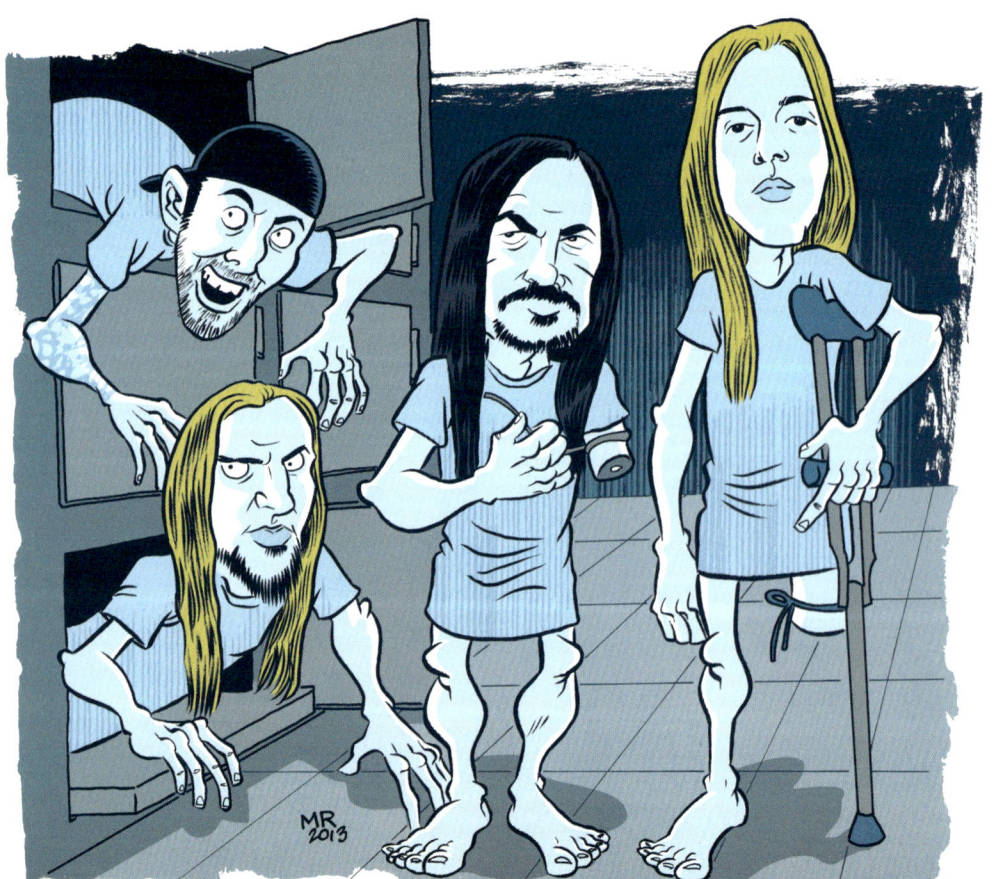

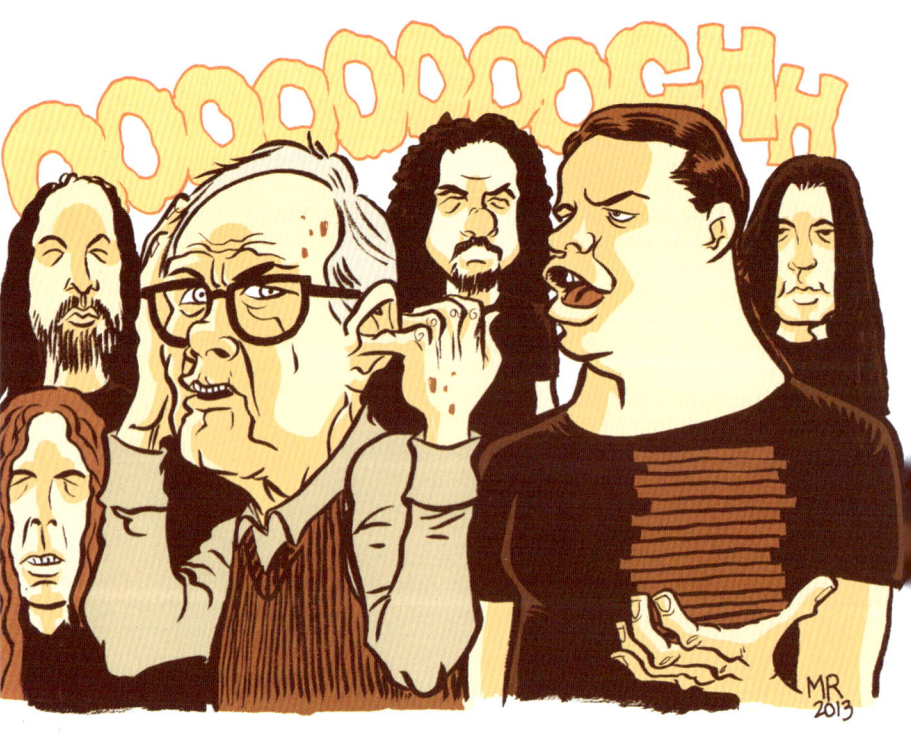

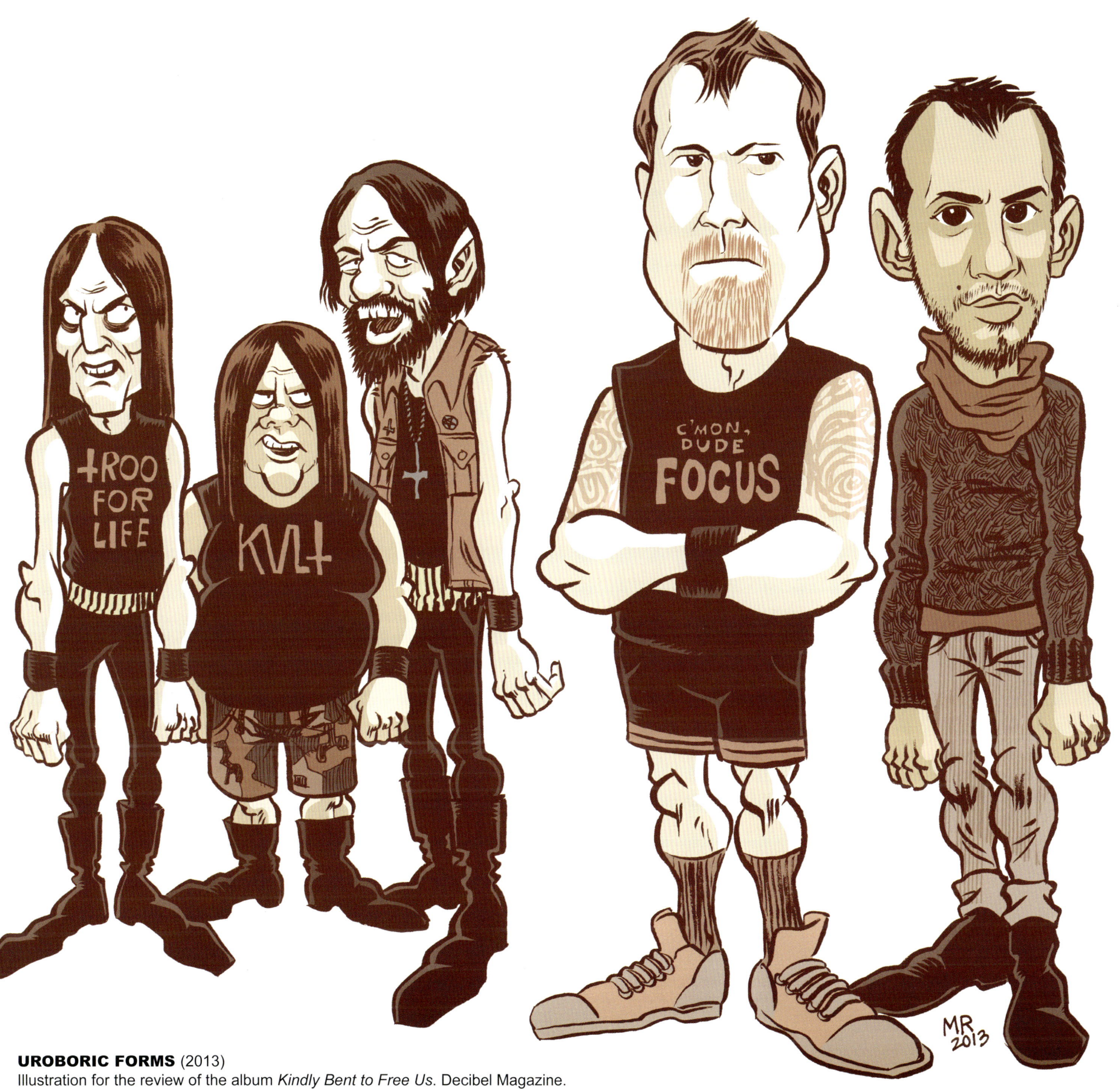

UROBORIC FORMS (2013)
Illustration for the review of the album *Kindly Bent to Free Us*. Decibel Magazine.

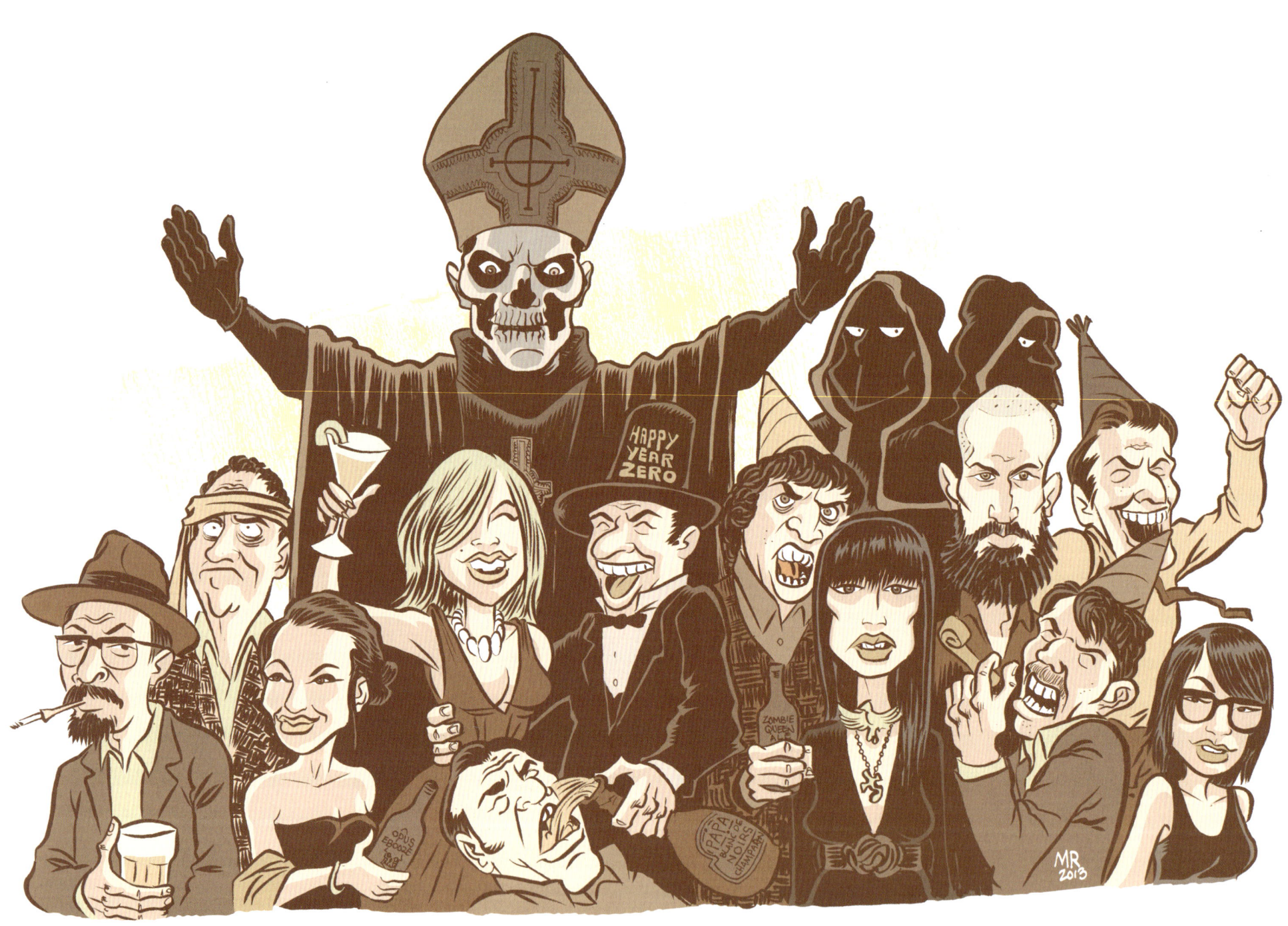

NEW YEAR, NEW PAPA (2013)
Illustration for a column from Papa Emeritus from Ghost about New Years resolutions. Originally appeared in Metal Hammer UK.

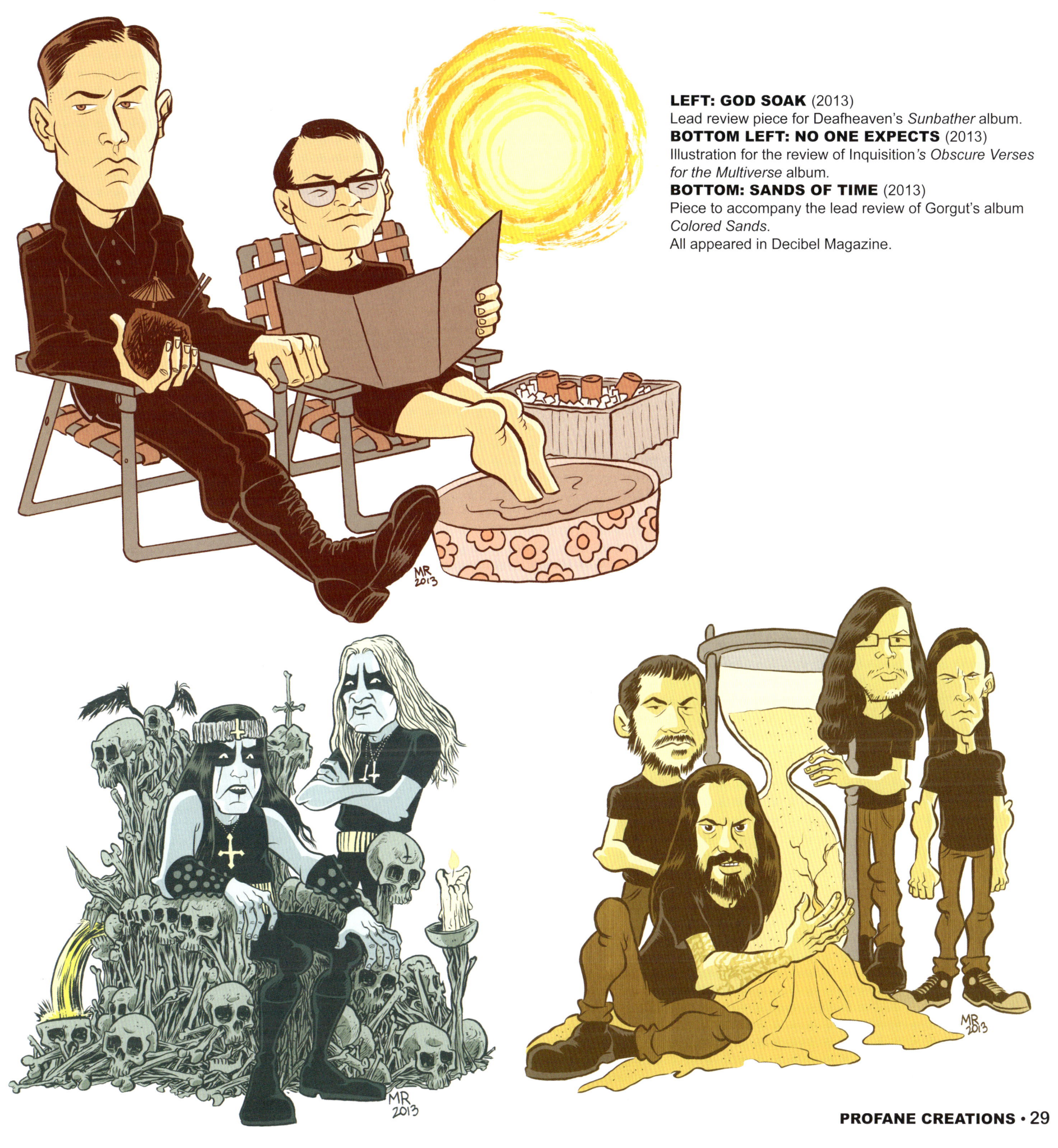

LEFT: GOD SOAK (2013)
Lead review piece for Deafheaven's *Sunbather* album.
BOTTOM LEFT: NO ONE EXPECTS (2013)
Illustration for the review of Inquisition's *Obscure Verses for the Multiverse* album.
BOTTOM: SANDS OF TIME (2013)
Piece to accompany the lead review of Gorgut's album *Colored Sands*.
All appeared in Decibel Magazine.

RIGHT: CORPORATE MASTERS (2013)
Illustration for a column by Jello Biafra about questioning our leaders from Metal Hammer UK.
BOTTOM LEFT: MUTOIDED (2013)
Illustration for the review of Mutoid Man*'s Bleeder* EP in Decibel Magazine.
BOTTOM RIGHT:
MAKEUP BREAKDOWN (2013)
Piece to accompany a column written by King Diamond about his various makeup looks. From Metal Hammer UK.

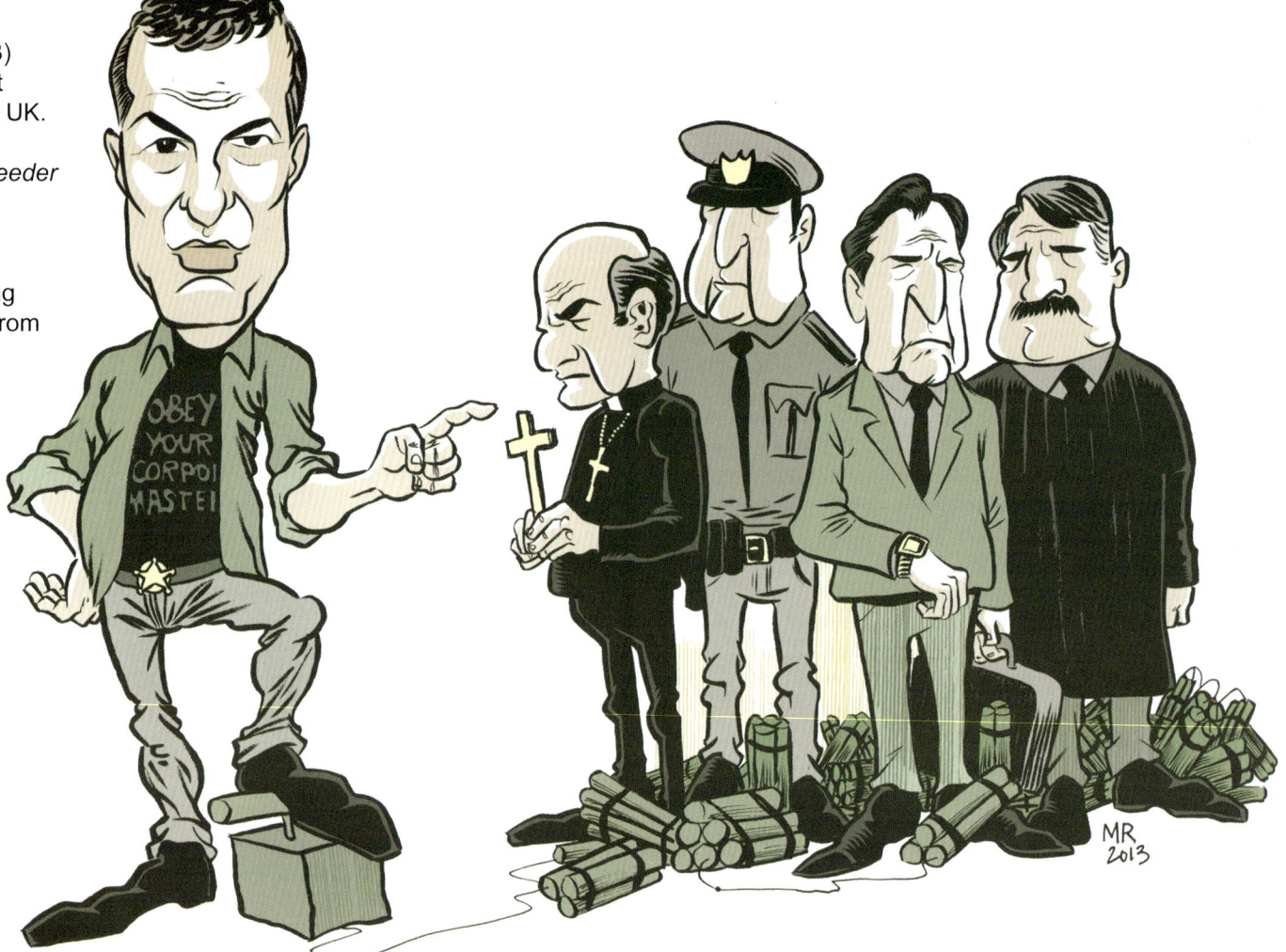

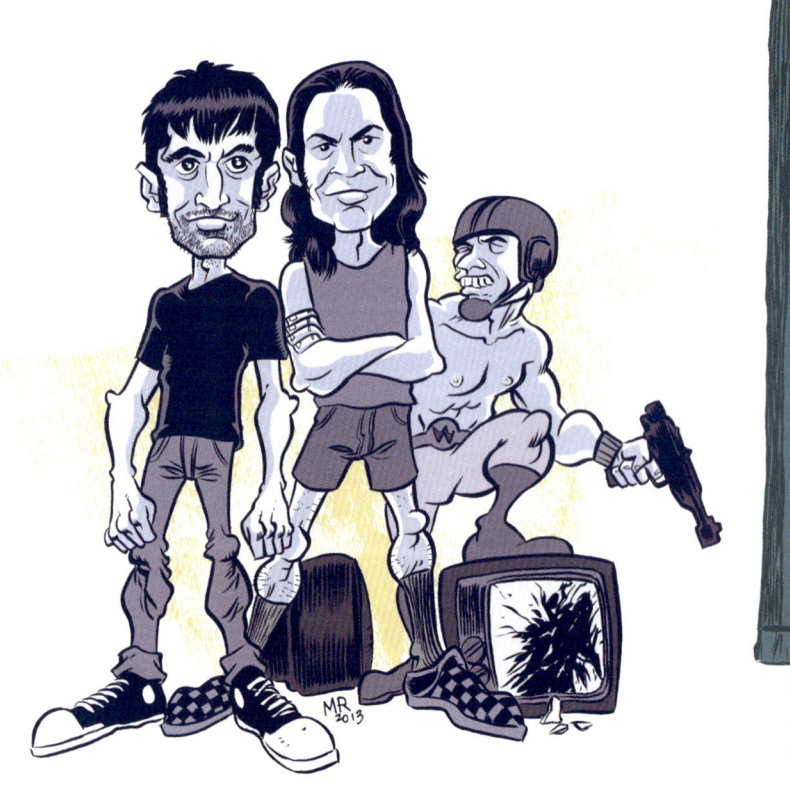

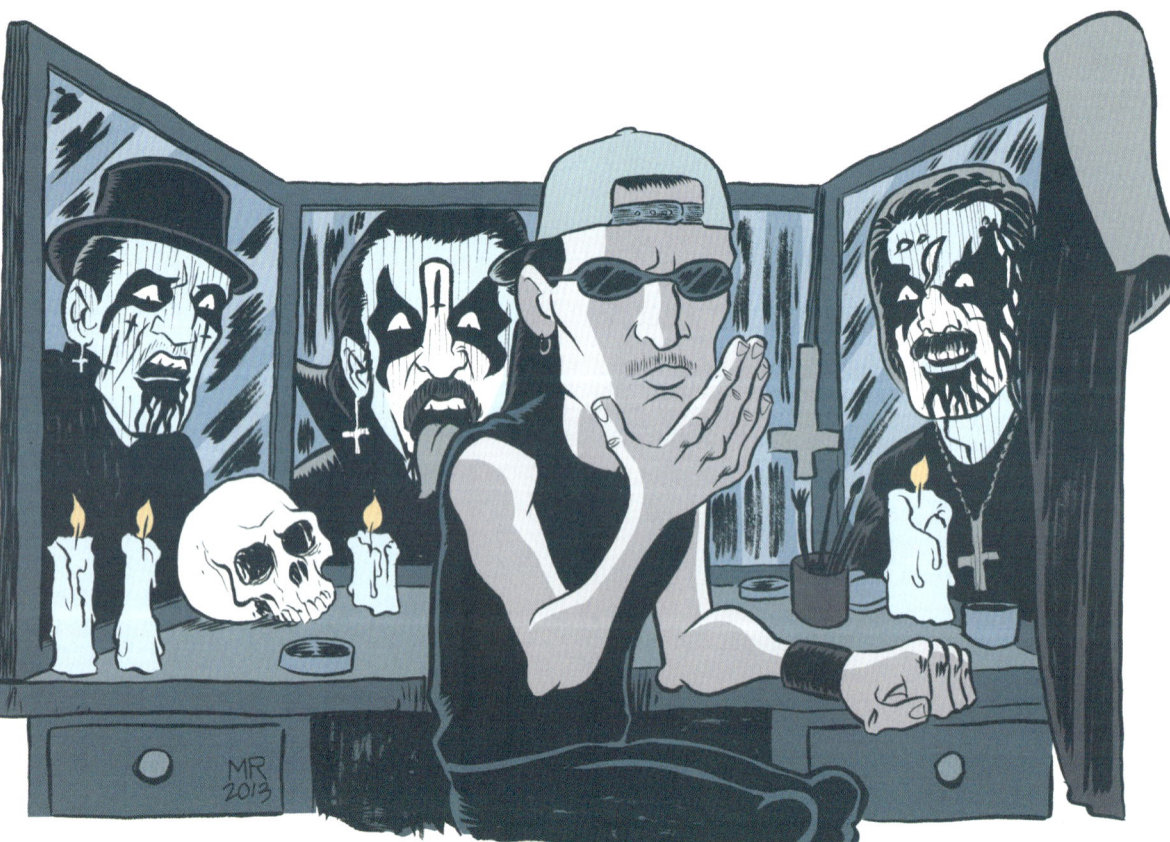

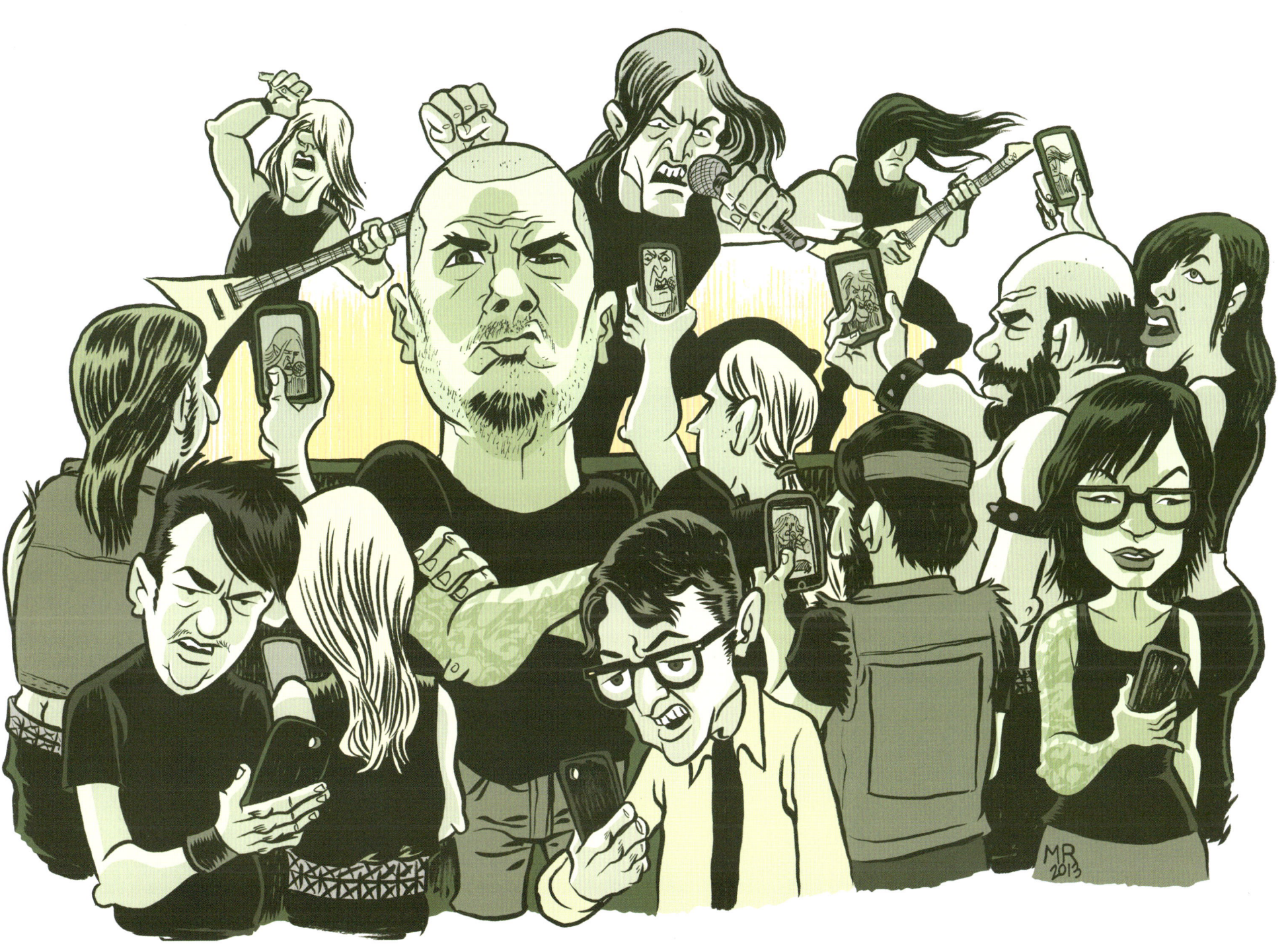

VISION THING (2013)
Illustration for a column written by Phil Anselmo about how cell phones are ruining the view at concerts.

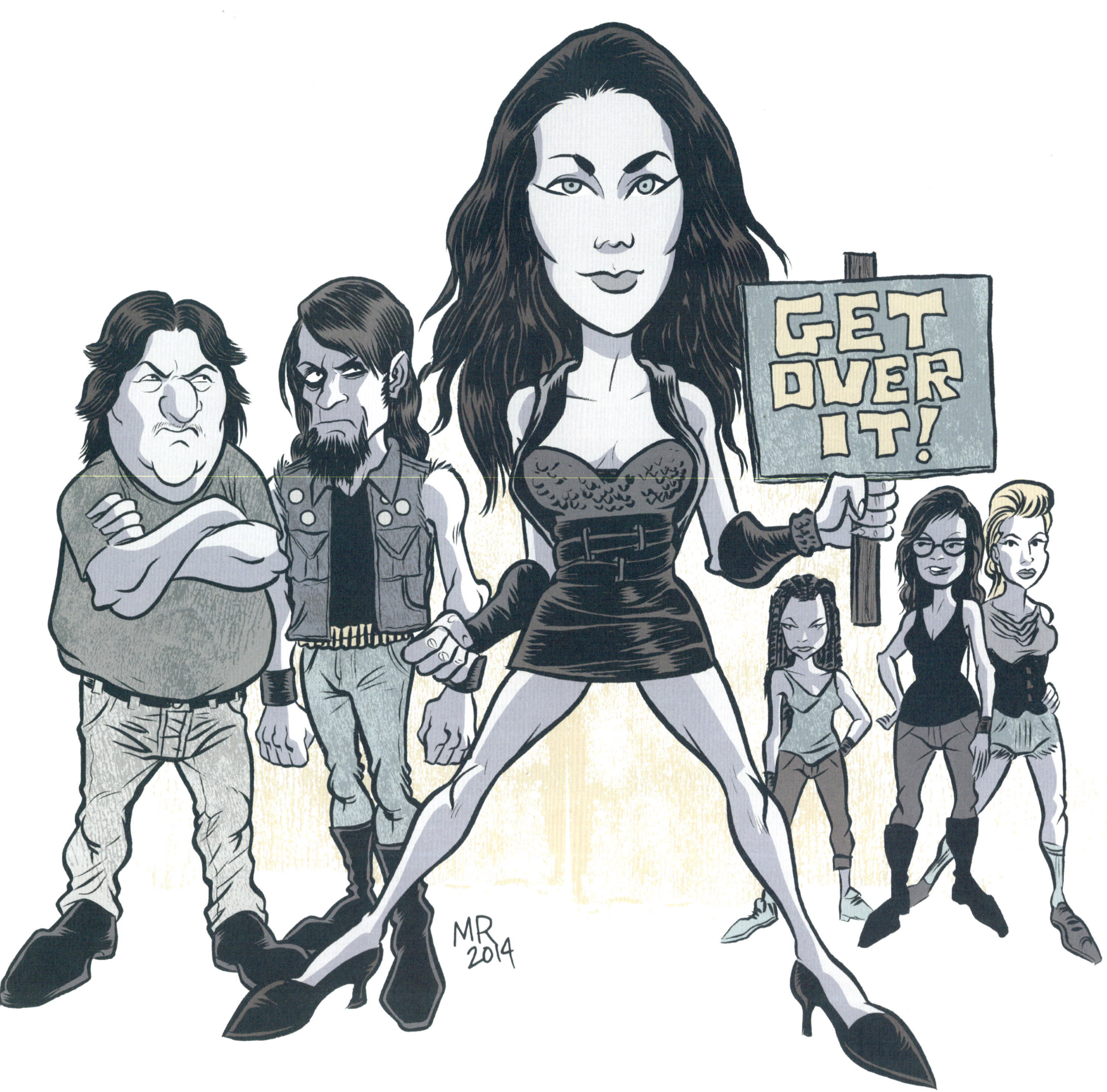

OVER-THE-TOP (2014)
Illustration for a column from Elize Ryd from Amaranthe about people being hung up on a woman fronting a metal band. Originally appeared in Metal Hammer UK.

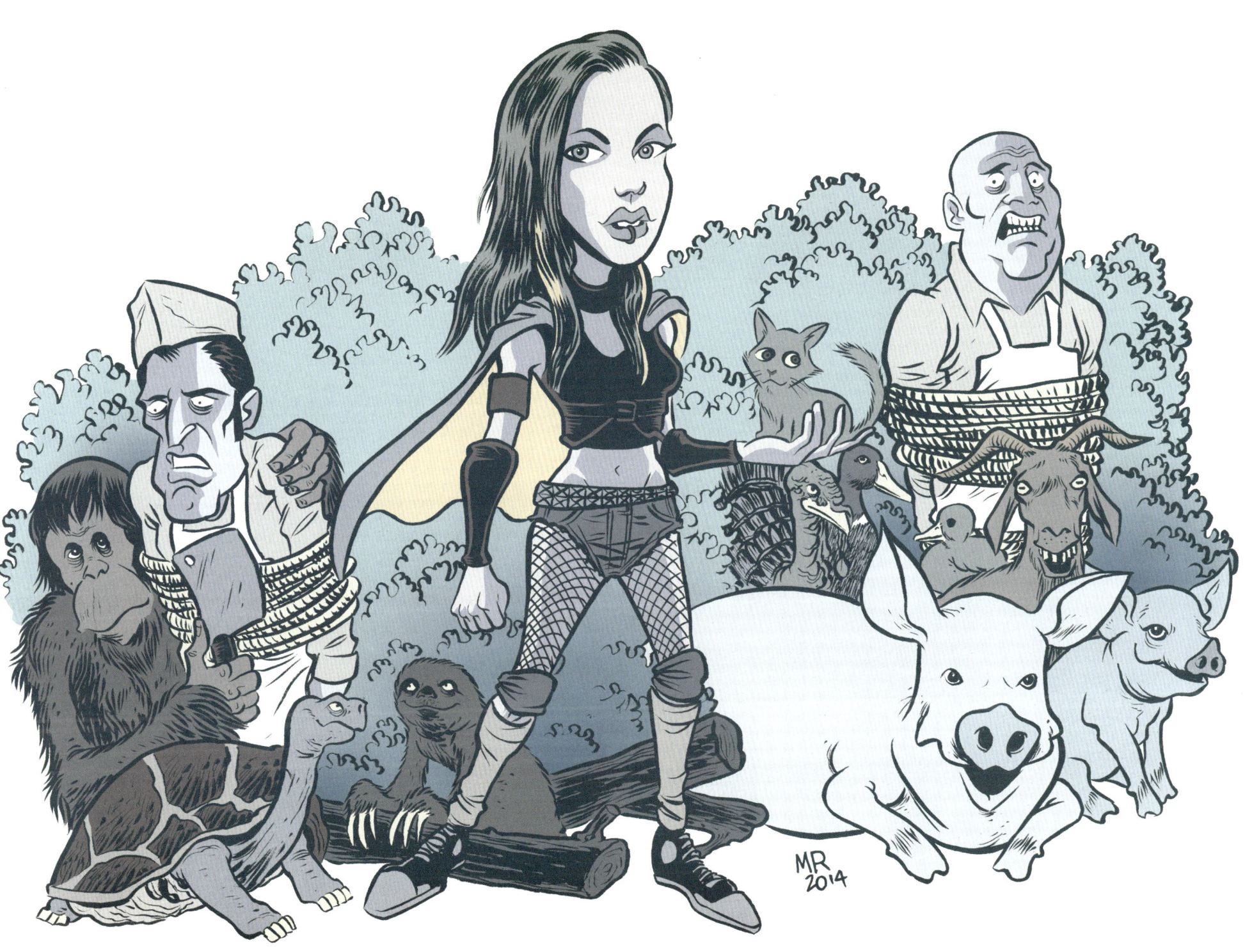

PEDIGREE BUTCHERY (2014)
Illustration for a column from Alissa White-Gluz from Arch Enemy about animal rights. Originally appeared in Metal Hammer UK.

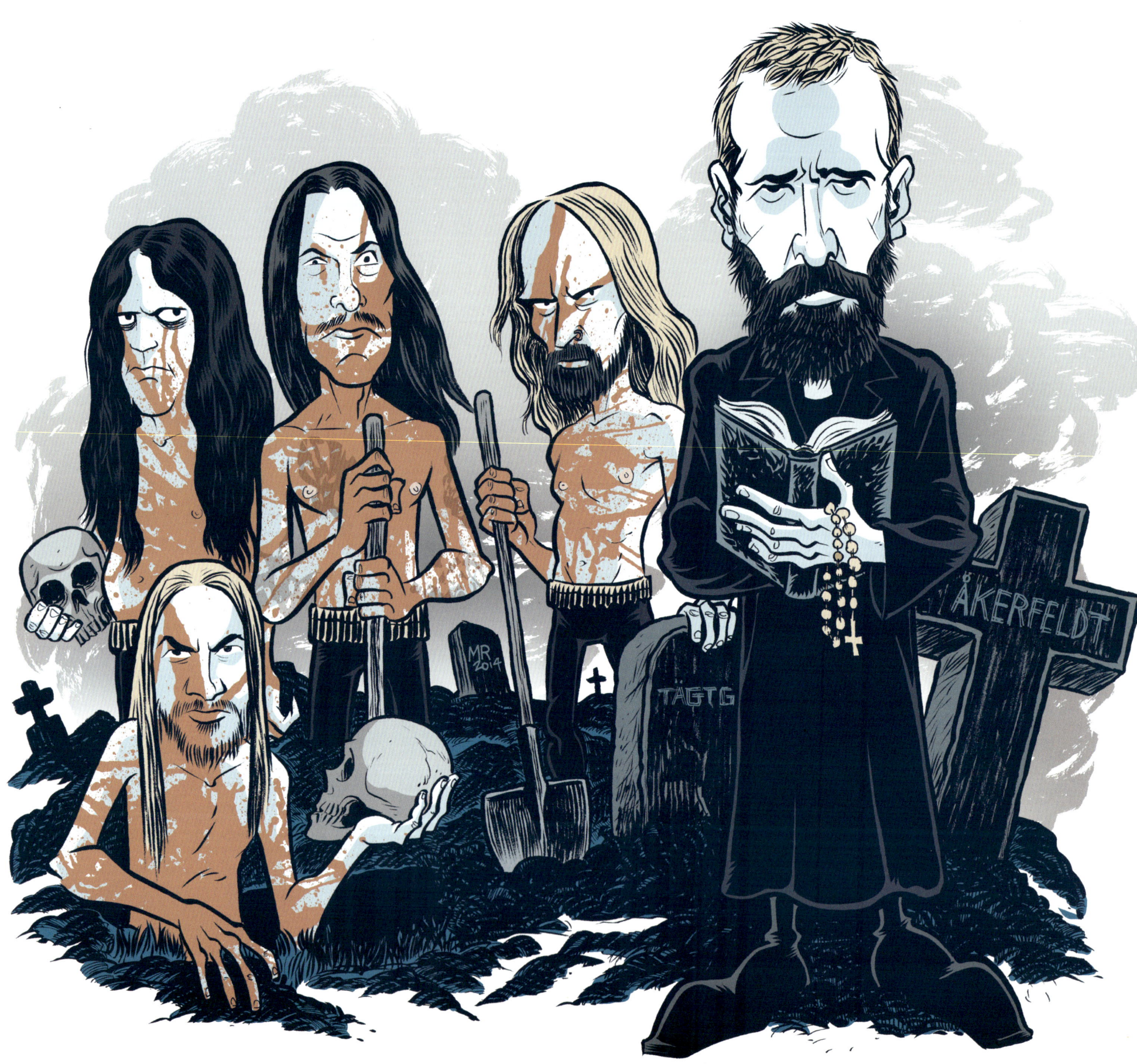

UNTIL THE GRAVE (2014)
Illustration for a review for Bloodbath's *Grand Morbid Funeral* album from Decibel Magazine.

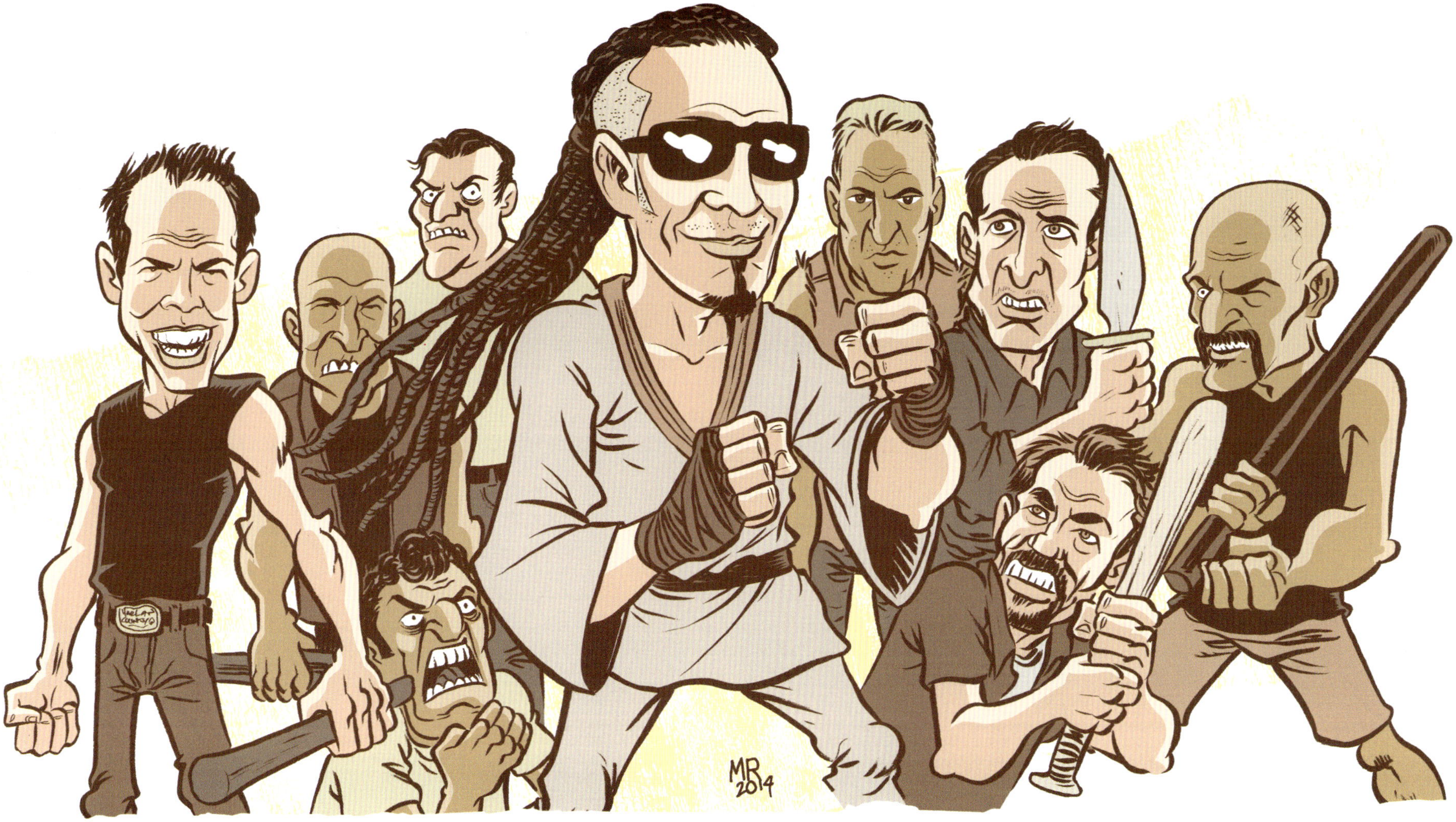

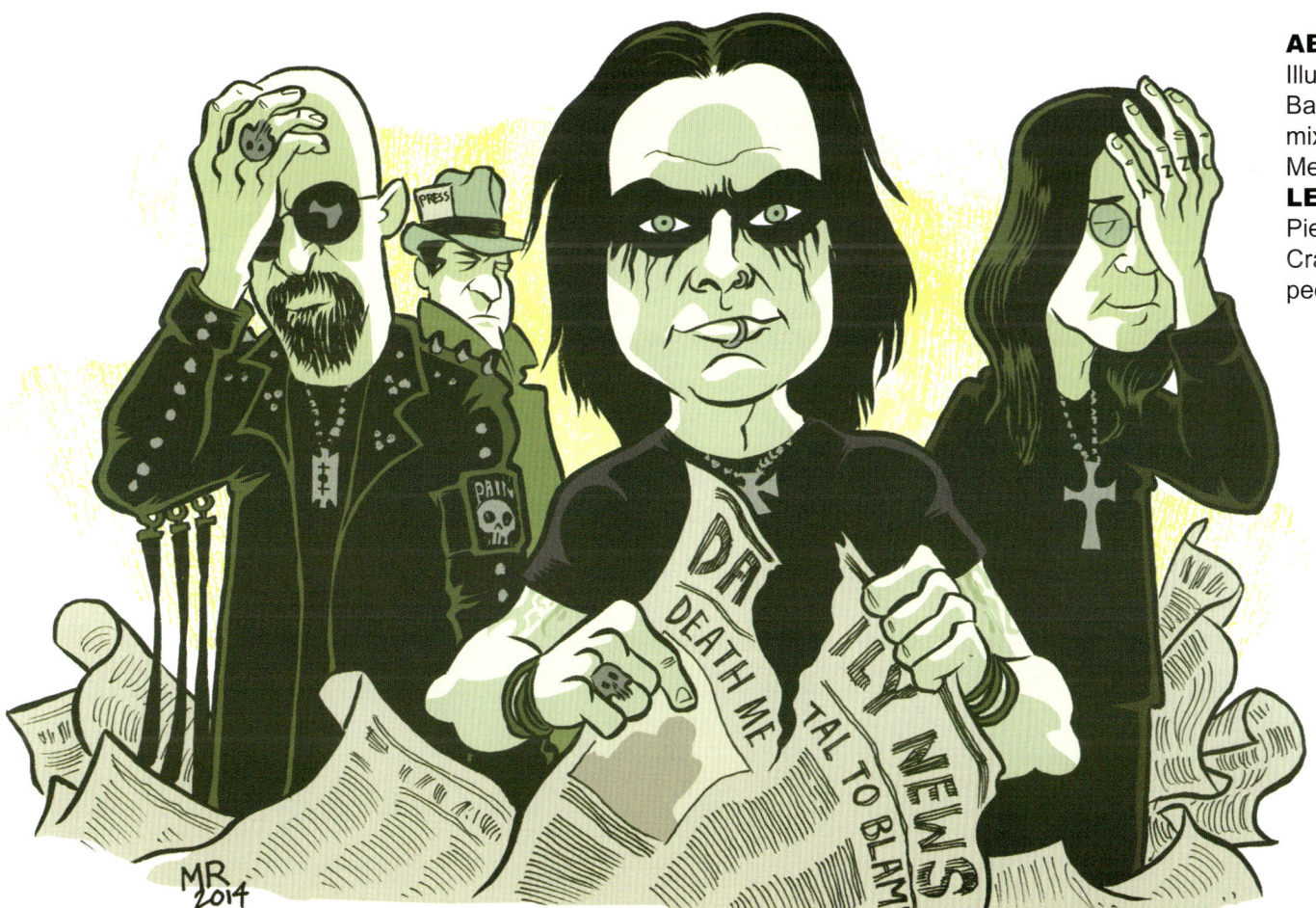

ABOVE: JUSTIFIED VIOLENCE (2014)
Illustration for a column written by Zoltan Bathory from Five Finger Death Punch about mixed martial arts that originally appeared in Metal Hammer UK.

LEFT: PASS THE BUCK (2014)
Piece for a column written by Dani Filth from Cradle of Filth about metal being blamed for people's bad behavior.

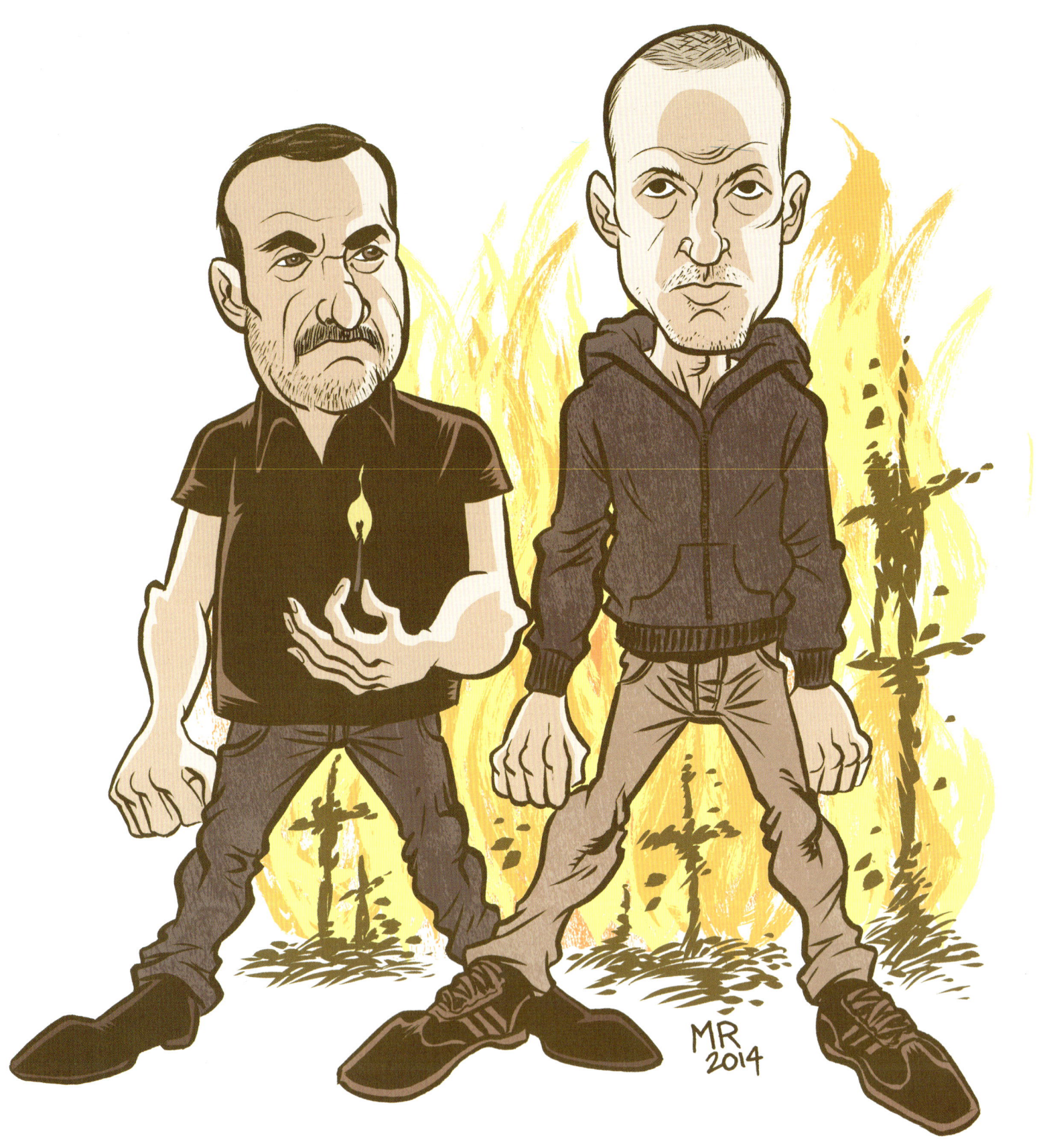

STREETCLEANING WITH FIRE (2014)
Illustration for a review of Godflesh's *A World Lit Only By Fire* album from Decibel Magazine.

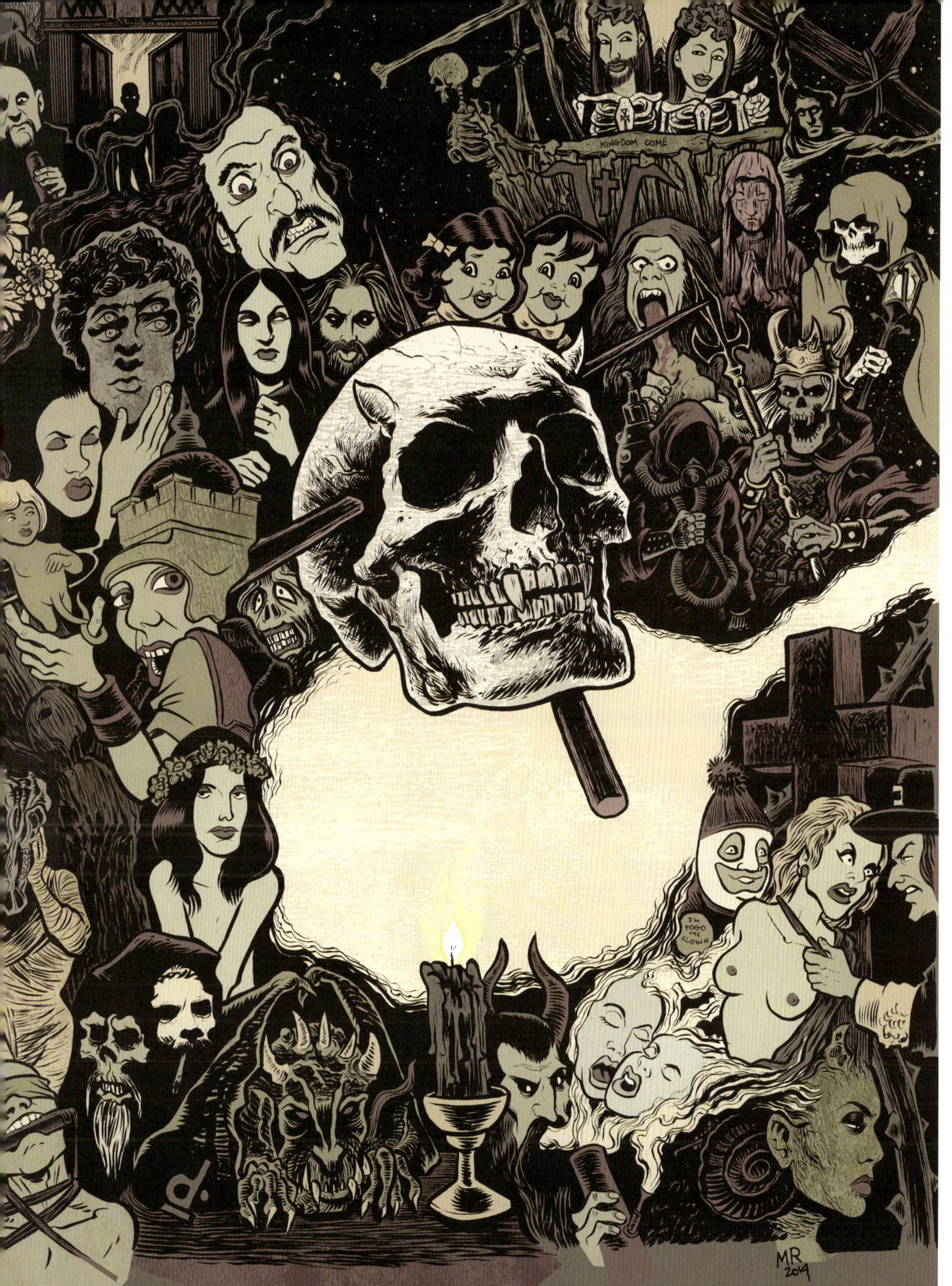

DOOM METAL (2014)
Cover illustration for Decibel's special Doom Metal issue. A montage of 35 different cover elements of the top 100 doom metal albums of all time.

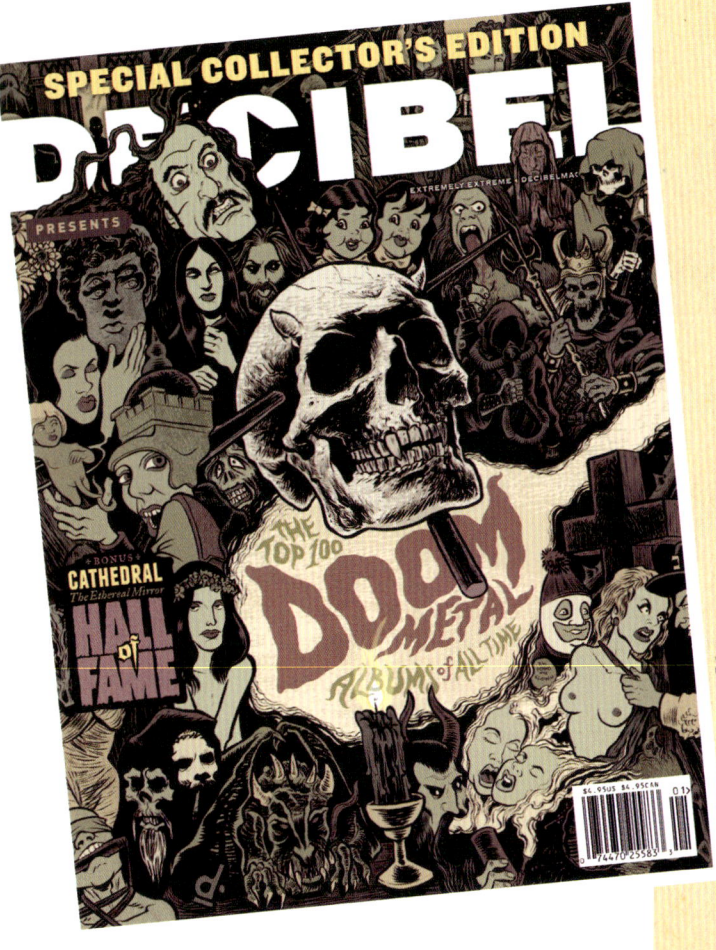

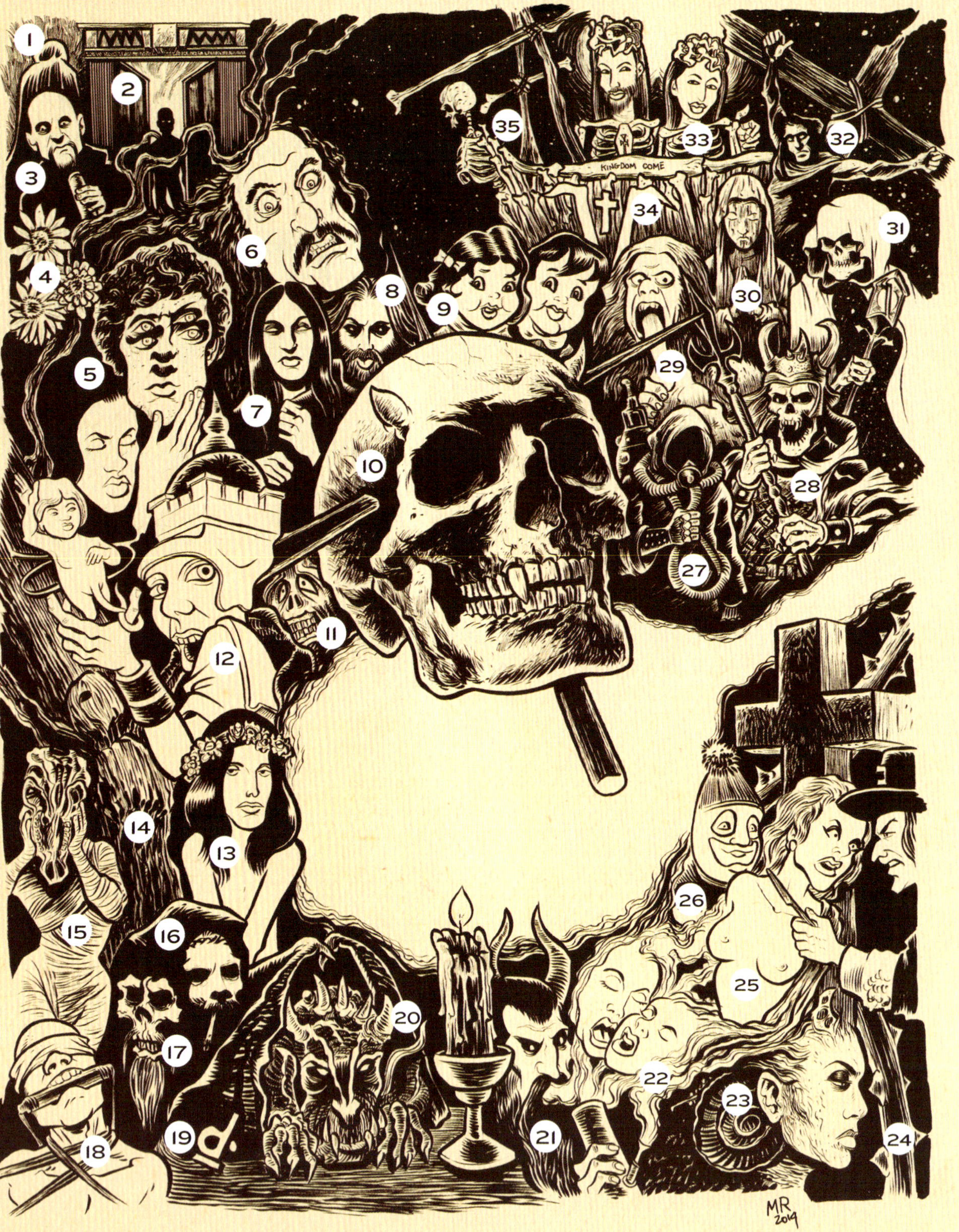

1. EVOKEN - Altra Mors
2. SOLITUDE AETURNUS - Beyond the Crimson...
3. ELECTRIC WIZARD - Come My Fanatics
4. TIAMAT - Wildhoney
5. PARADISE LOST - Icon
6. PENTAGRAM - Relentless
7. BLACK SABBATH - S/T
8. PAGAN ALTAR - Volume I
9. MELVINS - Gluey Porch Treatments
10. CANDLEMASS - Epicus Doomicus...
11. GRIEF - Come to Grief
12. CATHEDRAL - The Ethereal Mirror
13. EYEHATEGOD - Take as Needed...
14. TROUBLE - Psalm 9
15. ANATHEMA - Serenades
16. DOWN - NOLA
17. HOODED MENACE - Never Cross...
18. CONFESSOR - Condemned
19. DISEMBOWELMENT - Transcendence...
20. DREAM DEATH - Journey Into...
21. ELECTRIC WIZARD - Dopethrone
22. TYPE O NEGATIVE - Bloody Kisses
23. PARADISE LOST - Draconian Times
24. TYOE O NEGATIVE - October Rust
25. WITCHFINDER GENERAL - Death...
26. ACID BATH - When the Kite String...
27. SLEEP - Jerusalem
28. CIRITH UNGOL - King of the Dead
29. THE OBSESSED - Lunar Womb
30. MY DYING BRIDE - Turn Loose...
31. PALLBEARER - Sorrow and Extinction
32. PARADISE LOST - Gothic
33. CATHEDRAL - The Carnival Bizarre
34. SAINT VITUS - Born Too Late
35. Sir Lord Baltimore - Kingdom Come

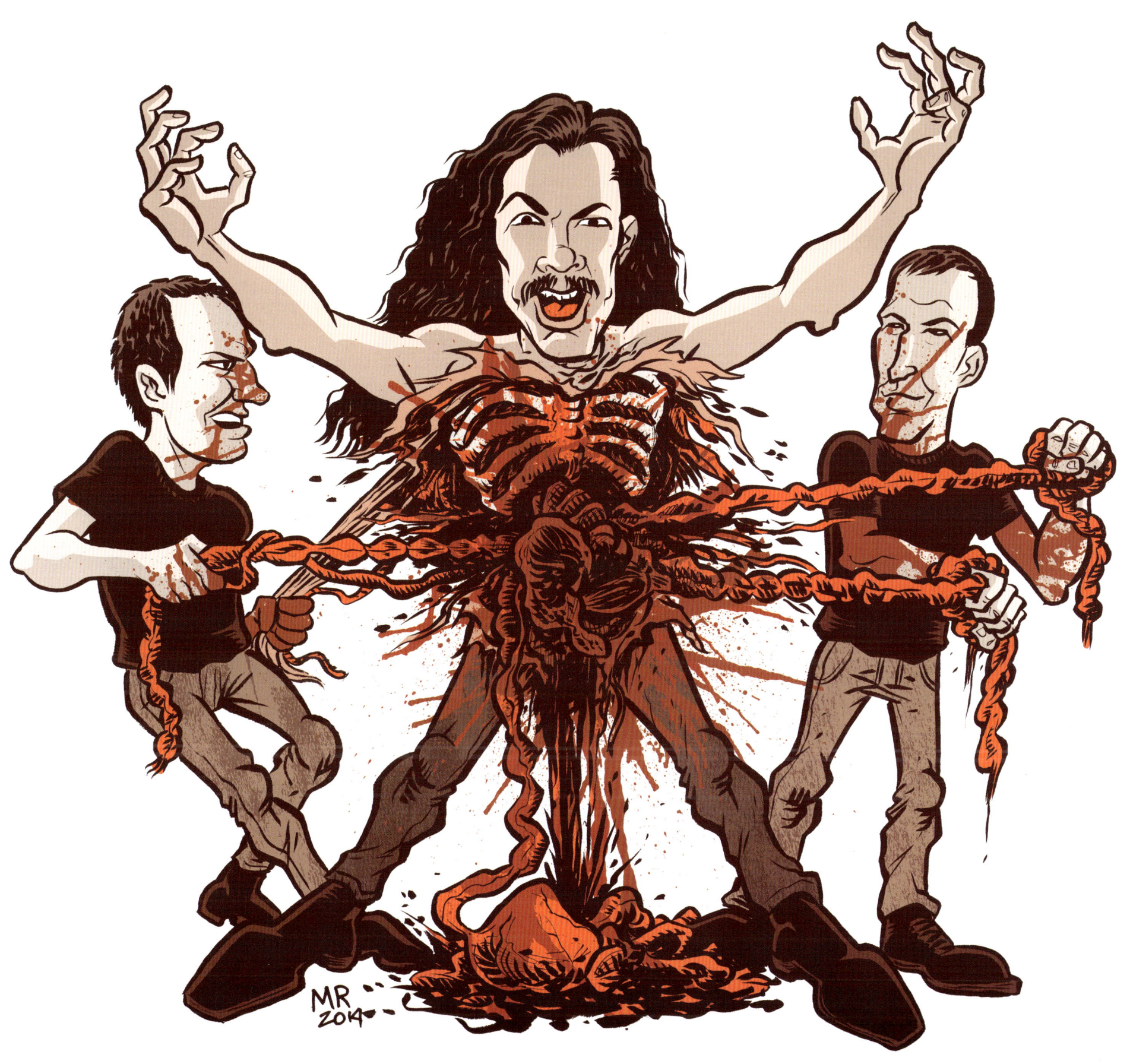

SLIT YOUR GUTS (2014)
Illustration for a review for Horrendous' *Ecdysis* album from Decibel Magazine.

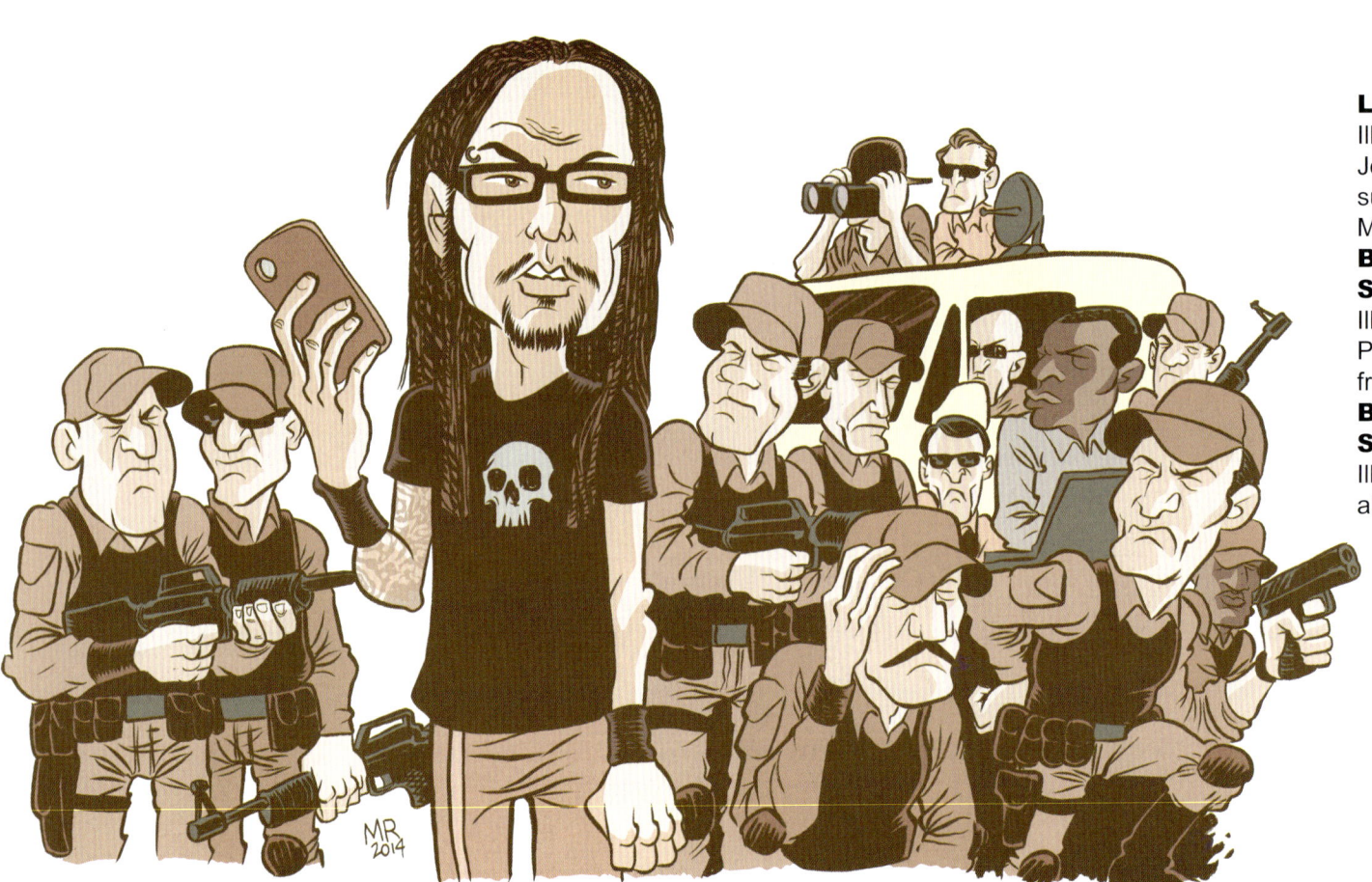

LEFT: PORNO CREEP (2014)
Illustration for a column written by Johnathan Davis from Korn about the surveillance state. Originally appeared in Metal Hammer UK.

BOTTOM LEFT:
STRONG FOUNDATION (2014)
Illustration for the lead review of Pallbearer's album *Foundations of Burden* from Decibel Magazine.

BOTTOM:
SUPPOSED TO ROT (2014)
Illustration for a review of Morbus Chron's album *Sweven* from Decibel Magazine.

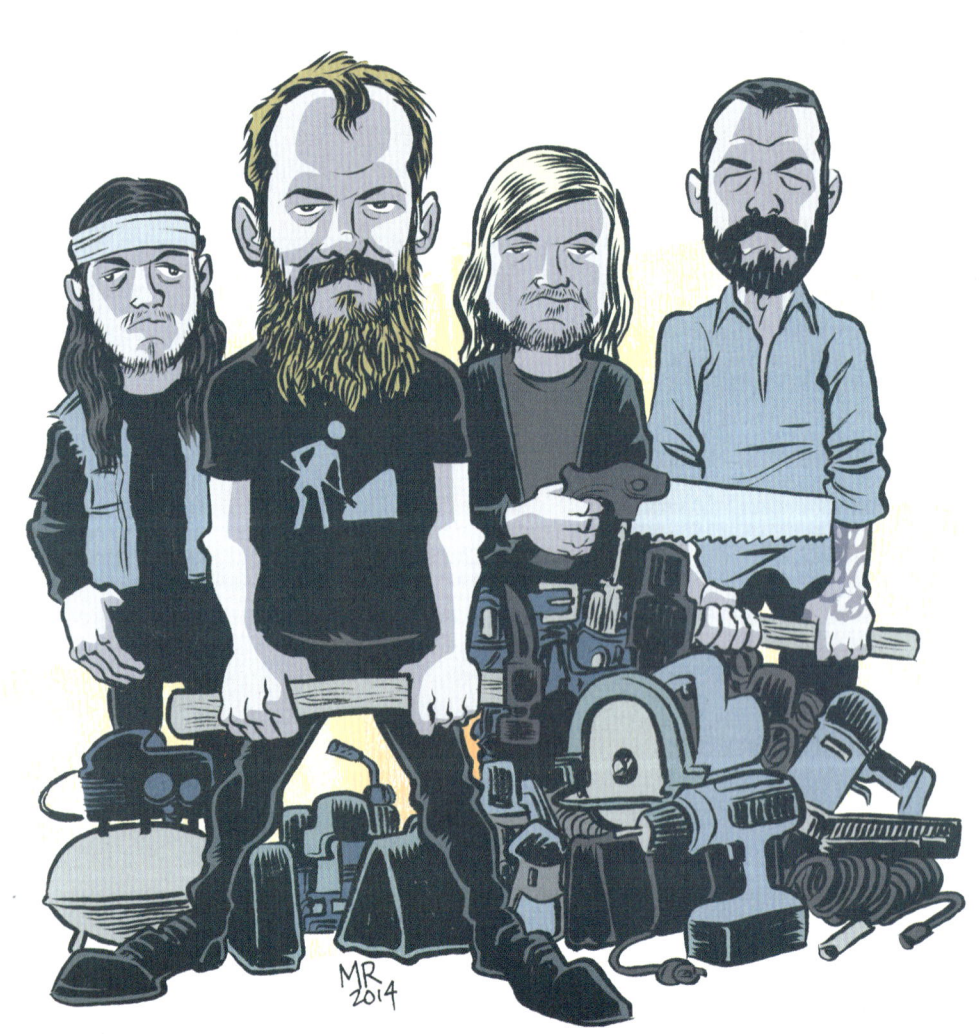

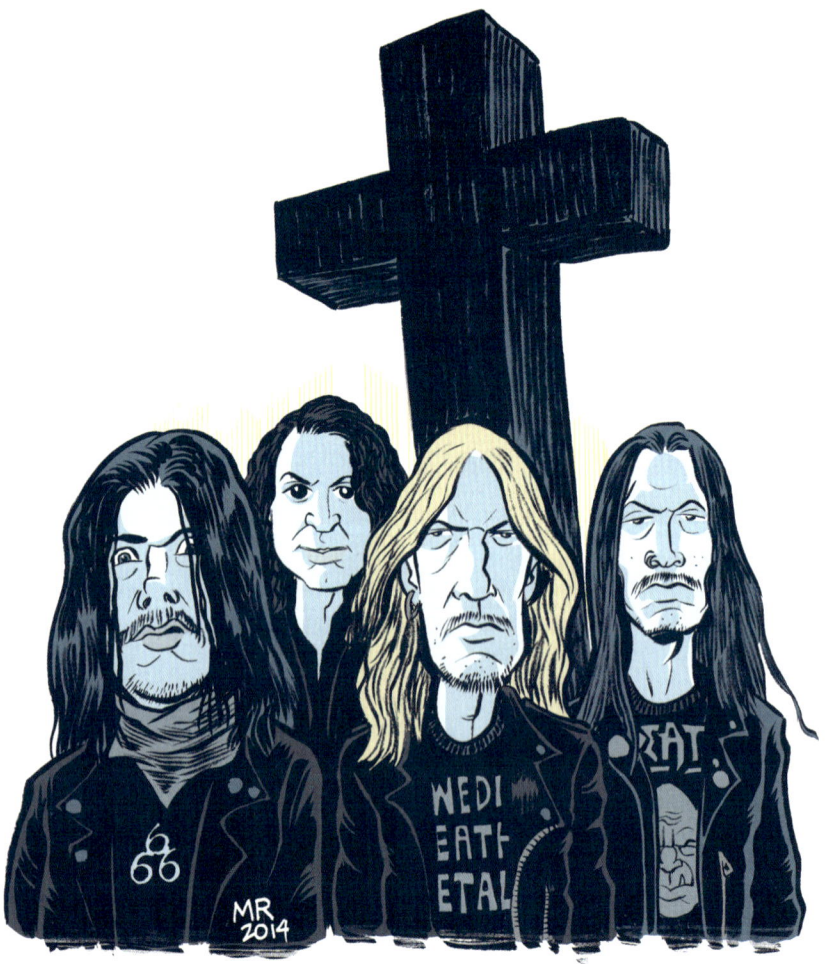

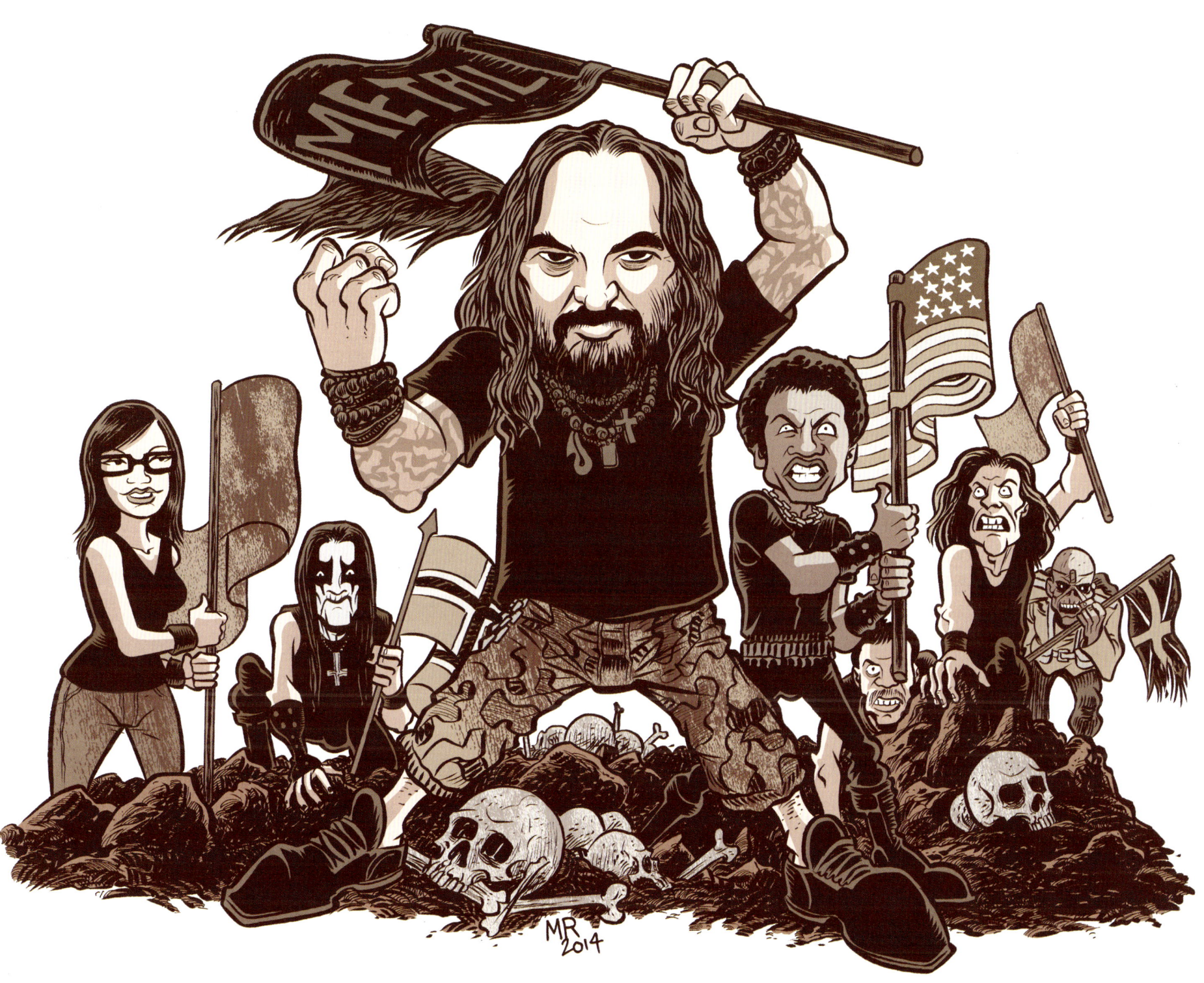

FLAG OF HATE (2014)
Illustration for a column Written by Max Cavalera about being united under the flag of metal.Originally appeared in Metal Hammer UK.

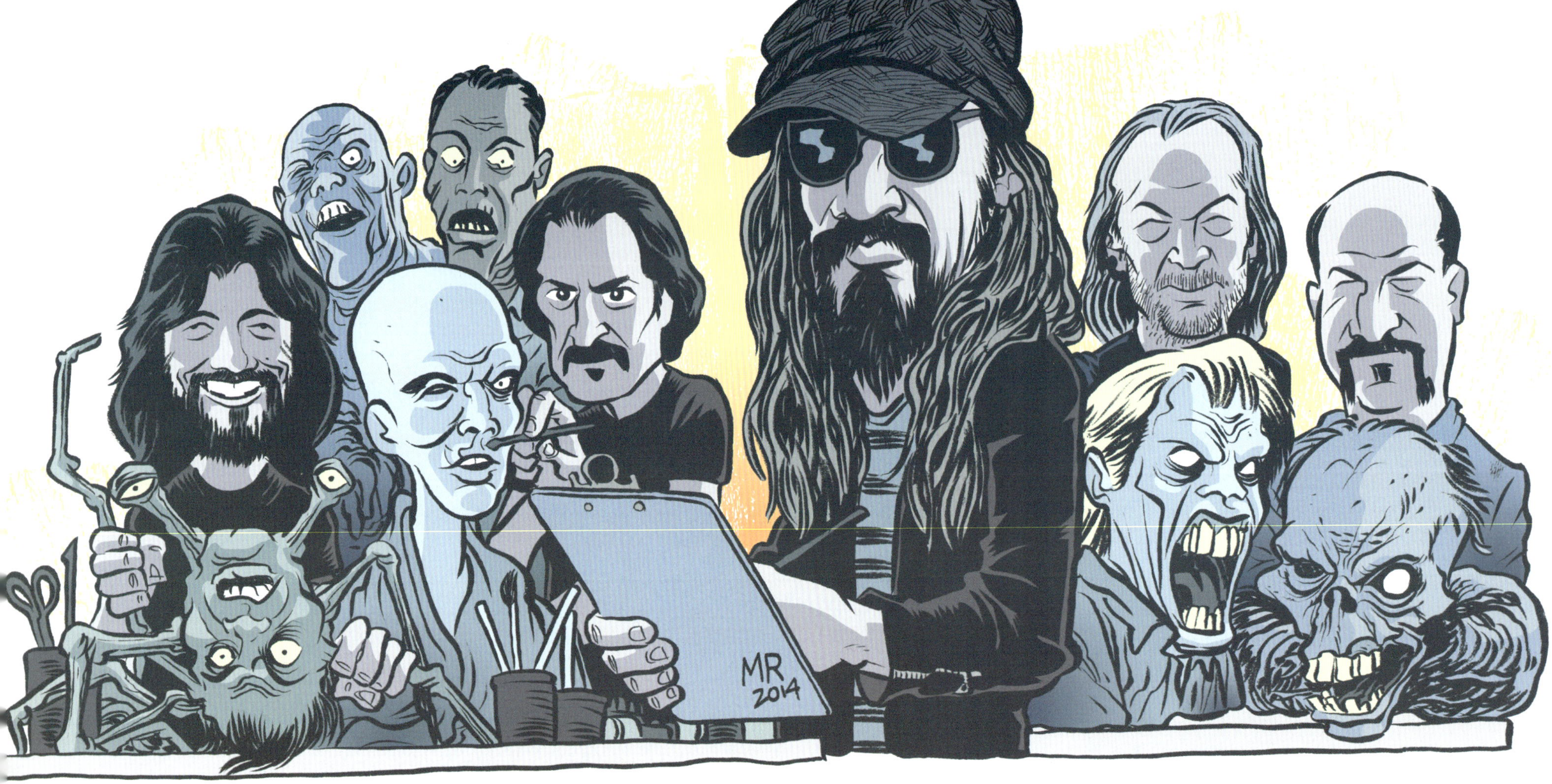

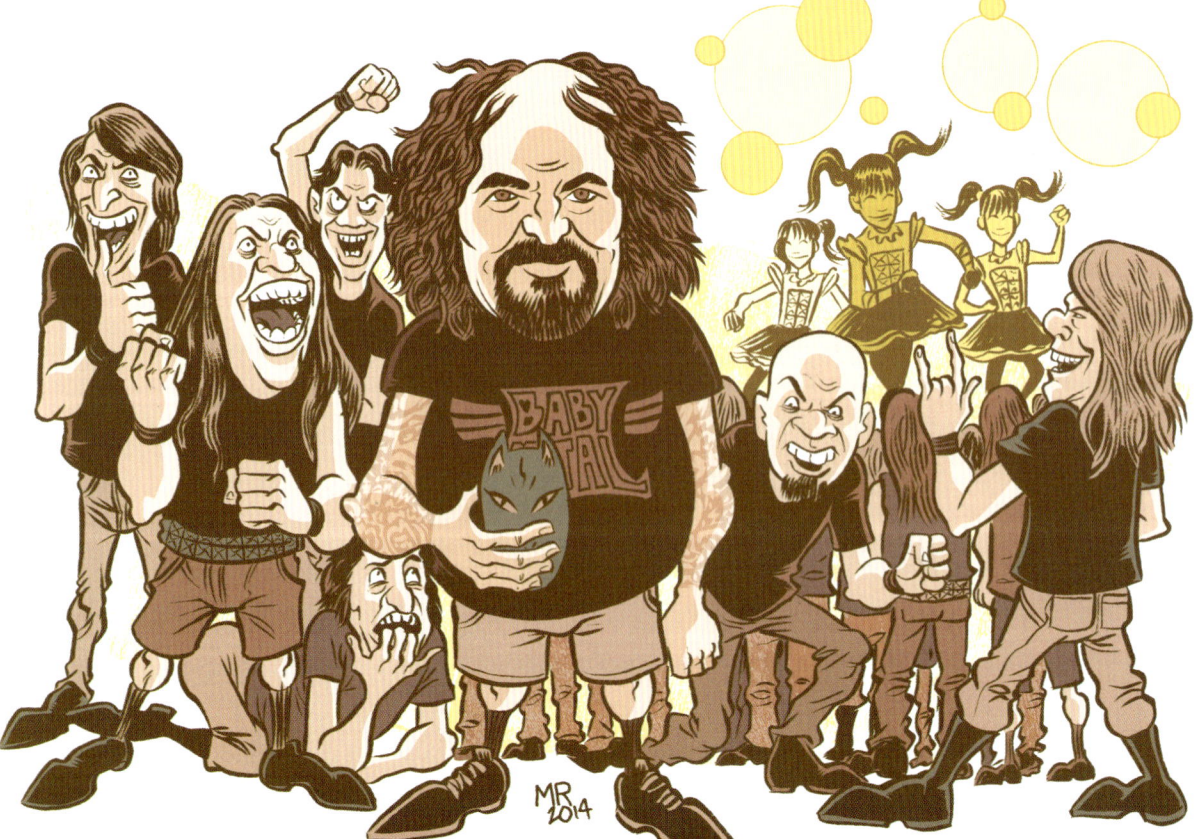

ABOVE: COVERGHOUL (2014)
Illustration for a column written by
Rob Zombie about the magic of analog
effects.
LEFT:
CHILD'S PLAY (2014)
A piece for a column written by Shane
Embury espousing his appreciation of
BABY METAL. Both originally appeared
in Metal Hammer UK.

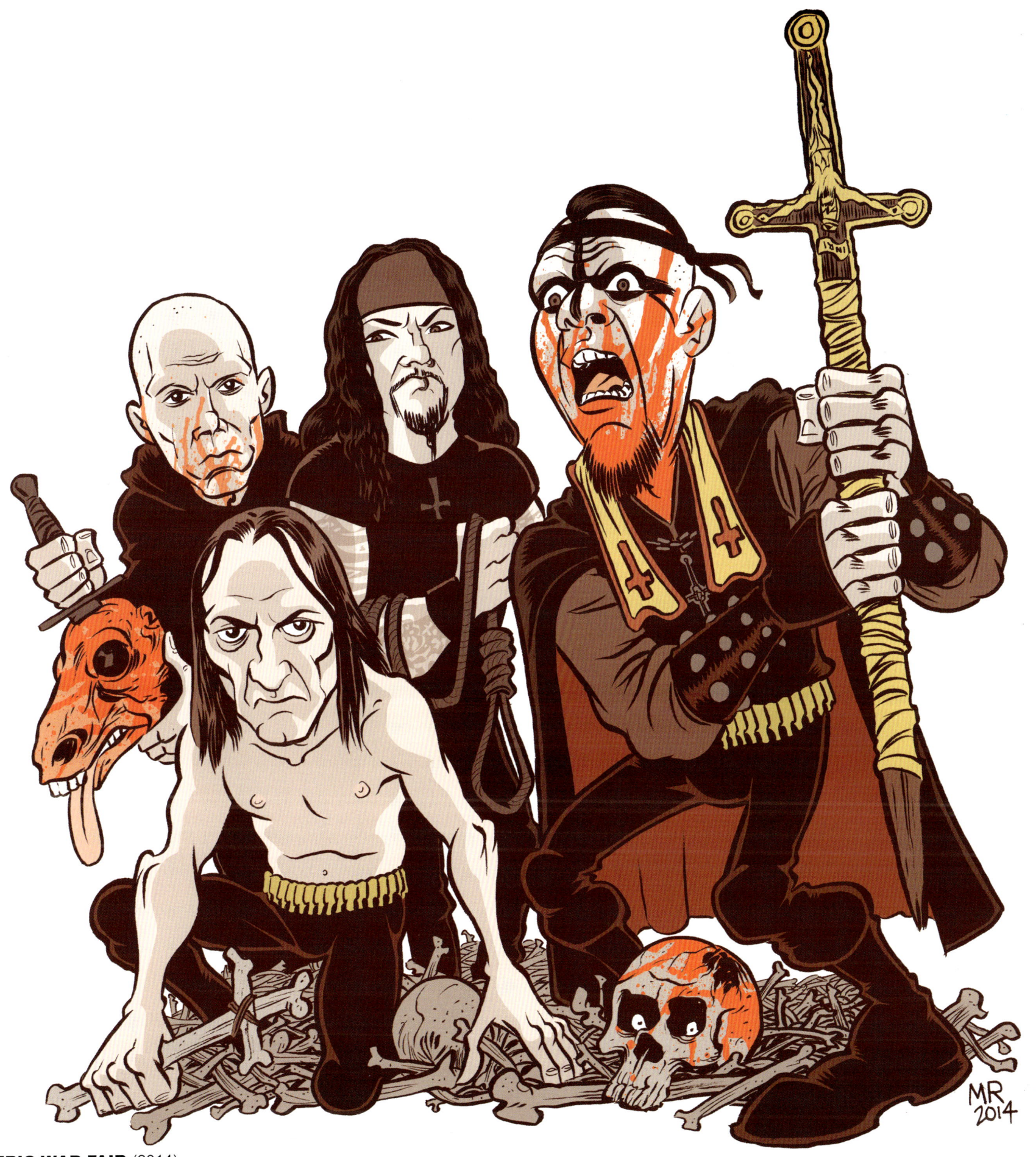

ESOTERIC WAR FAIR (2014)
Illustration for a review of Mayhem's *Esoteric Warfare* album from Decibel Magazine.

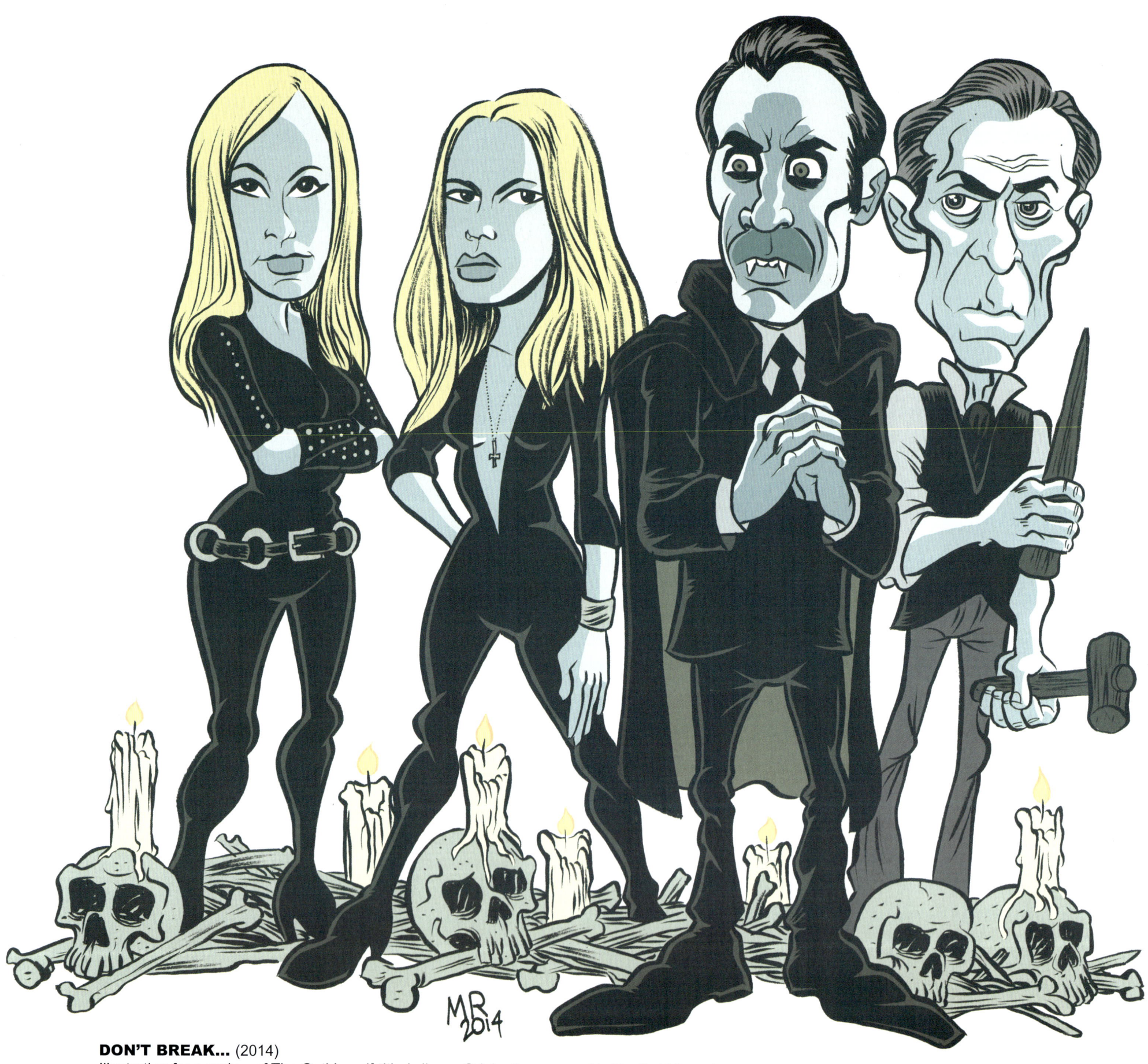

DON'T BREAK... (2014)
Illustration for a review of The Oath's *self-titled* album. Originally appeared in Decibel Magazine.

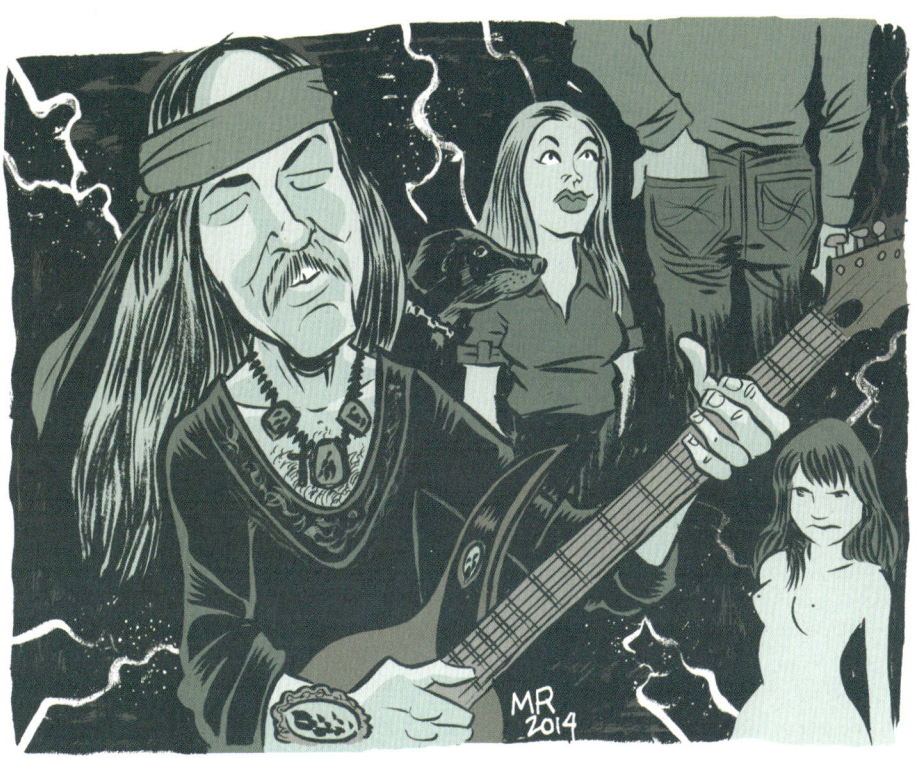

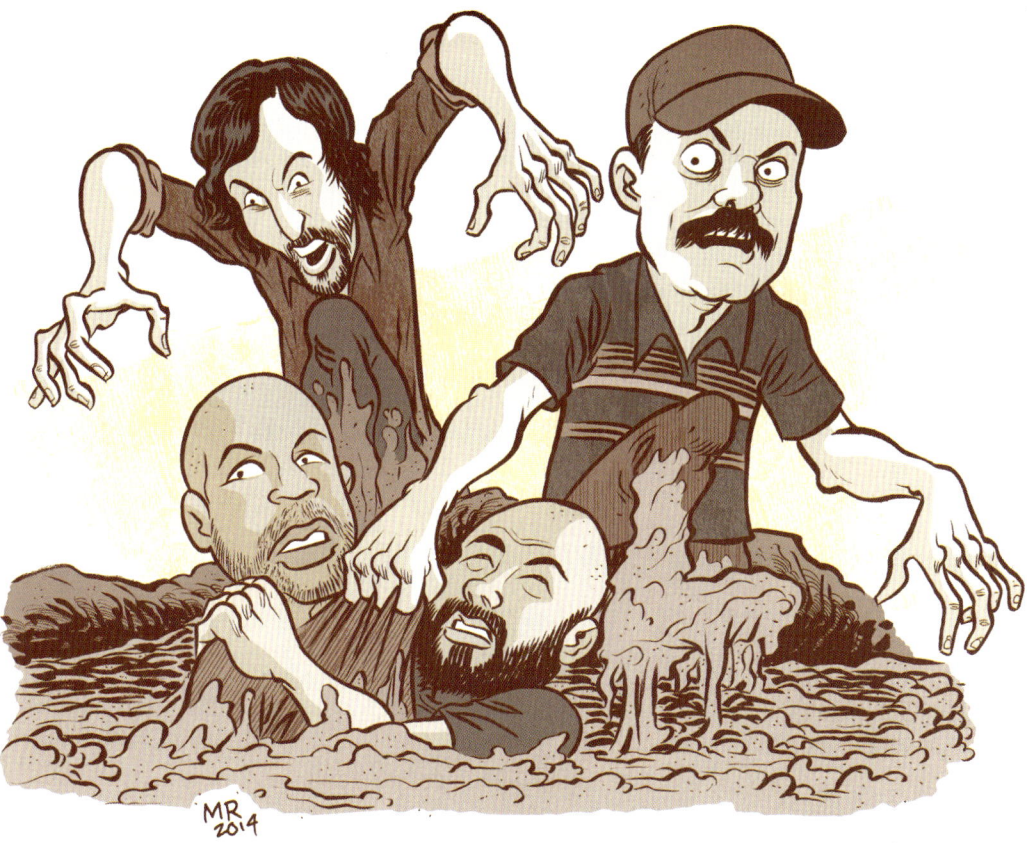

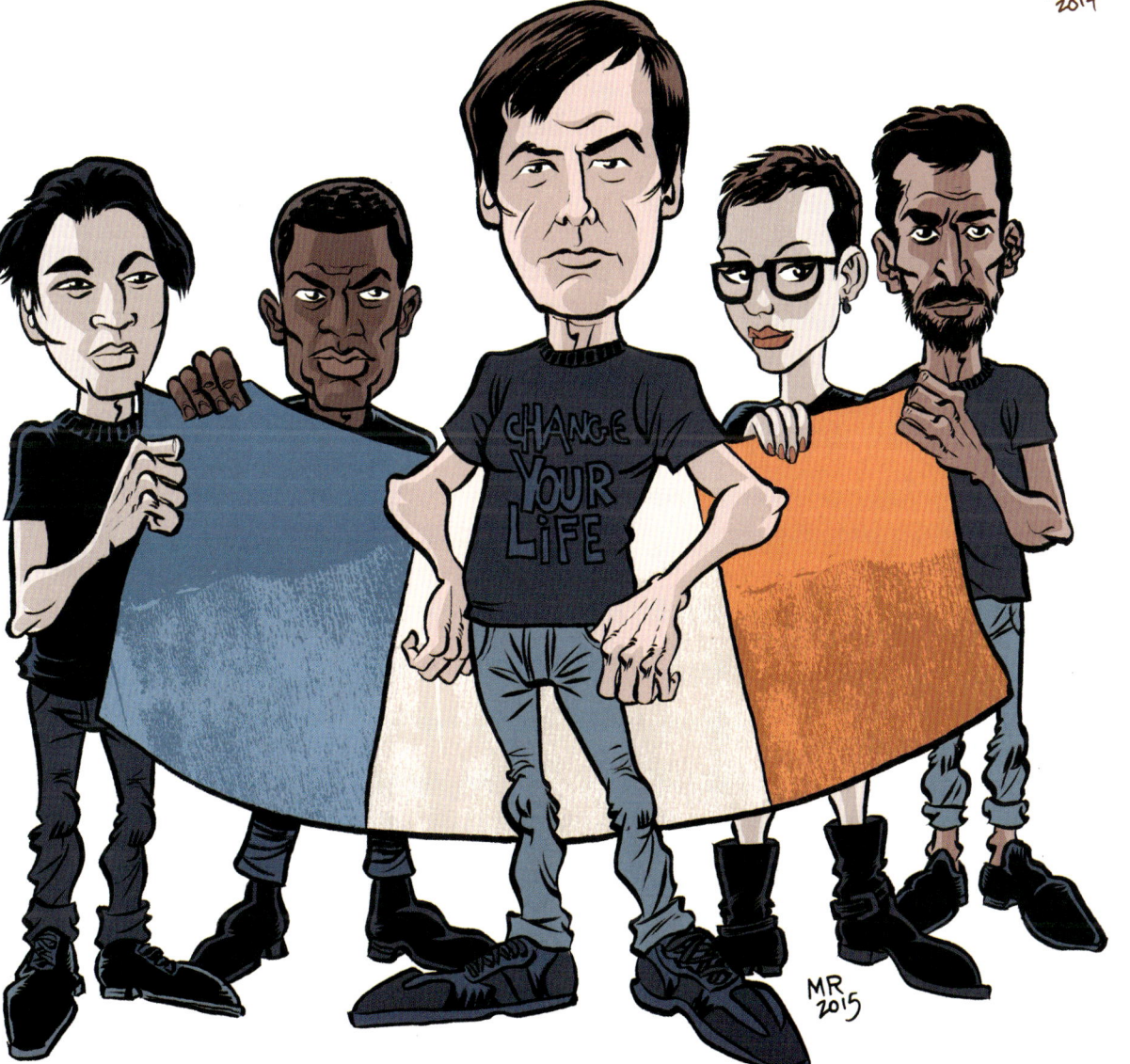

ABOVE LEFT: STRONG POLES (2014)
Illustration for the Southpole Dispatch column from Decibel Magazine discussing Uli Jon Roth's tenure in The Scorpions.

ABOVE: LIGHT IT (2014)
A piece for a review of Torche's album *Restarter*. Originally apperaed in Decibel Magazine.

LEFT: MELTING POT (2015)
An illustration for a column written by Barney Greenway about getting along with each other no matter our backgrounds. Originally appeared in Metal Hammer UK.

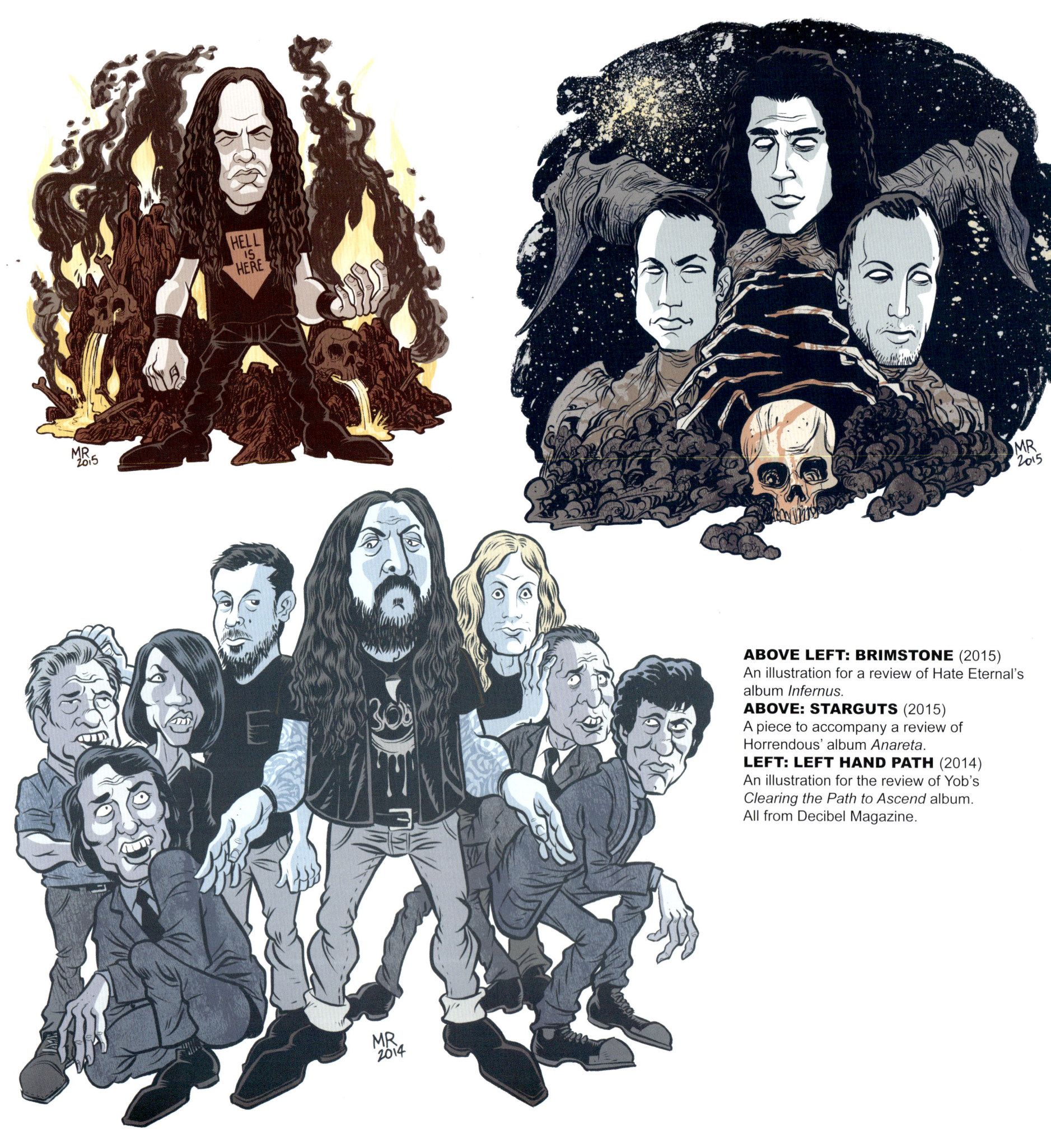

ABOVE LEFT: BRIMSTONE (2015)
An illustration for a review of Hate Eternal's album *Infernus*.
ABOVE: STARGUTS (2015)
A piece to accompany a review of Horrendous' album *Anareta*.
LEFT: LEFT HAND PATH (2014)
An illustration for the review of Yob's *Clearing the Path to Ascend* album.
All from Decibel Magazine.

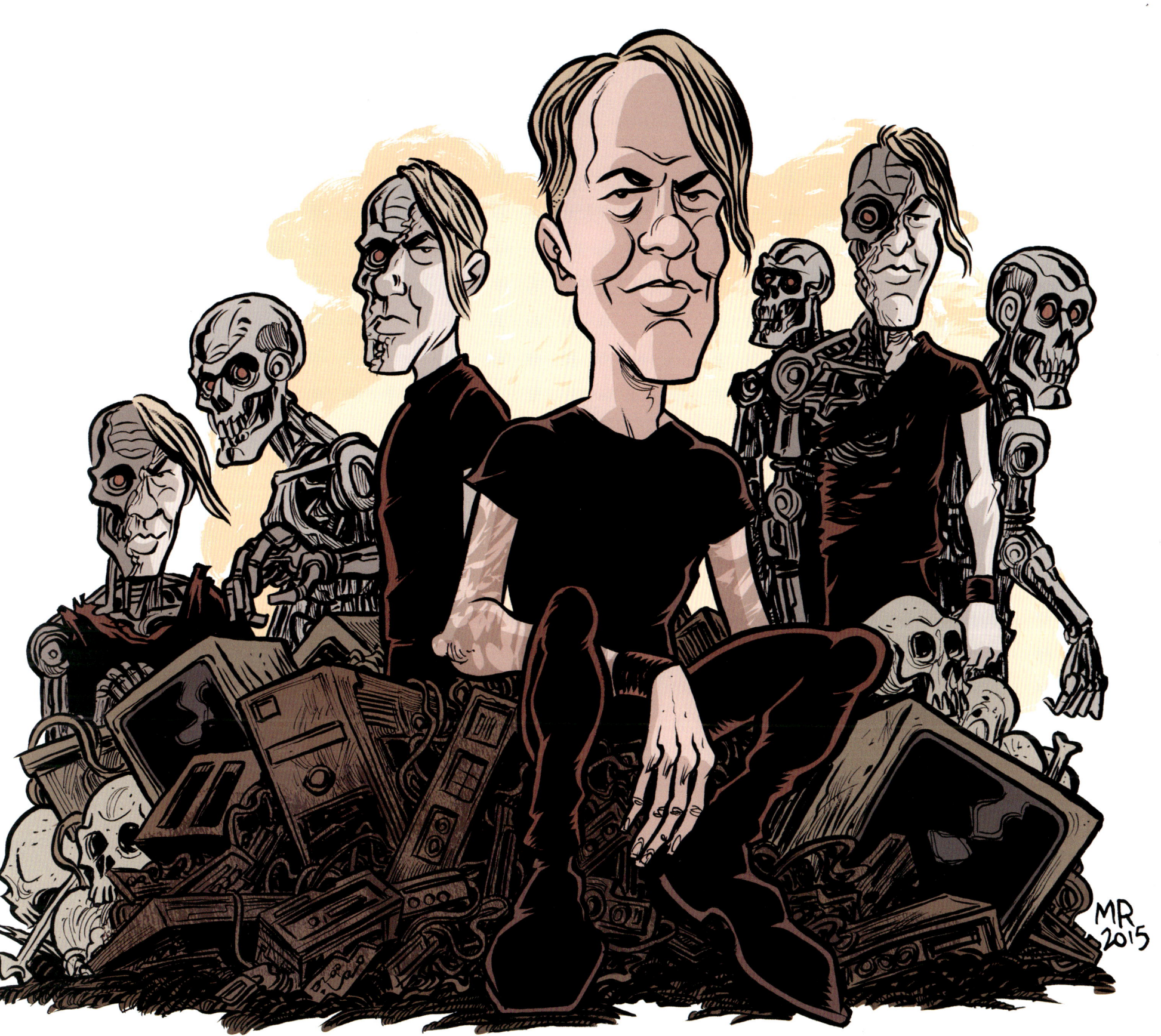

TECHNOLOGY REMANUFACTURE (2015)
Illustration from a column by Burton C. Bell of Fear Factory continuing to beat the drum of technology taking over the people who created it.

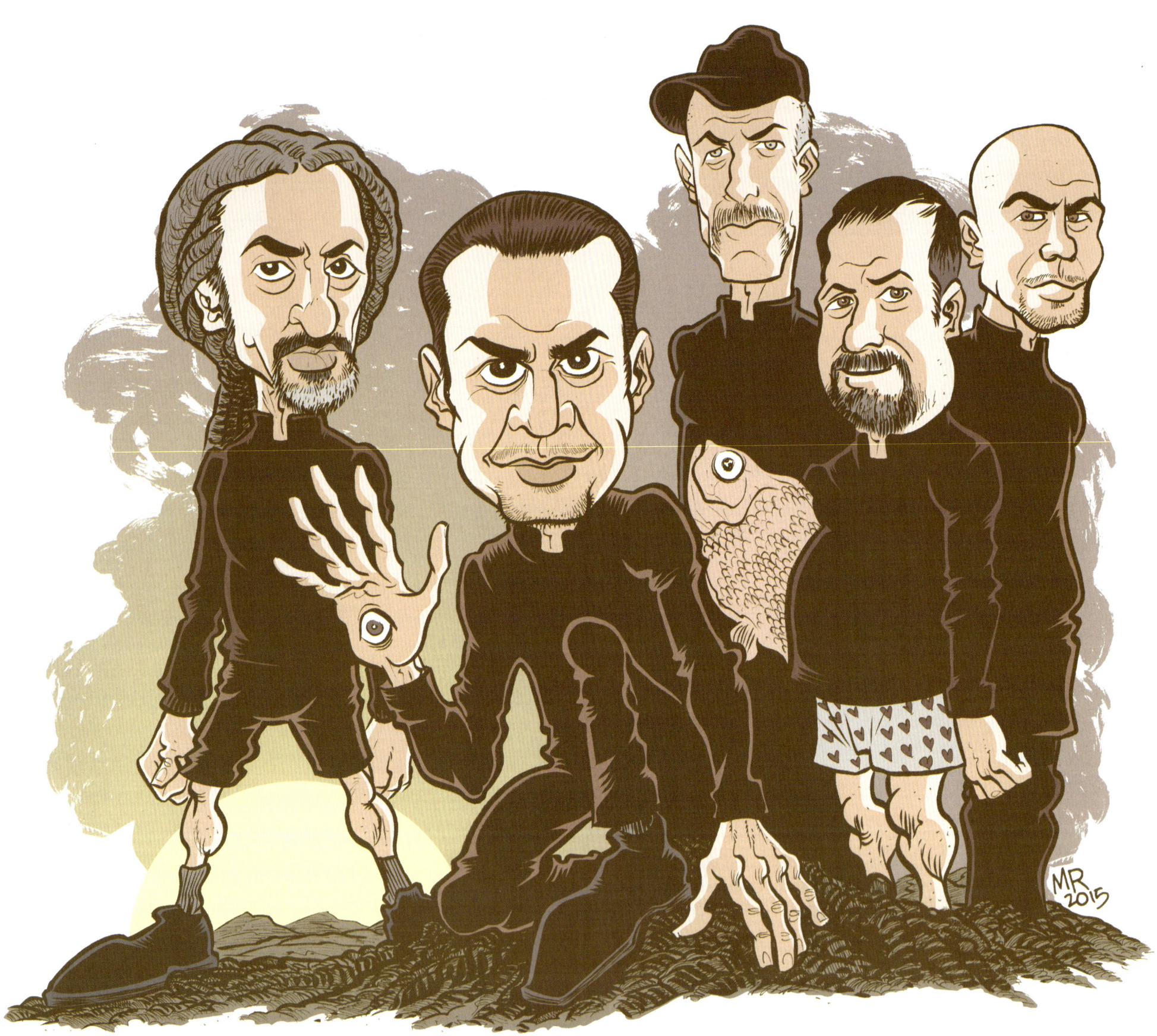

OUT OF NOWHERE (2015)
An illustration for a review of Faith No More's album *Sol Invictus.* Originally appeared in Decibel Magazine.

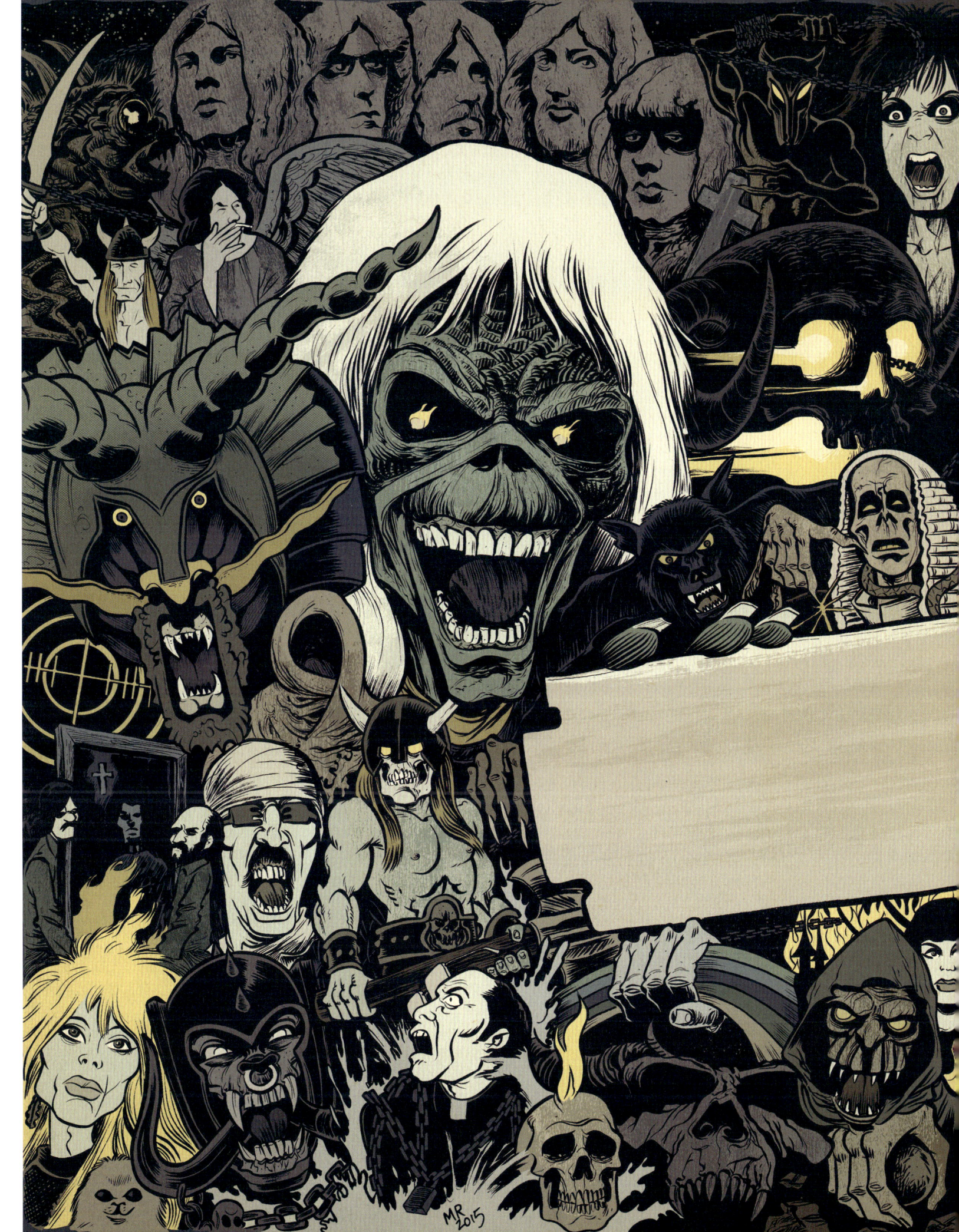

OLD-SCHOOL METAL
(2015)
Cover illustration for a
Decibel Magazine special
issue; The top 100
Old-School Metal Albums
of All Time. I used elements
from 27 different album
covers.

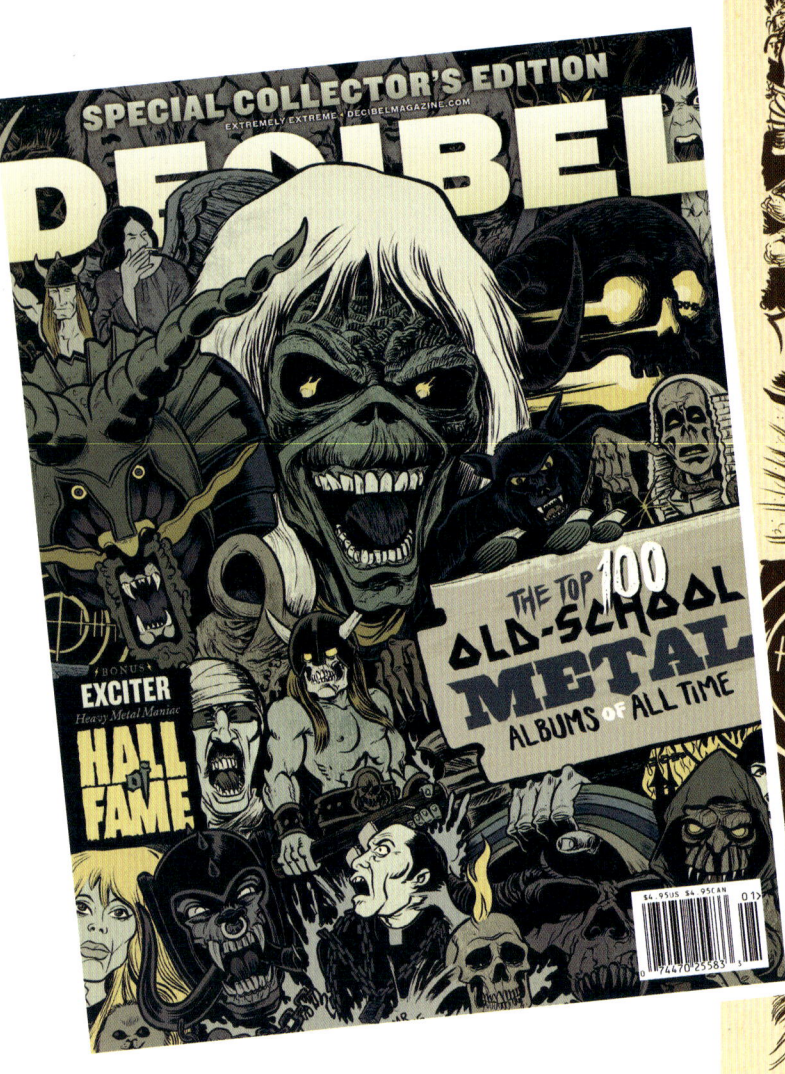

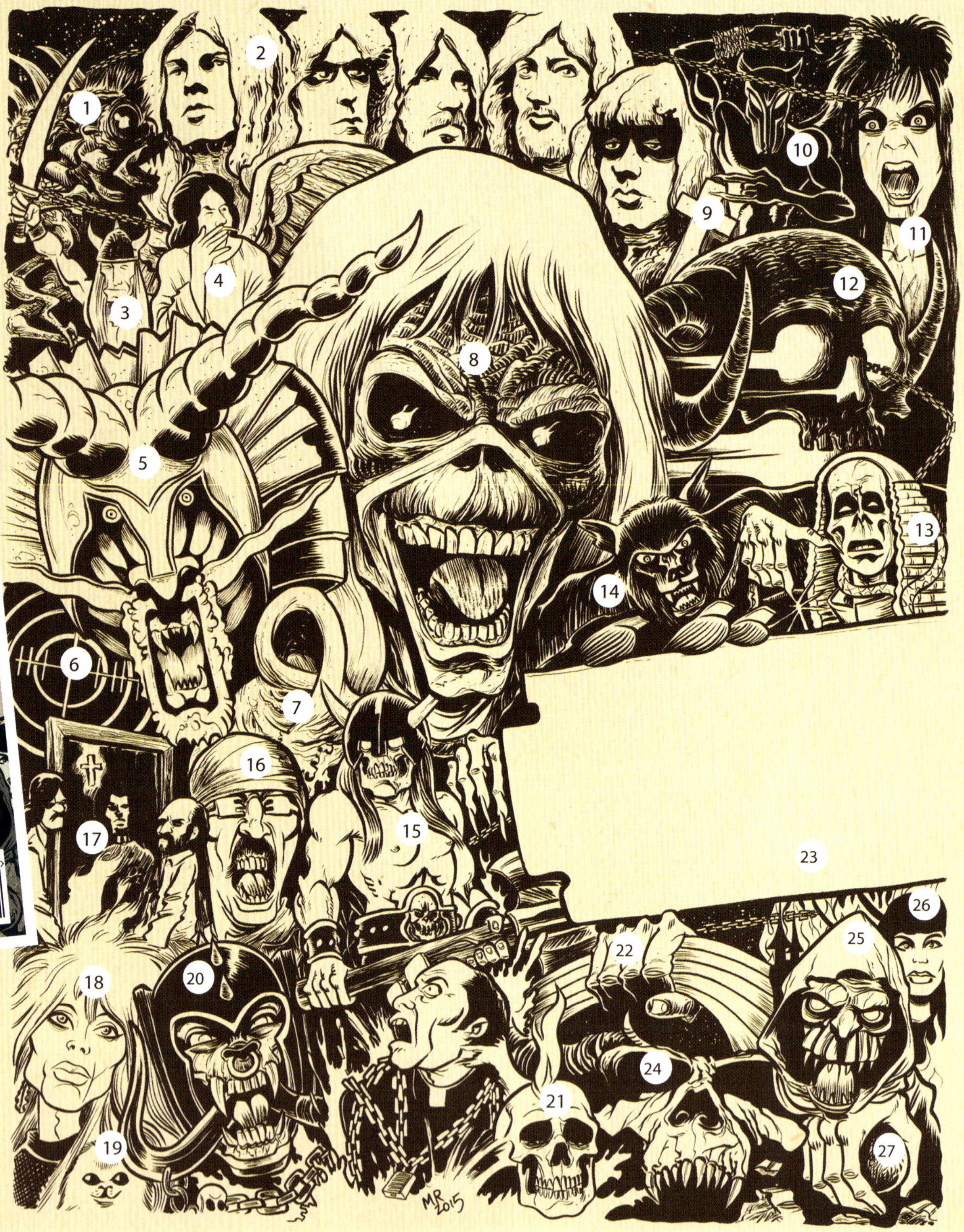

1. CIRITH UNGOL - One Foot In Hell
2. DEEP PURPLE - In Rock
3. MANILLA ROAD - Crystal Logic
4. BLACK SABBATH - Heaven & Hell
5. JUDAS PRIEST - Defenders of the Faith
6. DEF LEPPARD - Pyromania
7. BLACK SABBATH - Mob Rules
8. IRON MAIDEN - Number of the Beast
9. SCORPIONS - Taken by Force

10. DIO - Holy Diver
11. W.A.S.P. - W.A.S.P.
12. MERCYFUL FATE - Melissa
13. SATAN - Court in the Act
14. WITCH CROSS - Fit For Fight
15. OMEN - Battle Cry
16. SCORPIONS - Blackout
17. RUSH - Moving Pictures
18. HANOI ROCKS - Two Steps from the Move

19. RIOT - Fire Down Under
20. MOTÖRHEAD - Orgasmatron
21. OZ - Fire in the Brain
22. RAINBOW - Rising
23. JUDAS PRIEST - British Steel
24. DANZIG - Danzig
25. HELLOWEEN - Walls of Jericho
26. KING DIAMOND - Fatal Portrait
27. ACCEPT - Balls to the Wall

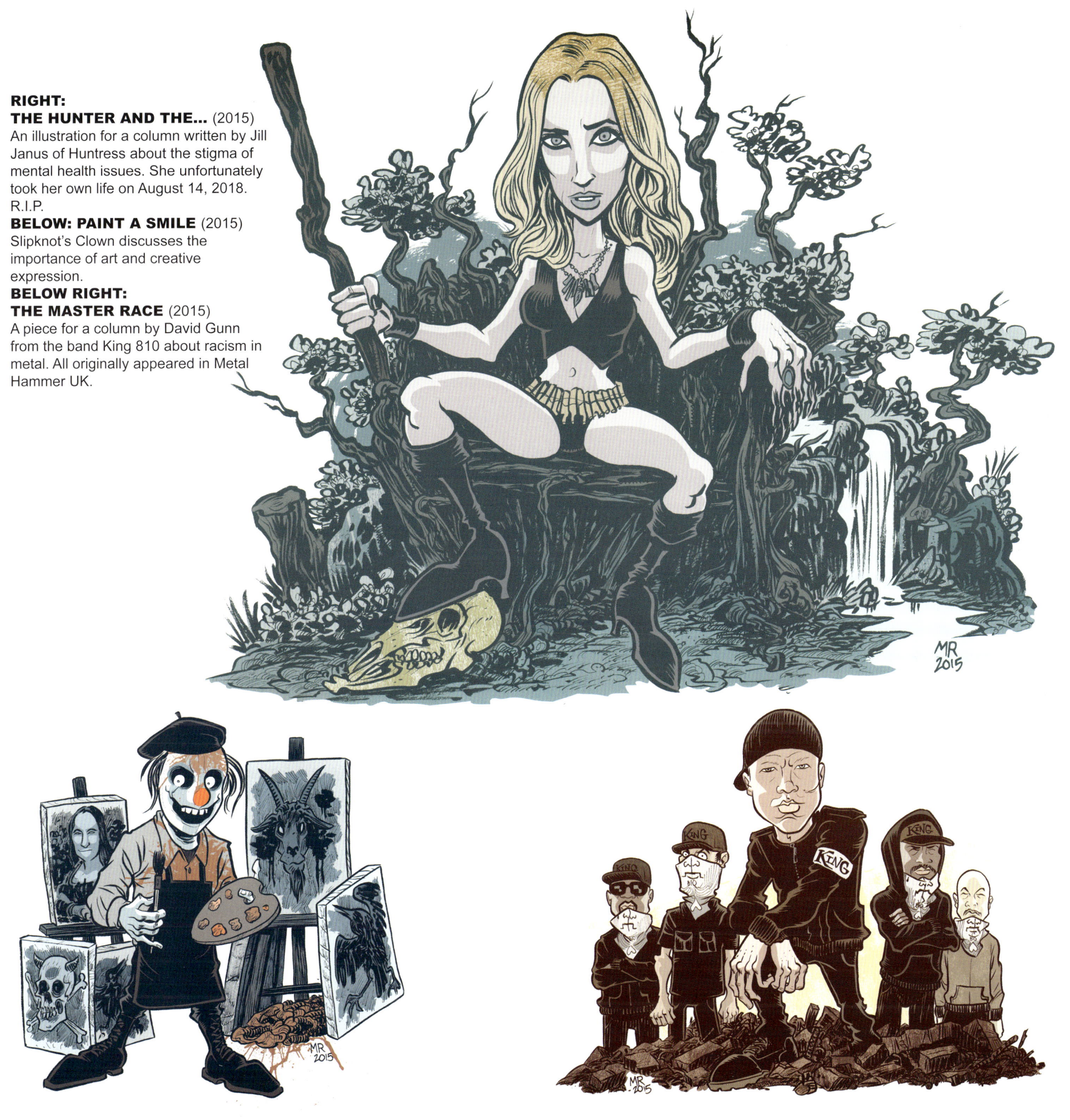

RIGHT:
THE HUNTER AND THE... (2015)
An illustration for a column written by Jill Janus of Huntress about the stigma of mental health issues. She unfortunately took her own life on August 14, 2018. R.I.P.
BELOW: PAINT A SMILE (2015)
Slipknot's Clown discusses the importance of art and creative expression.
BELOW RIGHT:
THE MASTER RACE (2015)
A piece for a column by David Gunn from the band King 810 about racism in metal. All originally appeared in Metal Hammer UK.

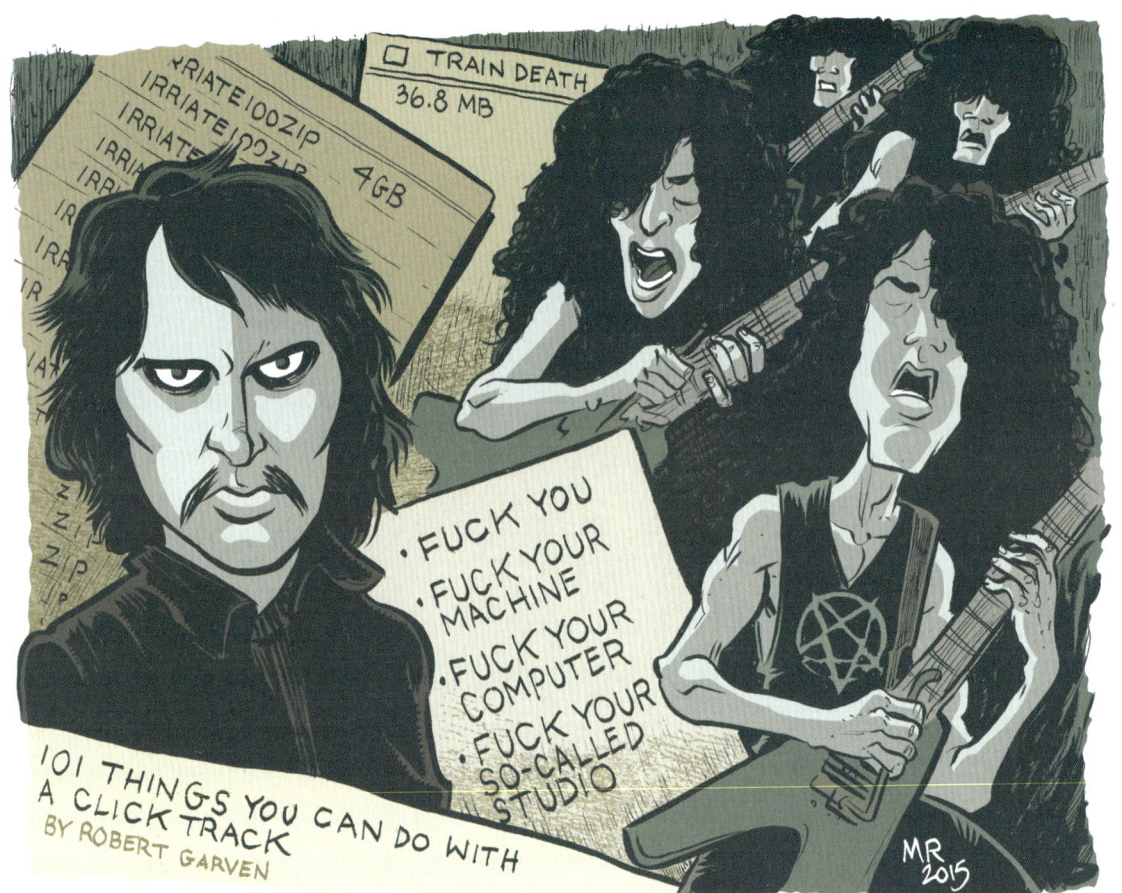

LEFT: FUCKERY 101 (2015)
A piece for the Southpole Dispatch column about Robert Garvin from Cirith Ungol's perceived hatred of click tracks. Also features Morbid Angel's Trey Azagthoth.

BELOW: ALL WORK... (2015)
A lead review illustration for Shining's album *IX – Everyone, Everything, Everywhere, Ends*.

BELOW LEFT: FINNISH THEM (2015)
An illustration for the review of Oranssi Pazuzu's *Värähtelijä* album.
All originally appeared in Decibel Magazine.

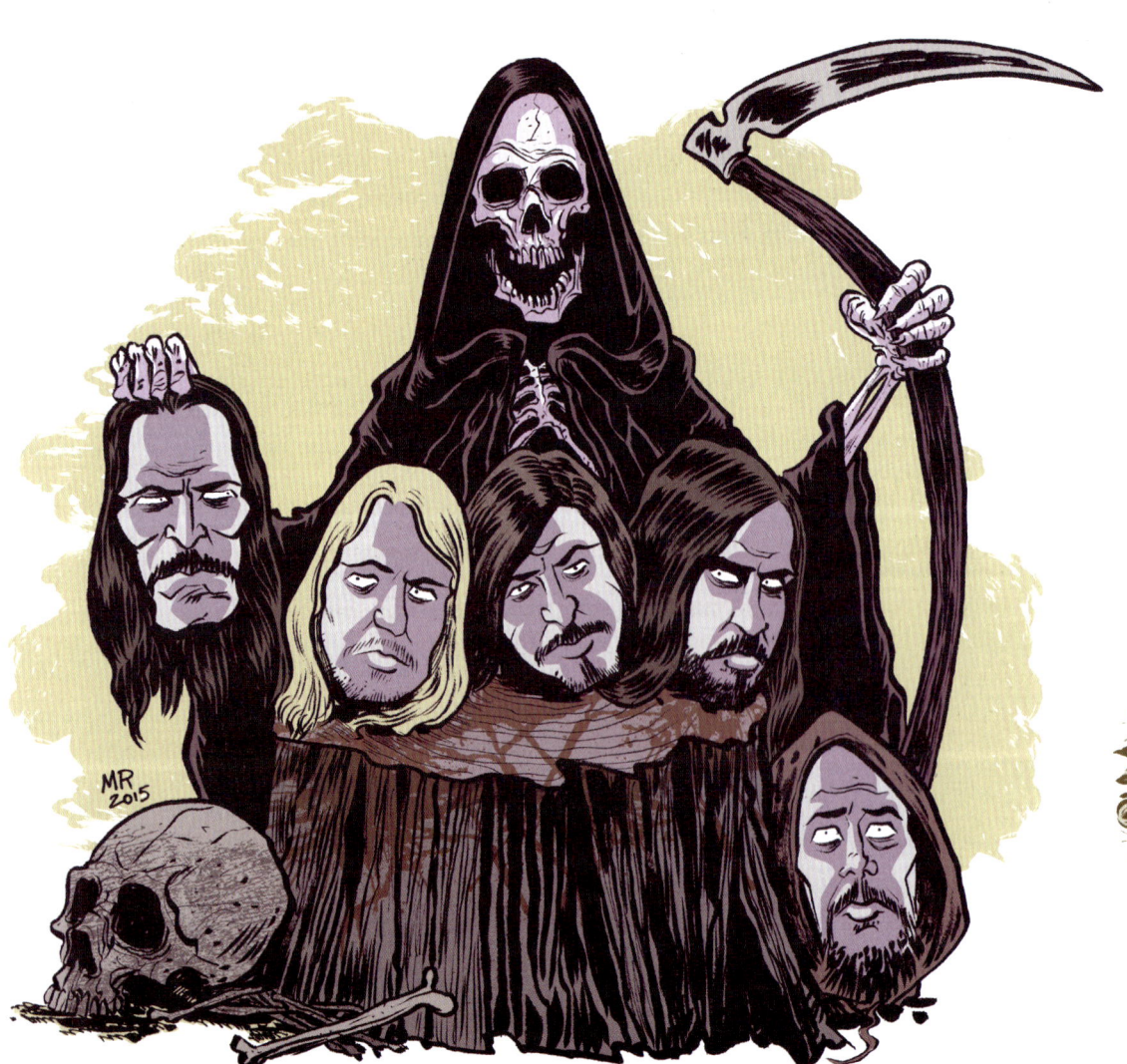

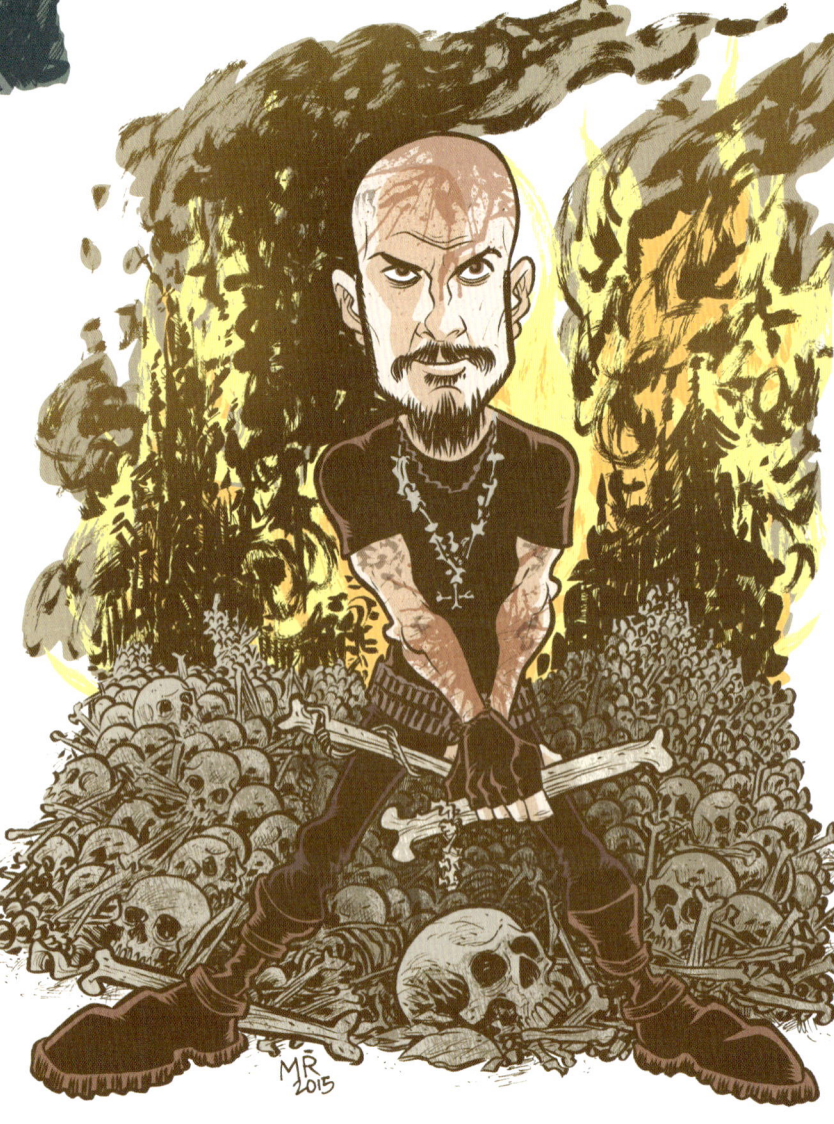

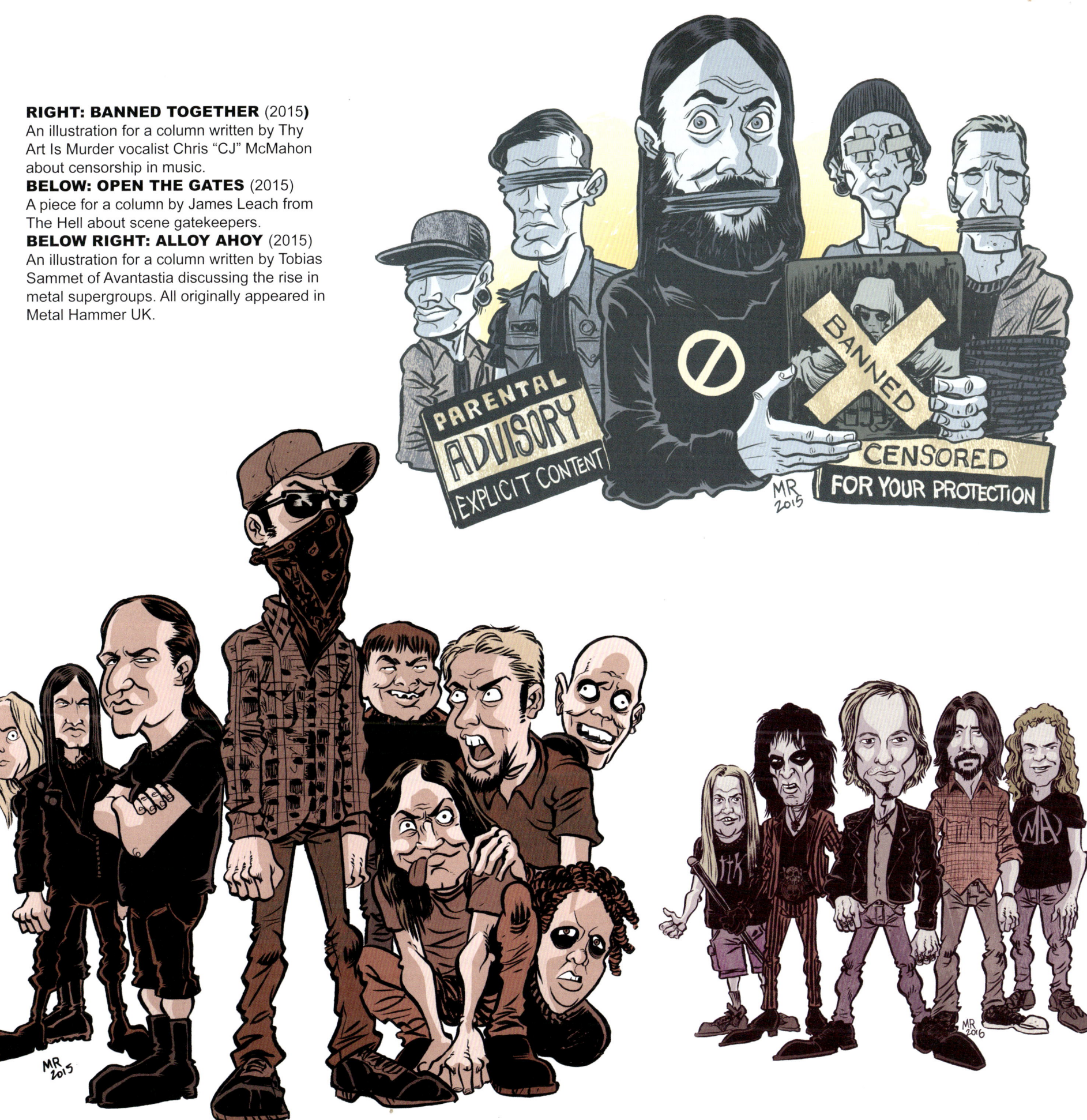

RIGHT: BANNED TOGETHER (2015)
An illustration for a column written by Thy Art Is Murder vocalist Chris "CJ" McMahon about censorship in music.

BELOW: OPEN THE GATES (2015)
A piece for a column by James Leach from The Hell about scene gatekeepers.

BELOW RIGHT: ALLOY AHOY (2015)
An illustration for a column written by Tobias Sammet of Avantastia discussing the rise in metal supergroups. All originally appeared in Metal Hammer UK.

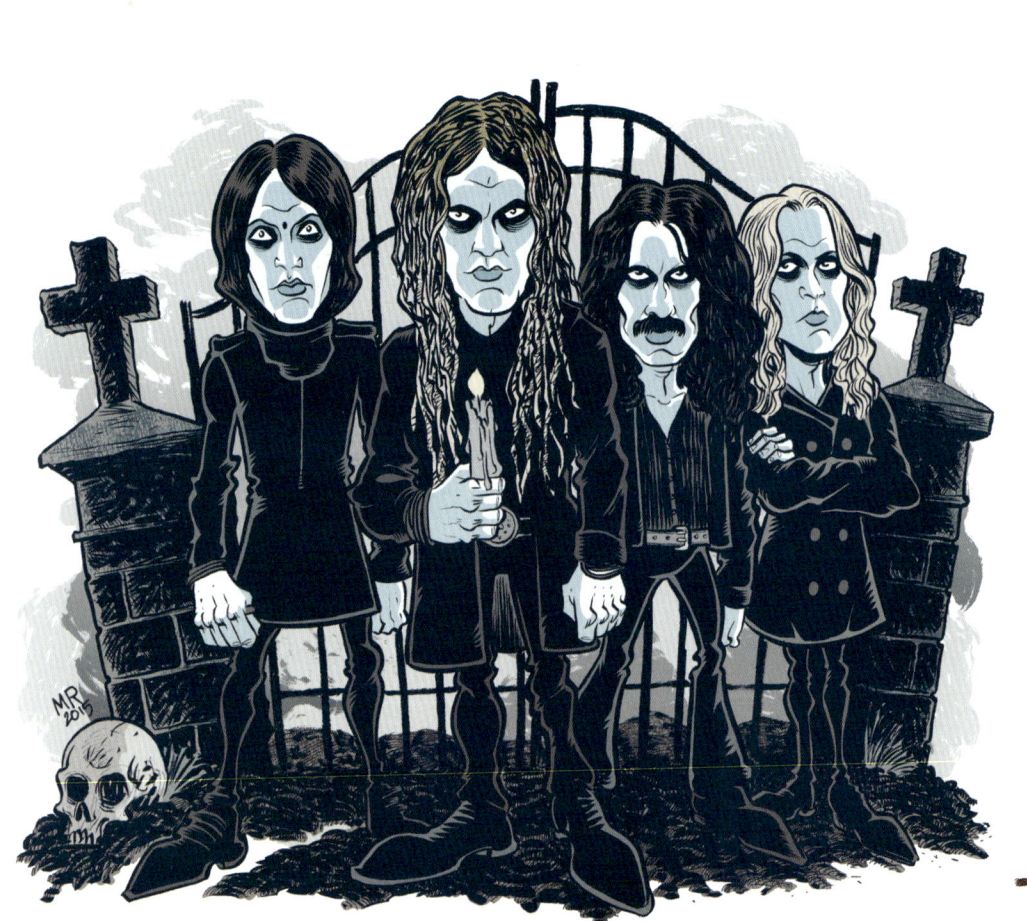

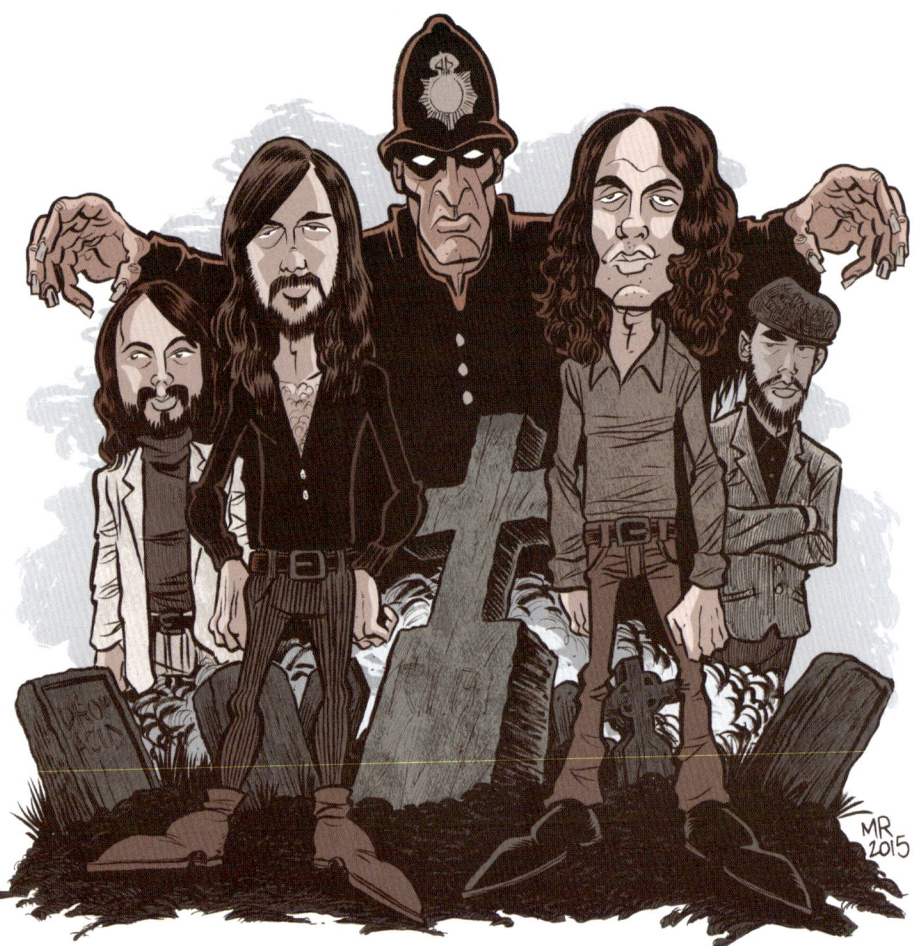

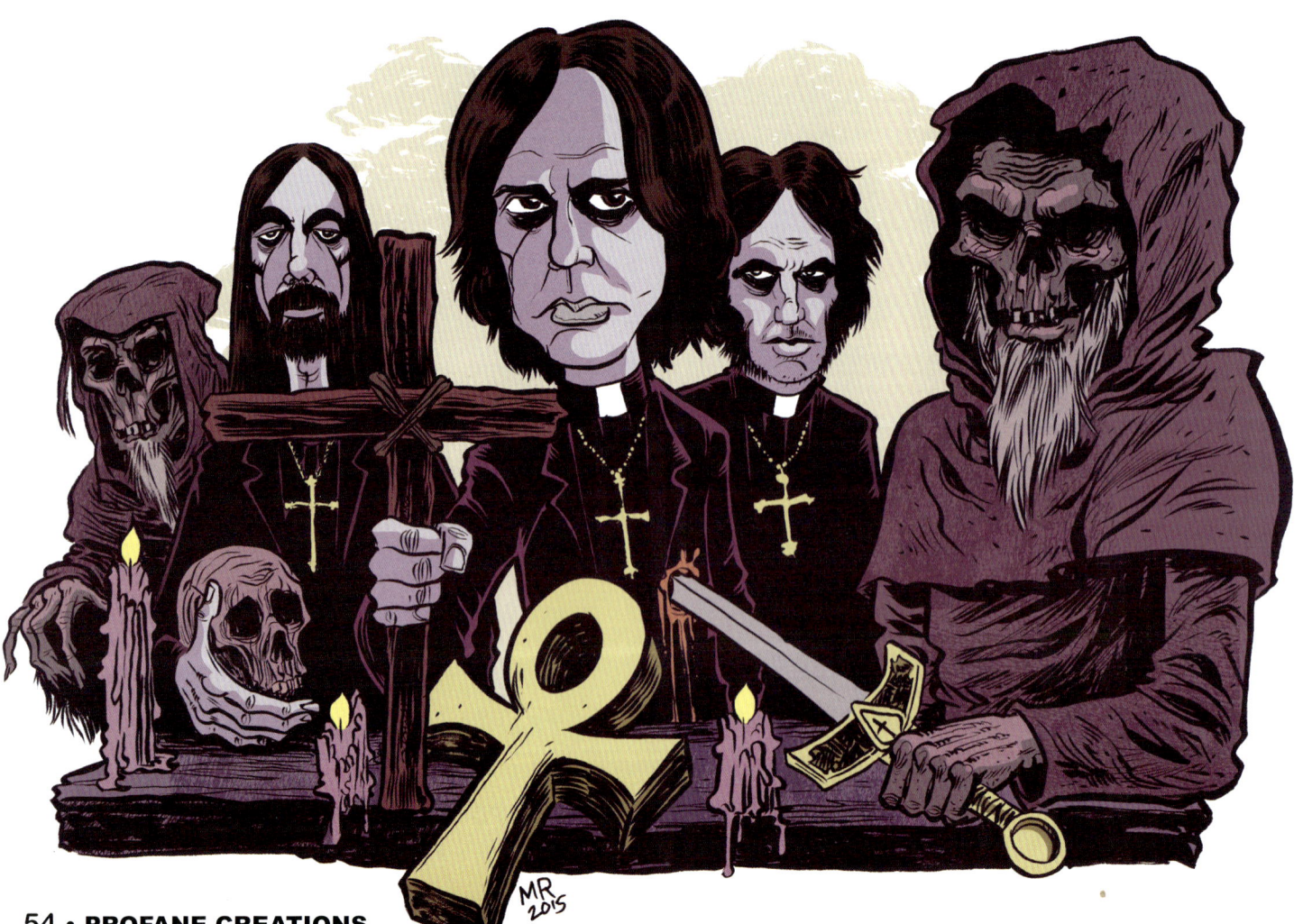

ABOVE LEFT:
GATEWAYS BECKON (2015)
An illustration for a review of Tribulation's album *The Children of the Night*.

ABOVE: CUT YOU DOWN (2015)
A piece for the review of Uncle Acid and the Deadbeats album *The Night Creeper*.

LEFT: BLIND DEAD (2015)
An illustration for the review of With The Dead's eponymous debut album. All appeared in Decibel Magazine.

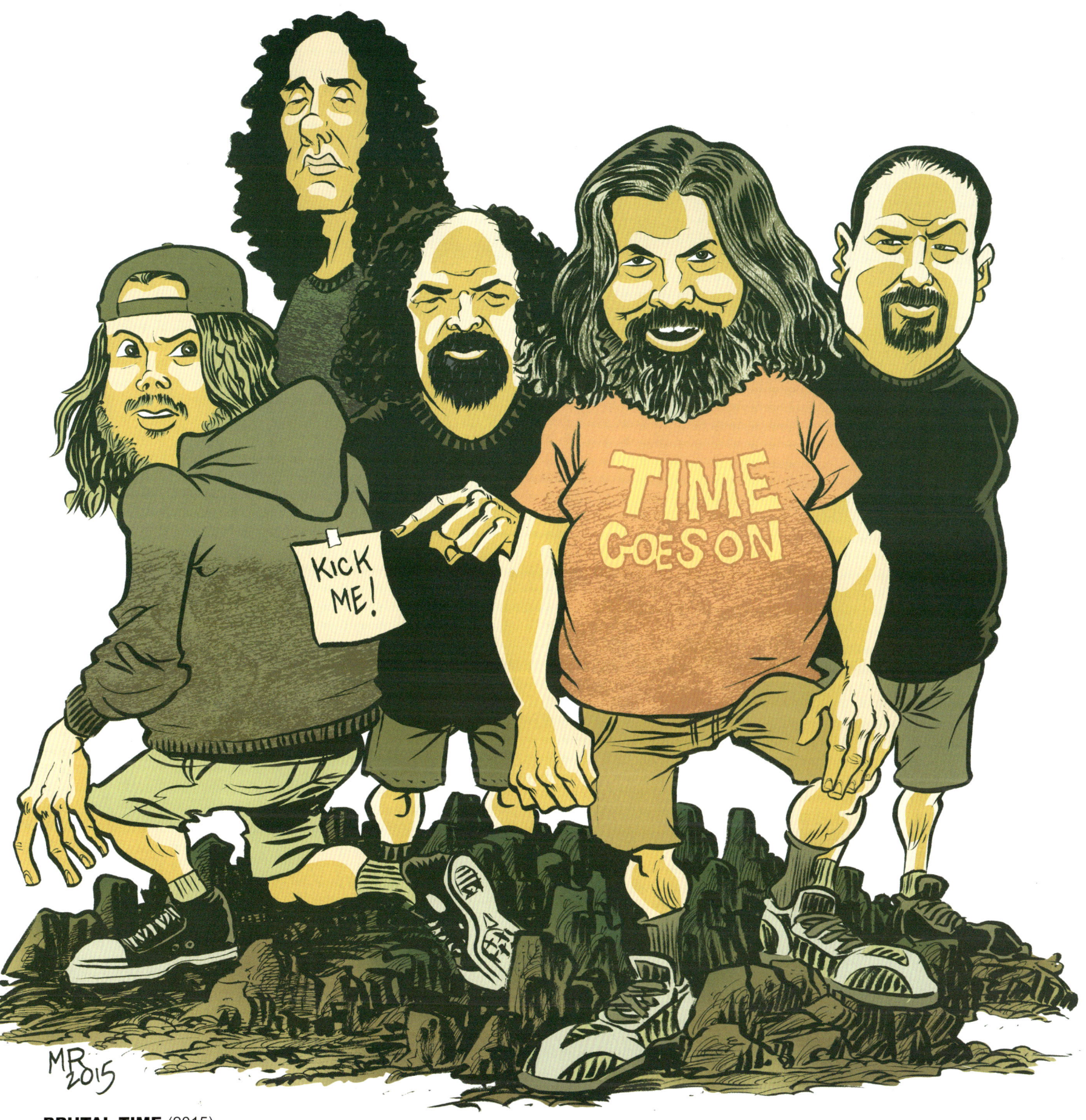

BRUTAL TIME (2015)
An illustration for a review of Venomous Concept's album *Kick Me Silly VCIII*. Originally appeared in Decibel Magazine.

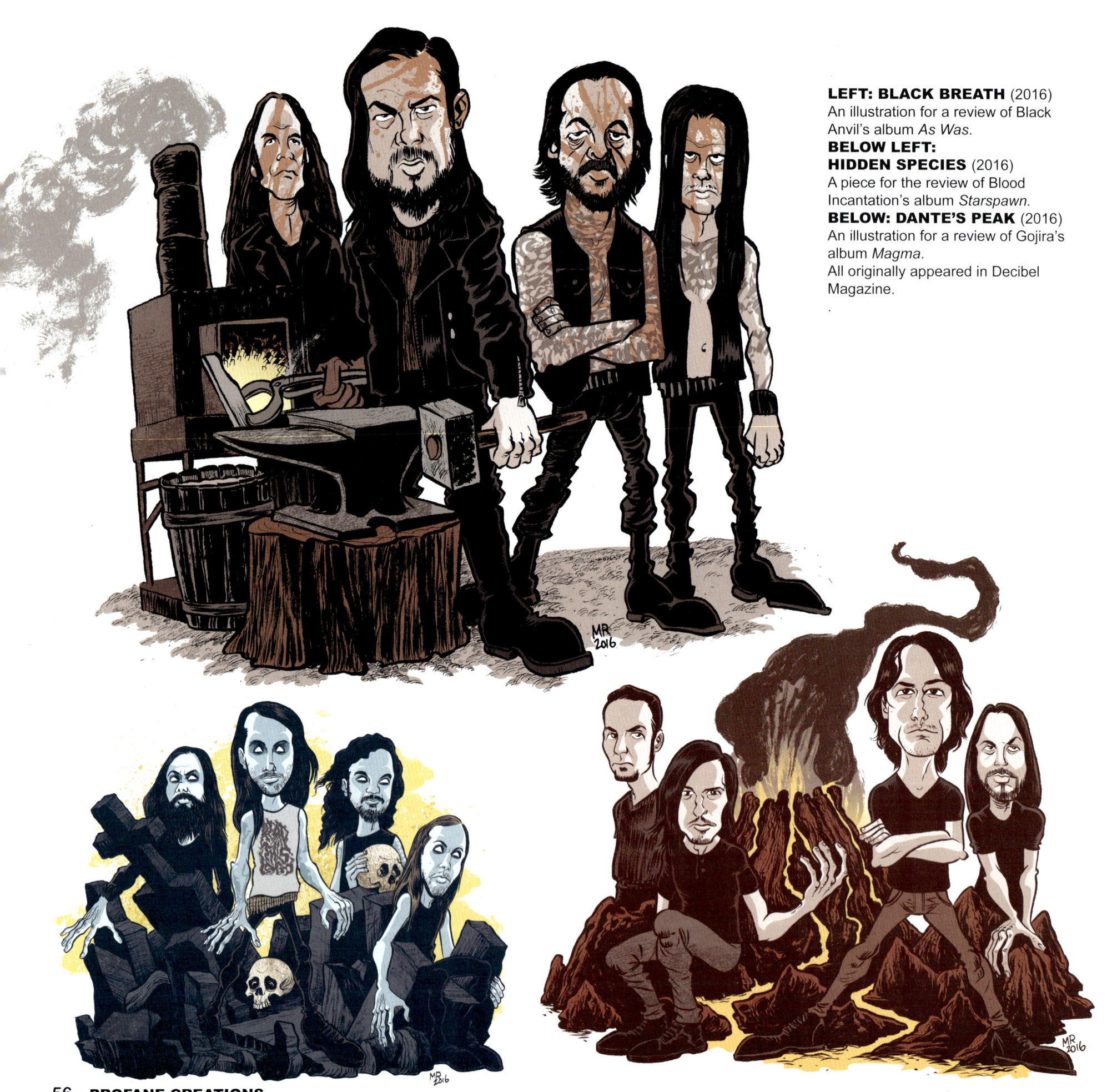

LEFT: BLACK BREATH (2016)
An illustration for a review of Black Anvil's album *As Was*.
BELOW LEFT:
HIDDEN SPECIES (2016)
A piece for the review of Blood Incantation's album *Starspawn*.
BELOW: DANTE'S PEAK (2016)
An illustration for a review of Gojira's album *Magma*.
All originally appeared in Decibel Magazine.
.

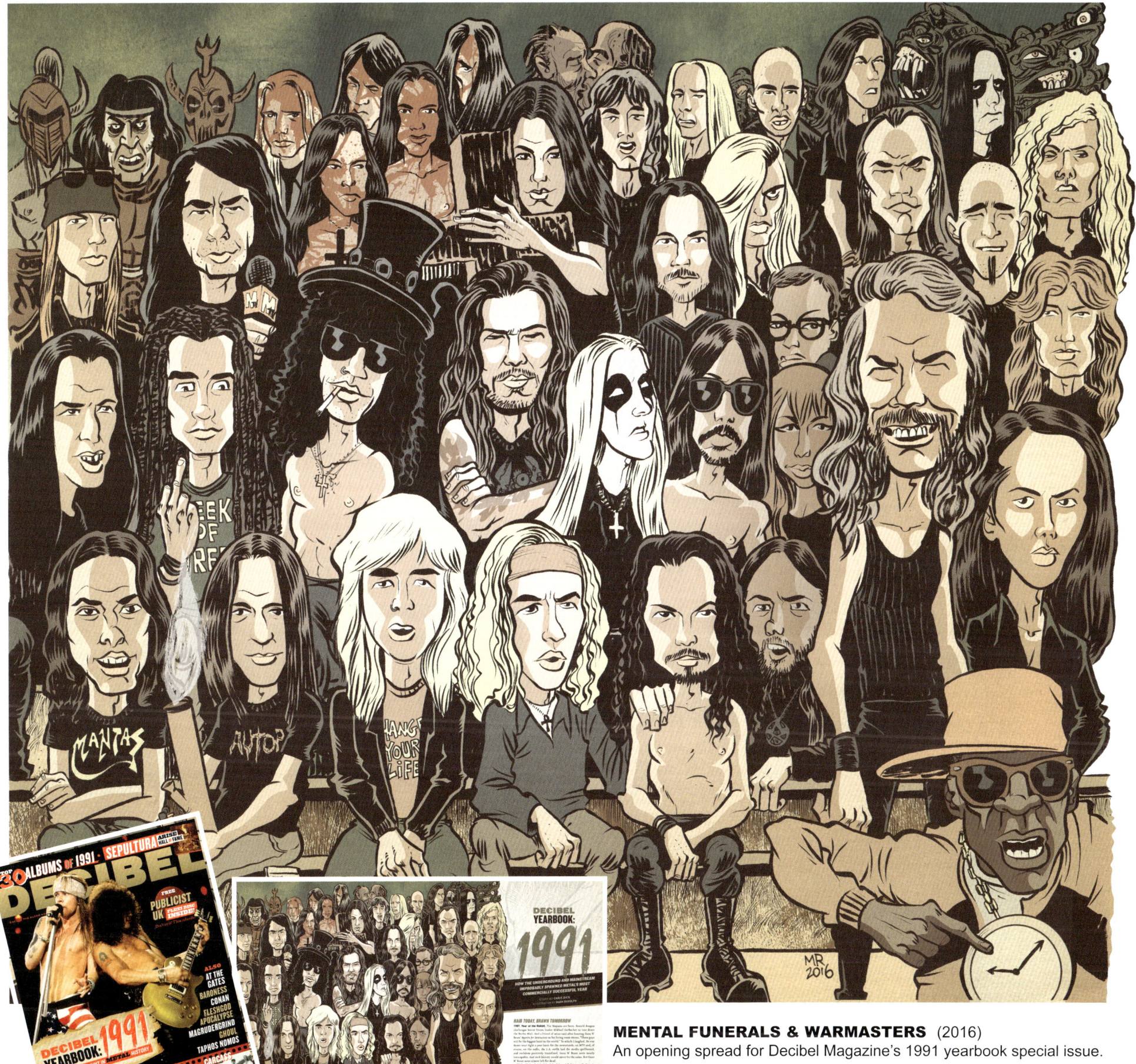

MENTAL FUNERALS & WARMASTERS (2016)
An opening spread for Decibel Magazine's 1991 yearbook special issue.

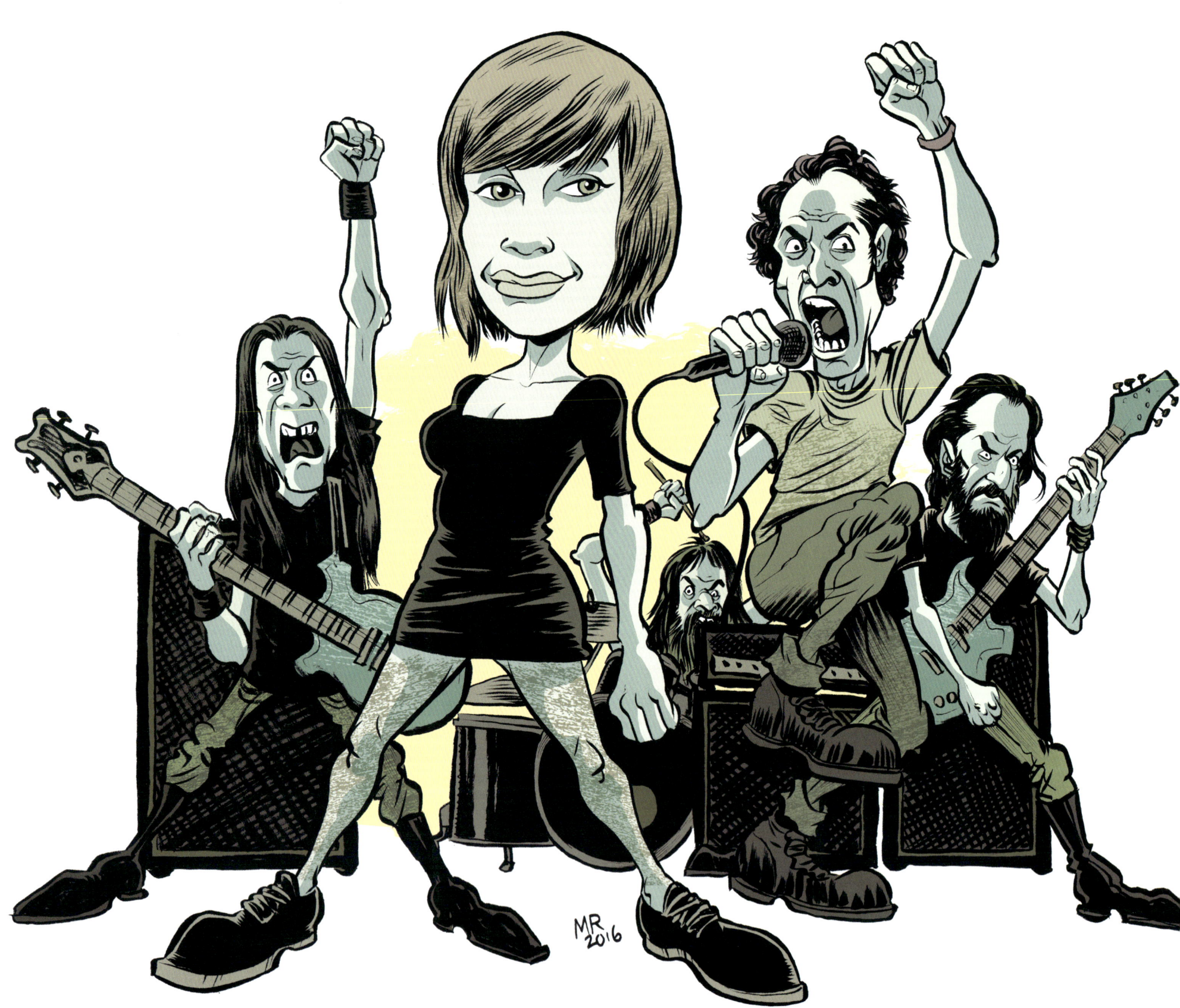

ABOVE: THAT'S HOW YOU... (2016)
An illustration for a column by Eva Spence of Rolo Tamassi about the importance of local scenes and having a DIY ethic.
Originally appeared in Metal Hammer UK.

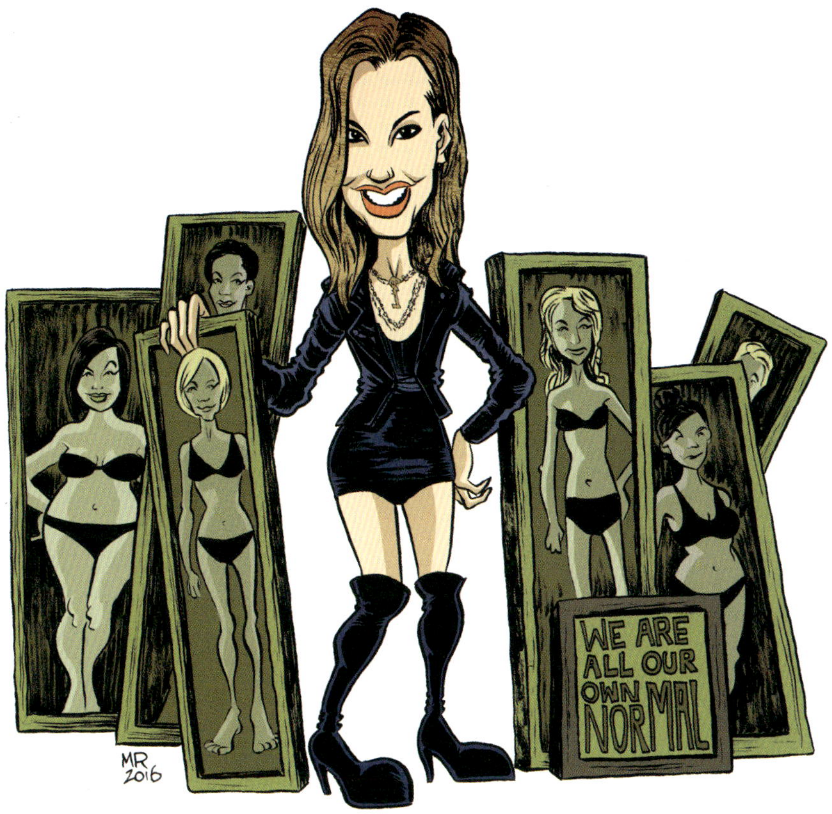

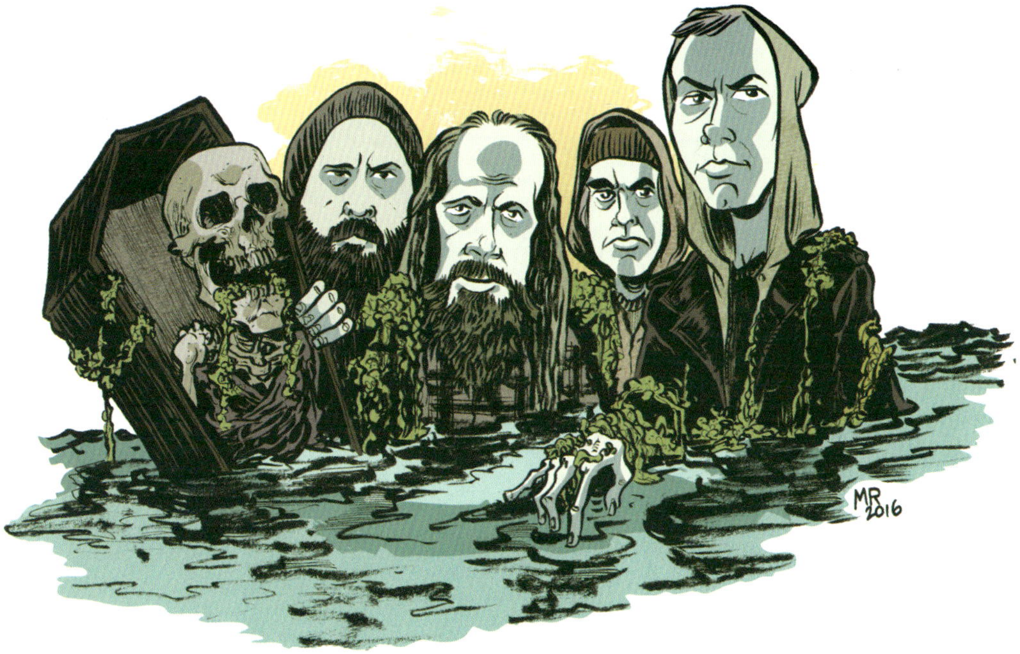

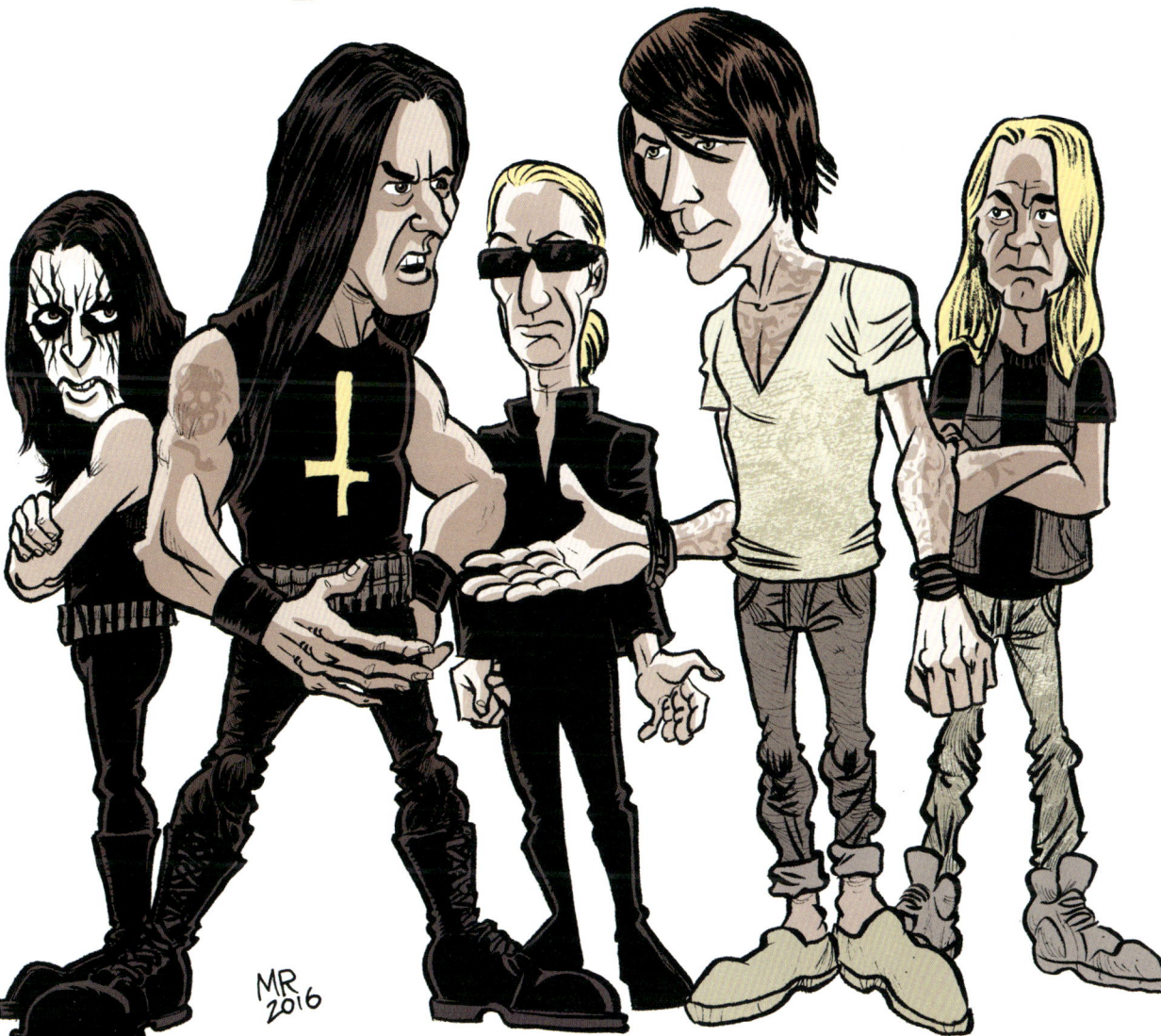

ABOVE LEFT: NORMAL (2016)
An illustration for a column written by Lzzy Hale of Halestorm discussing the normalization of different female body shapes. From Metal Hammer UK.

ABOVE:
DEADLY INNER SENSE (2016)
A piece for a review of Graves At Sea's album *The Curse That is*. Originally appeared in Decibel Magazine.

LEFT: GET OFF MY LAWN (2016)
An illustration for an article about different genres and generations of metal getting along. From Metal Hammer UK

RIGHT:
THE HANDS OF REASON (2016)
An illustration for the lead review of Iron Reagan's album *Crossover Ministry*. From Decibel Magazine.
BELOW: HANGMAN'S CHOIR (2016)
A piece for a review of Inter Arma's album *Paradise Gallows*. Originally appeared in Decibel Magazine.
BOTTOM RIGHT:
ART THERAPY? (2016)
An illustration for a column by John Dyer Baizley from Baroness about how art helped him overcome obstacles. From Metal Hammer UK.

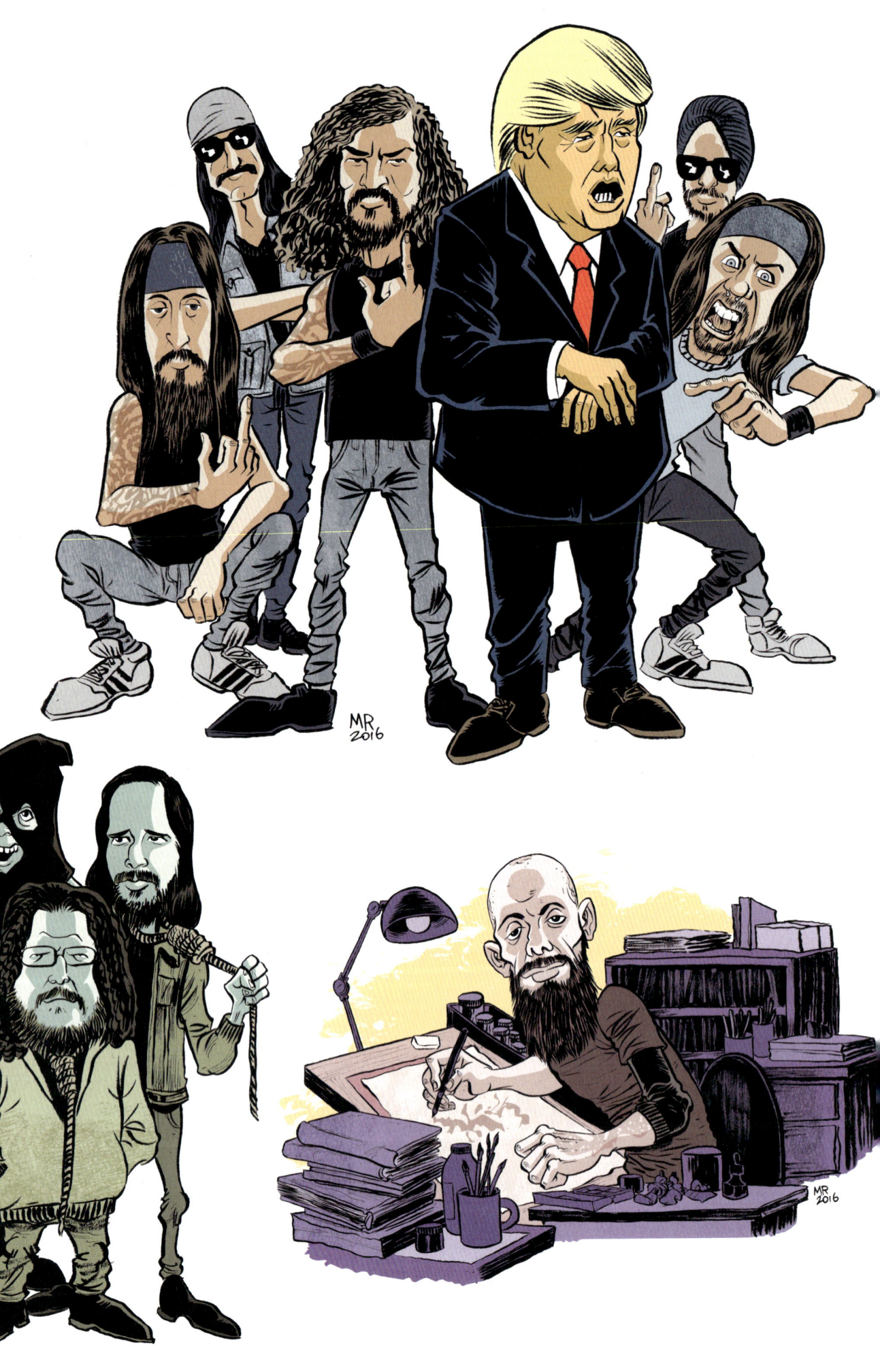

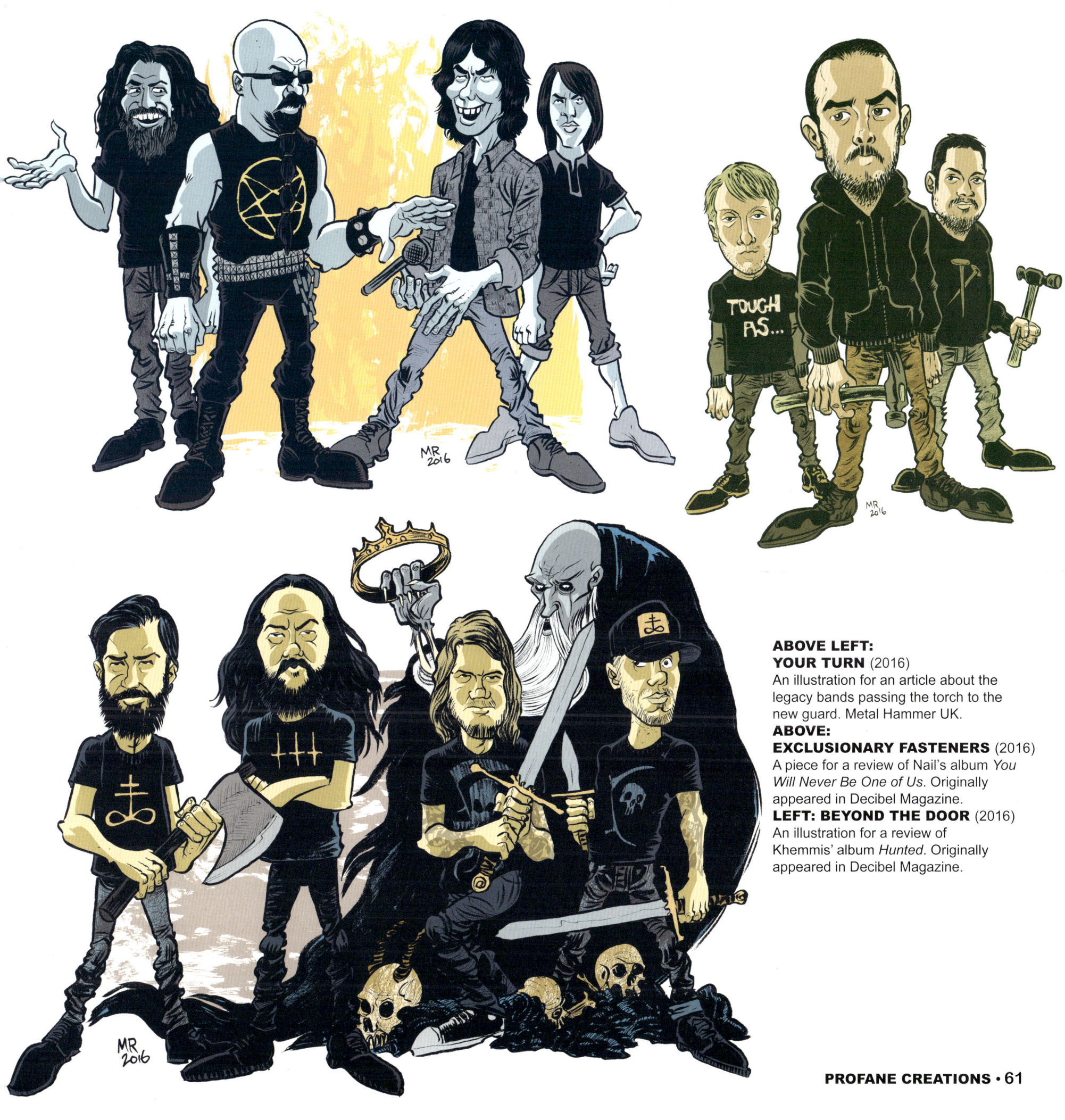

ABOVE LEFT:
YOUR TURN (2016)
An illustration for an article about the legacy bands passing the torch to the new guard. Metal Hammer UK.
ABOVE:
EXCLUSIONARY FASTENERS (2016)
A piece for a review of Nail's album *You Will Never Be One of Us*. Originally appeared in Decibel Magazine.
LEFT: BEYOND THE DOOR (2016)
An illustration for a review of Khemmis' album *Hunted*. Originally appeared in Decibel Magazine.

RIGHT:
THINK BEFORE YOU INK (2016)
An illustration for a column by Trivium's Matt Heafy
about tattoos as mindless fashion accessories or
personal expression. Metal Hammer UK.
BELOW:
STRAIGHT THROUGH THE HEART (2016)
A piece for a review of SubRosa's album *For This
We Fought The Battle of Ages*. Originally appeared
in Decibel Magazine.
BELOW RIGHT: ATTITUDE ERA (2017)
Illustration for an article about the absurdness of
mainstream metal in the 90s. Features: James
Hetfield, James "Munky" Shaffer, Wes Borland,
Peter Steele and Kerry King. Metal Hammer UK.

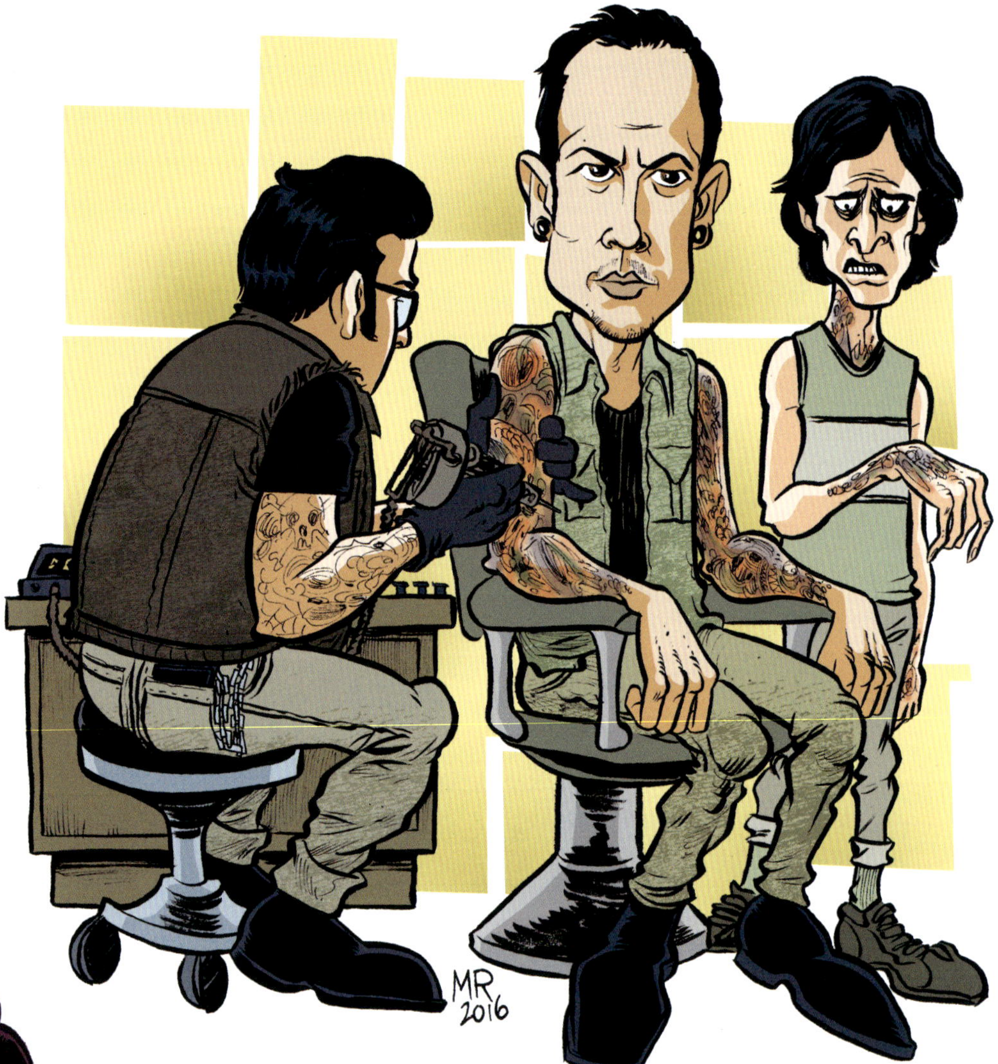

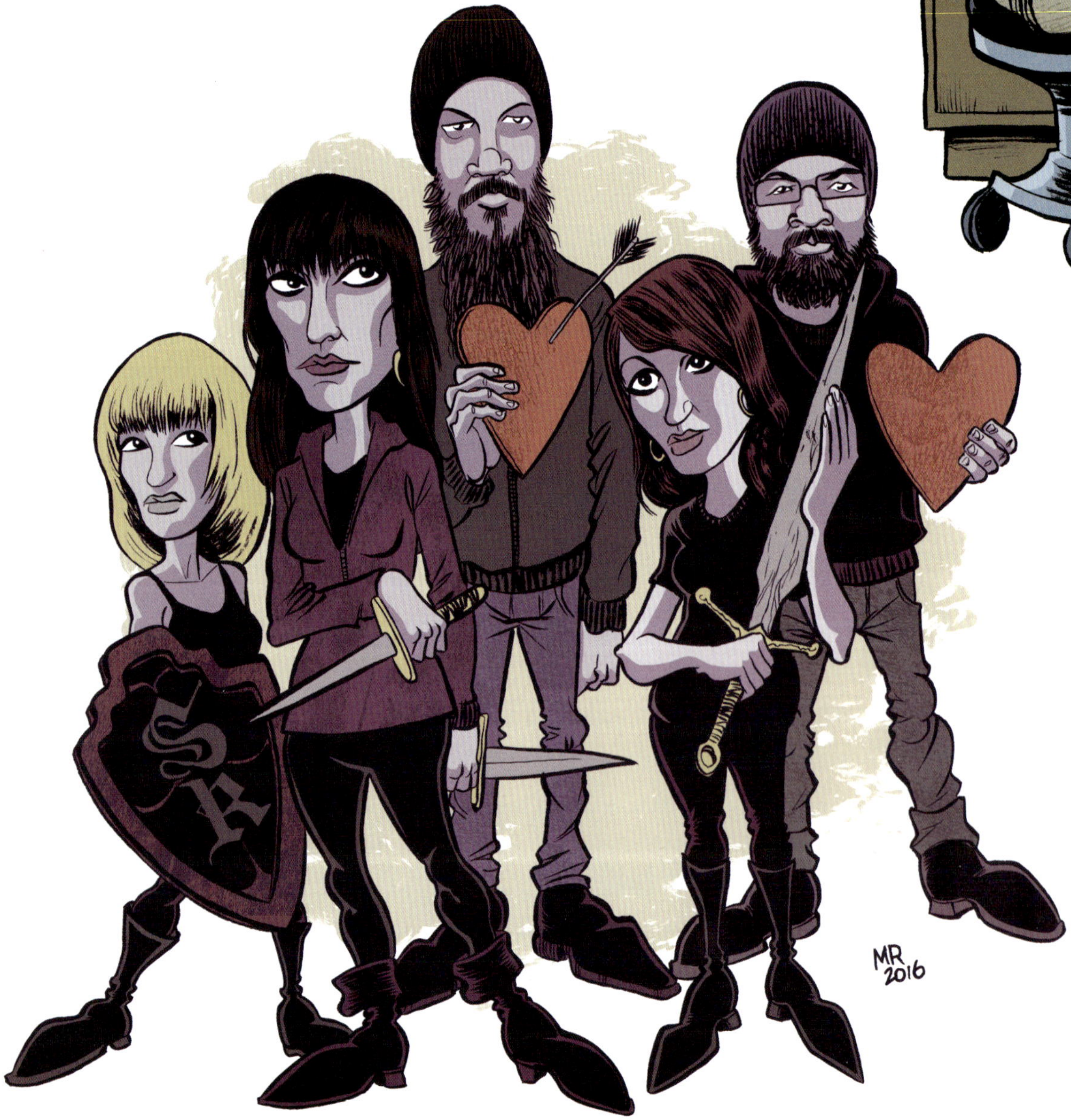

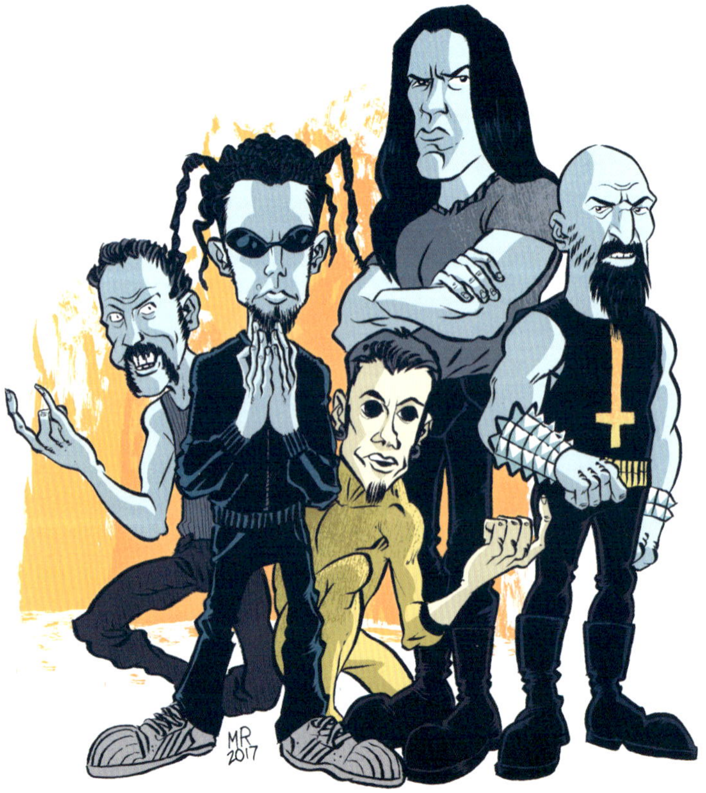

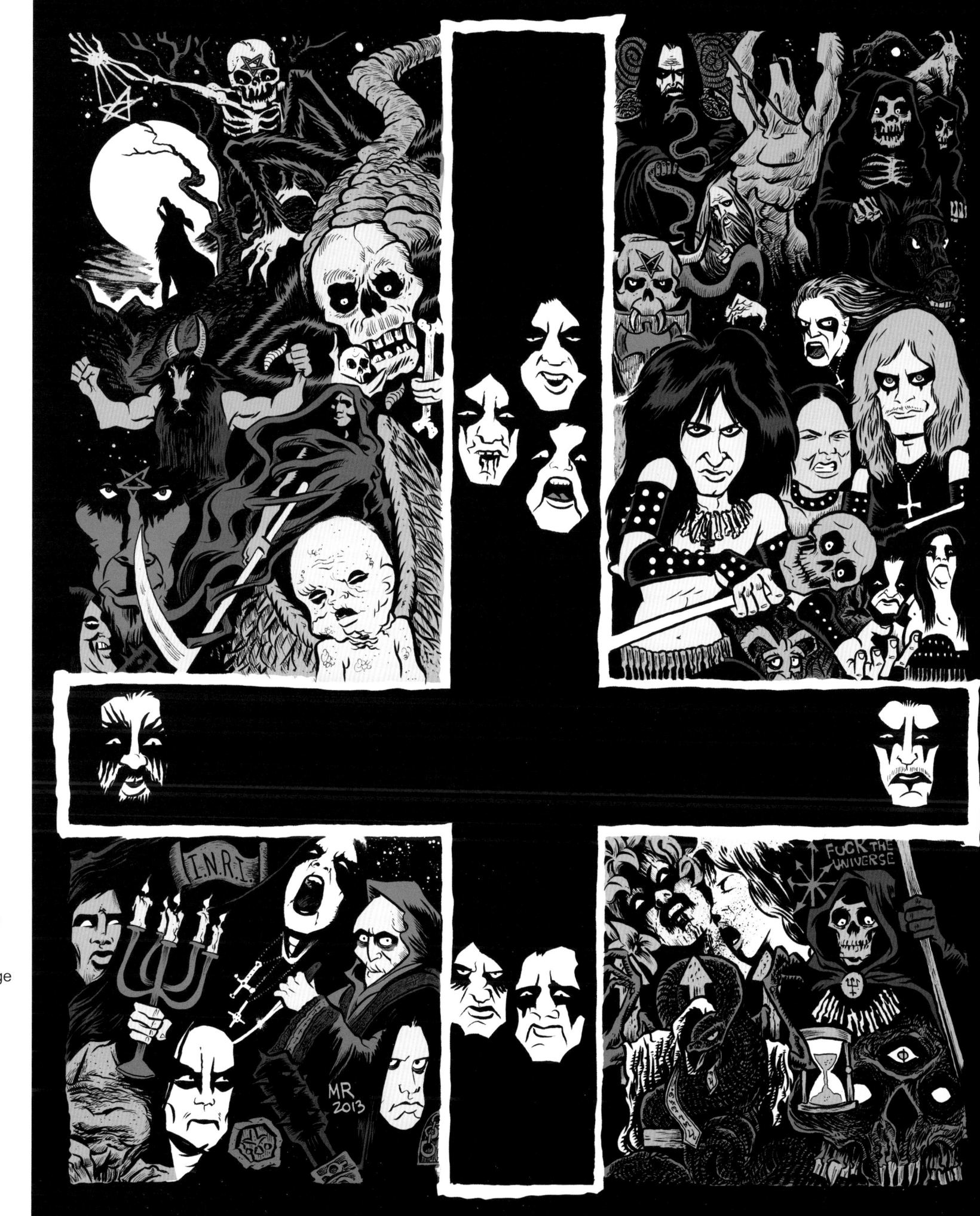

BLACK METAL (2017)
Cover illustration for Decibel's special Black Metal issue. It's a montage of 32 different cover elements of the top 100 Black metal albums of all time.

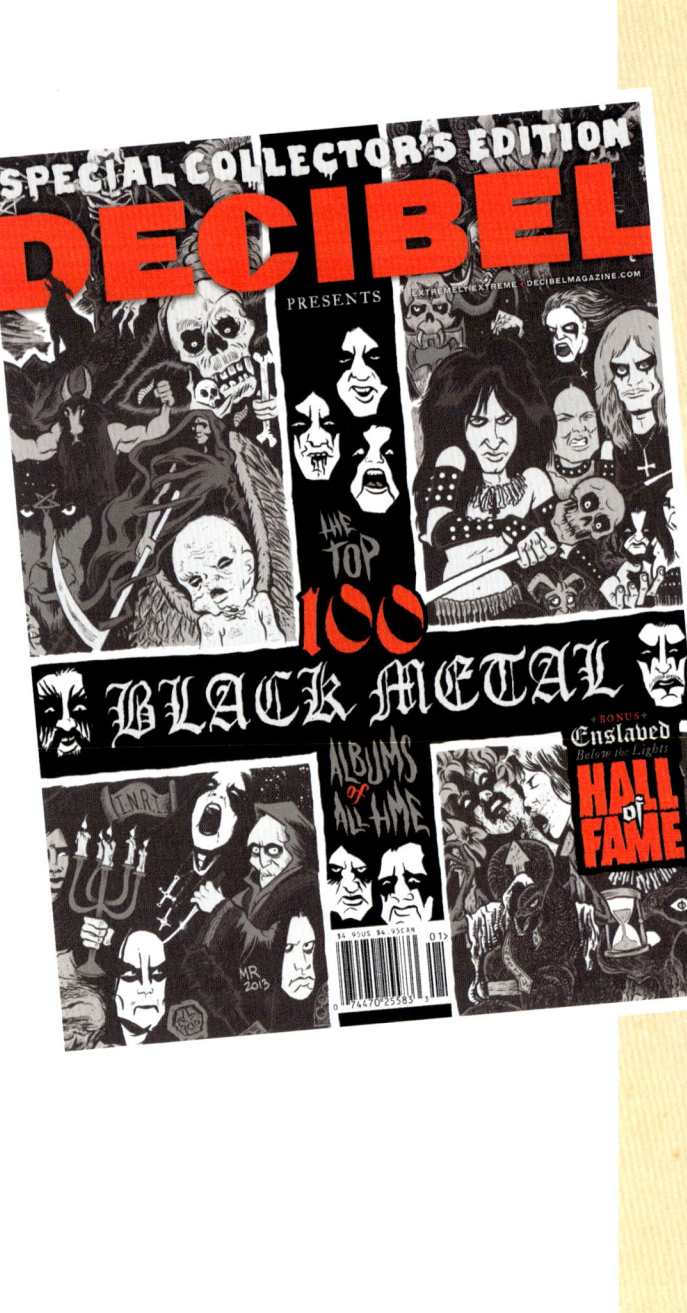
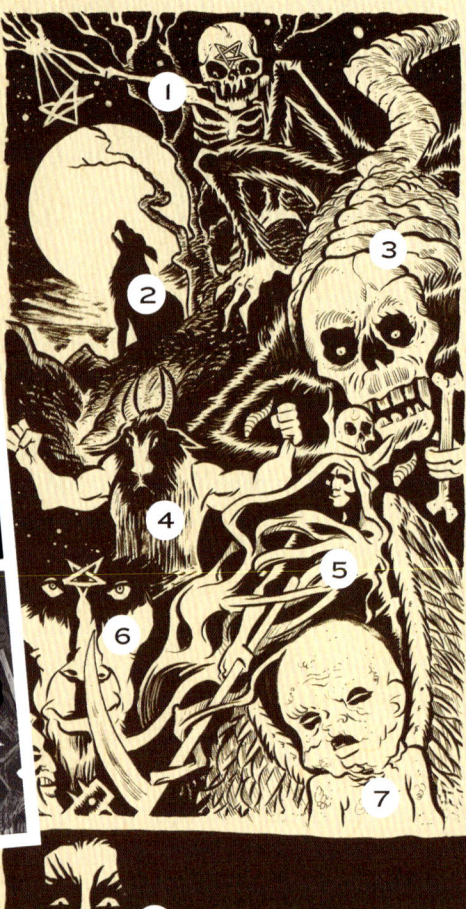
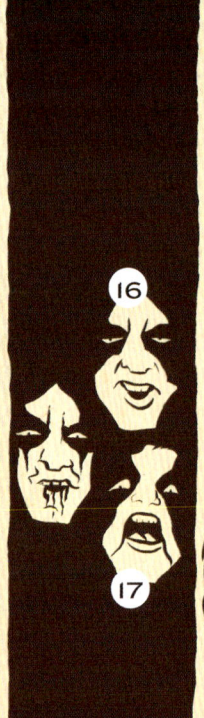
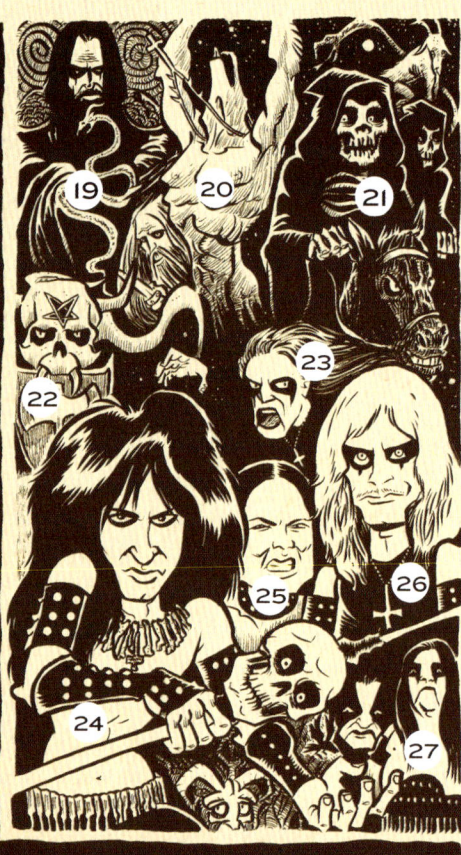
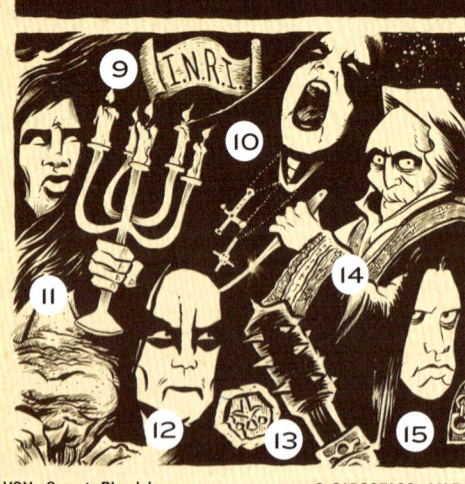
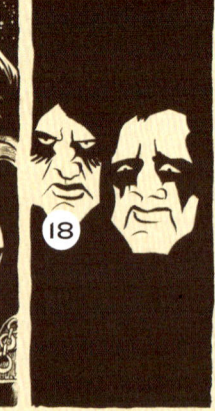
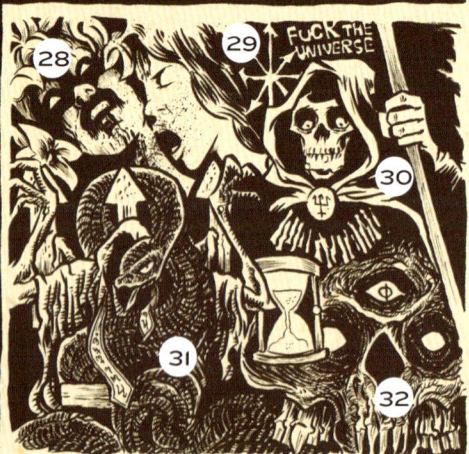

1. VON - Satanic Blood demo
2. ULVER - Nattens Madrigal
3. HELLHAMMER - Apocalyptic Raids
4. BATHORY - Under the Sign...
5. EMPEROR - In the Nightside Eclipse
6. VENOM - Black Metal
7. DEATHSPELL OMEGA - Si Monumentum...
8. ROOT - The Book

9. SARCOFAGO - I.N.R.I.
10. DARKTHRONE - Transilvanian Hunger
11. FUNERAL MIST - Maranatha
12. MAYHEM - De Mysteriis...
13. TORMENTOR - Anno Domini demo
14. SAMAEL - Blood Ritual
15. BURZUM - Filosofem
16. MAYHEM - Deathcrush
17. DIMMU BORGIR - Enthrone Darkness...

18. SATYRICON - Nemesis Divina
19. ABSU - Tara
20. MARDUK - Opus Nocturne
21. MARDUK - Those of the Unlight
22. MASTER'S HAMMER - Ritual
23. DARKTHRONE - A Blaze...
24. BATHORY - Bathory
25. VENOM - Welcome to Hell
26. CELTIC FROST - Morbid Tales

27. IMMORTAL - At The Heart of Winter
28. CRADLE OF FILTH - The Principle...
29. CRAFT - Fuck the Universe
30. DISSECTION - Storm of the Light's Bane
31. WATAIN - Sworn to the Dark
32. INQUISITION - Ominous Doctrines...

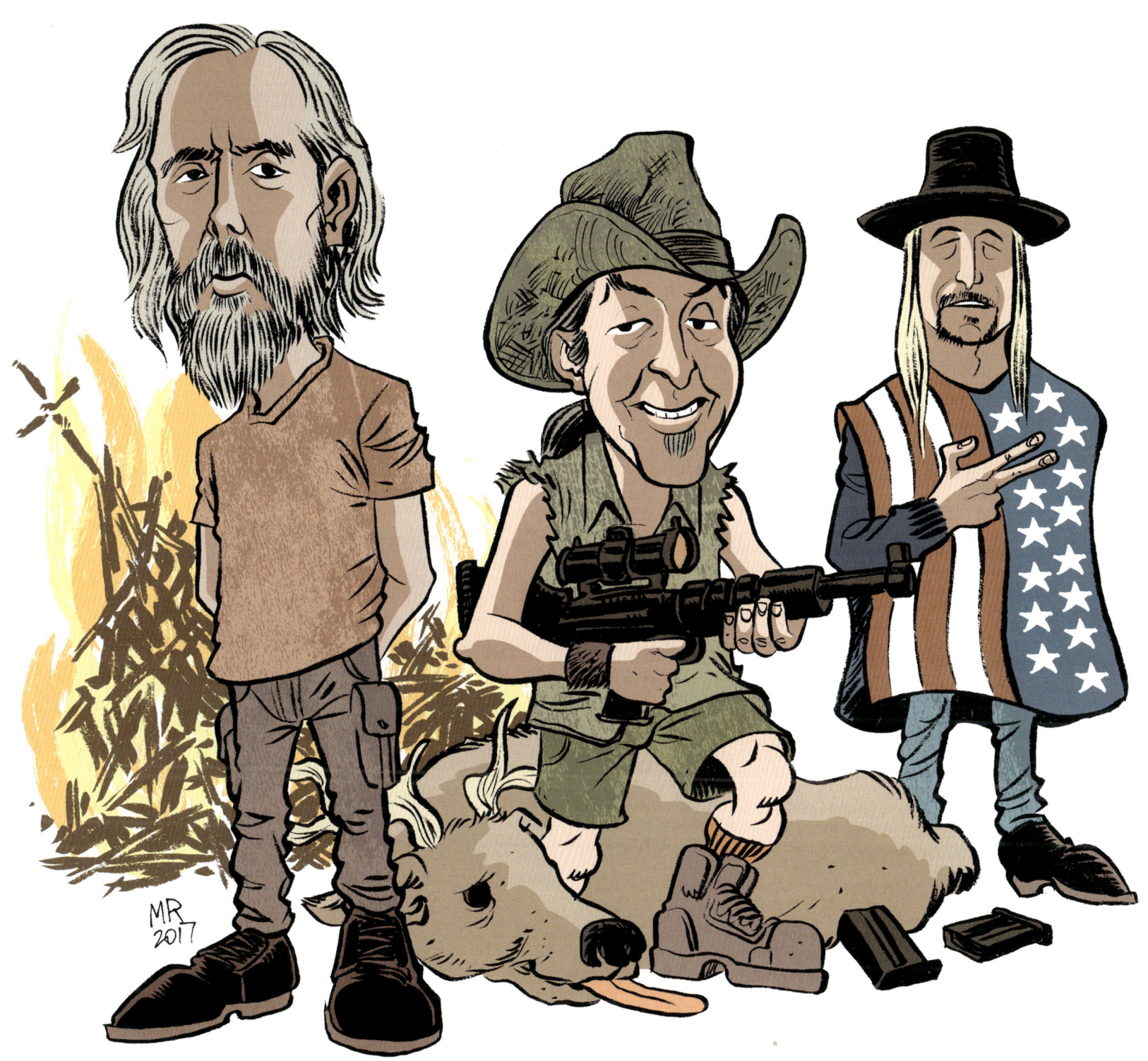

ART FROM THE ARTIST (2017)
An illustration for a column about seperating the art from the artist's personal beliefs and behaviour. Featuring: Kristian "Varg" Vikernes, Ted Nugent and Robert "Kid Rock" Ritchie. Originally appeared in Metal Hammer UK.

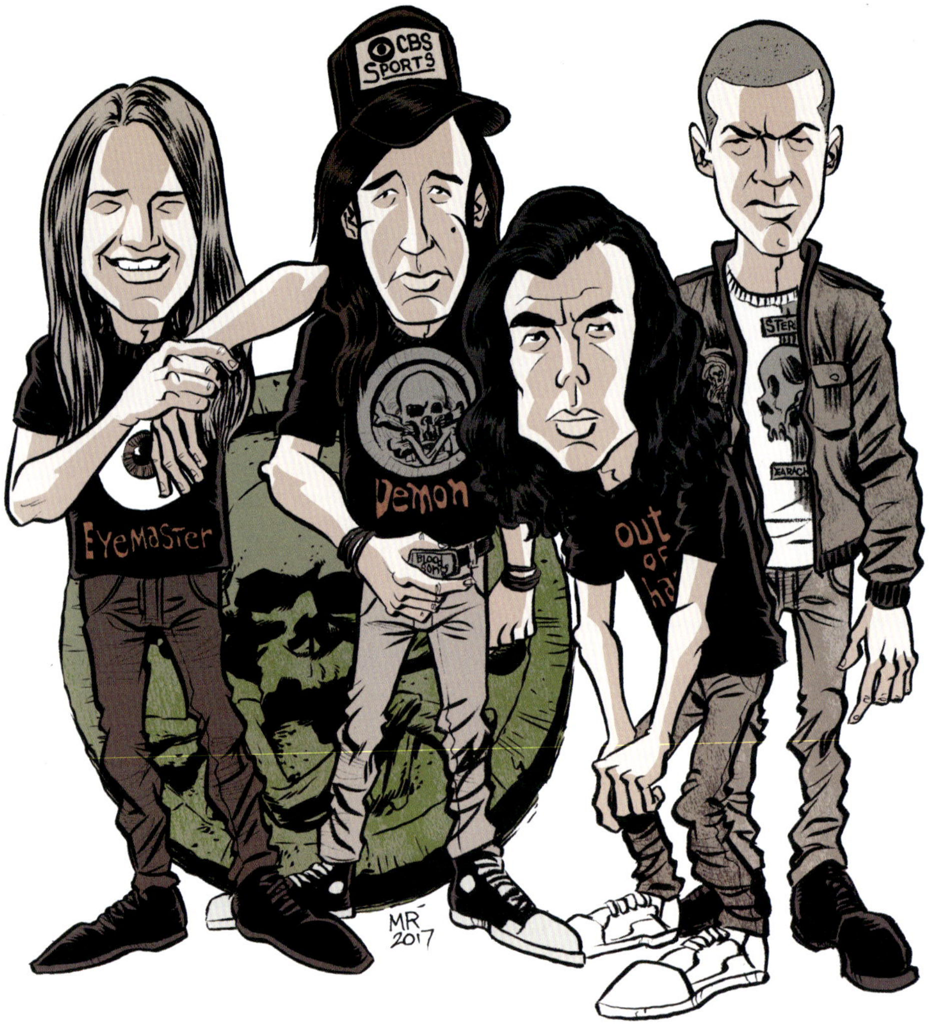

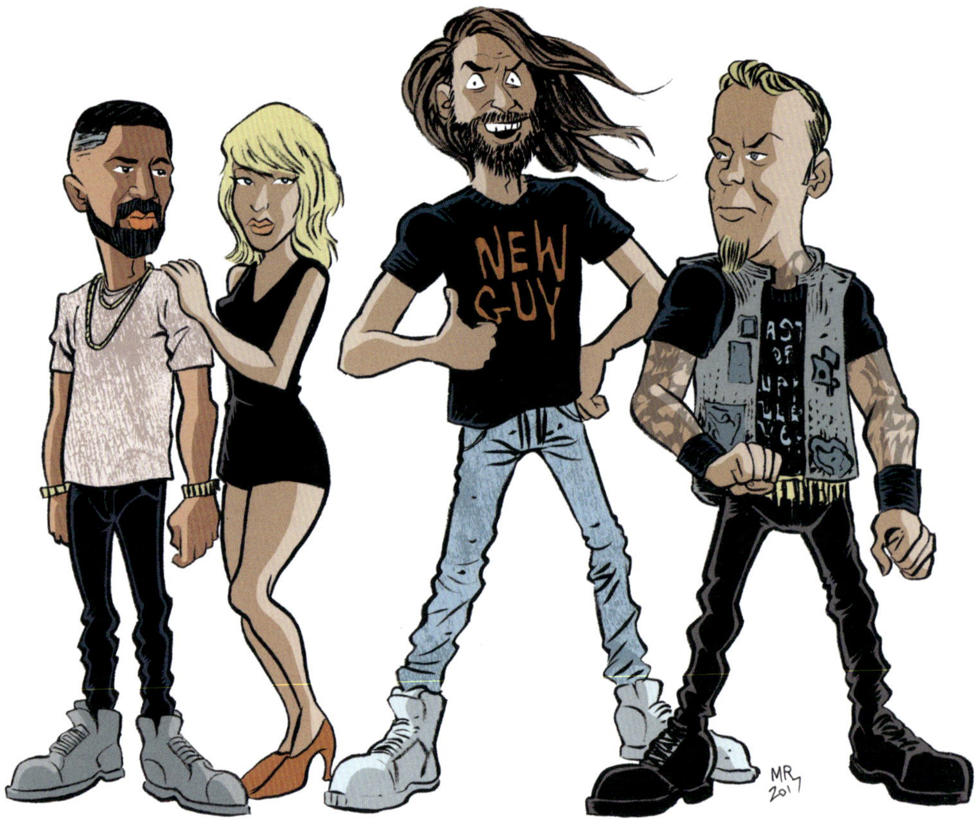

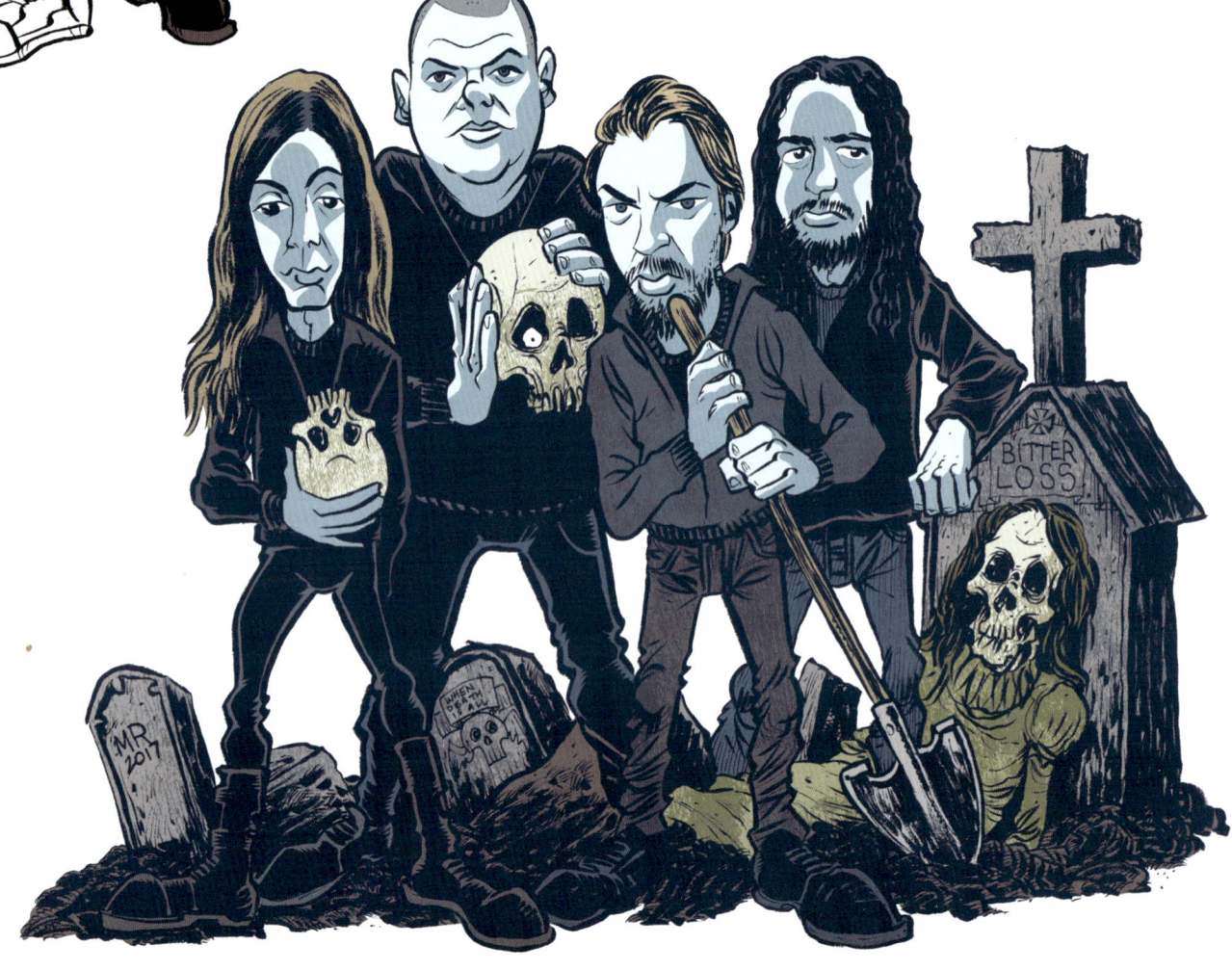

ABOVE: WALLS OF JERICHO (2017)
An illustration for the review of Full Of Hell's
Trumpeting Ecstasy album. Originally appeared
in Decibel Magazine.

ABOVE RIGHT:
SHADOWLIT FACADE (2017)
A piece for an article about the crossover of
metal aesthetic into mainstream music. Metal
Hammer UK.

RIGHT: BITTER LOSS (2017)
An illustration for the review of Loss' album
Horizonless. Decibel Magazine.

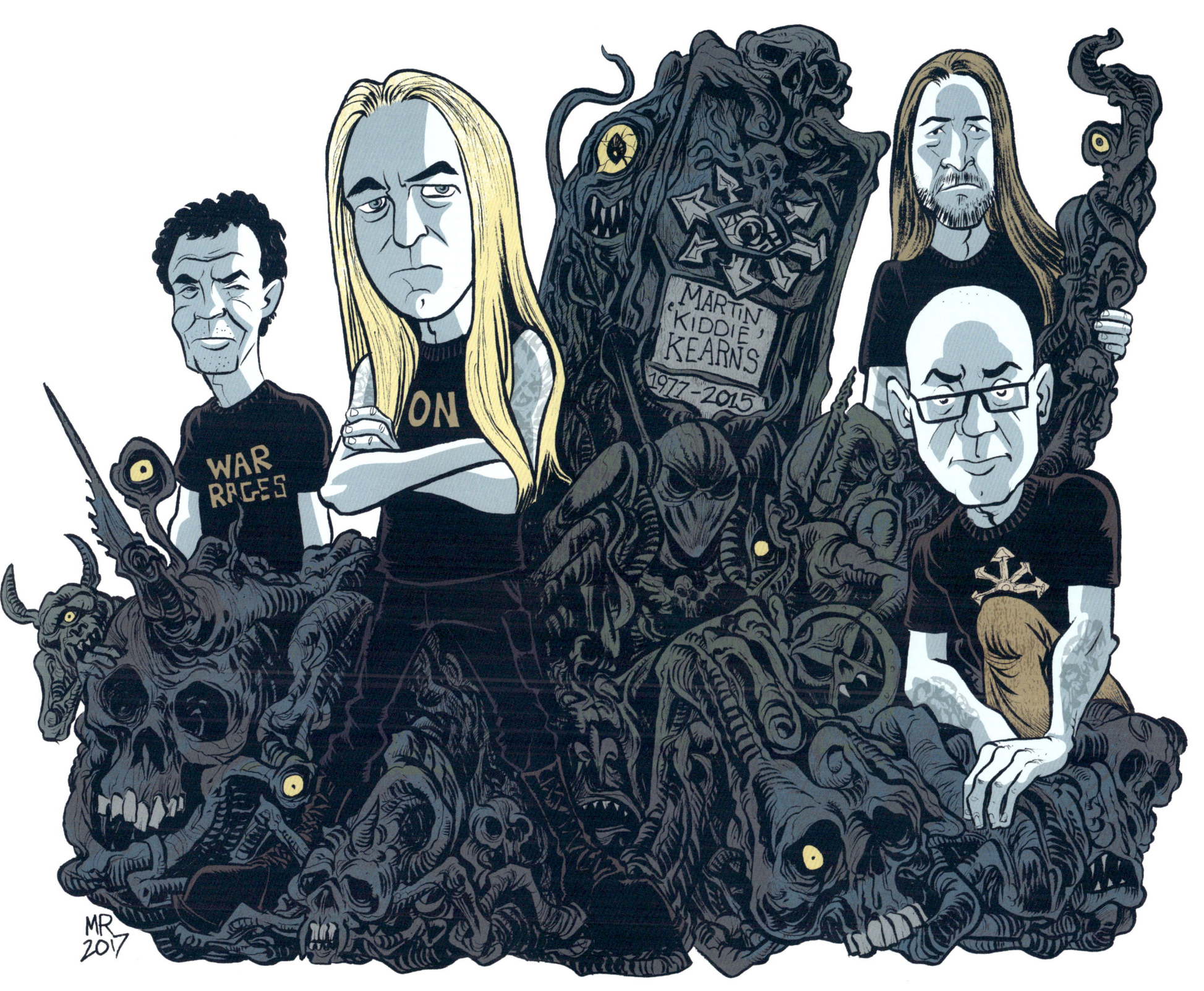

AS CANNONS FADE (2017)
An illustration for a review of Memoriam's *For The Fallen* album.

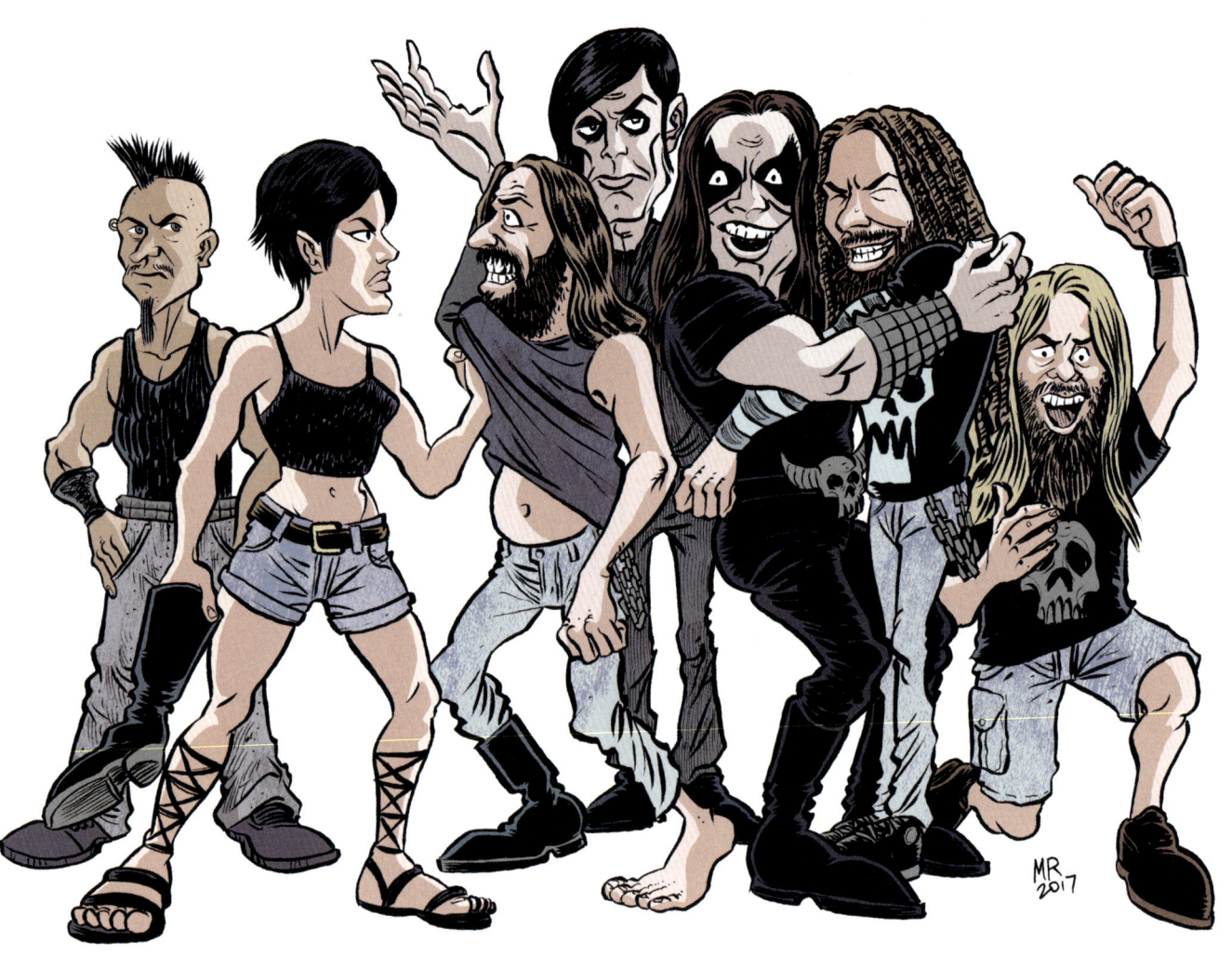

LEFT: METAL HEALTH (2017)
An illustration for a column about calling people out who are unsympathetic to those with mental health issues.

BOTTOM LEFT:
PAY FOR YOUR SINS (2017)
A piece for a column about paying for physical music formats.

BELOW: NO GODS, NO MEMBERS (2017)
An illustration for an article about bands with no original members. Featuring: Mikael Åkerfeldt (Opeth), Shane Embury (Napalm Death), Andreas Kisser (Sepultura) and Anders Fridén (In Flames).

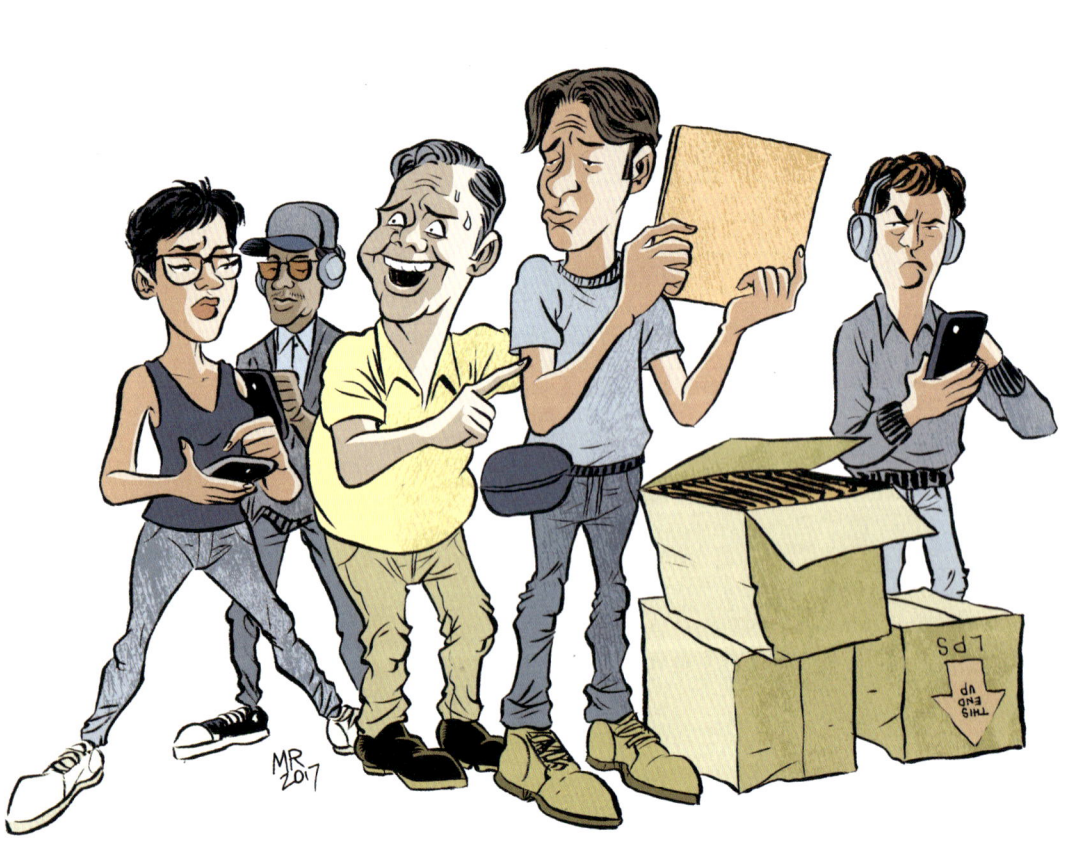

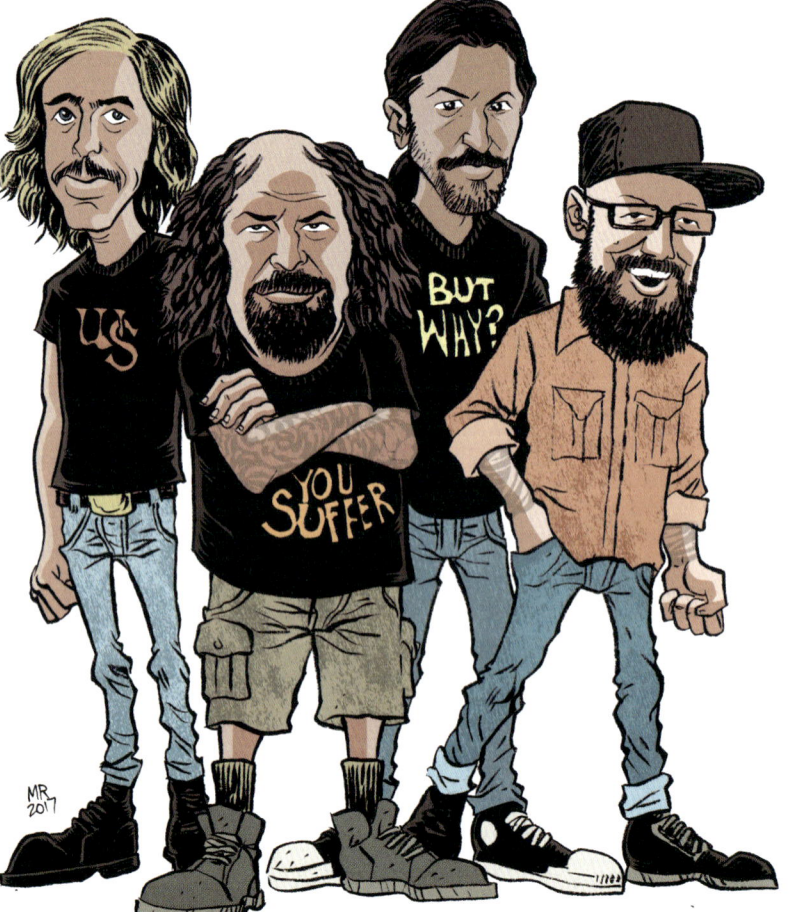

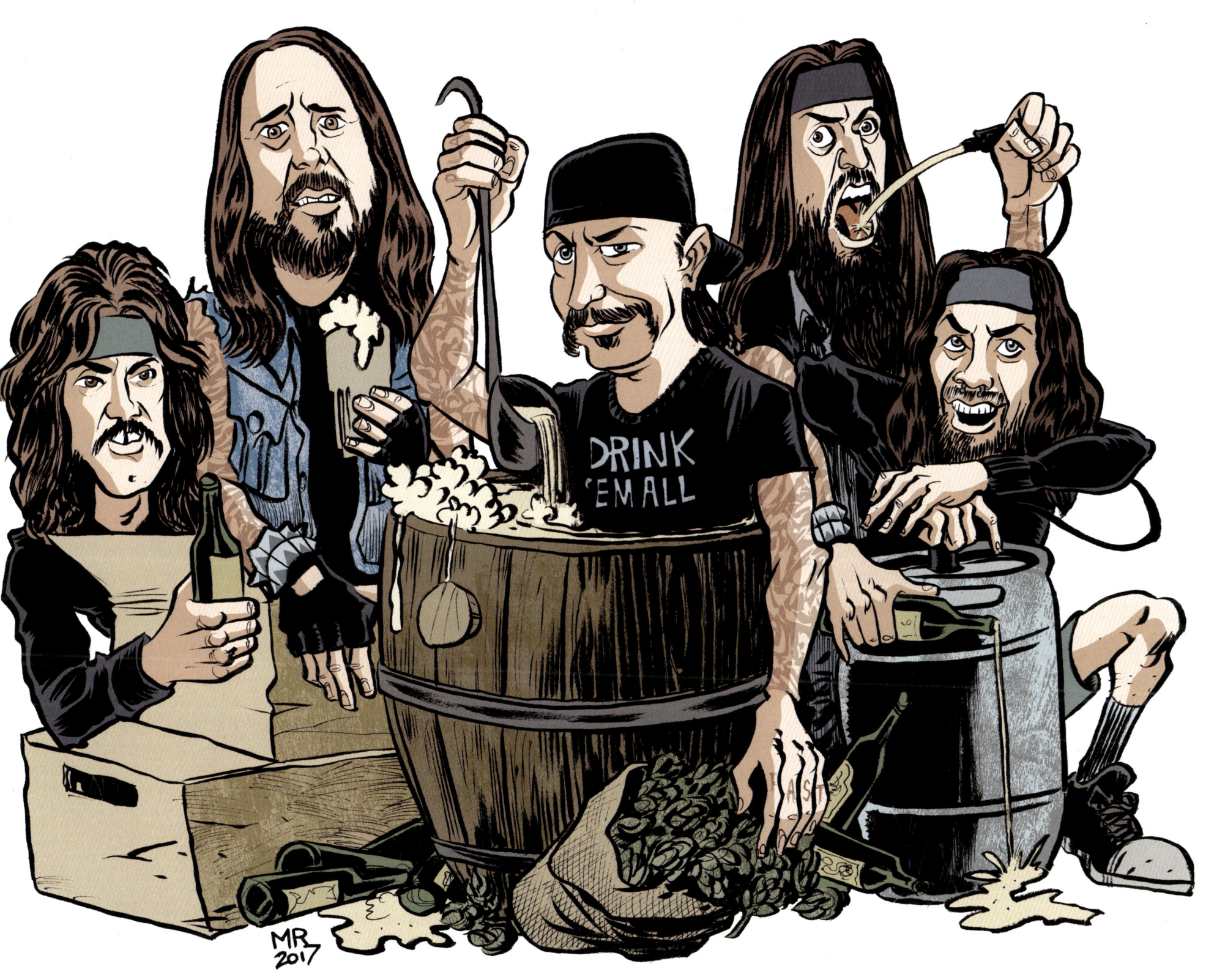

DRINK 'EM ALL (2017)
An illustration for the review of Municipal Waste's *Slime and Punishment* album. Originally appeared in Decibel Magazine.

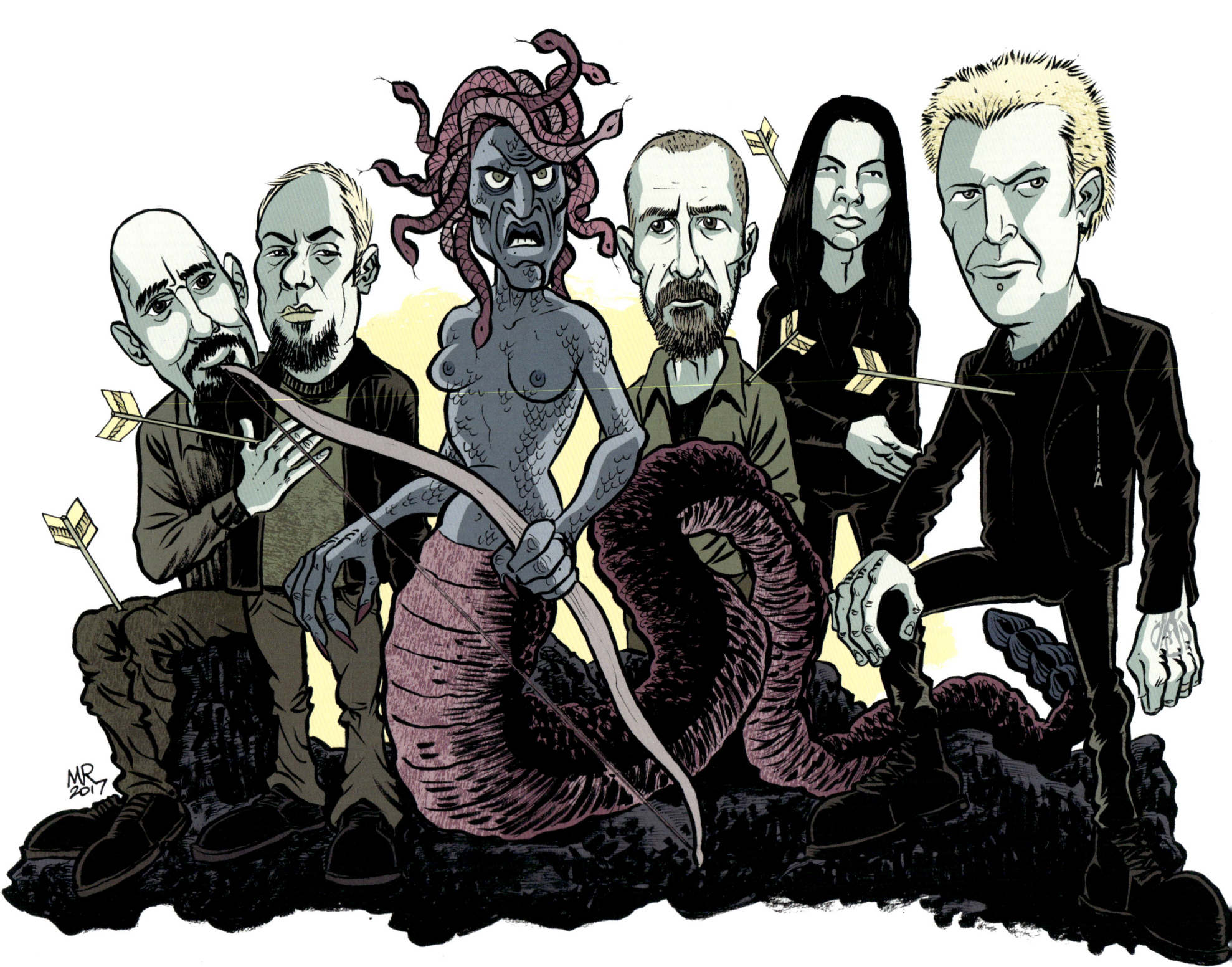

FOREVER AFTER (2017)
An illustration for the review of Paradise Lost's *Medusa* album. Originally appeared in Decibel Magazine.

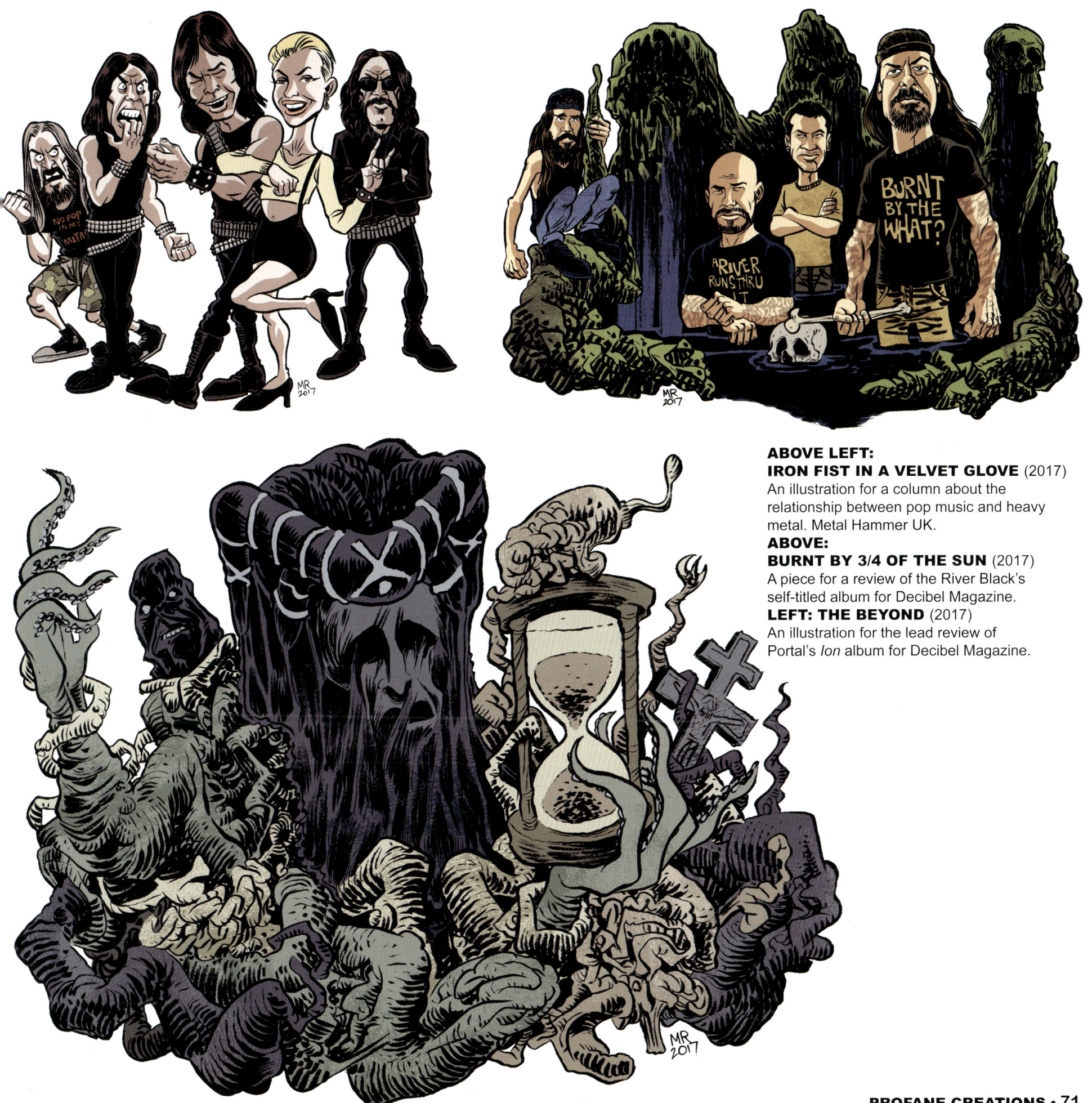

ABOVE LEFT:
IRON FIST IN A VELVET GLOVE (2017)
An illustration for a column about the relationship between pop music and heavy metal. Metal Hammer UK.
ABOVE:
BURNT BY 3/4 OF THE SUN (2017)
A piece for a review of the River Black's self-titled album for Decibel Magazine.
LEFT: THE BEYOND (2017)
An illustration for the lead review of Portal's *Ion* album for Decibel Magazine.

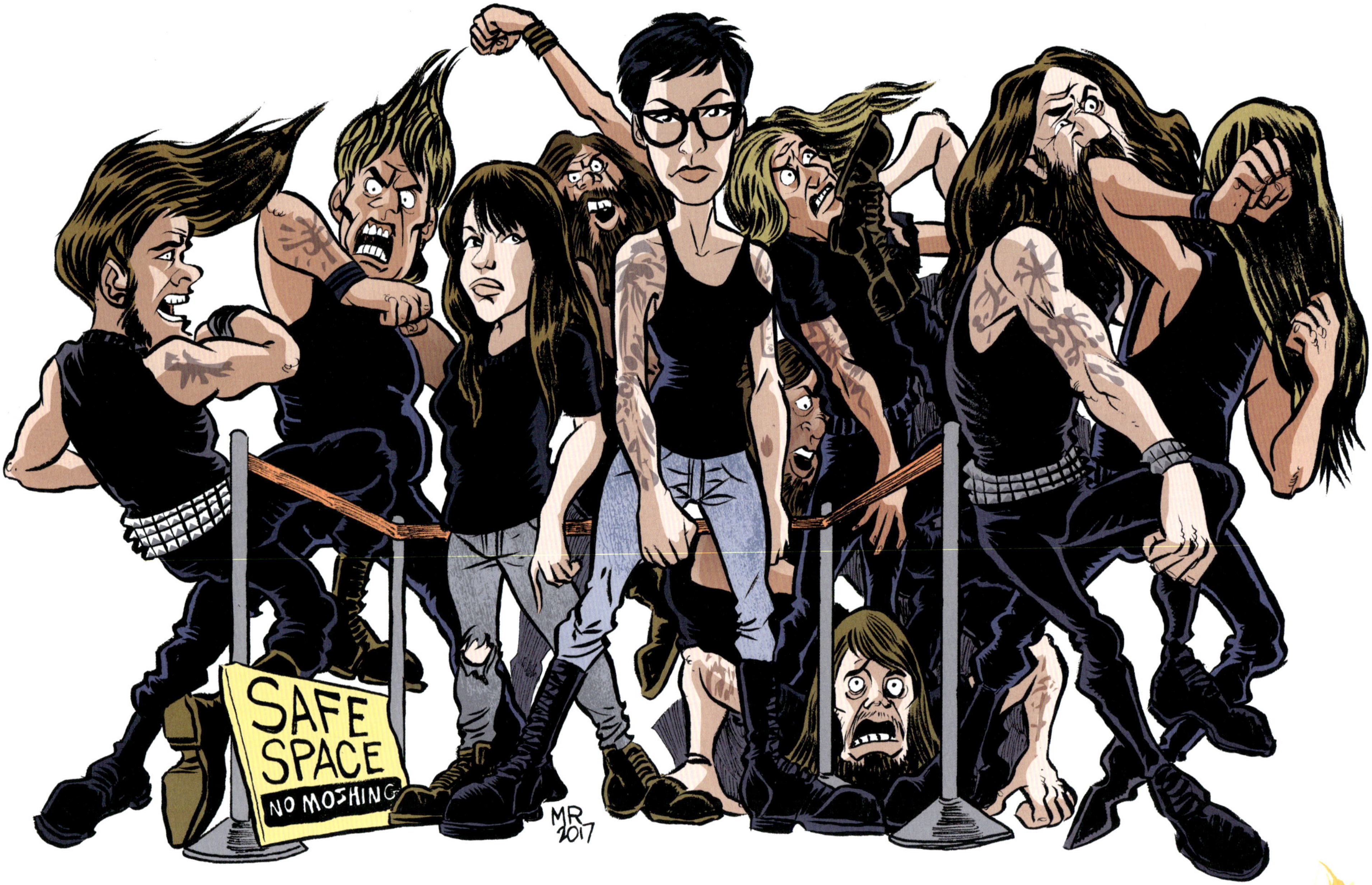

ABOVE: ACCEPT THE PAIN (2017)
An illustration for a column about "safe spaces" within the mosh pit.
RIGHT: OVER THE MADNESS (2017)
A piece for an article about metal bands that take their fantasy subject matter a little too serious.
Both originally appeared in Metal Hammer UK.

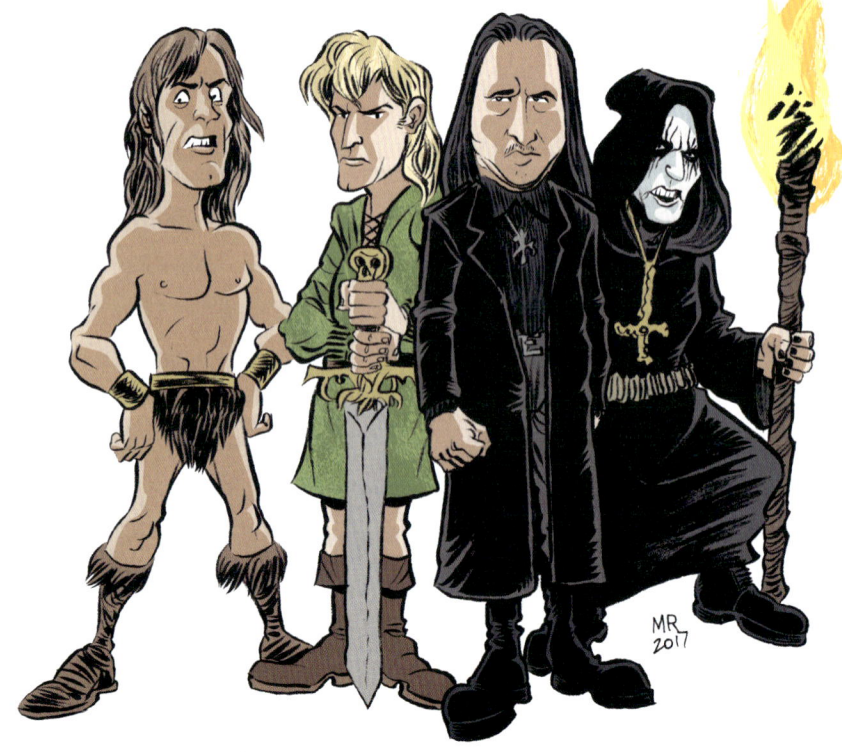

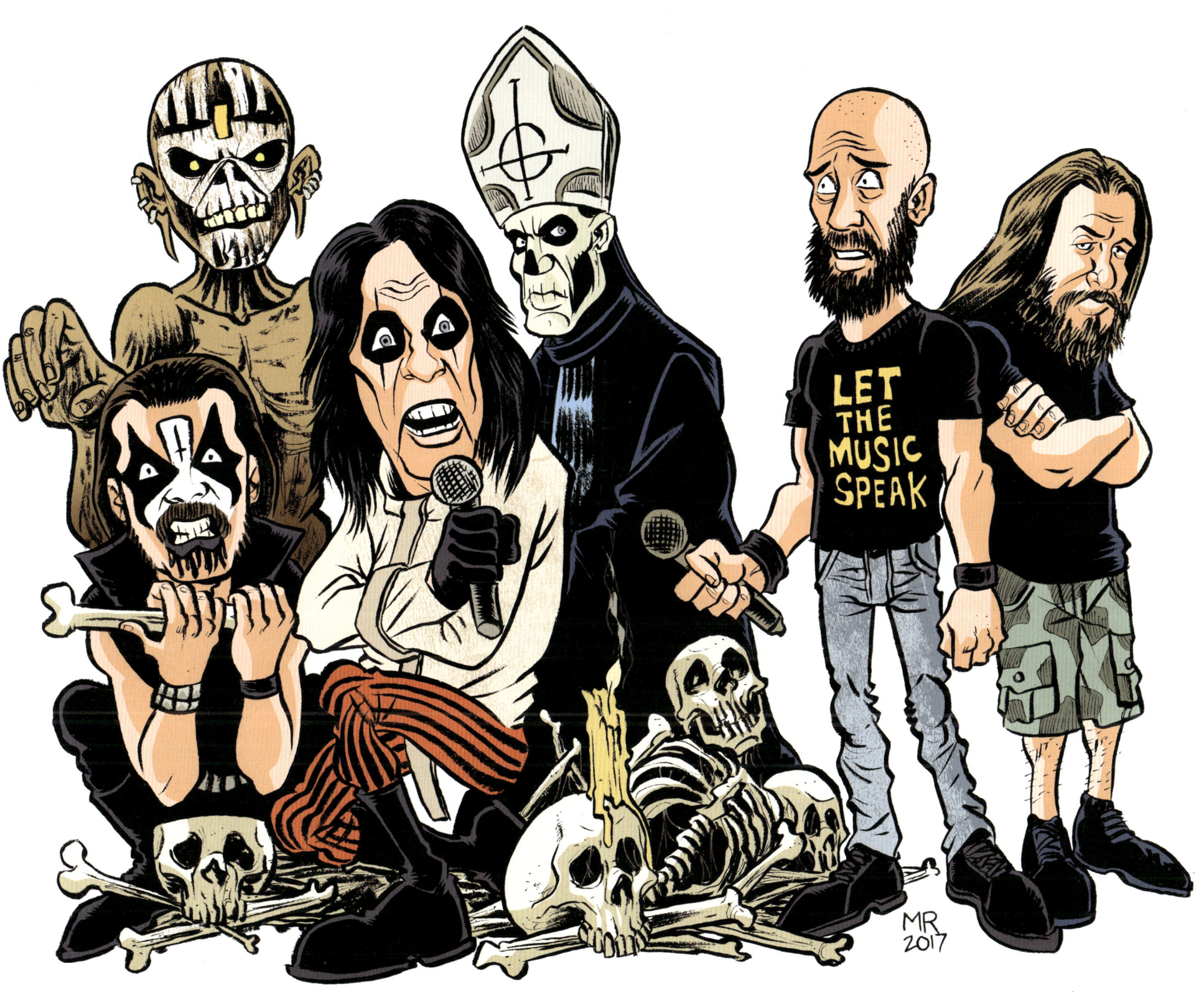

IN THIS WE DWELL (2017)
An illustration for a column about bands that use theatrics and those who let the music speak for itself. Metal Hammer UK.

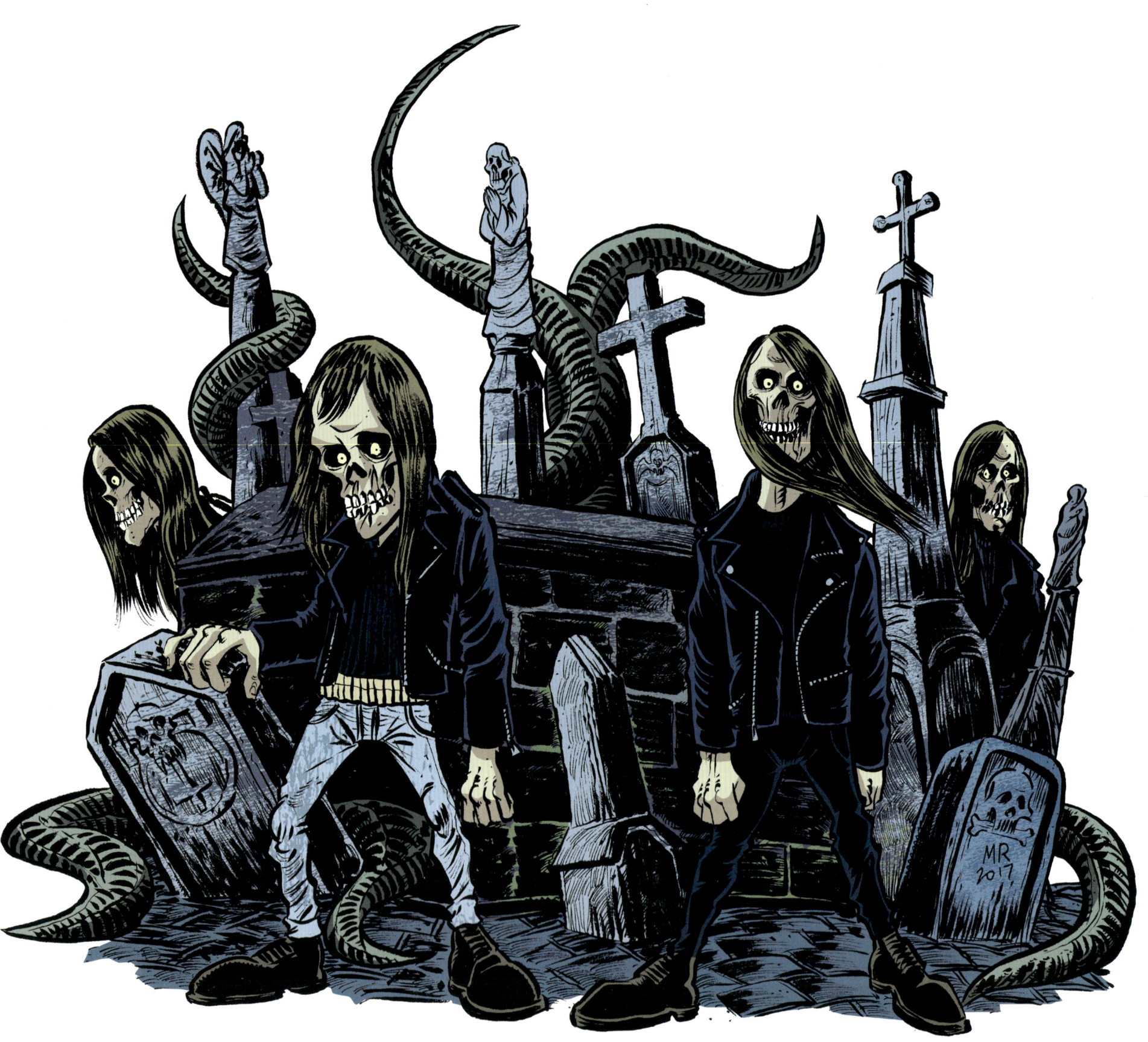

HONESTY IN DEATH (2017)
An illustration for a review of Spectral Voice's *Eroded Corridors of Unbeing* album. Decibel Magazine.

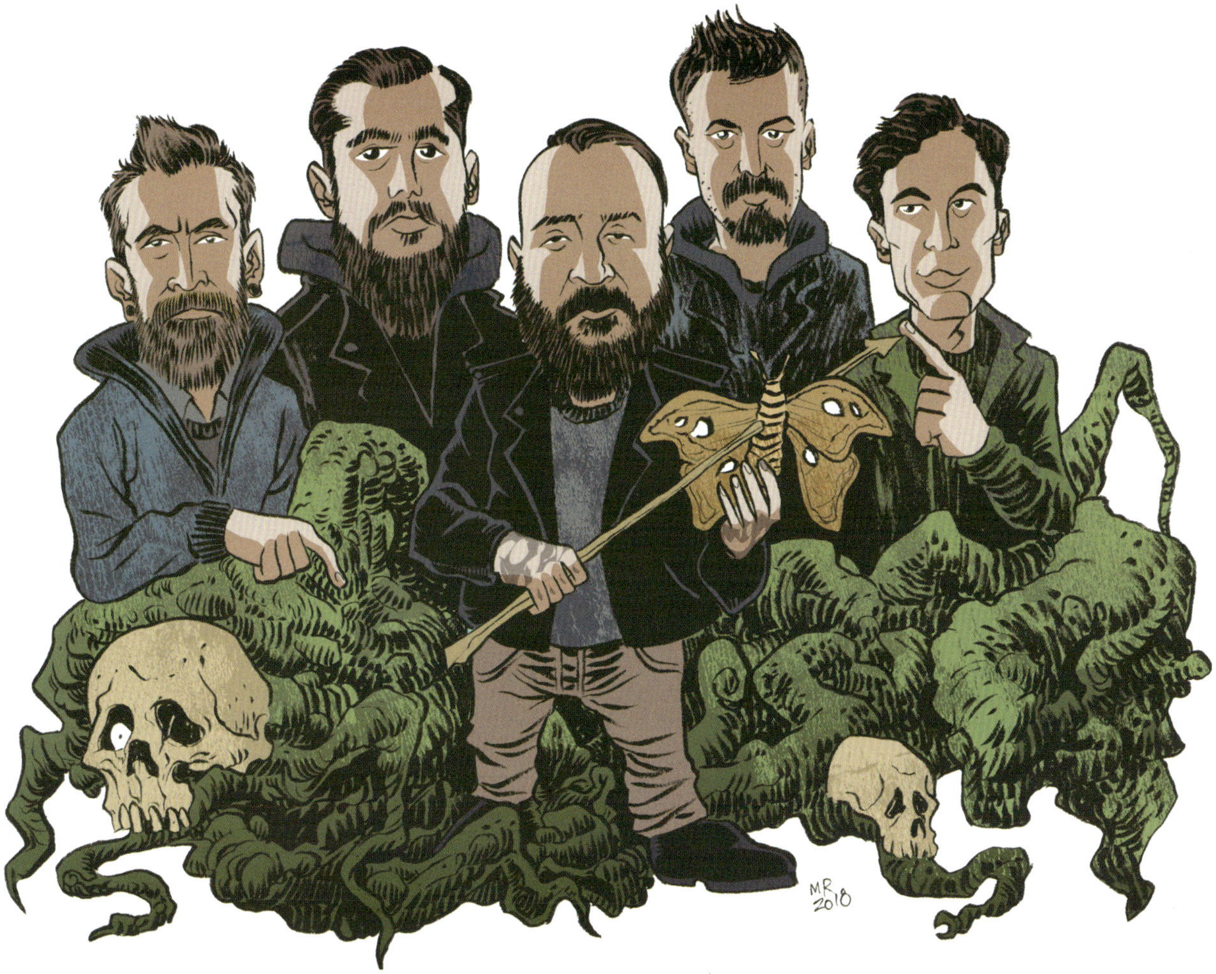

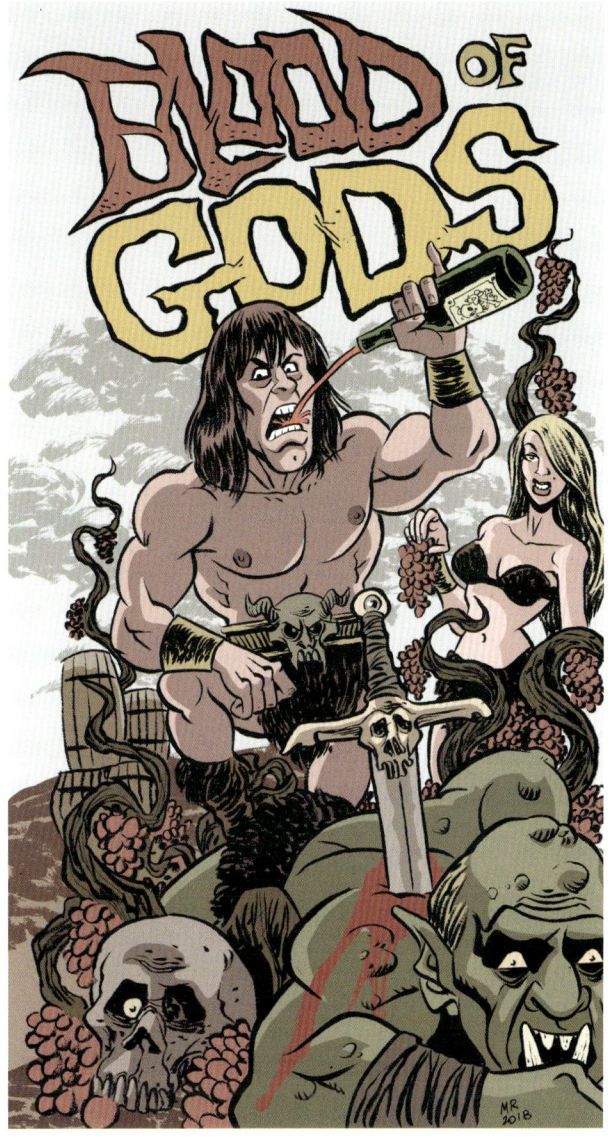

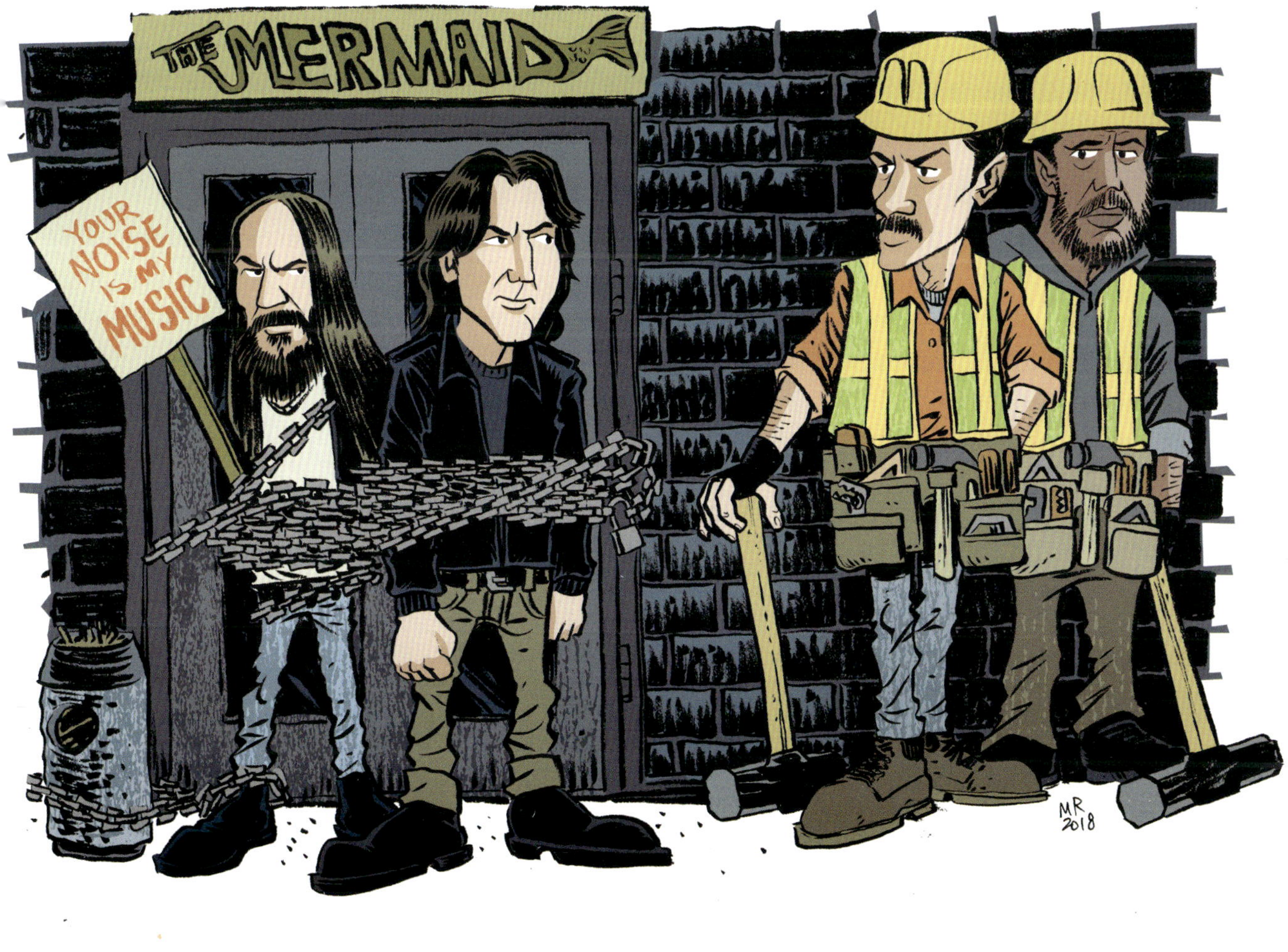

ABOVE LEFT: BLOOD & CHAOS (2018)
An illustration for a review of The Atlas Moth's
Coma Noir album. Decibel Magazine.

ABOVE: BARBARIAN OF GODS (2018)
A cover for the first issue of the metal and wine
magazine Blood of Gods.

LEFT: NO HOPE IN SIGHT (2018)
A piece for an article about what people can do
to save music venues. Originally appeared in
Metal Hammer UK.

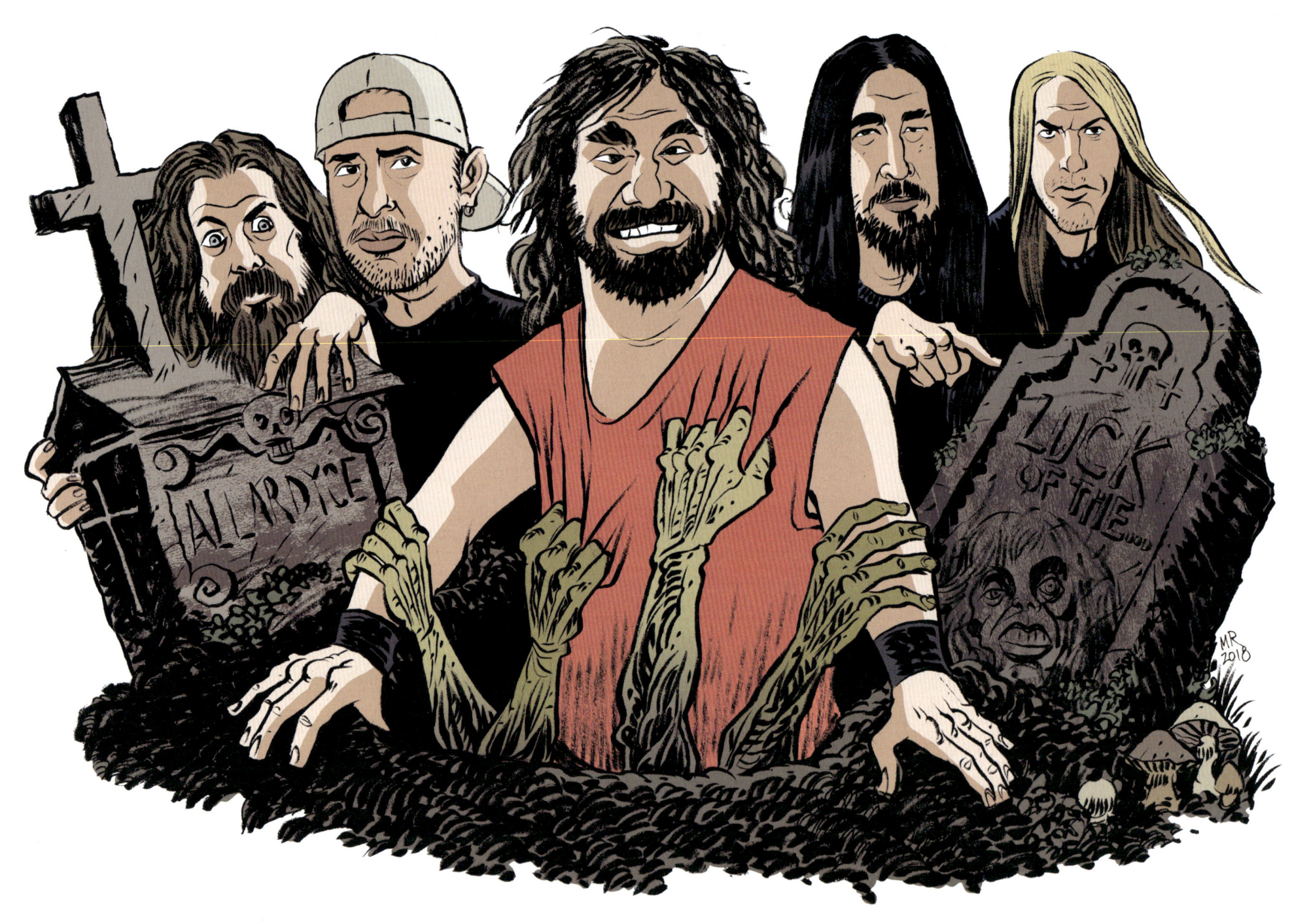

ROTTING MISERY (2018)
An illustration for a review of Deceased's *Ghostly White* album. Decibel Magazine.

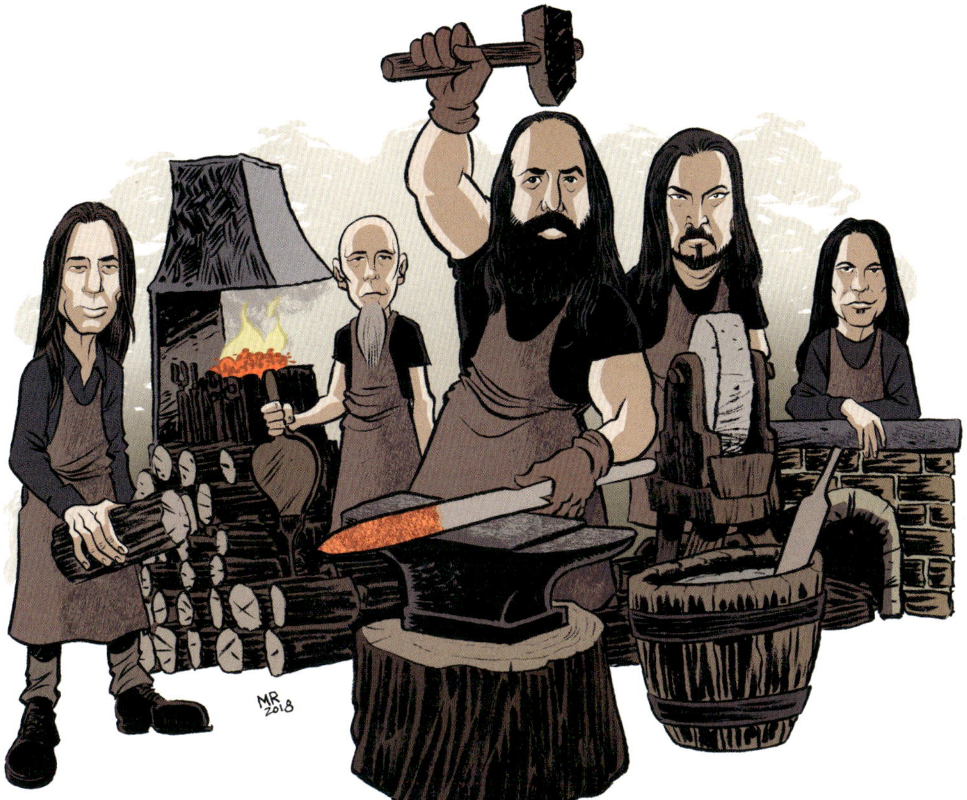

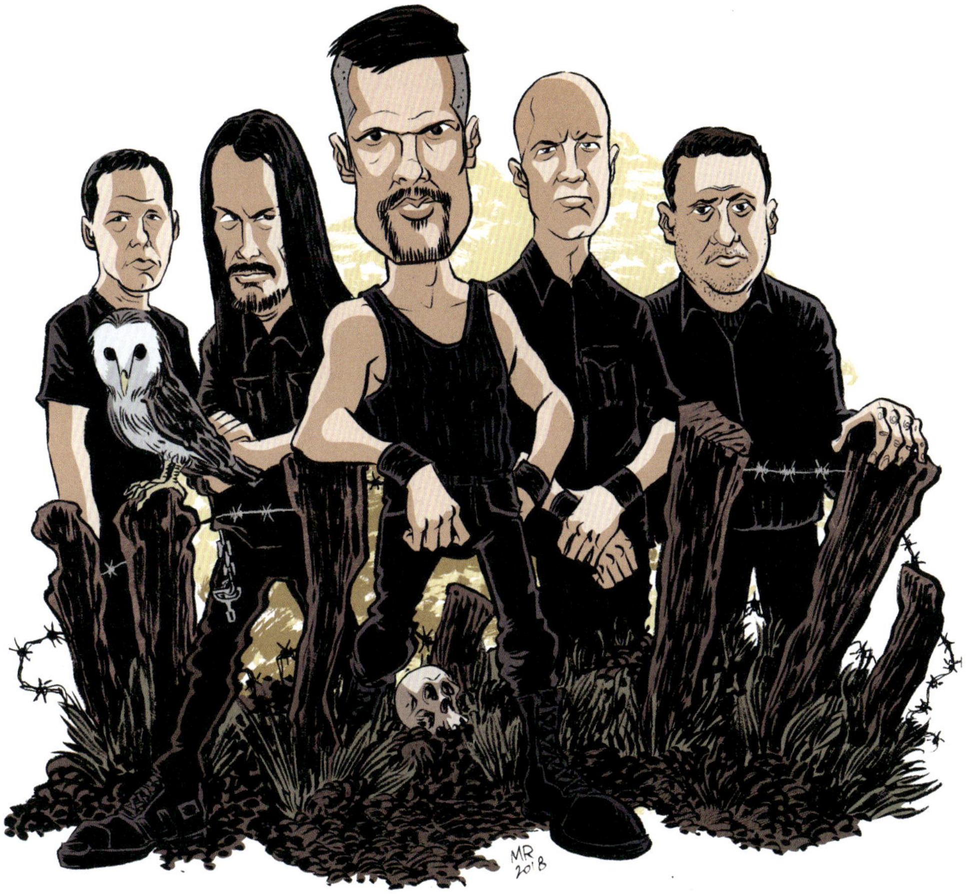

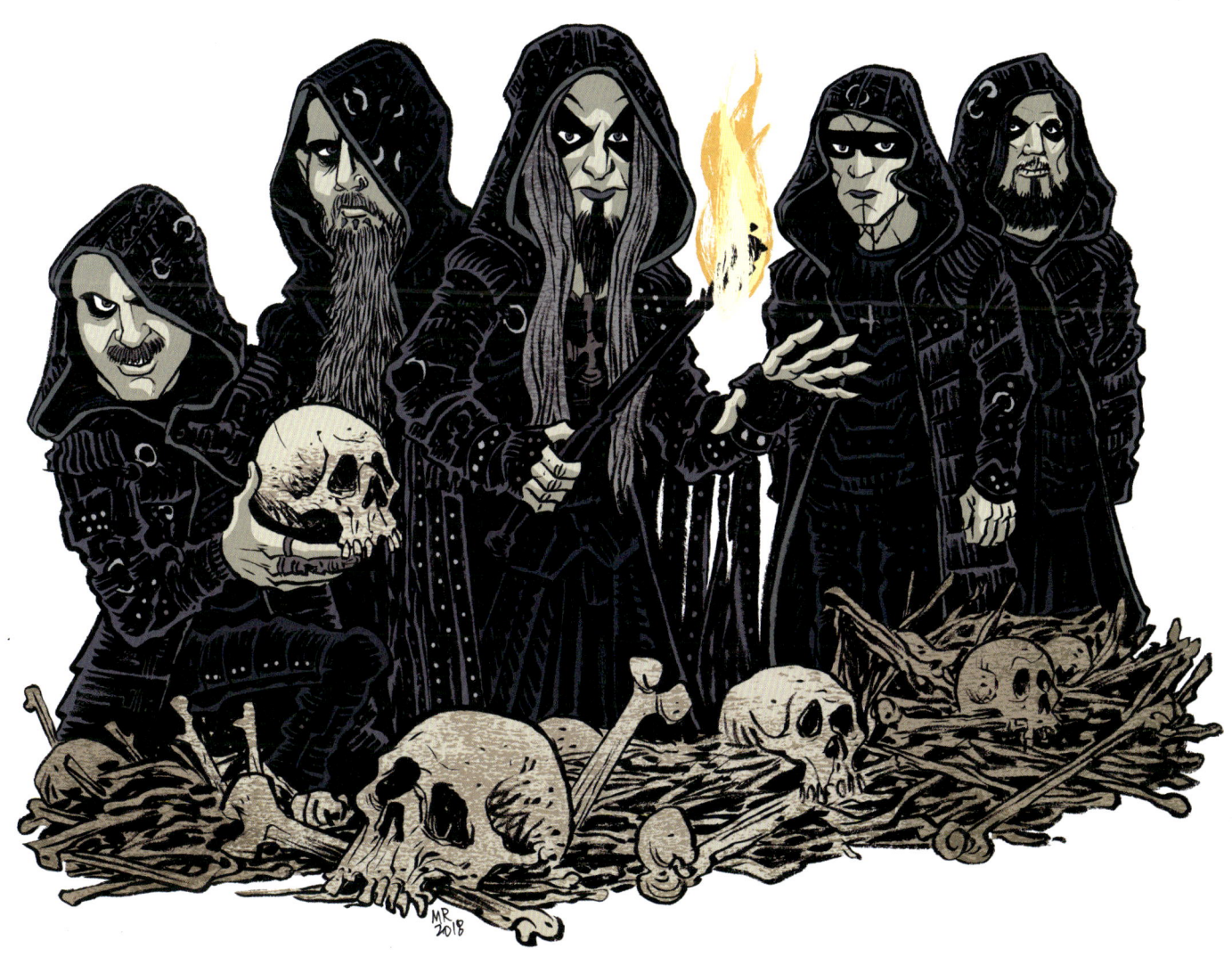

ABOVE: THE WORD MADE FLESH (2018)
An illustration for a review of Dream Theater's
Distance Over Time album.
ABOVE RIGHT:
YOUR HAND IN MINE (2018)
An piece for a review of Evoken's
Hypnagogia album.
RIGHT: FROZEN ILLUSION (2018)
An illustration for a review of Dimmu Borgir's
Eonian album.
All originally appeared in Decibel Magazine.

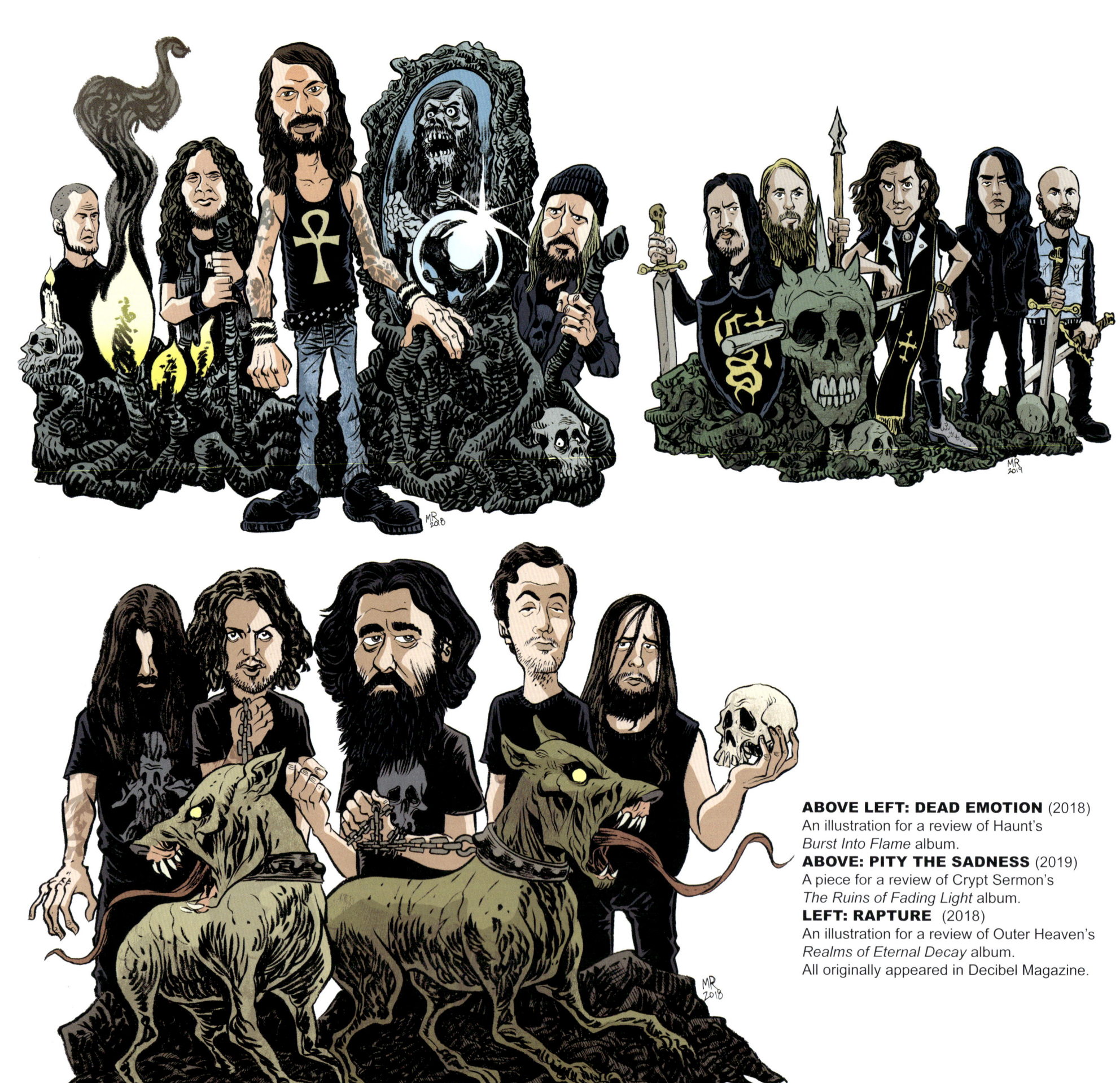

ABOVE LEFT: DEAD EMOTION (2018)
An illustration for a review of Haunt's
Burst Into Flame album.
ABOVE: PITY THE SADNESS (2019)
A piece for a review of Crypt Sermon's
The Ruins of Fading Light album.
LEFT: RAPTURE (2018)
An illustration for a review of Outer Heaven's
Realms of Eternal Decay album.
All originally appeared in Decibel Magazine.

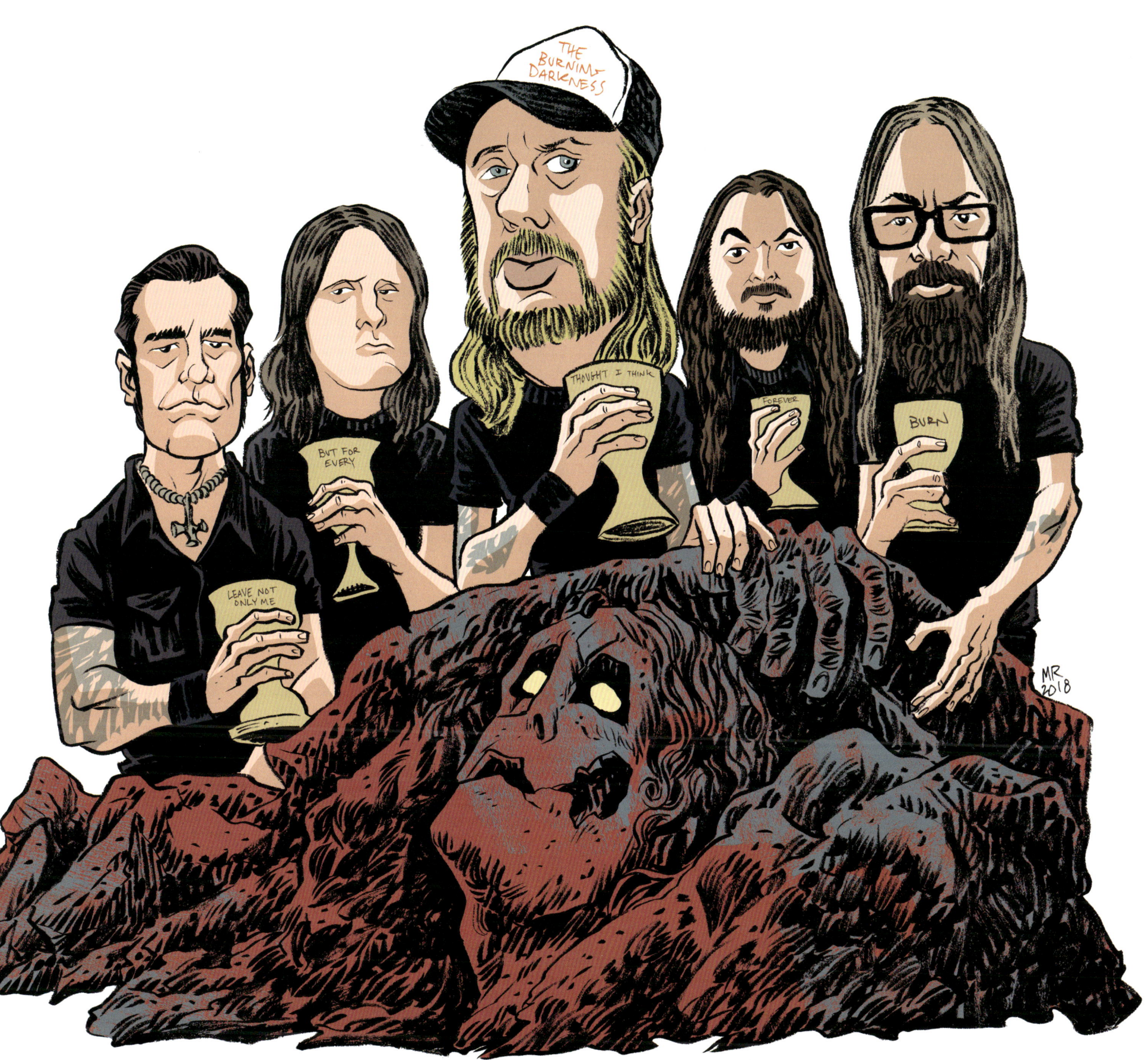

WEEPING WORDS (2019)
An illustration for a review for At The Gate's *To Drink From The Night Itself* album. Decibel Magazine.

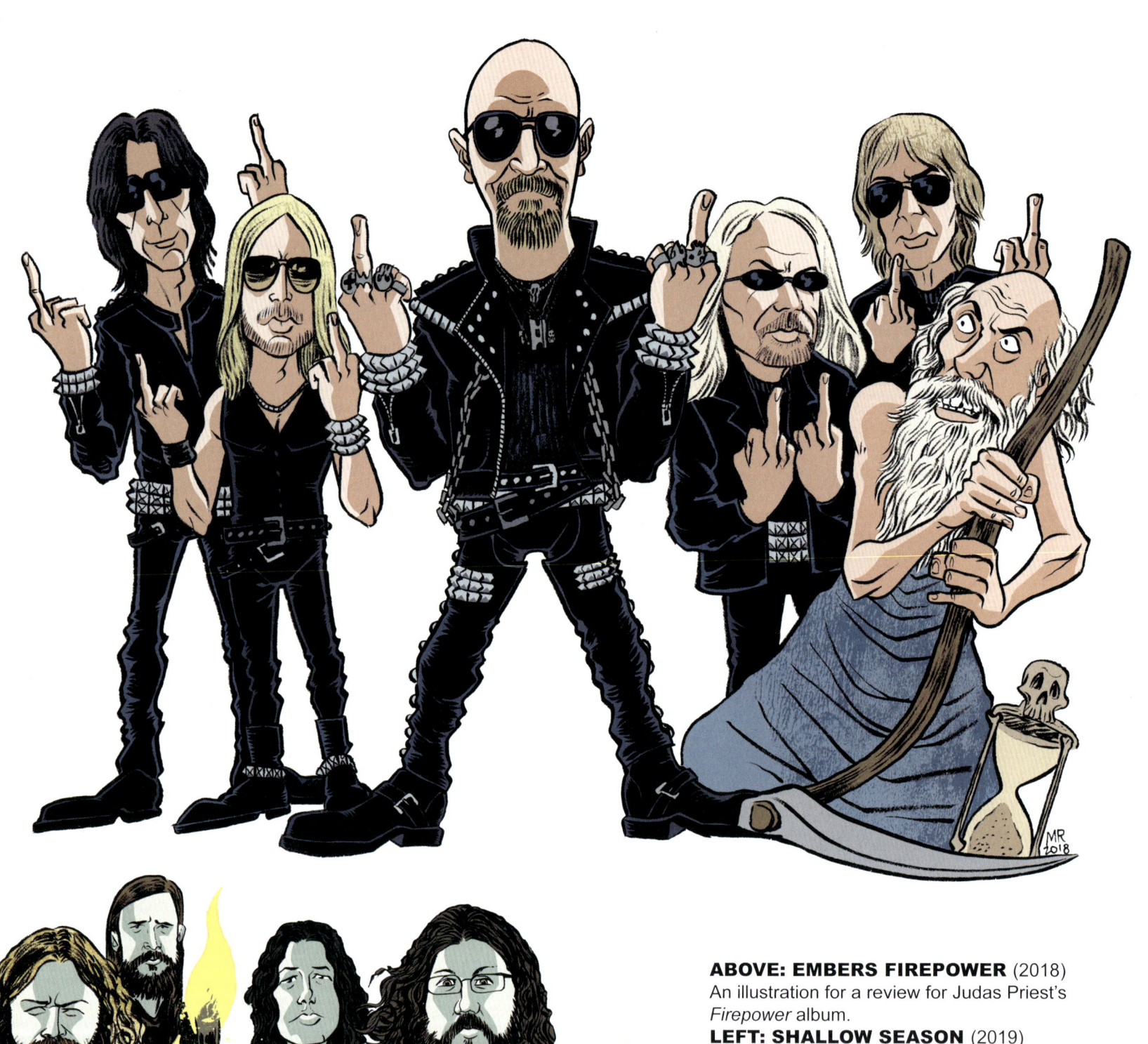

ABOVE: EMBERS FIREPOWER (2018)
An illustration for a review for Judas Priest's
Firepower album.
LEFT: SHALLOW SEASON (2019)
For a review for Inter Arma's *Sulphur English* album.
Both originally appeared in Decibel Magazine.

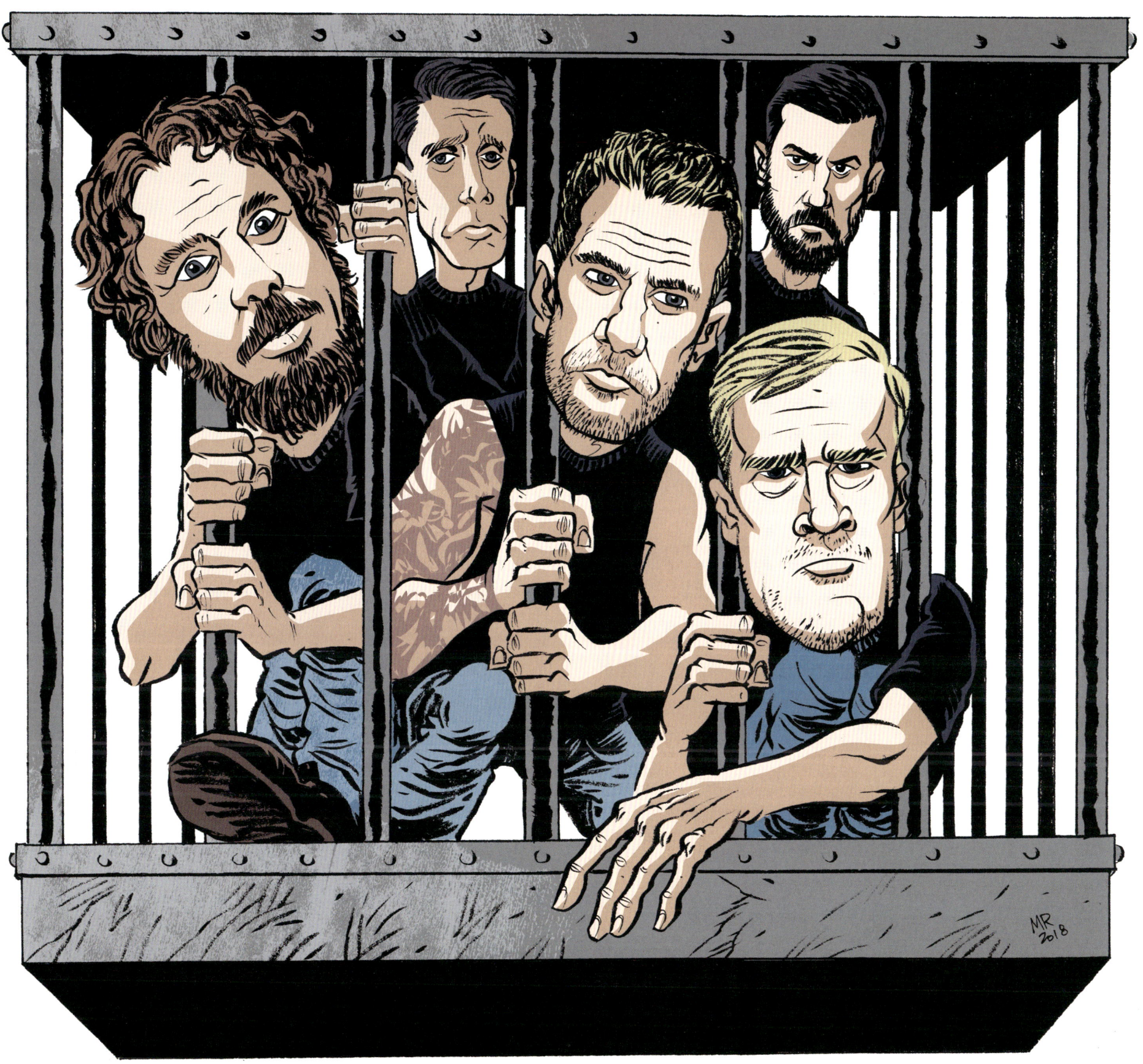

NOTHING SACRED (2018)
An illustration for a review for Pig Destroyer's *Head Cage* album. Decibel Magazine.

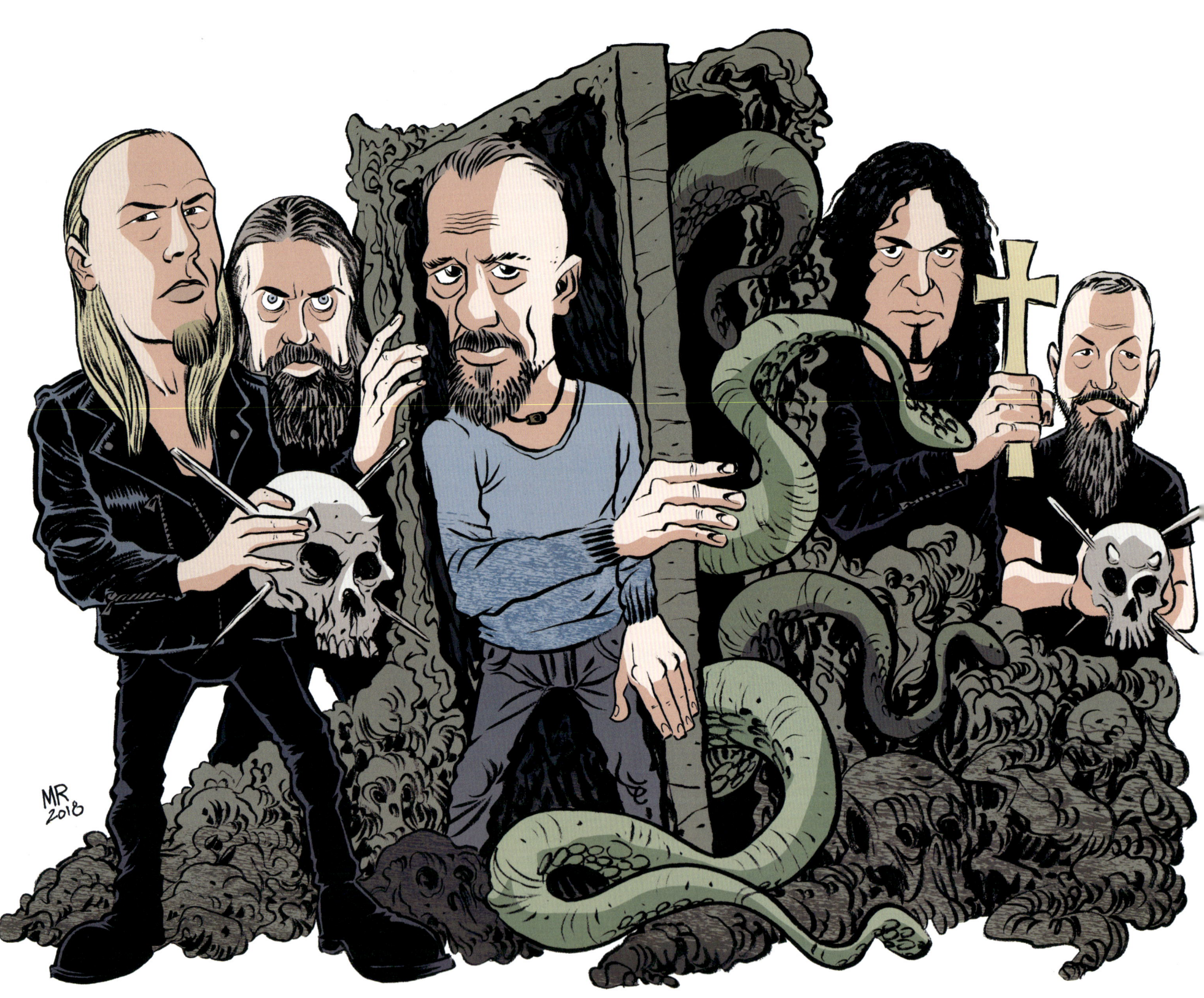

IN THROUGH THE DOOM DOOR (2018)
An illustration for a review for Candlemass' *The Door To Doom* album. Decibel Magazine.

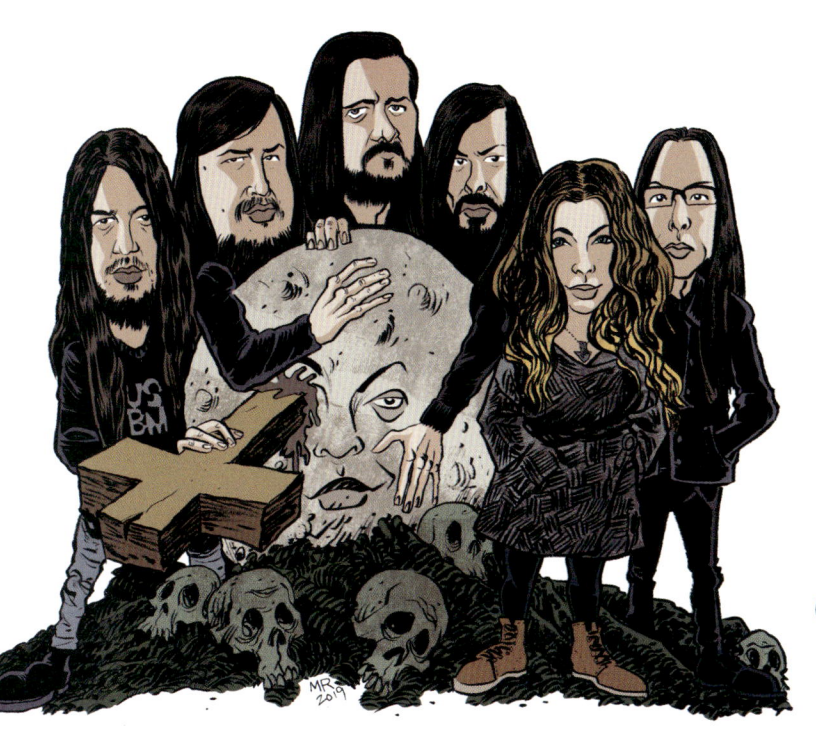

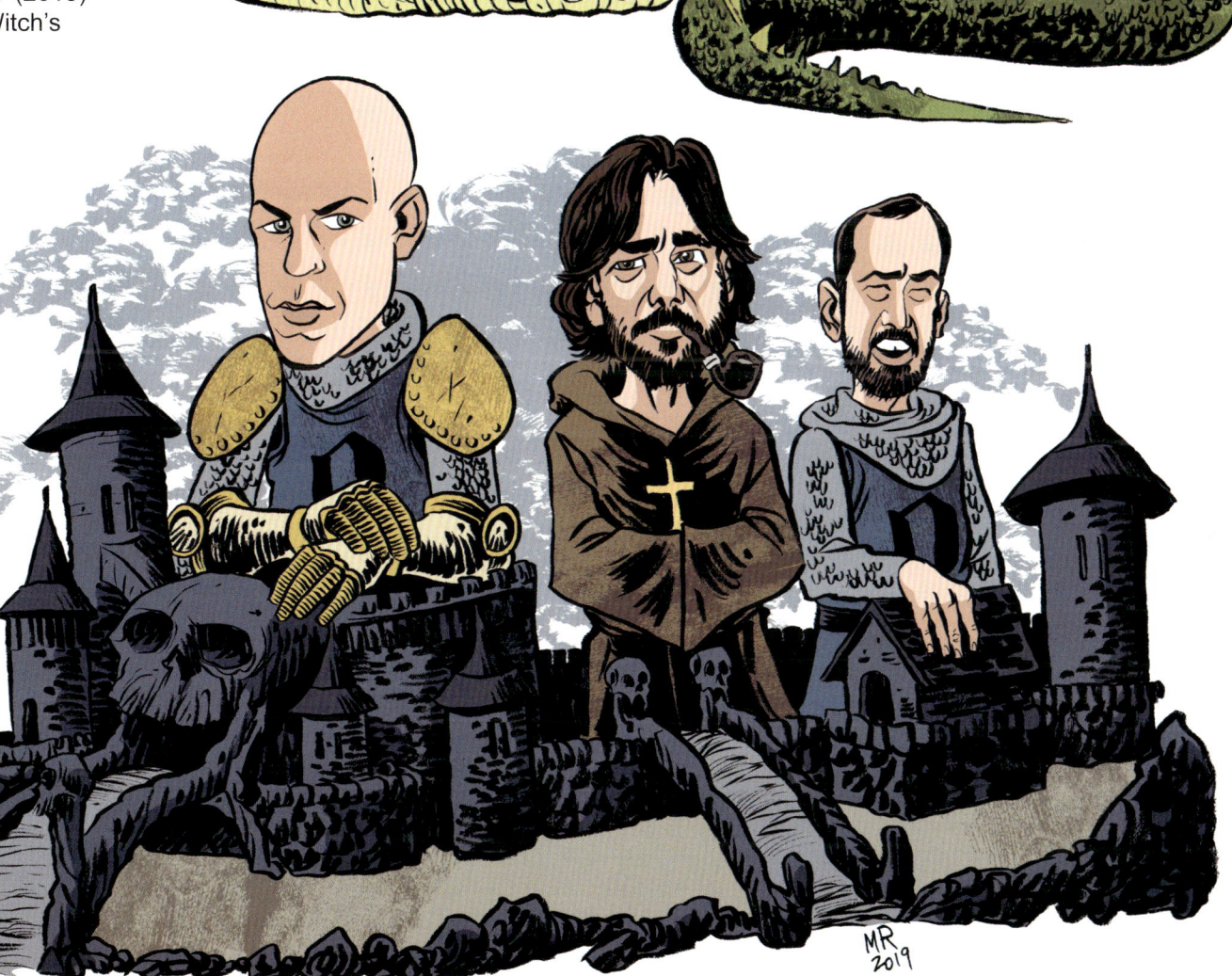

ABOVE: I AM NOTHING (2019)
For a review illustration for False's *Portent* album.
ABOVE RIGHT: SO MUCH IS LOST (2018)
An illustration for a review for Skeleton Witch's
Devouring Radiant Light album.
RIGHT: SHADOWKINGS (2019)
A piece for a review for Obsequiae's *The Palms of Sorrowed Kings* album.
All originally appeared in
Decibel Magazine.

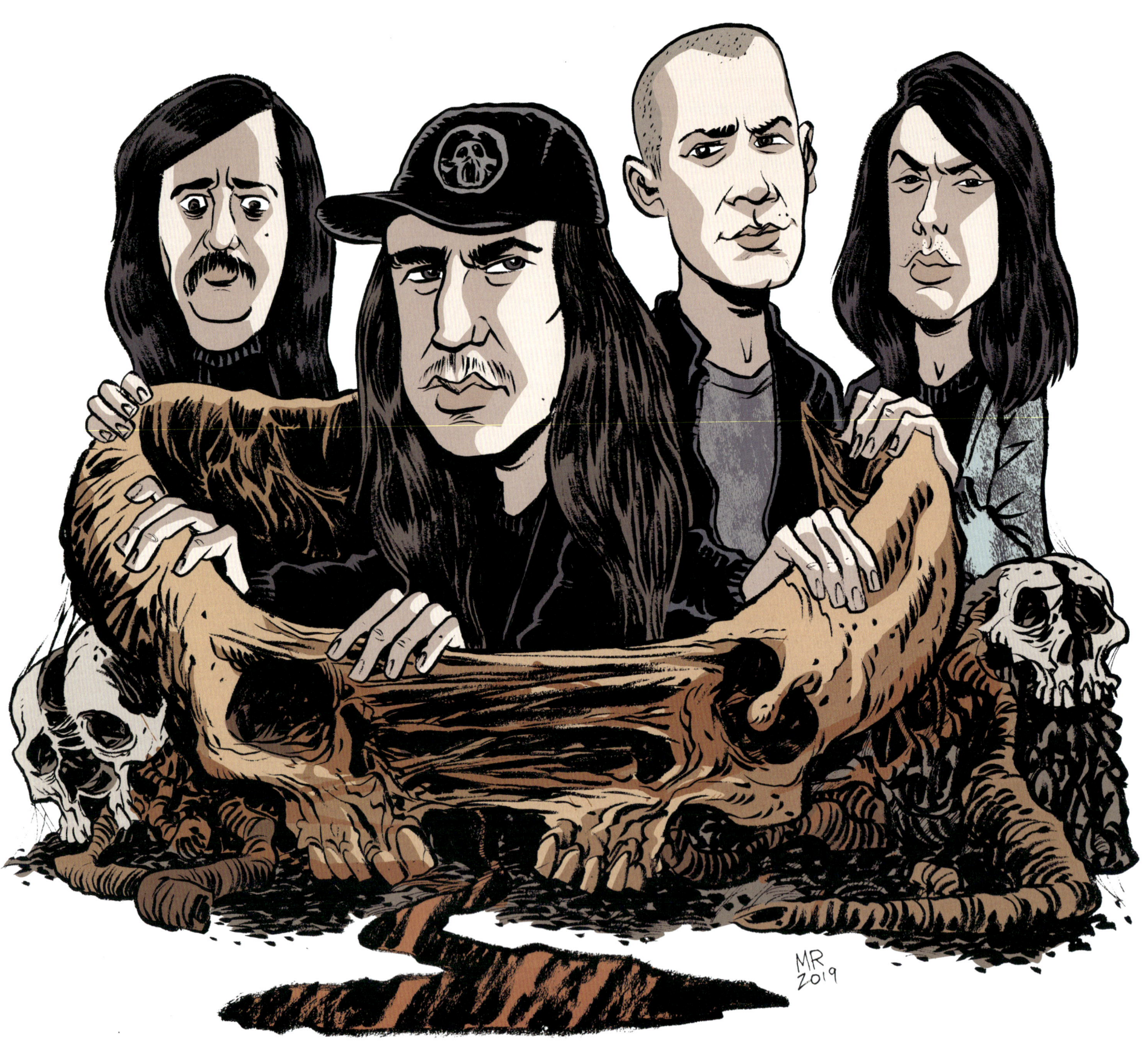

ROTTEN SOIL (2019)
An illustration for a review for Full Of Hell's *Weeping Choir* album. Decibel Magazine.

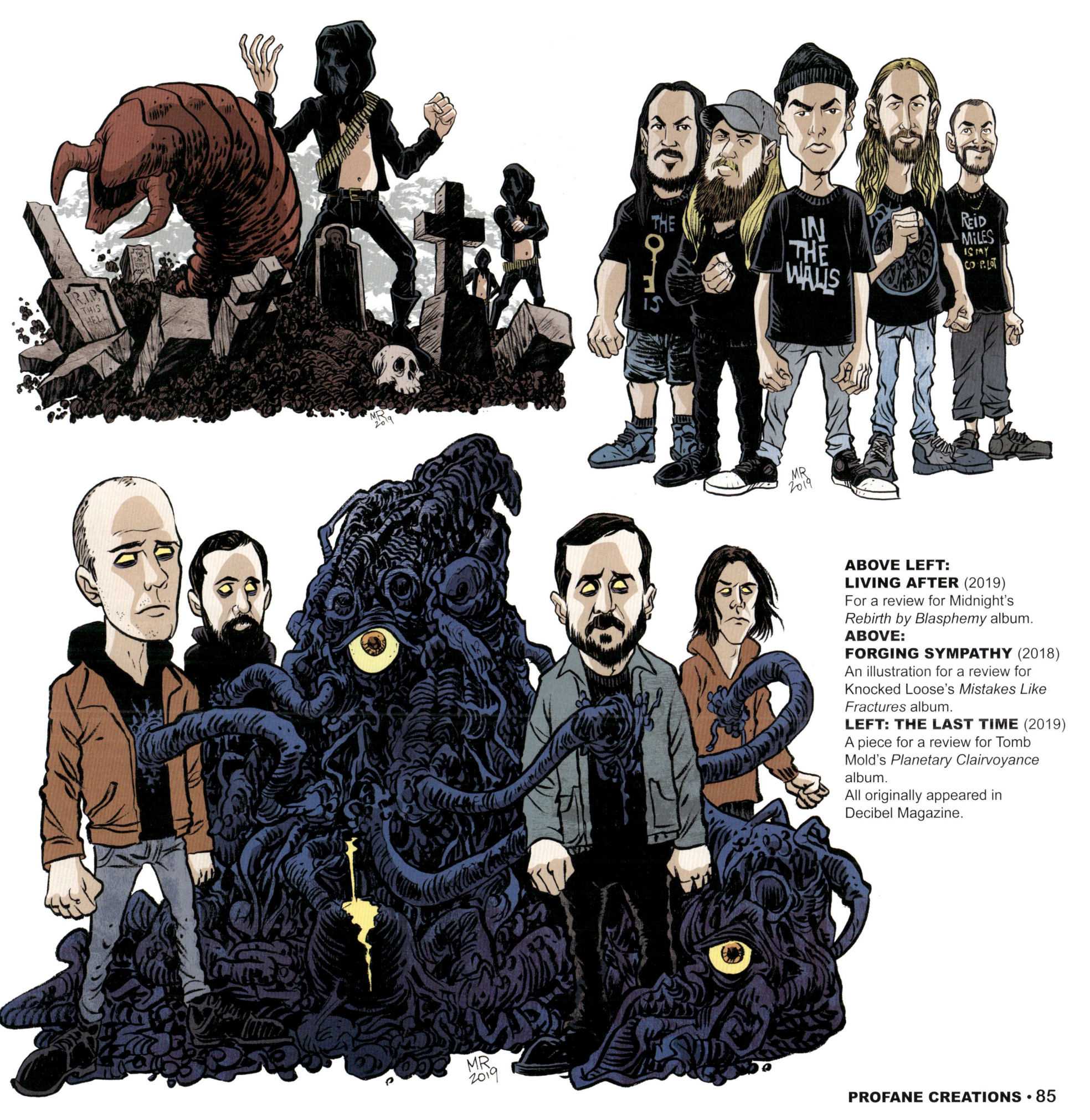

ABOVE LEFT:
LIVING AFTER (2019)
For a review for Midnight's *Rebirth by Blasphemy* album.
ABOVE:
FORGING SYMPATHY (2018)
An illustration for a review for Knocked Loose's *Mistakes Like Fractures* album.
LEFT: THE LAST TIME (2019)
A piece for a review for Tomb Mold's *Planetary Clairvoyance* album.
All originally appeared in Decibel Magazine.

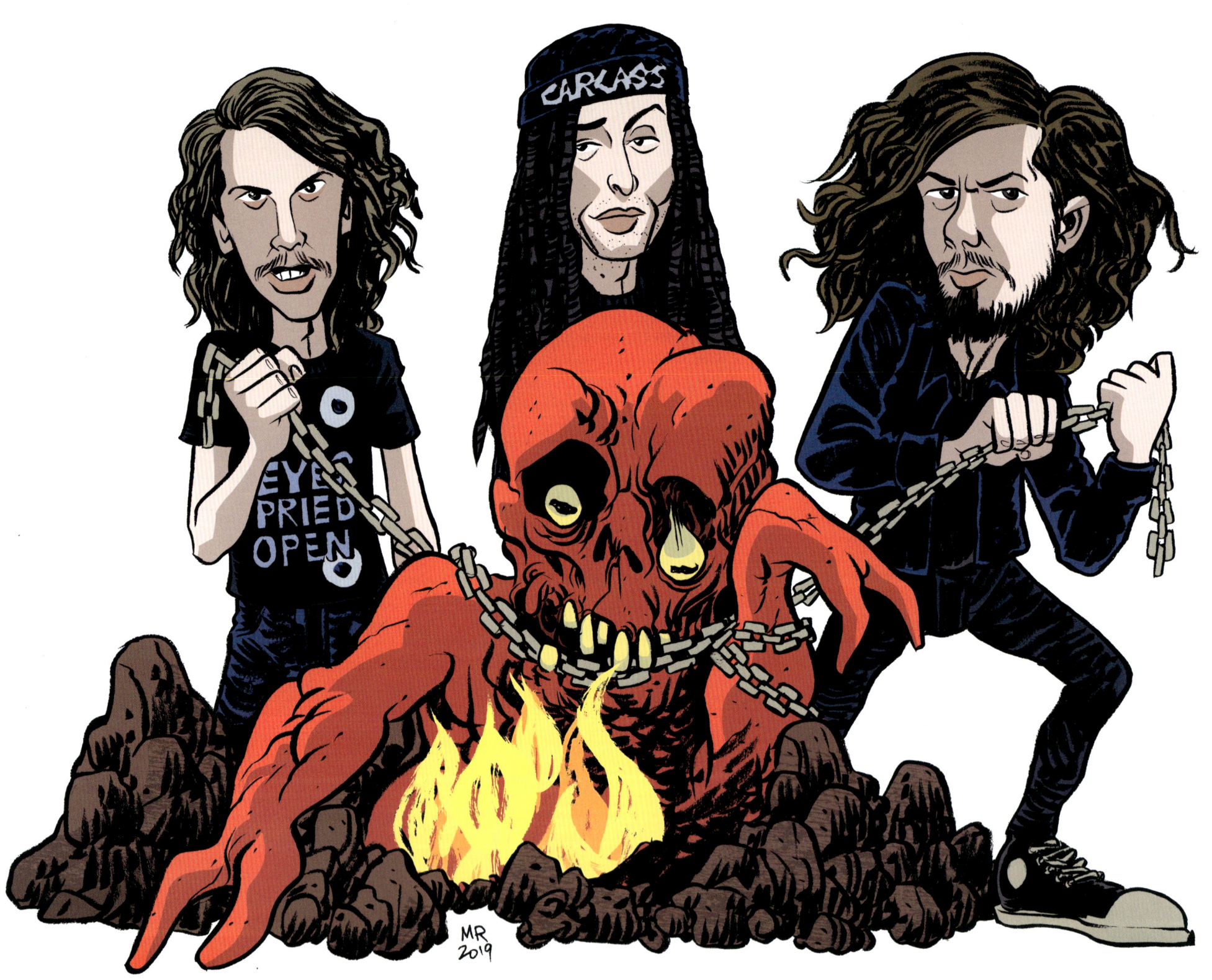

BLOOD OF ANOTHER (2019)
An illustration for a review of Noisem's *Cease to Exist album*. Decibel Magazine.

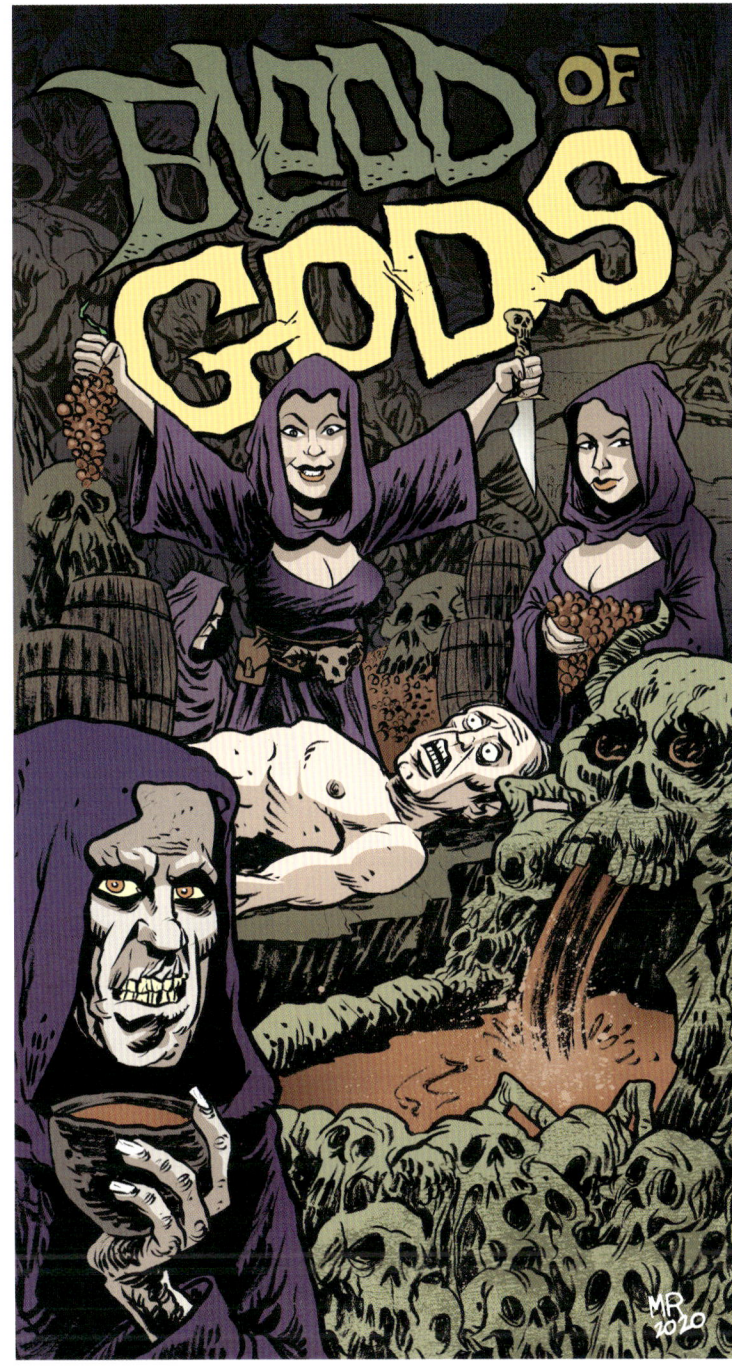

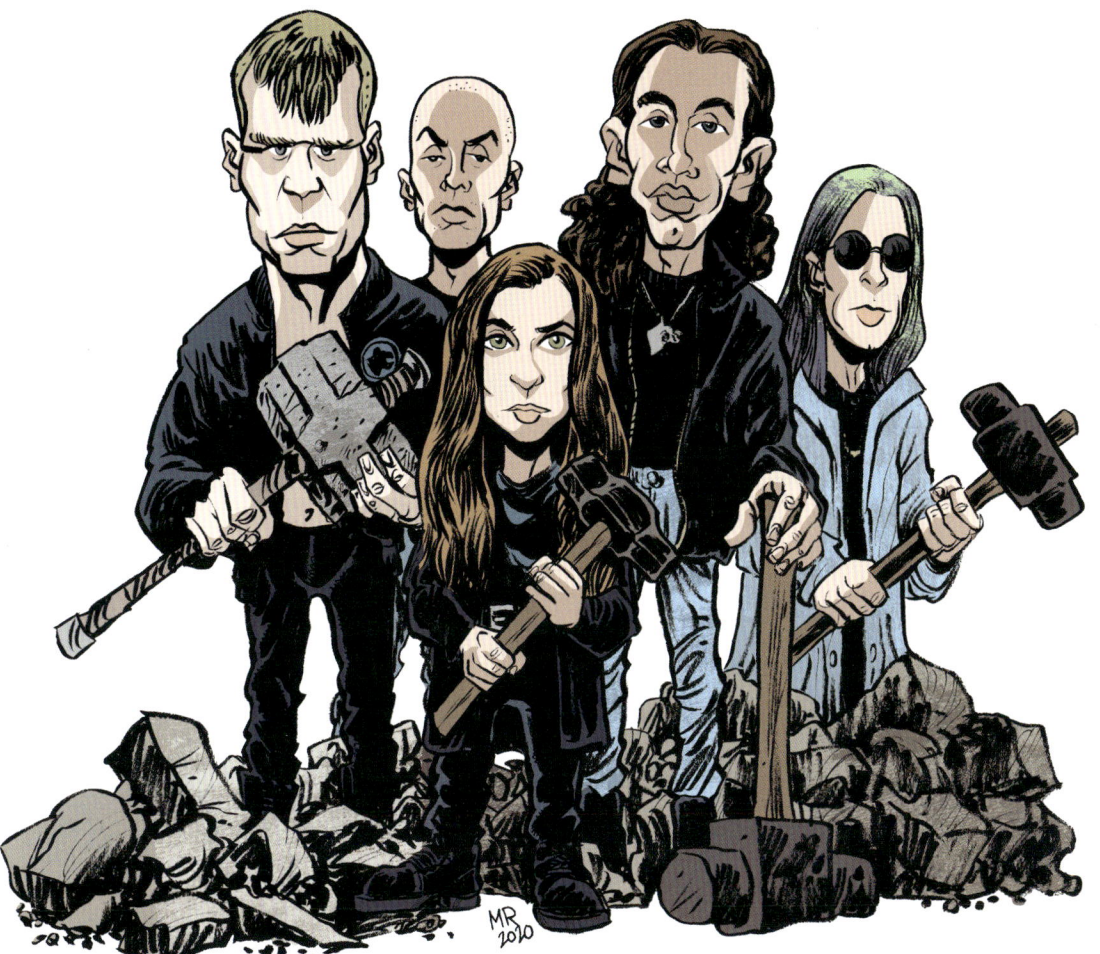

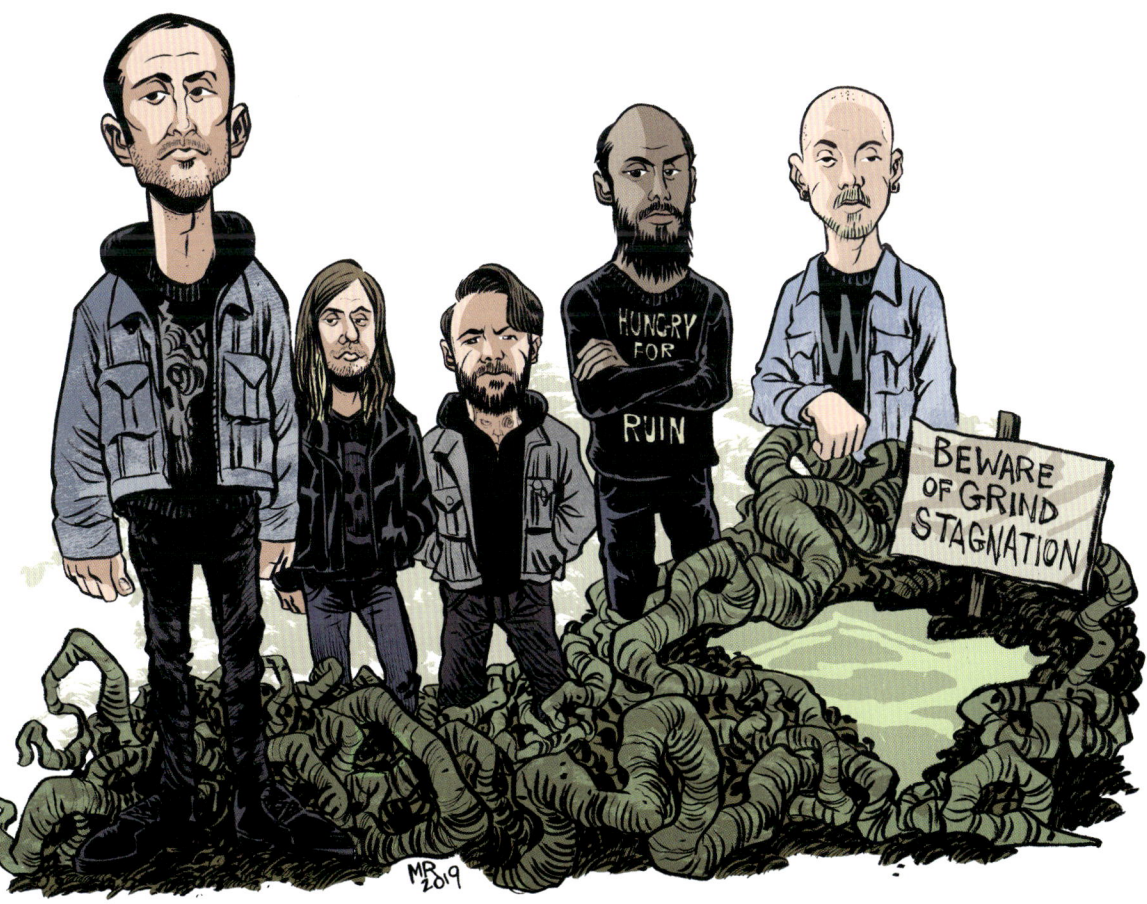

ABOVE: SACRIFICE OF GODS (2020)
The cover for Blood of Gods, a metal and wine magazine, issue two.

ABOVE RIGHT: SOMETHING REAL (2020)
An illustration for a review of Code Orange's *Underneath* album. Decibel Magazine.

RIGHT: CHANNEL FOR THE PAIN (2019)
A piece for a review of Wake's *Devouring Ruin* album. Decibel Magazine.

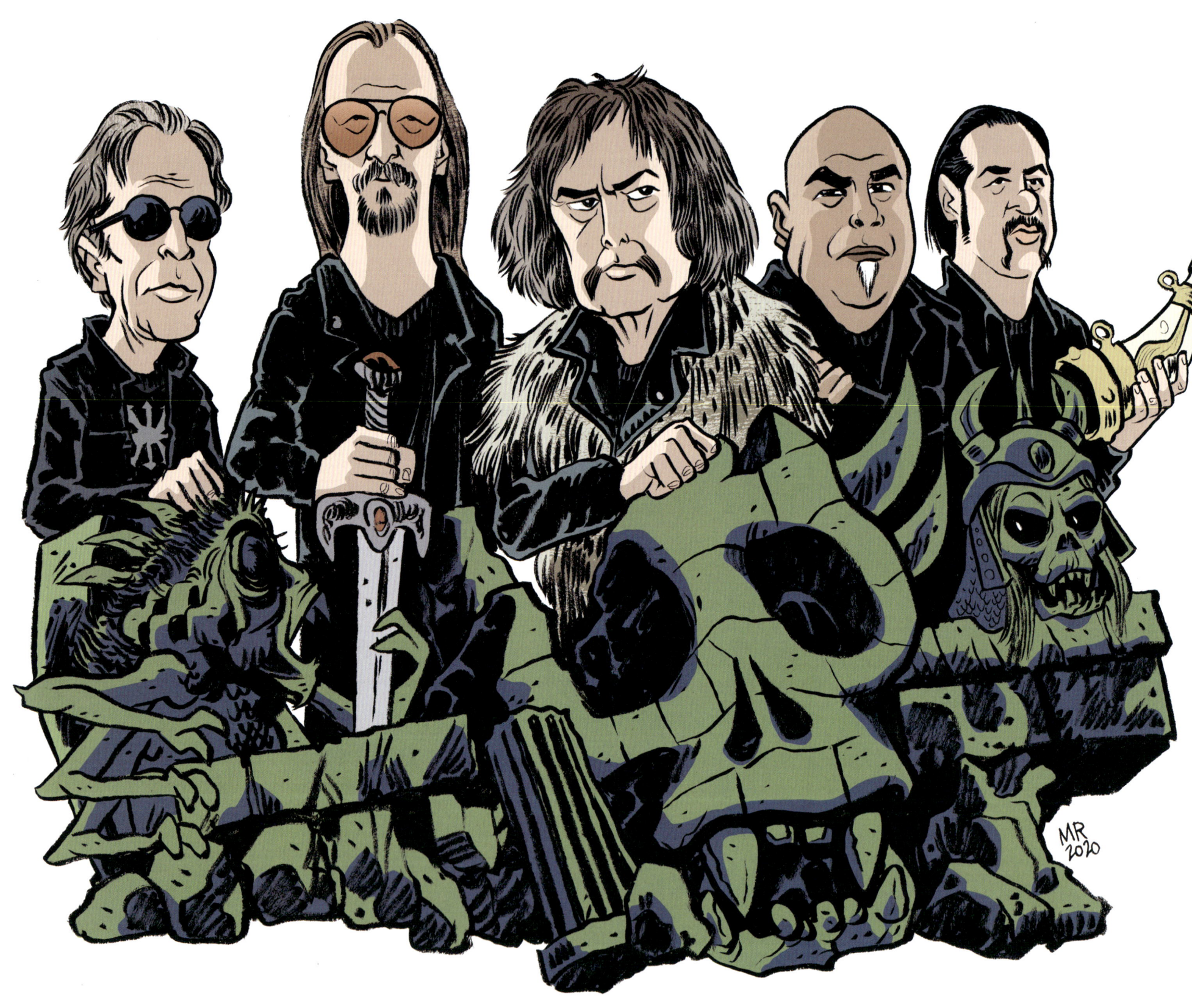

TO THE DARKNESS (2020)
An illustration for a review of Cirith Ungol's *Forever Black album*. Decibel Magazine.

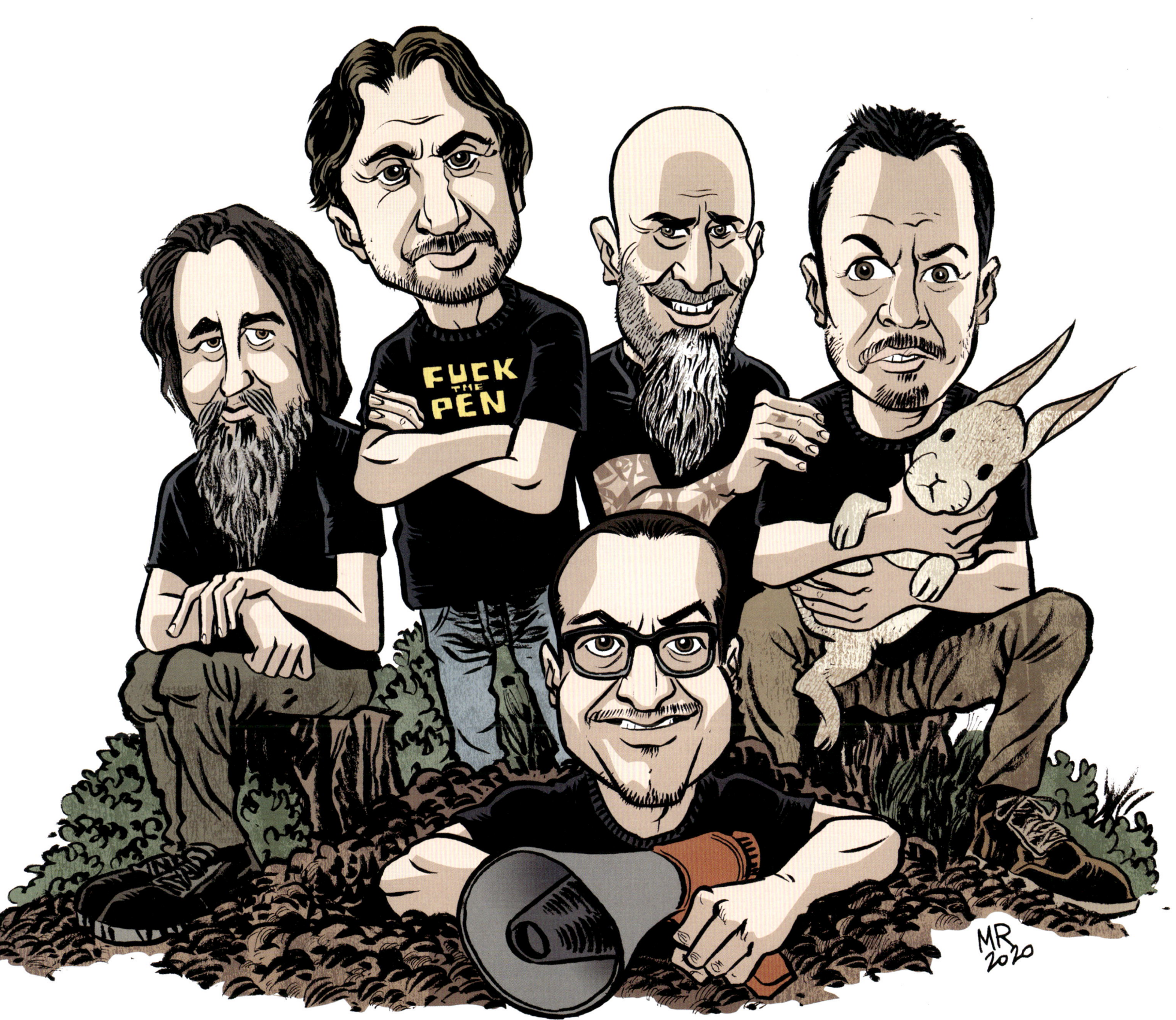

SYMBOLIC VIRTUE (2020)
An illustration for a review of Mr. Bungle's *The Raging Wrath of the Easter Bunny Demo*. Decibel Magazine.

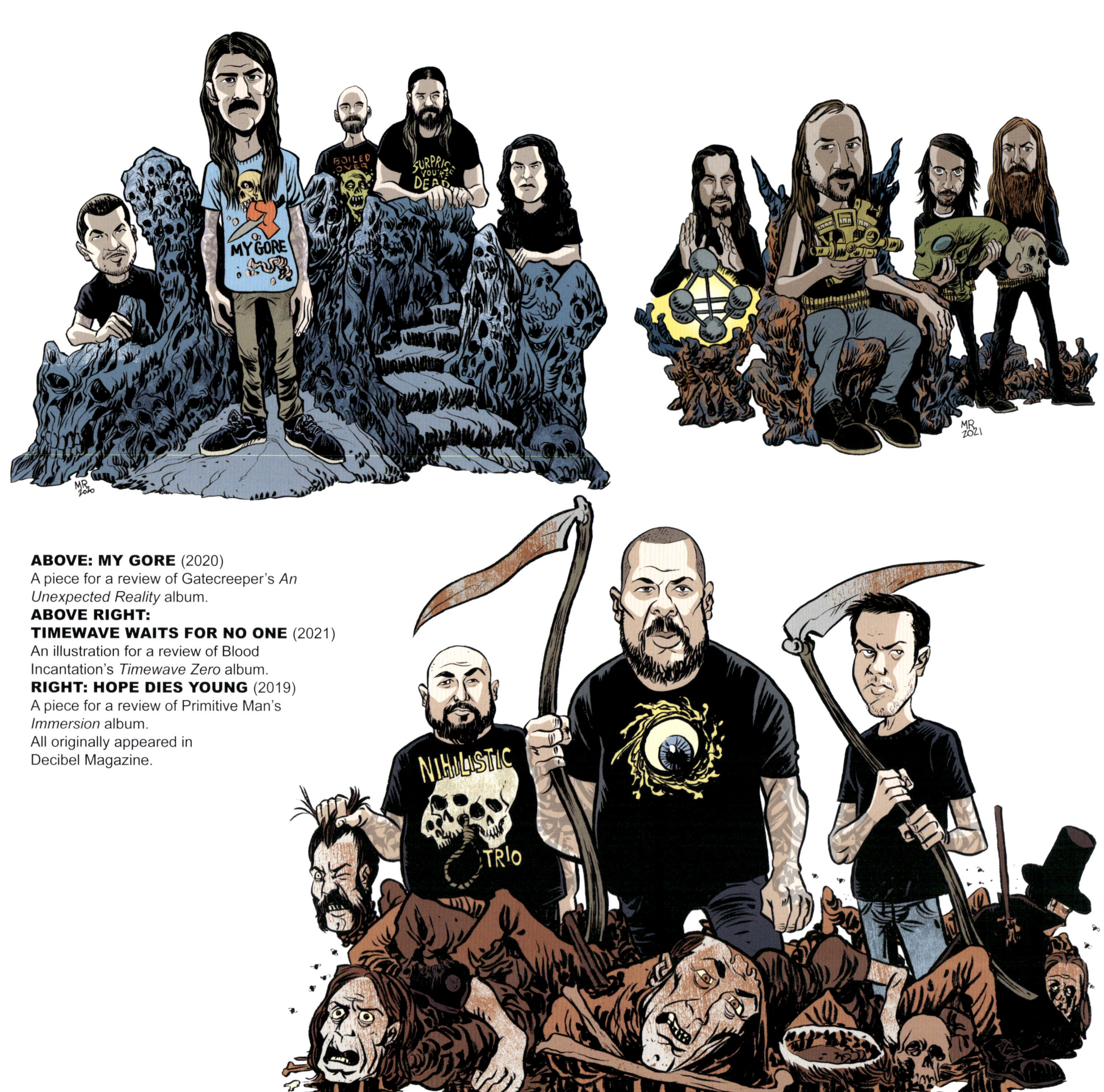

ABOVE: MY GORE (2020)
A piece for a review of Gatecreeper's *An Unexpected Reality* album.
ABOVE RIGHT:
TIMEWAVE WAITS FOR NO ONE (2021)
An illustration for a review of Blood Incantation's *Timewave Zero* album.
RIGHT: HOPE DIES YOUNG (2019)
A piece for a review of Primitive Man's *Immersion* album.
All originally appeared in Decibel Magazine.

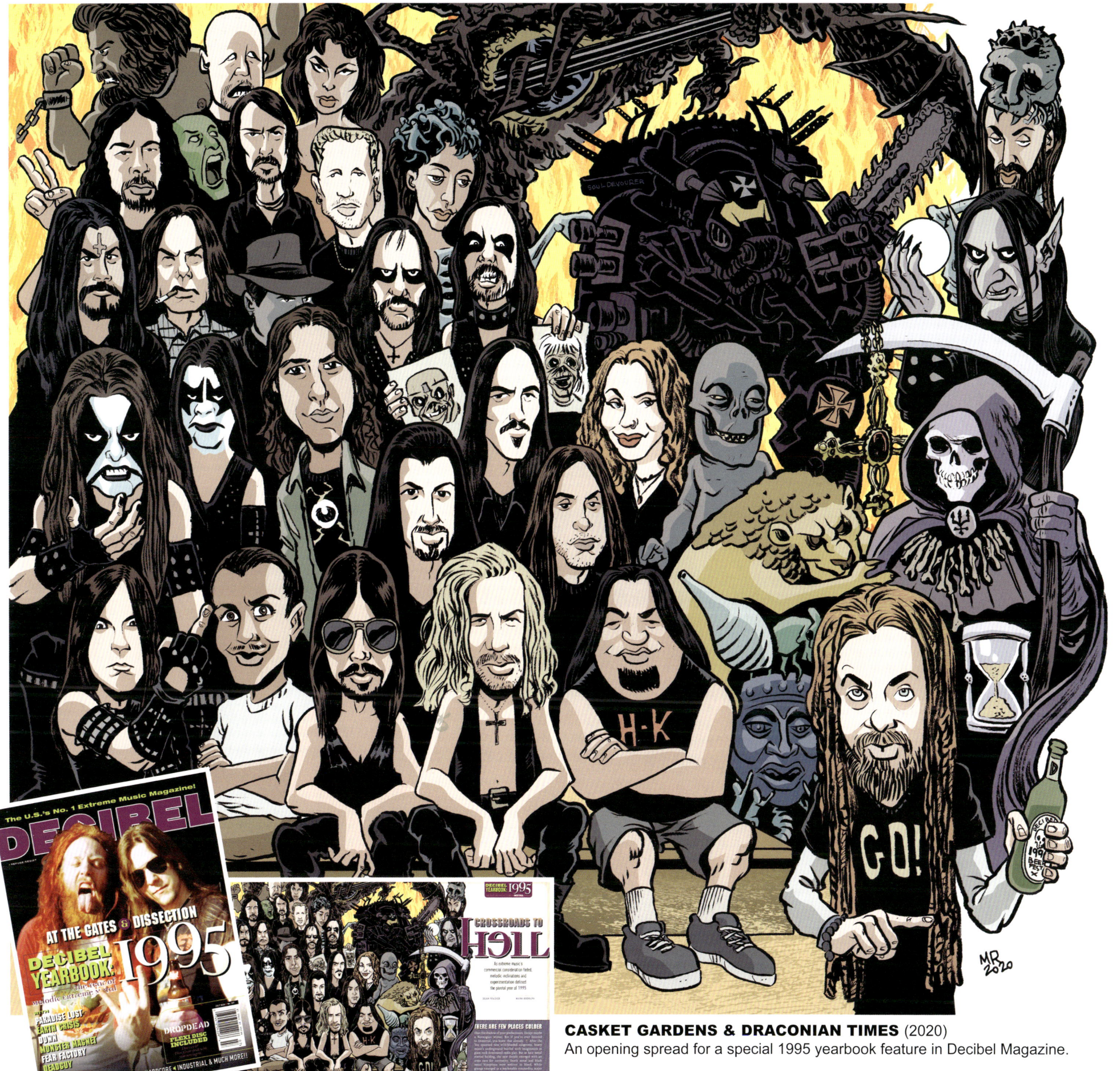

CASKET GARDENS & DRACONIAN TIMES (2020)
An opening spread for a special 1995 yearbook feature in Decibel Magazine.

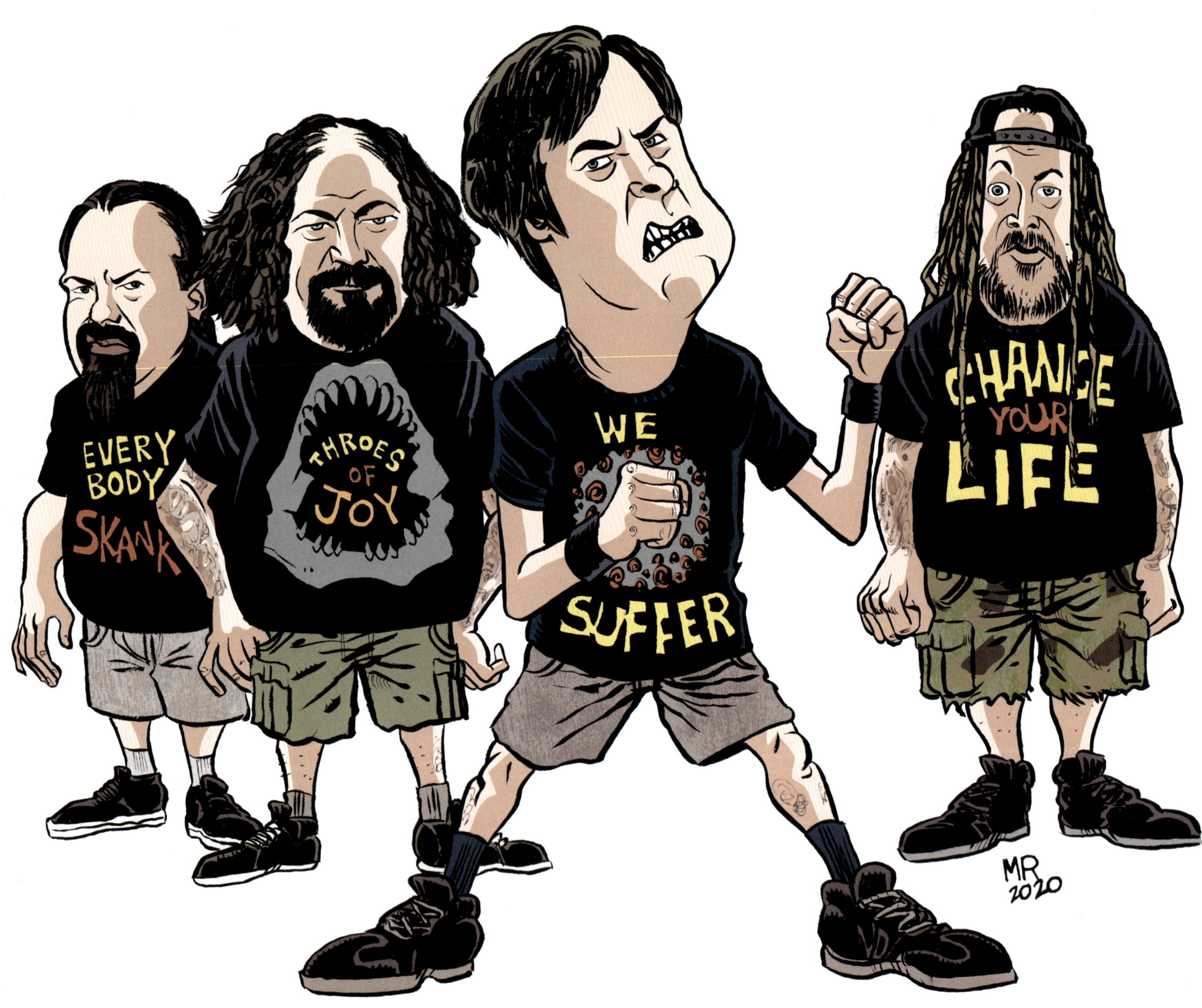

WE ALL SUFFER (2020)
An illustration for a review of Napalm Death's *Throes of Joy in the Jaws of Defeatism album*. Decibel Magazine.

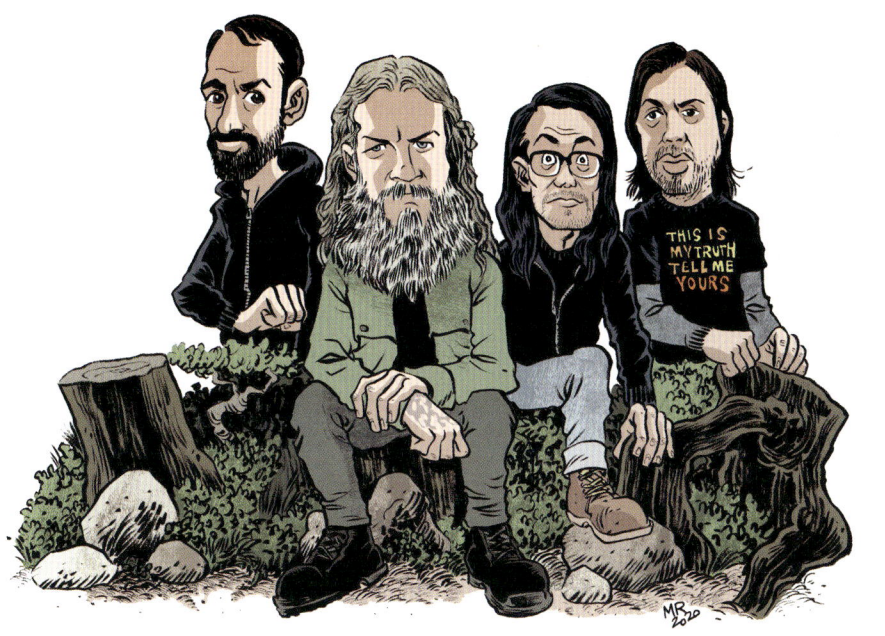

LEFT: TRUE BELIEF (2020)
A piece for a review of Old Man Gloom's *Seminar VIII: Light of Meaning* and *Seminar IX: Darkness of Being* albums.
BELOW: MORTALS WATCH THE DAY (2020)
An illustration for a review of Necrot's *Mortal* album.
Both originally appeared in Decibel Magazine.

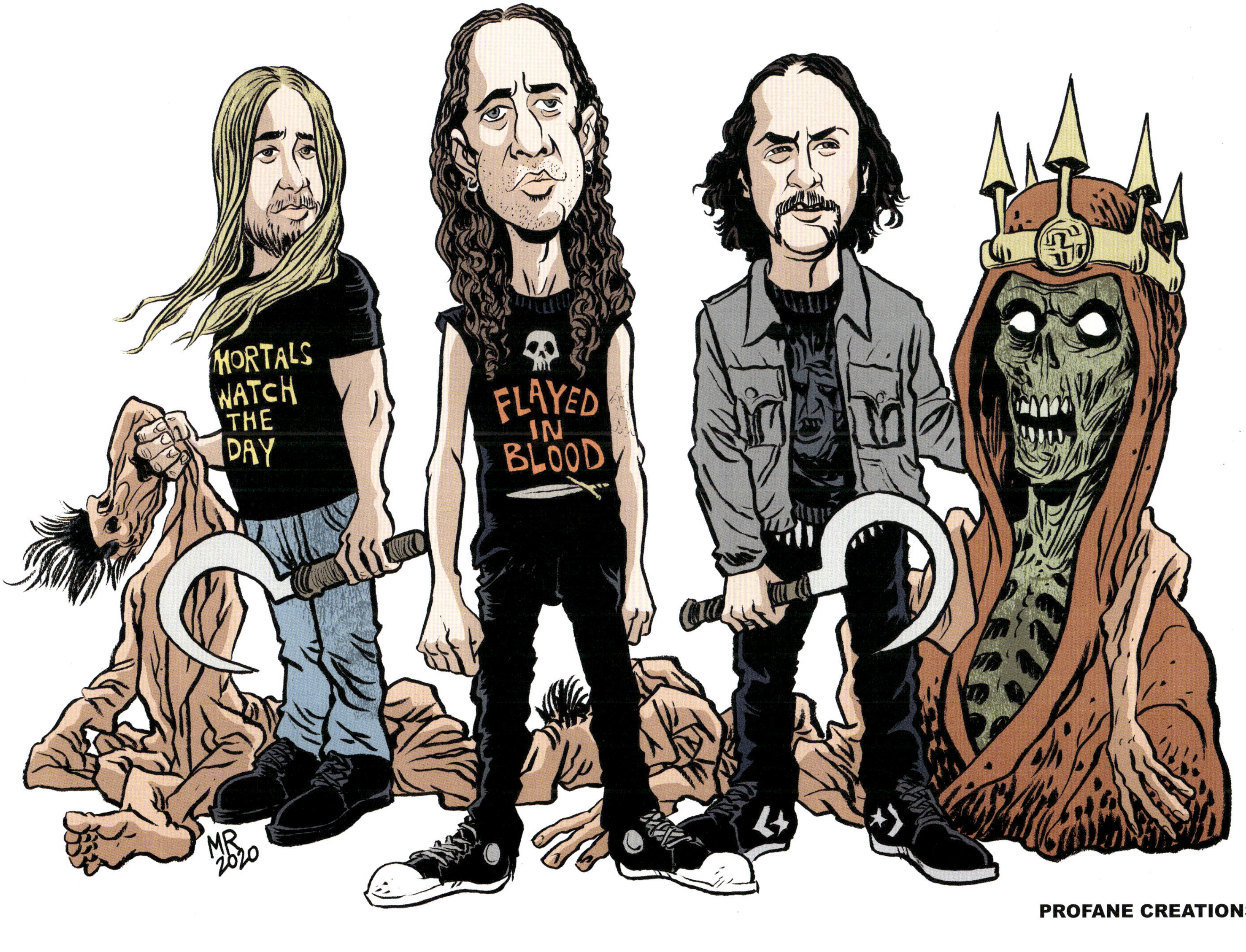

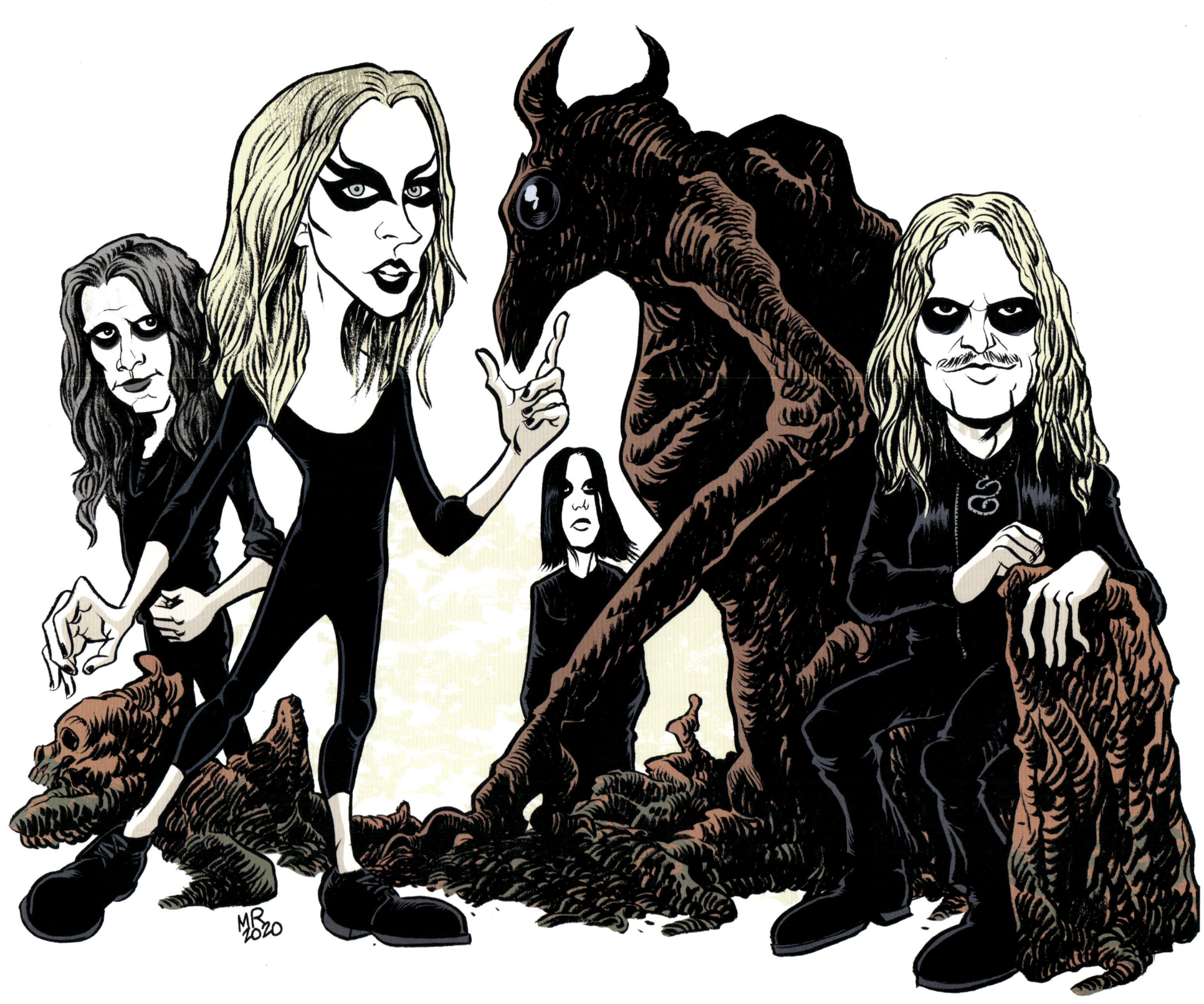

THE SUFFERER (2020)
An illustration for a review of Tribulation's *Where the Gloom Becomes Sound* album. Decibel Magazine.

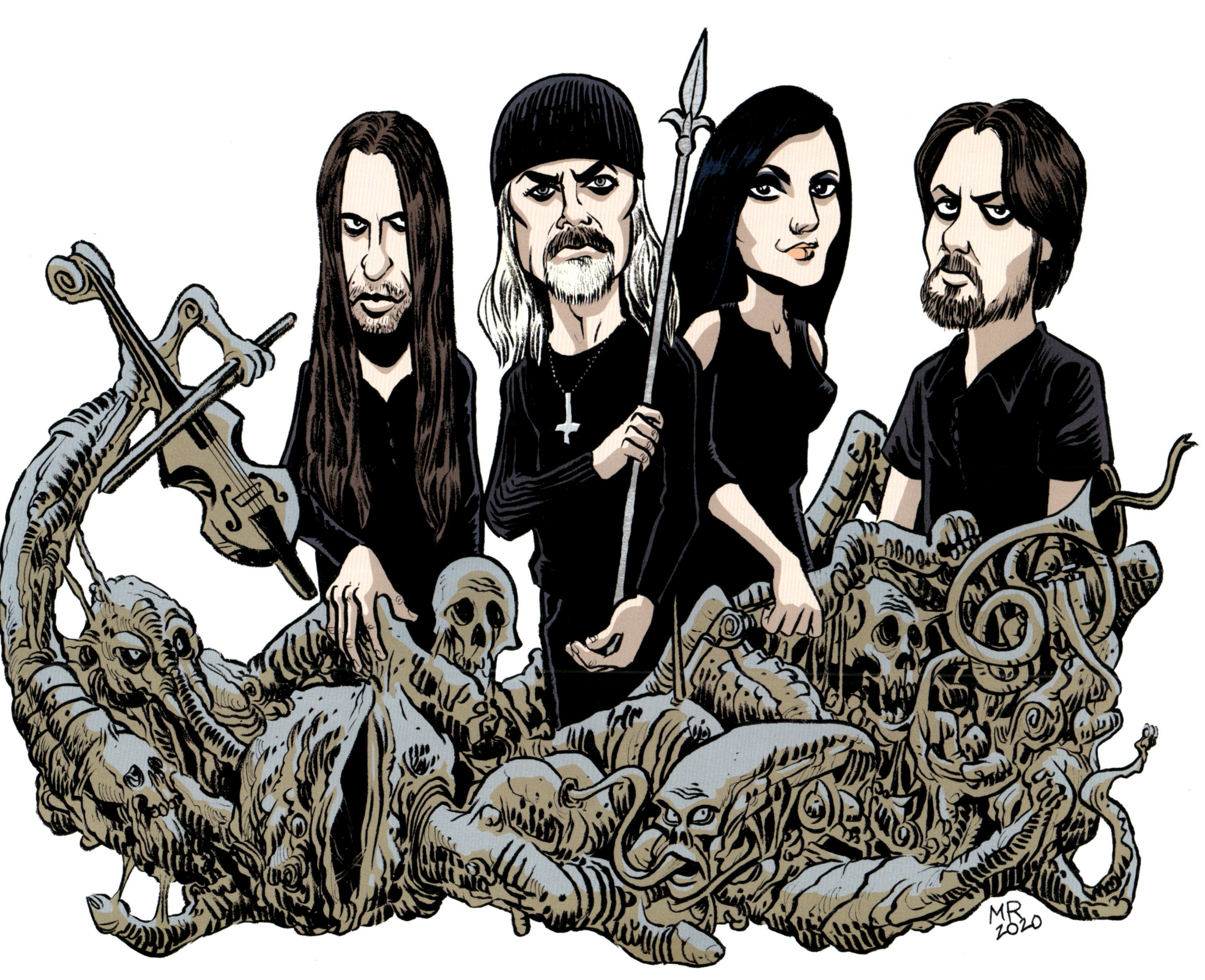

WORLD PRETENDING (2020)
An illustration for a review of Triptykon's *Requiem (Live at Roadburn 2019)* album. Decibel Magazine.

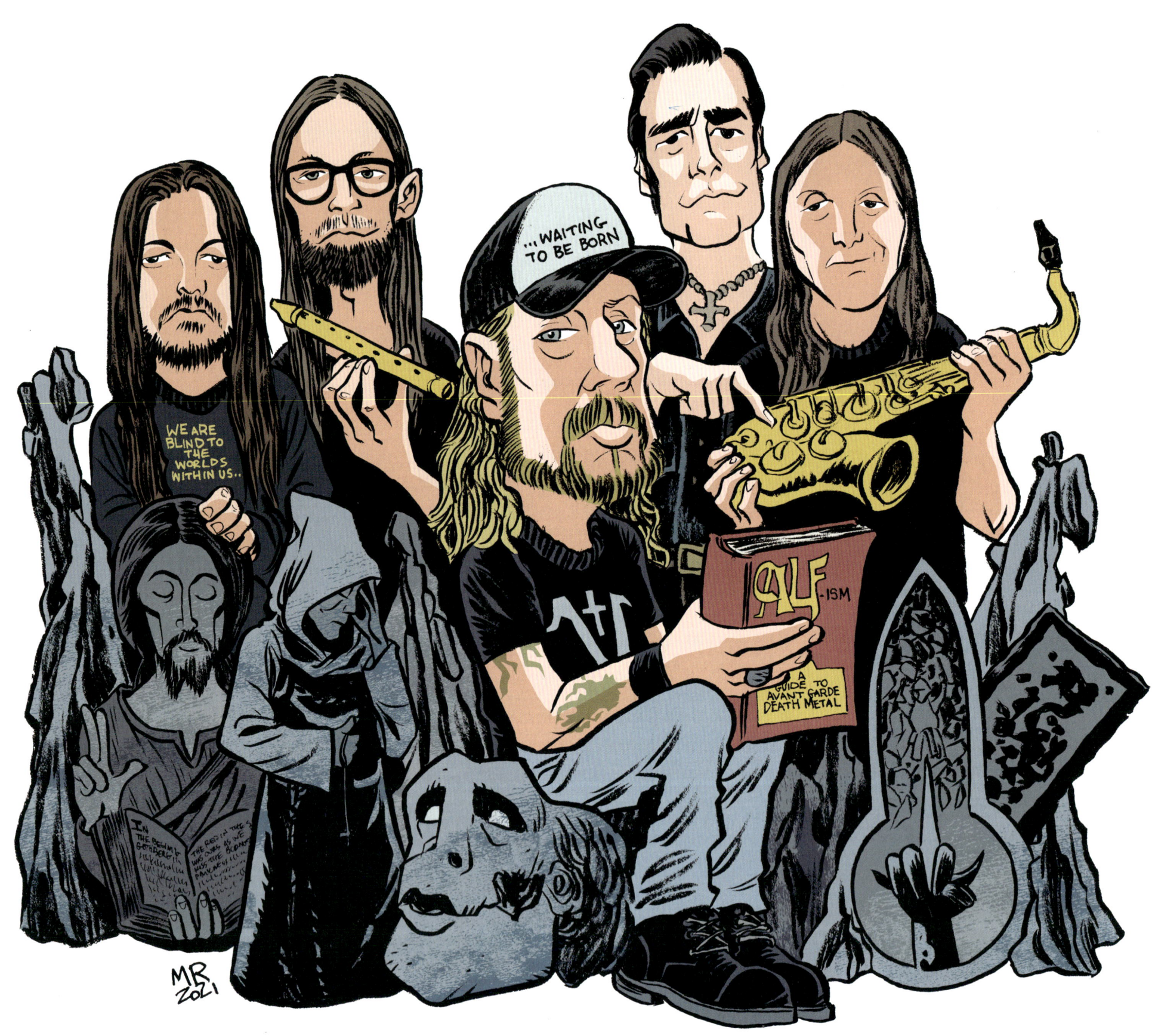

TWO WORLDS (2021)
An illustration for a review of At The Gate's *The Nightmare of Being* album. Decibel Magazine.

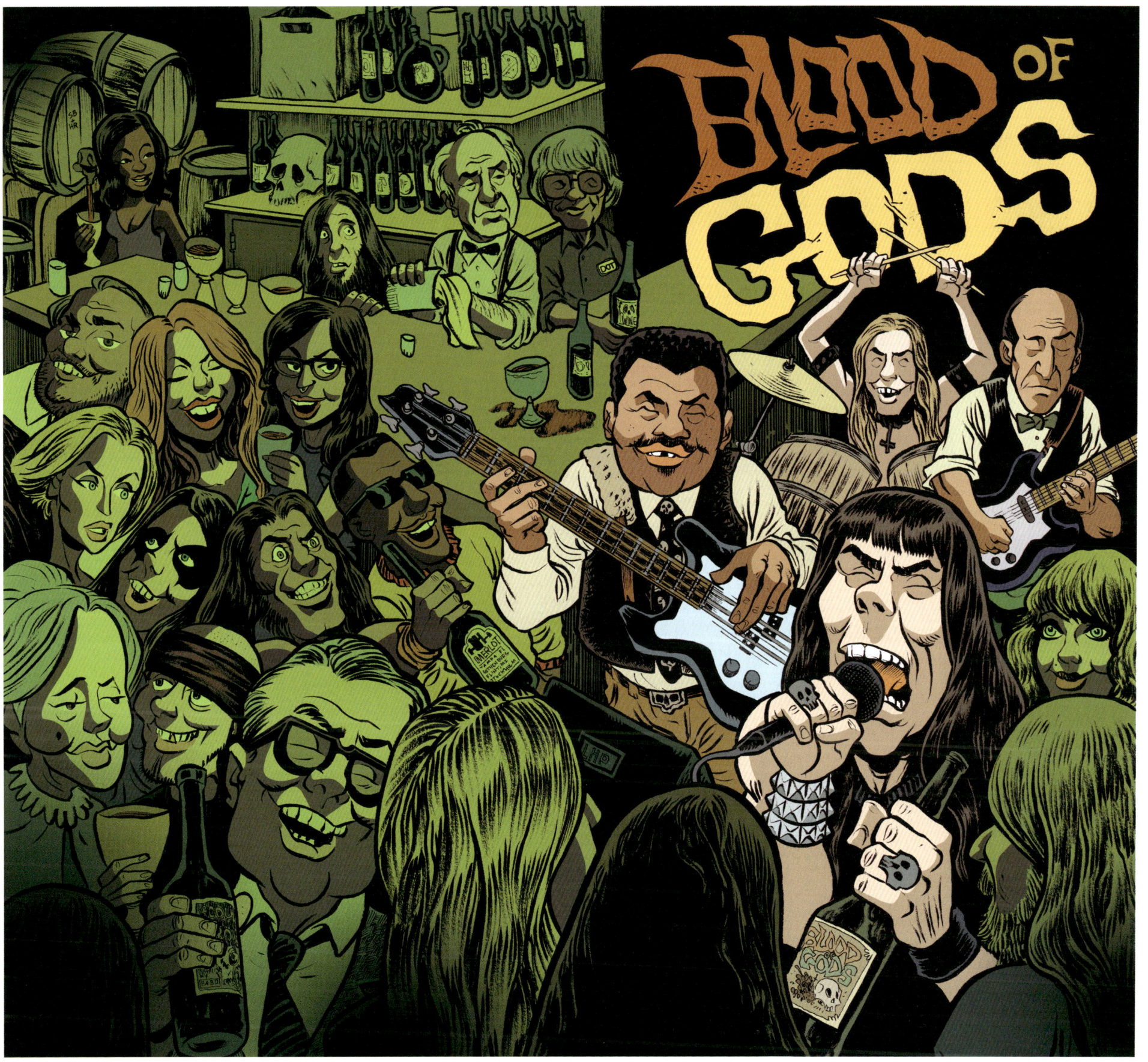

LOUNGE OF GODS (2021)
The cover for the third issue of Blood of Gods Magazine.

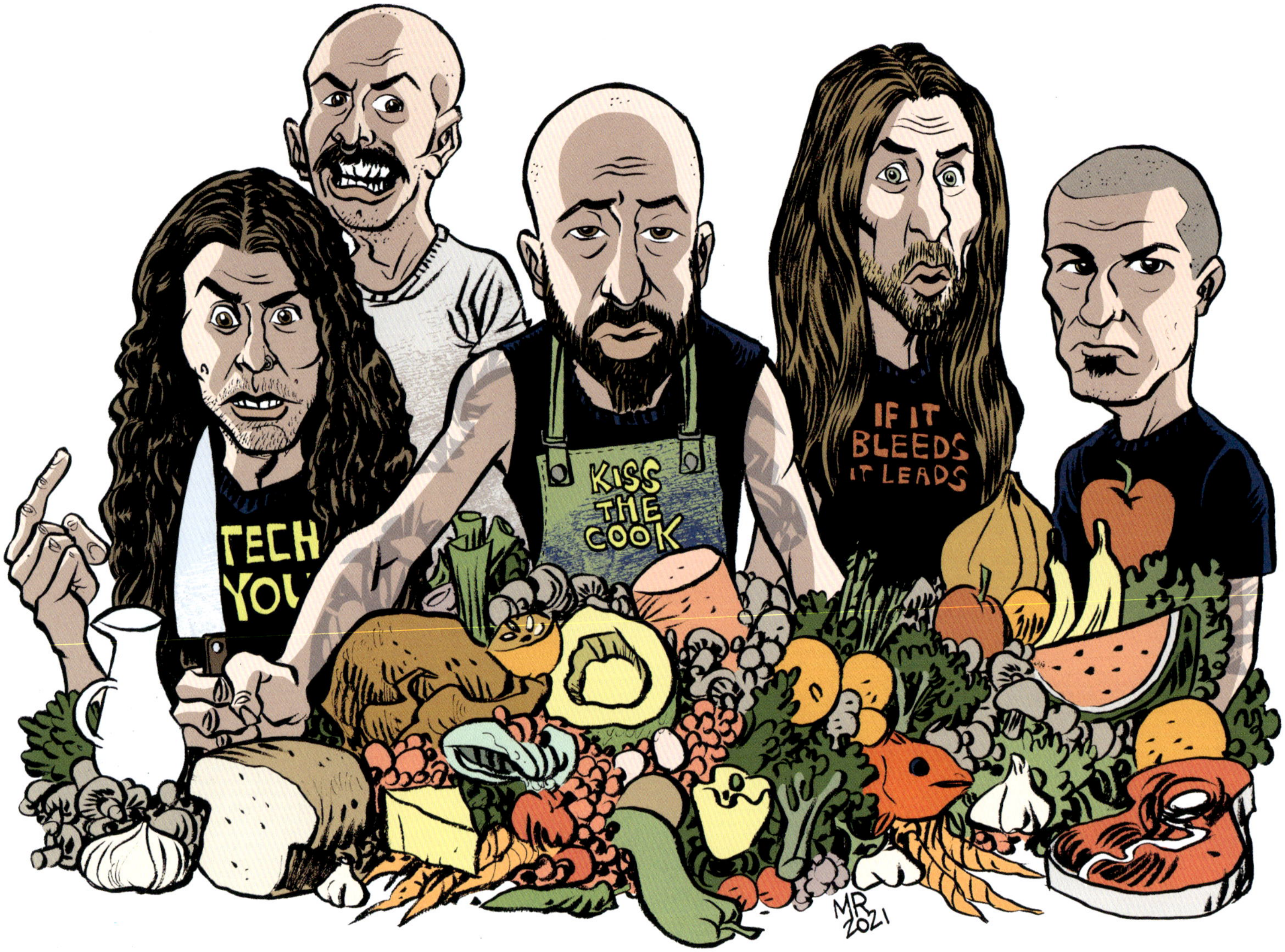

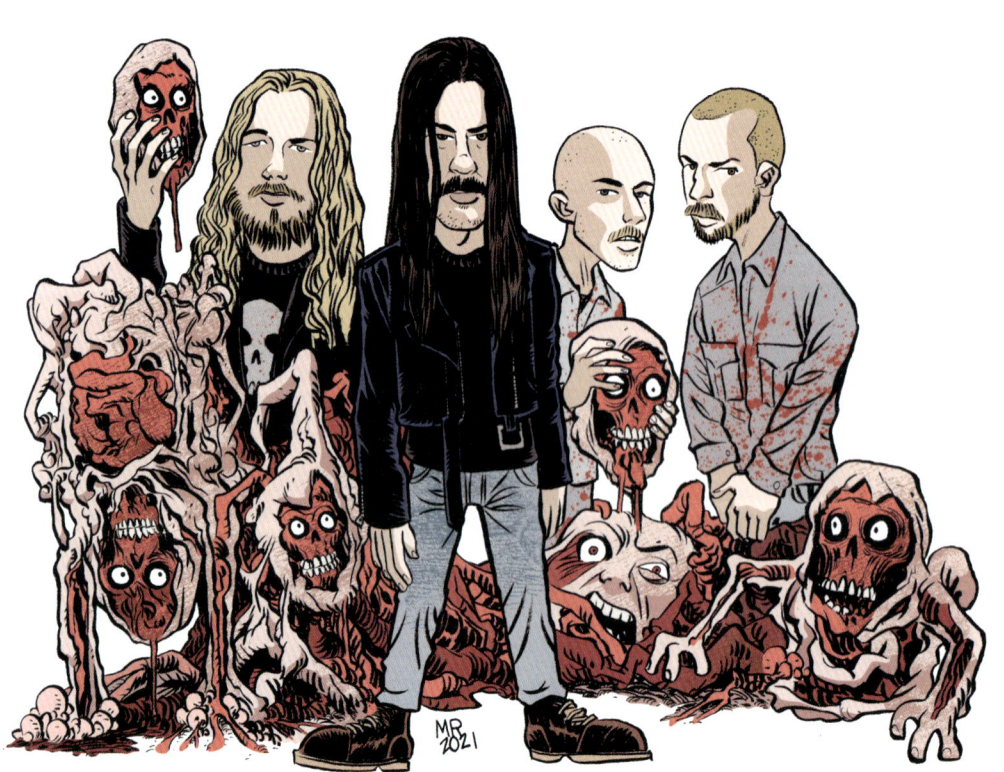

LEFT:
SEDATIVE GOD (2021)
A piece for a review of Archspire's *Bleed The Future* album.
BELOW LEFT:
CEREBRAL ROTTING MISERY (2021)
An illustration for a review of Cerebral Rot's *Excretion of Mortality* album.
BELOW:
AS HORIZONS END (2021)
A piece for a review of Vreid's *Wild North West* album.
All originally appeared in Decibel Magazine.

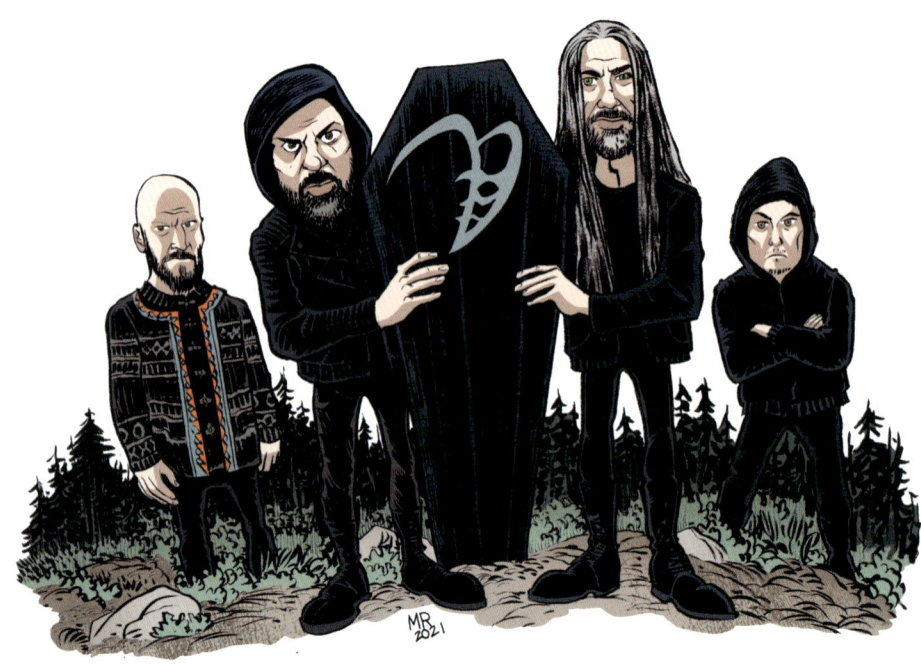

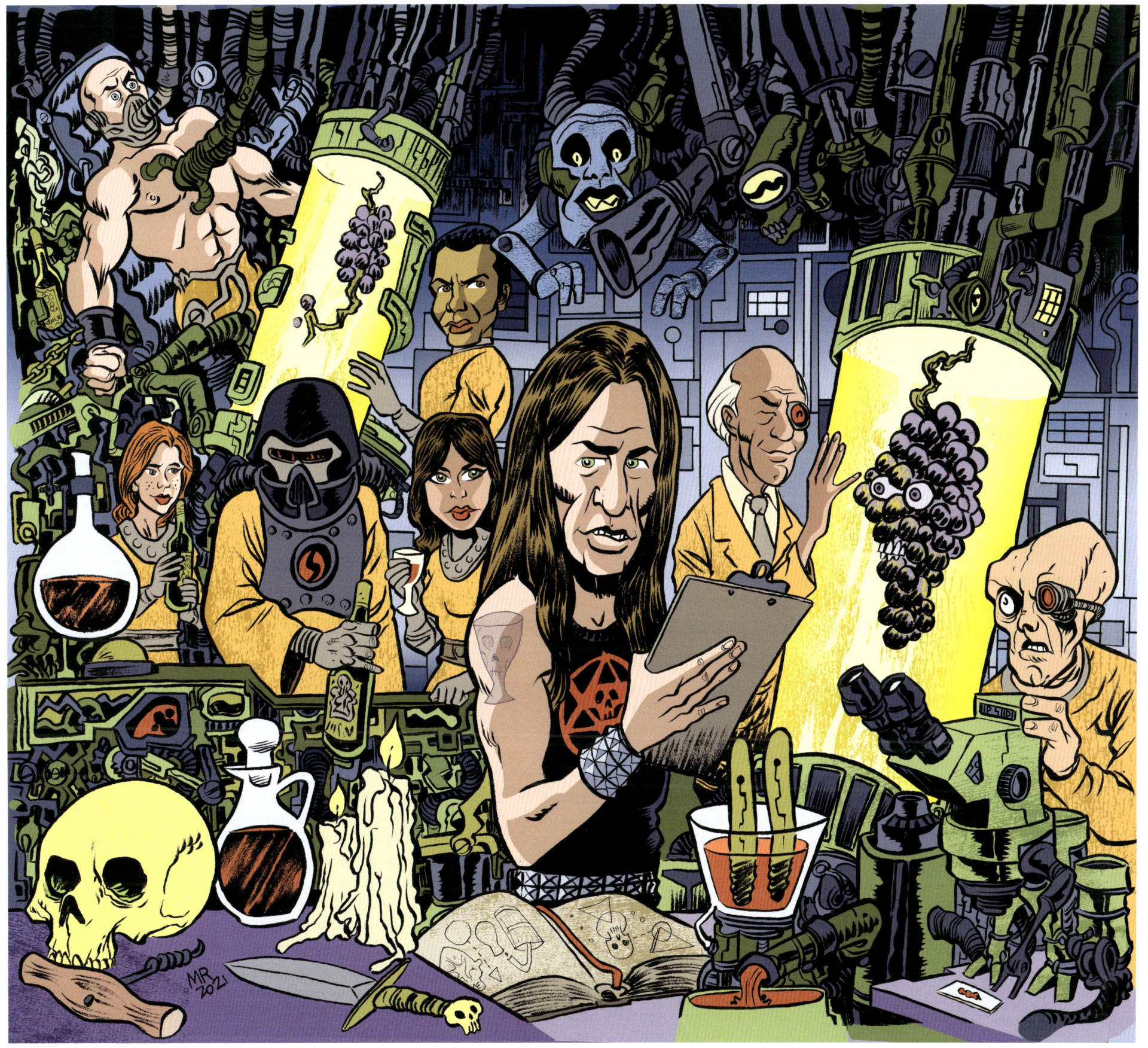

LAB OF GODS (2021)
The cover for the fourth issue of Blood of Gods Magazine.

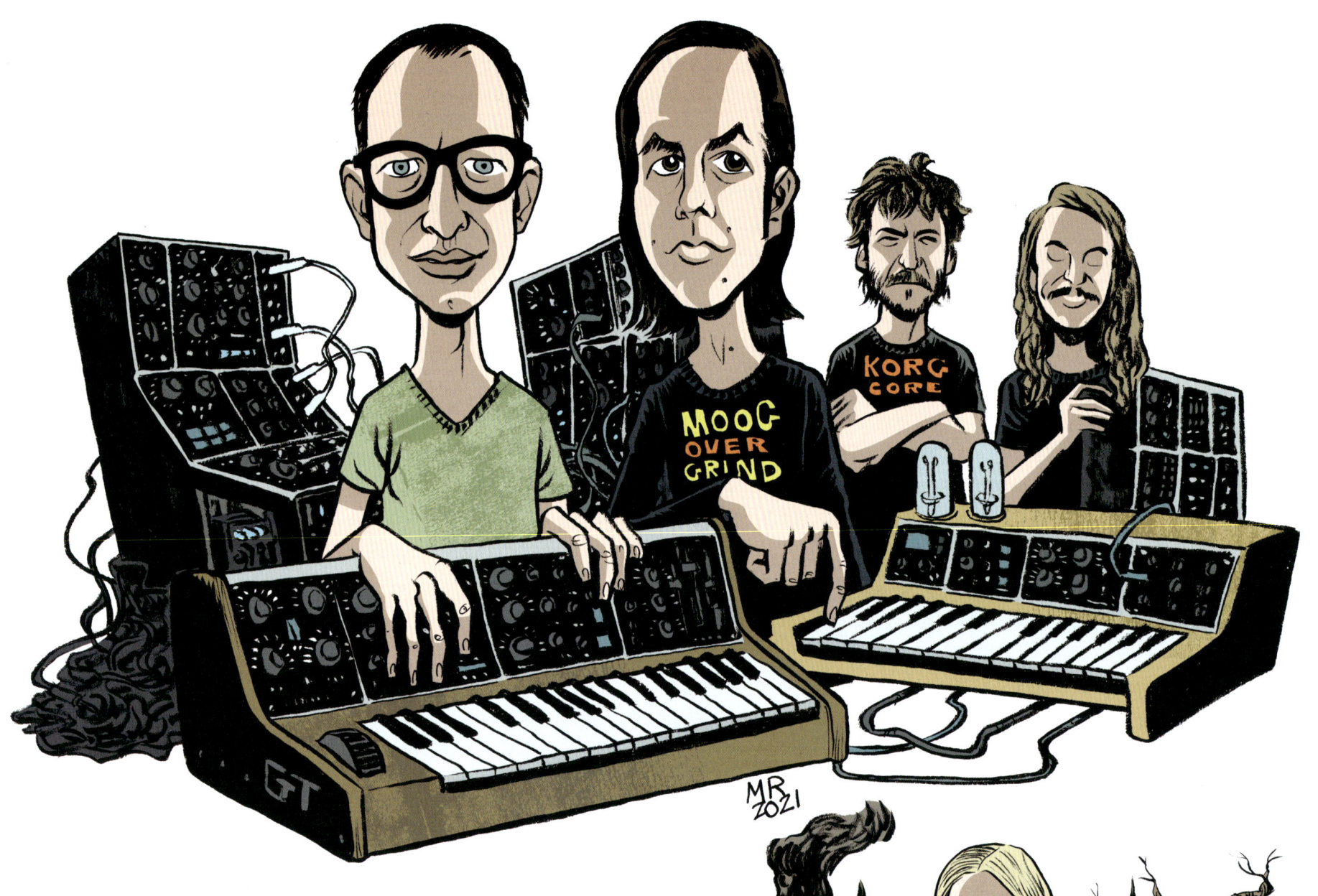

ABOVE: UNIVERSAL DREAM (2021)
A piece for a review of Genghis Tron's
Dream Weapon album.
RIGHT: FIRST LIGHT (2021)
An illustration for a review of Panopticon's
...And Again into the Light album.
Both originally appeared in
Decibel Magazine.

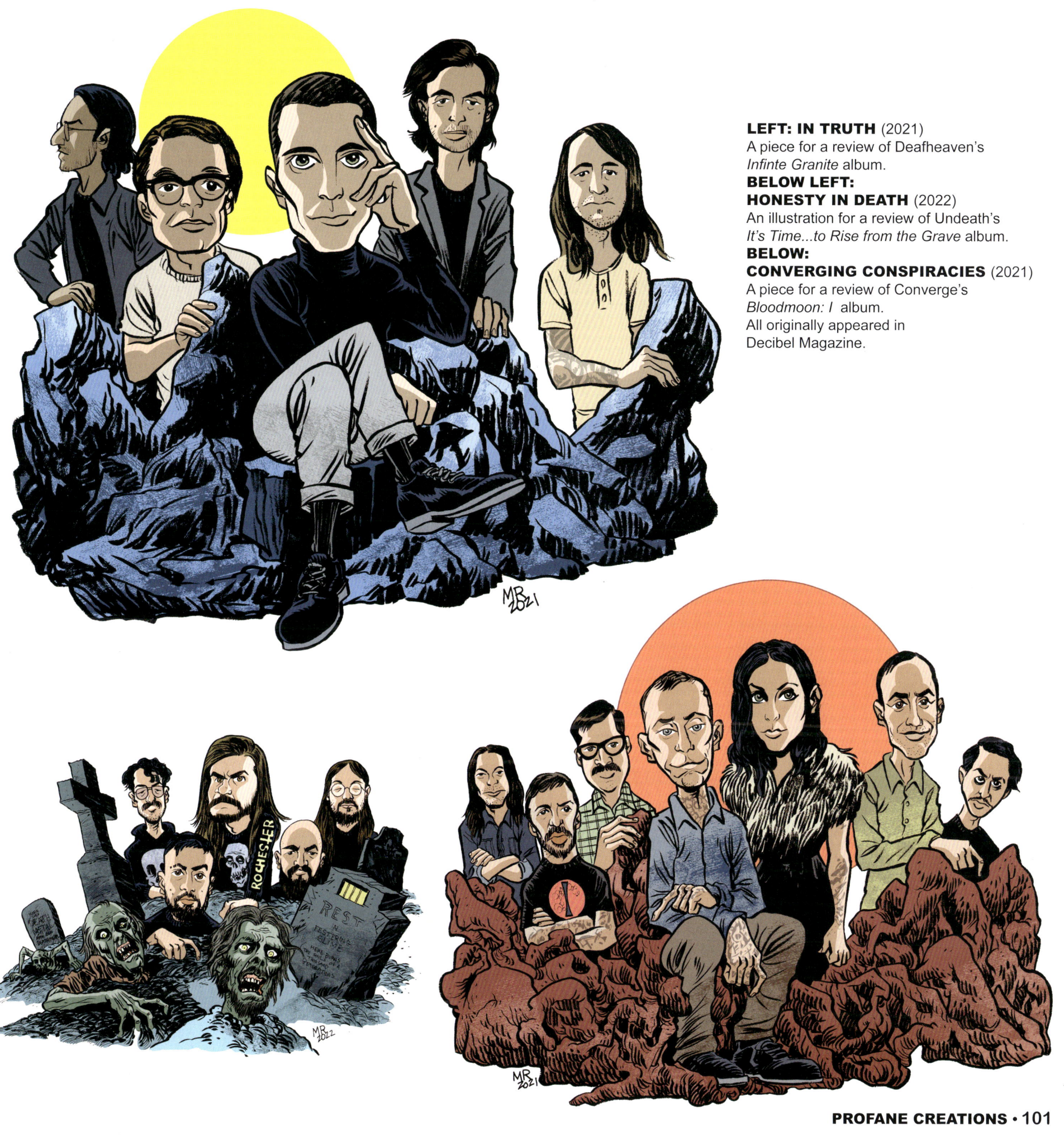

LEFT: IN TRUTH (2021)
A piece for a review of Deafheaven's
Infinte Granite album.
BELOW LEFT:
HONESTY IN DEATH (2022)
An illustration for a review of Undeath's
It's Time...to Rise from the Grave album.
BELOW:
CONVERGING CONSPIRACIES (2021)
A piece for a review of Converge's
Bloodmoon: I album.
All originally appeared in
Decibel Magazine.

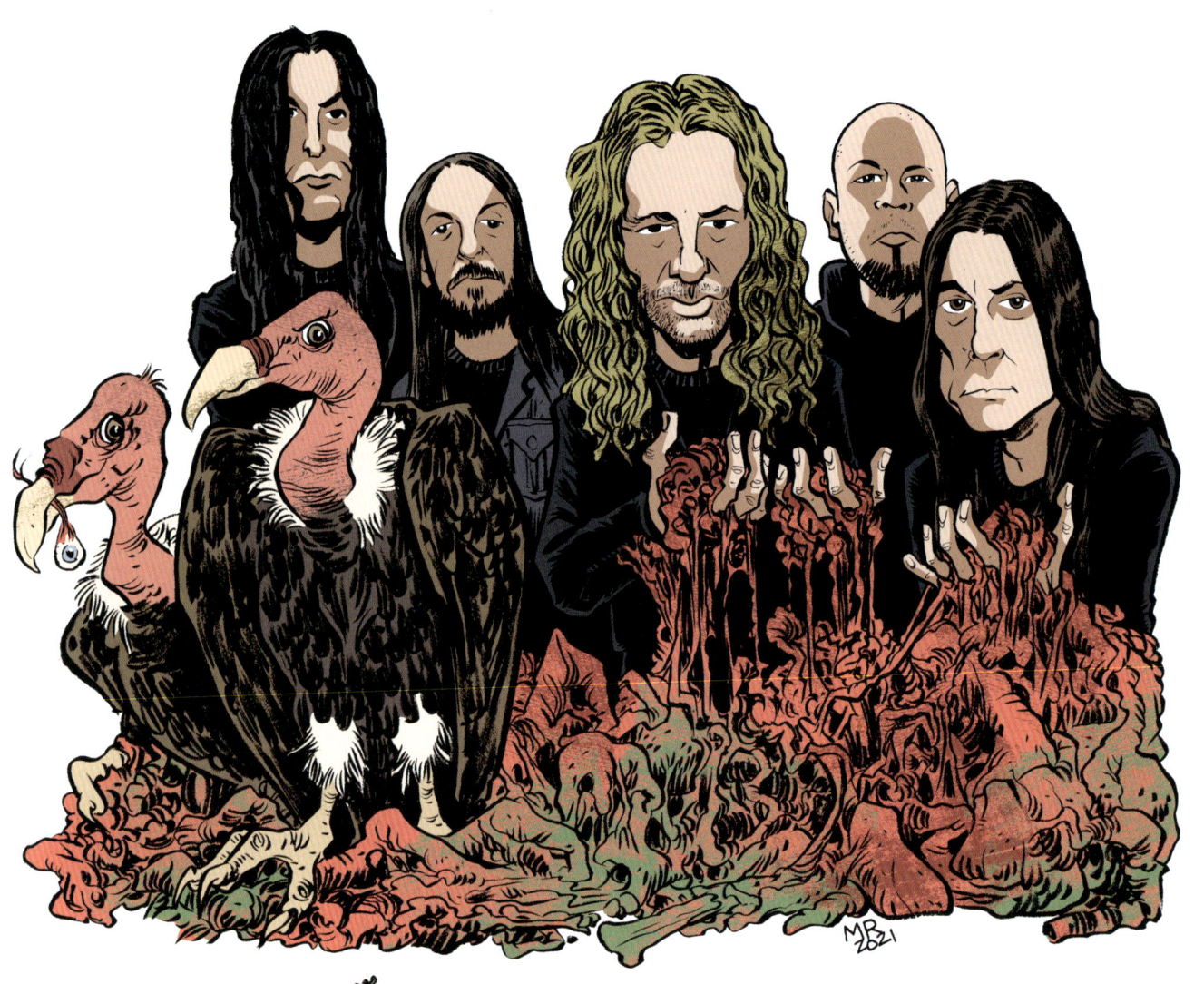

LEFT: BLOOD & CHAOS (2021)
An illustration for a review of Unanimated's *Victory in Blood* album.
BELOW LEFT:
WORTH FIGHTING FOR (2021)
A piece for a review of Dream Unending's album, *Song of Salvation*.
BELOW:
PUNISHMENT THROUGH TIME (2021)
An illustration for a review of Venom Prison's *Erebos* album.
All originally appeared in Decibel Magazine.

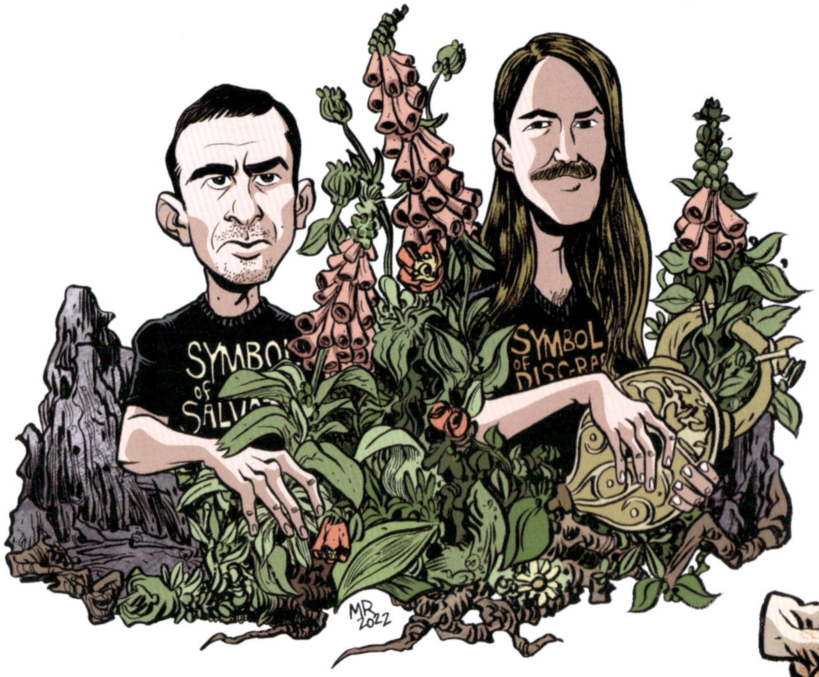

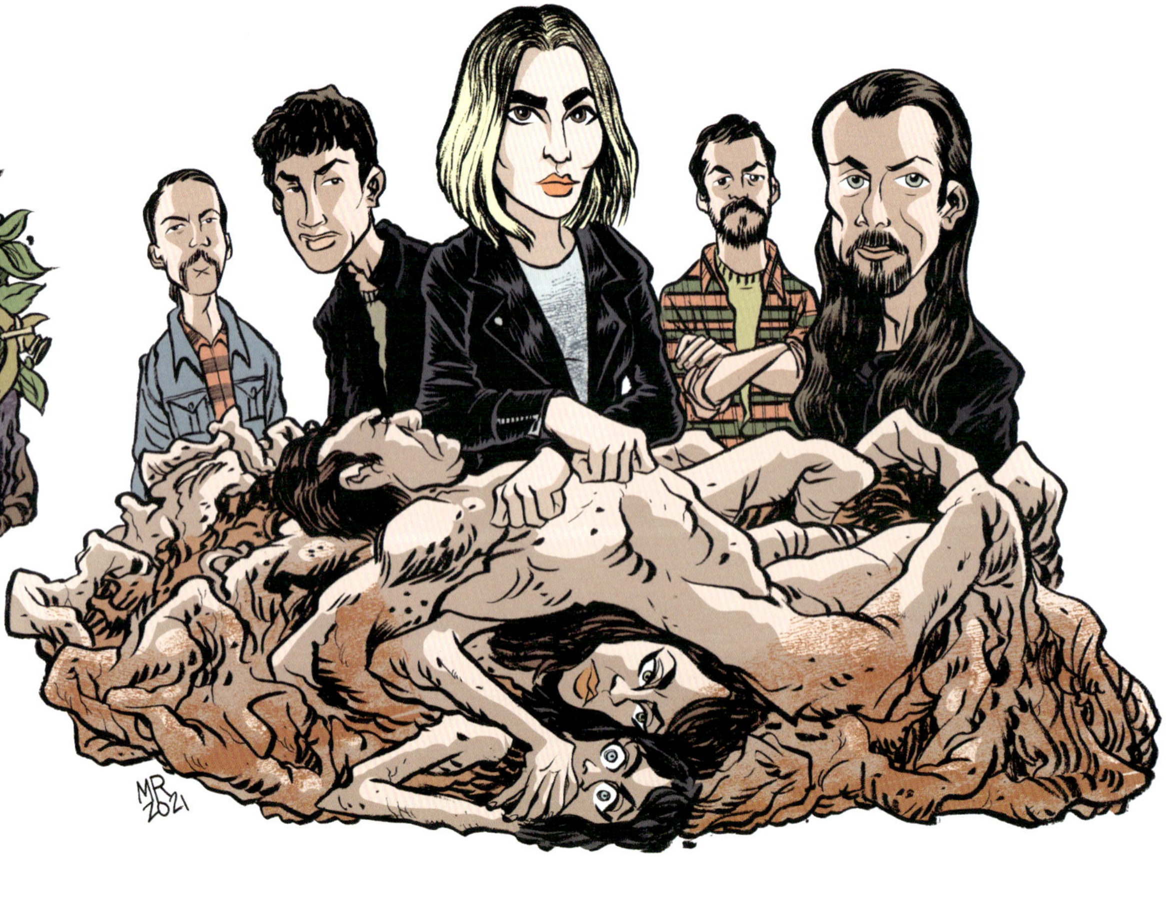

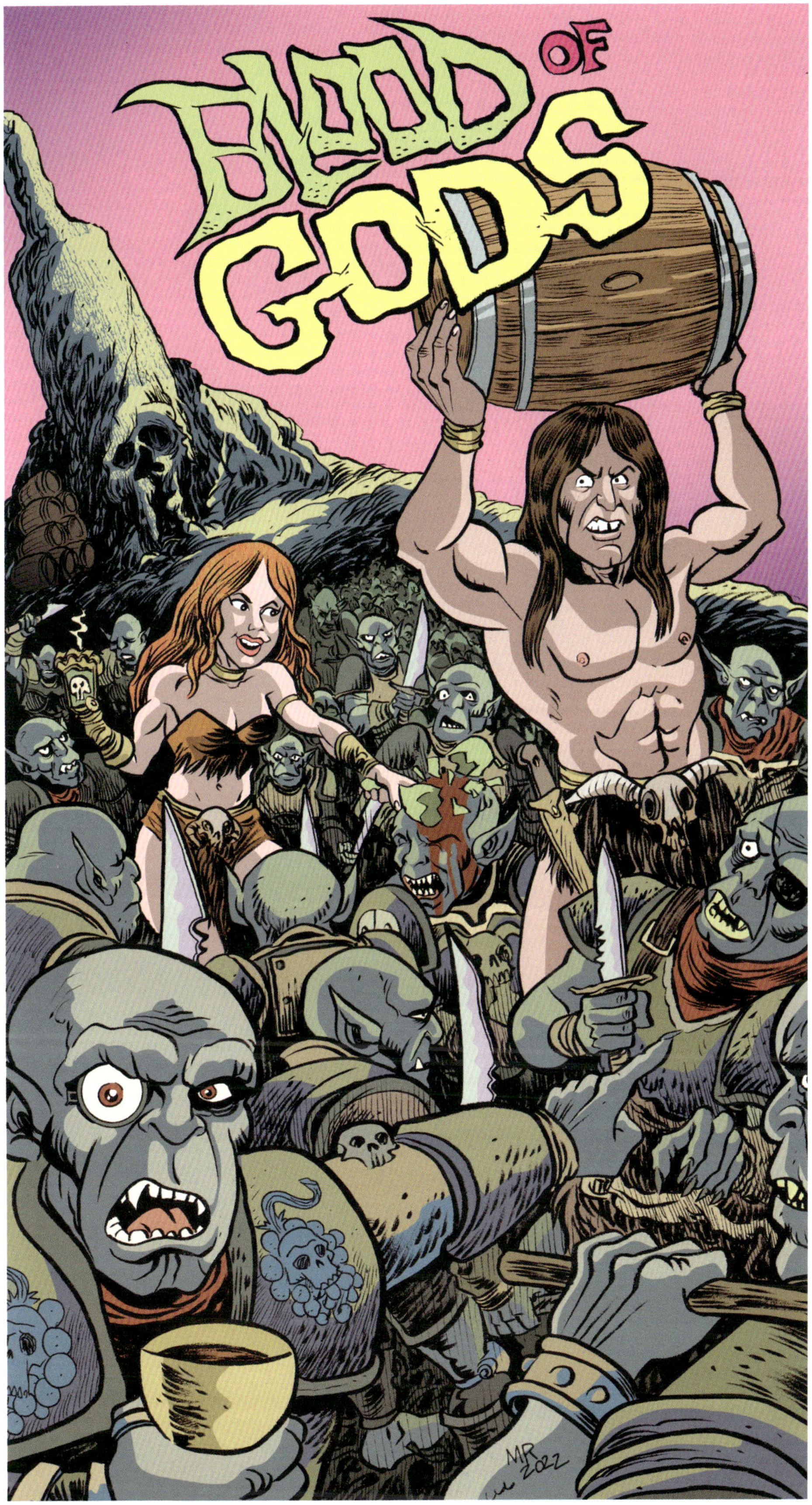

CASTLE OF GODS (2022)
Cover for issue number five of Blood of Gods Magazine.

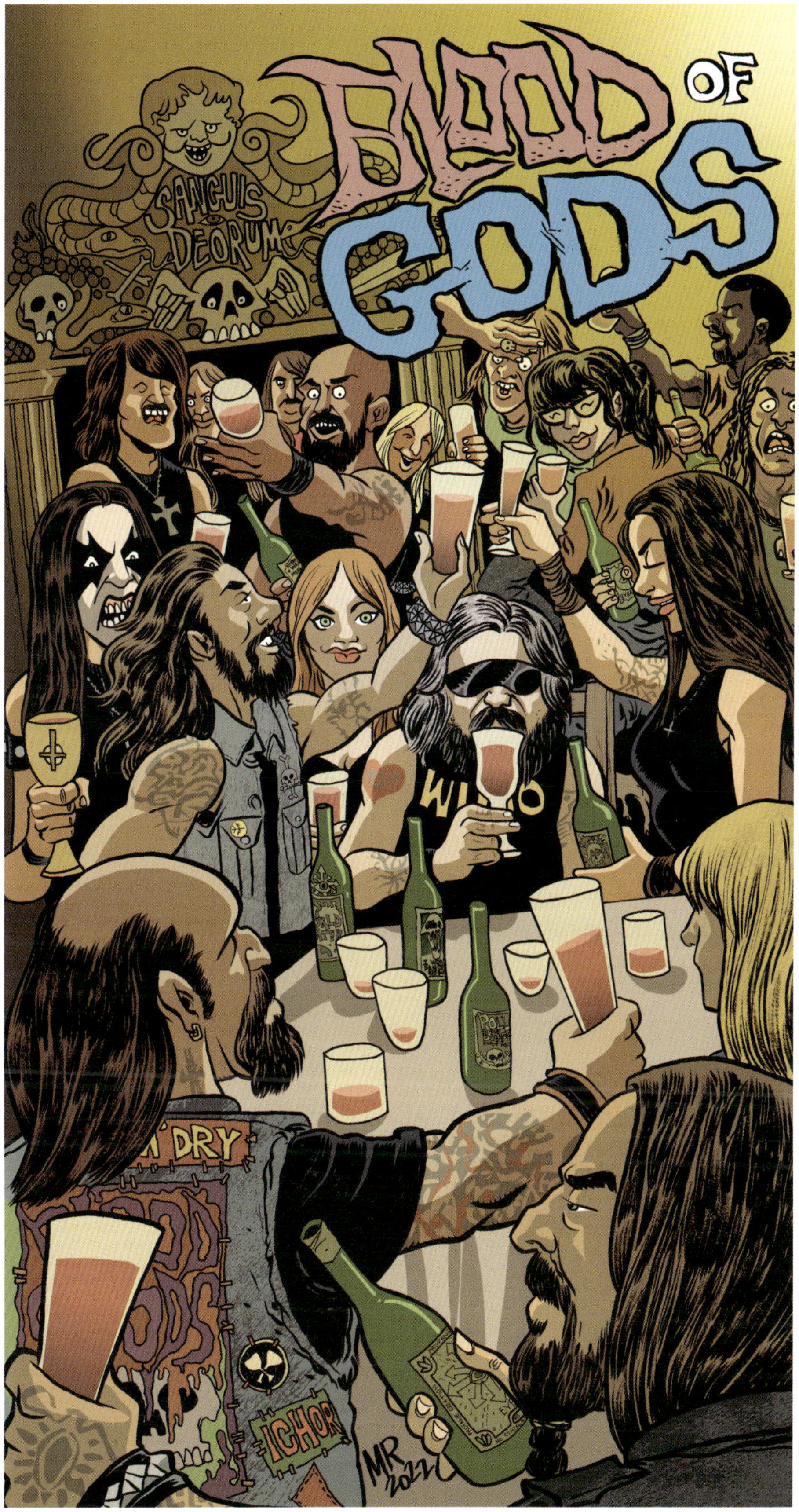

HALL OF GODS (2022)
Cover for issue number six of Blood of Gods Magazine.

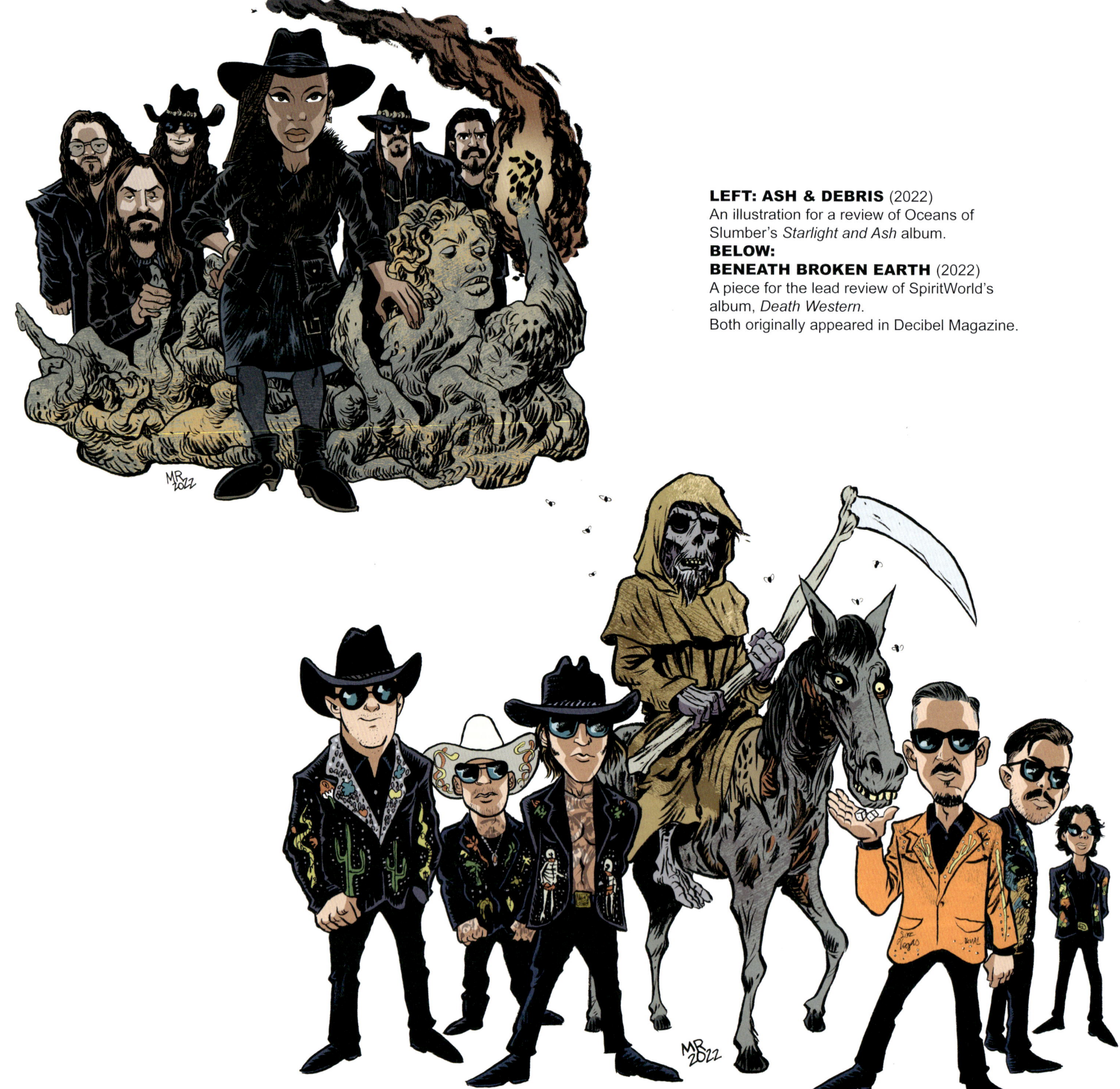

LEFT: ASH & DEBRIS (2022)
An illustration for a review of Oceans of Slumber's *Starlight and Ash* album.
BELOW:
BENEATH BROKEN EARTH (2022)
A piece for the lead review of SpiritWorld's album, *Death Western*.
Both originally appeared in Decibel Magazine.

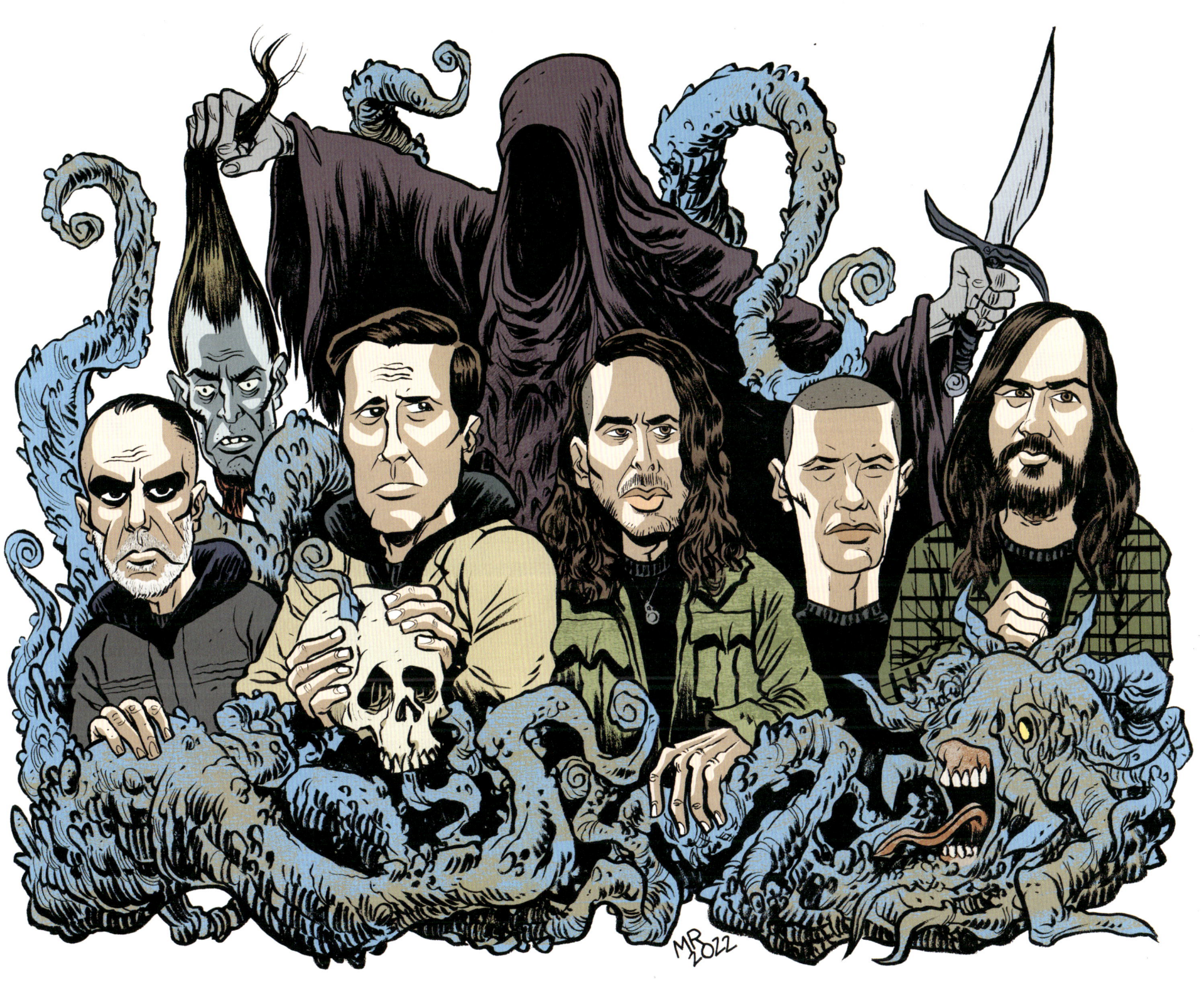

FACE THE SLAYER (2022)
An illustration for a review of Temple of Void's *Summoning The Slayer*. Originally appeared in Decibel Magazine.

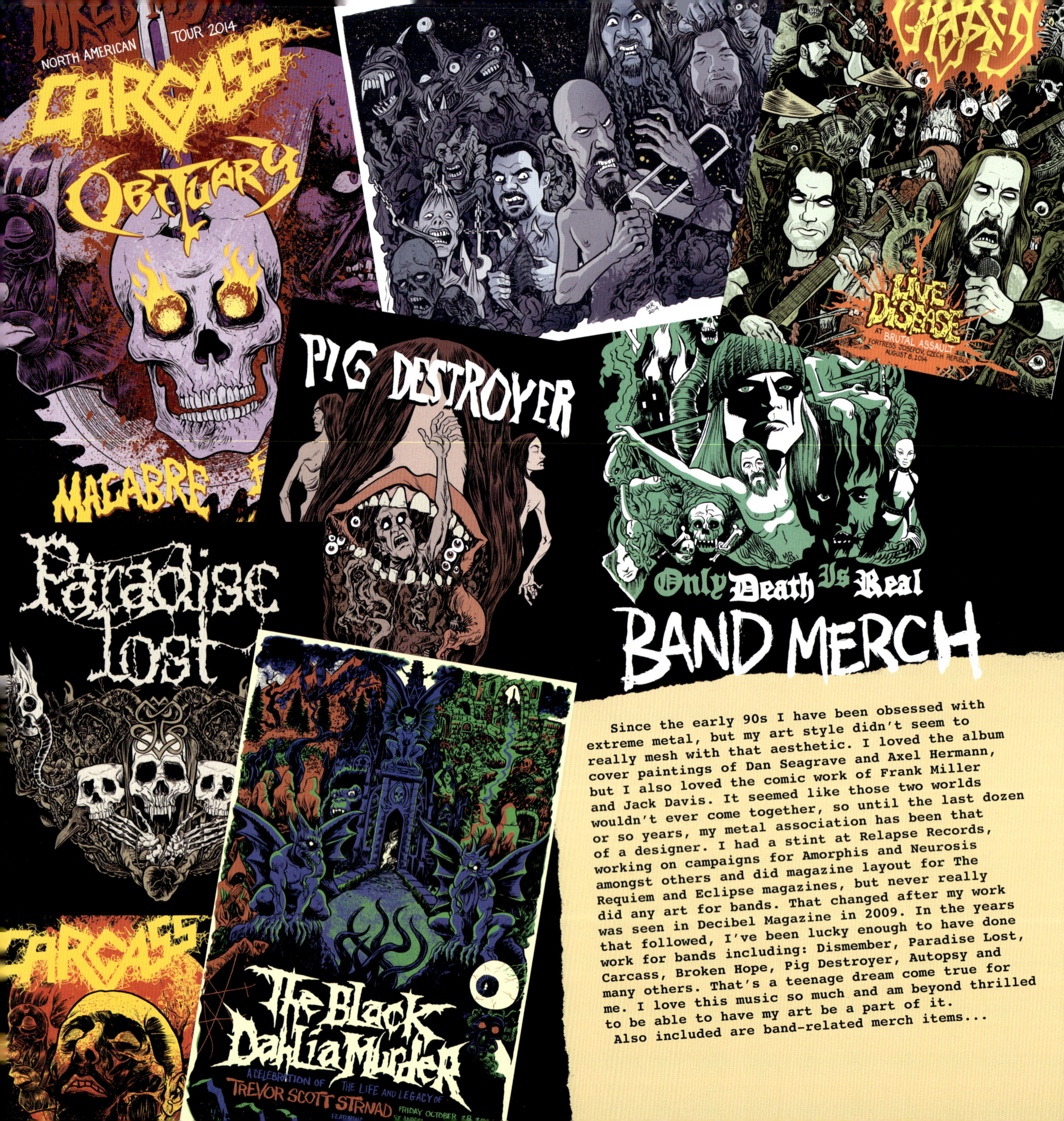

BAND MERCH

Only Death Is Real

Since the early 90s I have been obsessed with extreme metal, but my art style didn't seem to really mesh with that aesthetic. I loved the album cover paintings of Dan Seagrave and Axel Hermann, but I also loved the comic work of Frank Miller and Jack Davis. It seemed like those two worlds wouldn't ever come together, so until the last dozen or so years, my metal association has been that of a designer. I had a stint at Relapse Records, working on campaigns for Amorphis and Neurosis amongst others and did magazine layout for The Requiem and Eclipse magazines, but never really did any art for bands. That changed after my work was seen in Decibel Magazine in 2009. In the years that followed, I've been lucky enough to have done work for bands including: Dismember, Paradise Lost, Carcass, Broken Hope, Pig Destroyer, Autopsy and many others. That's a teenage dream come true for me. I love this music so much and am beyond thrilled to be able to have my art be a part of it.

Also included are band-related merch items...

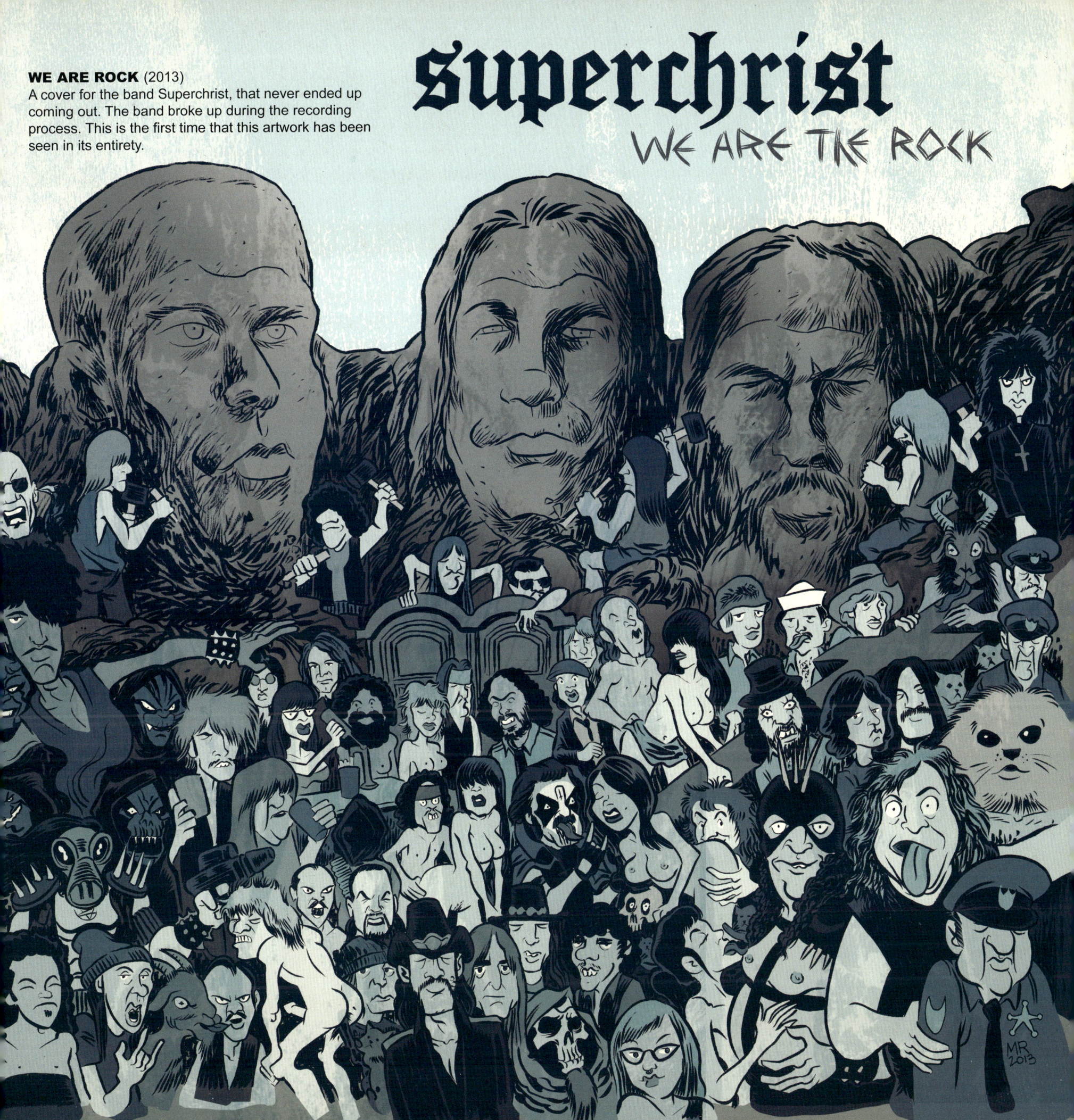

WE ARE ROCK (2013)
A cover for the band Superchrist, that never ended up coming out. The band broke up during the recording process. This is the first time that this artwork has been seen in its entirety.

superchrist
WE ARE THE ROCK

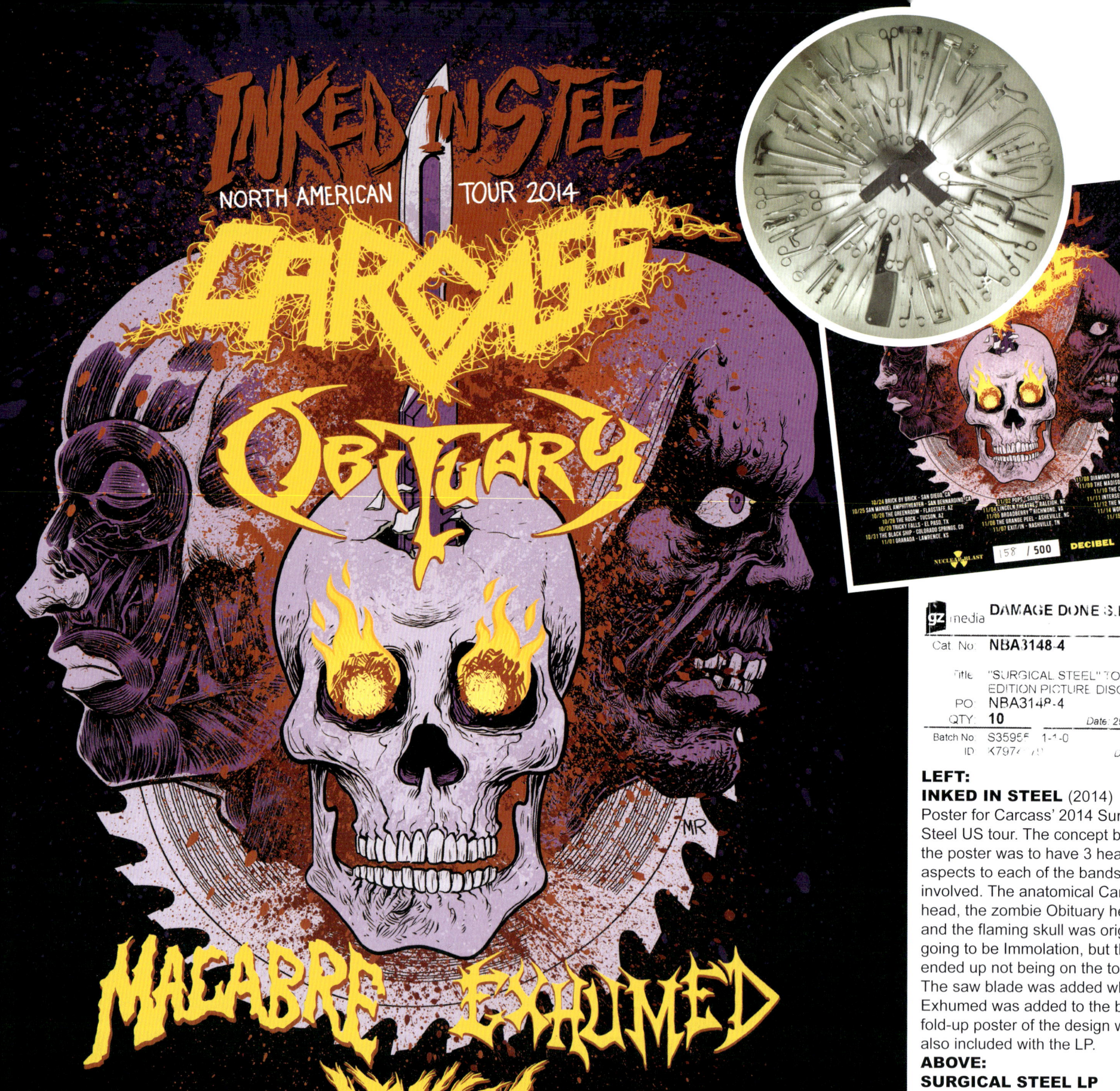

INKED IN STEEL
NORTH AMERICAN TOUR 2014

CARCASS
OBITUARY
MACABRE   EXHUMED
NOISEM

gz media **DAMAGE DONE S.R.O.**

Cat. No. NBA3148-4

Title "SURGICAL STEEL" TOUR
EDITION PICTURE DISC

PO NBA3148-4

QTY **10**   Date: 29.1.201

Batch No. S35955 1-1-0

ID K79747   DAMAG

LEFT:

INKED IN STEEL (2014)
Poster for Carcass' 2014 Surgical
Steel US tour. The concept behind
the poster was to have 3 heads/
aspects to each of the bands
involved. The anatomical Carcass
head, the zombie Obituary head
and the flaming skull was originally
going to be Immolation, but they
ended up not being on the tour.
The saw blade was added when
Exhumed was added to the bill. A
fold-up poster of the design was
also included with the LP.

ABOVE:

SURGICAL STEEL LP
The poster was also used on the
back of the limited US tour picture
disc. Below is the sticker that was
on the mailer box from the
manufacturer.

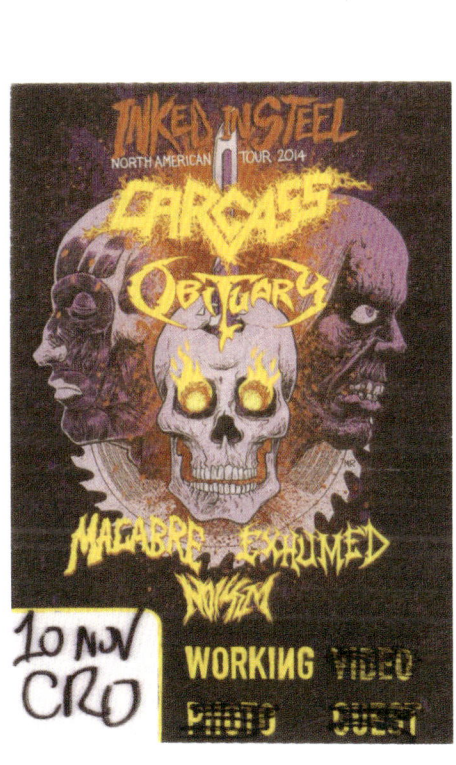

ABOVE:
INKED IN STEEL BADGE
Laminate for Carcass' 2014
US tour.
RIGHT:
INKED IN STEEL II (2014)
Poster for Carcass' 2014 Surgical
Steel show at The Crofoot in
Pontiac, Michigan. It was an
18x24, two color screen printed
poster that was sold only at the
show. Hand numbered and signed.

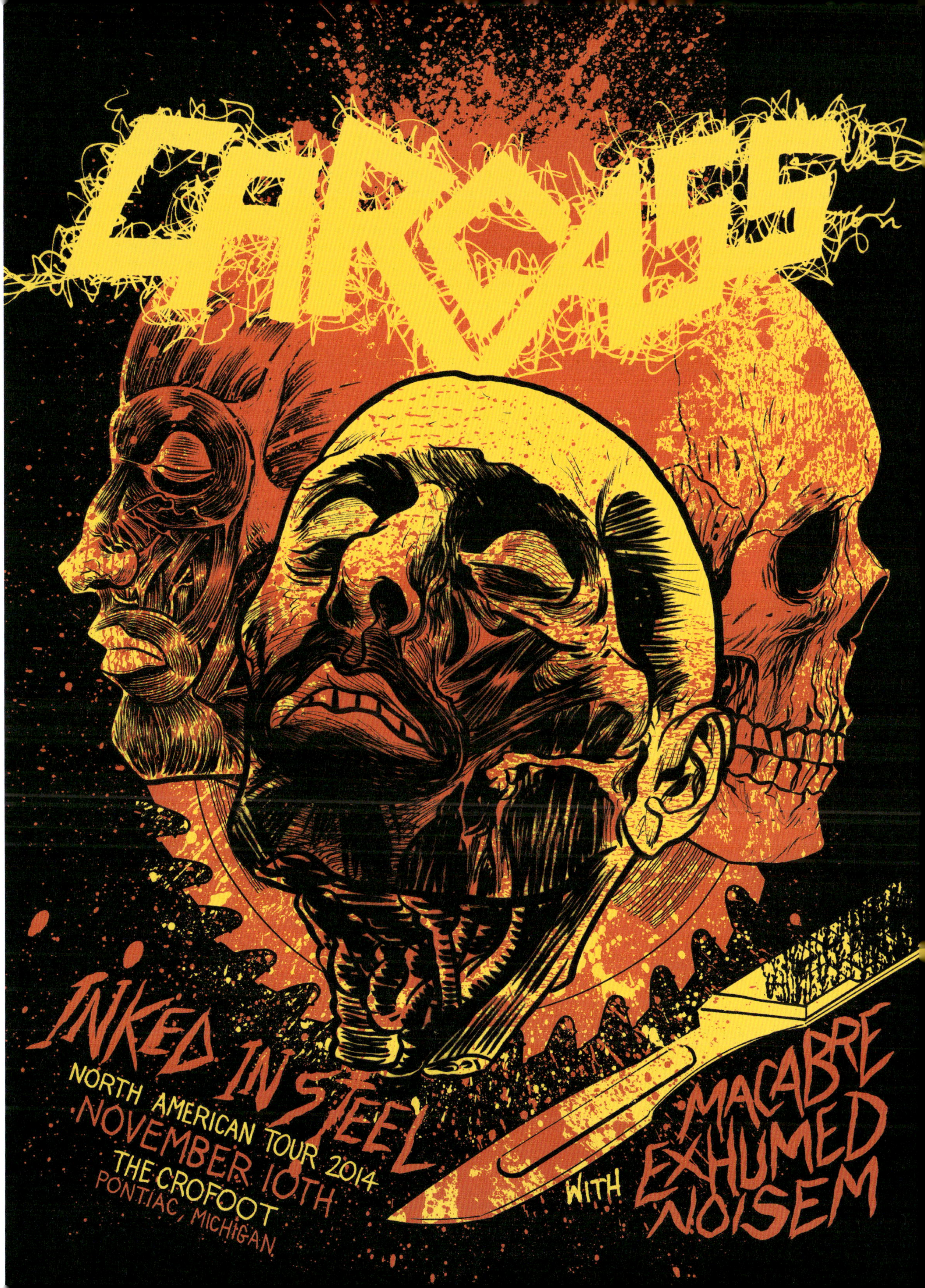

CARCASS

INKED IN STEEL
NORTH AMERICAN TOUR 2014
NOVEMBER 10TH
THE CROFOOT
PONTIAC, MICHIGAN
WITH MACABRE EXHUMED NOISEM

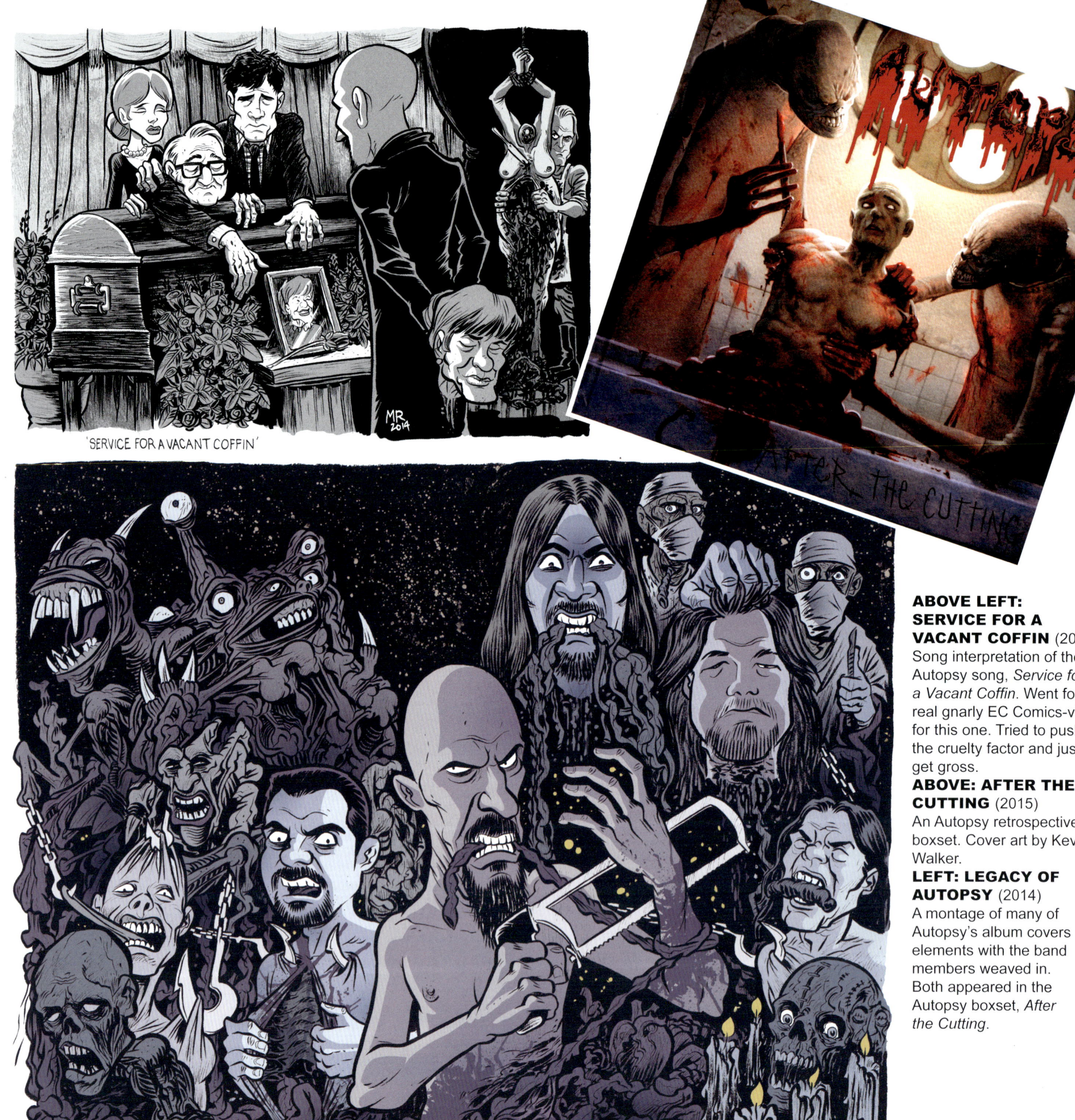

'SERVICE FOR A VACANT COFFIN'

ABOVE LEFT: SERVICE FOR A VACANT COFFIN (2014)
Song interpretation of the Autopsy song, *Service for a Vacant Coffin*. Went for a real gnarly EC Comics-vibe for this one. Tried to push the cruelty factor and just get gross.

ABOVE: AFTER THE CUTTING (2015)
An Autopsy retrospective boxset. Cover art by Kev Walker.

LEFT: LEGACY OF AUTOPSY (2014)
A montage of many of Autopsy's album covers elements with the band members weaved in. Both appeared in the Autopsy boxset, *After the Cutting*.

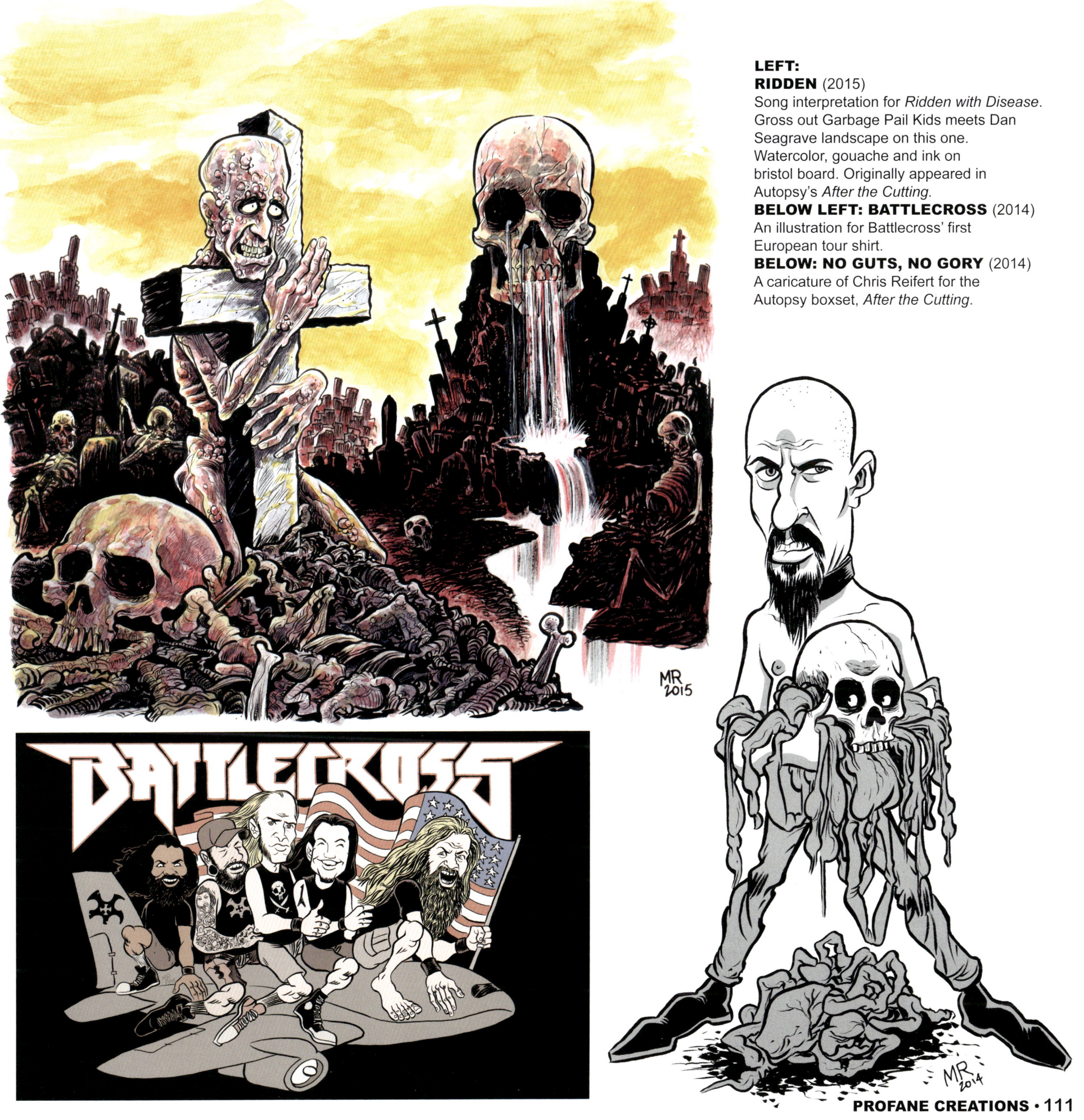

LEFT:
RIDDEN (2015)
Song interpretation for *Ridden with Disease*.
Gross out Garbage Pail Kids meets Dan
Seagrave landscape on this one.
Watercolor, gouache and ink on
bristol board. Originally appeared in
Autopsy's *After the Cutting*.
BELOW LEFT: BATTLECROSS (2014)
An illustration for Battlecross' first
European tour shirt.
BELOW: NO GUTS, NO GORY (2014)
A caricature of Chris Reifert for the
Autopsy boxset, *After the Cutting*.

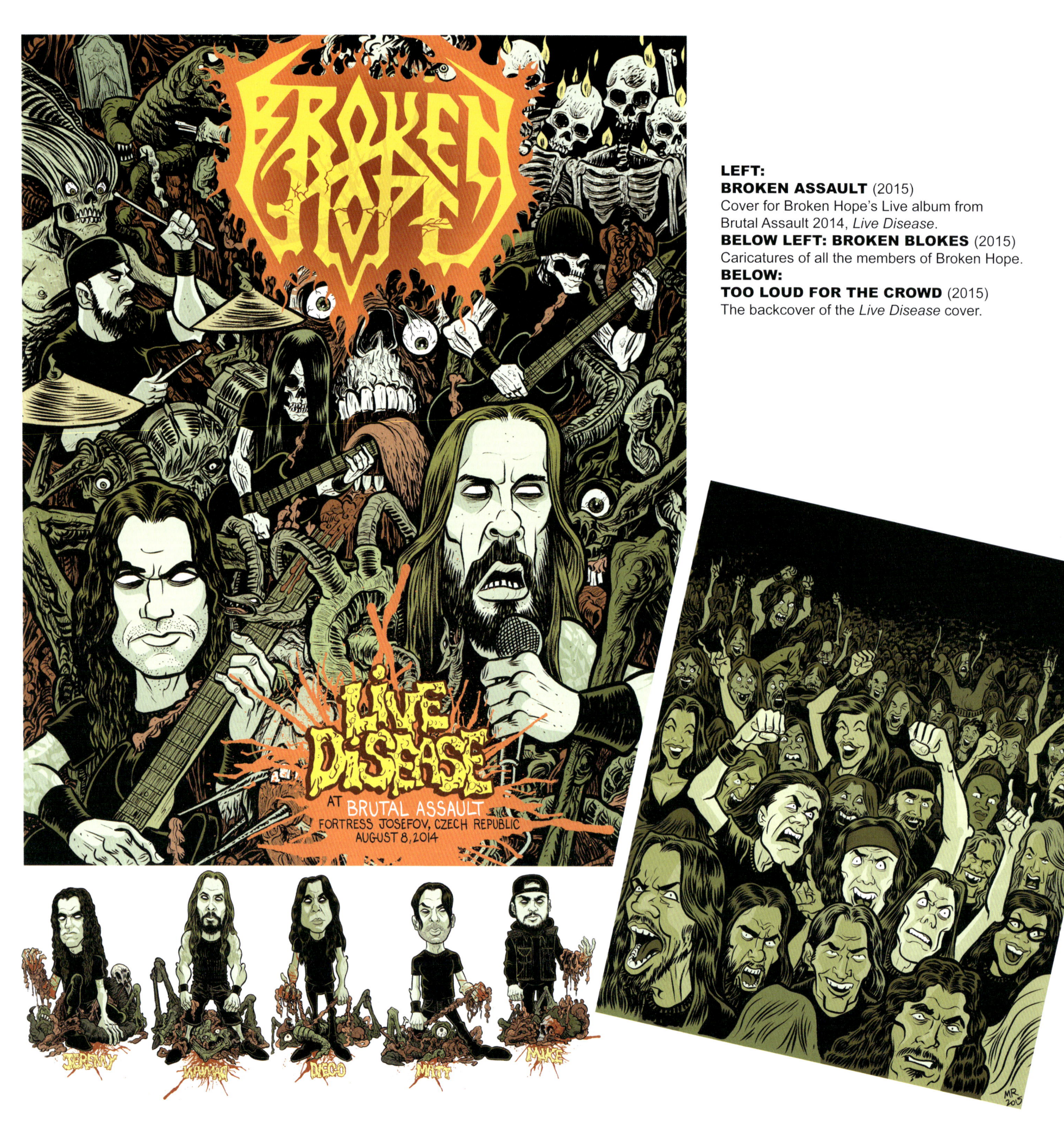

LEFT:
BROKEN ASSAULT (2015)
Cover for Broken Hope's Live album from
Brutal Assault 2014, *Live Disease*.
BELOW LEFT: BROKEN BLOKES (2015)
Caricatures of all the members of Broken Hope.
BELOW:
TOO LOUD FOR THE CROWD (2015)
The backcover of the *Live Disease* cover.

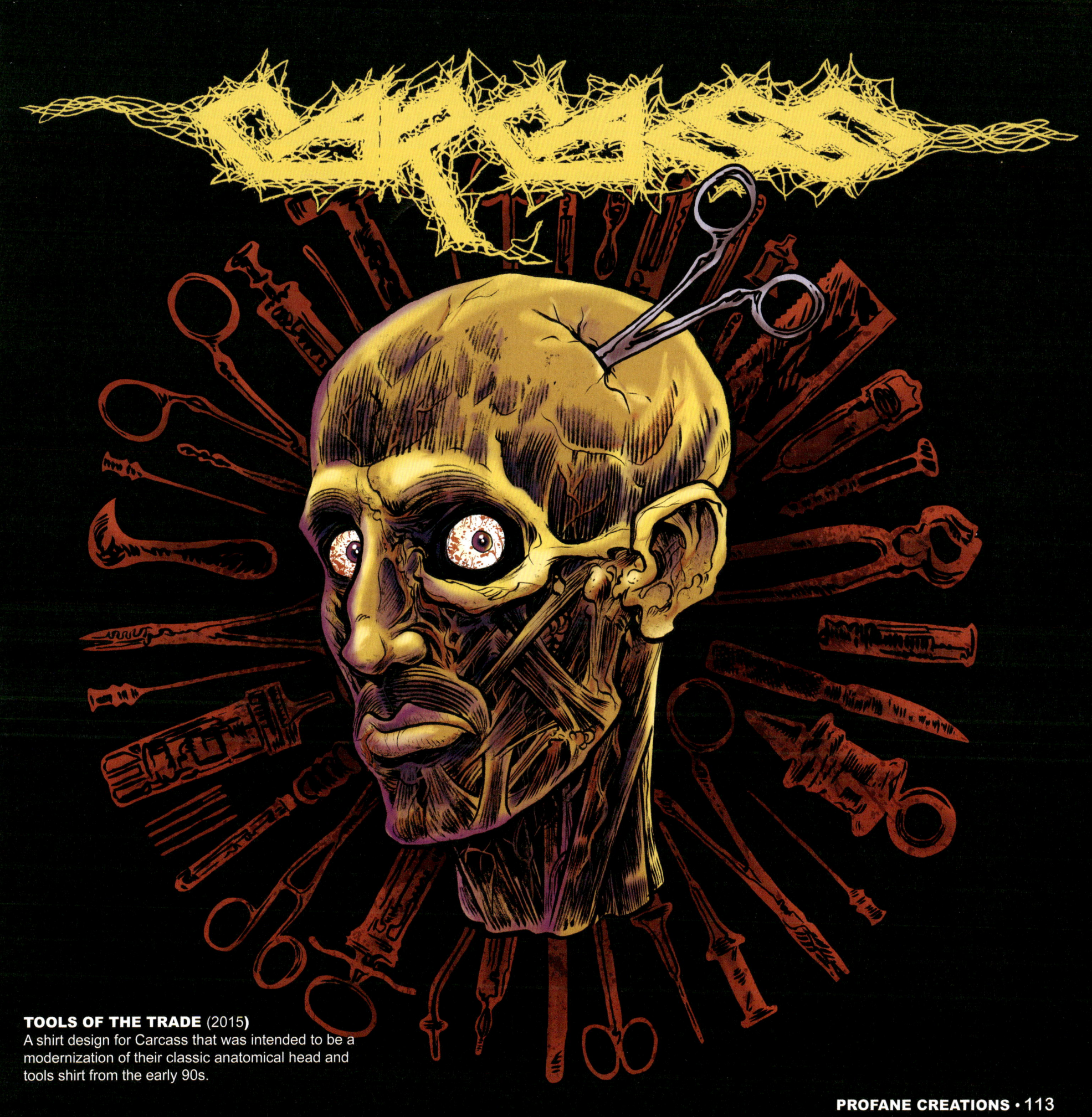

TOOLS OF THE TRADE (2015)
A shirt design for Carcass that was intended to be a modernization of their classic anatomical head and tools shirt from the early 90s.

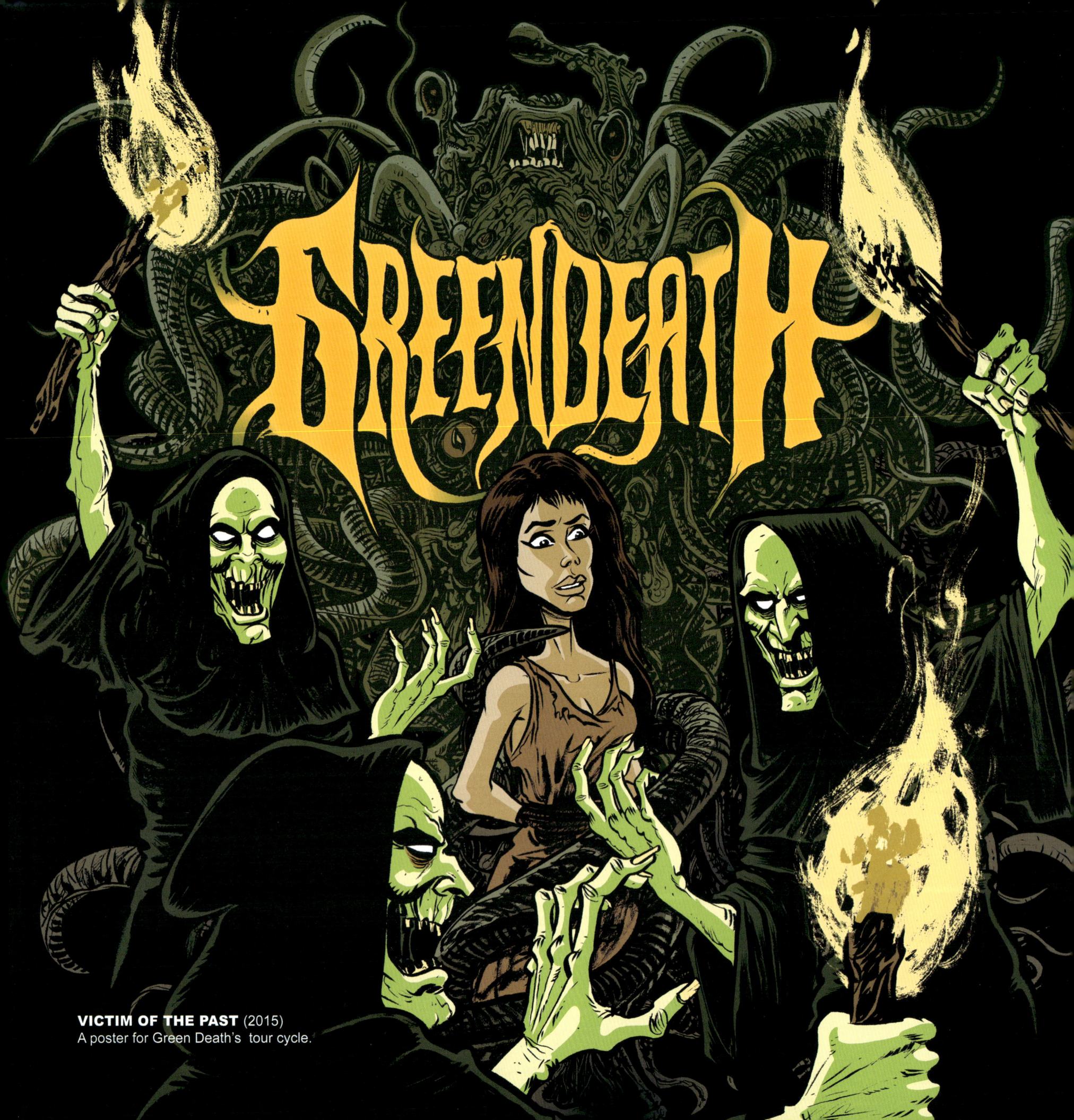

VICTIM OF THE PAST (2015)
A poster for Green Death's tour cycle.

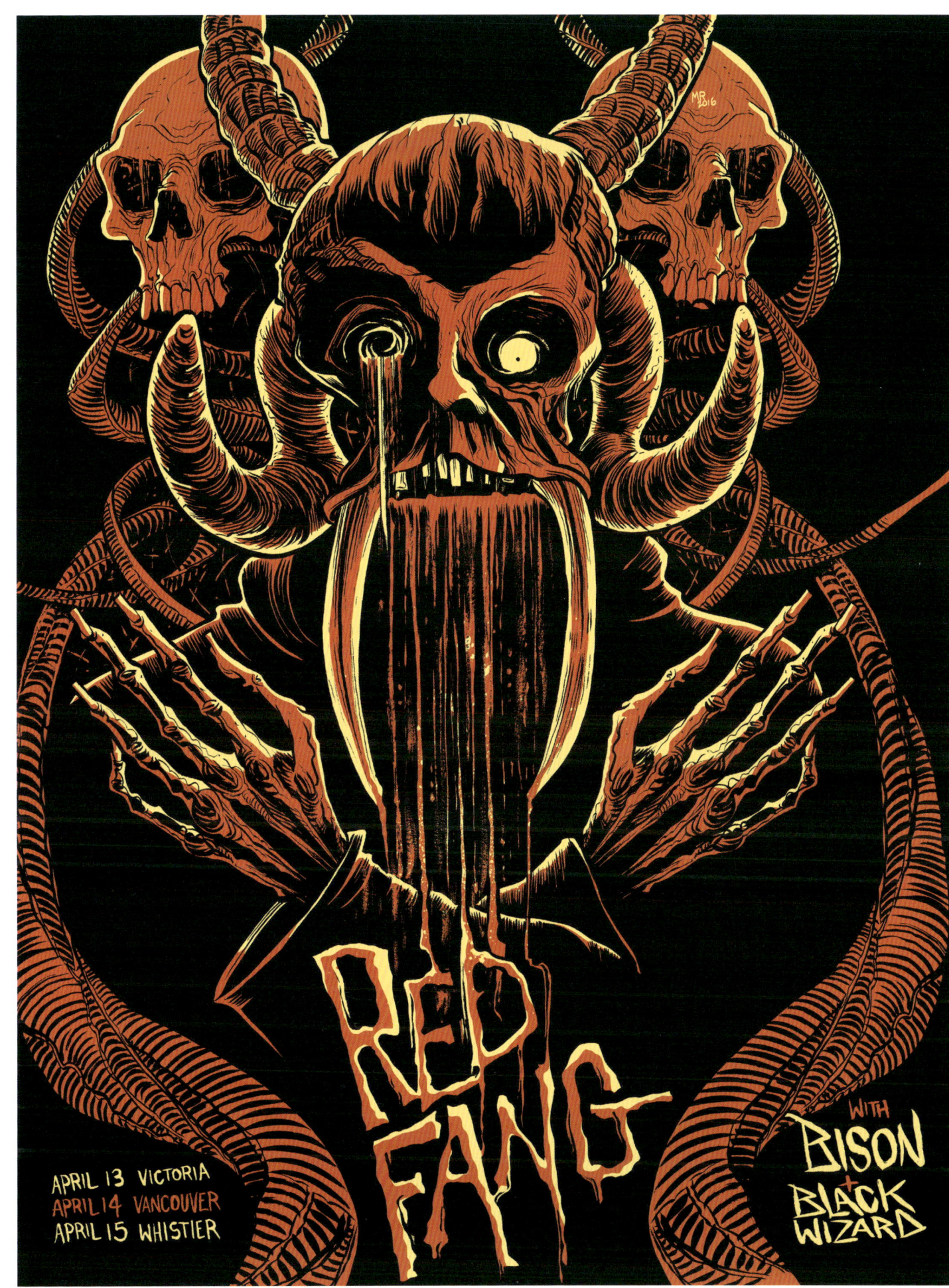

BLOOD TUSK (2016)
A poster for a three date Red Fang
Canadian tour. Was intended to be
a two color screen print.

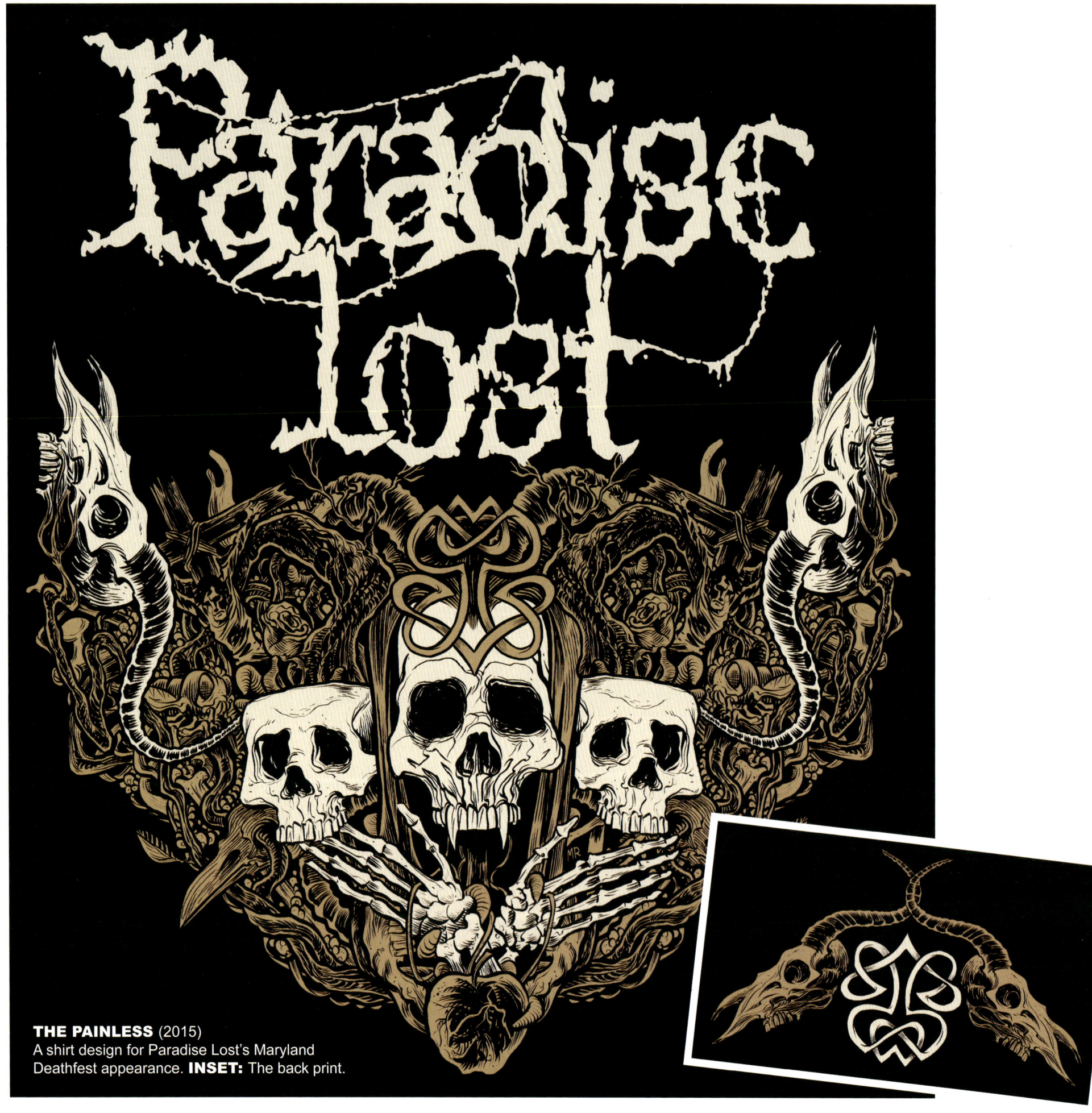

THE PAINLESS (2015)
A shirt design for Paradise Lost's Maryland
Deathfest appearance. **INSET:** The back print.

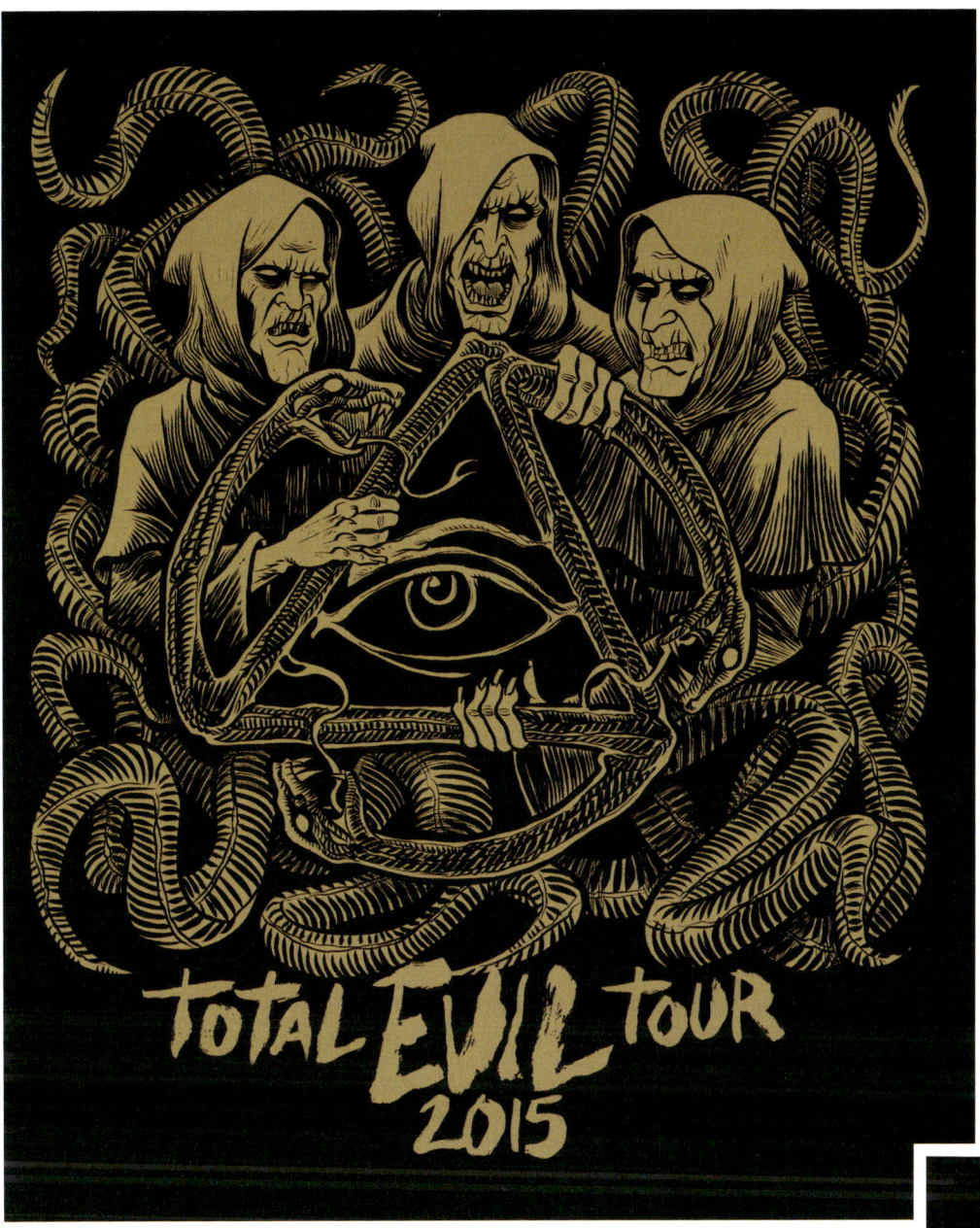

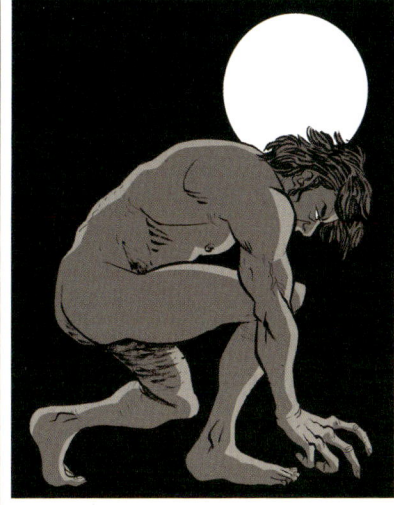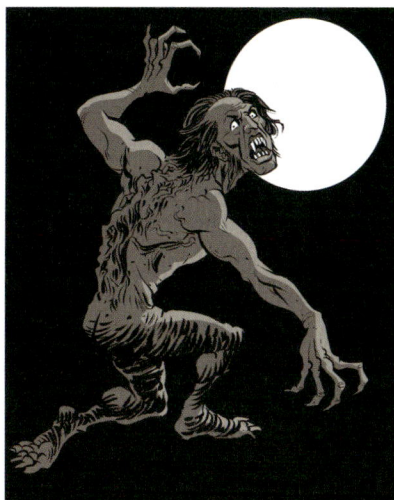

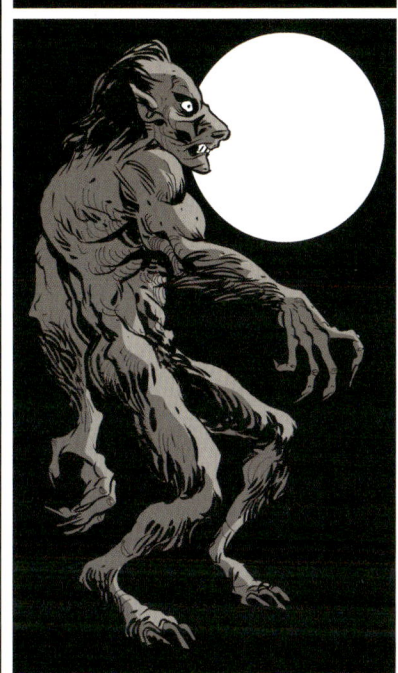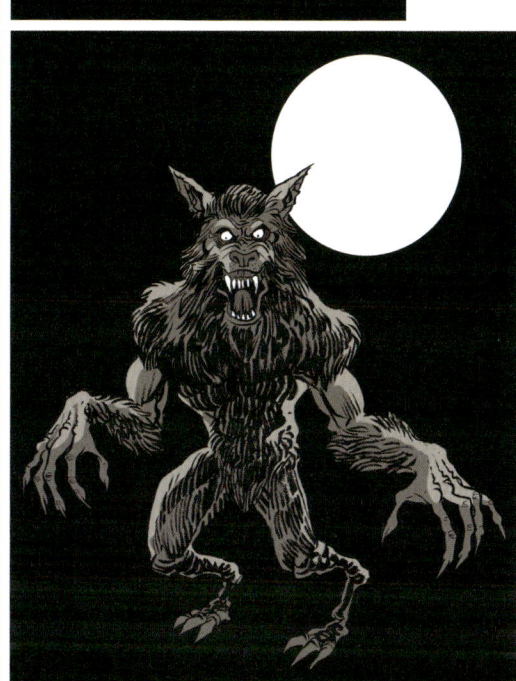

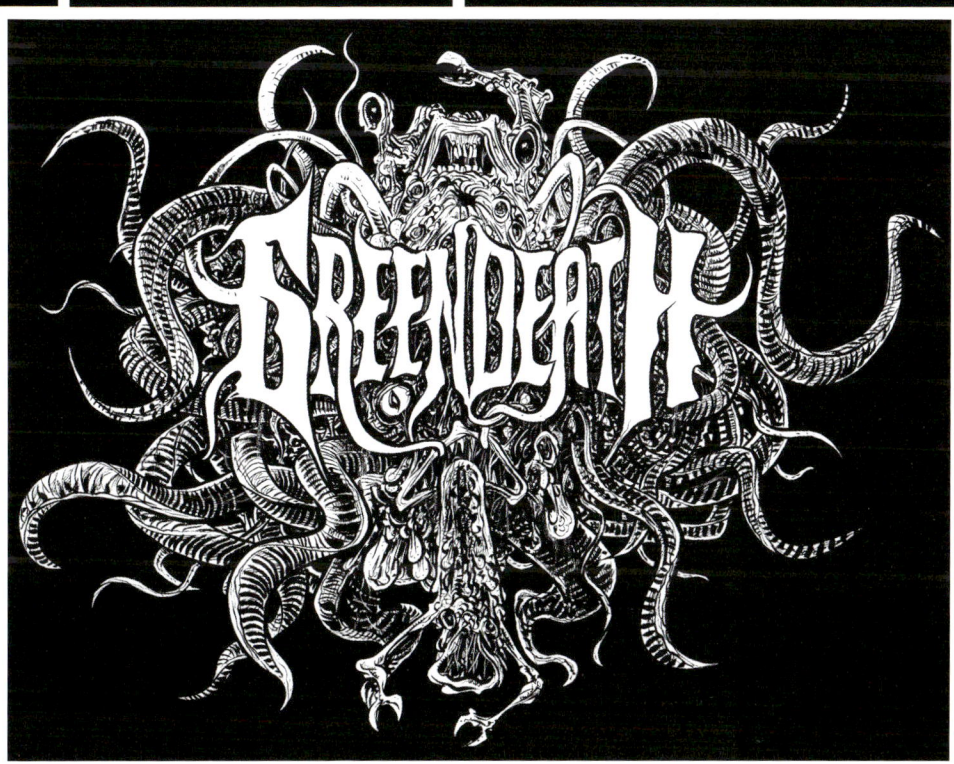

ABOVE: TOTAL EVIL (2015)
A poster for Green Death's 2015 tour.
ABOVE RIGHT:
OF WOLF AND MAN (2015)
A series of keyframes for a Green Death
video.
RIGHT:
LOVECRAFTIAN LOGO (2015)
A logo for a Green Death shirt.

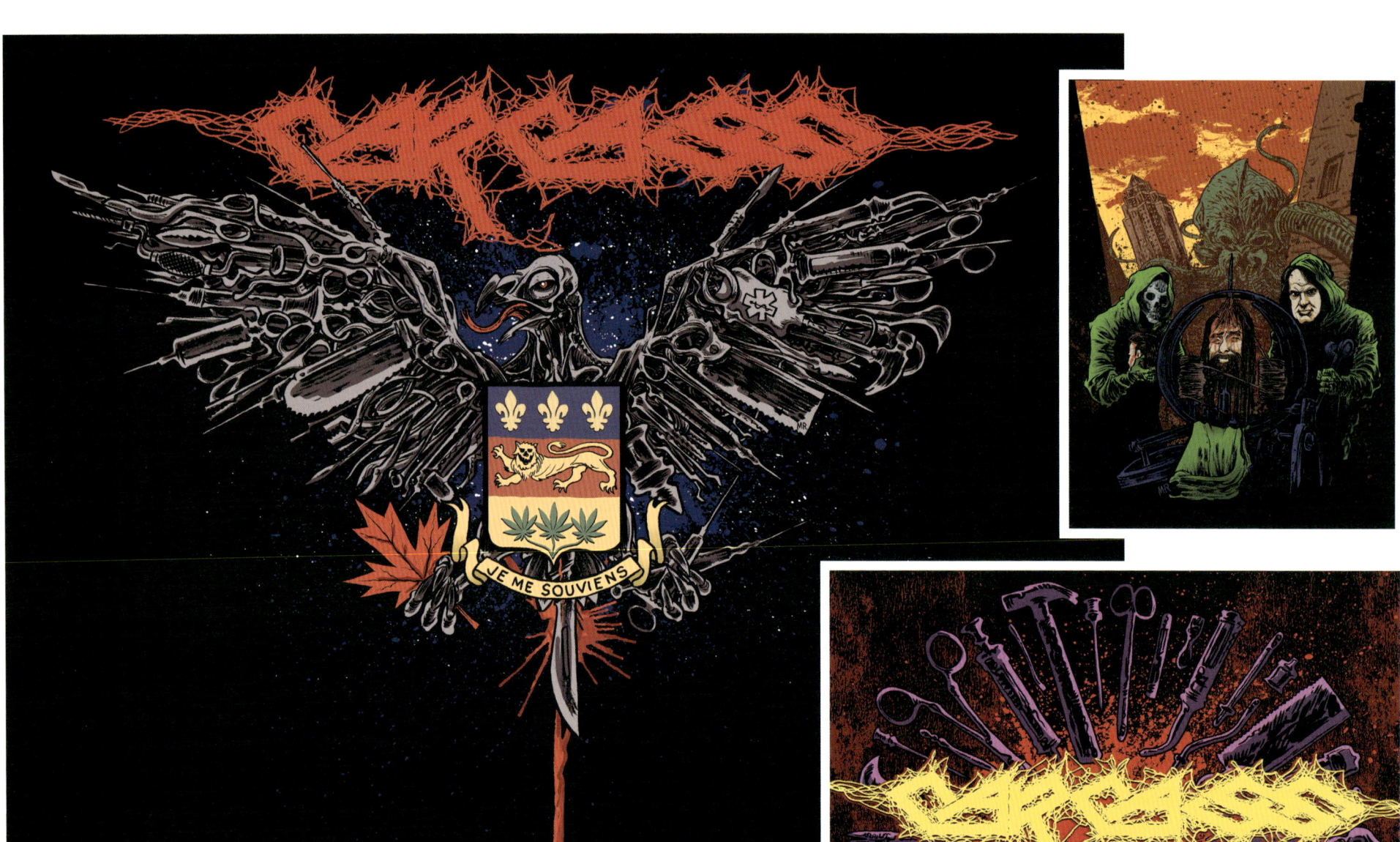

ABOVE: CANADIAN METAL (2016)
A design for Carcass' Canadian tour for their *Surgical Steel* album.
ABOVE RIGHT: FLESH FROM BONE (2016)
A poster design for Green Death's *Manufacturing Evil* record release show.
RIGHT: GRAVEYARD MONKS (2016)
A poster for Carcass' show in Des Moines, Iowa with Green Death.

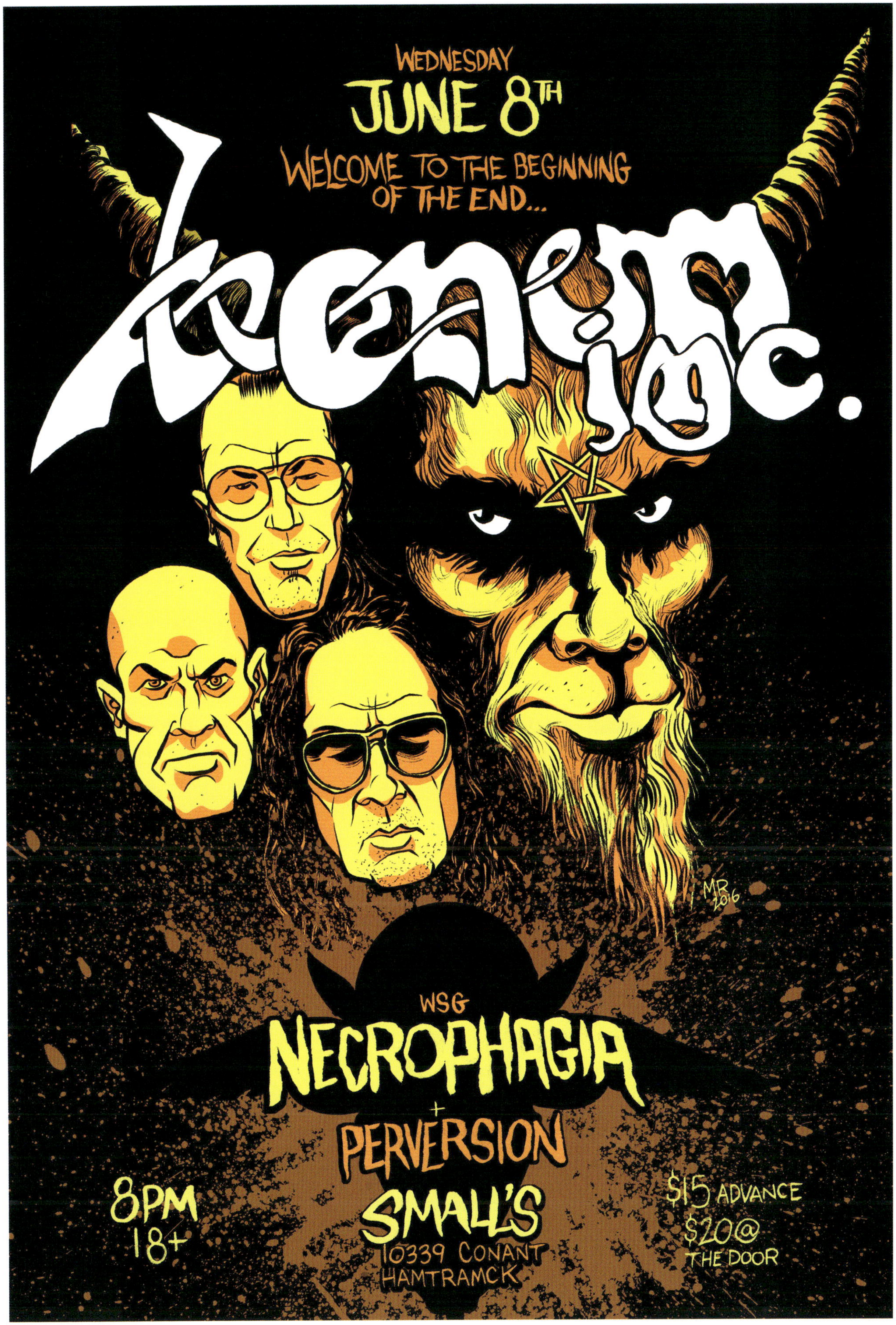

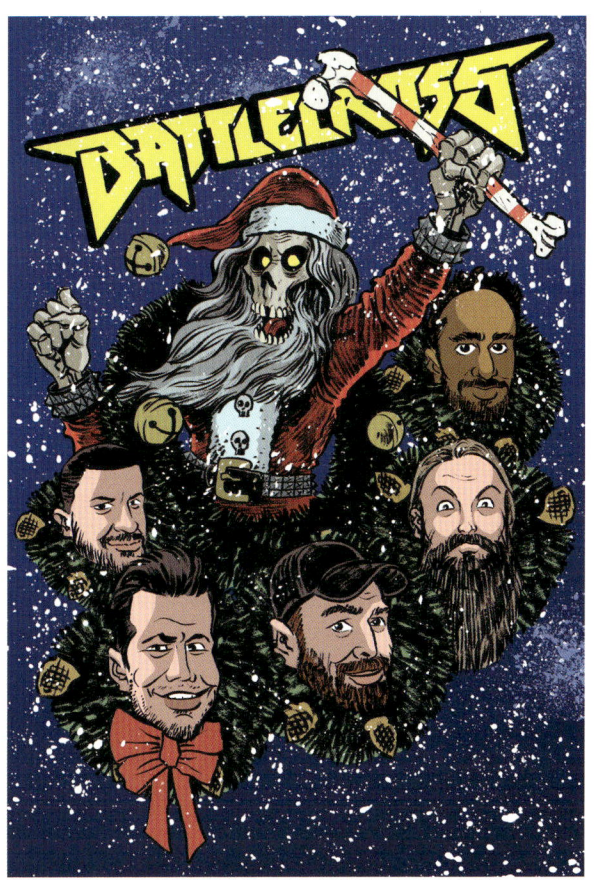

LEFT: SATAN INC. (2016)
A show poster for Venom Inc.'s Hamtramck, MI date. Killer show!

ABOVE: DEADLY NIGHT (2018)
A poster for Battlecross' annual Christmas show.

BELOW: NATASHA (2020)
A shirt design for Pig Destroyer based on the lyrics of Natasha.

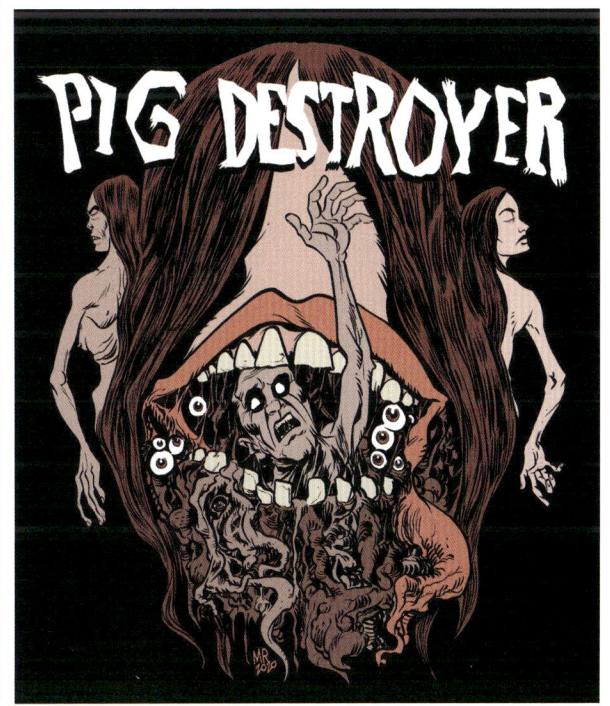

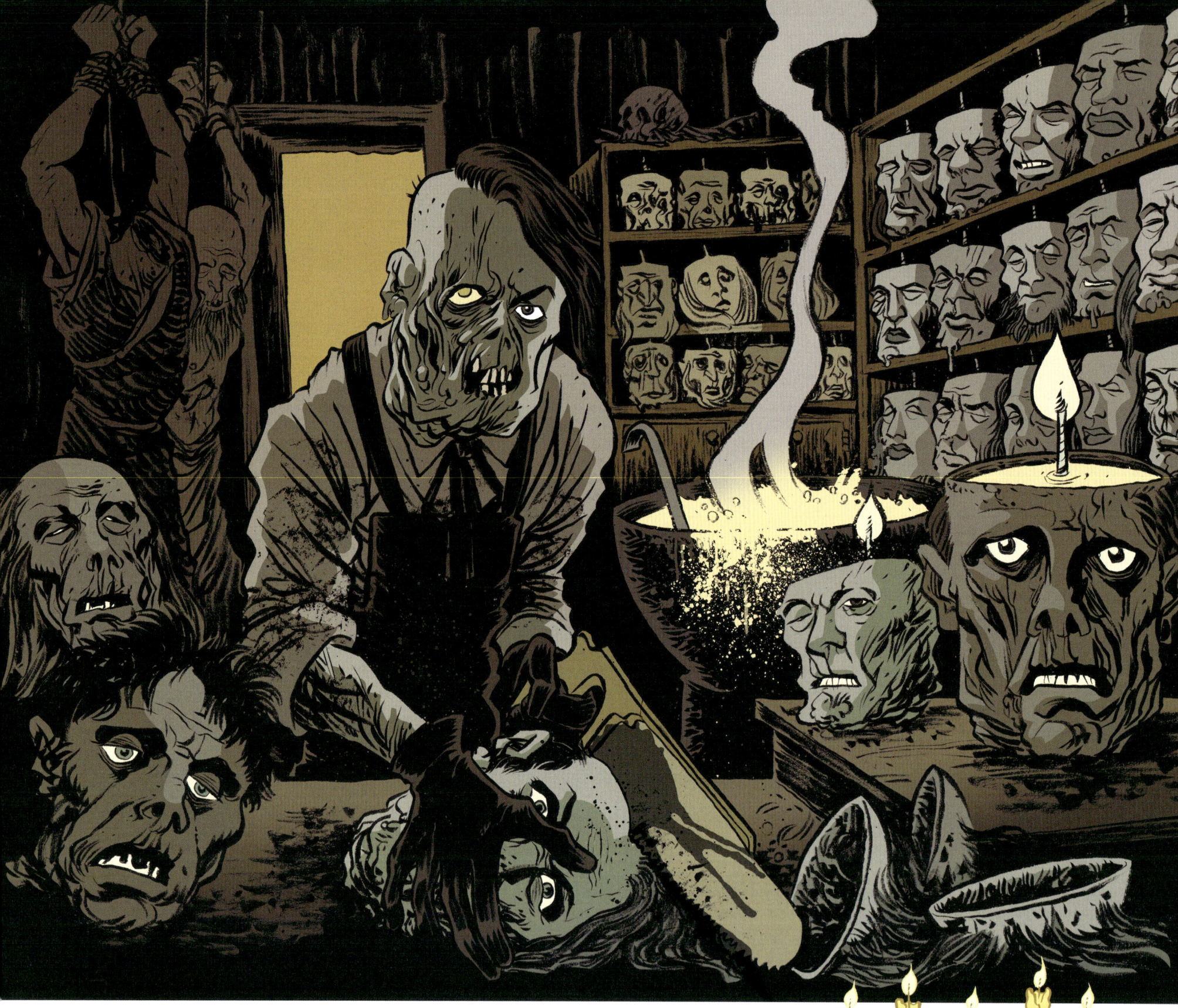

ABOVE: ONCE HALLOW (2018)

A show poster for *Hallow Massacre*, which was intended to be an annual Halloween-themed music festival in Des Moines, Iowa. The basic concept was described and I created the look and feel of this Crypt Keeper-type host. He murders people, saws off their skull cap, removes the contents and fills it full of wax. A morbid maker of human Jack-o'-lanterns. I tried to give it a Tobe Hooper vibe -- A filthy, depraved 70s exploitation feel to things. A character that lives outside of modern society and punishes those who break his twisted moral code. At one point I worked on making a latex mask of the character, but budgetary constraints prevented that from happening. Super fun project. The logo I created for the event on the right.

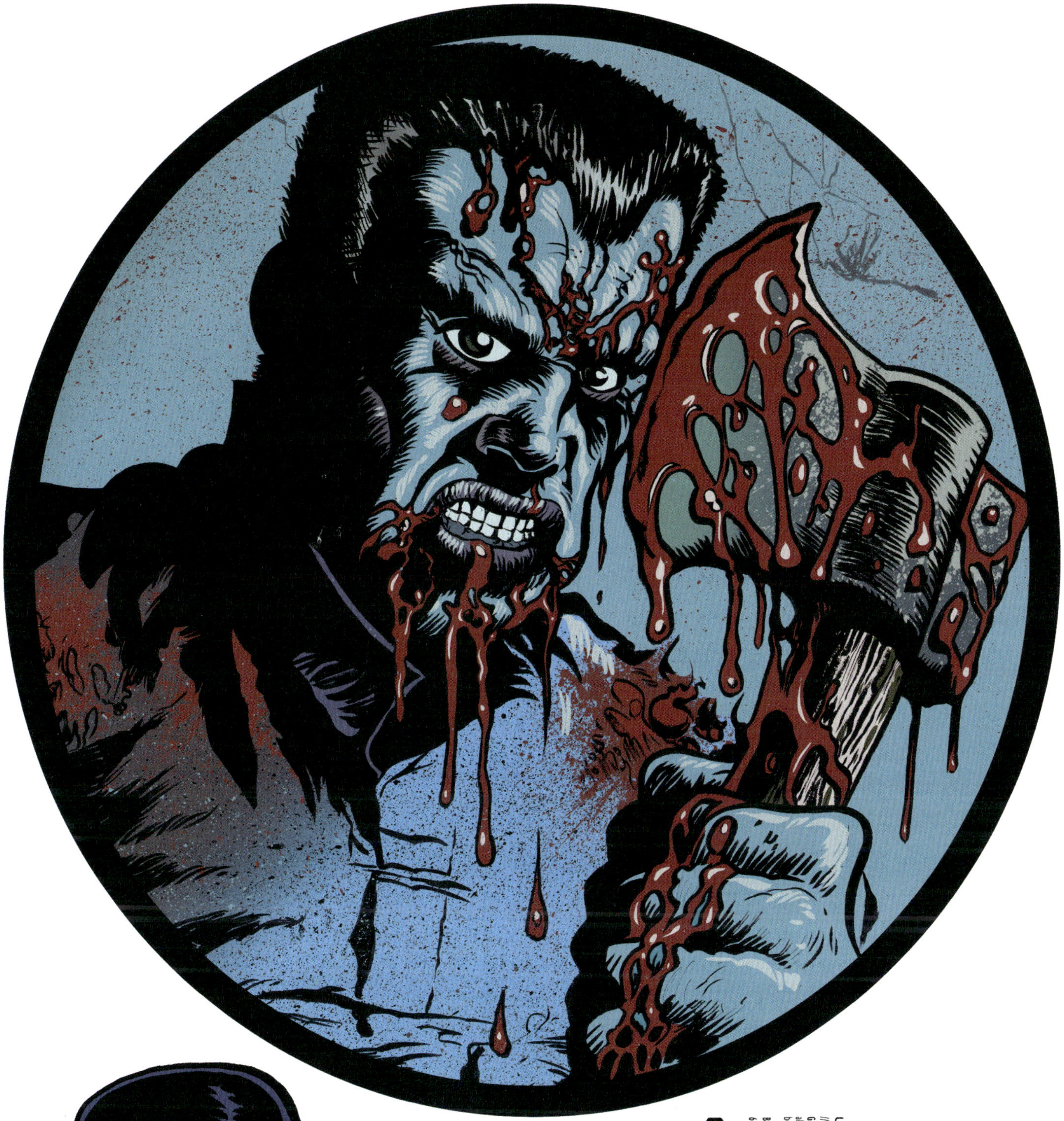

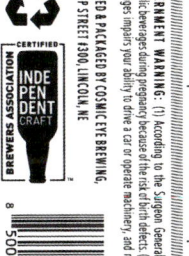

LEFT:
SKIN HER ALIVE (2021)
A recreation of Dismember's *Skin Her Alive* 7" picture disc from 1991 that was used as a shirt design.
BELOW: ALTE SCHULE (2022)
A shirt design, inspired by Dismember's *Reborn in Blasphemy* demo cover, for Deathevokation's *Alte Schule* beer release at Decibel Metal & Beer Fest 2022. Also see the beer label below. Created by Cosmic Eye Brewing.
BELOW LEFT:
SLAYTANIC SLAUGHTER (2022)
A patch based on the classic Slayer Slaytanic Wehrmacht shirt design.

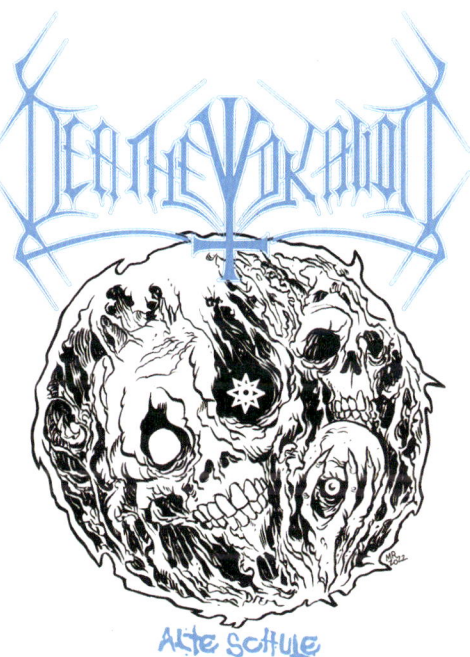

Alte Schule

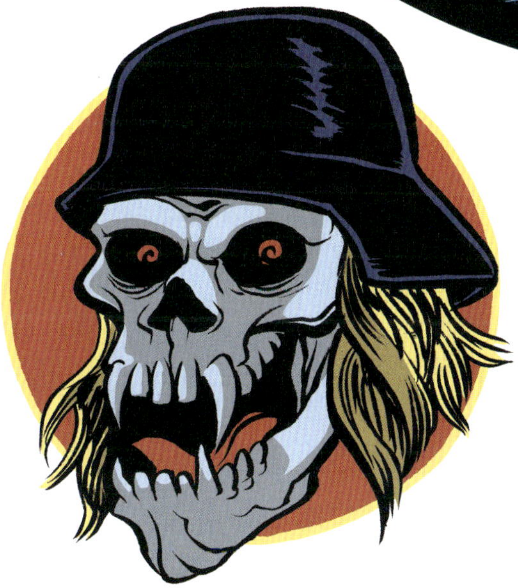

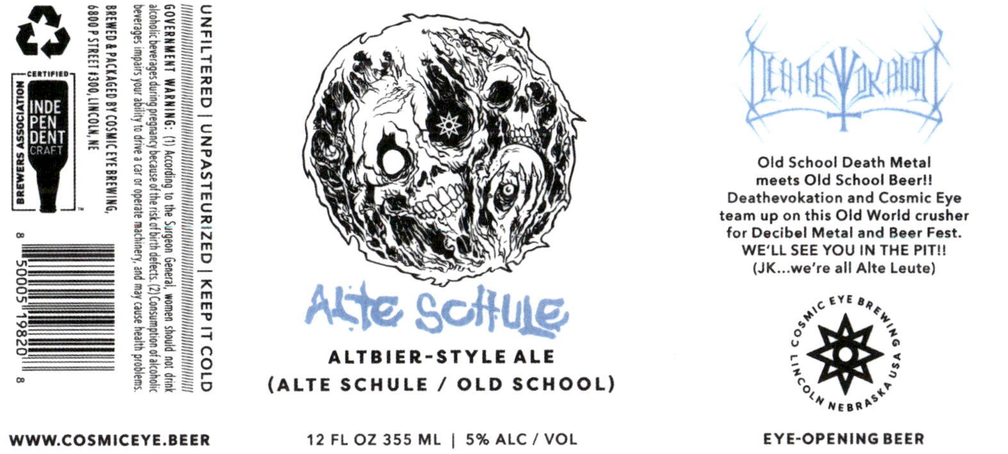

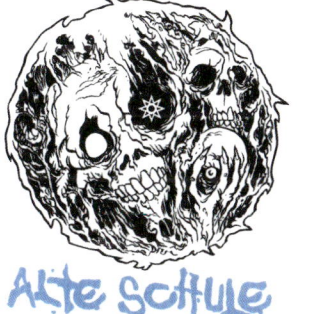

Alte Schule
ALTBIER-STYLE ALE
(ALTE SCHULE / OLD SCHOOL)

Old School Death Metal meets Old School Beer!! Deathevokation and Cosmic Eye team up on this Old World crusher for Decibel Metal and Beer Fest. WE'LL SEE YOU IN THE PIT!! (JK...we're all Alte Leute)

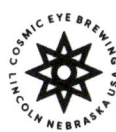

UNFILTERED | UNPASTEURIZED | KEEP IT COLD

GOVERNMENT WARNING: (1) According to the Surgeon General, women should not drink alcoholic beverages during pregnancy because of the risk of birth defects. (2) Consumption of alcoholic beverages impairs your ability to drive a car or operate machinery, and may cause health problems.

BREWED & PACKAGED BY COSMIC EYE BREWING, 6800 P STREET #300, LINCOLN, NE

INDEPENDENT CRAFT — CERTIFIED BREWERS ASSOCIATION

WWW.COSMICEYE.BEER

12 FL OZ 355 ML | 5% ALC / VOL

EYE-OPENING BEER

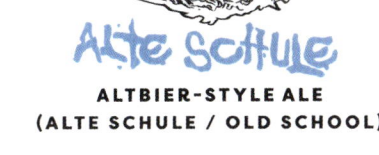

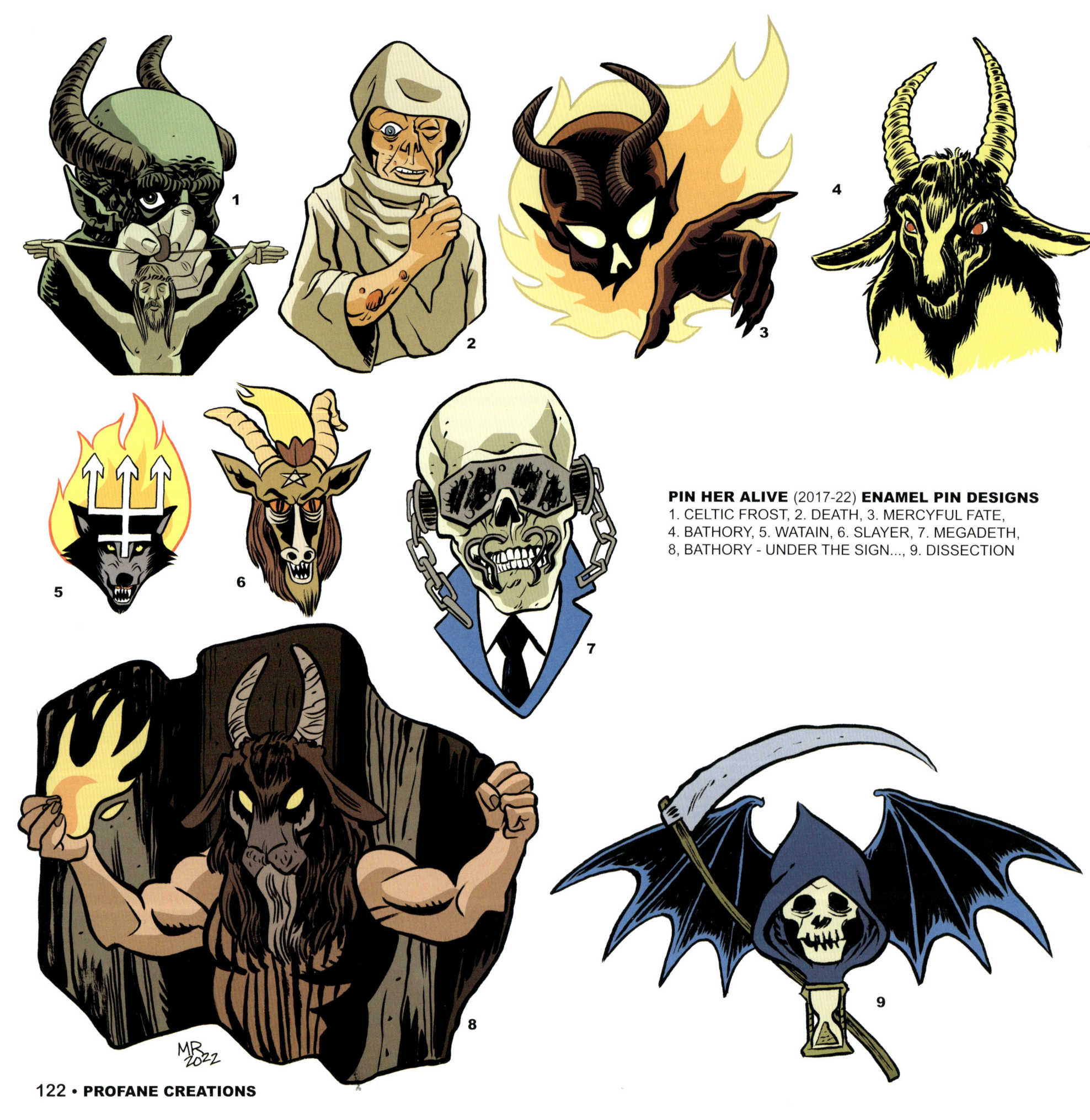

PIN HER ALIVE (2017-22) **ENAMEL PIN DESIGNS**
1. CELTIC FROST, 2. DEATH, 3. MERCYFUL FATE,
4. BATHORY, 5. WATAIN, 6. SLAYER, 7. MEGADETH,
8, BATHORY - UNDER THE SIGN..., 9. DISSECTION

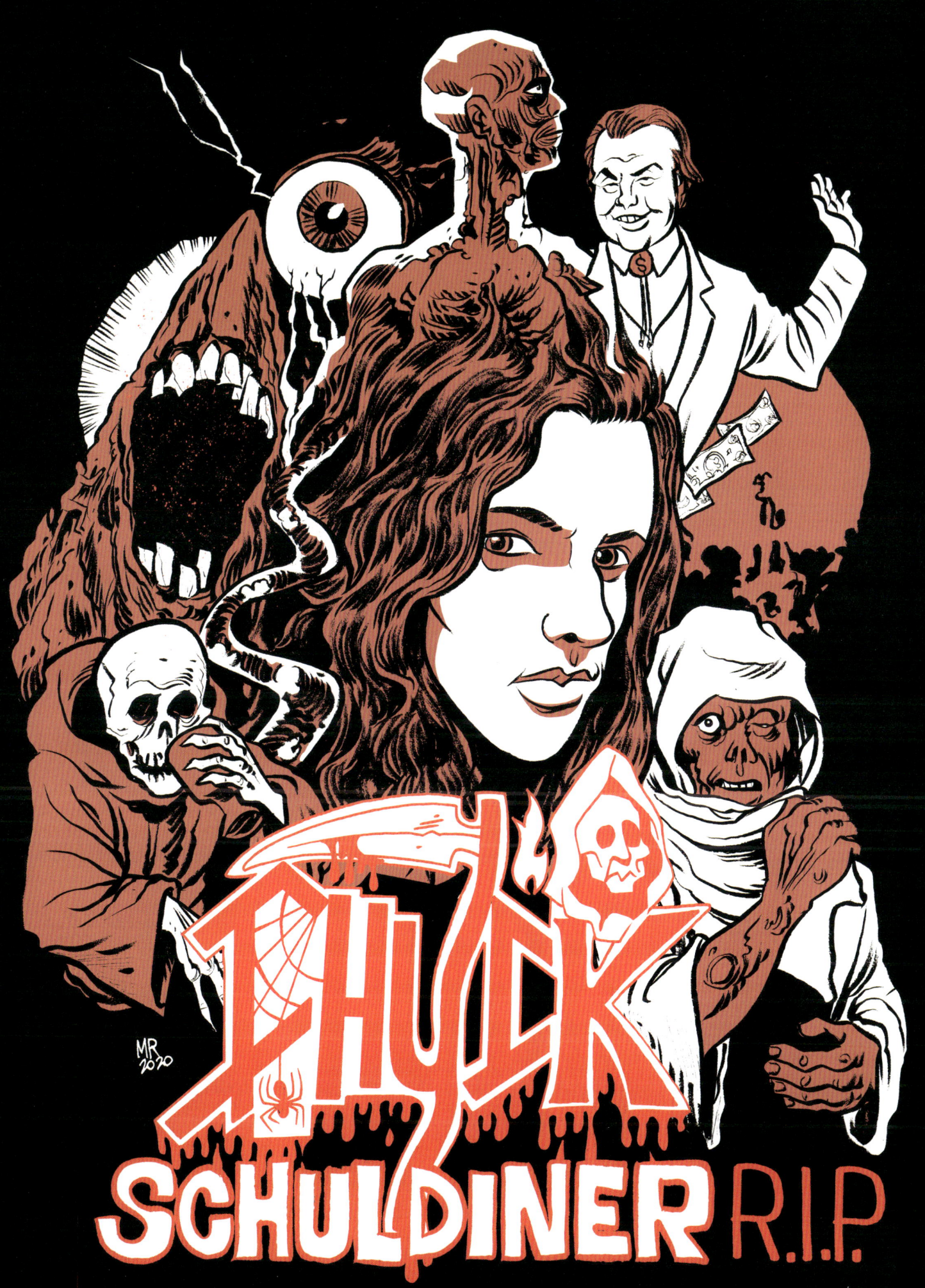

CHUCK SCHULDINER R.I.P.

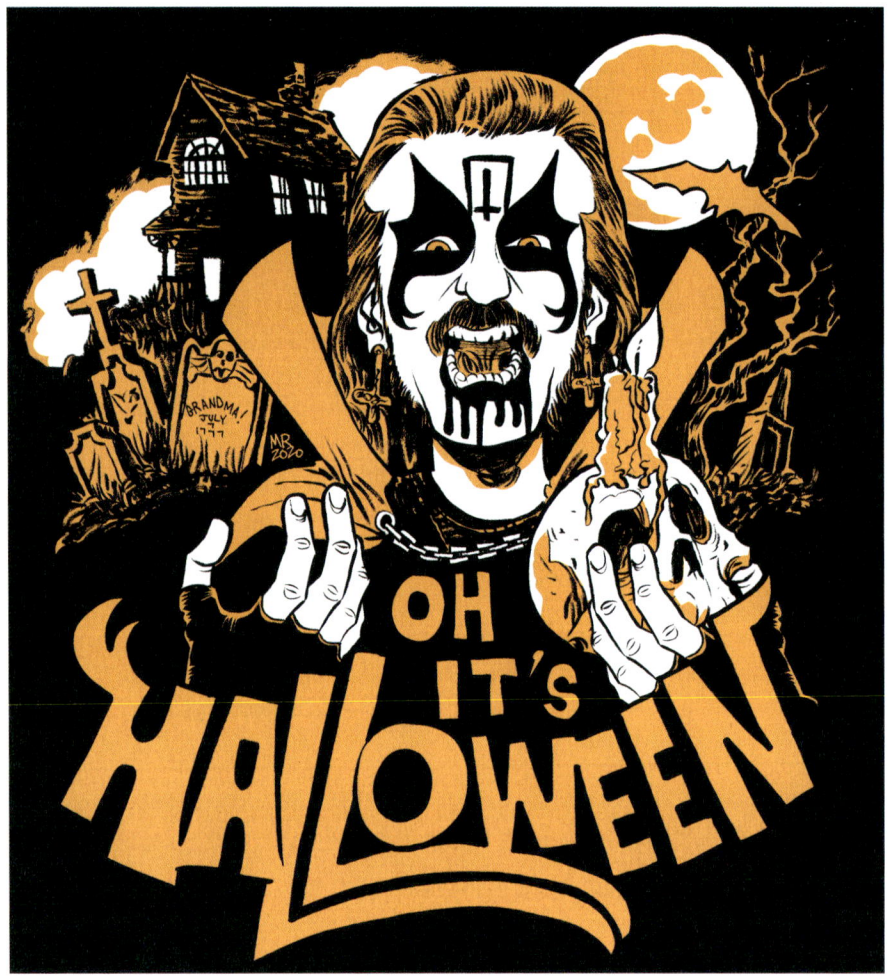

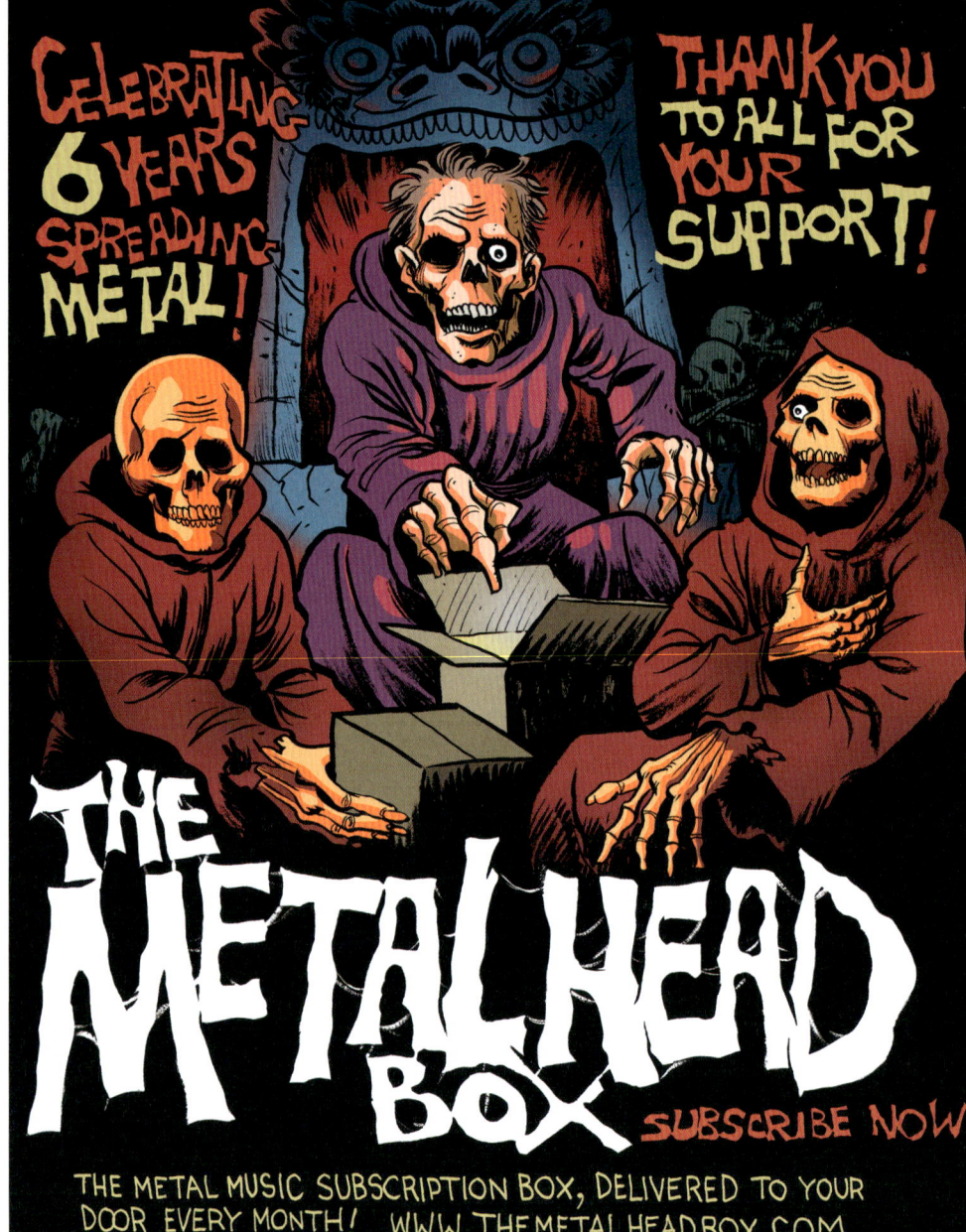

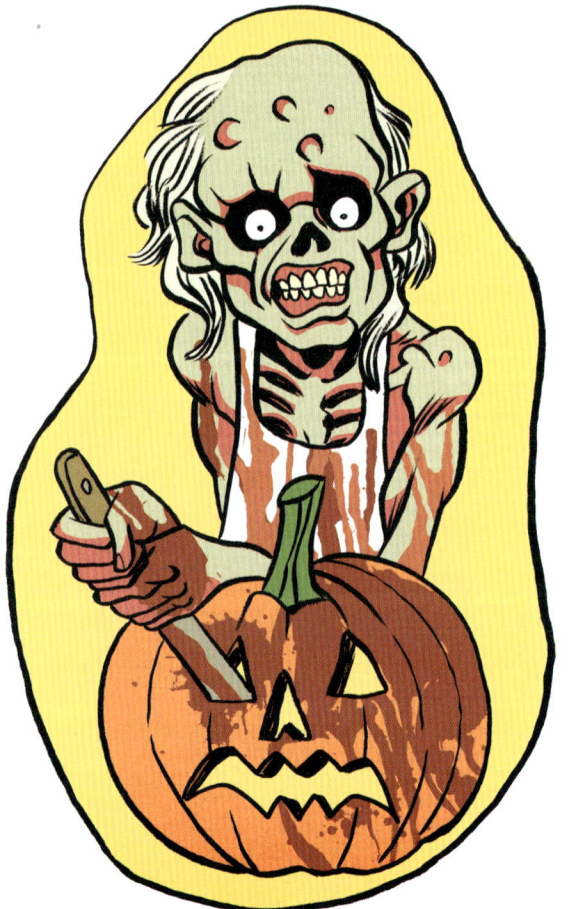

OPPOSITE PAGE: RIP CHUCK (2020)
A shirt design celebrating the life of Chuck Schuldiner.
ABOVE LEFT: HALLOWEEN (2020)
A design for a Halloween-themed King Diamond shirt.
ABOVE RIGHT: SCREAM BLOODY (2022)
A Death *Scream Bloody Gore* parody advertisement for The Metal Head Box,
LEFT: CANNIBAL HALLOWEEN (2022)
A keychain design parody of Cannibal Corpse's Butchered at Birth album character.

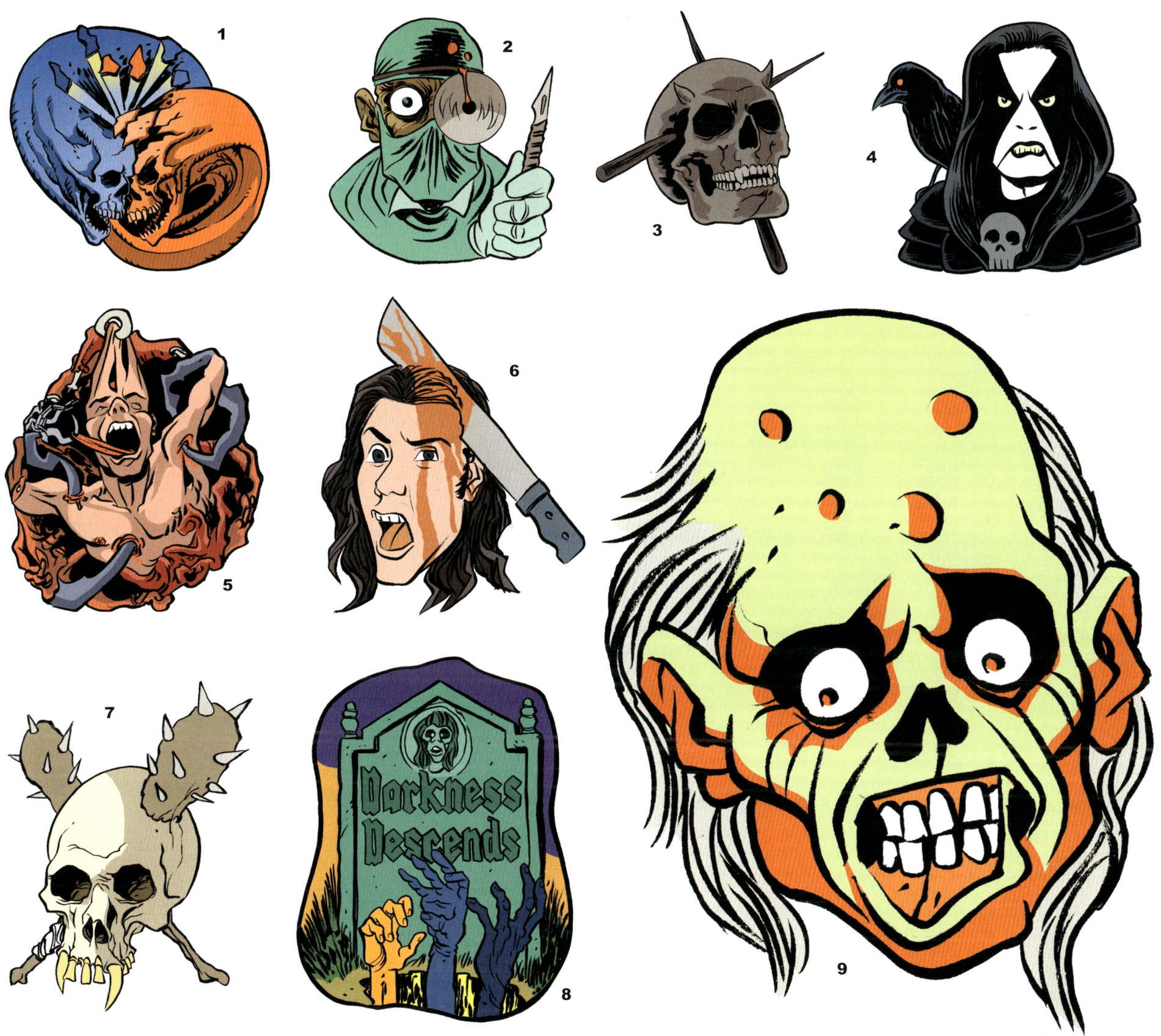

PIN HER ALIVE (2017-22) **ENAMEL PIN DESIGNS**
1. FORBIDDEN, 2. AUTOPSY, 3. CANDLEMASS, 4. ABBATH, 5. AUTOPSY - SEVERED SURVIVAL, 6. CANCER,
7. METALLICA, 8. DARK ANGEL, 9. CANNIBAL CORPSE

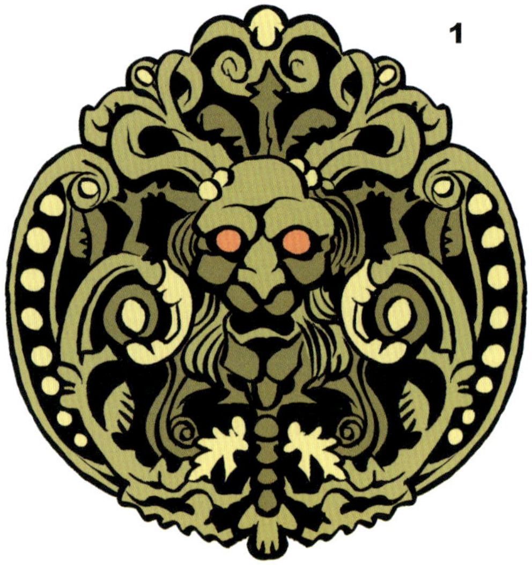

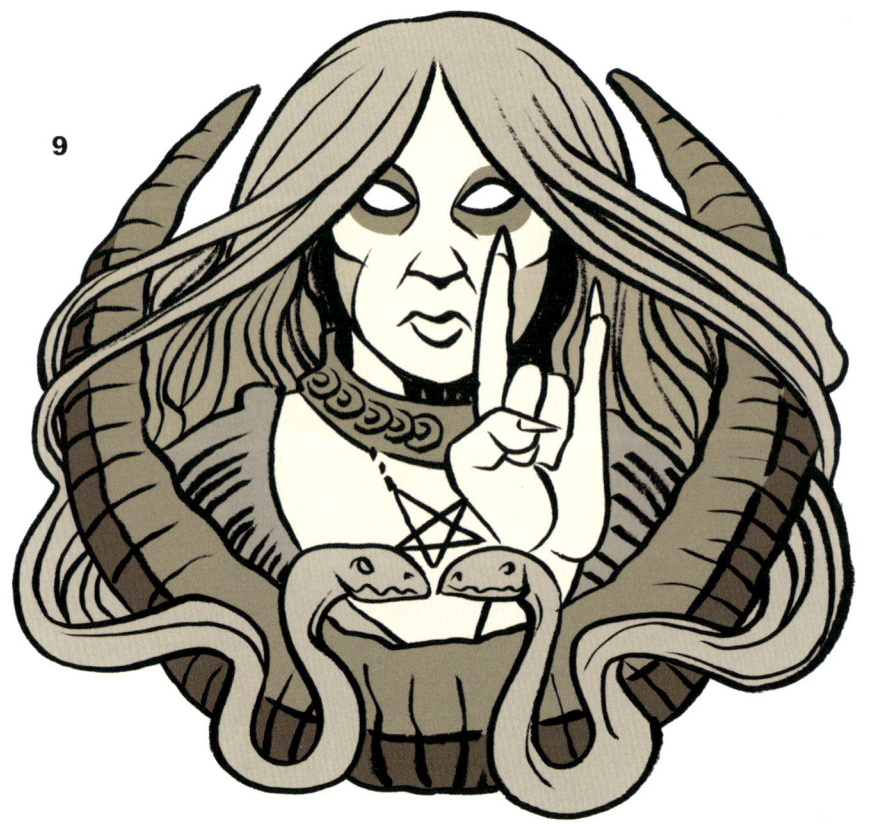

PIN HER ALIVE (2017-22) **ENAMEL PIN DESIGNS**
1. DEICIDE, 2. DEATH - SCREAM BLOODY GORE, 3. RONNIE JAMES DIO,
4. DEAD, 5. HAMMER SMASHED, 6. EURONYMOUS, 7. EXODUS,
8. JUDAS PRIEST, 9. EMPEROR

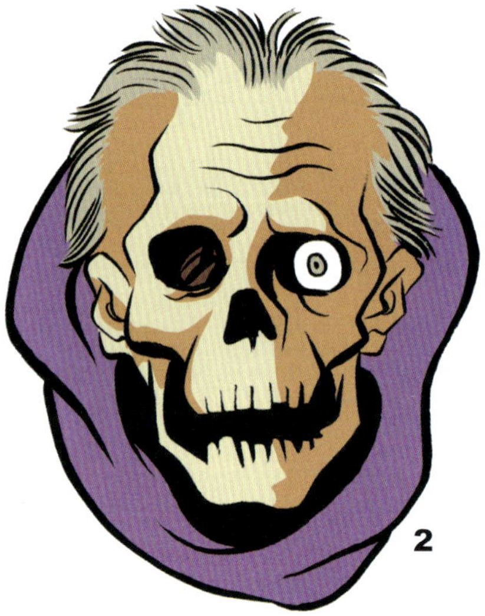

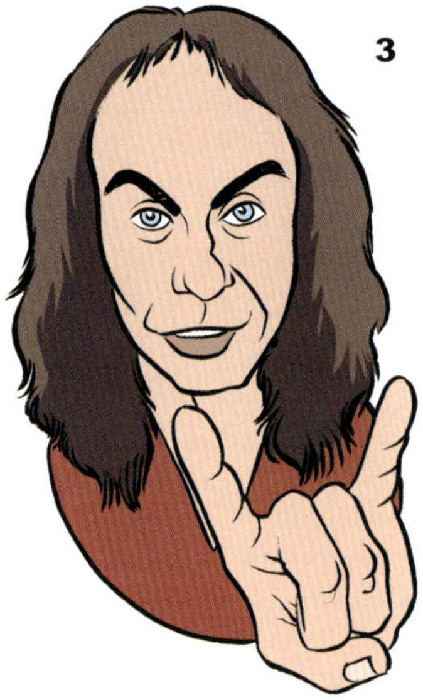

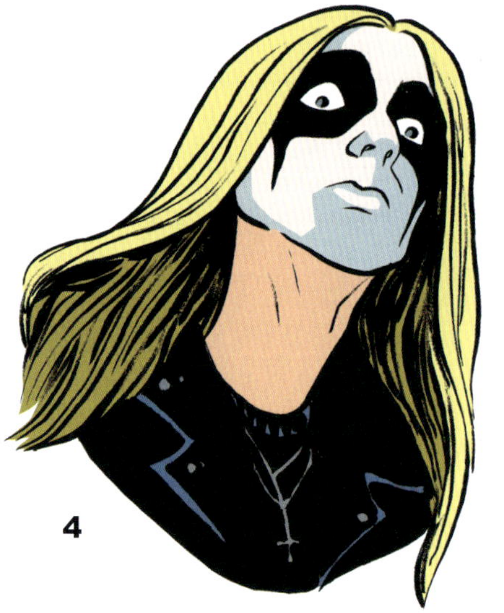

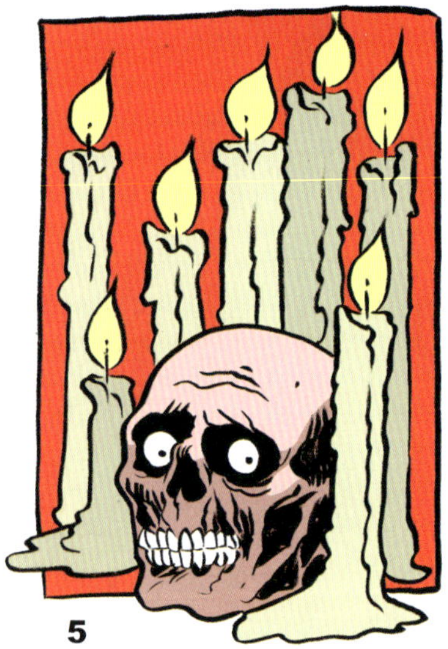

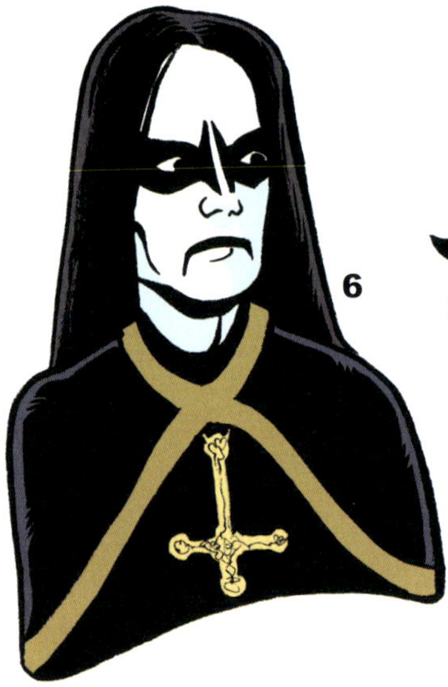

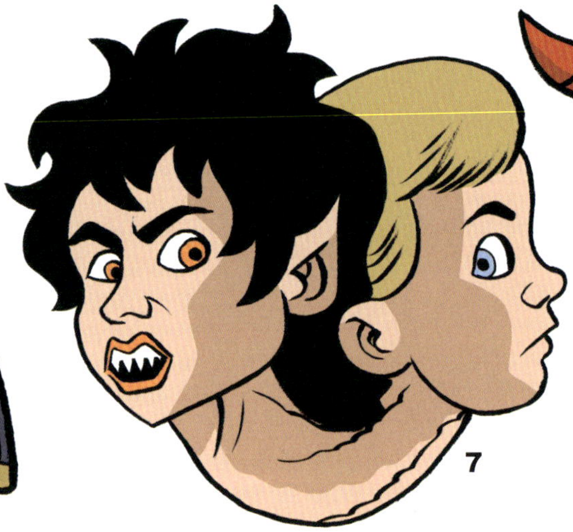

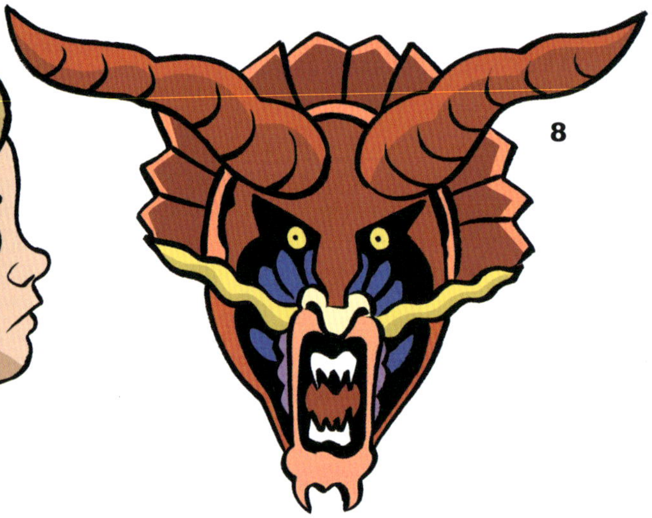

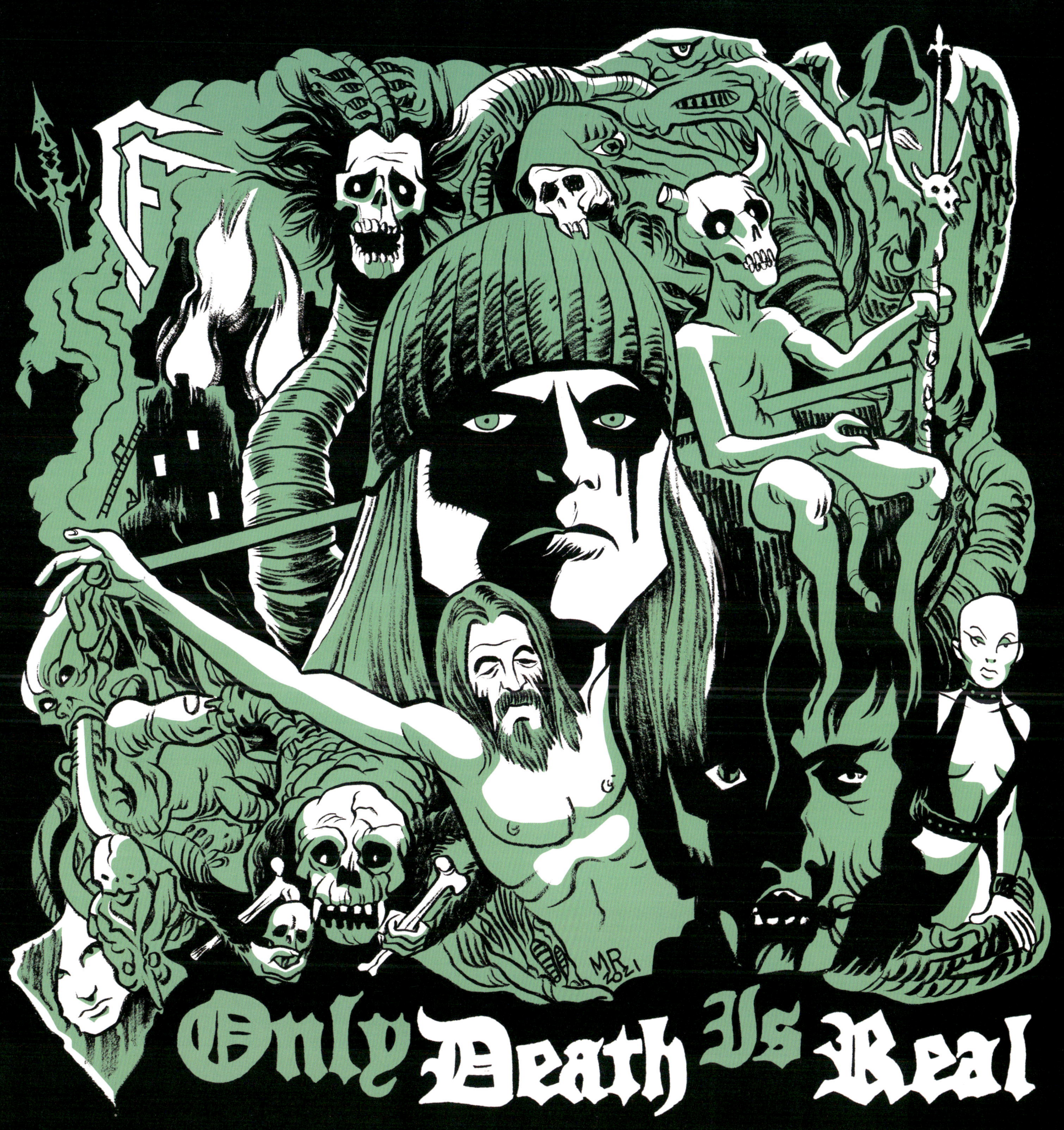

Only Death Is Real

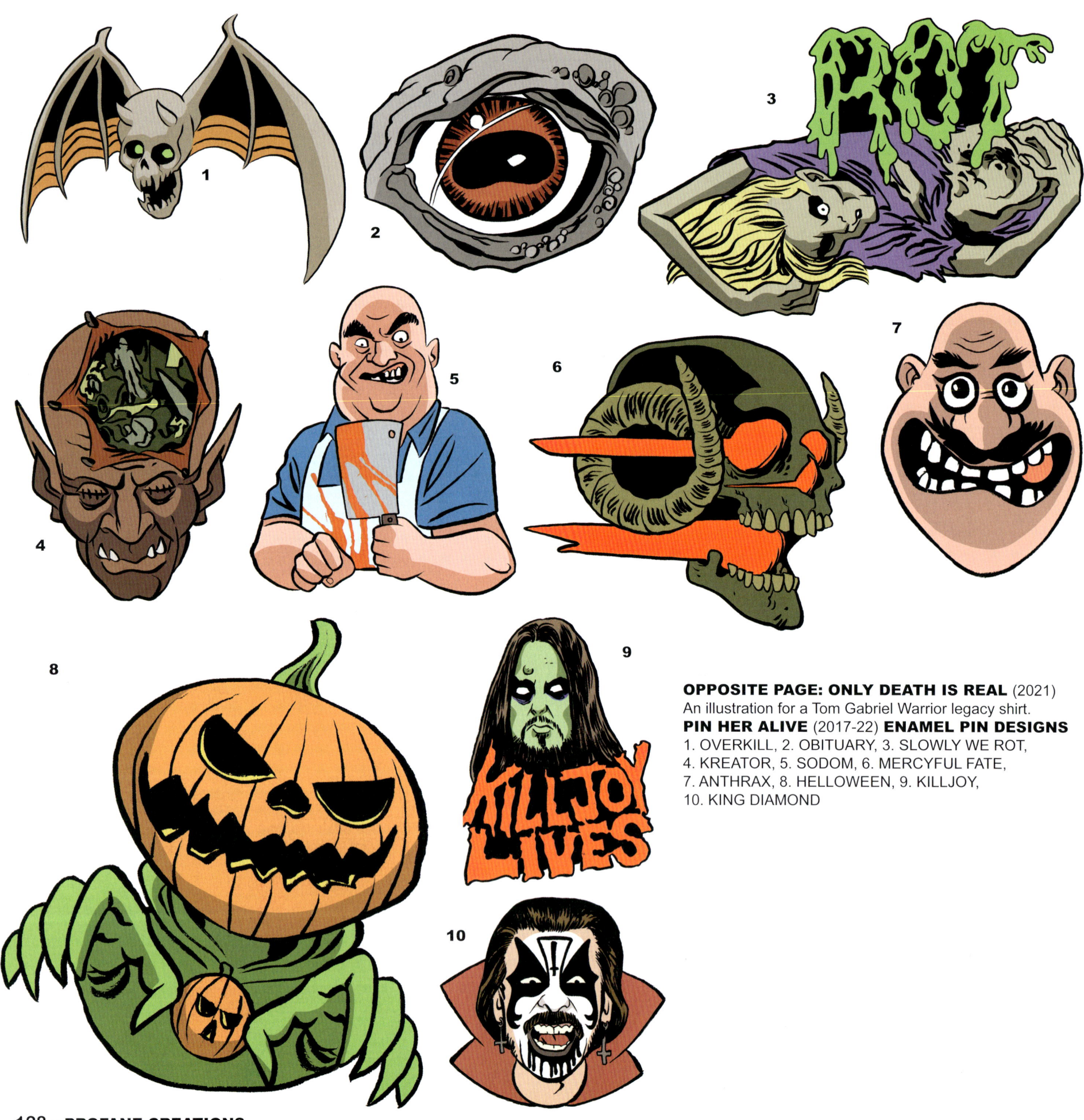

OPPOSITE PAGE: ONLY DEATH IS REAL (2021)
An illustration for a Tom Gabriel Warrior legacy shirt.
PIN HER ALIVE (2017-22) **ENAMEL PIN DESIGNS**
1. OVERKILL, 2. OBITUARY, 3. SLOWLY WE ROT,
4. KREATOR, 5. SODOM, 6. MERCYFUL FATE,
7. ANTHRAX, 8. HELLOWEEN, 9. KILLJOY,
10. KING DIAMOND

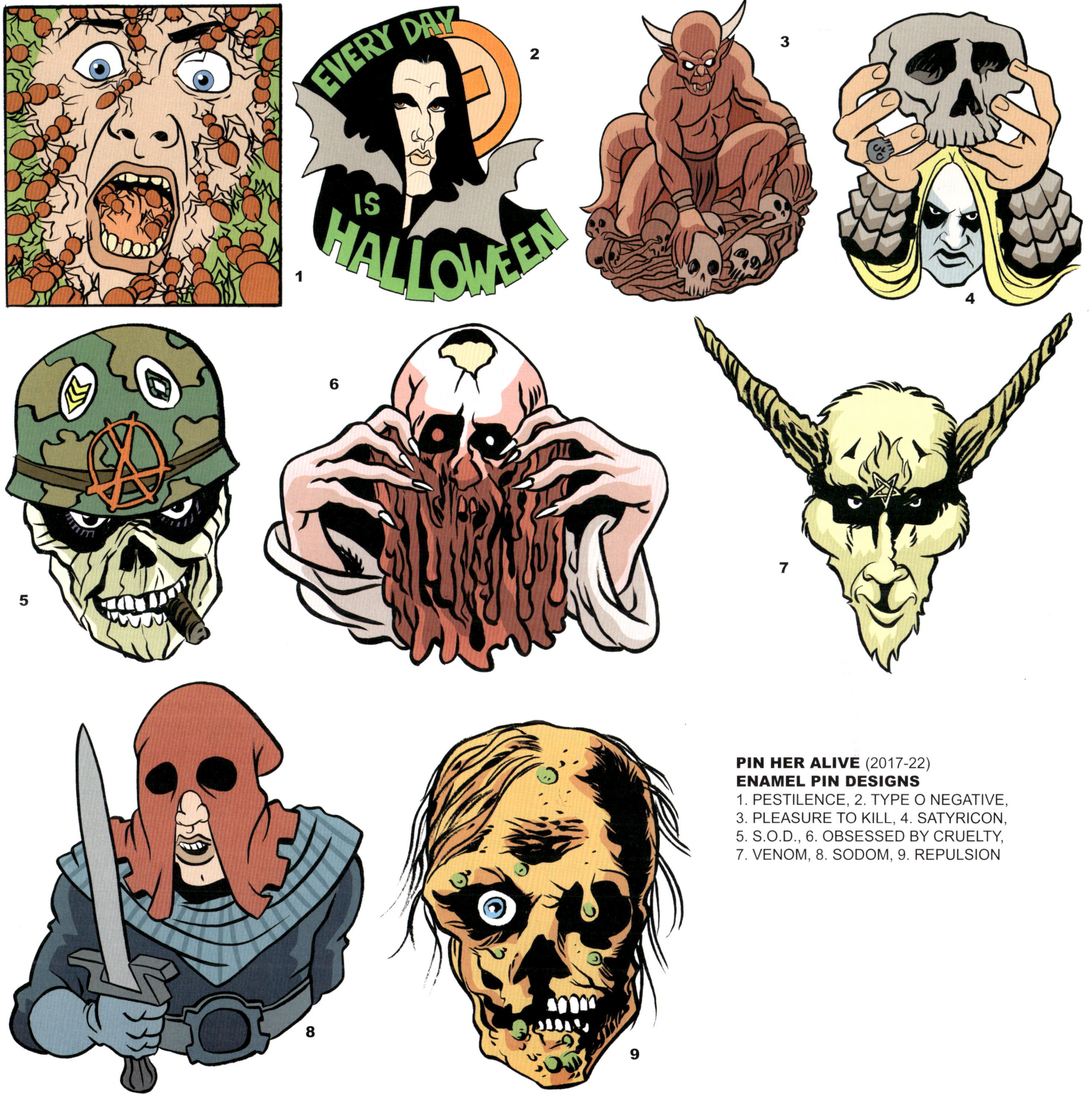

PIN HER ALIVE (2017-22)
ENAMEL PIN DESIGNS
1. PESTILENCE, 2. TYPE O NEGATIVE,
3. PLEASURE TO KILL, 4. SATYRICON,
5. S.O.D., 6. OBSESSED BY CRUELTY,
7. VENOM, 8. SODOM, 9. REPULSION

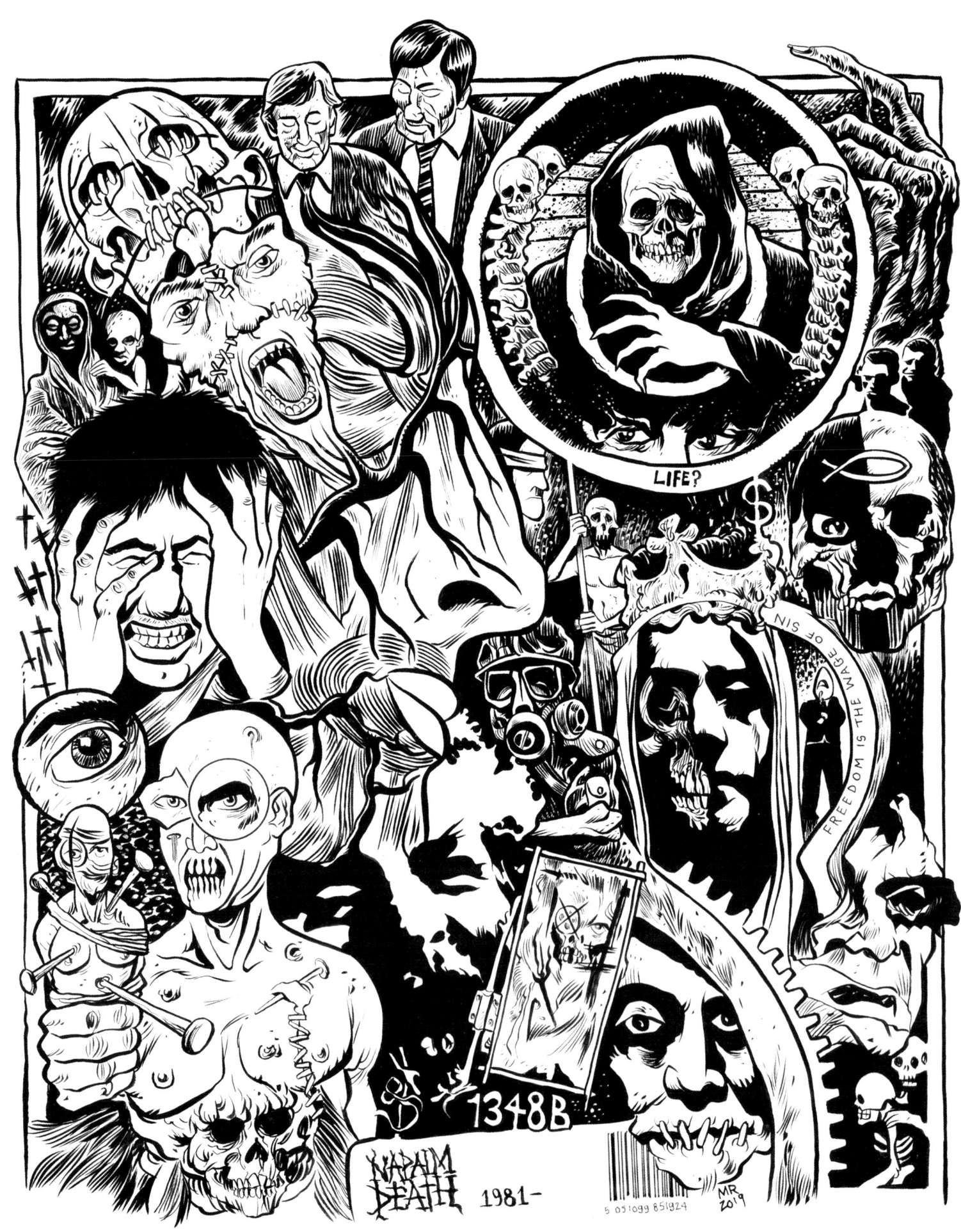

A LEGACY OF NAPALM (2019)
A piece chronicling every Napalm Death album from 1981-2019.

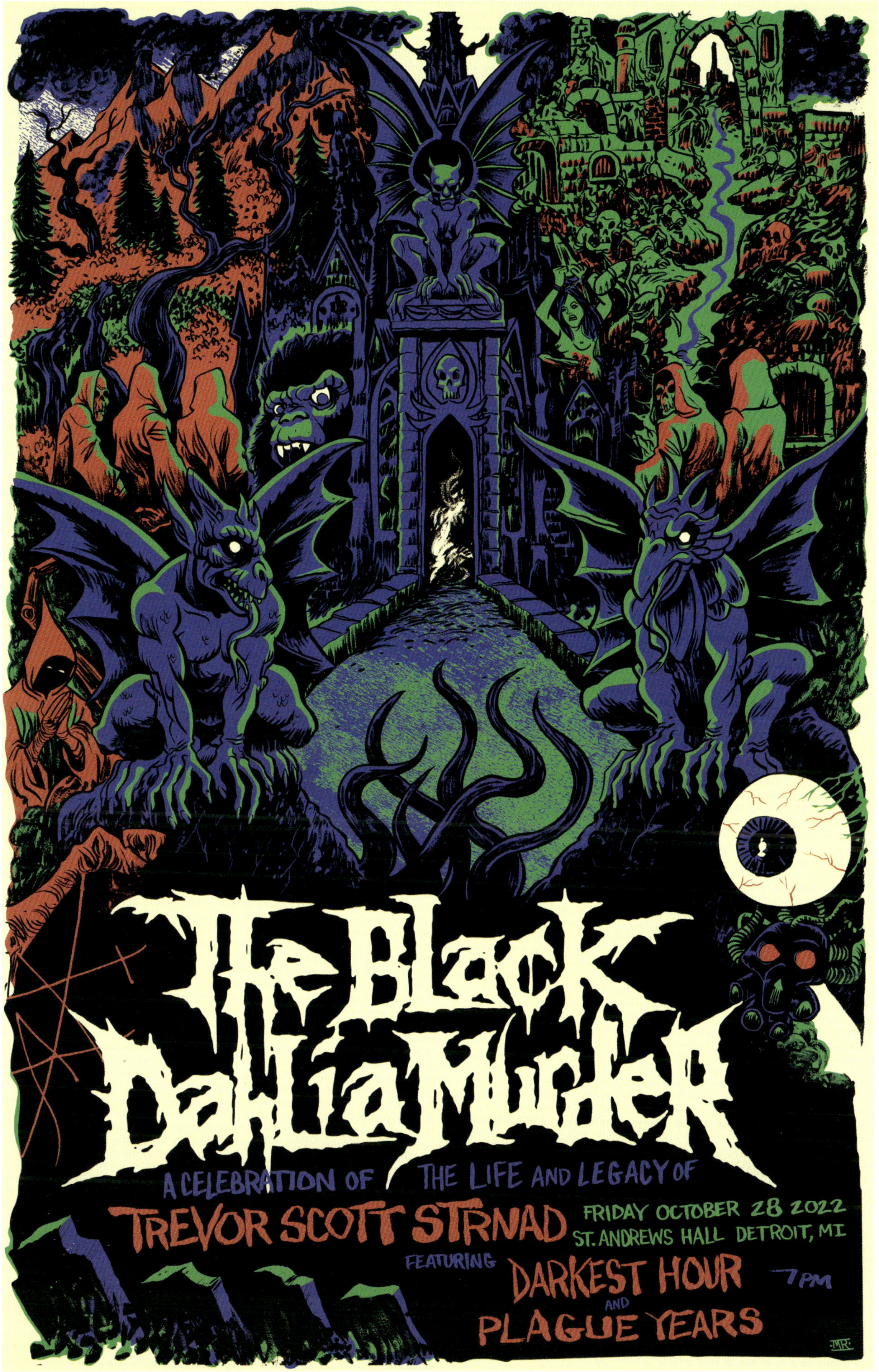

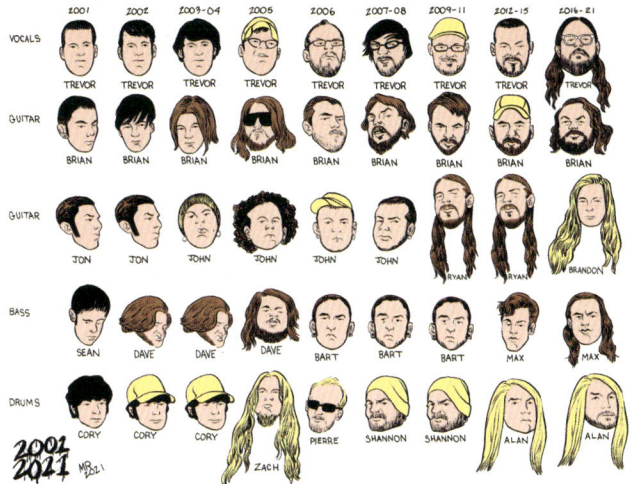

LEFT: STRNAD LEGACY (2022)
A poster for the first Black Dahlia Murder show with Brian Eschbach on vocals after the tragic death of previous frontman Trevor Strnad.

ABOVE: FAMILY TREE (2021)
A poster exclusively for the Black Dahlia Murder's Fan club. The poster was a parody of a similar themed poster showing the vast lineup changes in Black Flag.

BELOW: RAINBOW IN THE DARK (2018)
A poster and shirt design for a Dio-themed cancer charity.

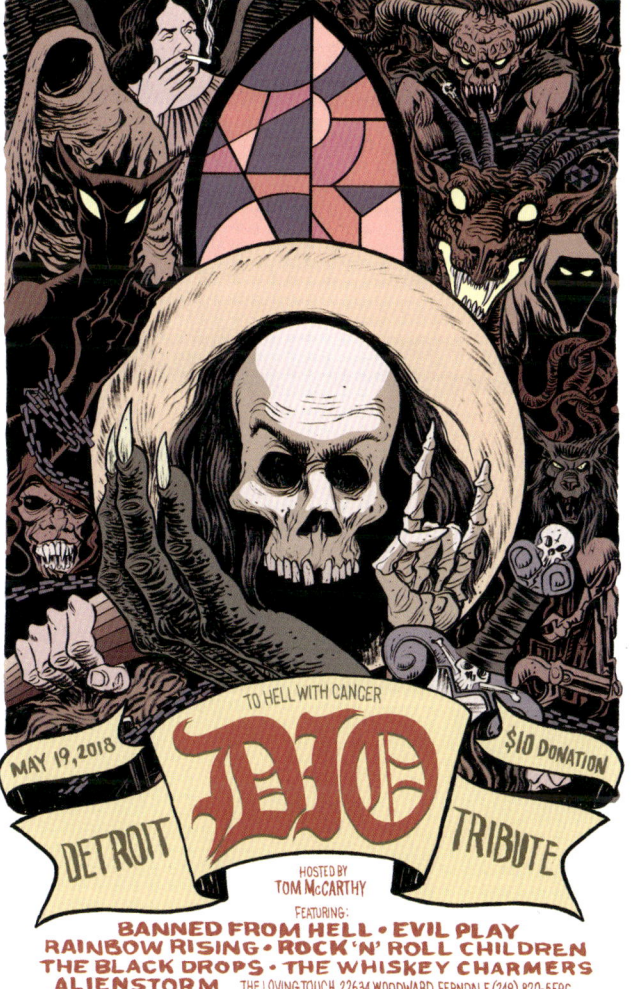

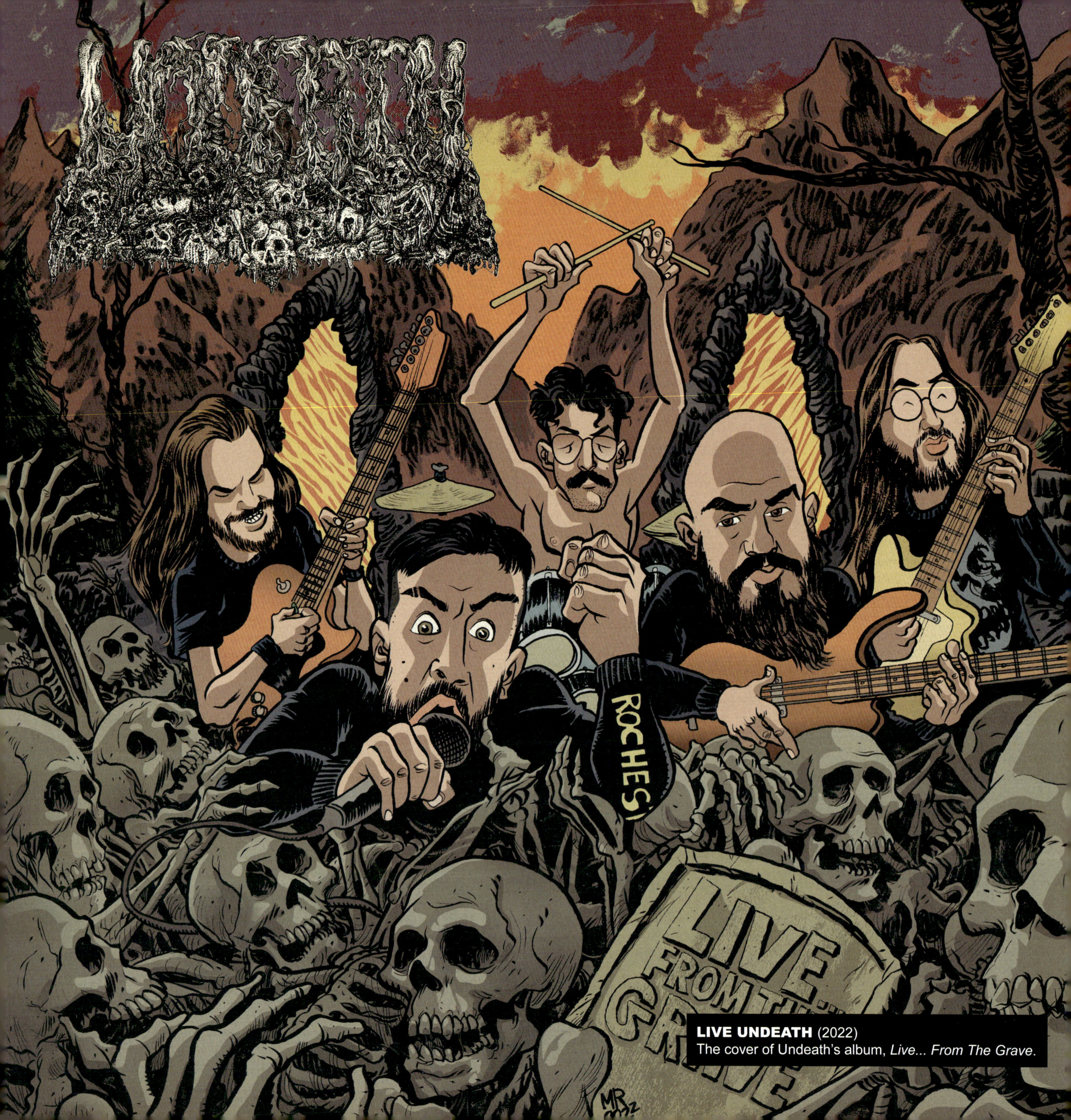

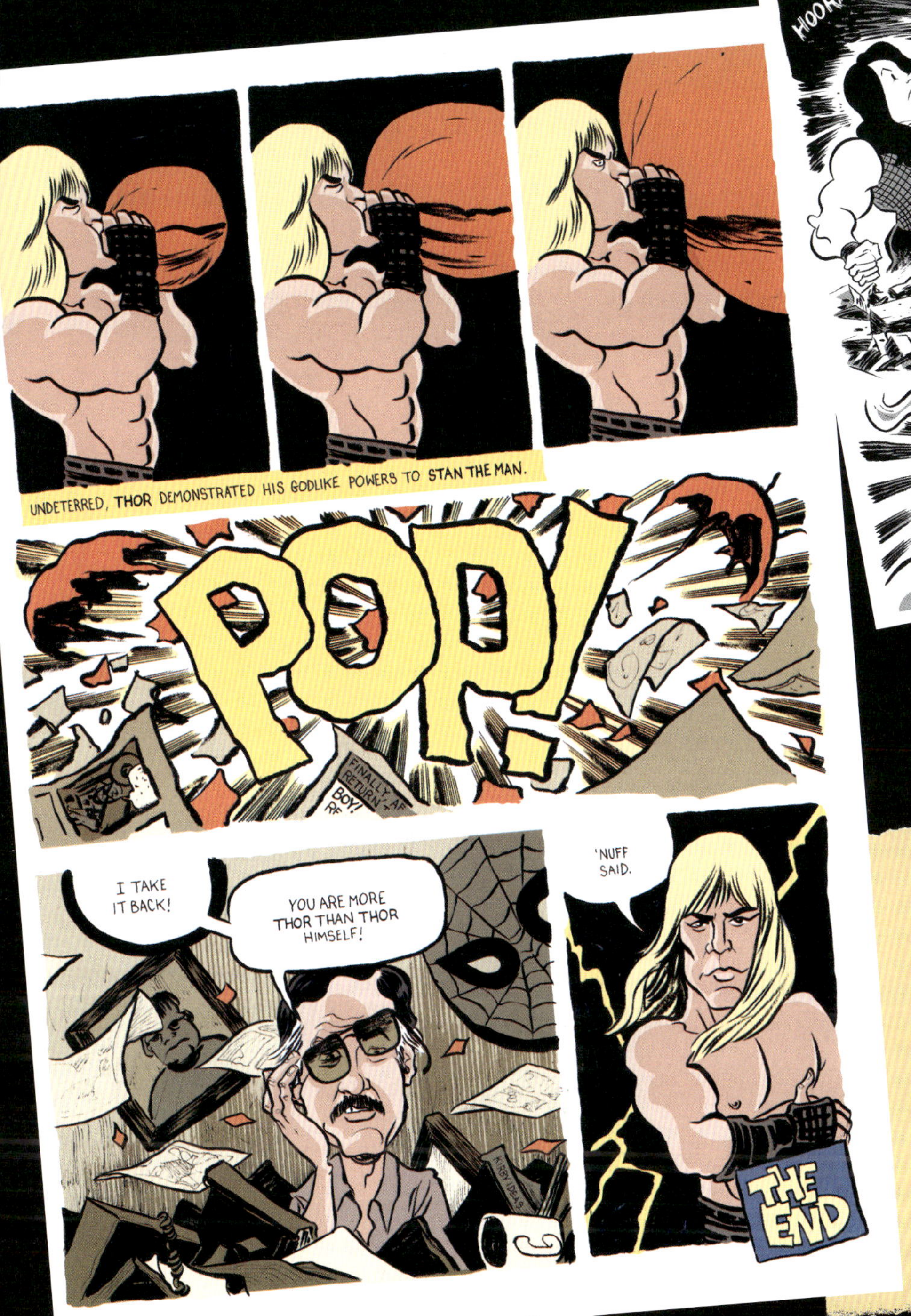

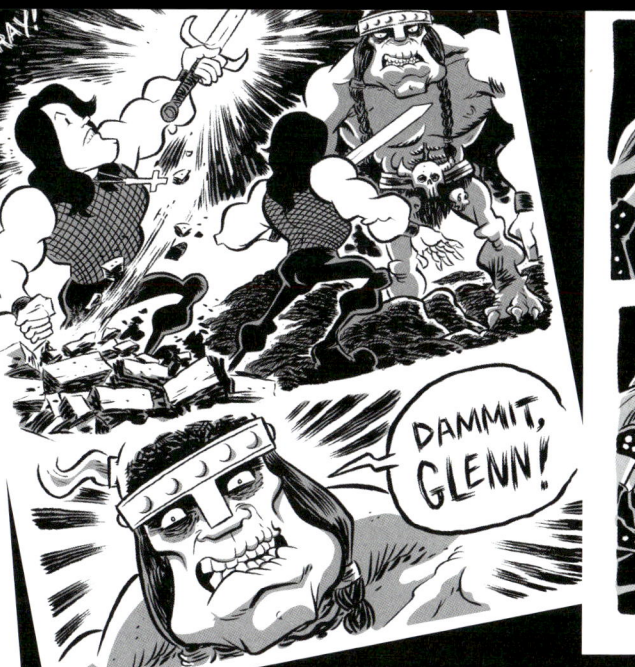

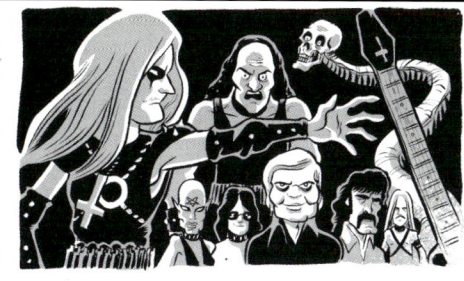

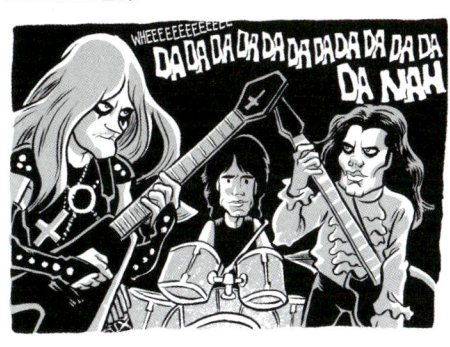

COMICS

Up until the last dozen or so years, my comics and metal obsession didn't ever really mix. Those two aspect of my creative life were always kept seperated by some artificial wall. Doing monthly work for Decibel Magazine changed that. It pointed out the doorway that had been there all along. In 2012 I was invited to participate in the Henry & Glenn Forever and Ever project, spearheaded by Tom Neely. That book and the monthly magazine work gave me the courage to put out my own metal-related comic, Satan Is Alive: A Tribute to Mercyful Fate. It combined my previous fanzine experience with comics and turned into a pretty unique series of books. The following pages are a selection of comics from those projects.

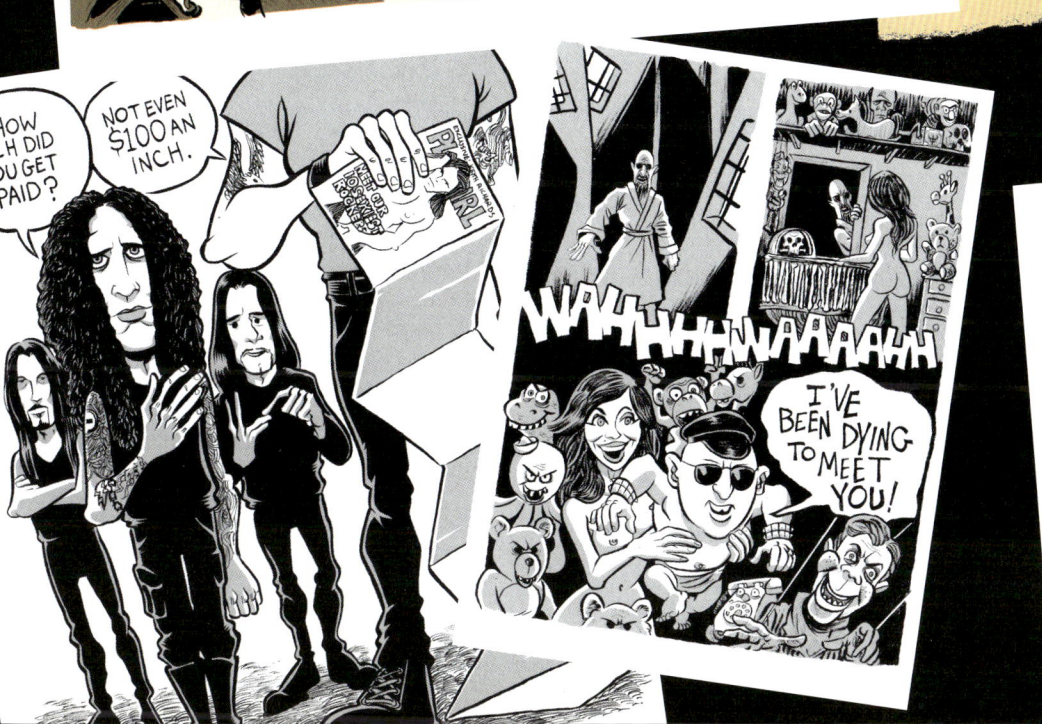

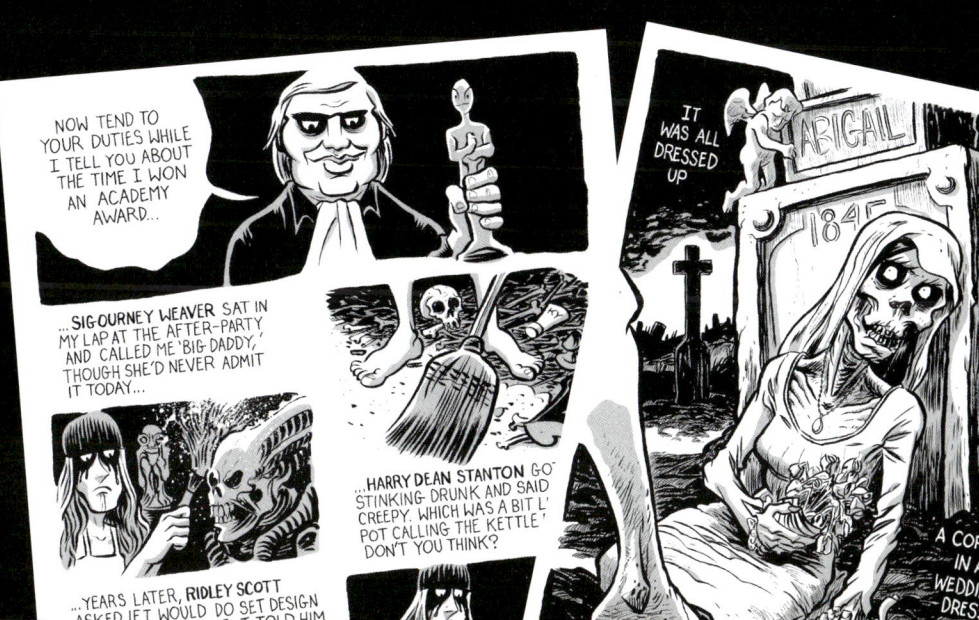

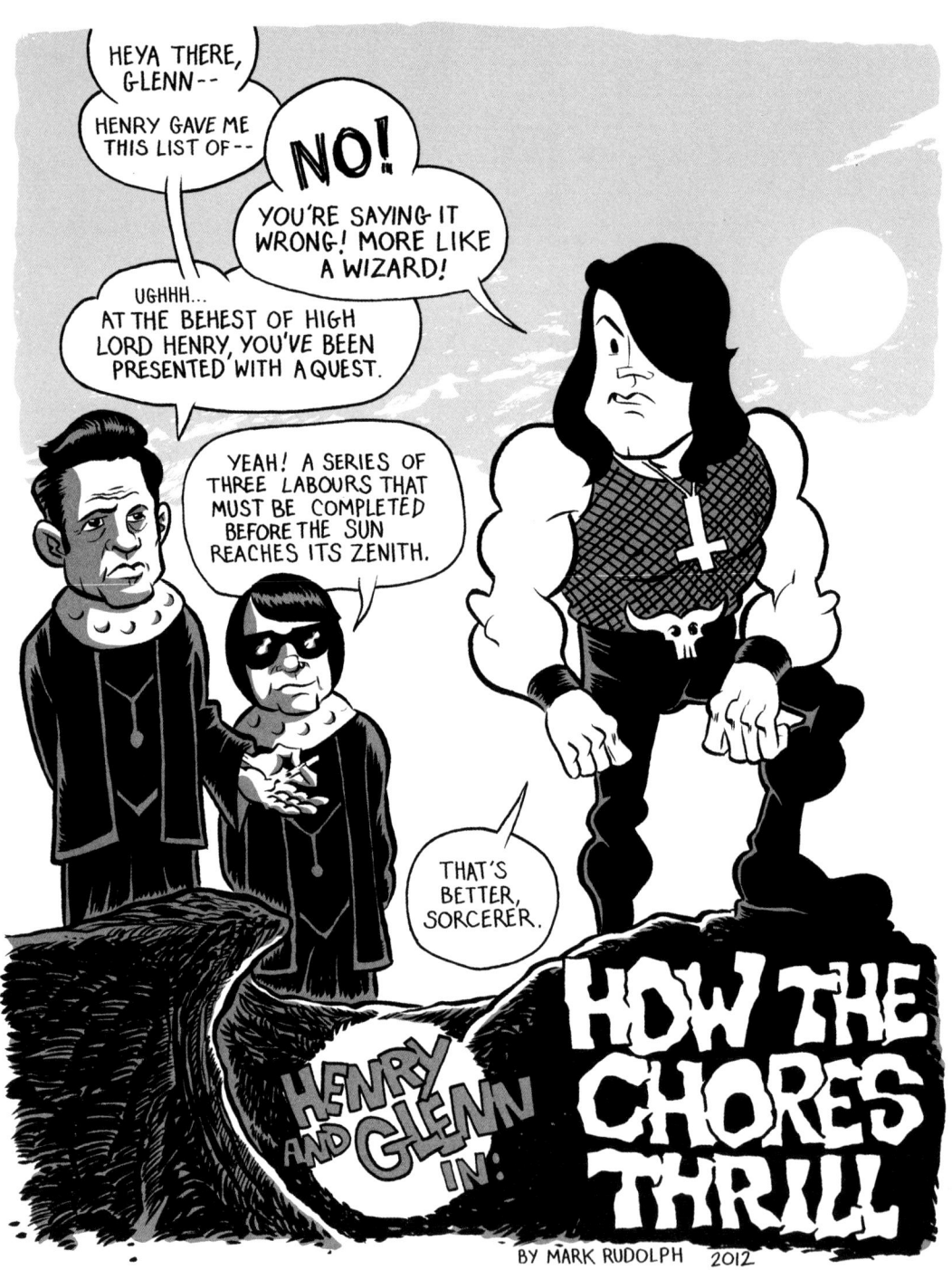

HOW THE CHORES THRILL (2012)
A comic for Tom Neely's Henry & Glenn Forever anthology.

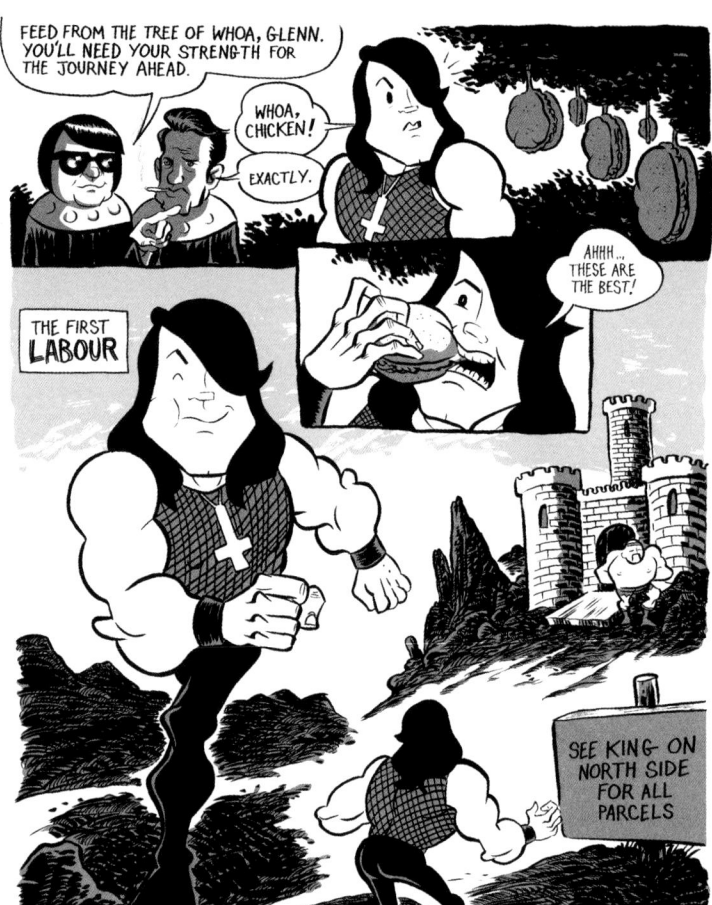

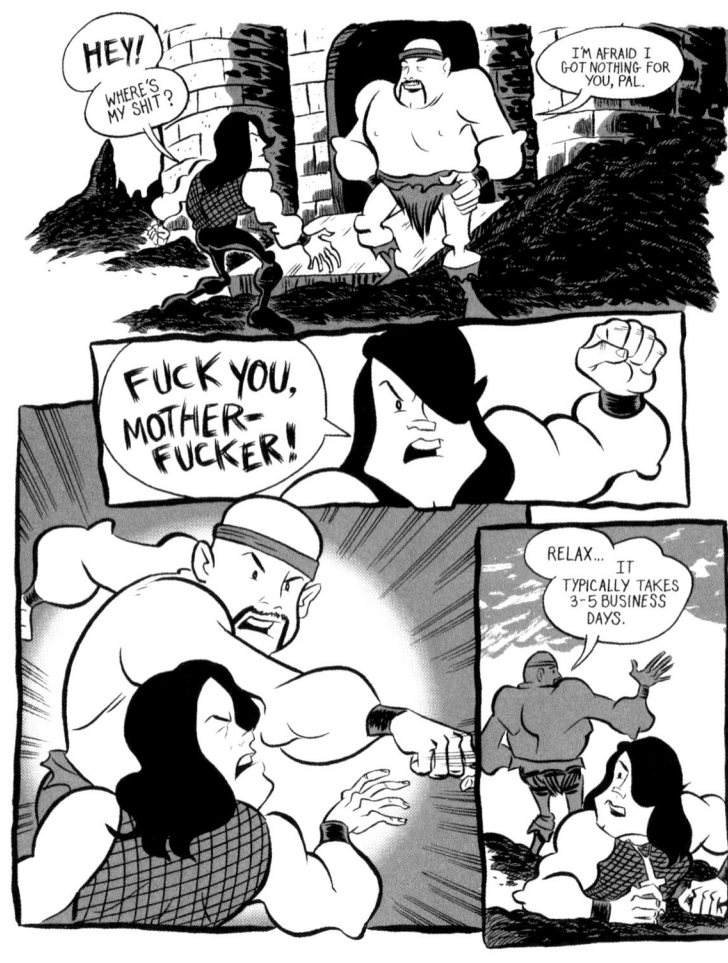

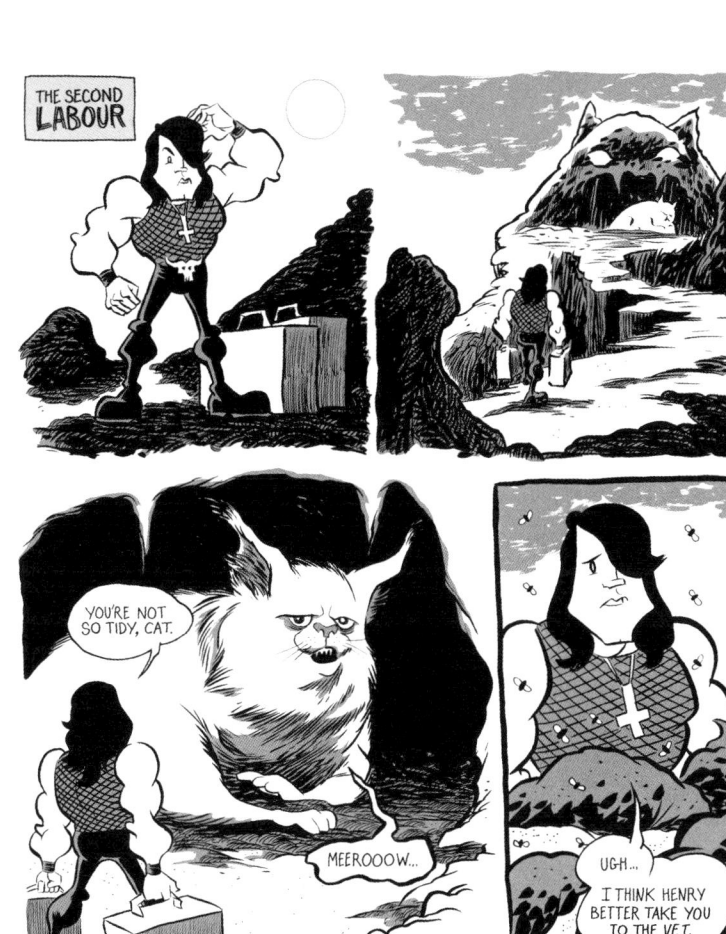

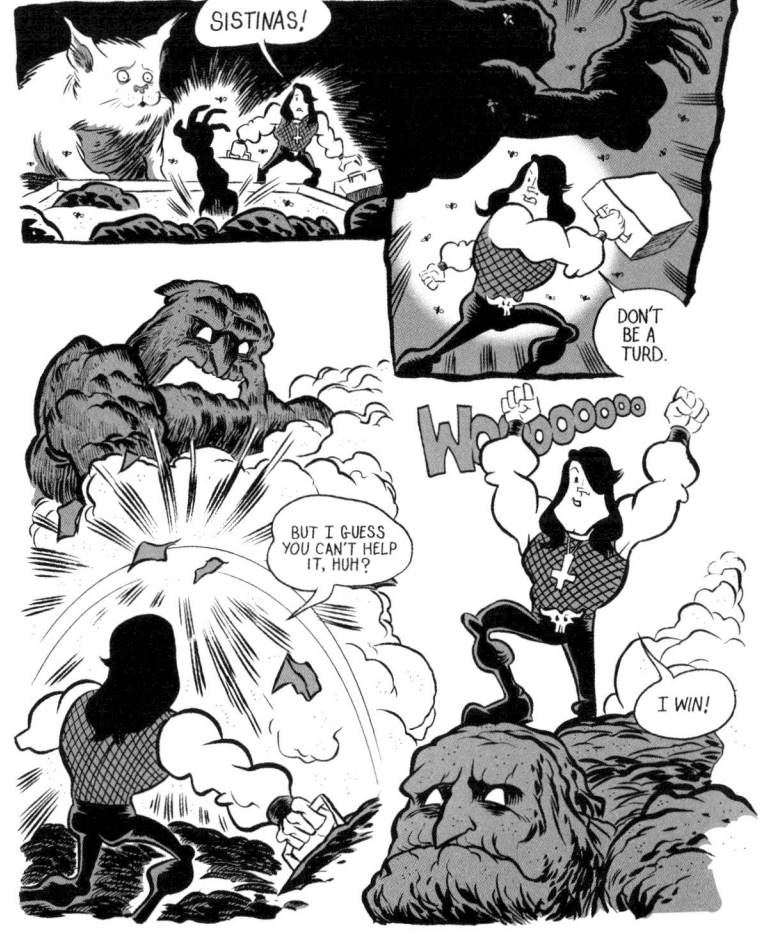

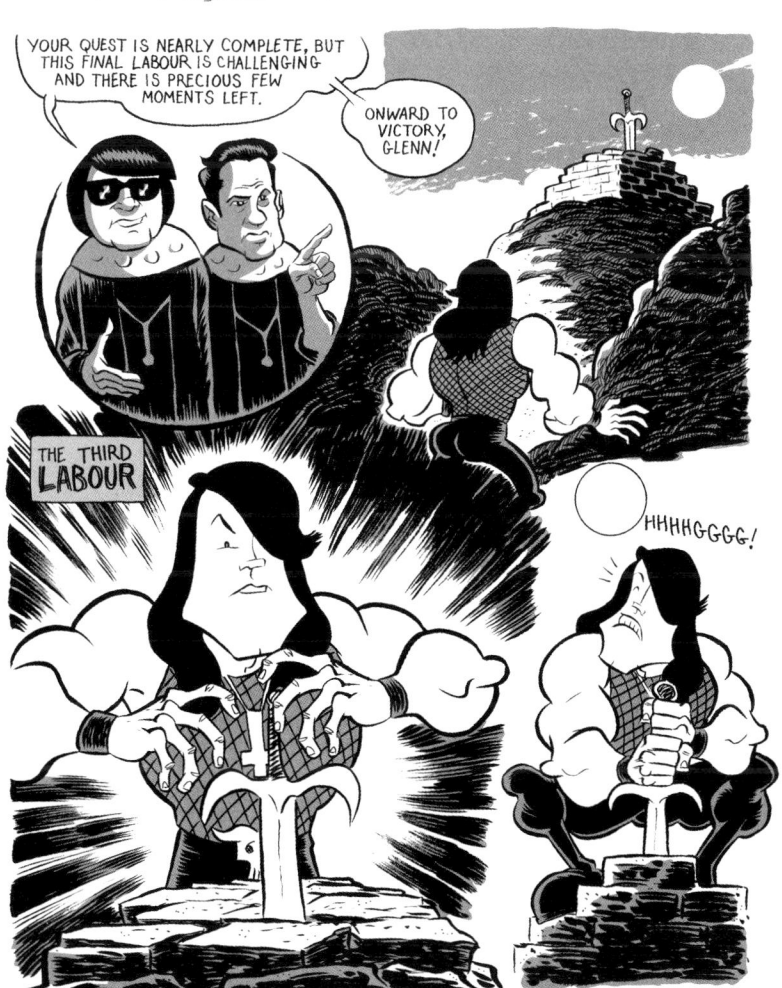

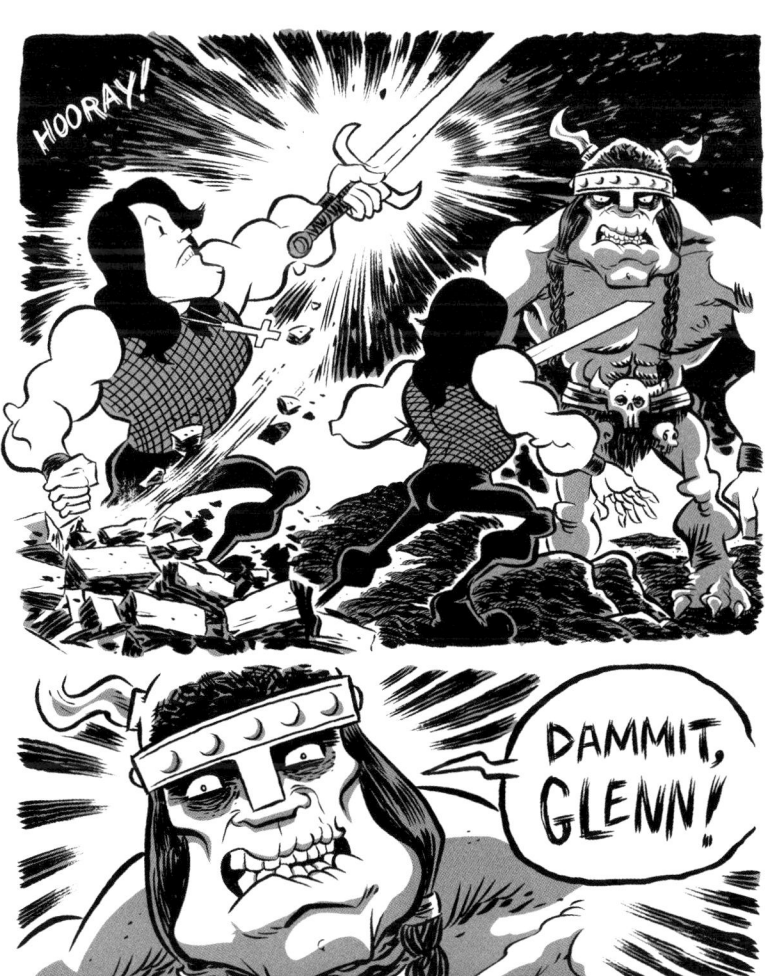

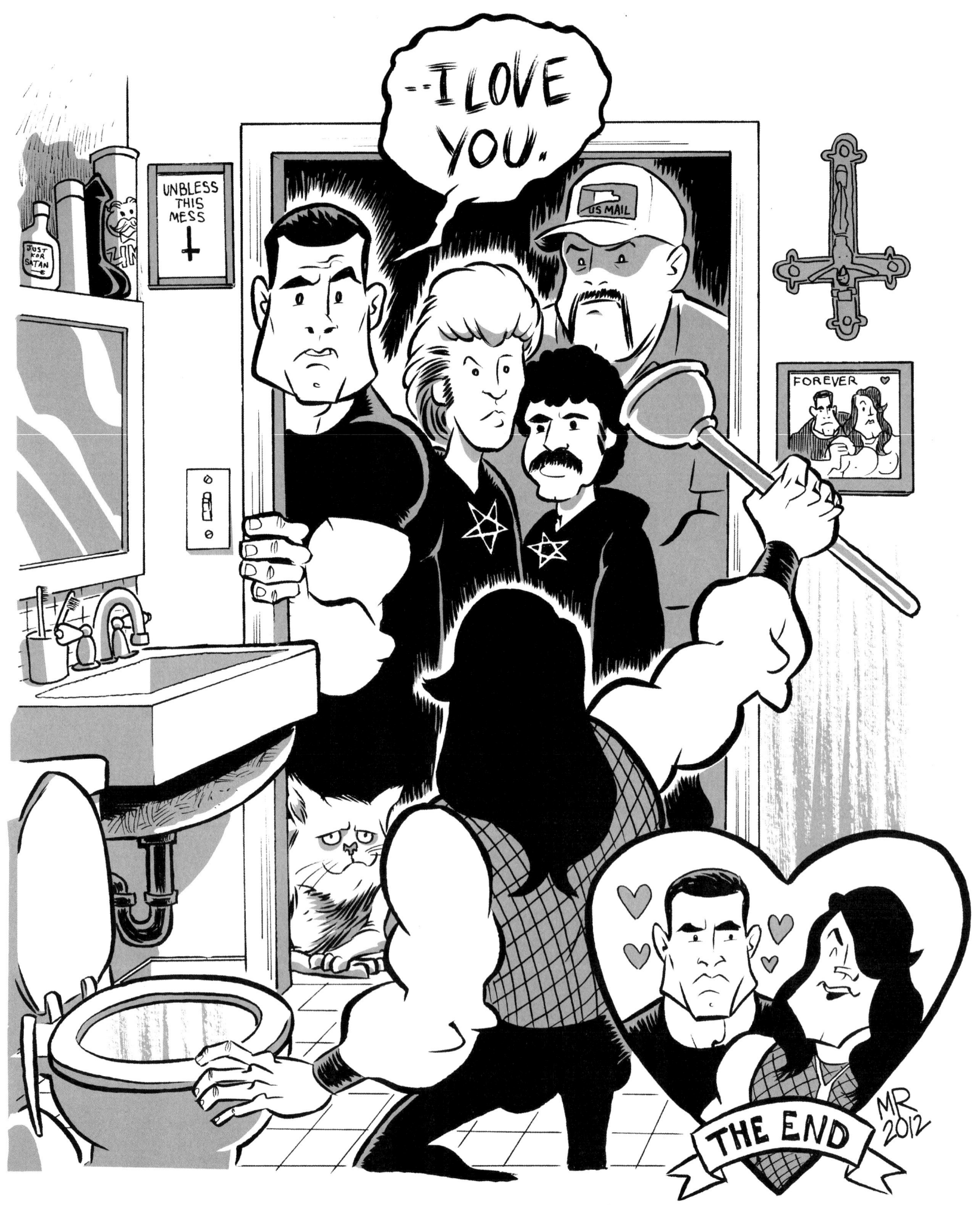

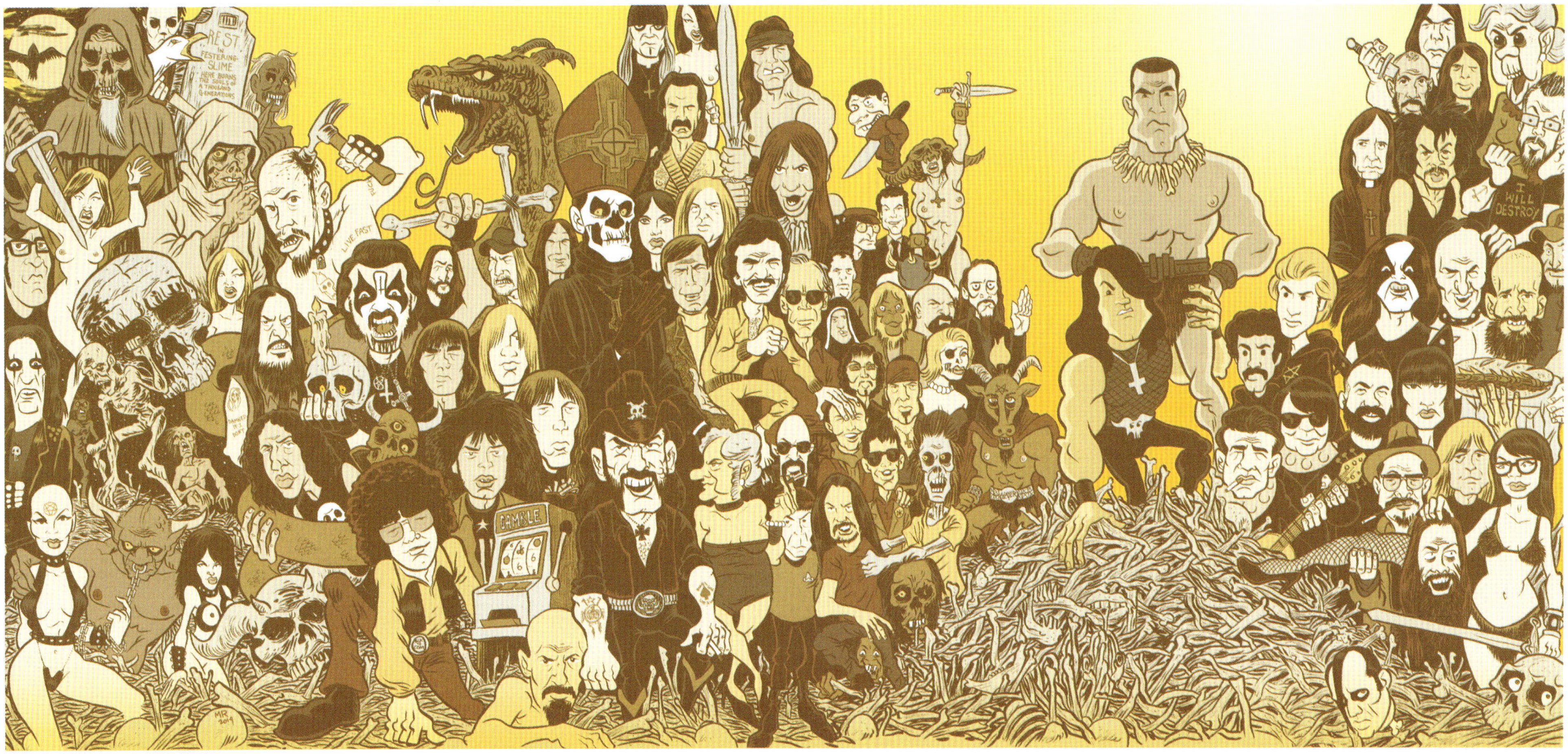

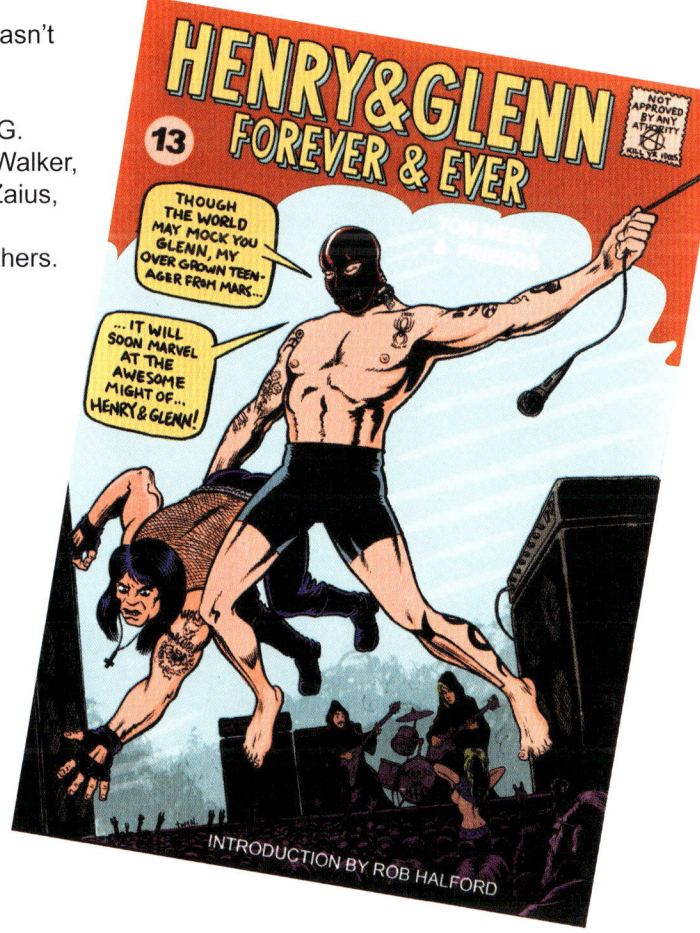

THE DEVIL EMBRACED (2012)

Originally intended to be a dust jacket for a collected edition of Henry & Glenn Forever anthology, but wasn't published until *The Complete Edition* in 2022. Included: Templar knight, Seagull, Michael Myers, Entombed, Butchered At Birth, Leper, G.G. Allin, Autopsy, Alice Cooper, Fenriz, Barry Thompson, L.G. Petrov, Gavin Ward, Papa, The MC5, Dan Lilker, Chris Reifert, Lemmy, Wild West Prostitute, Tom G. Warrior, Conan, Jo Bench, Karl Willets, Lee Majors, Burt Reynolds, Zardoz, Quorthon, Metal God, Jeff Walker, Spock, Lou Reed, Eddie, Omega Man, David Vincent, Black Flag, Danzig, Jello Biafra, Misfits, Doctor Zaius, Kerry King, Repulsion head, Johnny Cash, Roy Orbison, Hall and Oates, Ed Luce, J.T. Dockery, Abbath, Cronos, Mickey Dee, J. Bennett, Philthy Animal Taylor, Scott Carlson, Lee Dorrian and many others. RIGHT: The cover for Henry & Glenn Forever & Ever Complete Edition. Drawn by Tom Neely.

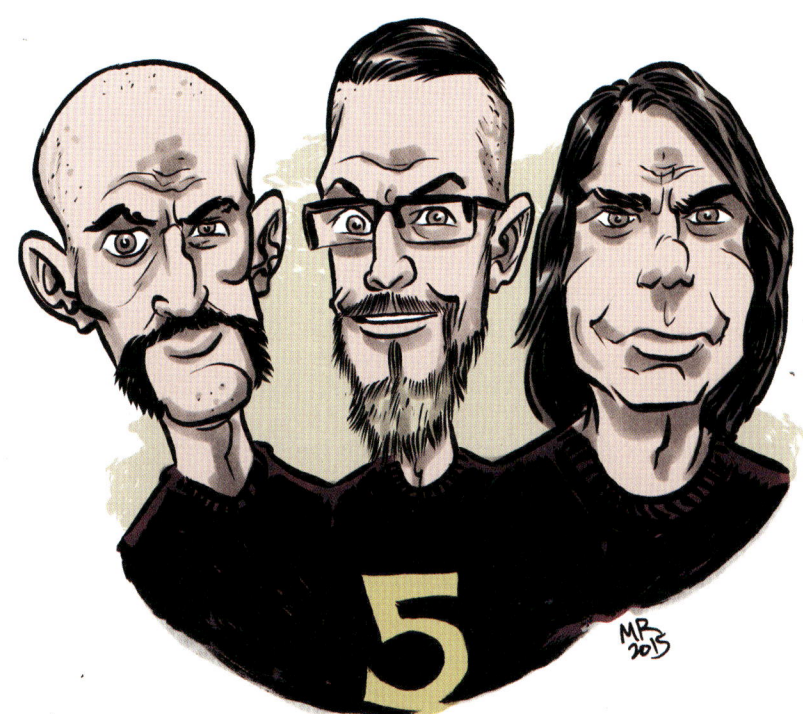

LEFT:
FIVE YEARS (2015)
J. Bennett (Writer), Tom Neely (cartoonist) and Scott Carlson (Musician) piece for their 5 years of DJing together.

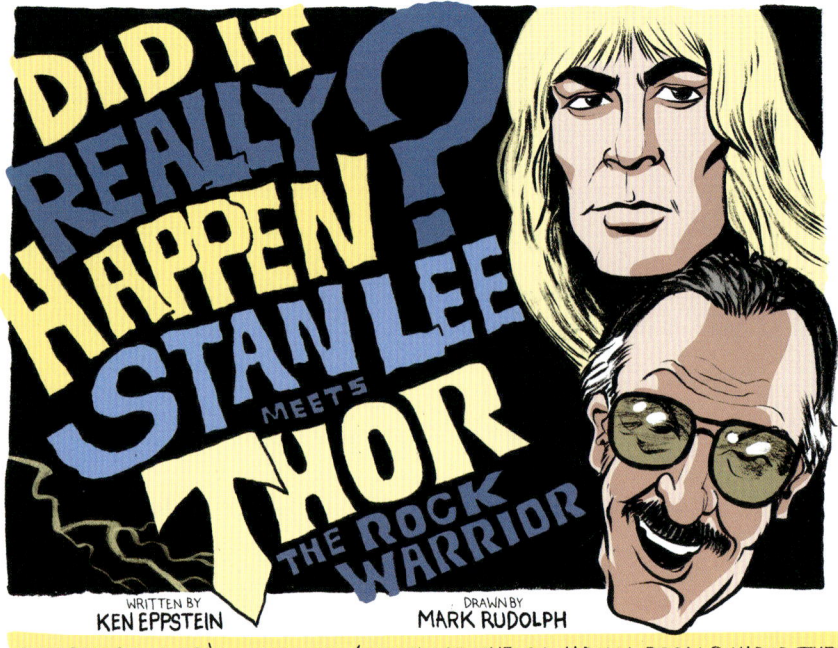

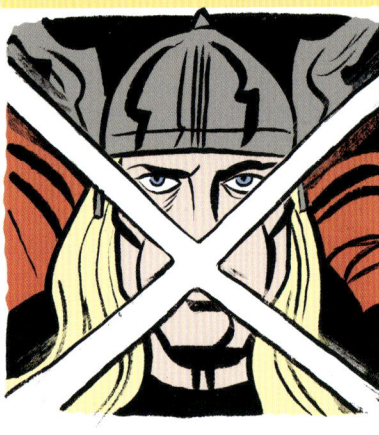

THANKS IN PART TO MARVEL COMICS SPOKESPERSON **STAN LEE**, WHEN MOST PEOPLE HEAR THE NAME **THOR**, THEY THINK OF A HAMMER SLINGIN' SUPERHERO.

WRITTEN BY KEN EPPSTEIN

DRAWN BY MARK RUDOLPH

BUT THOSE OF US 'IN THE KNOW' THINK OF THE CANADIAN BODY BUILDER TURNED ROCKSTAR, **JON MIKL THOR**, WHO WOWED AUDIENCES WITH HIS FEATS OF STRENGTH.

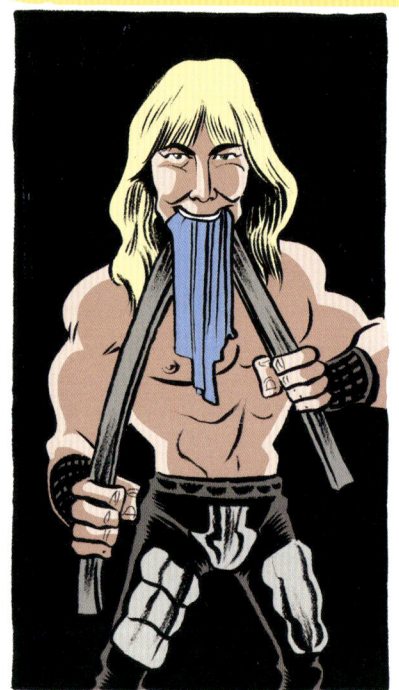

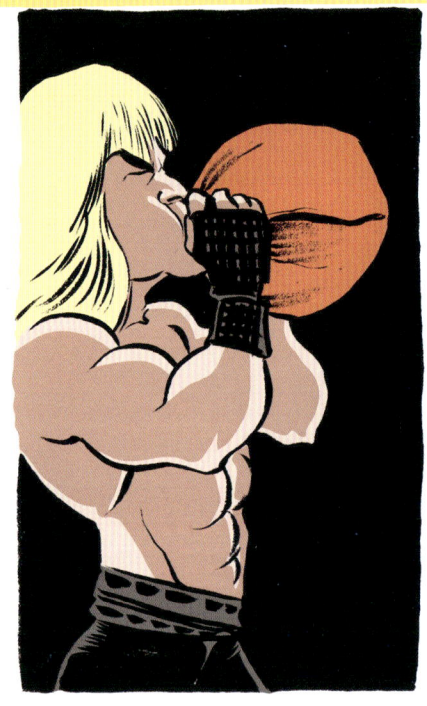

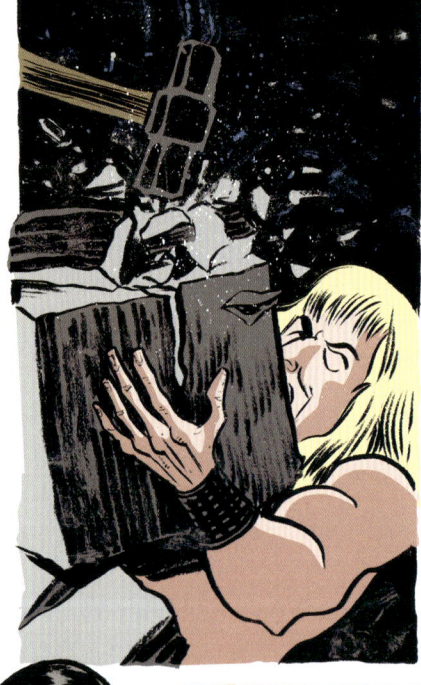

SO WHAT HAPPENED WHEN **THOR** FINALLY MET **STAN LEE**?

THERE IS ONLY ONE **THOR**, THE ONE **I** CREATED FOR **JOURNEY INTO MYSTERY** MAGAZINE IN 1962! *

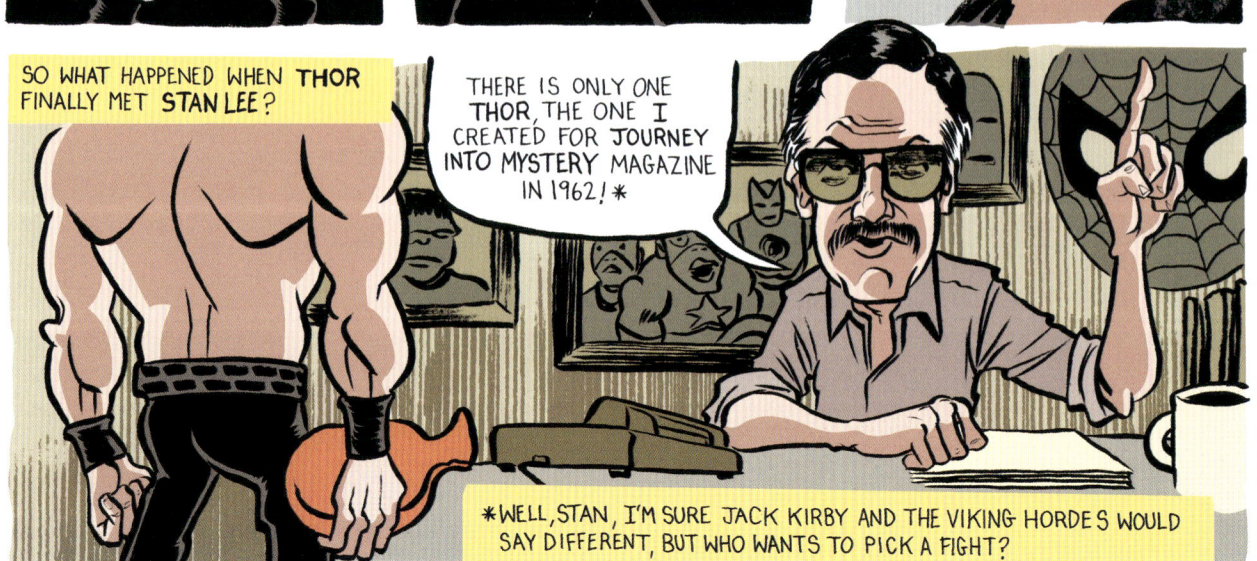

*WELL, STAN, I'M SURE JACK KIRBY AND THE VIKING HORDES WOULD SAY DIFFERENT, BUT WHO WANTS TO PICK A FIGHT?

THOR THE ROCK WARRIOR
(2016)
Nix Comics strip documenting the alleged first meeting of Jon Mikl Thor and Stan Lee.
Written by Ken Eppstein.

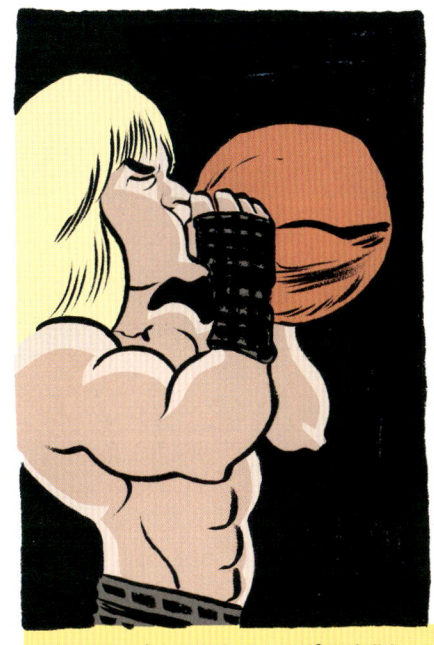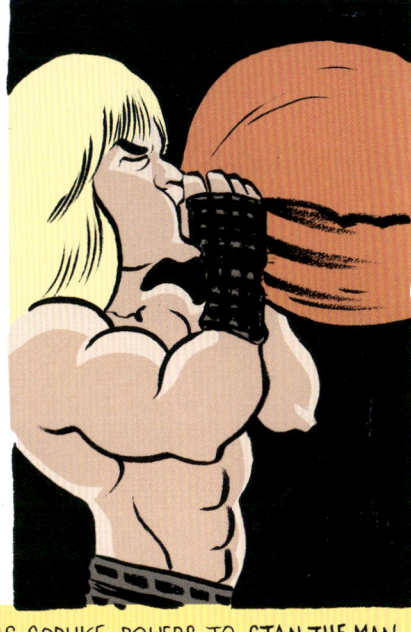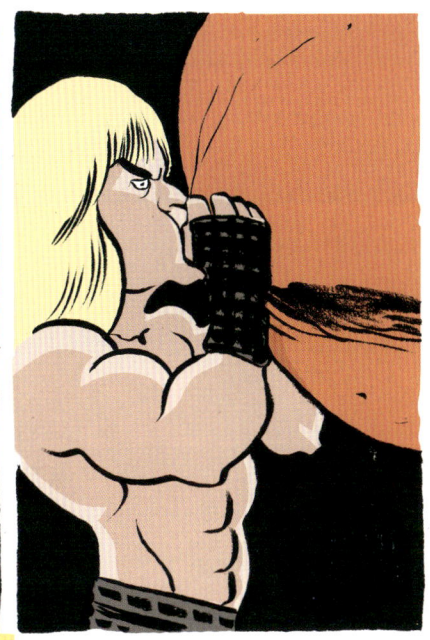

UNDETERRED, **THOR** DEMONSTRATED HIS GODLIKE POWERS TO **STAN THE MAN**.

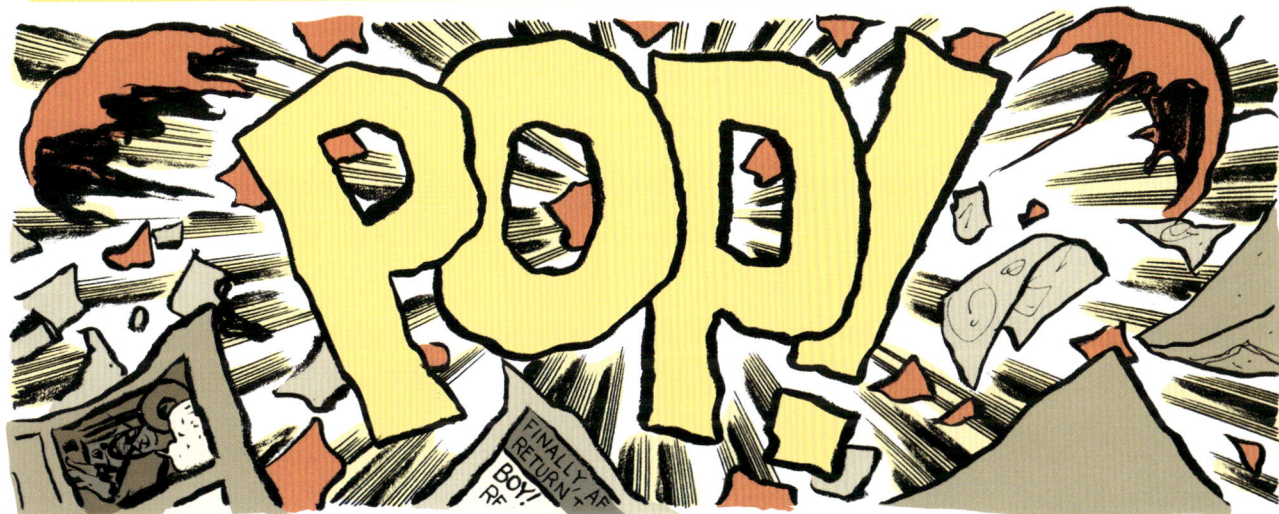

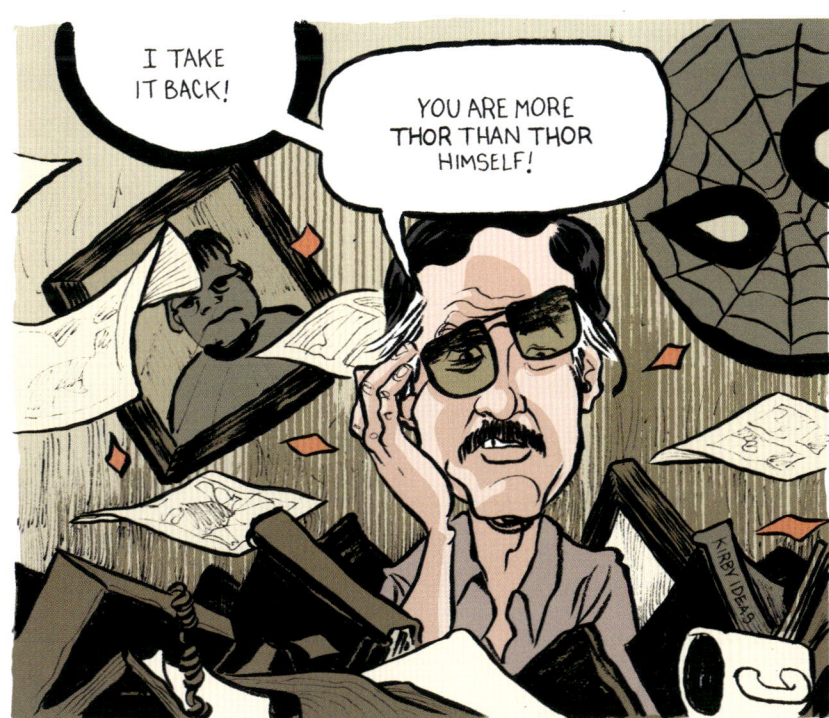

I TAKE IT BACK!

YOU ARE MORE THOR THAN THOR HIMSELF!

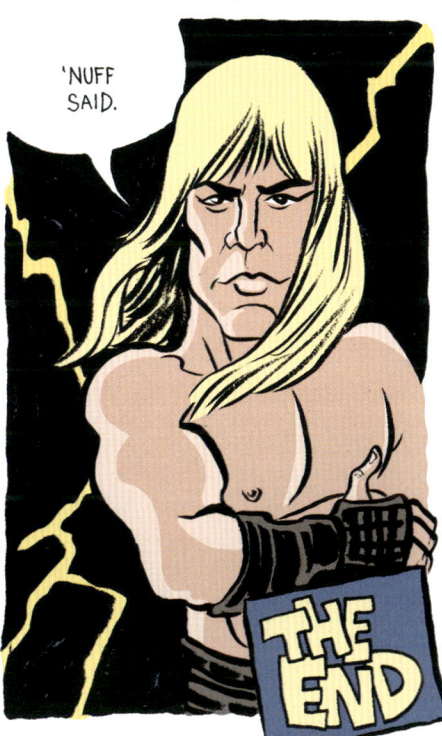

'NUFF SAID.

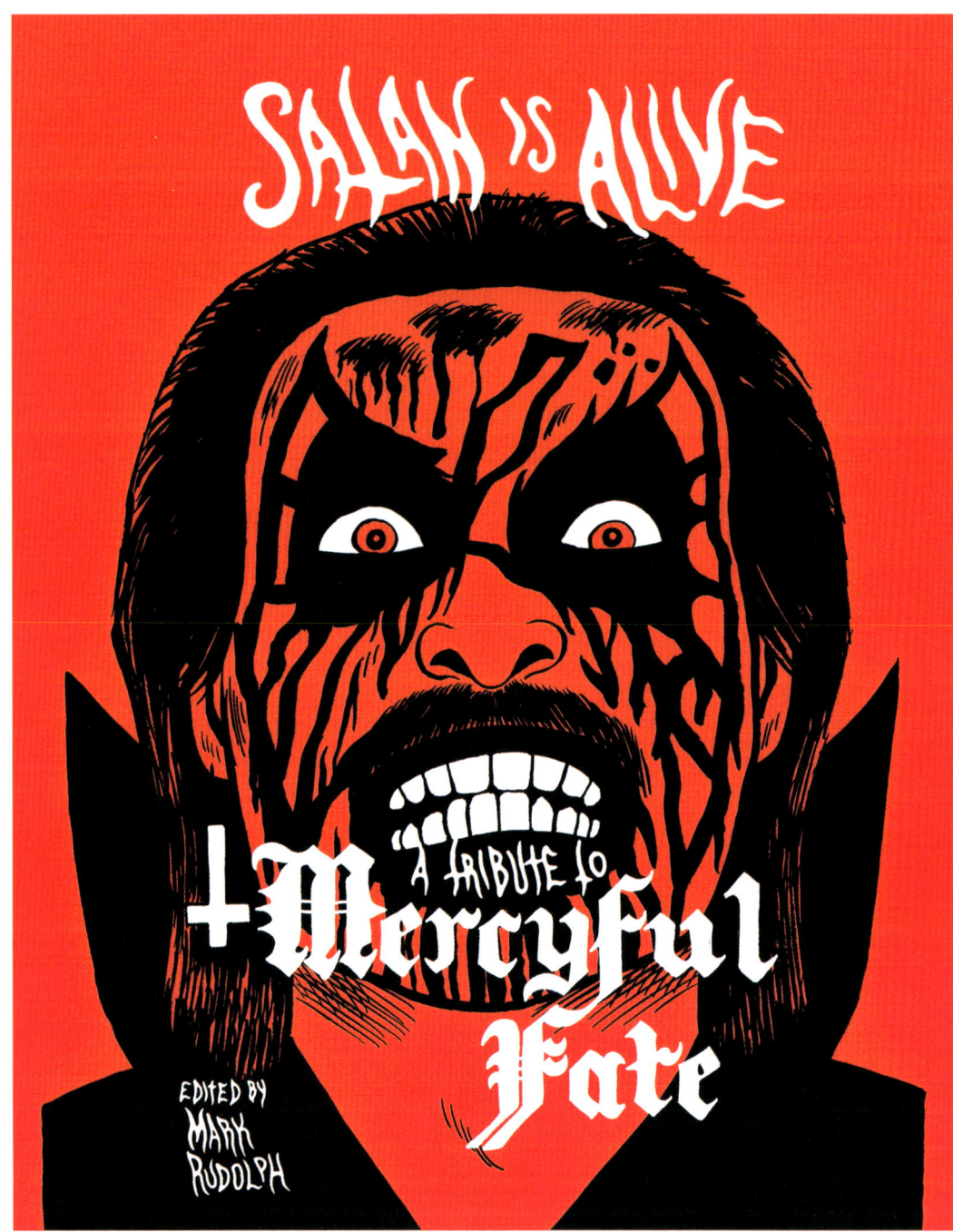

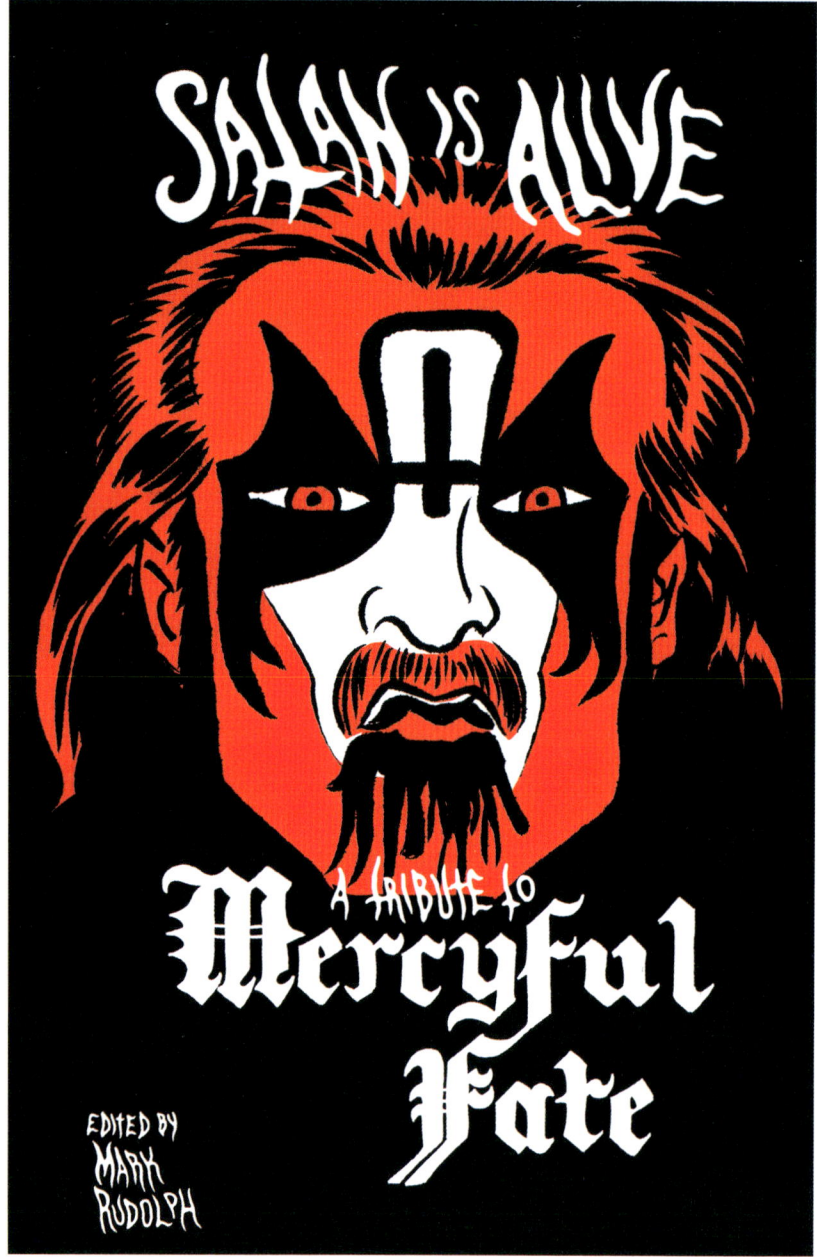

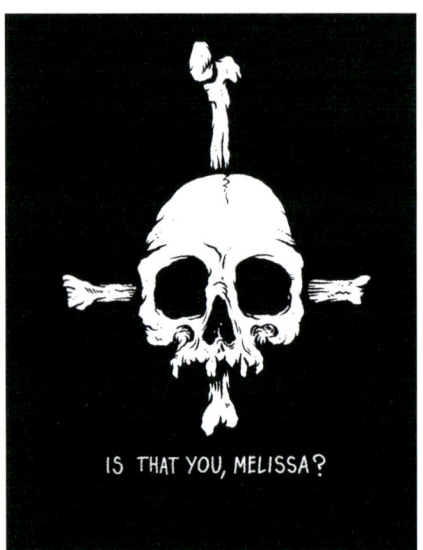

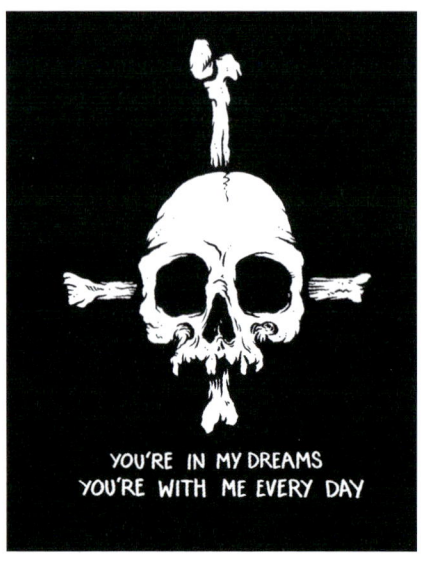

IS THAT YOU, MELISSA?

YOU'RE IN MY DREAMS
YOU'RE WITH ME EVERY DAY

ABOVE:
SATAN IS ALIVE PREPRODUCTION (2012)
Two versions of the book cover. On the left is a Johnny Ryan and the right is mine.
LEFT: MELISSA (2012)
The endpapers for the book. Illustration by Bruno Guerreiro and lettering by Mark Rudolph.

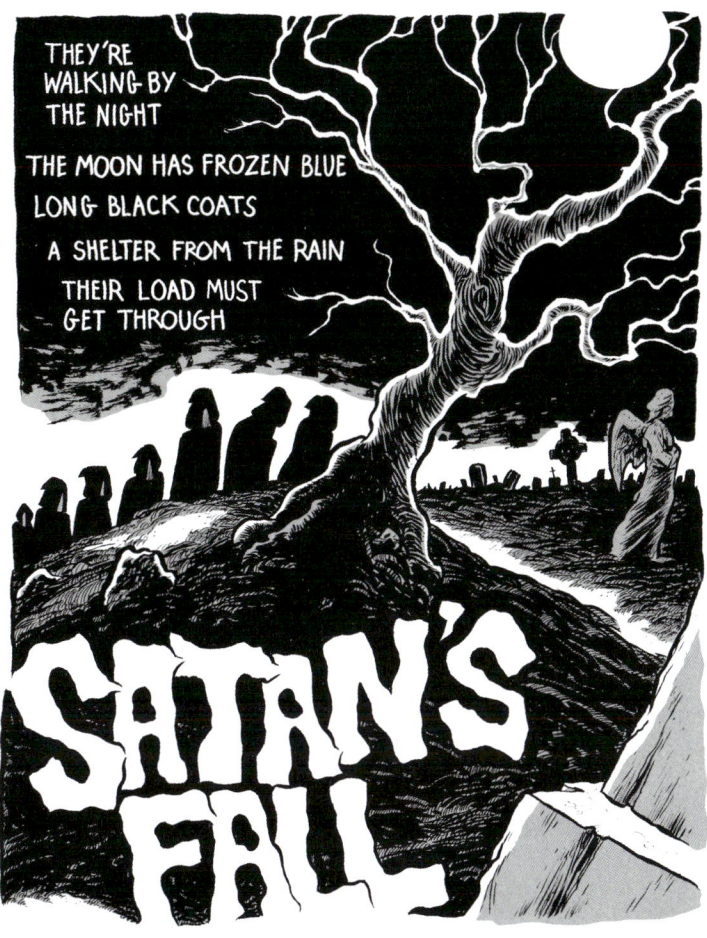

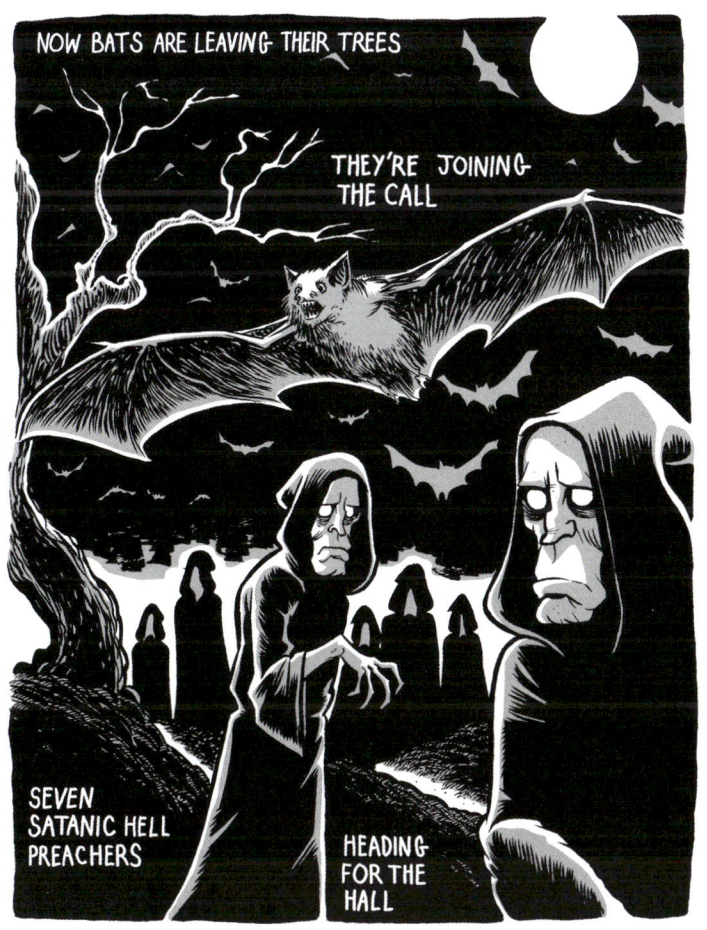

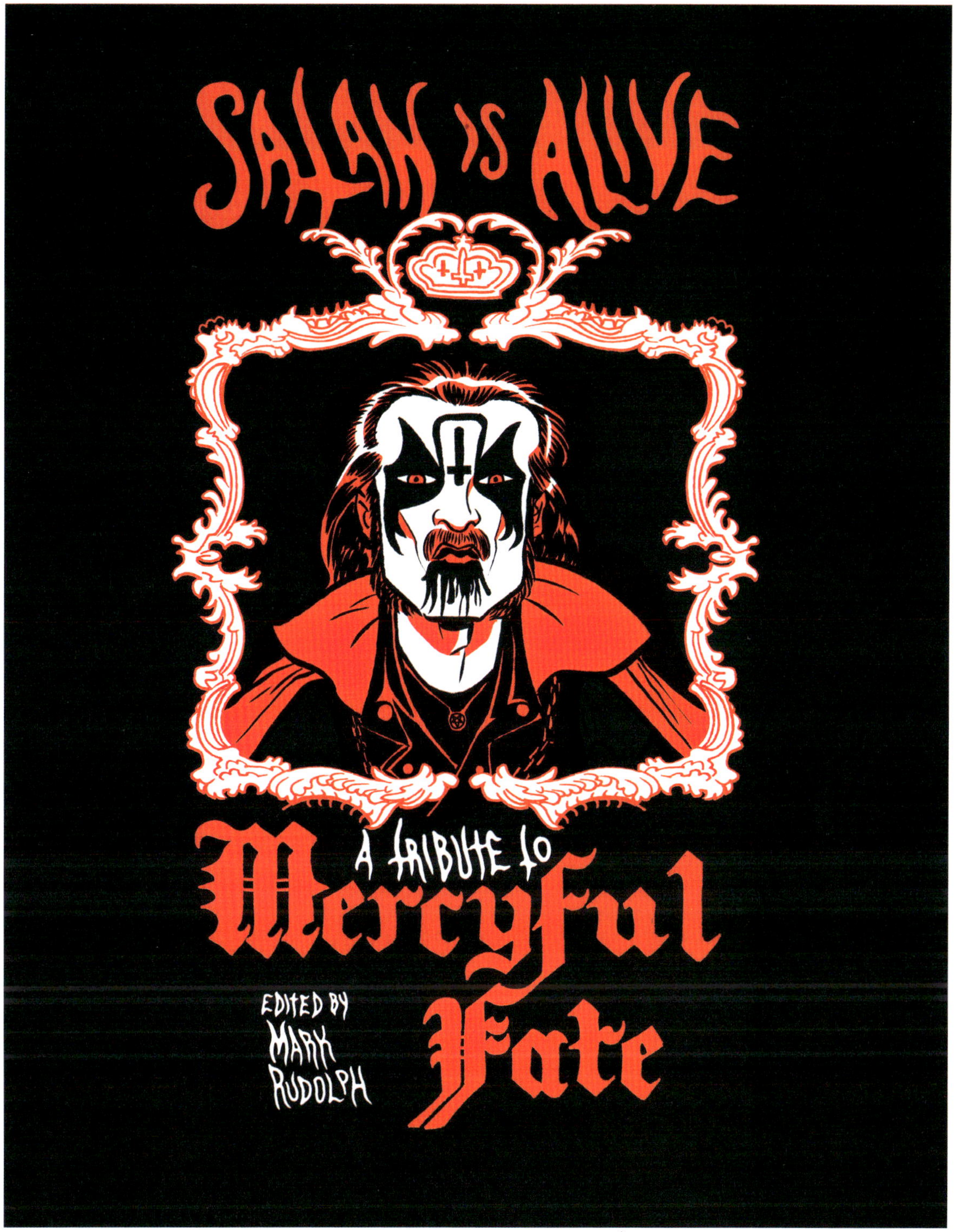

ABOVE: SATAN IS ALIVE. (2012)
The cover of the tribute to Mercyful Fate anthology comic.
LEFT: SATAN'S FALL (2012)
 A comic based on the lyrics to the Mercyful Fate song, *Satan's Fall*.

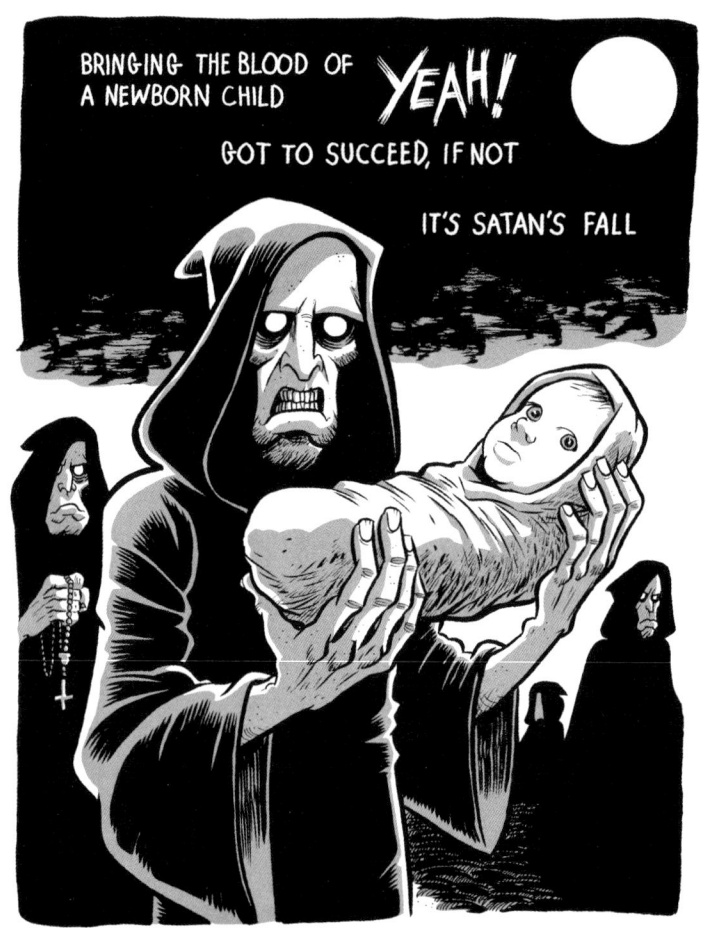

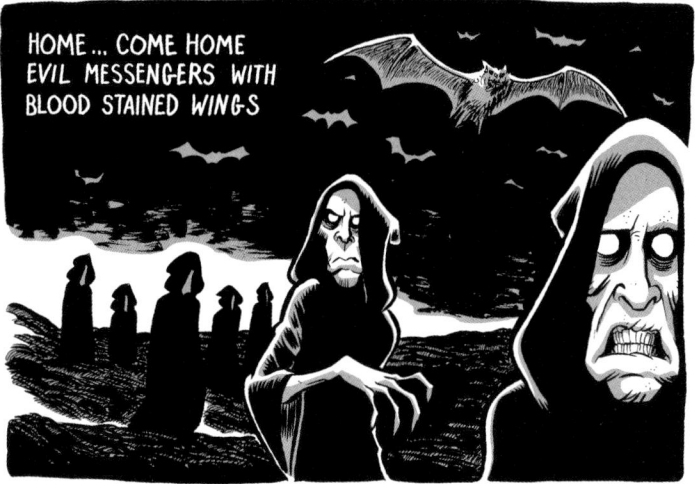

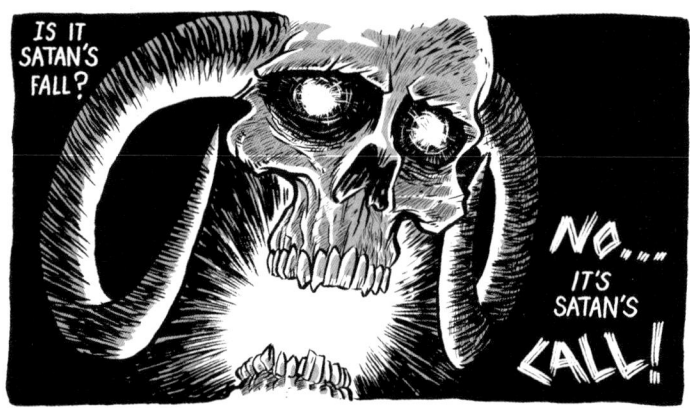

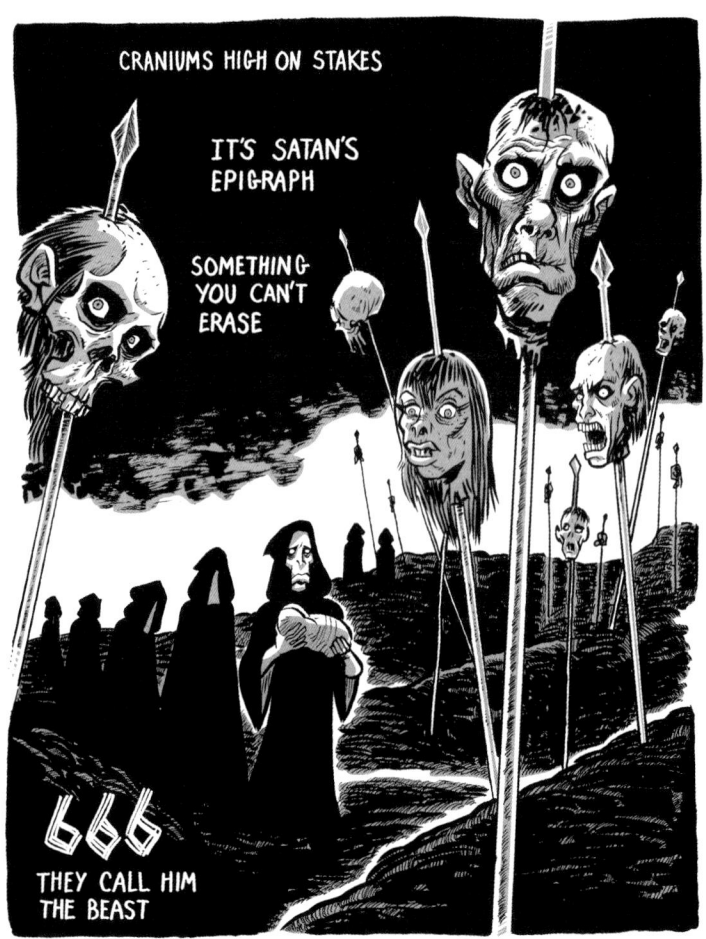

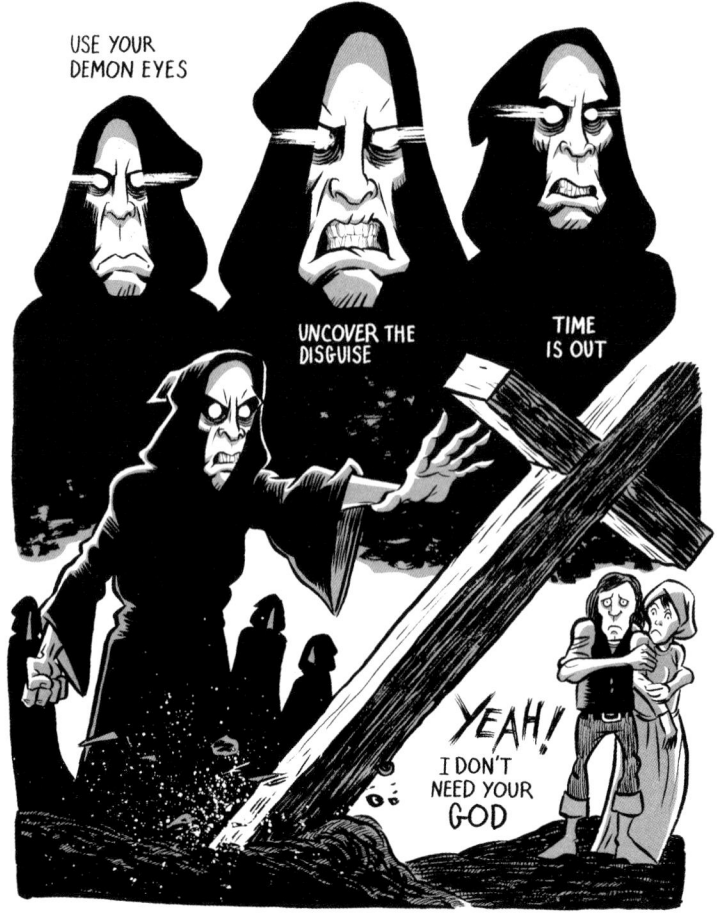

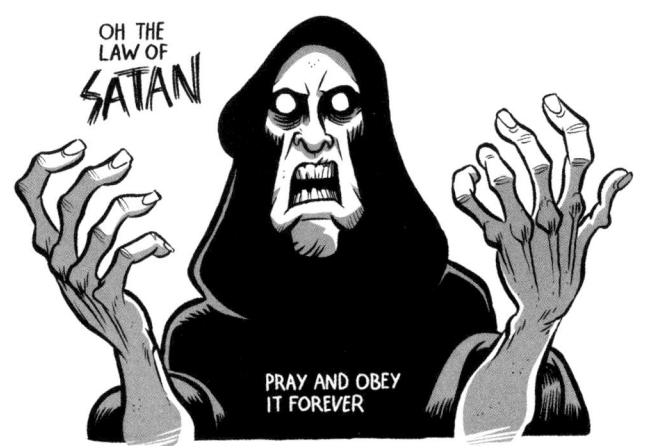

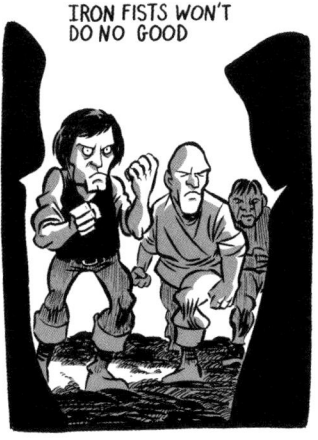

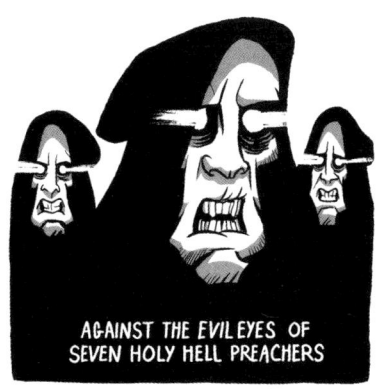

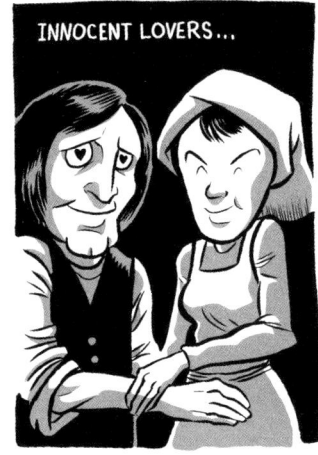

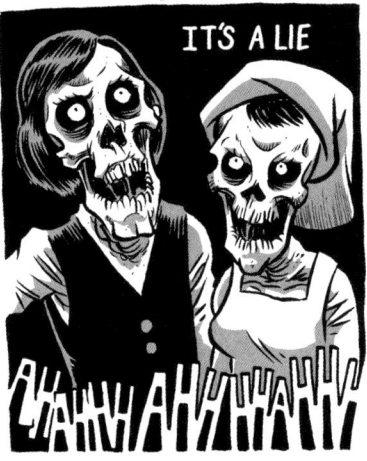

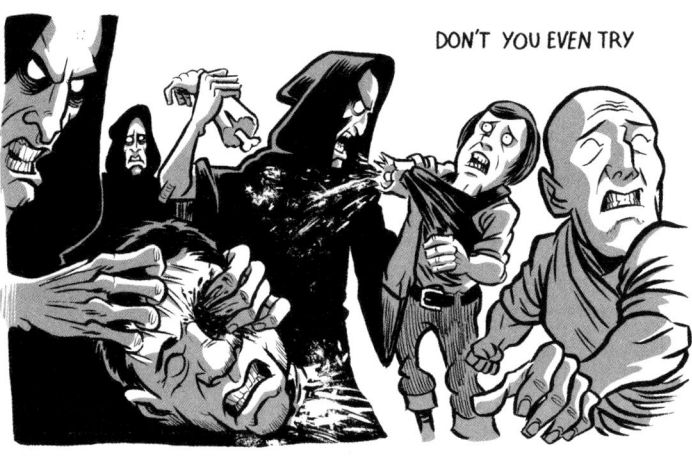

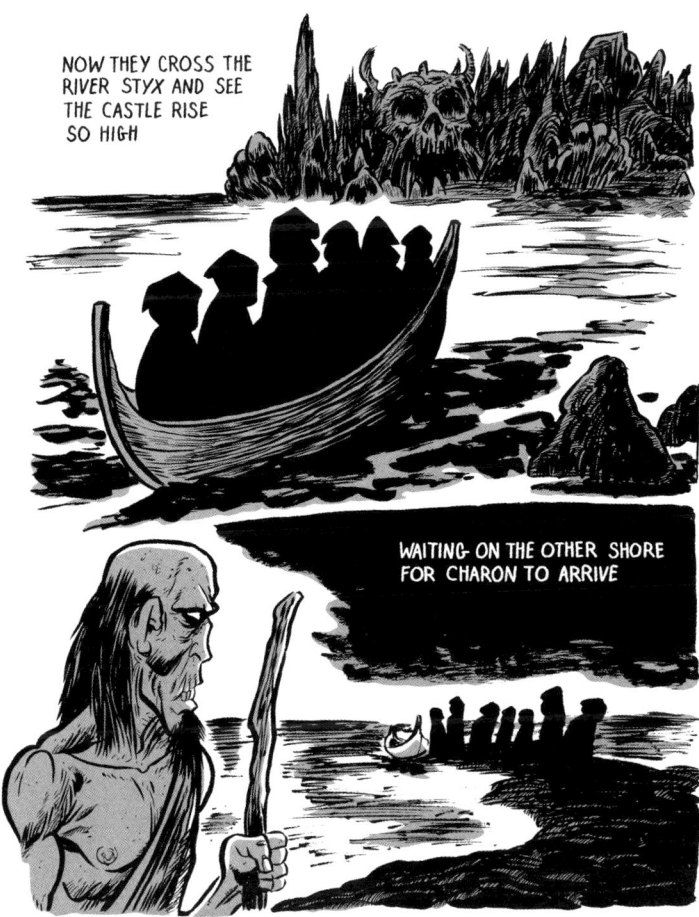

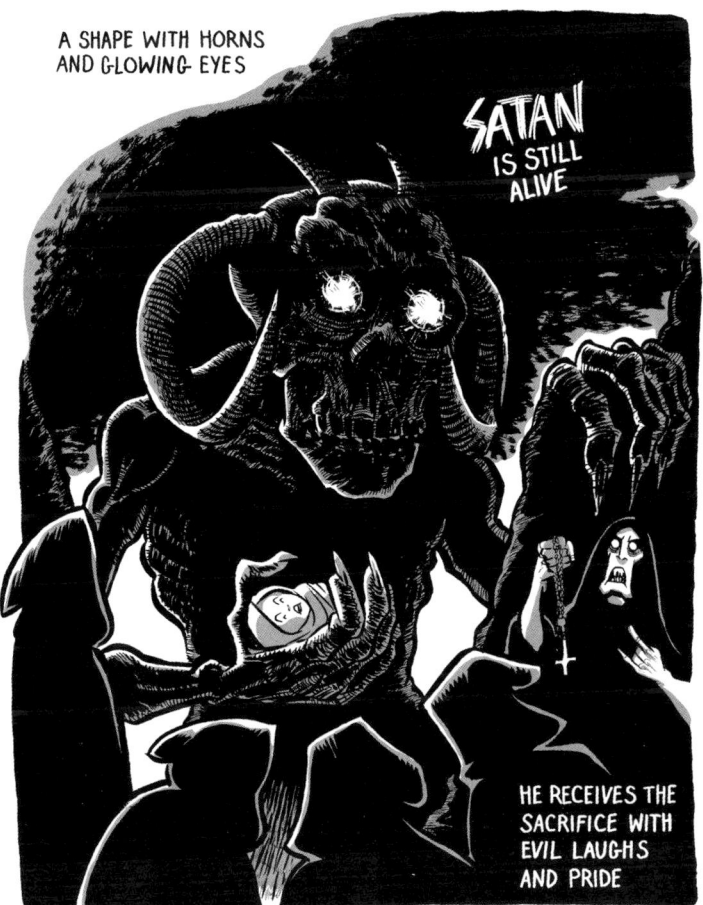

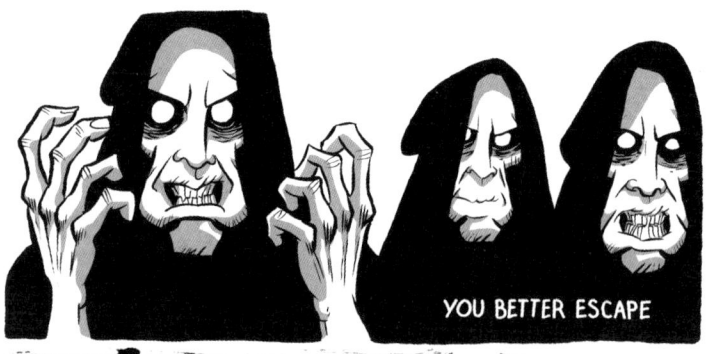

YOU BETTER ESCAPE

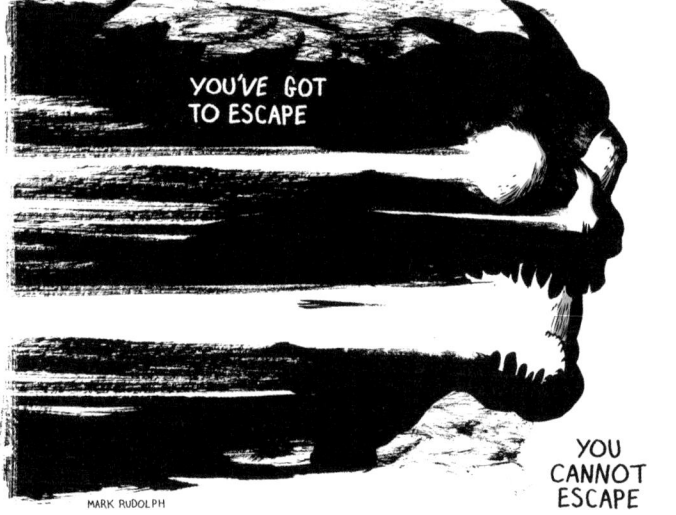

YOU'VE GOT TO ESCAPE

YOU CANNOT ESCAPE

MARK RUDOLPH

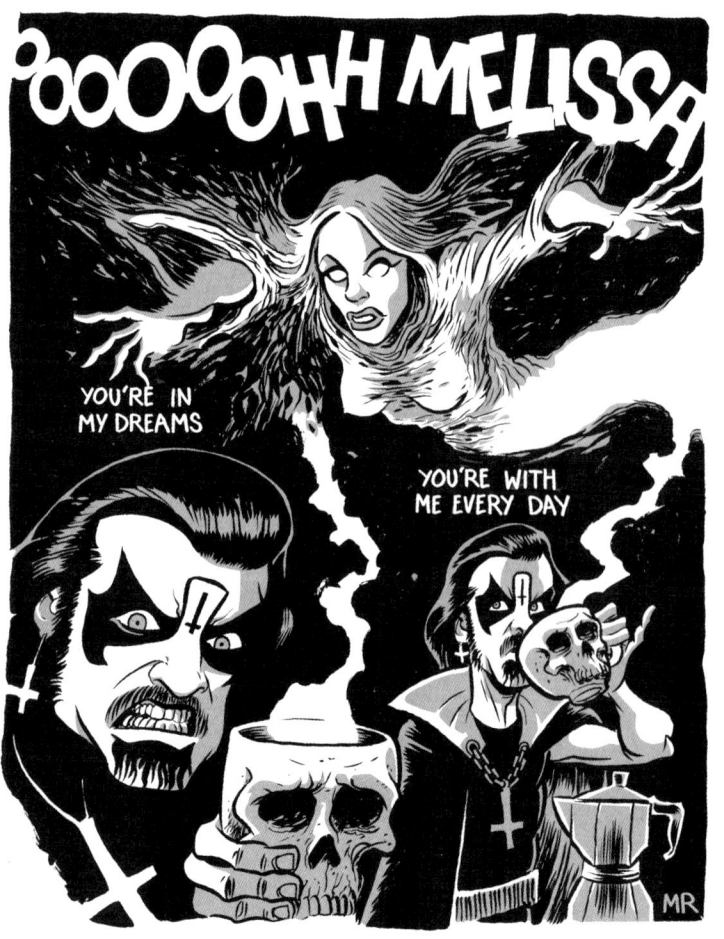

POOOOOHH MELISSA

YOU'RE IN MY DREAMS

YOU'RE WITH ME EVERY DAY

MR

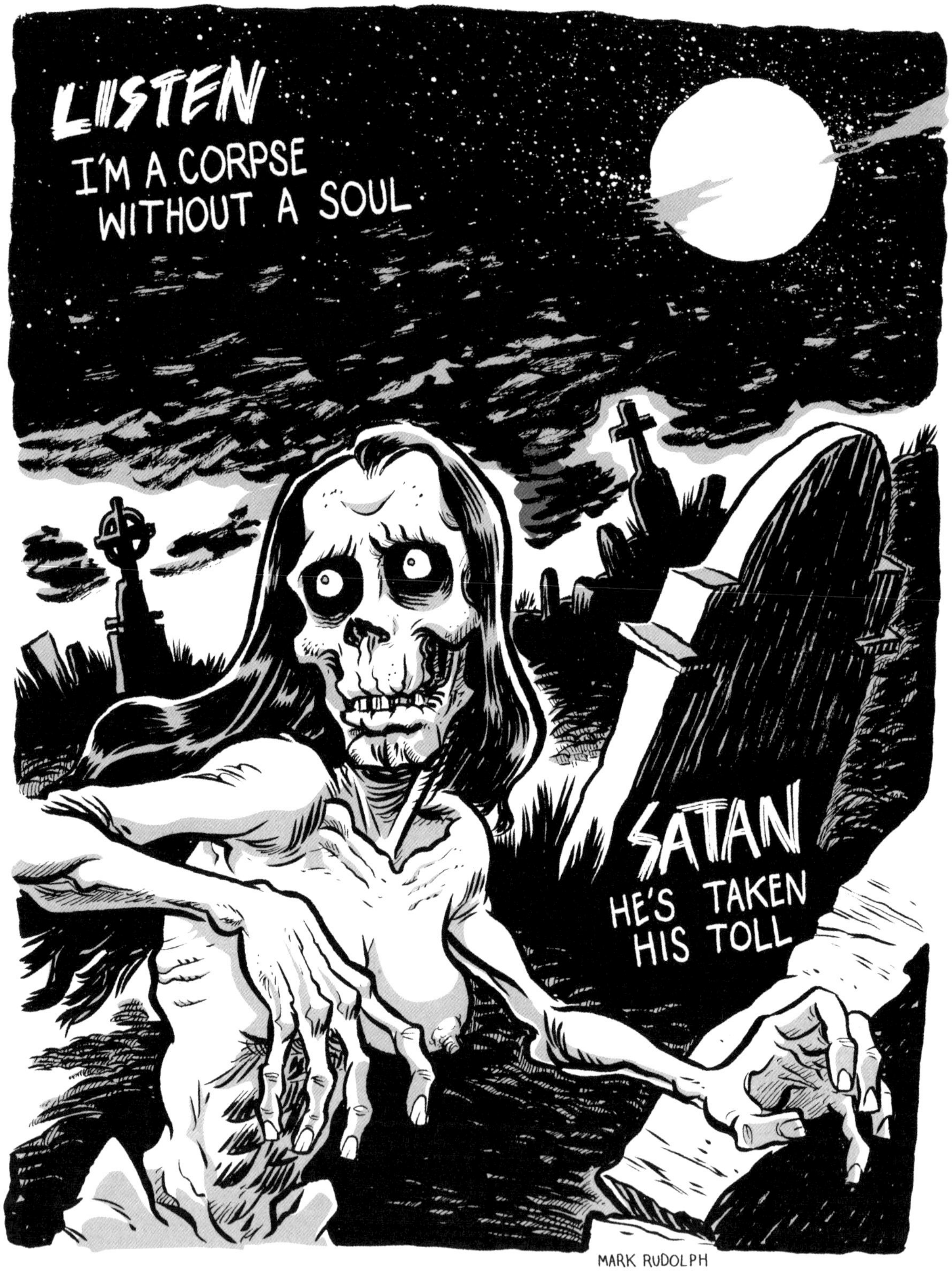

LISTEN

I'M A CORPSE WITHOUT A SOUL

SATAN HE'S TAKEN HIS TOLL

MARK RUDOLPH

ABOVE: CORPSE WITHOUT A SOUL (2012)
First page of a comic based on the lyrics of the Mercyful Fate song, *Corpse Without a Soul*.
LEFT: MELISSA COFFEE (2012)
A filler gag page for the book.

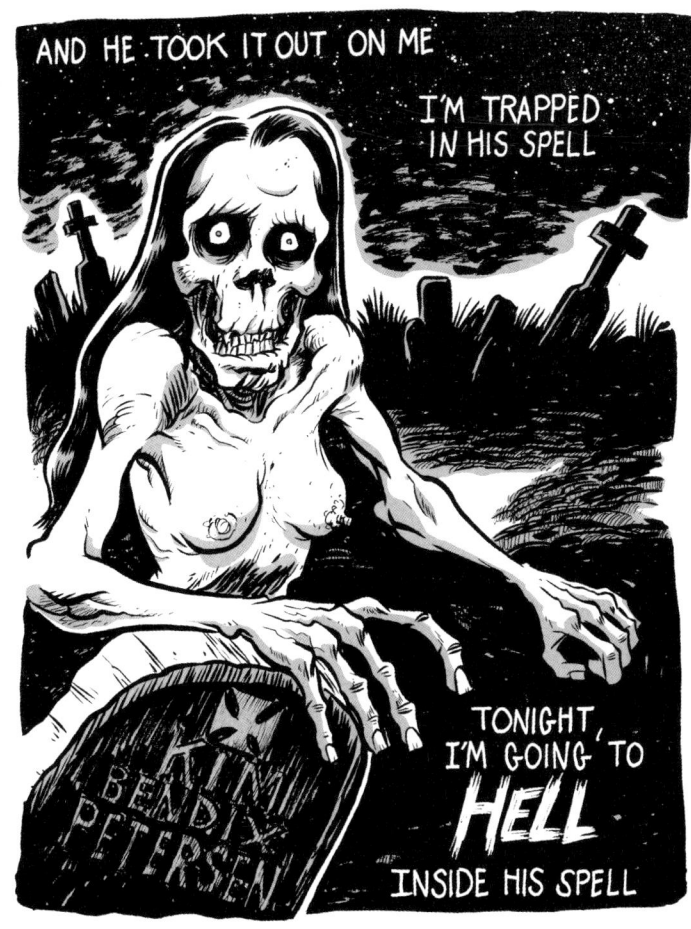

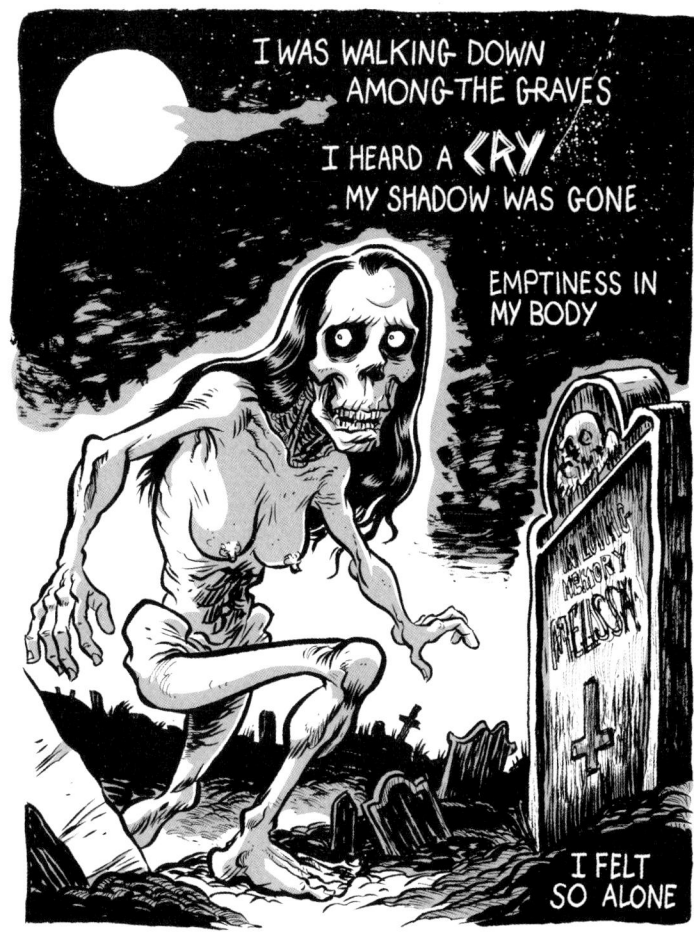

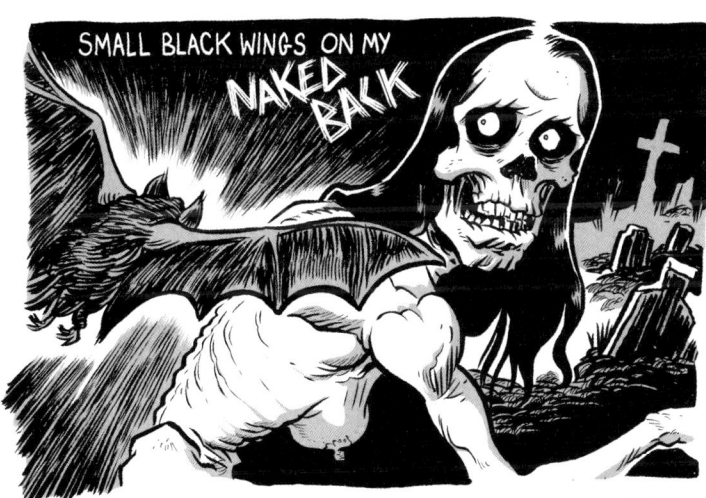

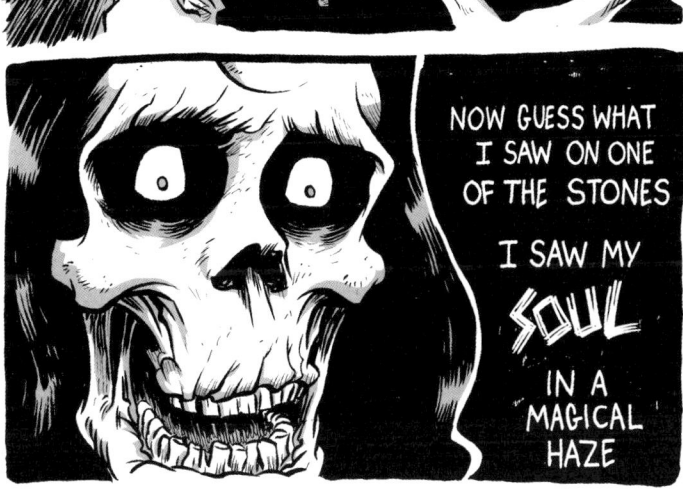

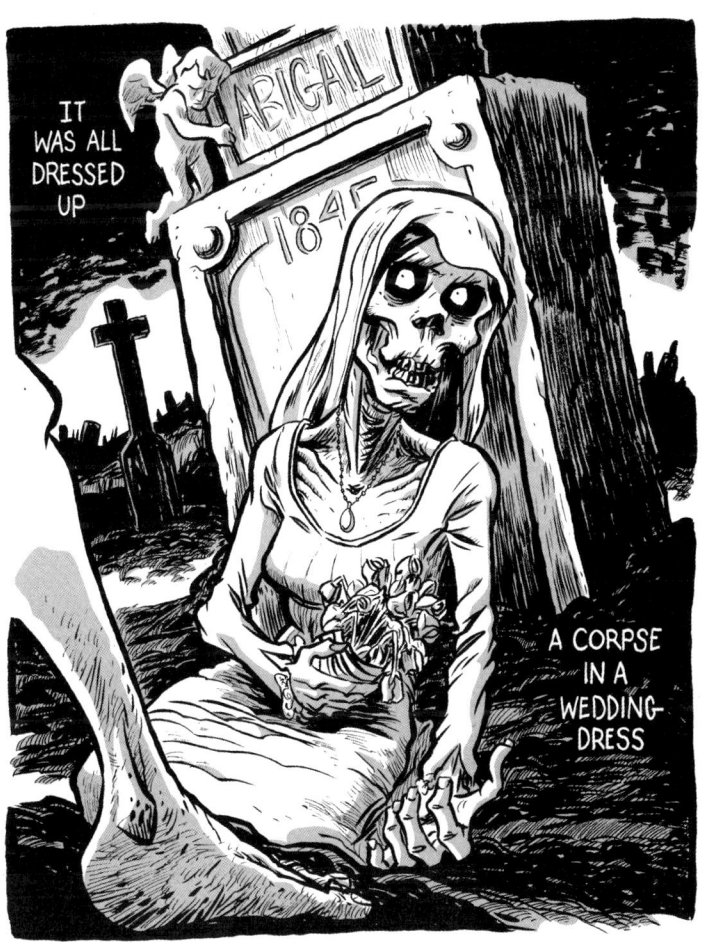

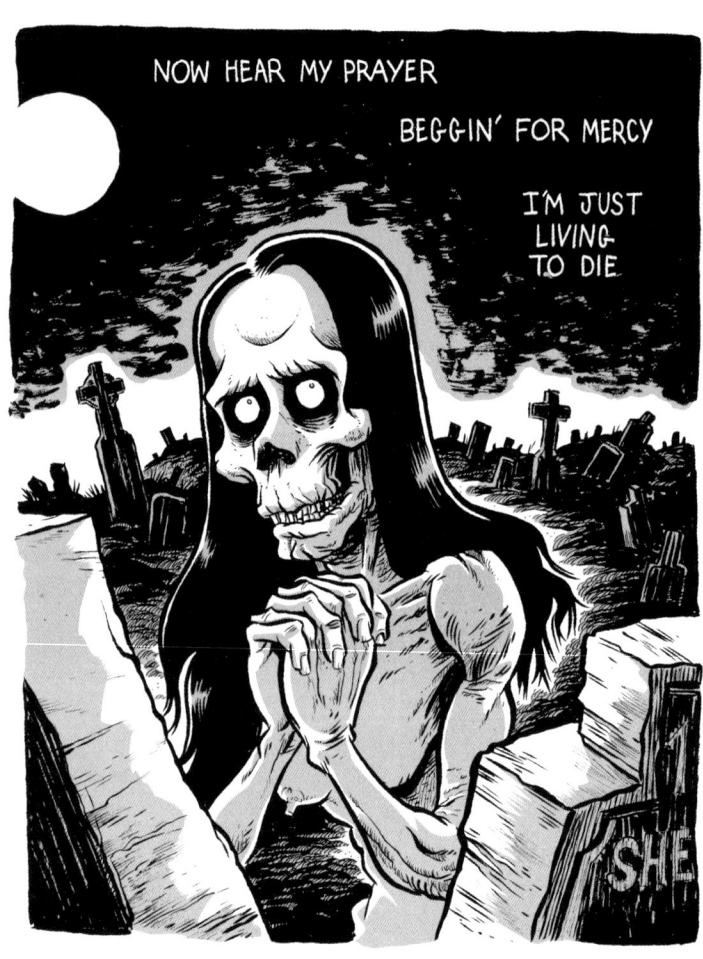

NOW HEAR MY PRAYER

BEGGIN' FOR MERCY

I'M JUST LIVING TO DIE

SHE

RIGHT: THE KING (2012)
A page from the Satan is Alive book and an advertisement for the book.

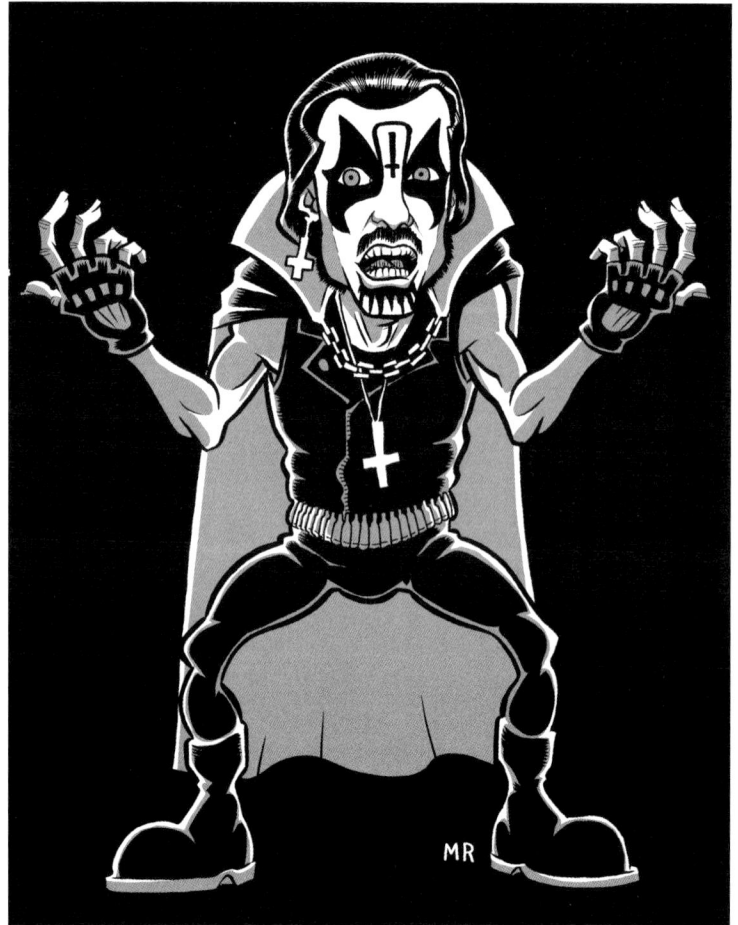

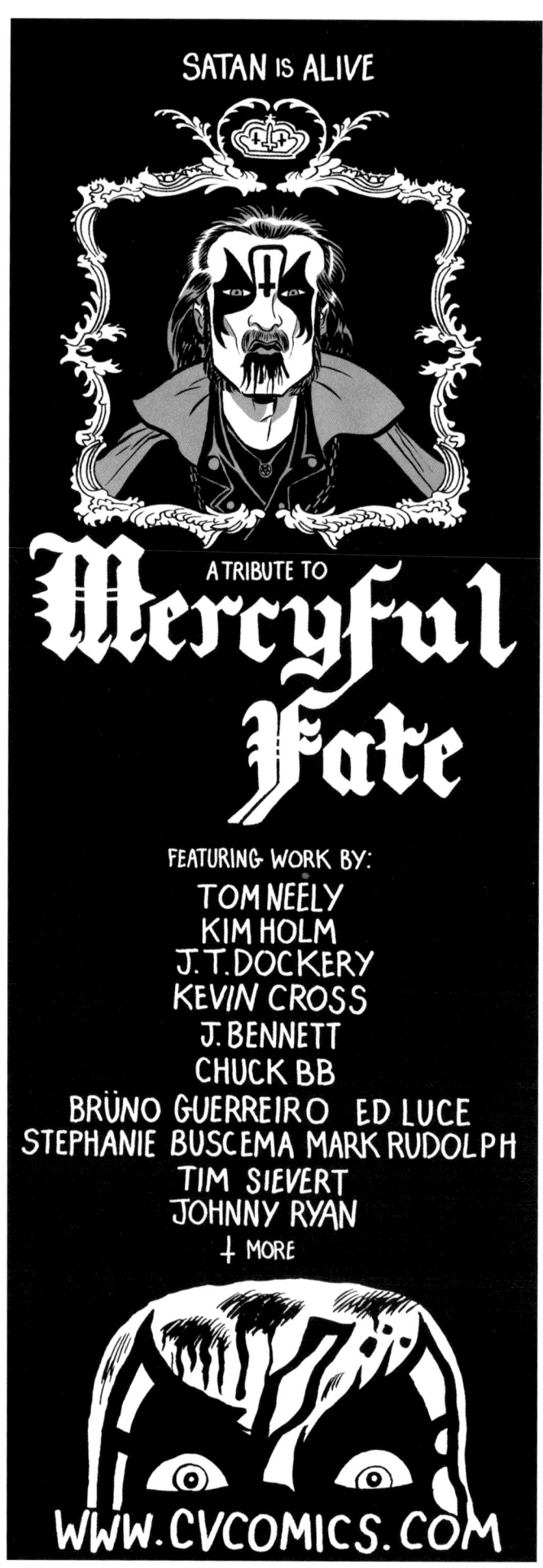

SATAN IS ALIVE

A TRIBUTE TO

Mercyful Fate

FEATURING WORK BY:

TOM NEELY
KIM HOLM
J.T. DOCKERY
KEVIN CROSS
J. BENNETT
CHUCK BB
BRÜNO GUERREIRO   ED LUCE
STEPHANIE BUSCEMA MARK RUDOLPH
TIM SIEVERT
JOHNNY RYAN
+ MORE

WWW.CVCOMICS.COM

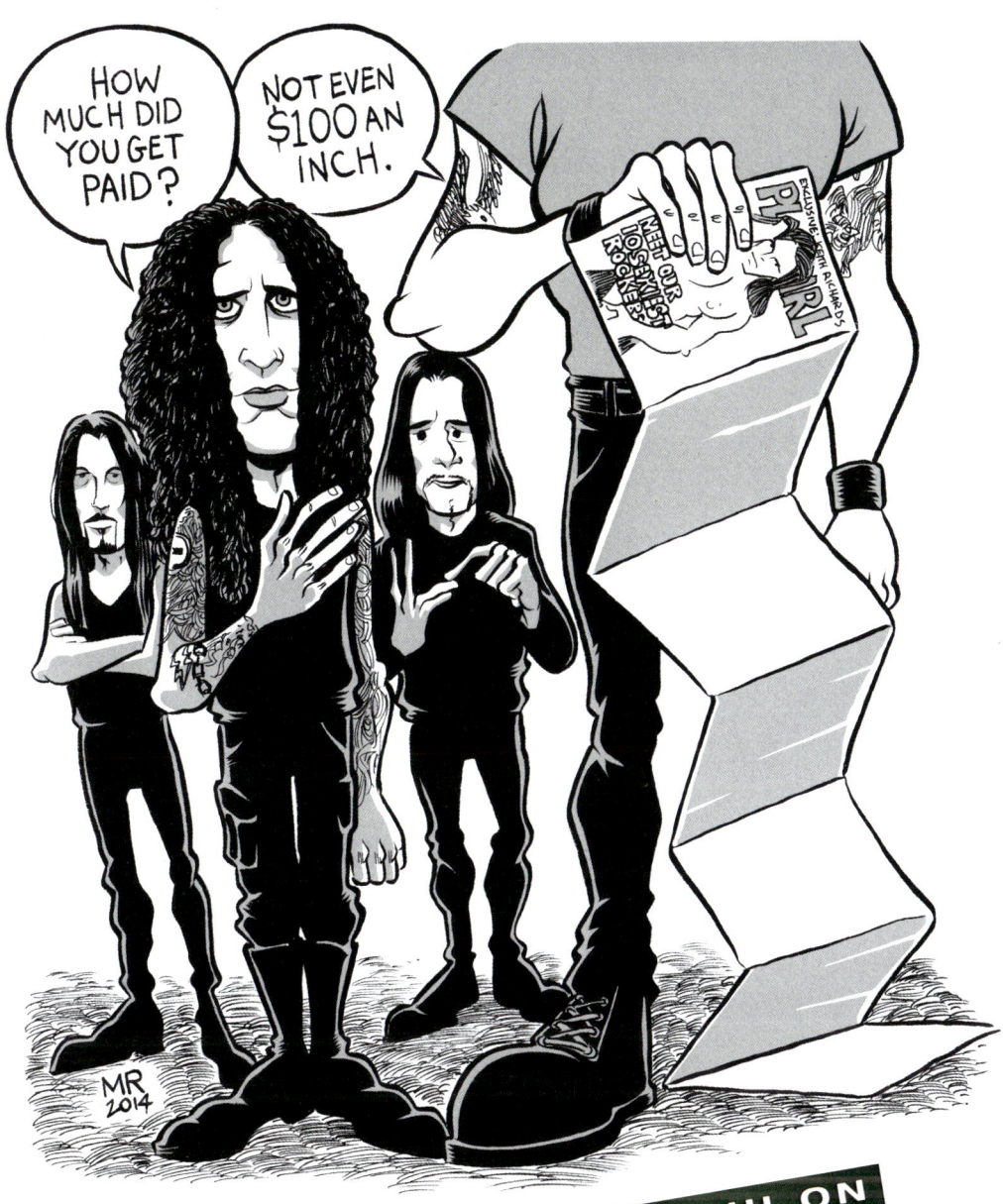

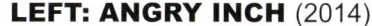

LEFT: ANGRY INCH (2014)
An illustration for the book *Soul On Fire - The Life And Music Of Peter Steele* by Jeff Wagner.
BELOW: OAF CRUSH (2014)
All of the Oaf's metal crushes. A pin-up for The Wuvable Oaf collected volume from Fantagraphic.
Includes: Steve Harris, Kevin Sharp, Kerry King, Rob Halford, GG Allin, Abbath, Horgh, Scotty Ian, Cronos, Eddie, Trevor Strnad, Vinnie Paul, King Diamond, Zakk Wylde, Kirk Windstein, Johan Hegg and a few others.

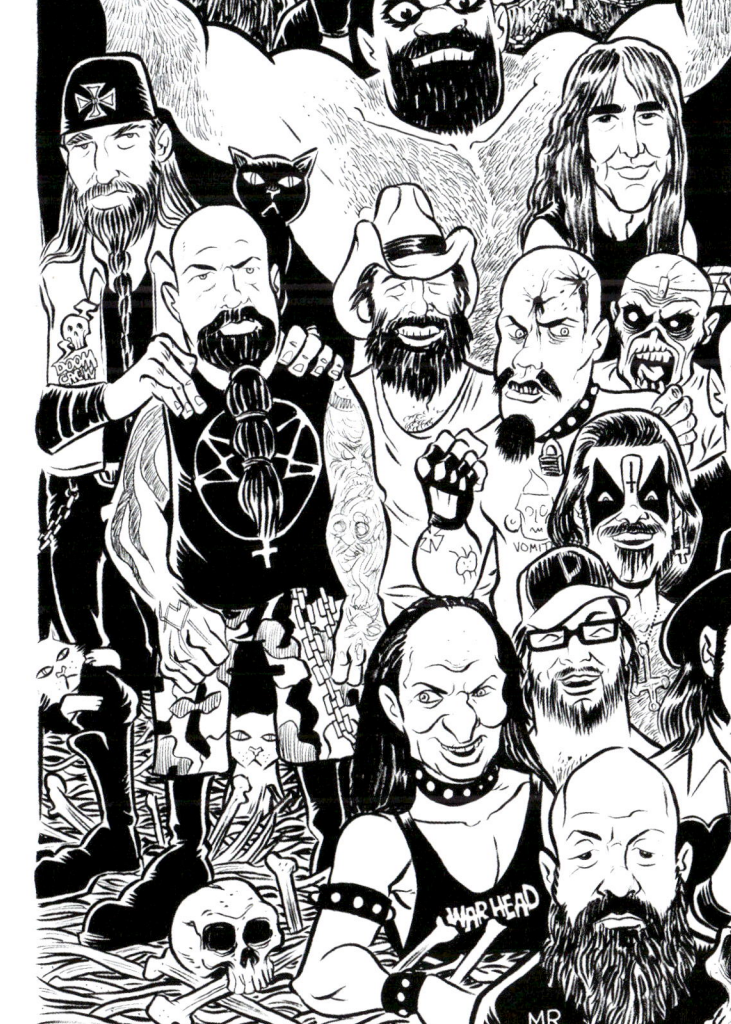

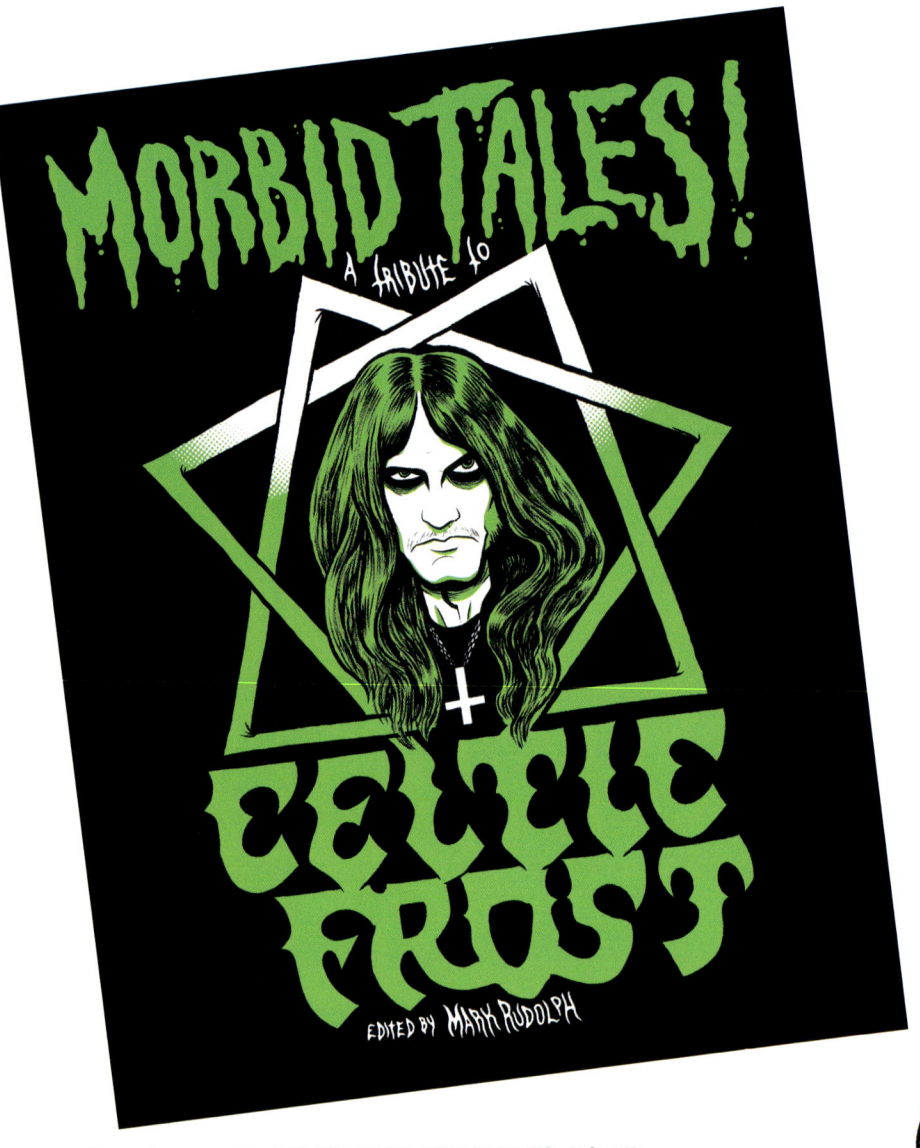

MORBID TALES!

A tribute to

CELTIC FROST

EDITED BY MARK RUDOLPH

I THINK **CELTIC FROST** IS ONE OF THE MOST INNOVATIVE HEAVY METAL BANDS OF ALL TIME. IN THE MID 80s I WAS TOTALLY INFLUENCED BY THEIR AVANTGARDE ATTITUDE. MORE OVER THEY OPENED MY INTEREST TOWARDS EXPERIMENTAL MUSIC AS WELL, WITH SONGS LIKE **DANSE MACABRE**. I CAN ONLY SAY A HUGE THANKS FOR **TOM G. WARRIOR** AND HIS BANDS FOR THE ETERNAL INSPIRATION!

ATTILA CSIHAR
MAYHEM

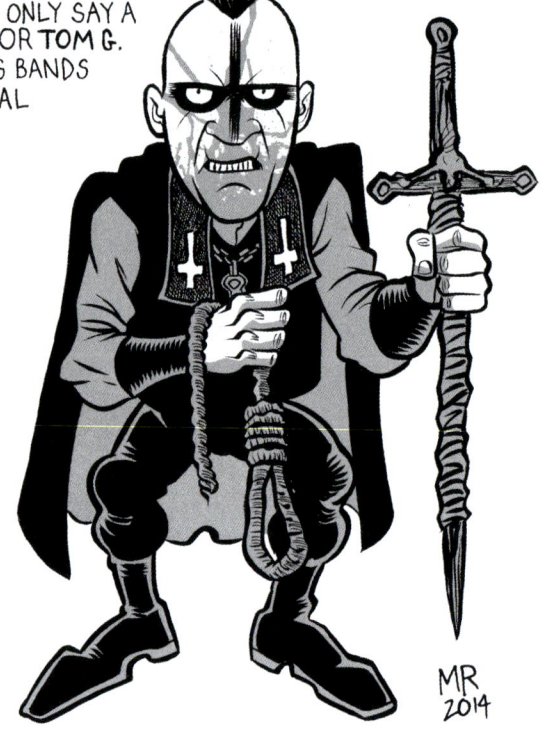

THOSE OF US WHO WERE ALREADY HIP TO **HELLHAMMER** AND THE DISSOLUTION THEREOF, WAITED WITH MAGGOT-BAITED BREATH FOR THE REBIRTH IN THE FORM OF **CELTIC FROST**. WHEN OUR EARS WERE TREATED TO THE RESULT, IT WAS A GLORIOUS THING. THOSE STRANGLED GUITARS, THOSE MANGLED VOCALS, THAT THUDDING BASS, THOSE CHOPPING BLOCK DRUMS... THAT SOUND! WE KNEW WE WERE IN GOOD HANDS, EVEN THOUGH THEY REACHED OUT TO CHOKE THE VERY LIFE OUT OF US AS WE LISTENED. DARKNESS ENSUED AND WE WERE TREATED TO THE SENSATION OF WATCHING THE ASHES OF OUR DISTORTION PUMMELED SKULLS FALL BEFORE OUR EYES INTO A SEA OF UTTER DESOLATION AND MORBIDITY. THE REAPER HAD COME AND THE SOUNDTRACK WAS PERFECT.

CHRIS REIFERT
AUTOPSY

I FIRST BECAME AWARE OF **CELTIC FROST** IN THE MID-80s WITH **MORBID TALES**. PRIOR TO THIS, I WAS PRIMARILY INTO PUNK MUSIC. A FEW OF THE PUNK BANDS I WAS INTO STARTED TO CROSS-OVER INTO METAL SLIGHTLY--SOME OF THIS BEING DUBBED CRUST. WHEN I HEARD **MORBID TALES** AND THEN RETROACTIVELY **APOCALYPTIC RAIDS** AND THE **HELLHAMMER** MATERIAL, I WAS ASTONISHED. TO ME, THIS REALLY BRIDGED THE GAP THAT EXISTED BETWEEN THE PUNK AND THE EXTREME METAL GENRES PERFECTLY. MY PATH IN MUSIC MAY HAVE BEEN COMPLETELY DIFFERENT WITHOUT THIS INTERVENTION, AND IT OPENED MY EYES TO DIFFERENT STYLES OF MUSIC THAT OTHERWISE I MAY HAVE IGNORED.

GREG MACKINTOSH
PARADISE LOST / VALLENFYRE

**ABOVE LEFT:
MORBID TALES** (2014)
The cover to the Celtic Frost tribute book, *Morbid Tales.* The other images are caricatures and testimonials that appeared in the book.

I WAS JUST ANOTHER HEAVY METAL KID INTO **PRIEST** AND **KISS** WHEN I BORROWED THREE ALBUMS I'D NEVER HEARD ABOUT BEFORE FROM A NEW FRIEND: ETERNAL DEVASTATION, HELL AWAITS AND MORBID TALES. **DESTRUCTION** AND **SLAYER** WERE OF COURSE MINDBLOWINGLY AWESOME IN THEIR OWN RIGHT, MAKING ME TEAR DOWN MY **IRON MAIDEN** POSTERS IN MINUTES. BUT **FROST** WAS ANOTHER BEAST ENTIRELY. THERE WAS SOMETHING BEYOND THE SHEER POWER OF THE MUSIC, SOMETHING ANCIENT, MYSTICAL AND HOWARDESIAN / LOVECRAFTESQUE THAT PROPELLED MY FRAGILE TEEN MIND INTO TWISTED WORLDS OF MACABRE GODS AND FORGOTTEN DREAMS.

'AND THE PERFECT CREATION CALLS. WHAT WILL THE WIND BRING THESE DAYS?'

WHAT, INDEED? WE LIVE IN A TIME WHEN EVERY KID AND HIS GRANDMA CAN RECORD THEIR BAND PROFESSIONALLY ON A LAPTOP, AUTOTUNE VOCALS AND TRIGGER THE DRUMS, OR REACH MILLIONS ON A METAL BLOG. TO ME, THE STRENGTH (AND OH, WHAT POWER THEY HELD) OF **CELTIC FROST** WAS ACTUALLY IN THEIR TECHNICAL SHORTCOMINGS, AND HOW THEY CONQUERED THEM. IT WAS NEVER ABOUT VIRTUOSITY OR SEASONED PROFESSIONALISM, BUT BENDING ALL YOUR LIMITATIONS TO YOUR WILL AND FROM THEM CRAFT SOME OF THE MOST CRUSHING AND MAJESTIC MUSIC THIS PLANET HAS EVER HEARD. I HONESTLY THINK WE SHOULD STOP GIVING INSTRUMENT LESSONS TO KIDS. JUST GIVE THEM A COPY OF MORBID TALES AND LOCK THEM IN A ROOM WITH A STEREO AND SOME OLD **SAVAGE SWORD** OF **CONAN** COMICS. THE WORLD OF MUSIC WILL NEVER BE THE SAME AGAIN.

ORVAR SÄFSTRÖM
NIRVANA 2002

HEARING **TRIUMPH OF DEATH** FROM **HELLHAMMER** FOR THE FIRST TIME REALLY MOLDED ME AS A MUSICIAN. THE FIRST MINUTE FOR EXAMPLE, APOCALYPTIC BENDS AND FEEDBACK AND THOSE SCREAMS SET THE BAR FOR HOW BRUTAL YOU CAN MAKE MUSIC. THEN CAME **CELTIC FROST** AND NOW **TRIPTYKON**, TOM G. IS JUST A GENIUS. UPON FINDING OUT THAT ALL THIS DARKNESS AND PAIN CAME FROM A REAL PLACE, HIM GROWING UP AS A CHILD UNDER SUCH HARSH CONDITIONS REALLY MAKES THE MUSIC EVEN MORE INTENSE. MY BAND **EVOKEN** WOULD NOT EXIST WITHOUT MR. WARRIOR SHOWING ME HOW IT'S DONE. I WILL FOREVER BE IN THAT MAN'S DEBT.

ONLY DEATH IS REAL.

JOHN PARADISO
EVOKEN

TRUE TESTIMONIAL
(2014) Some other testimonials from the Morbid Tales book.

I BELIEVE THAT IF YOU, AS AN ARTIST, REALLY WRENCH YOUR SOUL AND LAY IT ALL OUT IN YOUR ART, IT WILL SHINE THROUGH AND BE VISIBLE FOR THE SPECTATORS SO THAT THEY CAN CONNECT AND RESONATE WITH IT. BUT SELDOM HAS AN ARTIST GIVEN ME SUCH A STRONG FEELING THAN THE WORK OF LEGEND TOM G. WARRIOR. THE HAUNTING **HELLHAMMER**, THE COMPLEX **CELTIC FROST** AND THE TREMENDOUS **TRIPTYKON** ARE ALL FILLED WITH TRACE OF BARE SOULS LAYING NAKED FOR THE WORLD TO HURT AND HACK ON, OR TO EMBRACE AND ENJOY. THE COURAGE IT TAKES FOR A PERSON TO DO SUCH A THING YEAR AFTER YEAR, ALBUM AFTER ALBUM, IS NOTHING BUT INSPIRING AND RESPECTABLE. TOM WAS THE FIRST ARTIST I SENSED THIS WITH, AND HIS WORK OPENED THIS 'PORTAL' INTO MY MIND, SO THAT I STARTED LOOKING FOR IT IN ALL THE ART I EXPLORE.

THIS HAS BECOME THE BLUEPRINT IN MY ARTISTIC TASTE AND IS ALSO THE ONLY WAY I WANT TO CREATE ART MYSELF. WHEN PEOPLE TALK ABOUT 'TRUE' IT IS MY OPINION THAT YOU ARE TRUE TO YOURSELF, YOUR SOUL AND YOUR BLACK HEART. TO ME, **TOM G. WARRIOR** HAS PROVEN THROUGH ALL HIS ART THAT HE HAS A 'TRUE BLACK HEART.'

RAVN 1349

CELTIC FROST 'S HEAVY, MORBID, YET CATCHY SONGS ARE AMONG THE MOST INFLUENTIAL IN ALL OF METAL HISTORY. BUT TOM G. WARRIOR'S BOLDNESS AND DRIVE HAVE ALWAYS BEEN TWO OF HIS GREATEST STRENGTHS. EVEN AS **HELLHAMMER** WERE STILL LEARNING TO PLAY, THEY HAD TOTALLY PROFESSIONAL LOOKING PRESS RELEASES WITH COOL LOGOS AND ARTWORK FOR BOTH THE BAND AND THEIR **PROWLING DEATH** MANAGEMENT. THEY MADE GARGANTUAN LEAPS FROM STRENGTH TO STRENGTH. 'YOU THINK **HELLHAMMER** IS A JOKE (WRONG!) WHO CAN'T PLAY? LISTEN TO THIS, MOTHERFUCKERS!' AND **CELTIC FROST** IS BORN WITH TWO OF THE GREATEST AND HEAVIEST EPS EVER RELEASED! JUST WHEN WE THOUGHT WE KNEW WHO THEY WERE, THEY RELEASED ALBUM AFTER ALBUM OF SHOCKINGLY BOLD MUSIC. FRENCH HORNS, WALL OF VOODOO COVERS, LOOPS, SPOKEN WORD PIECES -- EVEN A HEAVY HANDED ATTEMPT AT GLAM ROCK ALL CAME IN RAPID SUCCESSION FROM A BAND THAT SHOWED NO FEAR OF JUDGEMENT OR REJECTION BY THE PRESS OR LISTENERS. THEY JUST KEPT ON DOING IT THEIR WAY. WHEN **CELTIC FROST** CAME BACK, THEY COULD HAVE GONE EASY ON THEMSELVES AND PRODUCED **MORBID TALES** 2. INSTEAD, THEY REINVENTED THEMSELVES INTO AN EVEN HEAVIER AND FORWARD-THINKING BAND. TOM HAS CARRIED THIS TRADITION OF NEVER RETREADING OLD WATERS AND ALWAYS CHALLENGING HIMSELF AND HIS LISTENERS WITH **TRIPTYKON**. FOR THIS REASON, I RESPECT EVERY PHASE OF TOM WARRIOR'S CAREER AND I LOOK FORWARD TO HEARING WHAT HE DOES NEXT.

MAY CHAOS REIGN!

SCOTT CARLSON
REPULSION

THE EXORCIST

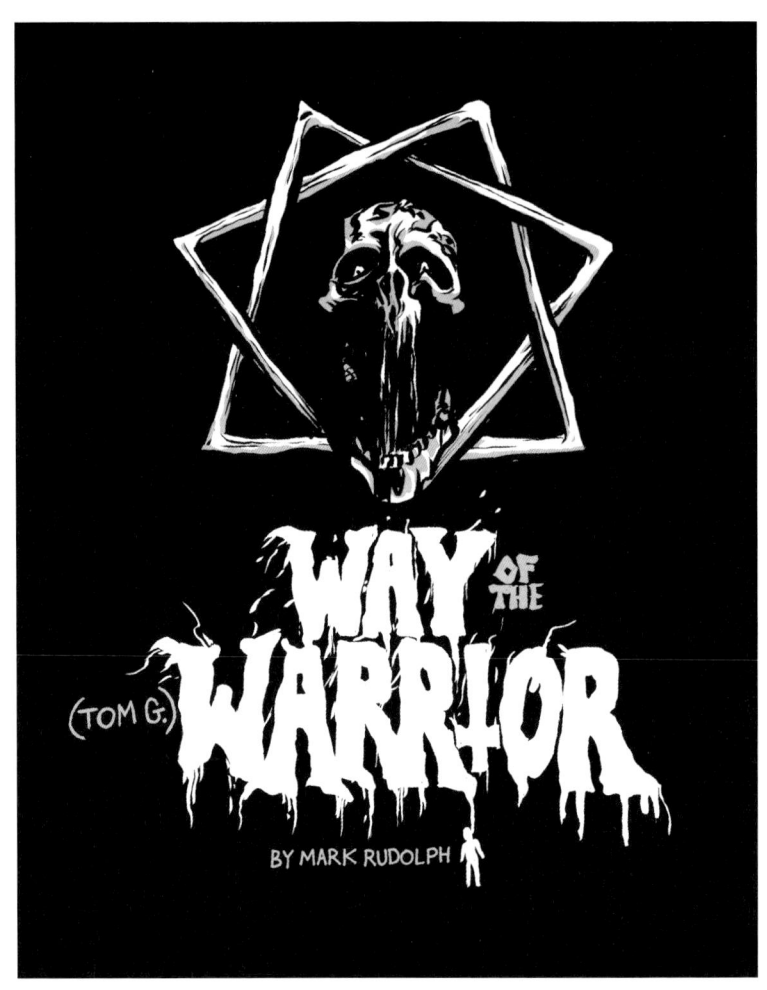

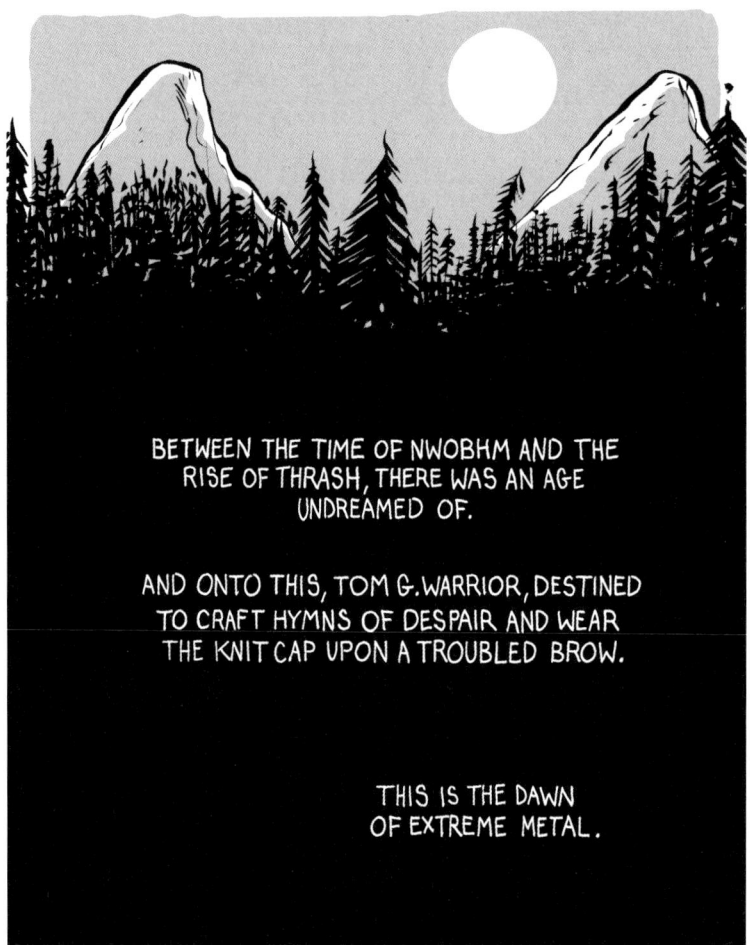

BETWEEN THE TIME OF NWOBHM AND THE RISE OF THRASH, THERE WAS AN AGE UNDREAMED OF.

AND ONTO THIS, TOM G. WARRIOR, DESTINED TO CRAFT HYMNS OF DESPAIR AND WEAR THE KNIT CAP UPON A TROUBLED BROW.

THIS IS THE DAWN OF EXTREME METAL.

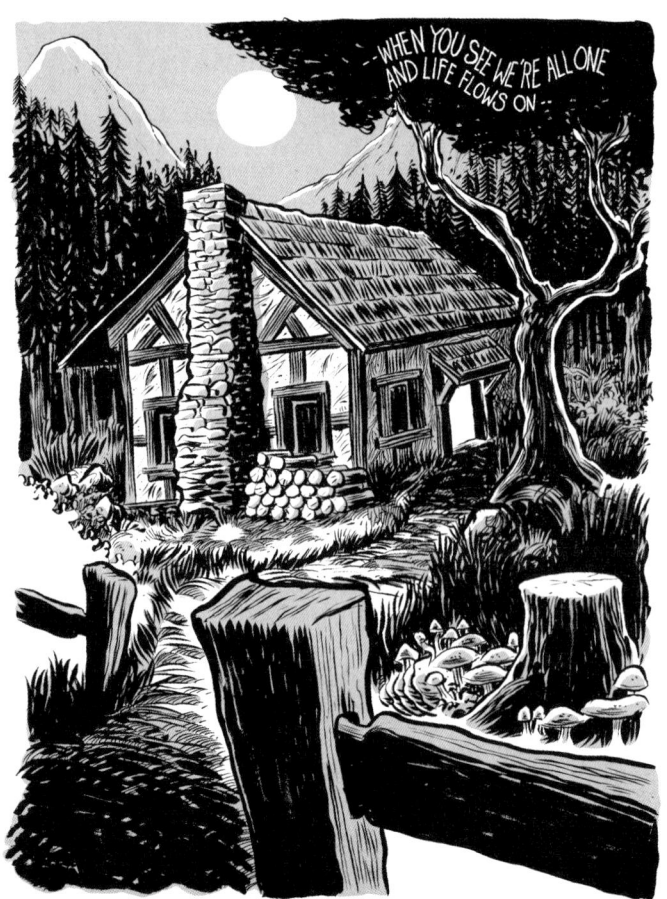

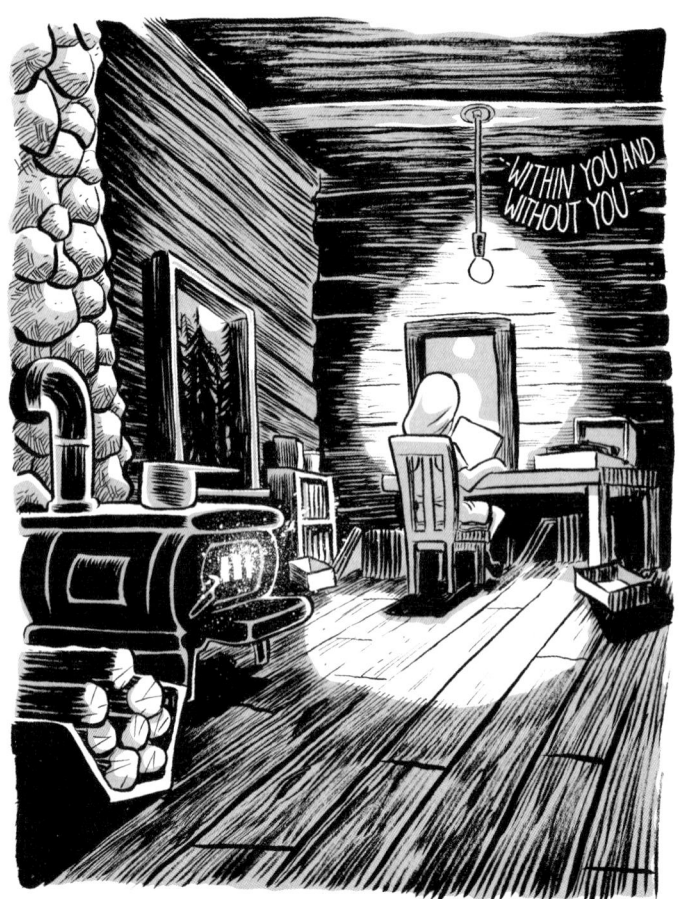

WAY OF THE WARRIOR
(2016)
A comic from Morbid Takes chronicalling the mythic history of Tom G. Warrior.

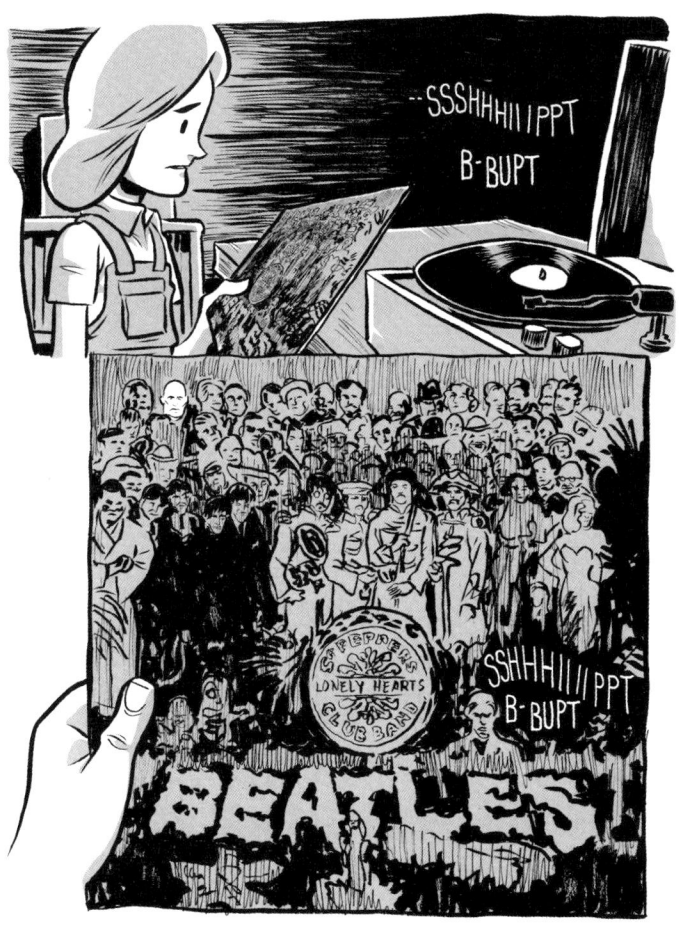

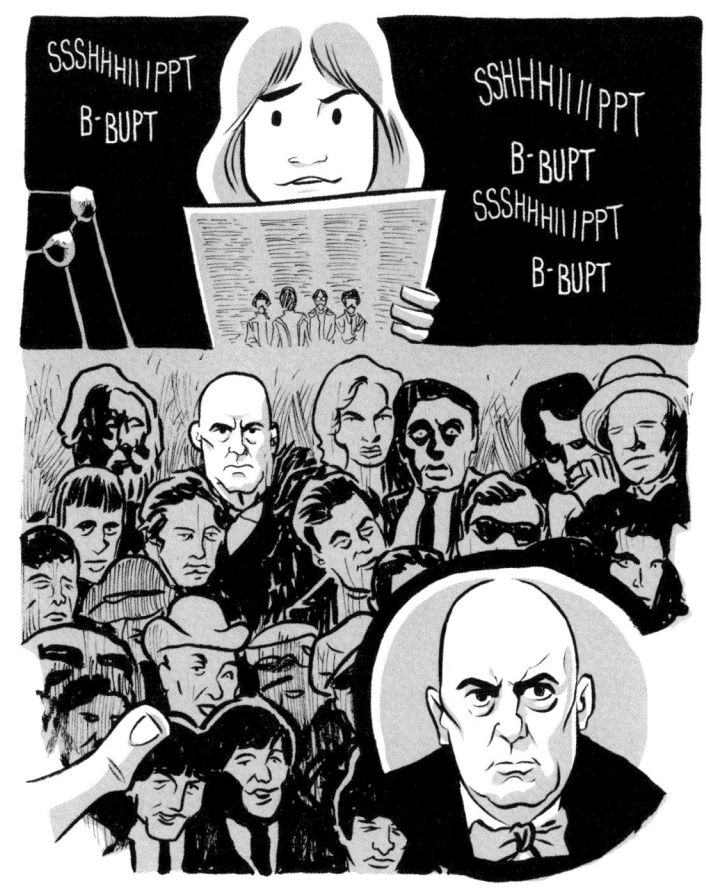

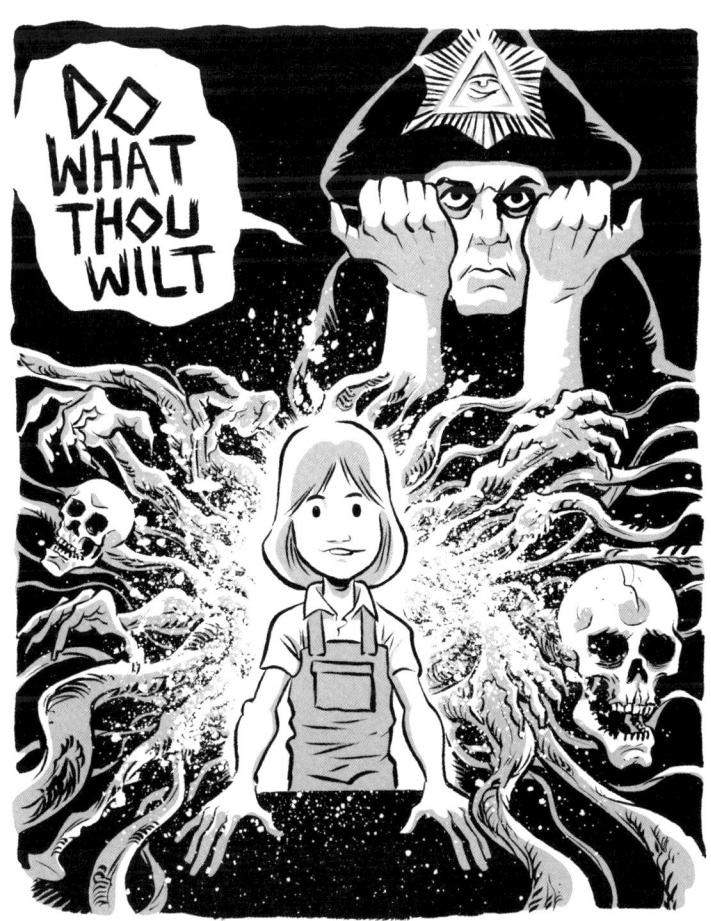

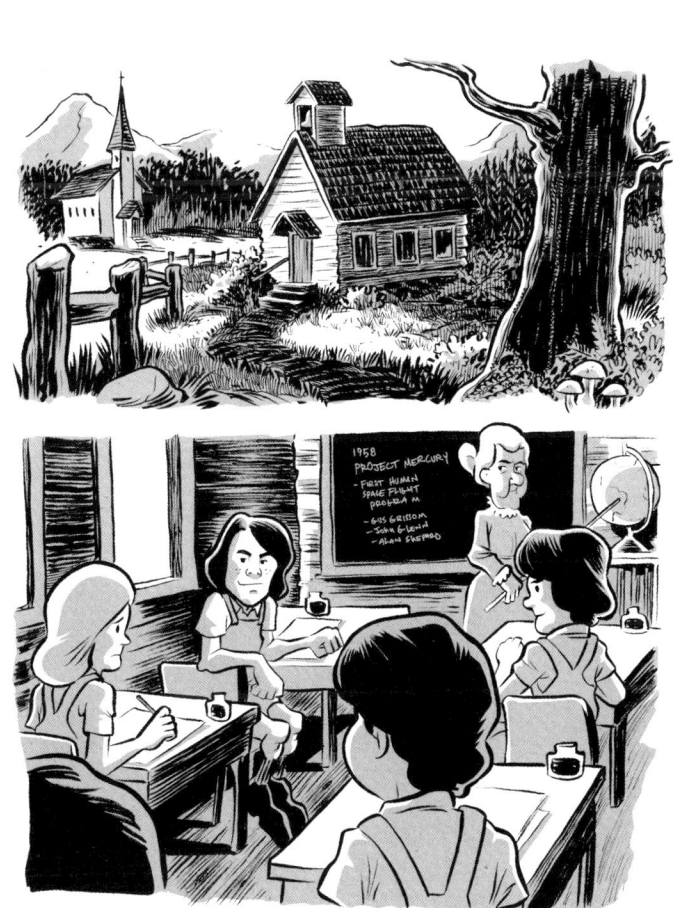

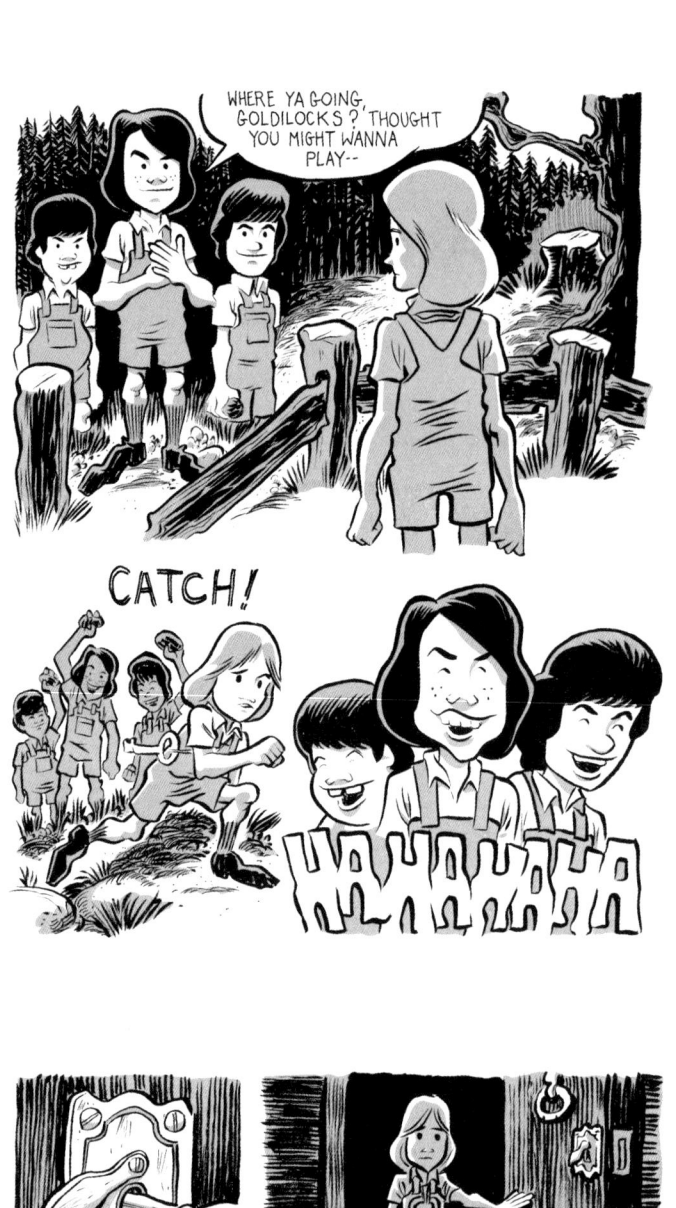

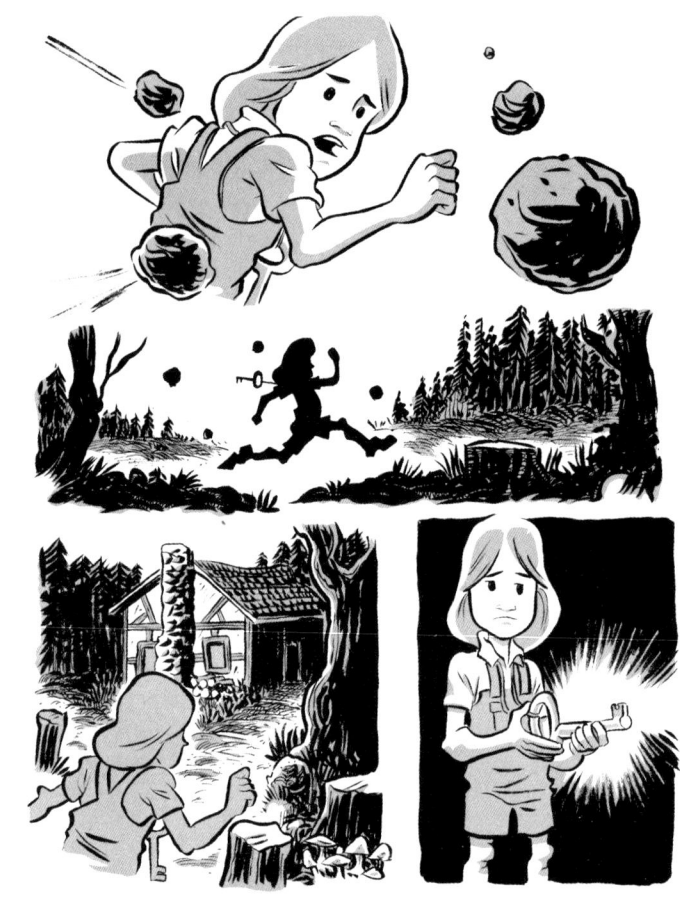

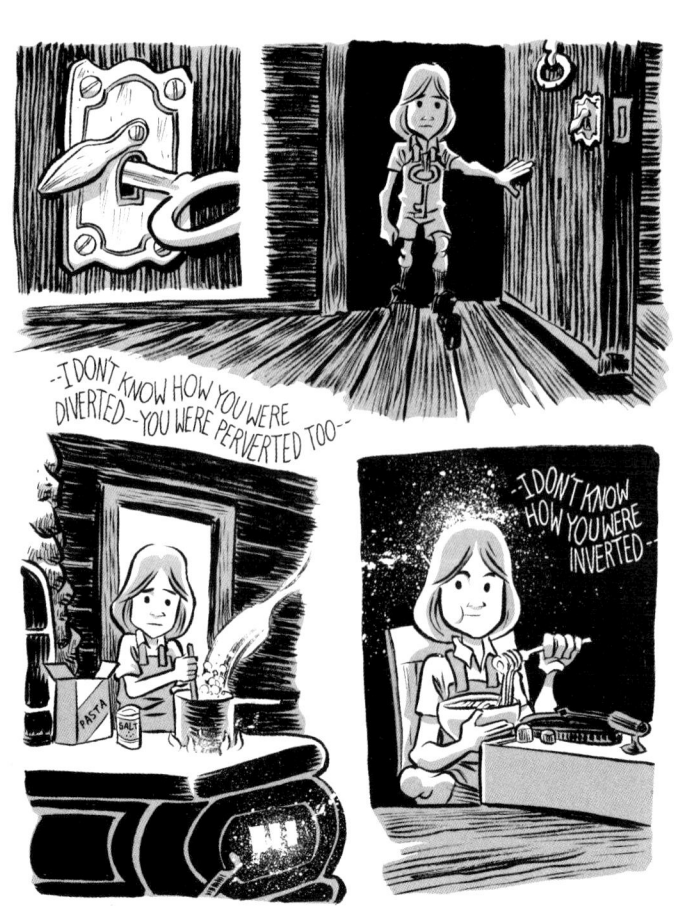

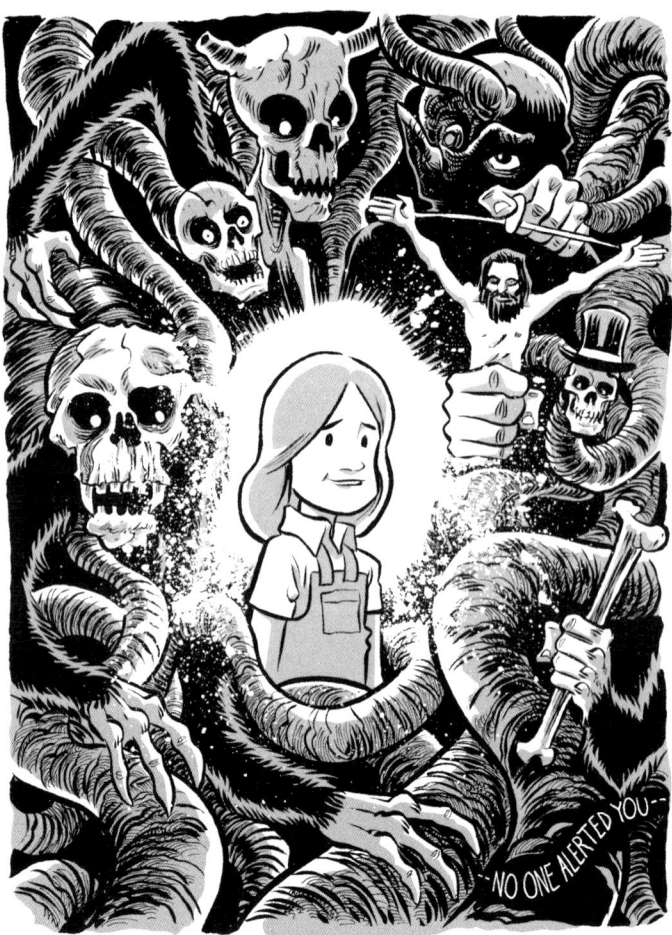

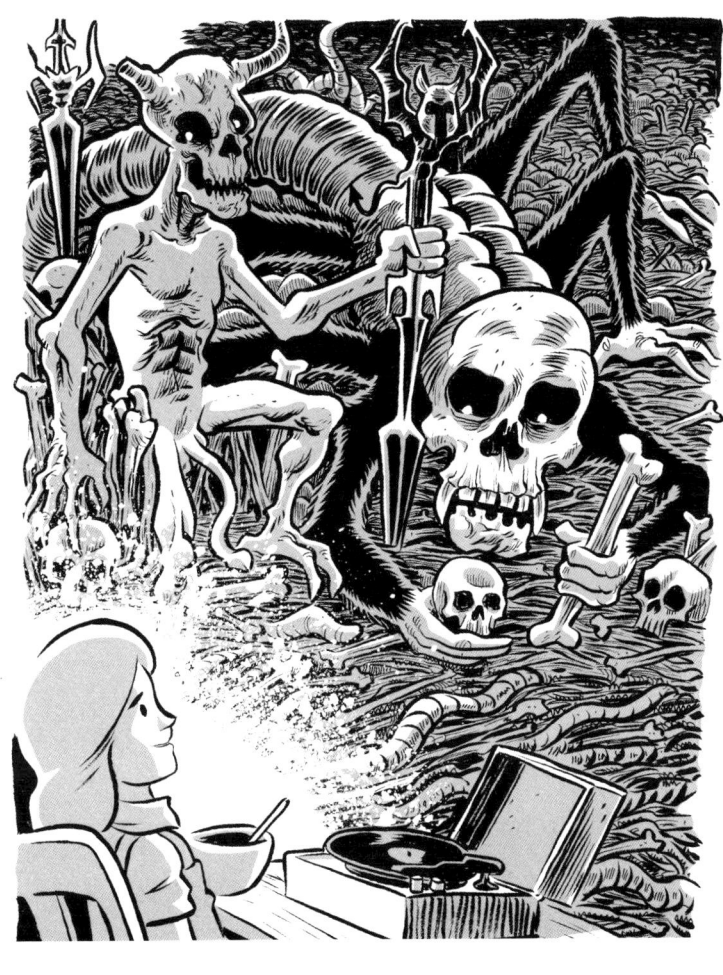

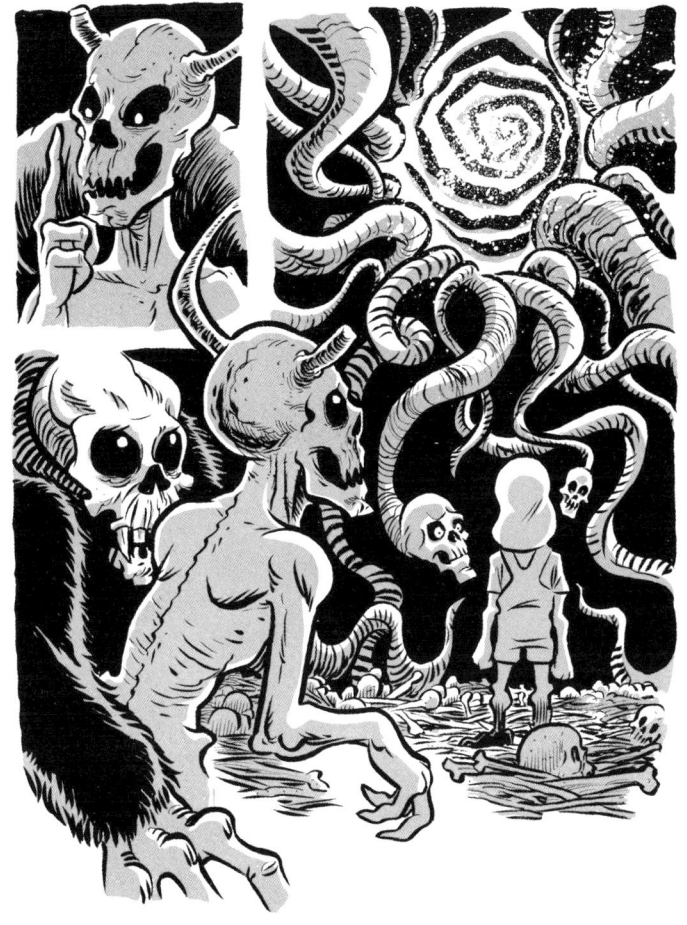

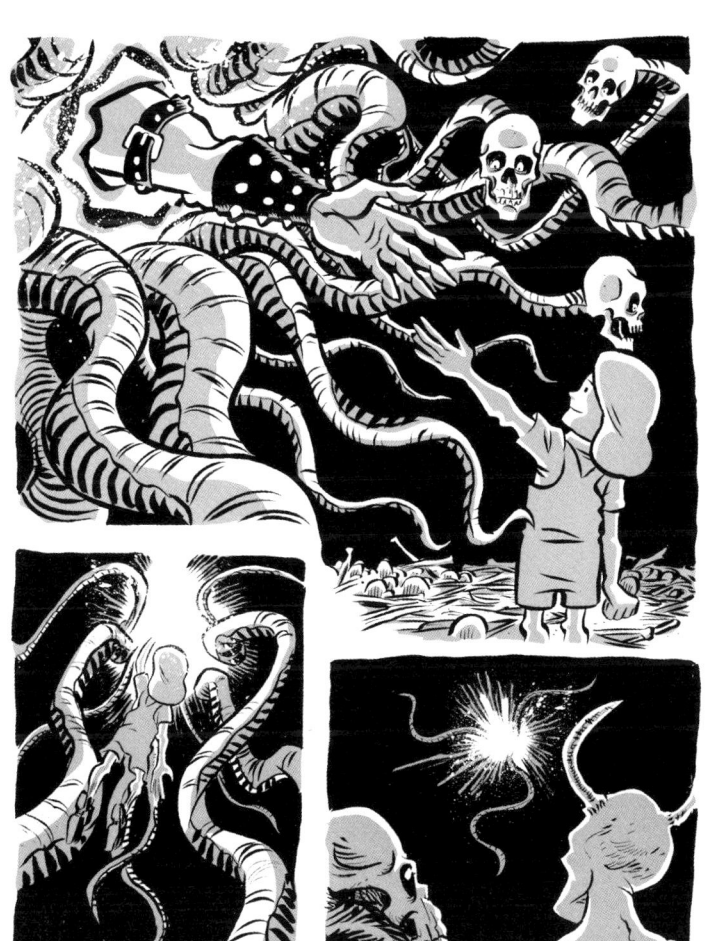

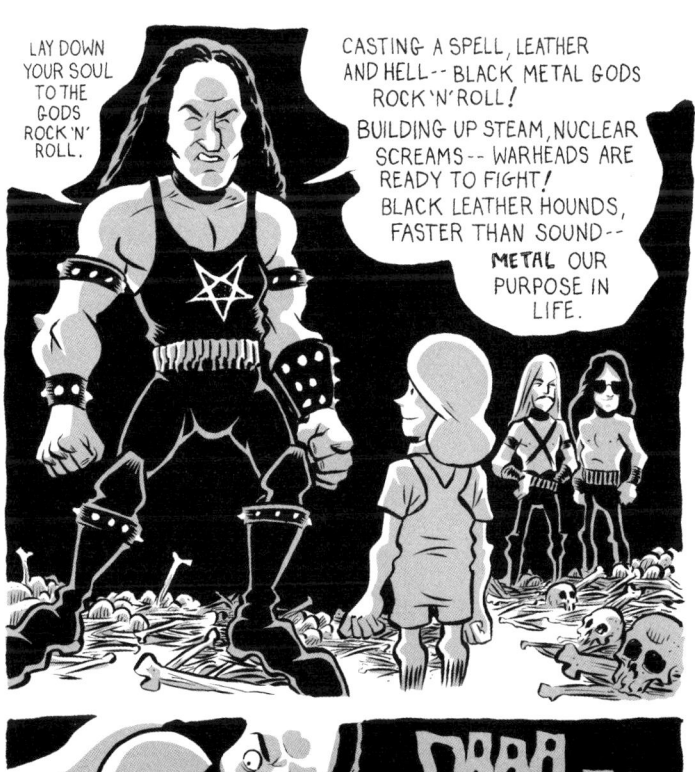

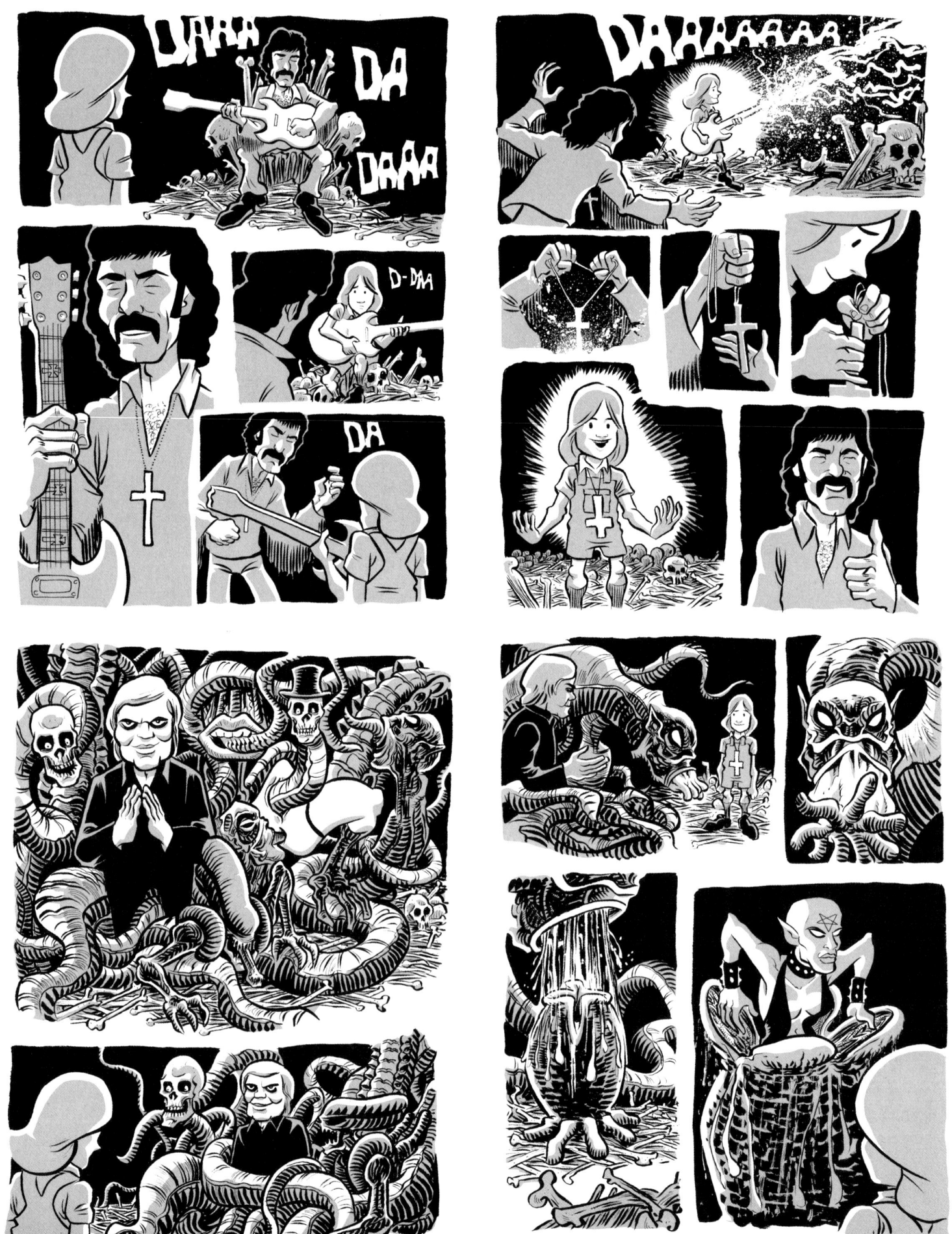

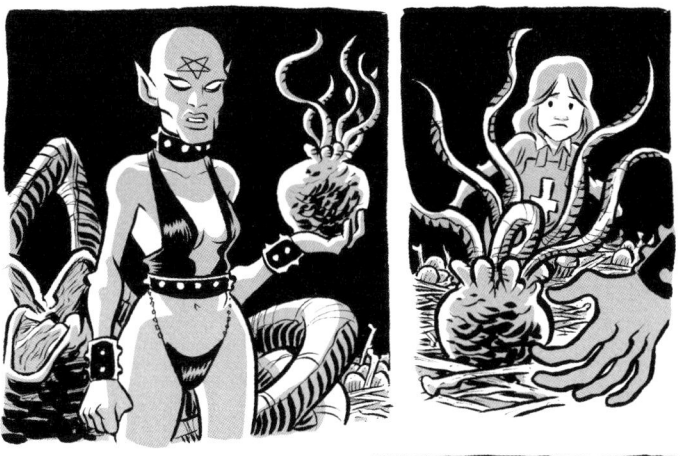

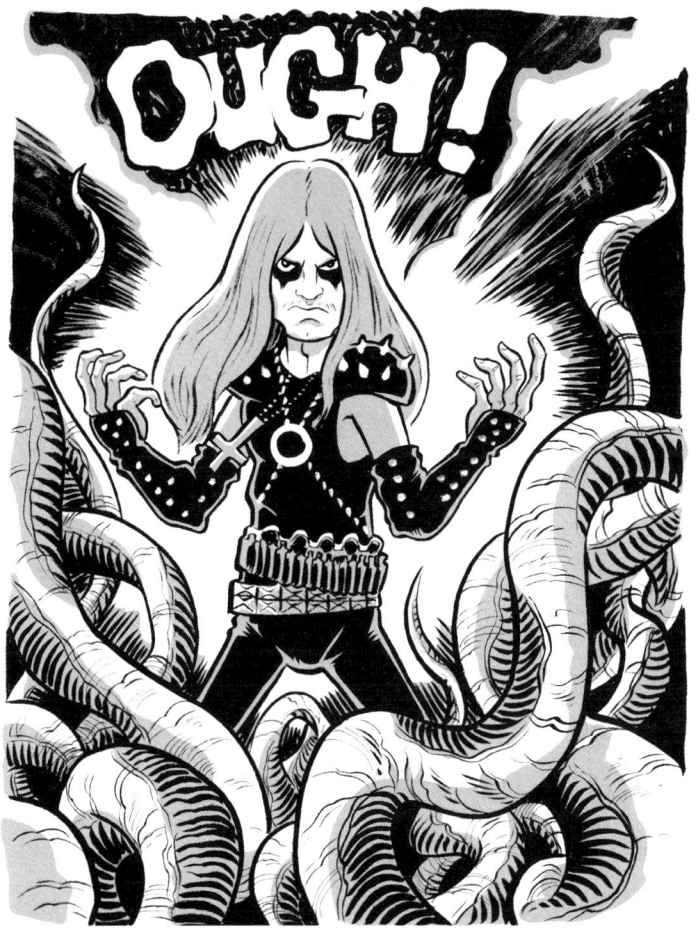

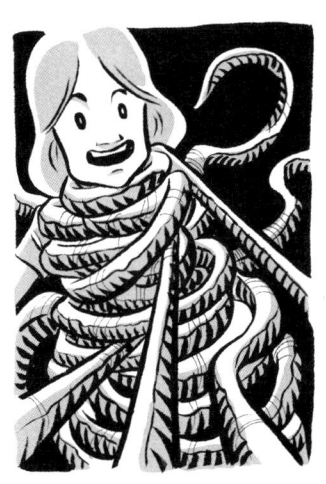

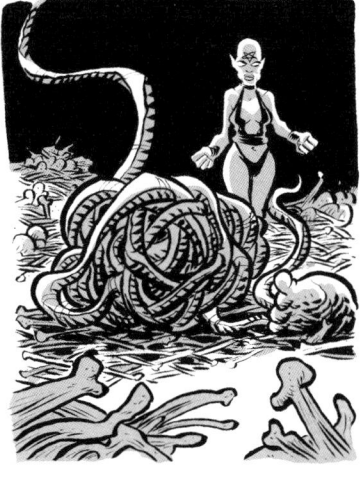

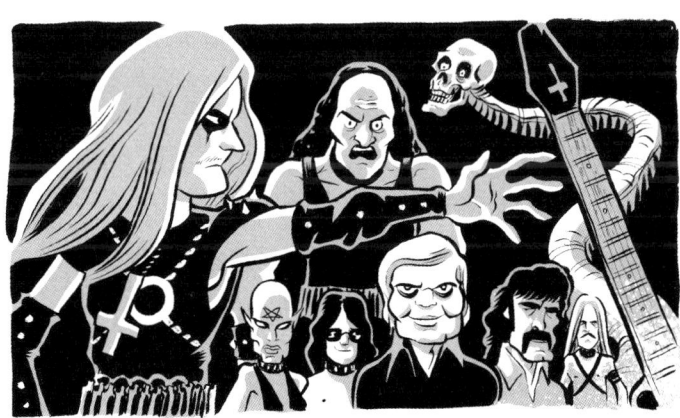

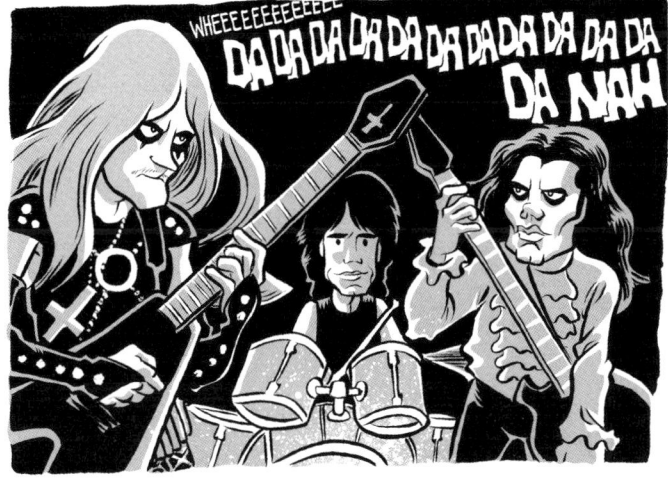

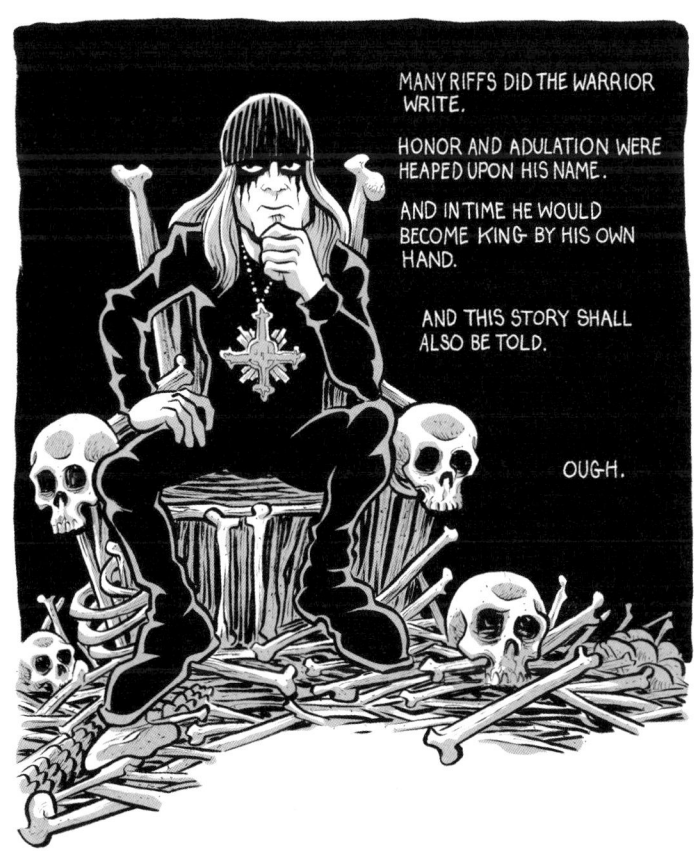

MANY RIFFS DID THE WARRIOR WRITE.

HONOR AND ADULATION WERE HEAPED UPON HIS NAME.

AND IN TIME HE WOULD BECOME KING BY HIS OWN HAND.

AND THIS STORY SHALL ALSO BE TOLD.

OUGH.

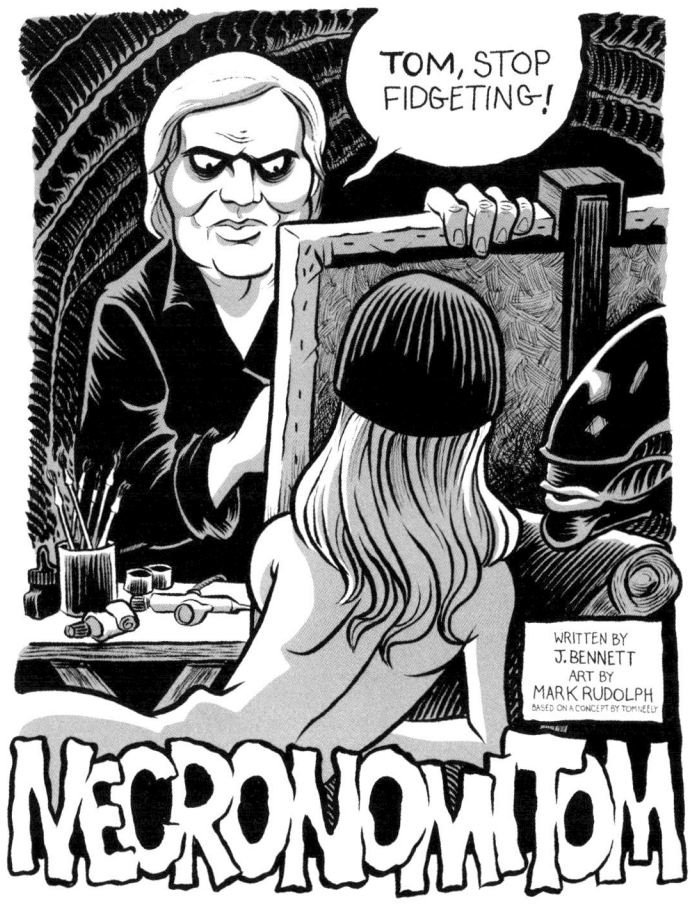

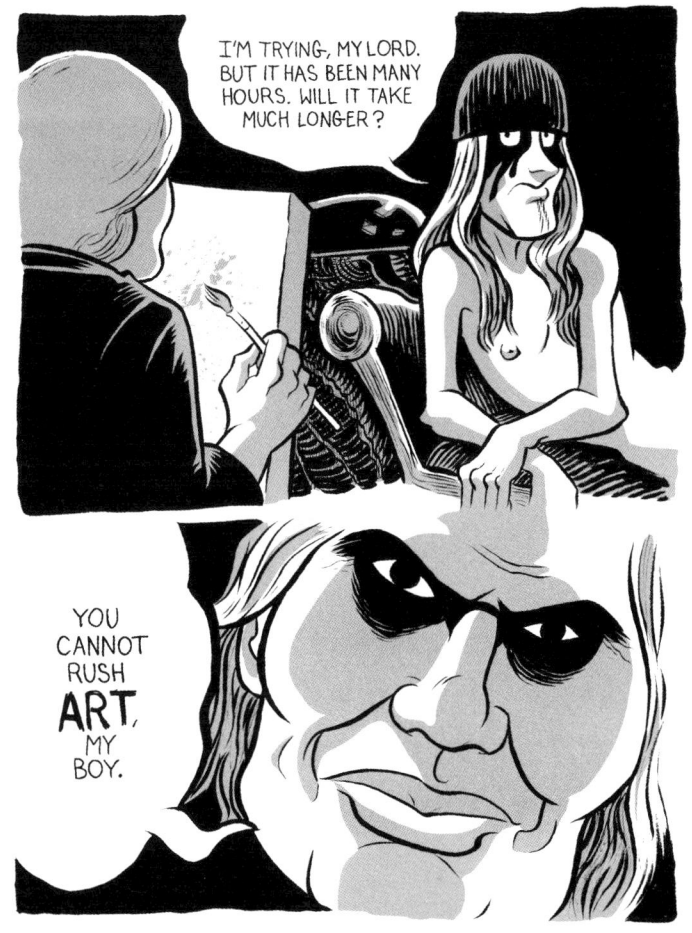

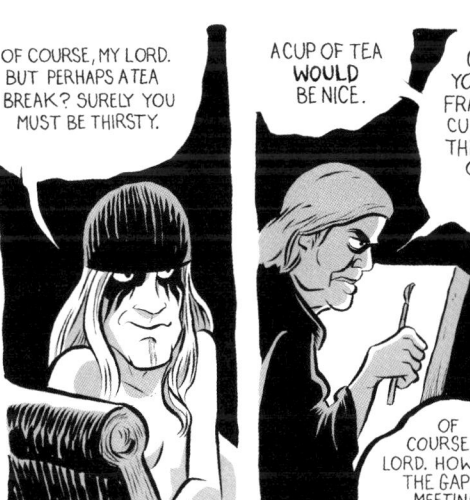

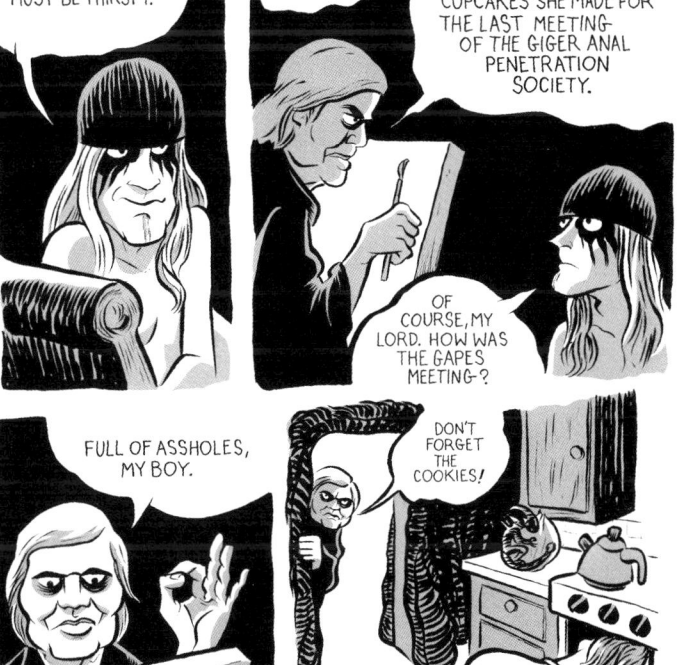

NECRONOMITOM
(2014)
A comic for Morbid Tales drawn by Mark Rudolph, written by J. Bennett.

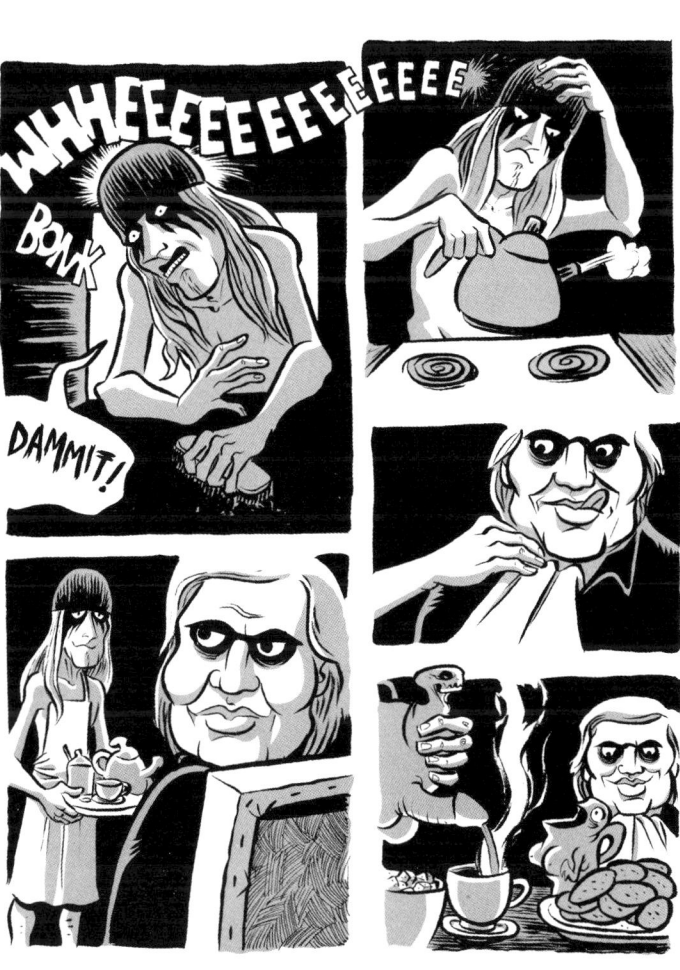

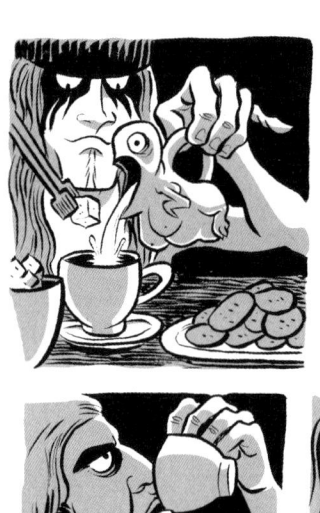
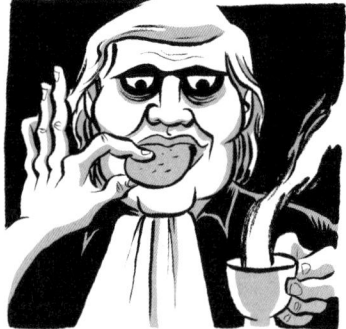
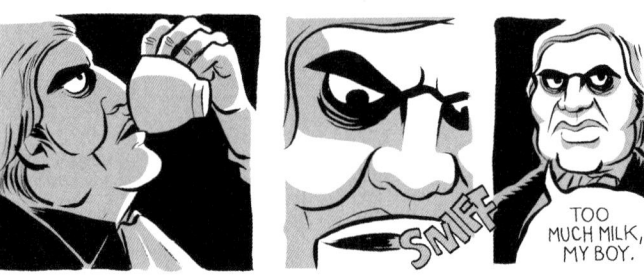
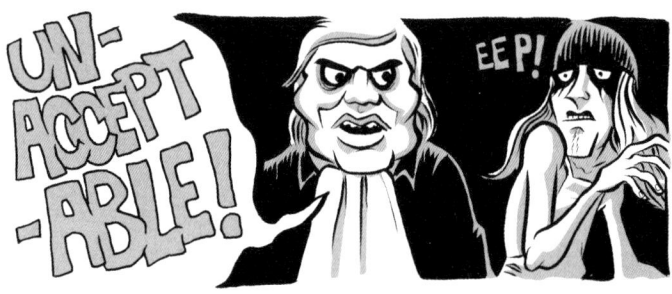
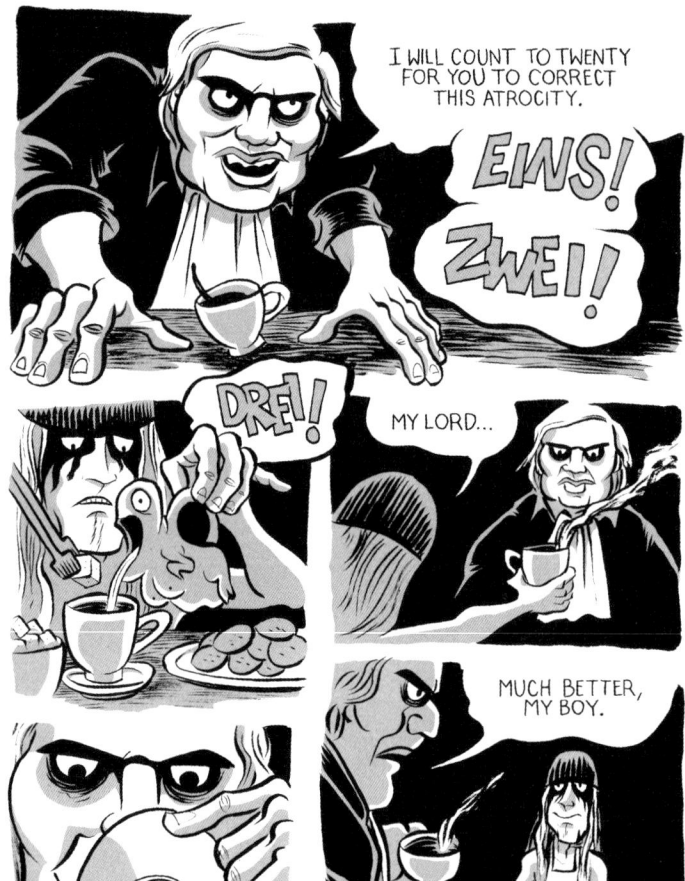
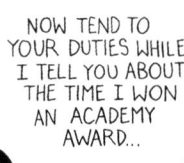
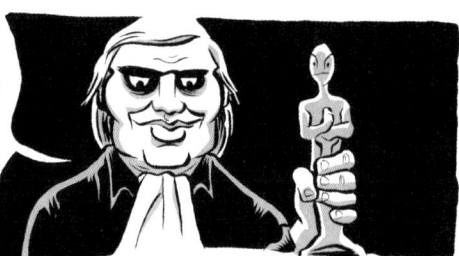
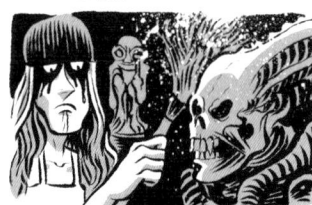
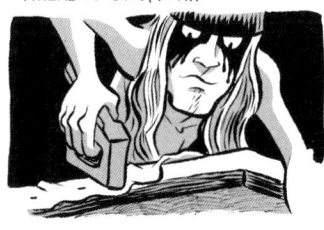
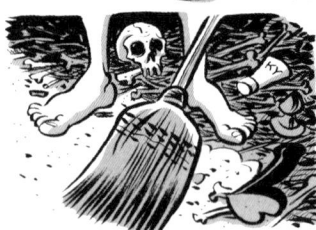
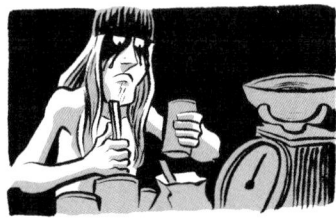
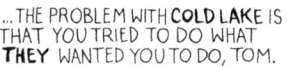
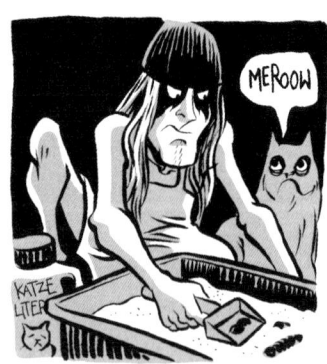
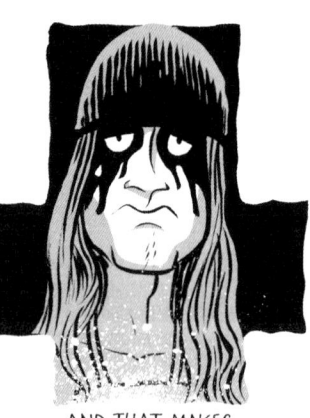
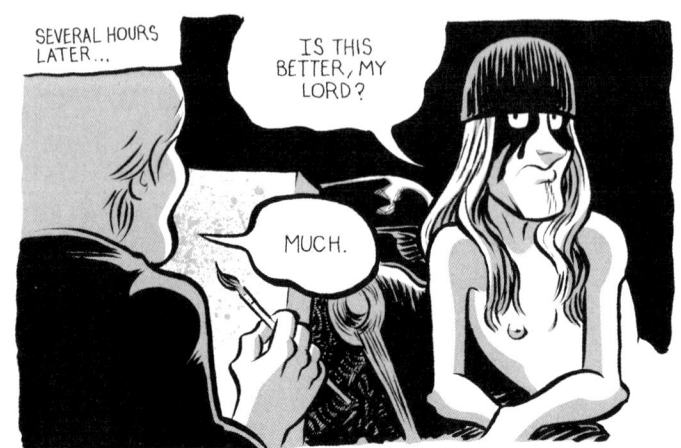

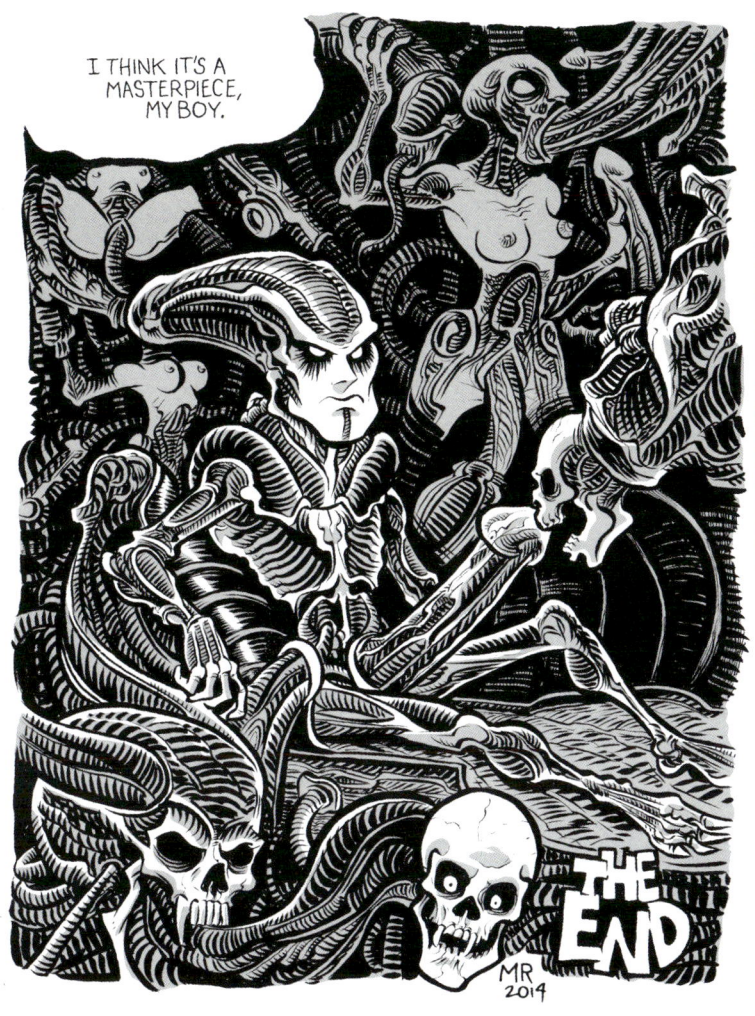

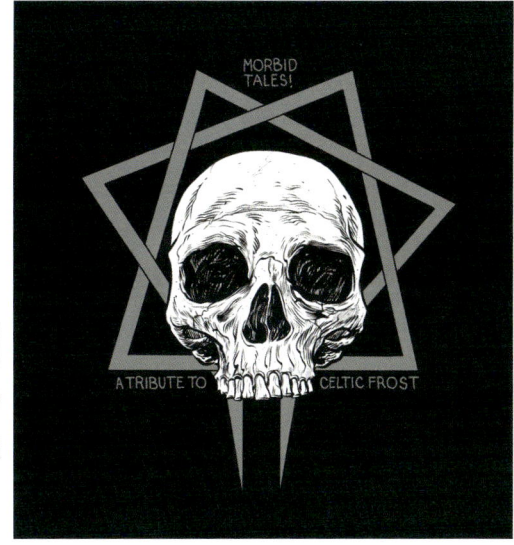

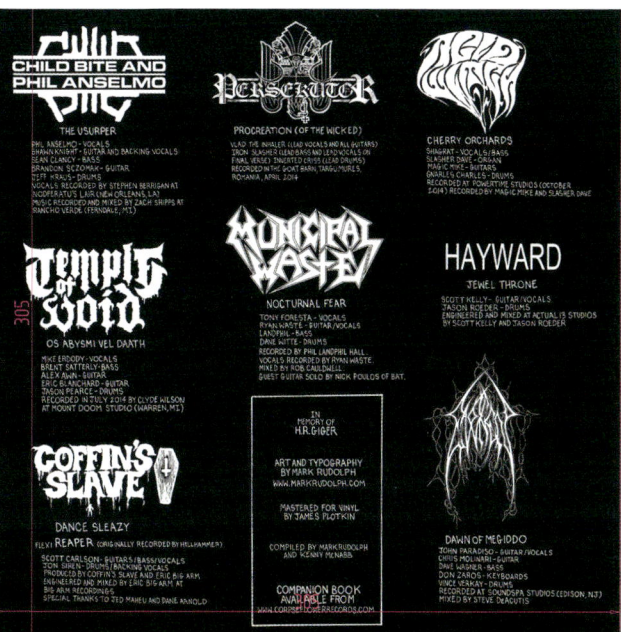

ABOVE: MORBID TALES INSERT (2015)
The LP insert for the *Morbid Tales* covers album.
BELOW: THE USURPER (2015)
The cover illustration for the LP was influenced by
H.R. Giger's biomechanical work through a comic
book lens.

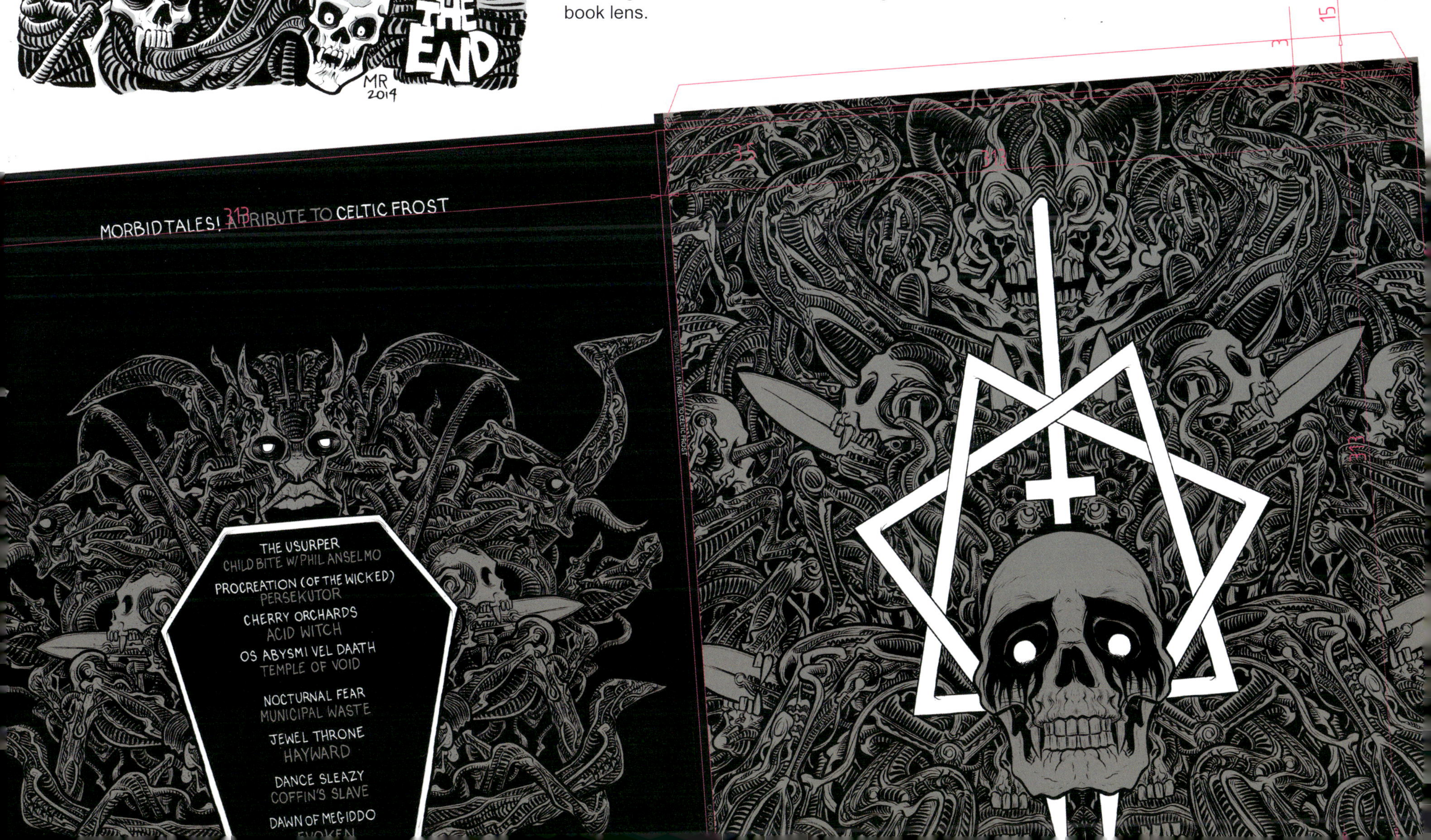

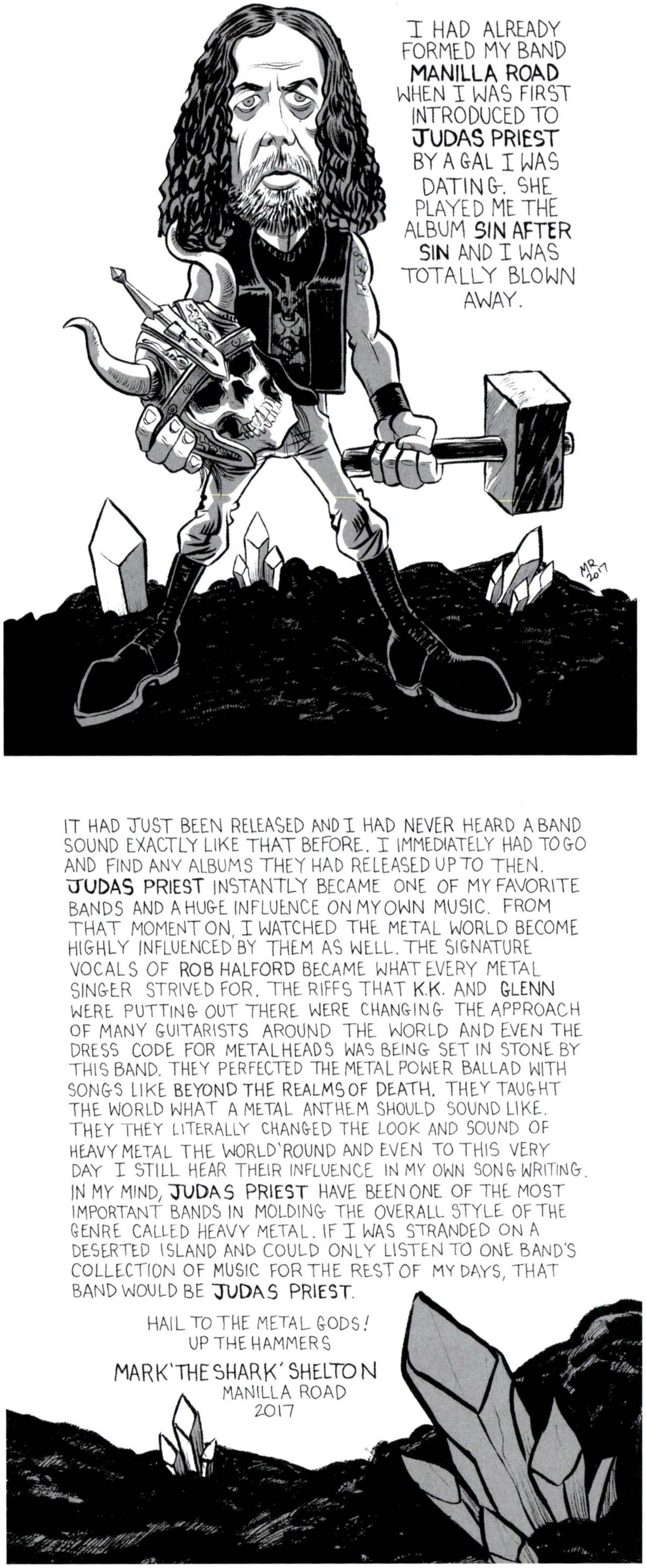

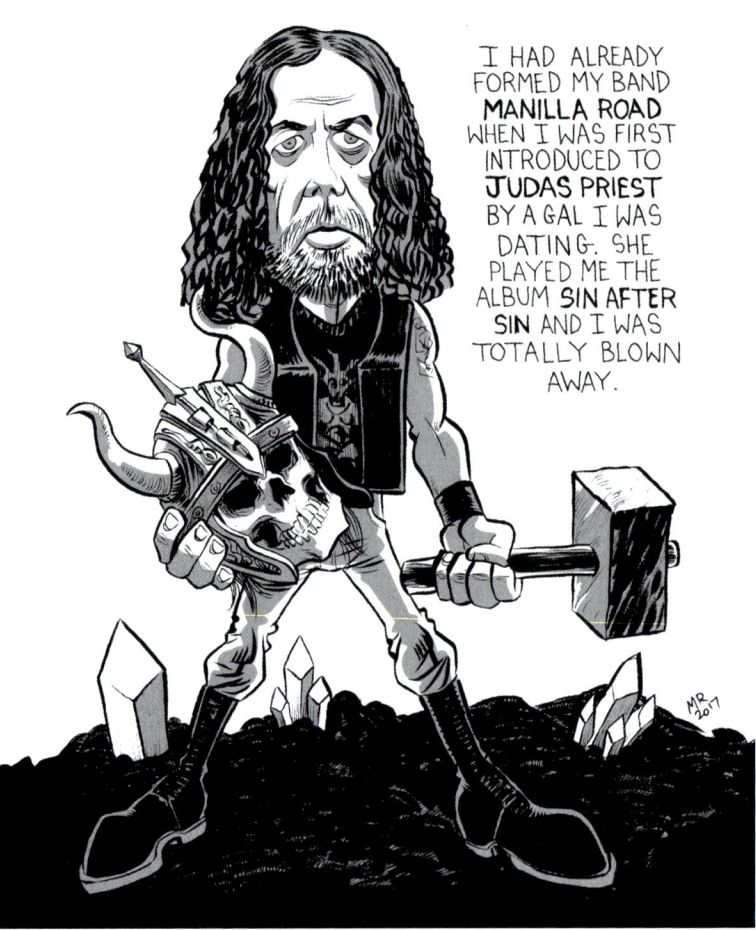

I HAD ALREADY FORMED MY BAND **MANILLA ROAD** WHEN I WAS FIRST INTRODUCED TO **JUDAS PRIEST** BY A GAL I WAS DATING. SHE PLAYED ME THE ALBUM **SIN AFTER SIN** AND I WAS TOTALLY BLOWN AWAY.

IT HAD JUST BEEN RELEASED AND I HAD NEVER HEARD A BAND SOUND EXACTLY LIKE THAT BEFORE. I IMMEDIATELY HAD TO GO AND FIND ANY ALBUMS THEY HAD RELEASED UP TO THEN. **JUDAS PRIEST** INSTANTLY BECAME ONE OF MY FAVORITE BANDS AND A HUGE INFLUENCE ON MY OWN MUSIC. FROM THAT MOMENT ON, I WATCHED THE METAL WORLD BECOME HIGHLY INFLUENCED BY THEM AS WELL. THE SIGNATURE VOCALS OF ROB HALFORD BECAME WHAT EVERY METAL SINGER STRIVED FOR. THE RIFFS THAT K.K. AND GLENN WERE PUTTING OUT THERE WERE CHANGING THE APPROACH OF MANY GUITARISTS AROUND THE WORLD AND EVEN THE DRESS CODE FOR METALHEADS WAS BEING SET IN STONE BY THIS BAND. THEY PERFECTED THE METAL POWER BALLAD WITH SONGS LIKE BEYOND THE REALMS OF DEATH. THEY TAUGHT THE WORLD WHAT A METAL ANTHEM SHOULD SOUND LIKE. THEY THEY LITERALLY CHANGED THE LOOK AND SOUND OF HEAVY METAL THE WORLD 'ROUND AND EVEN TO THIS VERY DAY I STILL HEAR THEIR INFLUENCE IN MY OWN SONG WRITING. IN MY MIND, **JUDAS PRIEST** HAVE BEEN ONE OF THE MOST IMPORTANT BANDS IN MOLDING THE OVERALL STYLE OF THE GENRE CALLED HEAVY METAL. IF I WAS STRANDED ON A DESERTED ISLAND AND COULD ONLY LISTEN TO ONE BAND'S COLLECTION OF MUSIC FOR THE REST OF MY DAYS, THAT BAND WOULD BE **JUDAS PRIEST**.

HAIL TO THE METAL GODS! UP THE HAMMERS

MARK 'THE SHARK' SHELTON
MANILLA ROAD
2017

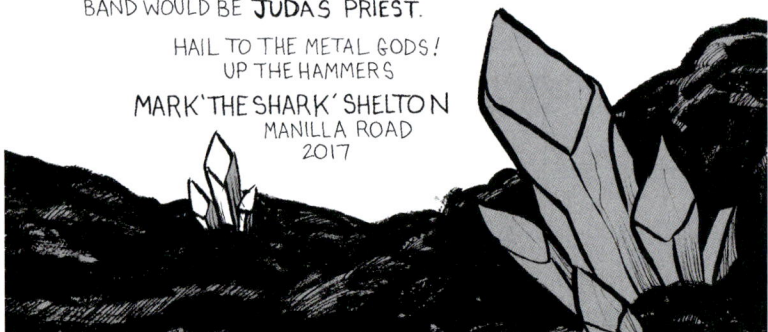

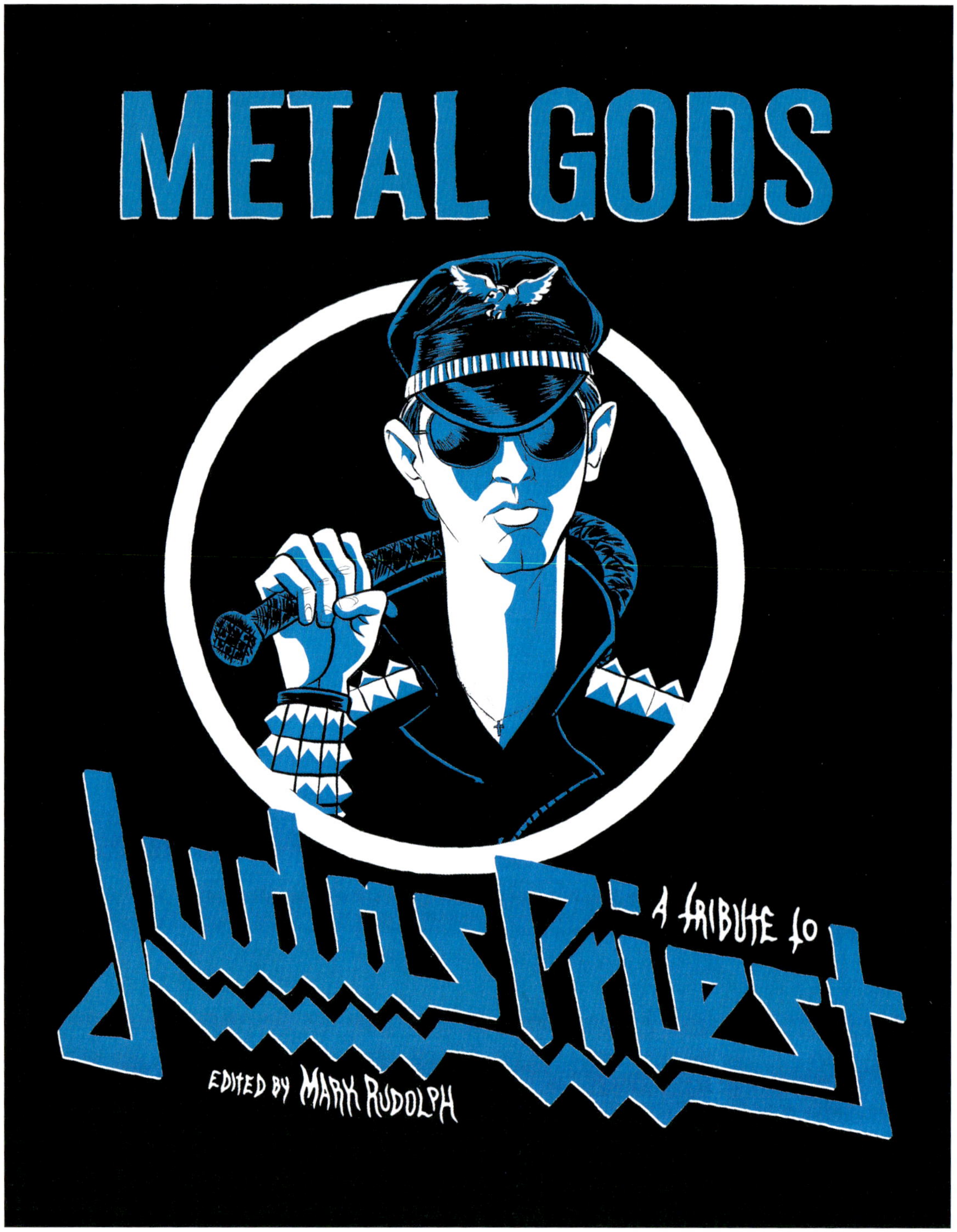

METAL GODS

A tribute to **Judas Priest**

EDITED BY MARK RUDOLPH

ABOVE LEFT: THE SHARK (2017)
A Judas Priest testimonial from the late great Mark "The Shark" Shelton.
ABOVE: BOW TO YOUR KNEES (2017)
The cover for *Metal Gods*: A Tribute to Judas Priest.
OPPOSITE PAGE: BEFORE THE DAWN (2017)
Comic written by Rachel Deering, drawn by Mark Rudolph.

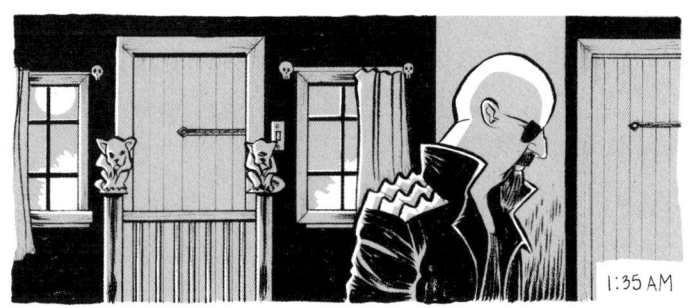

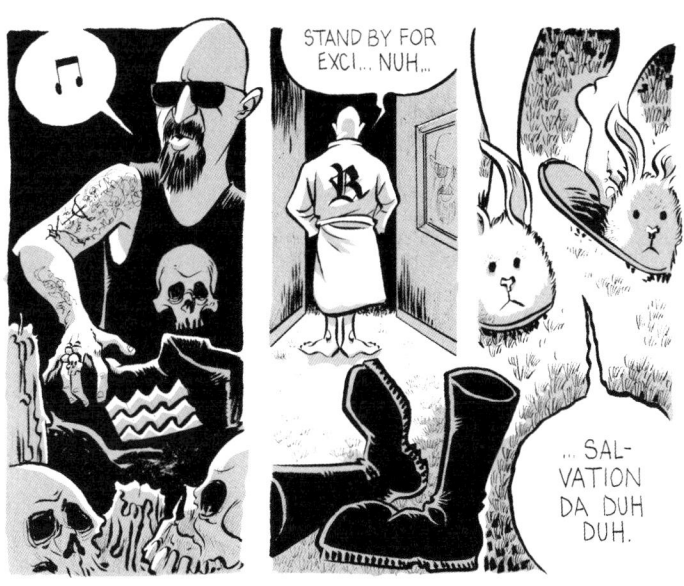

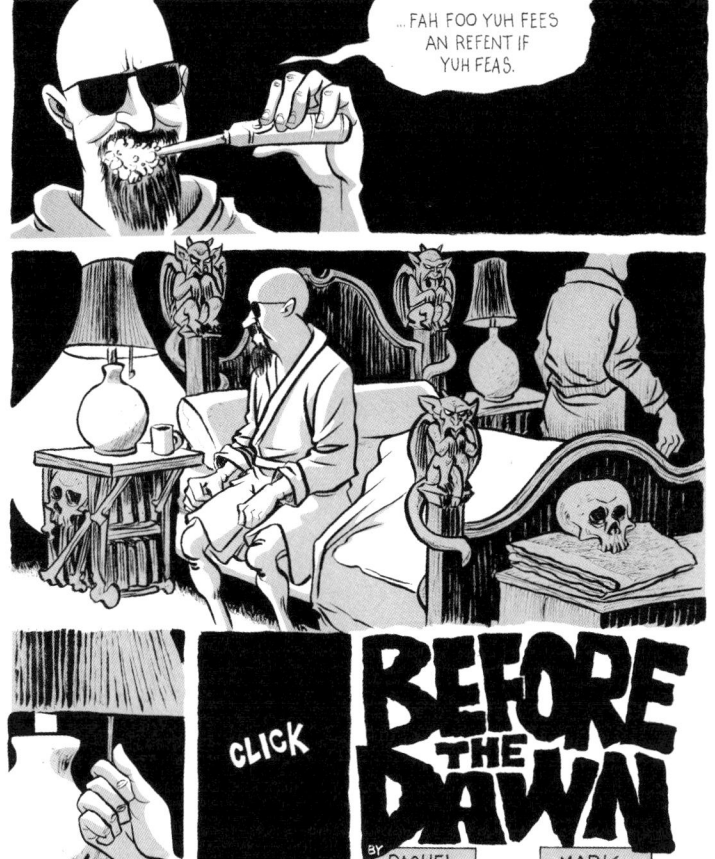

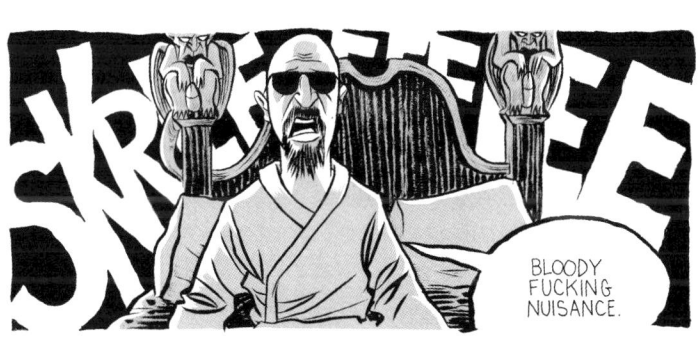

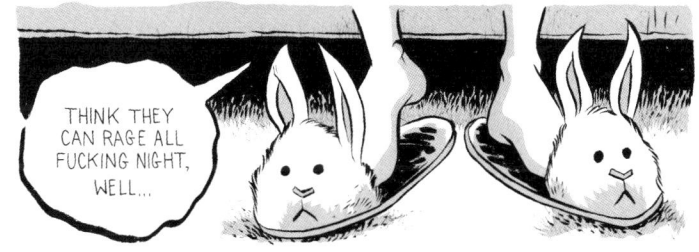

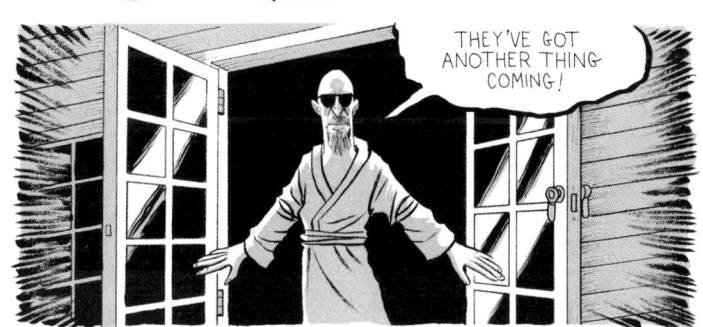

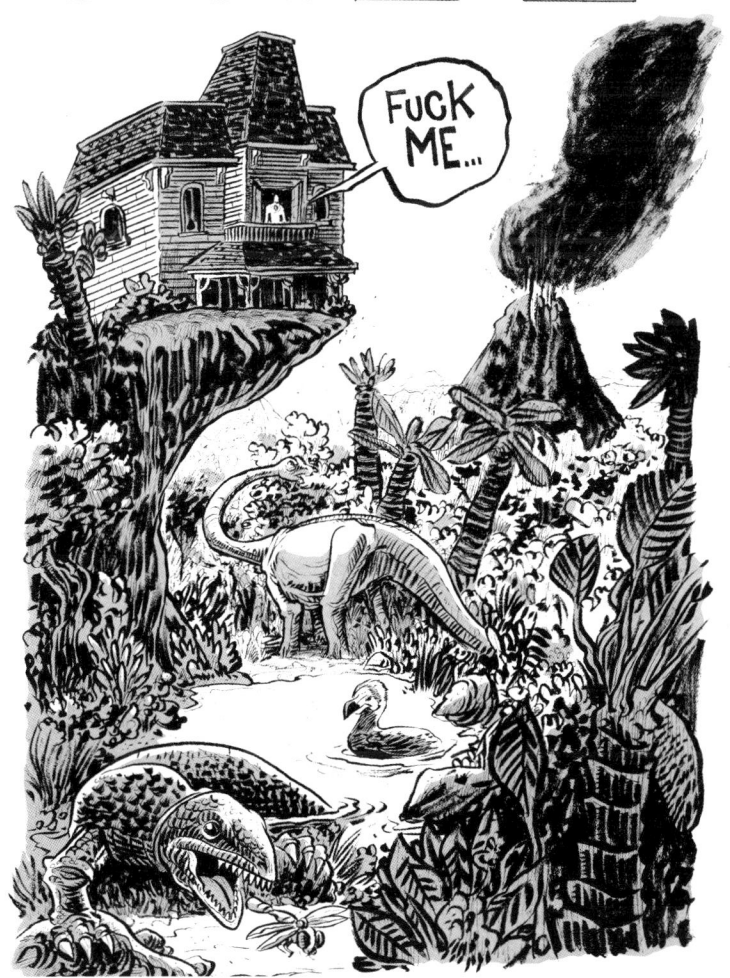

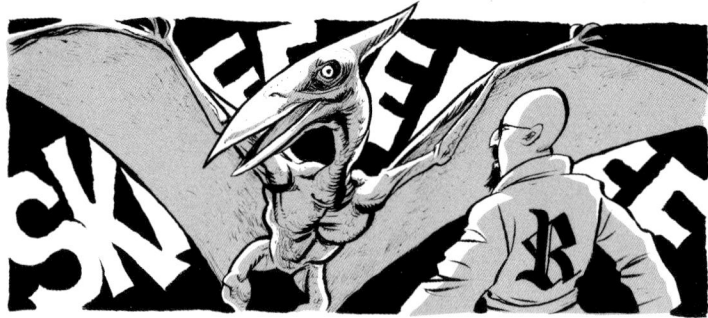

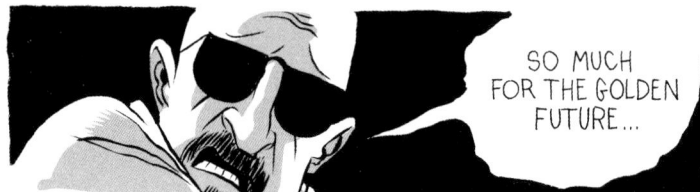

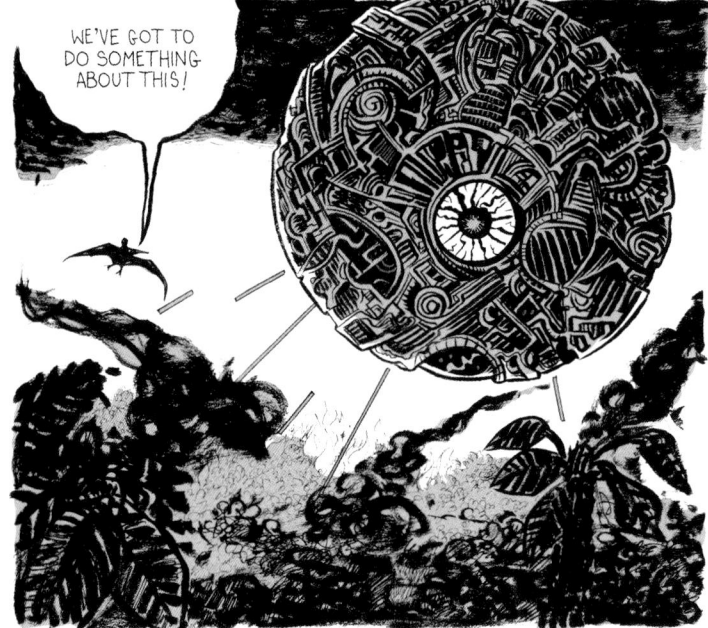

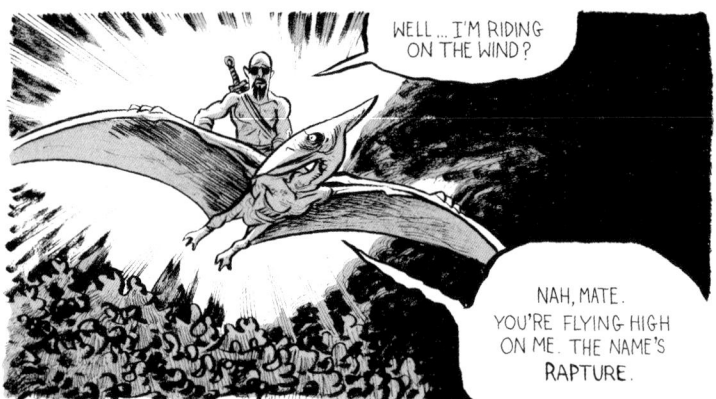

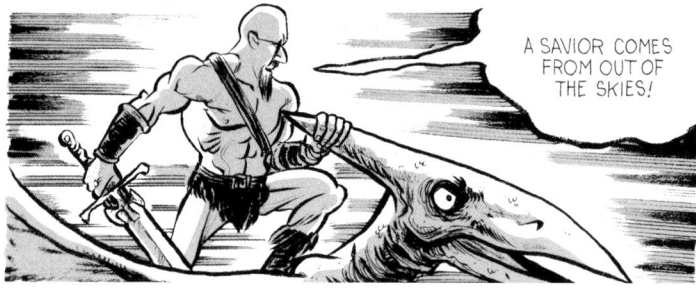

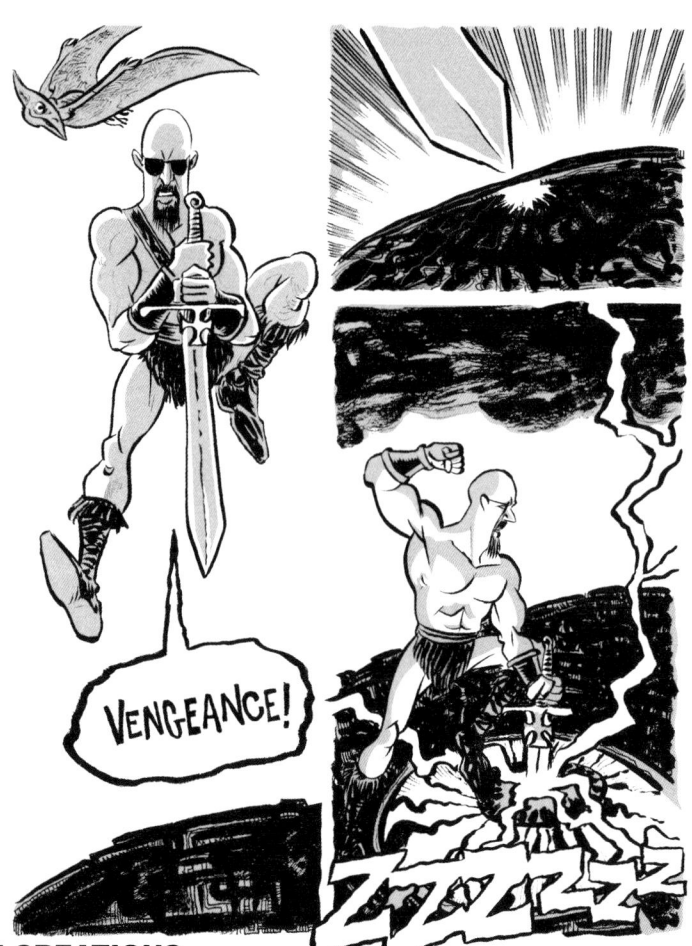

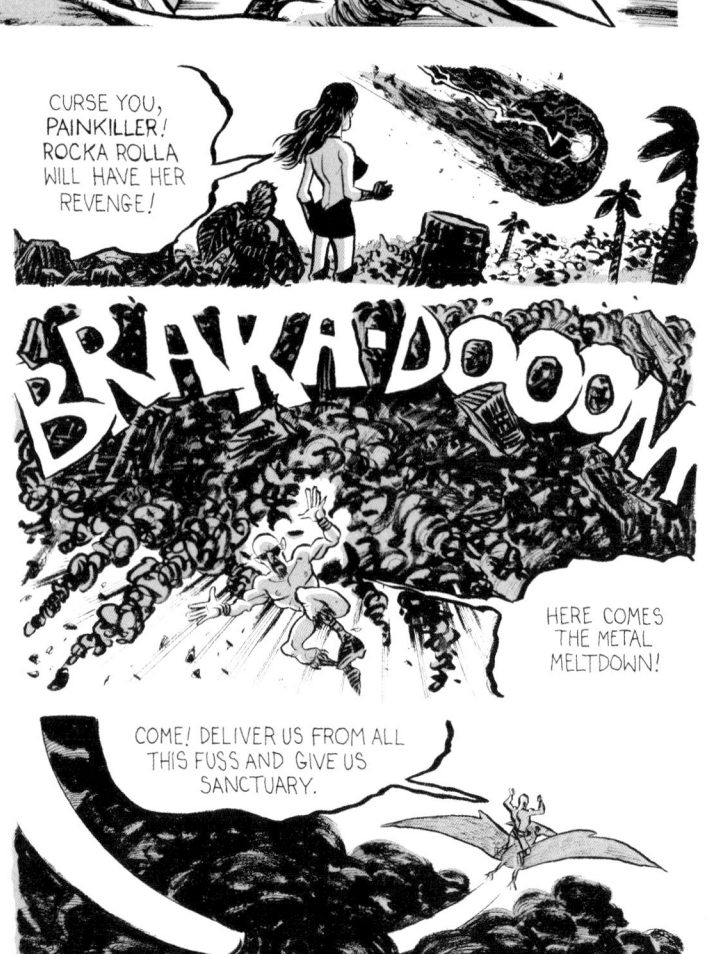

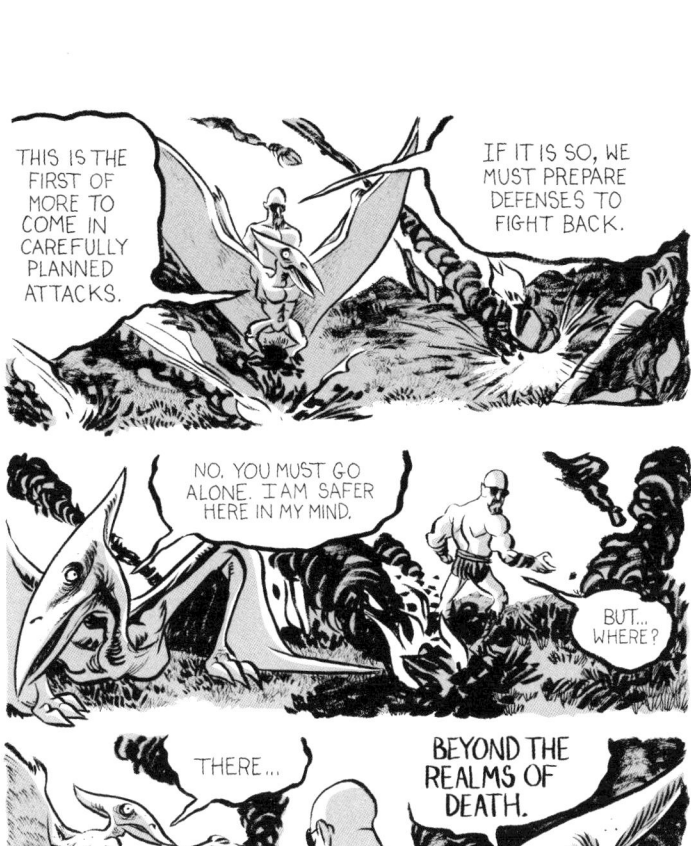

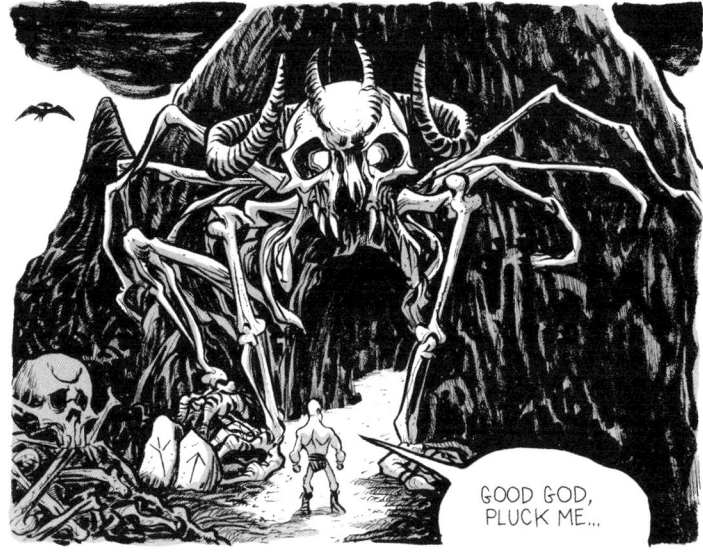

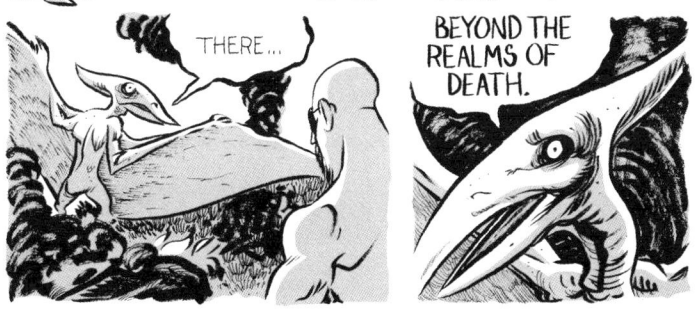

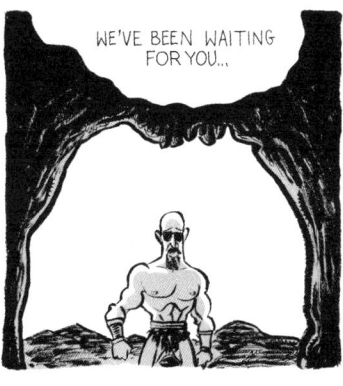

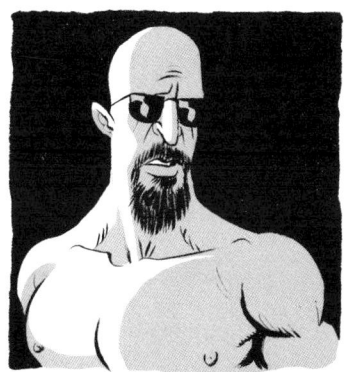

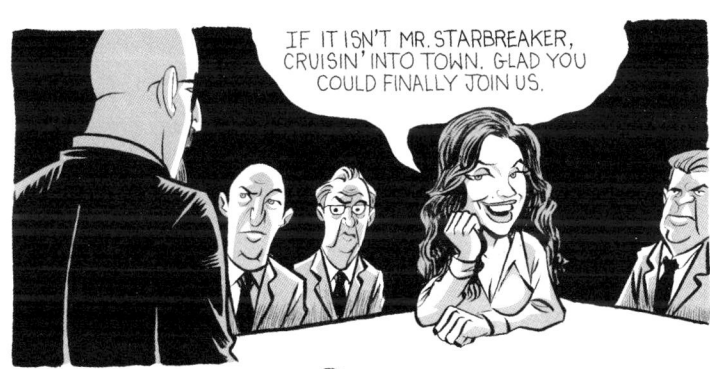

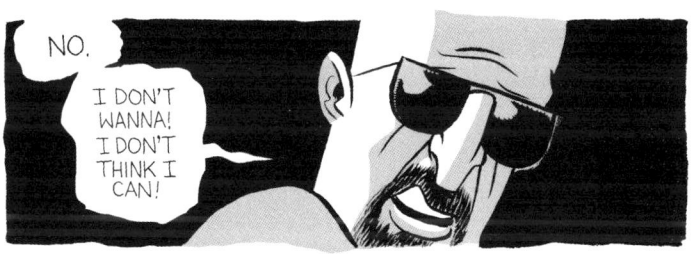

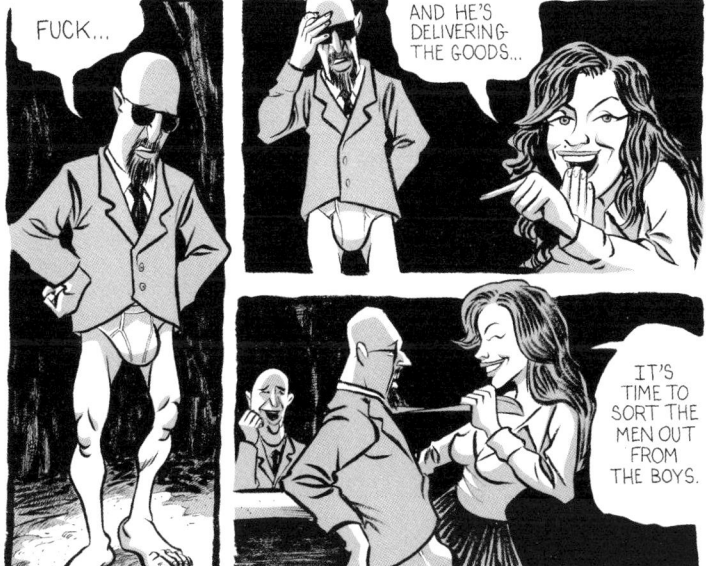

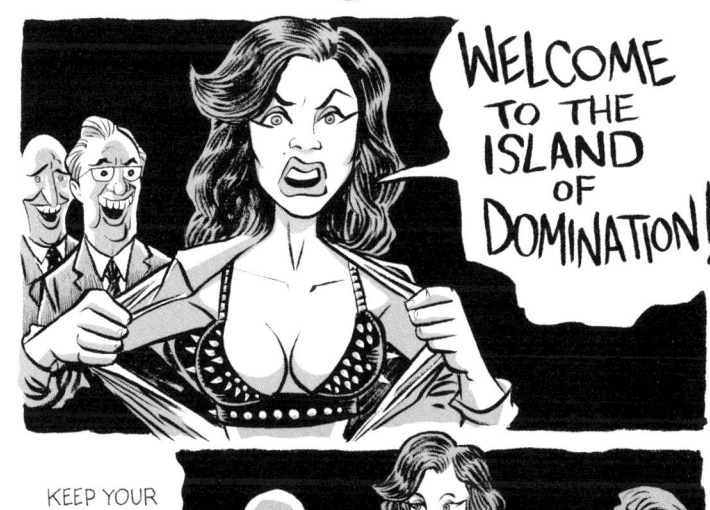

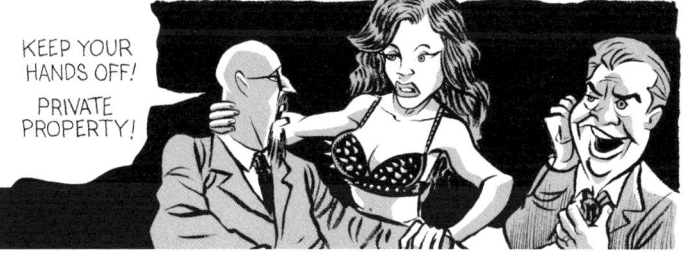

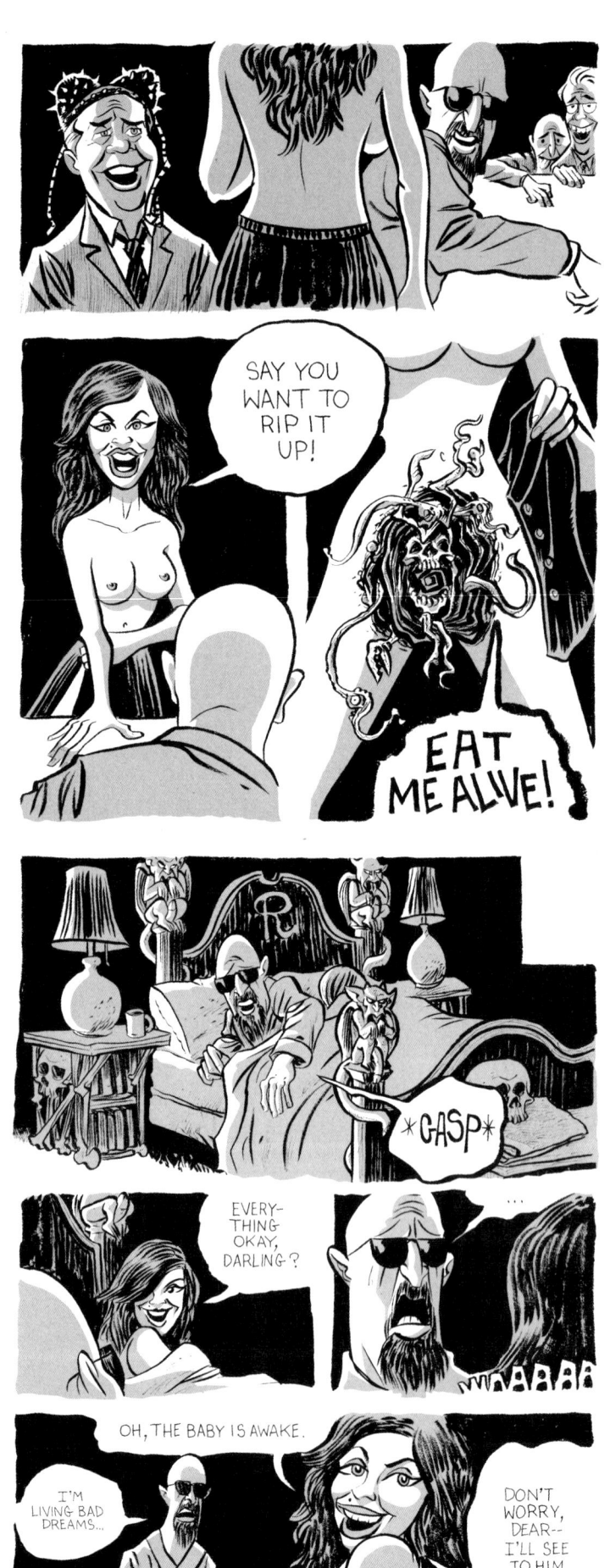

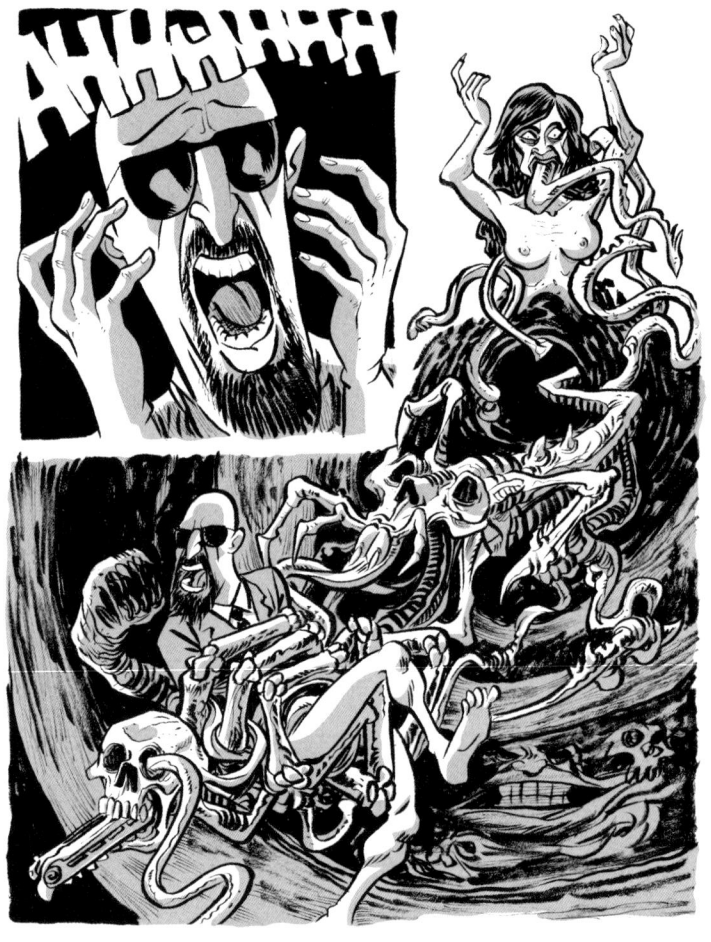

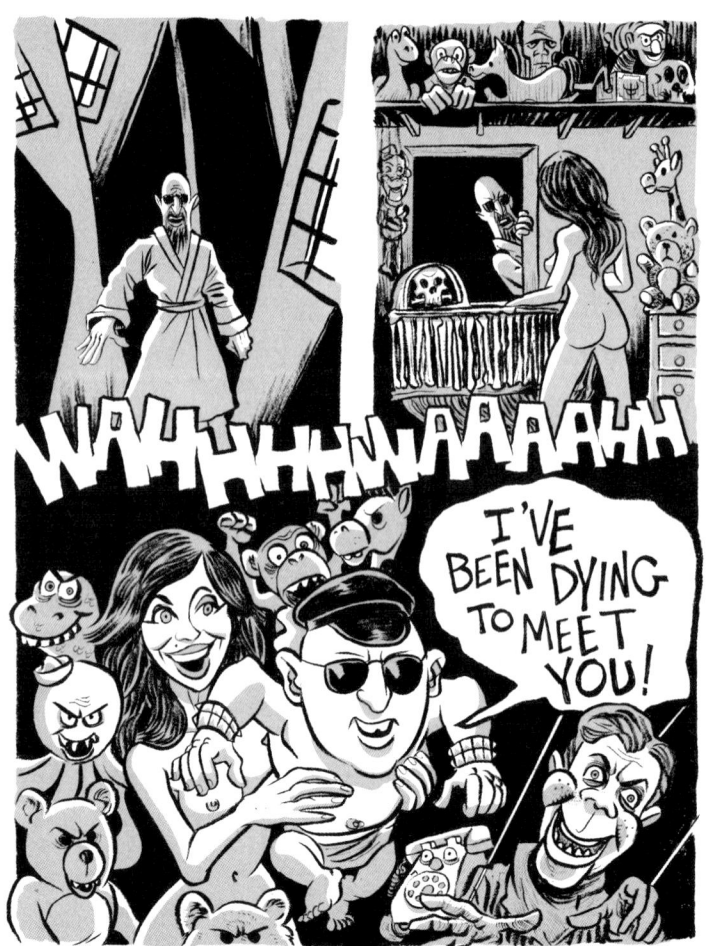

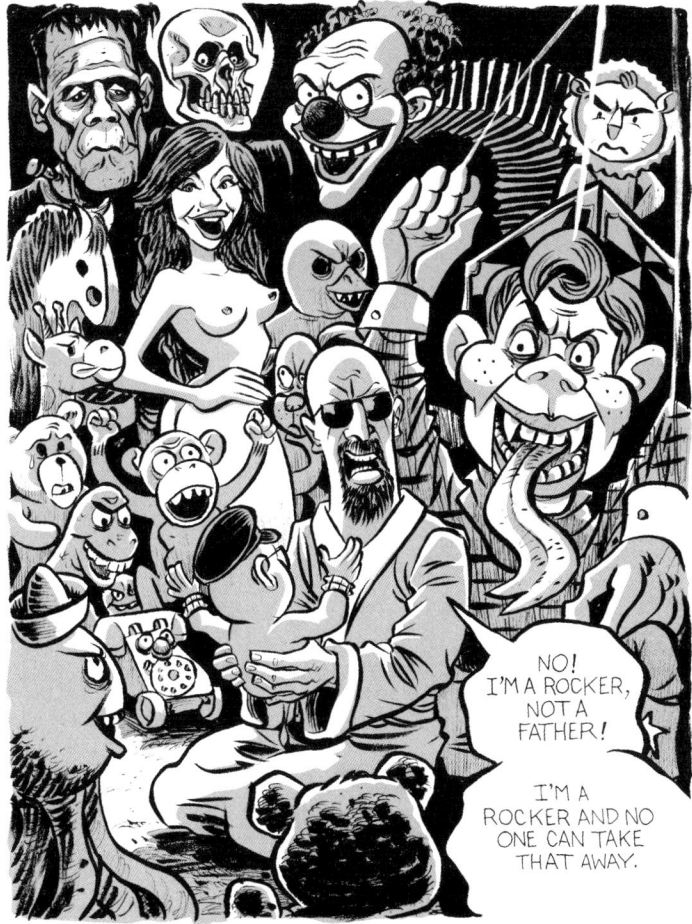

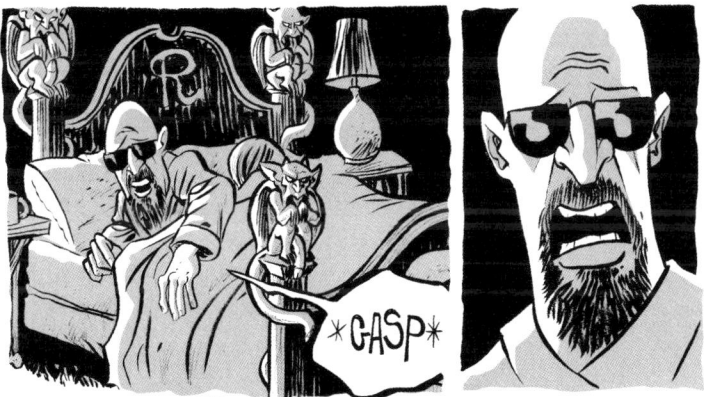

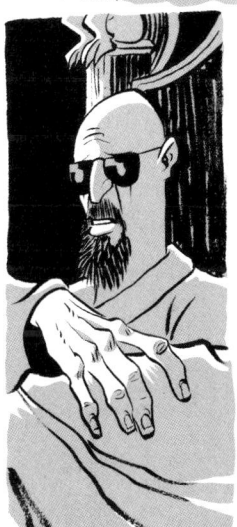

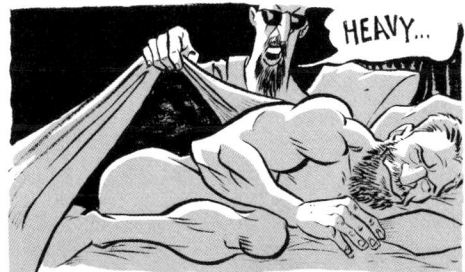

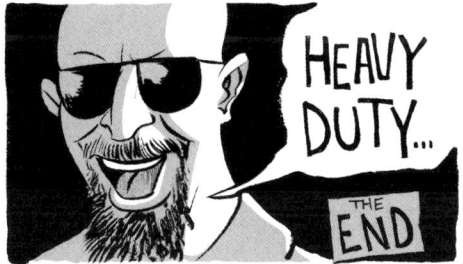

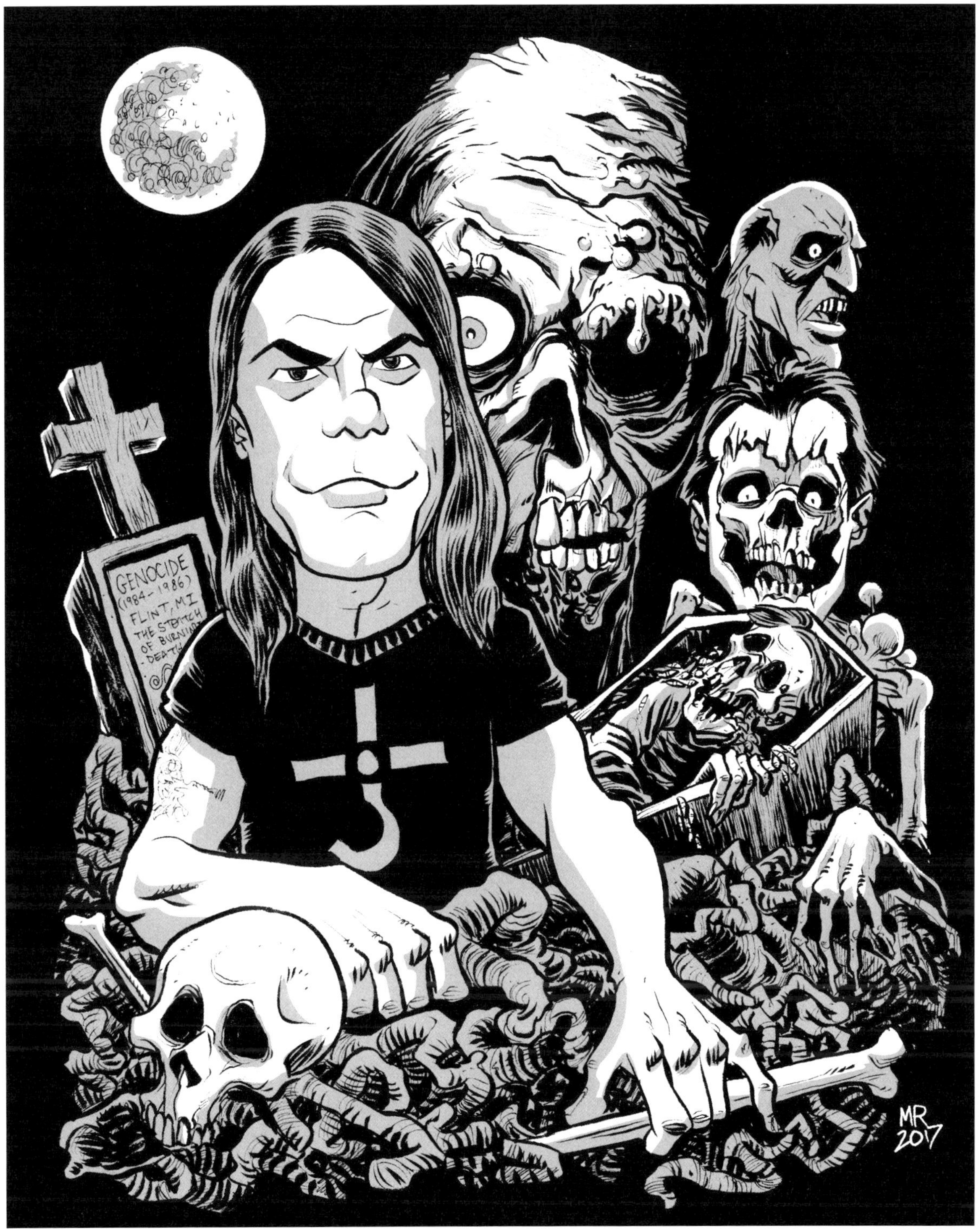

ABOVE: CALL FOR THE PRIEST (2017)
An illustration to accompany a Judas Priest
testimonial from Scott Carlson of Repulsion,
Cathedral, Septic Tank, Death Breath,
Superbees and Church of Misery.

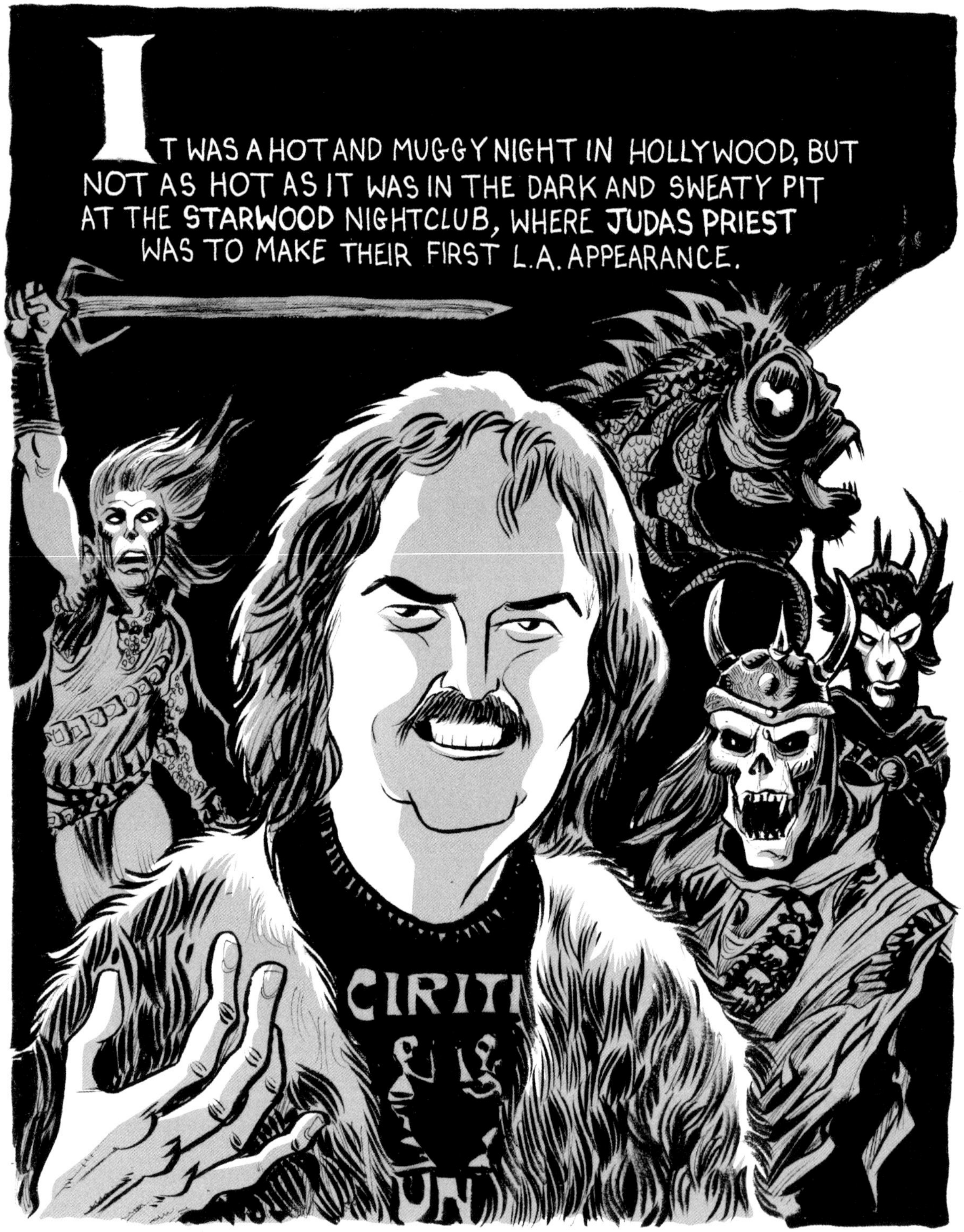

IT WAS A HOT AND MUGGY NIGHT IN HOLLYWOOD, BUT NOT AS HOT AS IT WAS IN THE DARK AND SWEATY PIT AT THE **STARWOOD** NIGHTCLUB, WHERE **JUDAS PRIEST** WAS TO MAKE THEIR FIRST L.A. APPEARANCE.

STARBREAKER (2017)
A comic written by Robert Garven's about his first experience seeing Judas Priest. Drawn by Mark Rudolph.

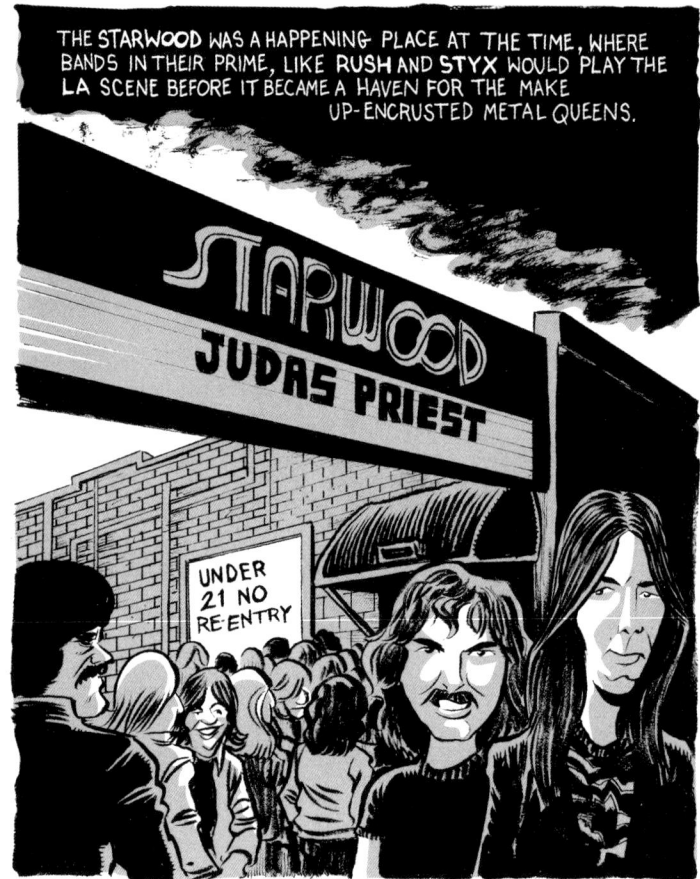

THE **STARWOOD** WAS A HAPPENING PLACE AT THE TIME, WHERE BANDS IN THEIR PRIME, LIKE **RUSH** AND **STYX** WOULD PLAY THE LA SCENE BEFORE IT BECAME A HAVEN FOR THE MAKE-UP-ENCRUSTED METAL QUEENS.

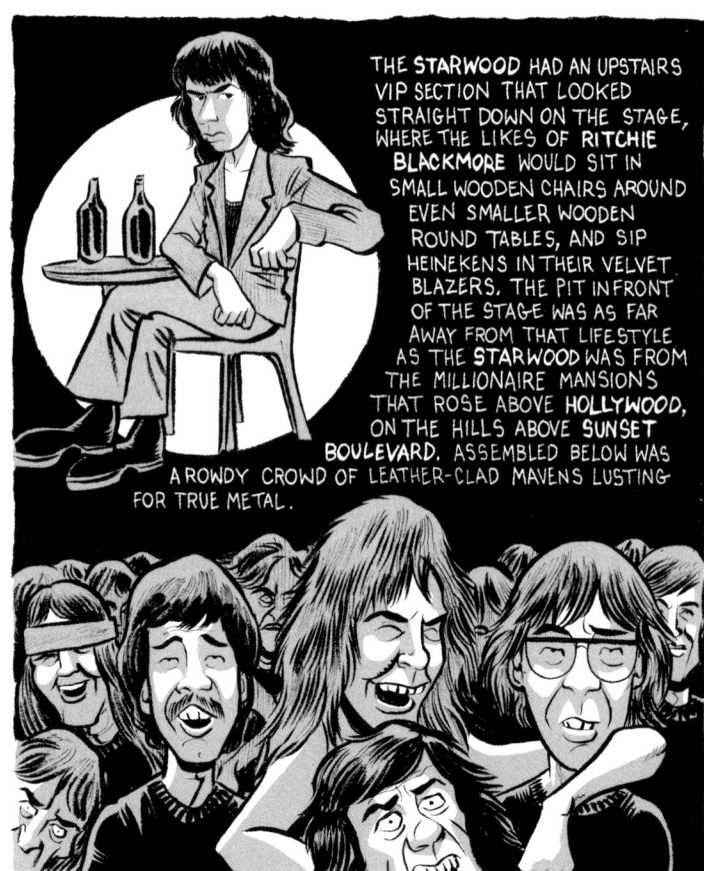

THE **STARWOOD** HAD AN UPSTAIRS VIP SECTION THAT LOOKED STRAIGHT DOWN ON THE STAGE, WHERE THE LIKES OF **RITCHIE BLACKMORE** WOULD SIT IN SMALL WOODEN CHAIRS AROUND EVEN SMALLER WOODEN ROUND TABLES, AND SIP HEINEKENS IN THEIR VELVET BLAZERS, THE PIT IN FRONT OF THE STAGE WAS AS FAR AWAY FROM THAT LIFESTYLE AS THE **STARWOOD** WAS FROM THE MILLIONAIRE MANSIONS THAT ROSE ABOVE **HOLLYWOOD**, ON THE HILLS ABOVE **SUNSET BOULEVARD**. ASSEMBLED BELOW WAS A ROWDY CROWD OF LEATHER-CLAD MAVENS LUSTING FOR TRUE METAL.

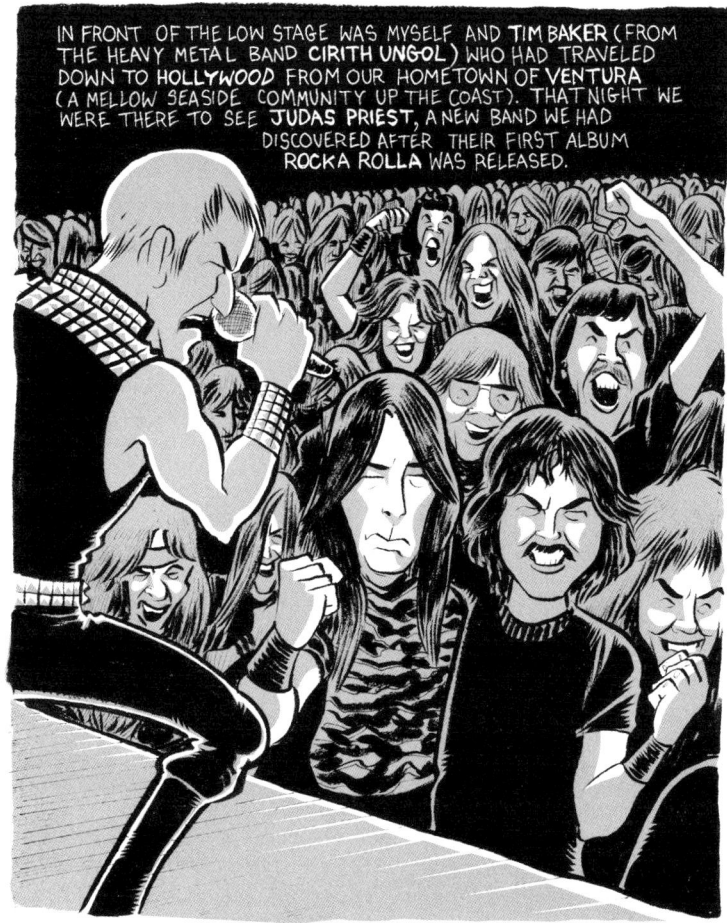

IN FRONT OF THE LOW STAGE WAS MYSELF AND **TIM BAKER** (FROM THE HEAVY METAL BAND **CIRITH UNGOL**) WHO HAD TRAVELED DOWN TO **HOLLYWOOD** FROM OUR HOMETOWN OF **VENTURA** (A MELLOW SEASIDE COMMUNITY UP THE COAST). THAT NIGHT WE WERE THERE TO SEE **JUDAS PRIEST**, A NEW BAND WE HAD DISCOVERED AFTER THEIR FIRST ALBUM **ROCKA ROLLA** WAS RELEASED.

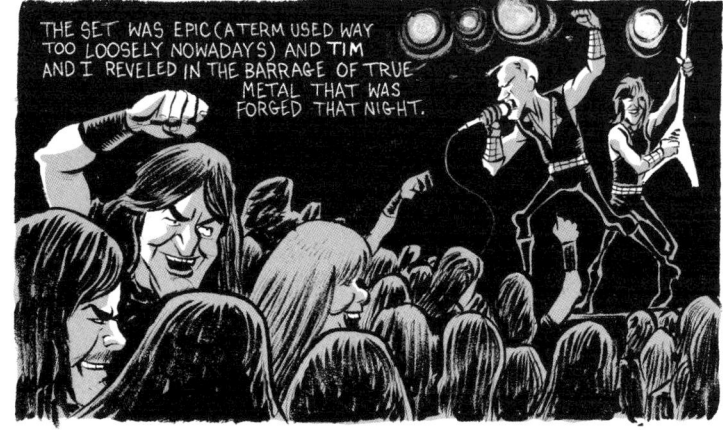

THE SET WAS EPIC (A TERM USED WAY TOO LOOSELY NOWADAYS) AND **TIM** AND I REVELED IN THE BARRAGE OF TRUE METAL THAT WAS FORGED THAT NIGHT.

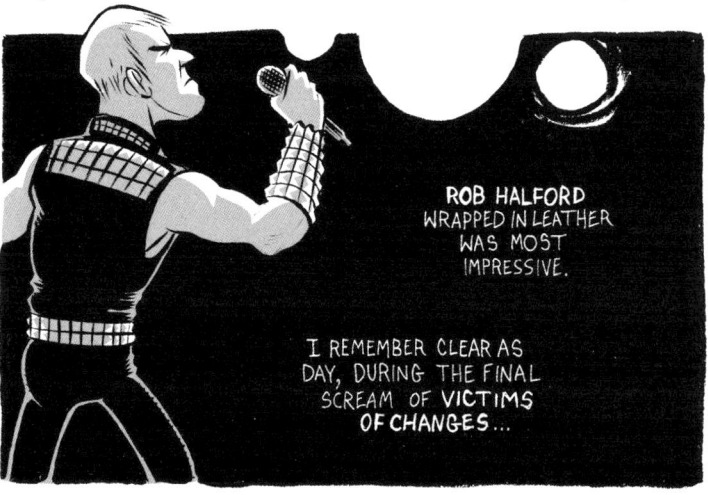

ROB HALFORD WRAPPED IN LEATHER WAS MOST IMPRESSIVE.

I REMEMBER CLEAR AS DAY, DURING THE FINAL SCREAM OF **VICTIMS OF CHANGES**...

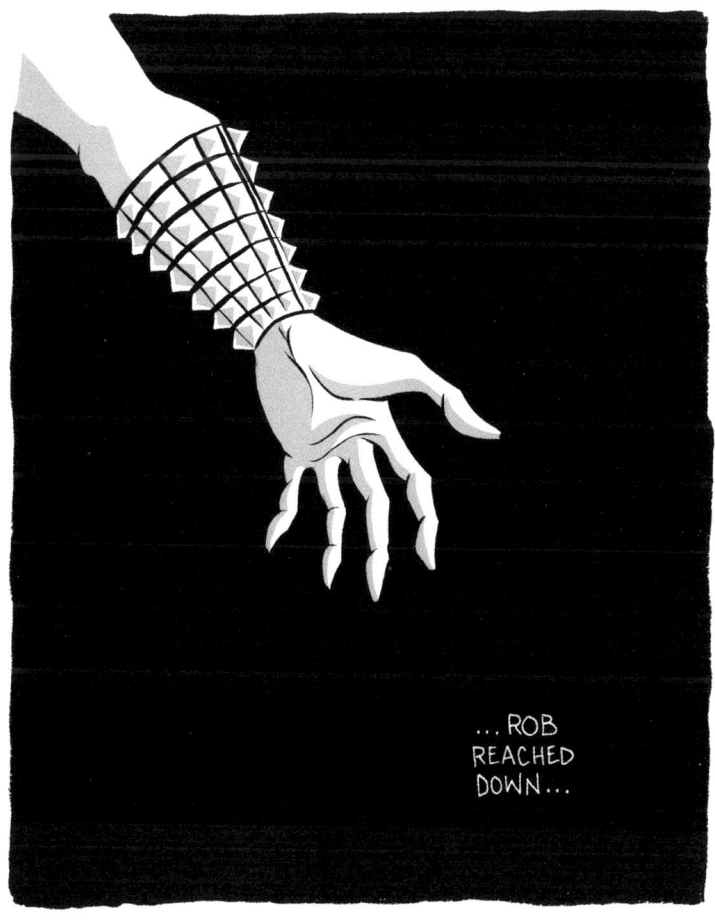

...ROB REACHED DOWN...

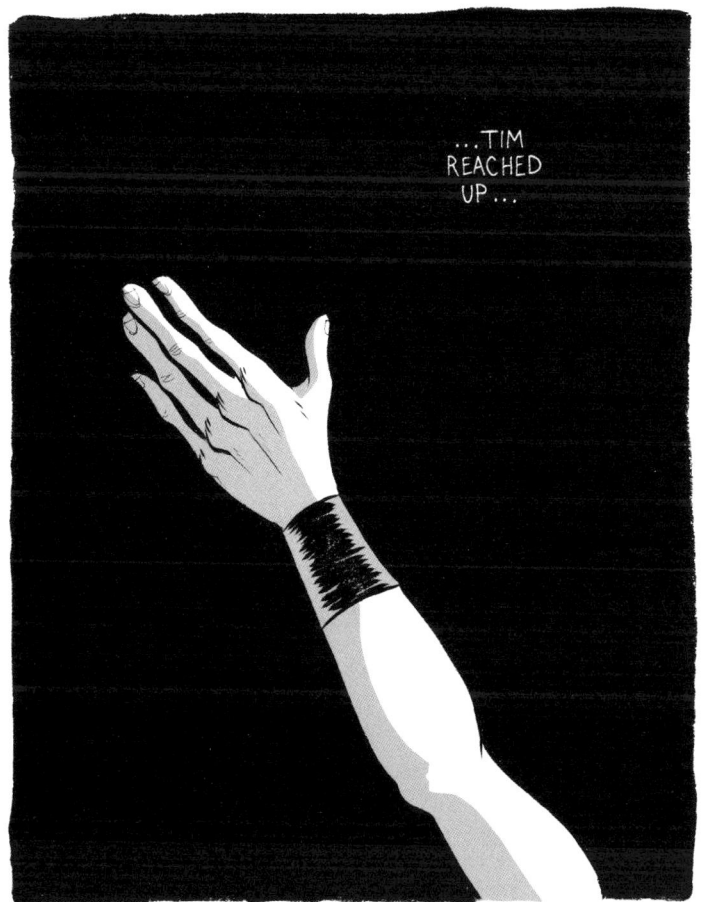

...TIM REACHED UP...

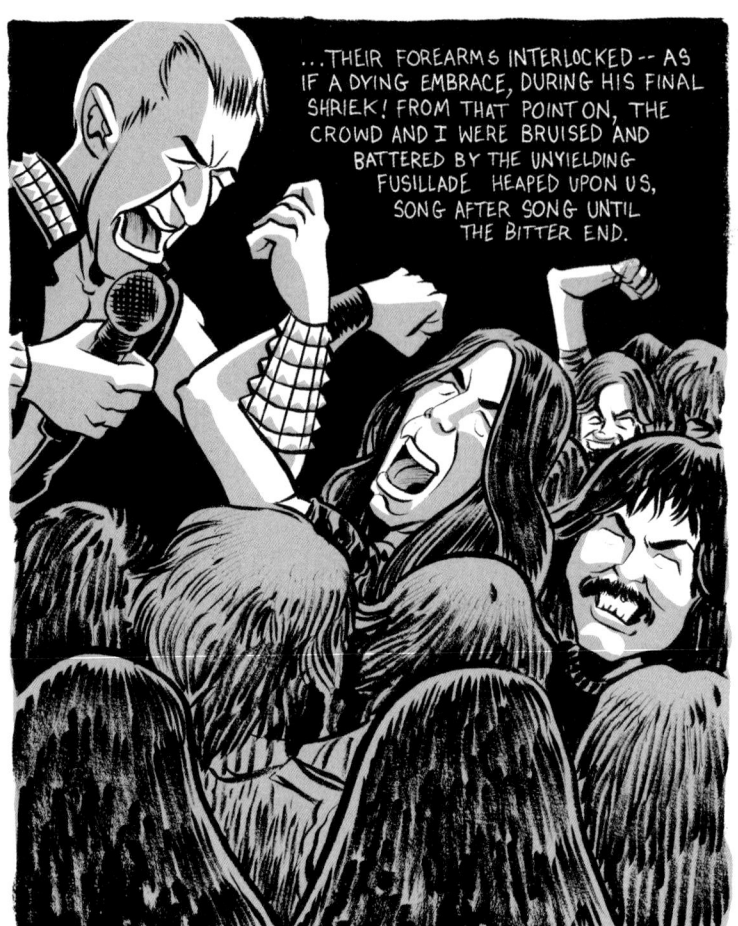

...THEIR FOREARMS INTERLOCKED -- AS IF A DYING EMBRACE, DURING HIS FINAL SHRIEK! FROM THAT POINT ON, THE CROWD AND I WERE BRUISED AND BATTERED BY THE UNYIELDING FUSILLADE HEAPED UPON US, SONG AFTER SONG UNTIL THE BITTER END.

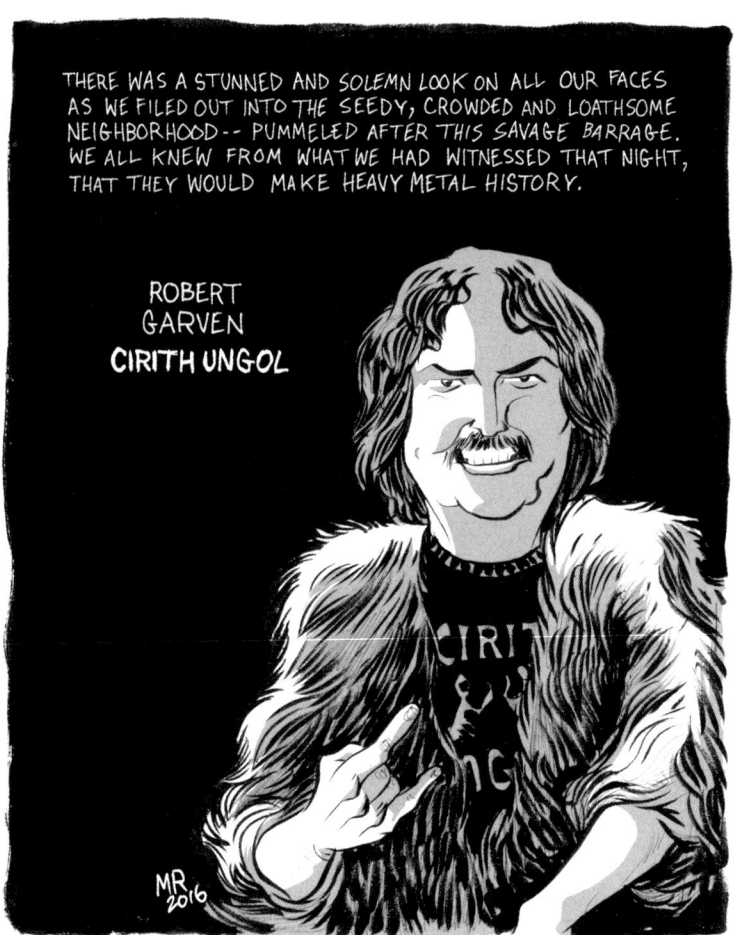

THERE WAS A STUNNED AND SOLEMN LOOK ON ALL OUR FACES AS WE FILED OUT INTO THE SEEDY, CROWDED AND LOATHSOME NEIGHBORHOOD -- PUMMELED AFTER THIS SAVAGE BARRAGE. WE ALL KNEW FROM WHAT WE HAD WITNESSED THAT NIGHT, THAT THEY WOULD MAKE HEAVY METAL HISTORY.

ROBERT GARVEN
CIRITH UNGOL

MR 2016

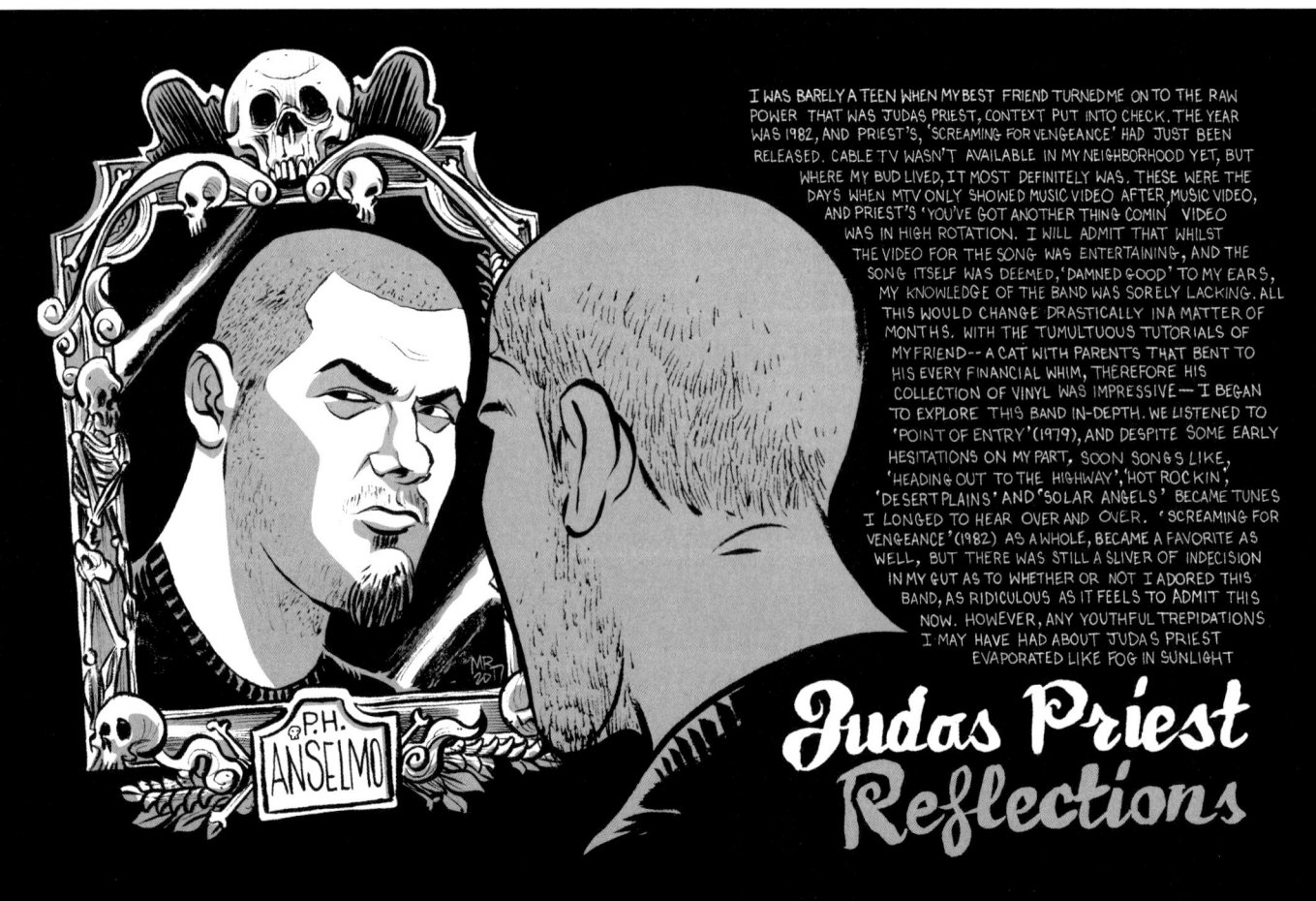

I WAS BARELY A TEEN WHEN MY BEST FRIEND TURNED ME ON TO THE RAW POWER THAT WAS JUDAS PRIEST, CONTEXT PUT INTO CHECK. THE YEAR WAS 1982, AND PRIEST'S, 'SCREAMING FOR VENGEANCE' HAD JUST BEEN RELEASED. CABLE TV WASN'T AVAILABLE IN MY NEIGHBORHOOD YET, BUT WHERE MY BUD LIVED, IT MOST DEFINITELY WAS. THESE WERE THE DAYS WHEN MTV ONLY SHOWED MUSIC VIDEO AFTER MUSIC VIDEO, AND PRIEST'S 'YOU'VE GOT ANOTHER THING COMIN' VIDEO WAS IN HIGH ROTATION. I WILL ADMIT THAT WHILST THE VIDEO FOR THE SONG WAS ENTERTAINING, AND THE SONG ITSELF WAS DEEMED, 'DAMNED GOOD' TO MY EARS, MY KNOWLEDGE OF THE BAND WAS SORELY LACKING. ALL THIS WOULD CHANGE DRASTICALLY IN A MATTER OF MONTHS. WITH THE TUMULTUOUS TUTORIALS OF MY FRIEND -- A CAT WITH PARENTS THAT BENT TO HIS EVERY FINANCIAL WHIM, THEREFORE HIS COLLECTION OF VINYL WAS IMPRESSIVE — I BEGAN TO EXPLORE THIS BAND IN-DEPTH. WE LISTENED TO 'POINT OF ENTRY' (1979), AND DESPITE SOME EARLY HESITATIONS ON MY PART, SOON SONGS LIKE, 'HEADING OUT TO THE HIGHWAY','HOT ROCKIN', 'DESERT PLAINS' AND 'SOLAR ANGELS' BECAME TUNES I LONGED TO HEAR OVER AND OVER. 'SCREAMING FOR VENGEANCE' (1982) AS A WHOLE, BECAME A FAVORITE AS WELL, BUT THERE WAS STILL A SLIVER OF INDECISION IN MY GUT AS TO WHETHER OR NOT I ADORED THIS BAND, AS RIDICULOUS AS IT FEELS TO ADMIT THIS NOW. HOWEVER, ANY YOUTHFUL TREPIDATIONS I MAY HAVE HAD ABOUT JUDAS PRIEST EVAPORATED LIKE FOG IN SUNLIGHT

P.H. ANSELMO

Judas Priest
Reflections

LEFT:
REFLECTIONS (2017)
A testimonial by Phil Anselmo about his love for Priest.

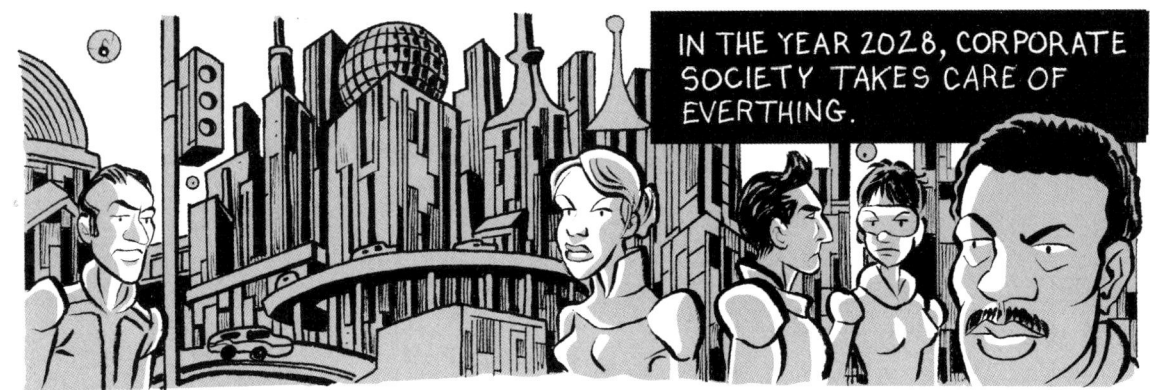

IN THE YEAR 2028, CORPORATE SOCIETY TAKES CARE OF EVERTHING.

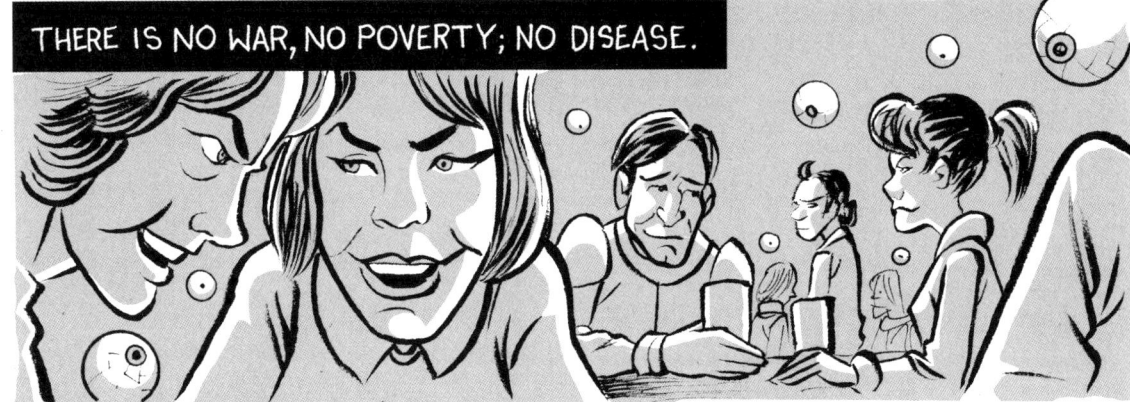

THERE IS NO WAR, NO POVERTY; NO DISEASE.

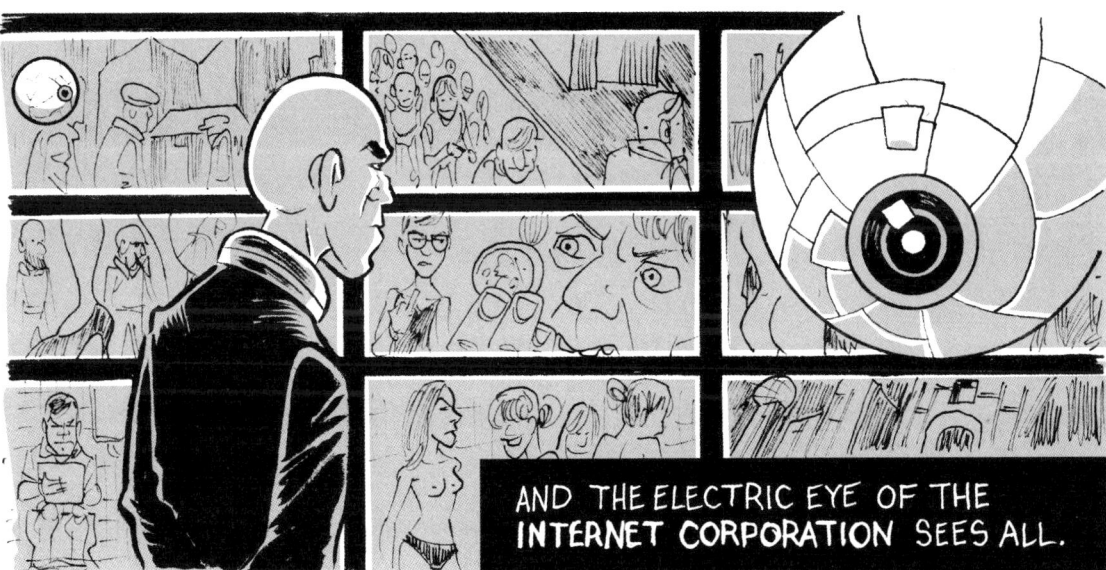

AND THE ELECTRIC EYE OF THE INTERNET CORPORATION SEES ALL.

LEFT: SATAN INC. (2017)
A comic written by J. Bennett (metal writer/musician),
drawn by Mark Rudolph with nods to 1975's *Rollerball*.

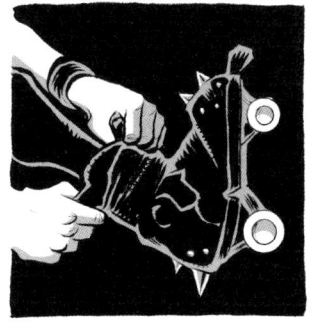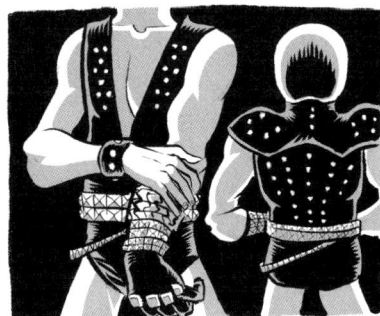

IN LIEU OF BATTLEFIELD VIOLENCE, THERE IS THE BLOODSTONE.

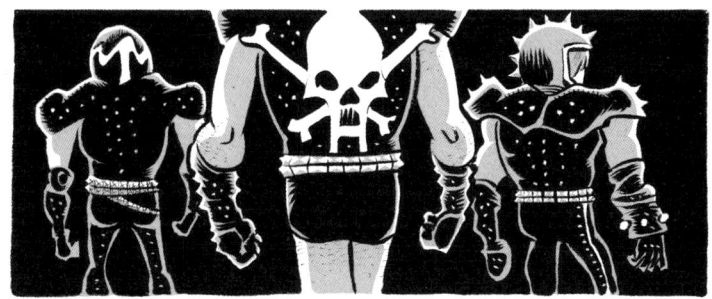

THE PINNACLE OF GLADIATORIAL COMBAT, THE BLOODSTONE SERVES A DEFINITE SOCIAL PURPOSE.

THE AUDIENCE DEMANDS MORE SPEED, MORE DANGER, MORE AGGRESSION. SOMETIMES THEY DEMAND BLOOD.

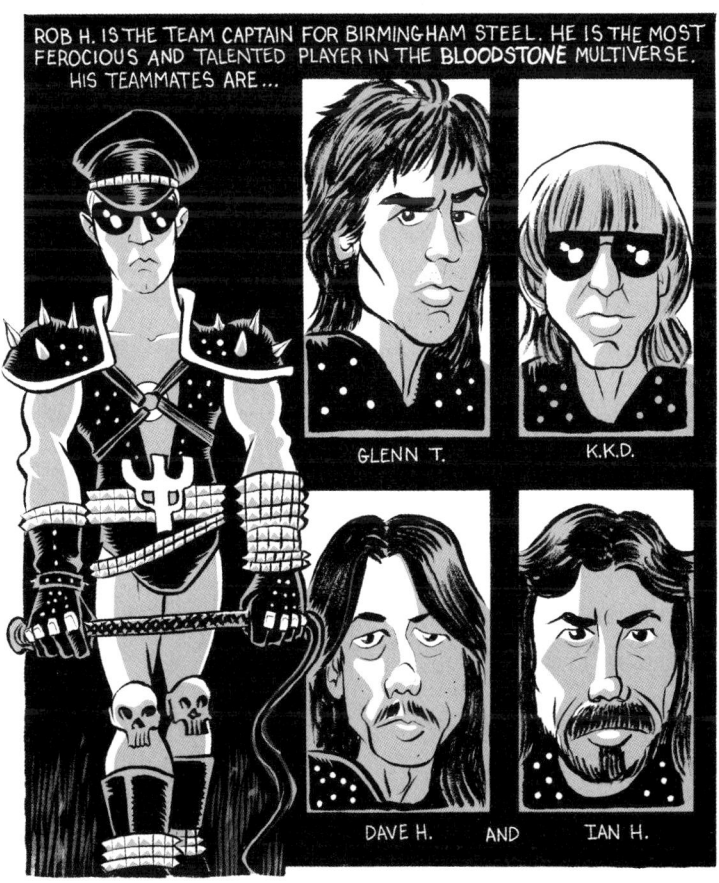

ROB H. IS THE TEAM CAPTAIN FOR BIRMINGHAM STEEL. HE IS THE MOST FEROCIOUS AND TALENTED PLAYER IN THE BLOODSTONE MULTIVERSE. HIS TEAMMATES ARE...

GLENN T.   K.K.D.

DAVE H.   AND   IAN H.

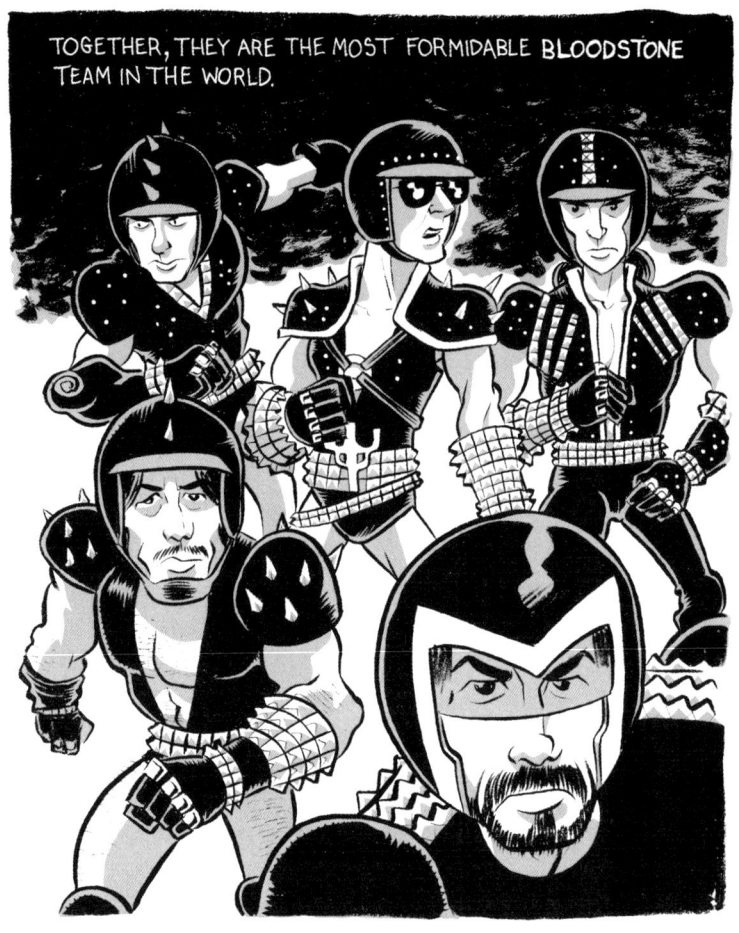

TOGETHER, THEY ARE THE MOST FORMIDABLE **BLOODSTONE** TEAM IN THE WORLD.

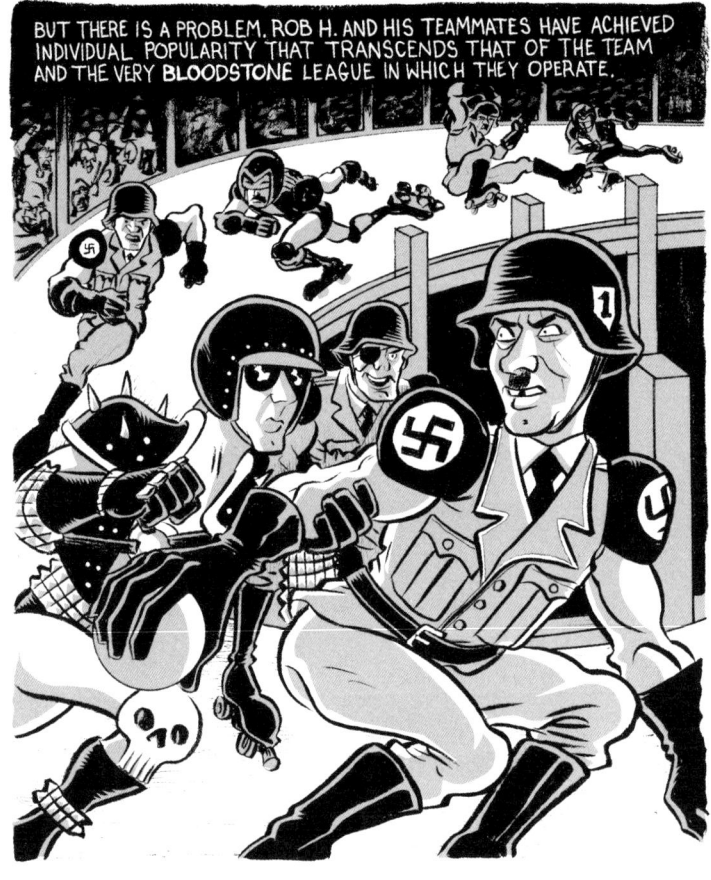

BUT THERE IS A PROBLEM. ROB H. AND HIS TEAMMATES HAVE ACHIEVED INDIVIDUAL POPULARITY THAT TRANSCENDS THAT OF THE TEAM AND THE VERY **BLOODSTONE** LEAGUE IN WHICH THEY OPERATE.

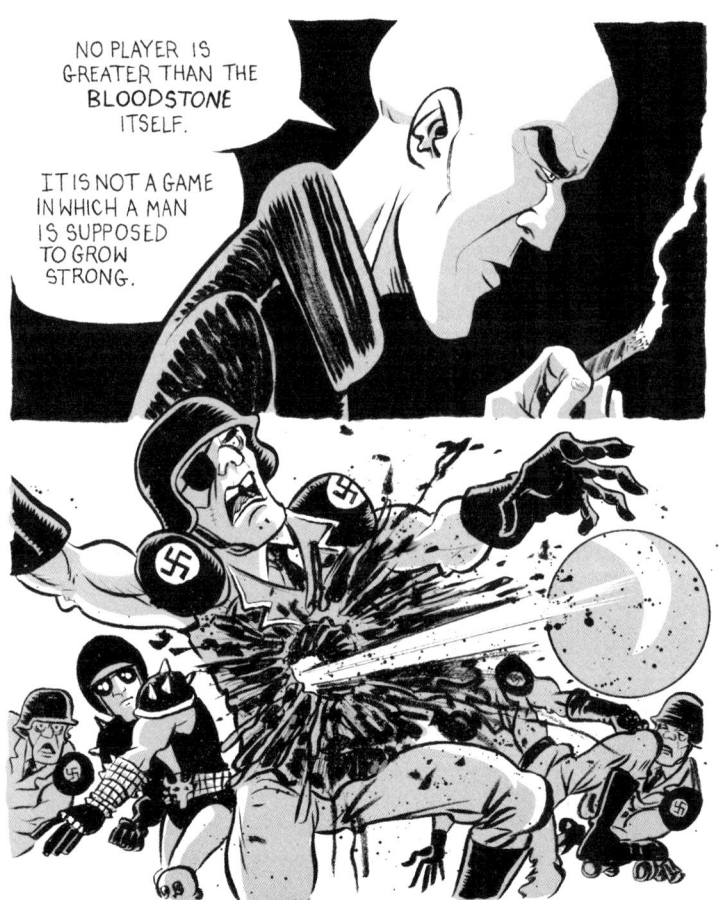

NO PLAYER IS GREATER THAN THE **BLOODSTONE** ITSELF.

IT IS NOT A GAME IN WHICH A MAN IS SUPPOSED TO GROW STRONG.

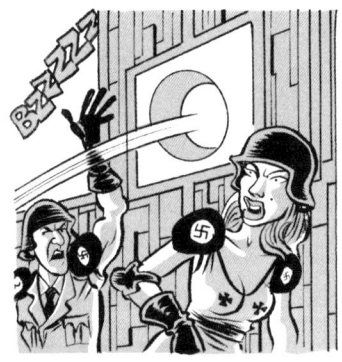 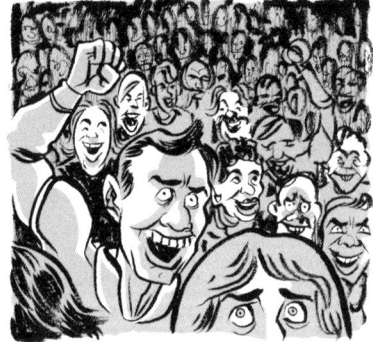

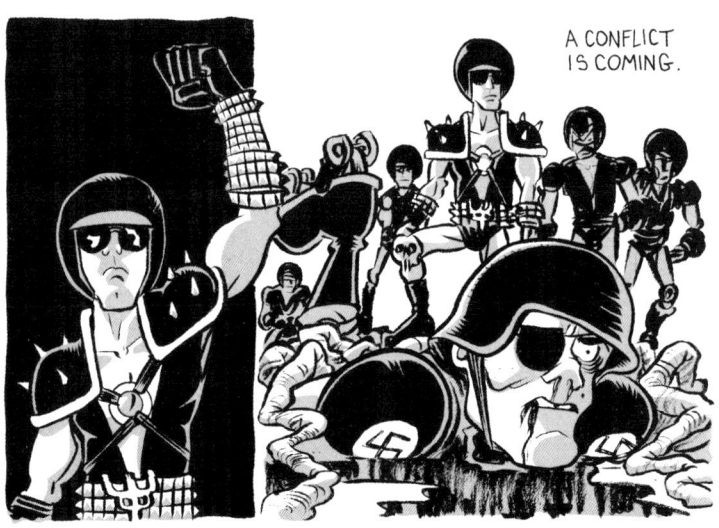

A CONFLICT IS COMING.

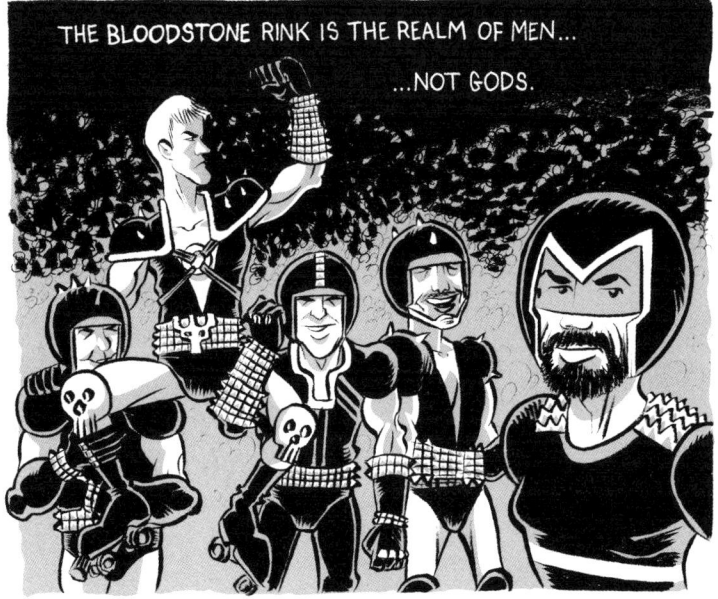

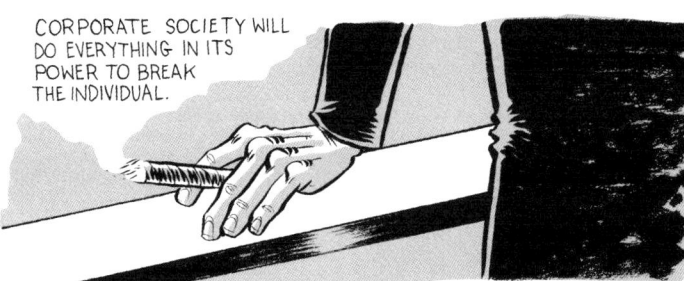

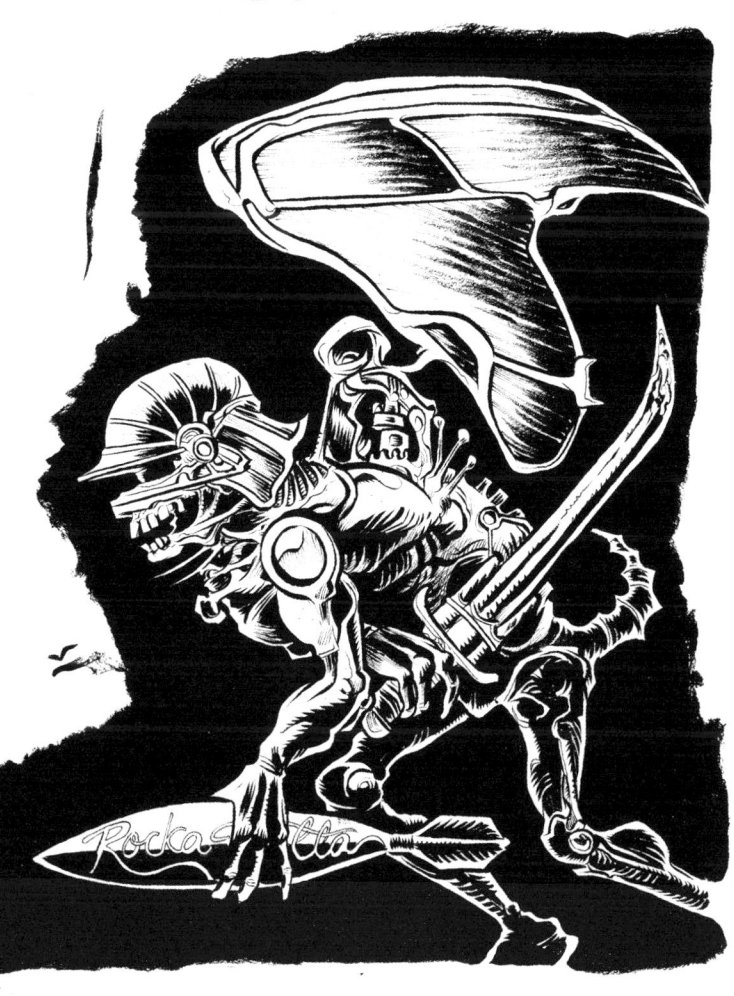

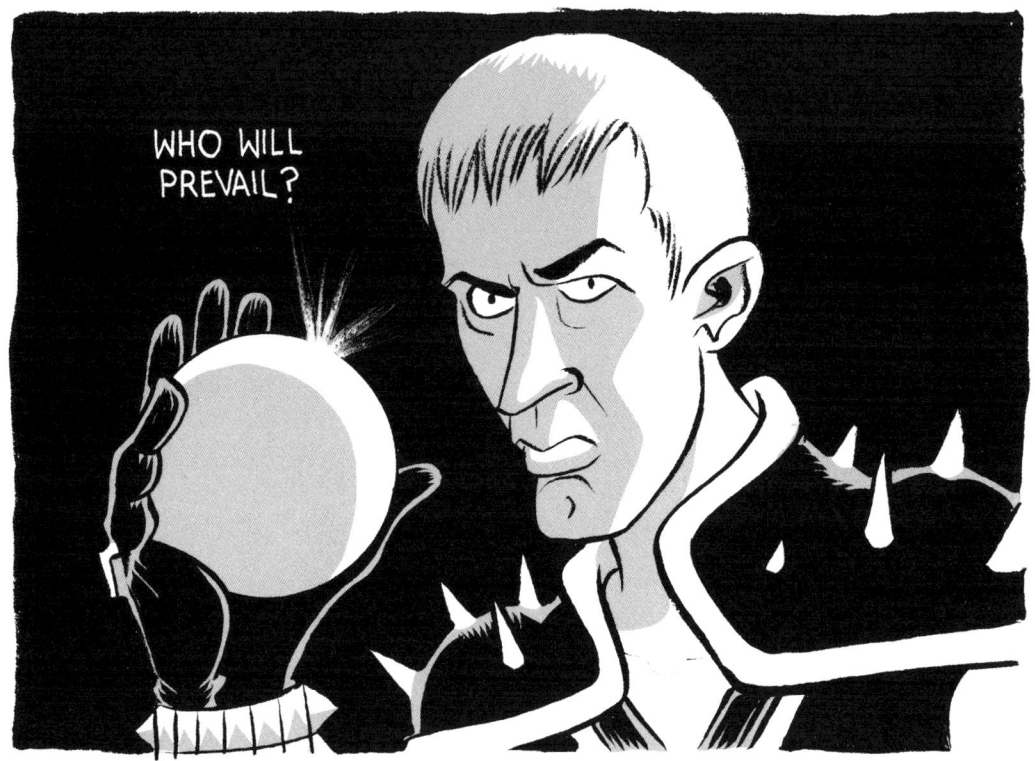

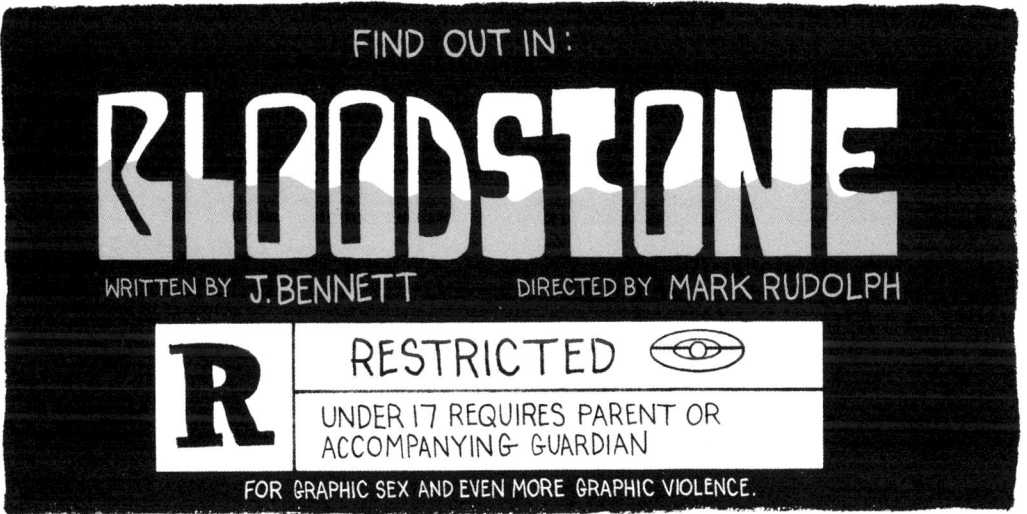

LEFT: ROCKA ROLLA (2017)
A drawing of the 1984 RCA re-issue of Rocka Rolla alternate cover art.
Was used in the history piece in the *Metal Gods* book.

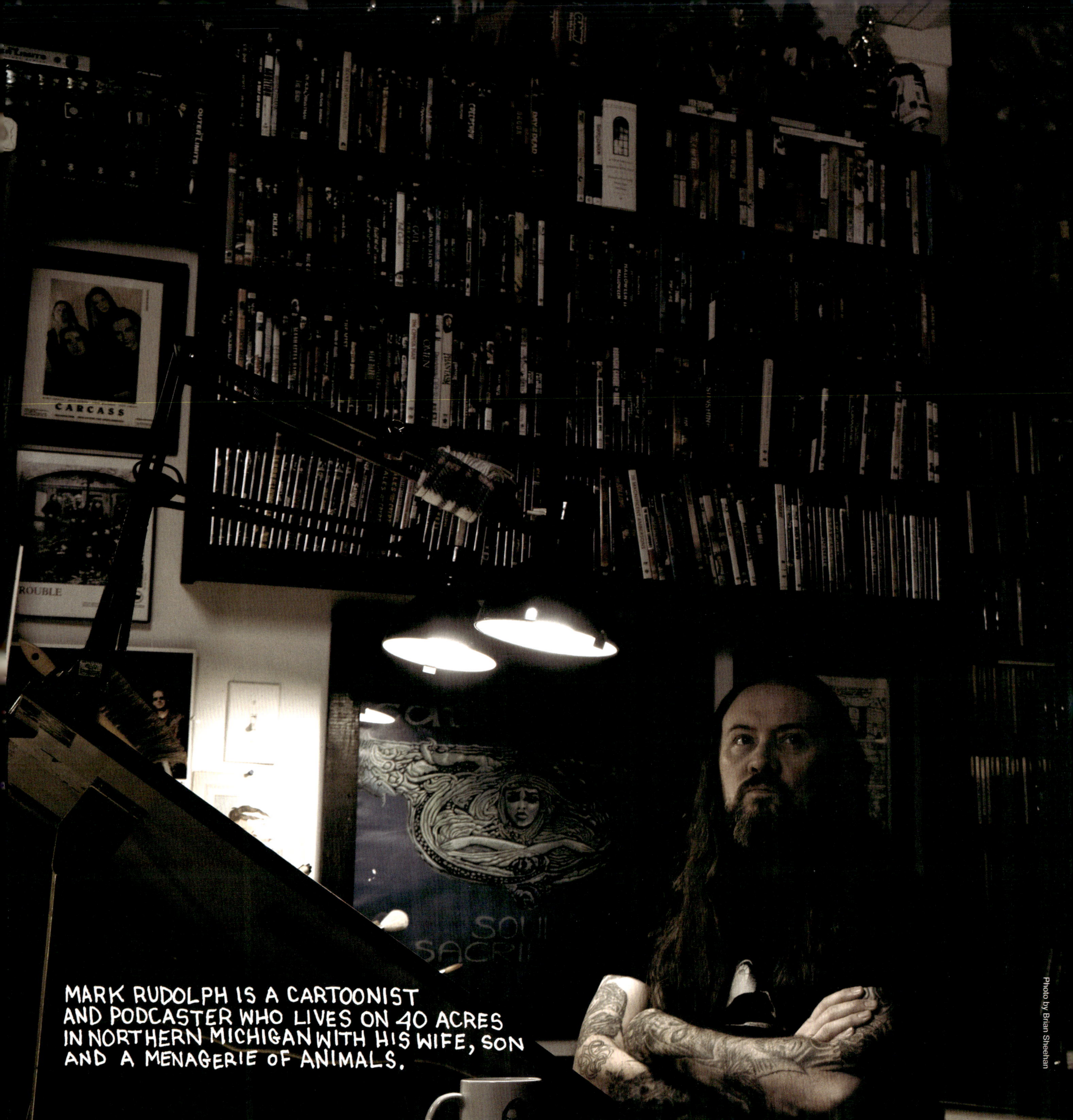

MARK RUDOLPH IS A CARTOONIST
AND PODCASTER WHO LIVES ON 40 ACRES
IN NORTHERN MICHIGAN WITH HIS WIFE, SON
AND A MENAGERIE OF ANIMALS.